ADVERTISING COPYWRITING

3rd Edition

By
Philip Ward Burton

4666 Indianola Avenue
Columbus, Ohio 43214

L.S.B.N. NO. 0-88244—042-X

Third Printing

FOREWORD

It had always seemed strange to me that no one had written a good, definitive book on advertising copywriting. Imagine how embarrassing it was to find that there not only was one, but that it was written by my very own former advertising professor. Obviously, this occurred several centuries ago at Syracuse University.

Writing a book on advertising copywriting must be, in some ways, like writing a how-to-do-it book on sex. You can choose to be very brief and general, and therefore of little practical use to anyone except as a kind of cheerleader, or you can be thorough and detailed. Having made the latter choice, however, you had better be right in what you say. And you had better not leave out anything that counts.

In this third and extensively revised edition of "Advertising Copywriting," I am happy to report that the author has left out almost nothing that I believe is important. And the details, as well as the overall focus, seem right to me.

Like any thorough text, this one provides far more answers than the novice has questions. What makes a good headline? What about body copy? Should your commercial be produced on film or tape? What's the *maximum* number of words in a 30-second spot? What about music?

These and all the other answers unfold, in their proper context, in a book that is notably lucid and well-organized.

Those persons who are not cut out to be copywriters (and they are legion) need read no further than the first chapter.

However, the thorough reader will find intelligent analysis of what makes good copy (and there are many different kinds); of the disciplined thinking required to write good copy; of the dynamic but delicate relationship between the writer and art director and how important this team-work is to single-minded advertising.

In telling detail, the book also shows how the copywriter works with account people, clients, researchers, and even lawyers. Does this make the copywriter's job sound difficult and complex? Well, it is. Otherwise, there would not be such a shortage of really good professionals.

In the second edition of this book the authors made many astute judgments that stood the test of time. For example, they correctly sensed a trend toward believability in advertising. Today, as this third edition appears, that trend has turned into a stampede, not only because advertising people are smarter, but so are consumers. And let's not forget the Government (a not-quite-disinterested-enough bystander that seems to be turning into an over-active participant).

As you would expect, this new book contains many outstanding examples of print and broadcast advertising. Most of them are current; some are classic. There are also new sections on farm advertising and different forms of business and professional advertising. The book also covers retail advertising and direct mail, and manages to do it without being superficial.

Overall, I don't know of anyone in advertising who could not learn something from reading this book. (And I know some fairly smart, and very successful, people.) Its value to the novice, therefore, should be enormous — and to a professional, whether practitioner or professor or both, should be substantial. Anyone who takes the trouble to understand what is in this book can save himself a lot of work, a lot of problems, and perhaps, at some point, even his job.

As any copywriter knows, that's a strong selling argument for any book.

Anthony C. Chevins
President
Cunningham & Walsh, Inc.

PREFACE

Copywriting is an anonymous activity. The copywriter works in behalf of someone else. Only a few persons know who did the writing of any advertisement. Yet, copywriting, more than any other advertising activity, provides an opportunity for personal expression. In the words of the body copy, in the headline, and in the art ideas conveyed to the artist, the copywriter unmistakably stamps his personality, or his lack of it since the copy may be stylized, inventive, deft, pedestrian, eloquent, persuasive, enthusiastic, lackluster.

Authors of books on copywriting likewise put more of their personal stamp upon those books than authors of other books on advertising such as those on media, research, principles, and budgeting, for example. Most often the author of a copywriting book is telling you what has worked for him. The style he favors is his style and the copy appeals he lists are those that he has worked into his own advertisements. It is unthinkable, in fact, that the author of a copywriting book could avoid putting so much of himself into a book on the subject since he has been living in the field or, more prosaically, working in it.

So it is with the third edition of this book. There are some decided changes in the book because, as I have continued to write advertising copy, I have continued to learn more about it. These more recently-learned facets of writing copy appear in the pages. This is a craft in which you learn more as you do, no matter how long you practice it.

Other changes appear in this new edition because I have continued to learn more about the teaching of advertising copywriting. As more students appear in your classrooms, one continues to discover how certain subject matter arouses student interest and speeds up learning. Ways of presenting this subject matter can make a significant difference in the process. Some immensely skilled practitioners of copywriting cannot convey their skill to the beginner because they cannot think like students. Theirs is an intuitive ability, based on quick, swift judgments. It is difficult, if not impossible, for them to work on the level of the uninformed, plodding learner. Yet, much of a book on advertising copywriting, must be addressed to this person. It must recognize his limitations and it must bring him along step by step.

Despite this talk of change in the book, it is a striking fact to see as one revises a book on advertising copywriting, how much about advertising copywriting stays timeless and constant. Most of the suggestions, made many years ago by such old masters as John Caples, are applicable today. Many, many suggestions appearing in the first edition of this new edition are likewise valid today. Since copywriters write for people and since the basic "people" appeals stay largely constant, a book written in recognition of this fact is not going to discard all the original material in succeeding editions.

Still, the third edition does present some rather pronounced changes. As an example, the first three chapters in the first two editions have been eliminated although some of the material from those chapters appears elsewhere.

Because of the dynamic character of television, and because of its ever-growing importance to the copywriter, the chapter on television advertising has undergone some changing and much strengthening. Many more examples of actual commercials have been reproduced to *show* the learner how commercials are done.

Although most of the second edition chapter concerned with the legal aspects of advertising was wholly valid in today's legalistic world some changes were made to reflect the role of the consumer in advertising decisions. Consumerism has become a much stronger force since the second edition when the word was not in the vocabulary of the working copywriter. Now the advertising writer, especially for certain products, looks warily over his shoulder as he writes. He feels more accountable than did the copywriter of a few years ago.

So it goes. Major changes and minor changes appear in chapter after chapter even though, to repeat, there was no need to change much of the book. The unchanged material has stood the test of the years.

Above all, this has become a more useful and more usable book. It is more *useful* to the novice who has everything ahead of him, and to the practitioner looking for ideas and for a reaffirmation of principles that he can apply in his work.

For the teacher it is a more *usable* book. In it, he will find more material, especially in the extensive appendix, that will help him in classroom instruction.

ACKNOWLEDGMENTS

Special thanks must be given to Sidney A. Diamond, authority on communications law, and a member of the law firm of Kaye, Scholer, Fierman, Hays and Handler. Mr. Diamond wrote the original chapter on advertising law. He has contributed likewise to the revised chapter "Copywriting and The Law." The revision reflects the latest legal developments as they affect creative people. Especial attention is given the impact on advertising, legally speaking, of the consumerism movement.

In addition, I would like to thank the following five advertising specialists who were acknowledged as major consultants in the book as first written. Much of what they contributed at that time has been retained in this revision:

Albert E. Ametrano
Melvin H. Goodrode
Rosemary Smith
Joseph Sollish
Richard S. Taylor

Many people were generous in supplying material—print and broadcast—used in this book. I have been very grateful for their help. Although I'm expressing gratitude to the following persons and/or companies for their contributions, I do not want to imply that they necessarily endorse everything written in this book:

T. F. Aherne, Cotton, Inc.; Douglas J. Alspaugh, Aetna Life & Casualty; Joel Alwine, NIBCO, Inc.; Carlo Ammirati, Lord & Taylor; L. C. Angelini, Teletype Corporation; Adolph Auerbacher, Better Homes & Gardens; Jack T. Baron, B. T. Credit Co., Inc.; Fred Bartlett, Jr., Holiday Inns, Inc.; Robert F. Beine, Abbott Laboratories; Eveylyn J. Benson, Parker Manufacturing Company; T. A. Best, T. A. Best, Inc.; Marilyn Biales, Timex Corporation; Richard A. Bigelow, Howard Johnson's Grocery Products Division; Gwen Birchenough, C.A.A., Inc; D. O. Bolander, Career Institute; R. G. Booth, Metropolitan Life; Gerald Broderick, J. Walter Thompson Company; Robert Van Brundt, Underwriters' Laboratories, Inc.; Frank J. Byrne, Jr., Lewis and Gilman, Incorporated; T. K. Cahill, R. J. Reynolds Tobacco Company; Robert W. Caldwell, Robert W. Caldwell, Inc.; Sydney M. Cassell, John F. Murray Advertising Agency; Thomas W. Chapman, Foote, Cone & Belding; G. Scott Conner, Campbell Soup Company; Joseph M. Cooper, Xerox Corporation; John P. Crichton, Rockwell Manufacturing Company; John R. Cuneo, Flair: The Gillette Company, Paper Mate Division; Phillip G. DeLong, American Telephone & Telegraph Company; Sidney A. Diamond, Kaye, Scholer, Fierman, Hays & Handler; J. Carson Eddings, William Cook Advertising, Inc.; Robert J. Ferguson, Sperry & Hutchinson Company; M. A. Fitzgerald, William Wrigley, Jr. Company; Jerome Frank, Sorgel Electric Corporation; H. A. Frediani, Bristol Laboratories; Jane Fry, formerly Lando Inc.; D. M. Furman, Bic Pen Corporation; Nic Goeres, Eastman Kodak, Inc.; Robert Green, T. A. Best, Inc.; William C. Gleason, Dancer Fitzgerald Sample, Inc.; Lawrence A. Glucs, McCann-Erickson, Inc.; Mary Joan Glynn, Bloomingdale Bros.; C. A. Grupp, E. W. Edwards, Inc.; John P. Hahn, Cunningham & Walsh, Inc.; Sheldon Harris, Doyle Dane Bernbach, Inc.; Hesston Corporation; Peter R. Hewett, PPG Industries; Thomas Hickey, New York Life Insurance Company; J. M. Hughlett, Jr., Armstrong Cork Company; Richard A. Jacobs, Joseph Jacobs Advertising, Inc.; Joseph Jankow, Sales Management Magazine; Robert H. Jurick, FALA: Mailmen Marketing Group; Richard Kabbon, Jack Byrne Advertising; Edward Keenan, Rochester Monotype Composition Co.; Laura Keye, J. L. Hudson Company; Estin Kiger, Parma Advertising; Phyllis Klein, Clairol, Inc; Peter Klinkenberg, Harrington's; Karl K. Koss, General Electric Company; T. J. Kucharik, Cast Combustion Engineering, Inc.; Lambert Brothers;

Richard Lansin, Richard Lansin Advertising; W. H. LeComte, GTE Sylvania; W. P. Leeder, International Harvester Company; Herbert A. Lehrter, Hiram Walker Incorporated; Robert H. Levenson, Doyle Dane Bernbach, Inc.; Edward H. Lewis, Jr., Armstrong Cork Company; John W. Loose, Corning Glass Works; John H. Lowden, International Telephone & Telegraph Corporation; Robert Lustgarten, Colorite Plastics Company; George Maniscalco, Avon Products, Inc.; Peter Manley, Sullivan, Stauffer, Colwell & Bayles, Inc.; John L. Massa, Hillyard Chemical Company; James B. McGraw, Lancaster Newspapers, Inc.; Frank McGuire, Daniel Starch & Staff, Inc.; Howard McIntyre, Plough, Inc.; A. P. Meaume, Amoco Oil Company; Lawrence Mintz, Schieffelin & Co.; T. H. Mooney, Jr., Philadelphia Electric Company; Ben Morris, Merling Marx & Seidman, Inc.; William R. Morrisey, Ogilvy & Mather, Inc.; T. S. Muller, Warner-Lambert Products Division; Jack Myers, Mutual Transit Sales; Christopher Orlie, Foote, Cone & Belding; M. W. Page, The Goodyear Tire & Rubber Company; Joseph Palastak; The Transit Advertising Association, Inc.; Richard Papke, D'Arcy-MacManus & Masius; Betty Phillips, Hunt-Wesson Foods; William F. Pinsak, American Motors Corp.; Steven R. Polcyn, Jr., Zenith Radio Corporation; PPG Industries, Inc.; James Pollak, J. Walter Thompson Company; William Pruett, The Coca-Cola Company; Joseph F. Puglisi, Lea & Perrins, Inc.; Allan Rakoff, Fairfield Noble Corp.; W. E. Richcreek, The Minster Machine Company; Lee F. Riley, Loehmann's, Inc.; John Robinson, Bergdorf Goodman; Terry L. Rosenquist, Sullivan, Stauffer, Colwell & Bayles; Allen G. Rosenshine, Batten, Barton, Durstine & Osborn; Susan Rothschild, Ogilvy & Mather, Inc.; Thomas M. Rouen, Fay's Drug Company, Inc.; Barbara K. Sadtler, Leslie Fay; Paul Schumucker, Green Giant Company; Lawrence M. Schopp, Clairol; Marvin Schwartz, New York Subways Advertising Co.; William L. Sekuler, Benton & Bowles; Roberta Signorile, Congoleum; Norman Simpton, Richards of Course, Inc.; Larry Sjulin, Inter-State Nurseries, Inc.; Donald T. Smith, Linen Supply News; Michael D. Speed, Terminix International, Inc.; Marcella Ann Stapor, Bristol-Myers Company; Don Stepp, Ames Division, McDonough Company; Fred Stines, Successful Farming; Jack N. Stoops, Nabisco, Inc.; Alfred M. Street, Jenkins Bros.; D. D. Thompson, Zenith Sales Company; Clifford R. Tolles, George H. Bullard Co., Inc.; Mrs. Eileen Tschida, Readex, Inc.; Paul Tully, Dancer Fitzgerald Sample, Inc.; Maurice Villency Interiors; Theodore N. Voss, Polaroid Corporation; Gail Wheeler, I. Miller; M. John White, Metropolitan Bank; T. R. Whittlesey, Doyle Dane Bernbach; C. Donald Williams, C. Donald Williams Advertising, Inc.; E. S. Williams, L. L. Bean, Inc.; Janis K. Wilson, Metro Transit Advertising; Mrs. Virginia S. Woodward, Olay Company, Inc.; Ford B. Worthing, Allen & Dorward, Inc.; Jean Yates, Bonwit Teller.

Finally, I would like to thank Helen Kleshinski, the art director for Grid, who created the design and layout for the book.

A WORD TO THE READER

Can anyone learn about copywriting by reading a book on copywriting?

Yes. And No.

Yes—he can learn to distinguish good copy from bad copy. He will learn the do's and don'ts that can save him time and trouble on the job.

Yes—he can learn the terminology of the field of copywriting, and of advertising.

Yes—he can learn what motivates people to buy and what appeals will motivate them.

Yes—he can learn the technical requirements that are peculiar to the different media so that he can proceed confidently whether he is writing a 10-second television commercial, a 4-color magazine spread, or a 24-sheet outdoor poster.

Yes—he can learn the special requirements of the different forms of advertising such as retail, mail order, industrial, professional, trade, and others.

Yes—he can learn what a copywriter must know about research and law, and how a copywriter can write advertising that is in keeping with the tenets of consumerism, yet can sell efficiently for the advertiser.

Yes—he can learn how a copywriter cooperates with, and learns from, artists and production men.

No—he cannot learn from a book the germinating of the inspirational idea that forms the basis of an outstanding campaign, or of a memorable, award-winning advertisement. Some people have a heaven-sent ability to germinate ideas and to think creatively and originally. They have this, book or no book. A copywriter can be trained but there are some who are "born" with recognizable talent, just as there are artists, poets, and musicians born with such talent.

No—he cannot learn from this, or any book, how to write "first-draft" copy speedily and under pressure. Such speed is learned on the job and is developed from constant practice.

A book on copywriting can point you in the right direction. It can give you a helping hand in a course in advertising copywriting, and it can help you enormously during those first days on the job. It can even help you after you've gained working experience because all writers need to go back to the fundamentals occasionally.

You will notice in this preface the stress on the words "learn" and "help." Learning is a constant process in advertising and in copywriting. This book will be part of that process. Above all, it is intended to be a helpful book because the copywriter, brash or confident as he may be in general, has those moments of doubt and insecurity. Perhaps this book can help him get through such moments.

TABLE OF CONTENTS

1.

Just What Is Copy?

Many persons in and out of advertising find it easy to define advertising copy. They call it "salesmanship in print." A great many advertising men and economists do not agree with this definition of copy, and have said so in books, magazines, and newspaper articles. They usually base their opposition to the definition upon the great number of advertisements which have nothing tangible to offer the public and thus nothing tangible to "sell." According to the views of these people, advertising copy that does not present a product to the public for purchase and does not offer reasons why the purchaser should buy, is not salesmanship, but subtle persuasion and impression-building. Others maintain that the salesmanship-in-print definition is too narrow-that it reduces the advertising man to the role of merchandise peddler. They point to advertising's place in the total marketing process. Advertising properly used is, they say, a force for mass consumer education, and a tool for effecting social change. It is almost insulting to the copywriter, they add, to assume that his only interest in writing copy is to sell something, or somebody.

These viewpoints are interesting, challenging, and possibly debatable. Yet, it hardly seems questionable that the overall objective of almost all advertising copy is to sell. Rarely is an advertisement found that does not have a sales motive *somewhere* behind its writing. True, as one looks at many advertisements it is difficult to find any obvious sales message. Many advertisements , for example, that appear in print media, or in broadcast media, are written to build a feeling of good will, to strengthen public opinion, or to break down a possible *negative* public opinion. Such advertisements, often called institutional advertisements, normally do not offer products or services for sale. The copy, nevertheless, is *selling* copy just as surely as is product-selling copy. It is merely selling something different. If you are a salesman and you invite a customer or a prospective customer to dinner, to play golf, or to see a ball game, you are engaged in a form of selling. Perhaps you aren't actually clinching your order-possibly you make no attempt to talk business—but you are selling your company or yourself, or both, and the impression you create in the mind of your client is almost certain to have an important bearing upon the ultimate signing of the order.

So it is with advertising copy. In almost any *type* of advertisment you are asked to write, remember that you have *something* to sell to your readers. Otherwise, there would be little reason to spend thousands of dollars, or anything at all, for the space or time in which to deliver your message.

COPY FURTHER DEFINED

Can we, accordingly, agree that copy *is* merely salesmanship in print? Is that as far as the definition goes? No—it isn't half defined—especially as far as you, the copywriter, are concerned.

Copy *can* be the voice of the advertiser, boasting about his product, shouting its merits in bald, unlovely terms, damning the competition, gaining attention through sheer weight of words and extravagant claims, making the most noise.

Or copy can be the voice of a friend—a trusted adviser offering help to the consumer in his purchasing problems—clear, arresting, interesting, honest.

Copy can be the enthusiasm of *salesmen*—echoing their words, reflecting their pride in their products, opening doors for them, easing their jobs. It can be your contribution to the merchant who knows what he wants to say but doesn't know how to say it. It can be a primer for the dealer, the jobber, and the distributor, a means of preconditioning their selling. Copy can be an instrument of better living, easier living, happier living. Through copy that stimulates mass sales, the whole economy of a field of enterprise may be improved by price-reduction and product-refinement. Copy is a social and an economic force. And the way *you* create it is the true way it may be defined.

WHAT COPY MEANS TO DIFFERENT PEOPLE

It is well, at the outset, to establish a *literal* interpretation of the word "copy." To the newspaper reporter, "copy" is simply the text of his story. It is the only thing he is responsible for. He needn't worry about headlines, subheadings, typography, illustrations. "Copy," to him, is what he writes—the main body text of his article.

Advertising has a different idea of copy. Copy now becomes everything that appears in an advertisement. When you are asked to prepare copy for an advertisement, you are expected to write everything required for the complete advertisement. If the man or woman to whom you turn over your finished job asks you, "Is the copy ready?", he, or she, expects that you have completed headline, subheadings, body text, captions, blurbs, signatures, and even copyright notices. To you, "copy" means every word that is to appear in your finished advertisement, depending upon its format. (This all-inclusive interpretation of copy in a few cases also embraces layout. In some advertising agencies and advertising departments, you might hear people referring to an entire advertisement as "copy." If you were asked to "get the copy" for some particular advertisement, in such an organization, you would be expected to come back with everything, including the layout. This is not very common—most advertising people keep layout separate in their thinking—but it does occur here and there.)

COPY ELEMENTS

To those of you who have already had experience in creating, or helping to create, advertising, the following definitions will probably be familiar. It is essential, however, for the beginner to know such terminology before he is faced with the writing of rush advertisements. Although each of these copy breakdowns will be discussed fully in later chapters, you will do well to familiarize yourself right now with the trade terms you will be using and hearing daily.

Occasionally you will find one advertisement that contains all the different elements of copy. This is rare. Normally, your advertisements will be made up of two or three of the common copy elements. You may sometimes find it necessary to employ all of them, but very seldom. There is certainly no rule of thumb by which you can predetermine exactly which elements you'll use and which you'll not need.

When preparing a campaign for a client, or a prospective client, a copywriter may often need but two elements of the complete advertisement in order to convey the basic campaign idea or approach. These elements are the headline and the illustration. A number of layouts may be prepared that show the client different headlines and illustrations. If he approves the campaign idea, as demonstrated in these layouts, the copywriter will then supply the body copy for the advertisements, plus the subheads, or captions, or other elements needed to complete the advertisements.

The headline

The copy element that is possibly the most important, and certainly the best known to the layman, is the headline. This is the part of your copy that is displayed in larger type than the rest and is designed, along with the illustration, to attract the attention of the reader. Normally, the headline of an advertisement will present a selling idea or will otherwise serve to intrigue the prospective purchaser into a further and more exhaustive reading of your advertisement.

Headlines can and do fall into many varied patterns. It is not necessary, for instance, for a headline to be *big*. Some headlines—notably in newspaper advertisements—are set in very large type and in general resemble regular newspaper headlines. Others, however, may be quite small in type size, and qualify as headlines by their leading position in the advertisement. Still another common form of headline is the blurb or balloon, in which a character is supposed to be speaking. Headlines do not even have to say anything. A company name, for instance, might be used as a headline. So might a familiar brand or signature. But practically all advertisements *have* headlines of one sort or another, and their primary function is to attract immediately the attention of the reader.

The overline

Sometimes called the "lead-in," the overline is an introductory heading that is placed over the headline. An example follows:

Overline:	How to beat the high cost of decorating
Headline:	DYE–CRAFT WITH RIT.

In this instance, as in most uses of the overline, it is set in smaller type than the main headline. Thus, it is very useful if the copywriter finds that it is difficult to put over a complete message in the main headline if the latter must be limited in length because of it being set in large, attention-getting type.

Another example:

Overline:	To anyone interested in saving money
Head:	Our interest rates are the highest in the state

The subhead

In writing an advertisement you will often have some important facts you wish to telegraph to your reader, but which require more space than you care to use in the display of the headline, or possibly they are not quite so appealing as attention-attracters. When such information is displayed in smaller type than the headline, yet larger than the body text of the advertisement, it is known as a subhead. Subheads may be three or four lines of copy underneath the headline, or they may be display lines throughout the text, or in other places in the advertisement.

In our nation of quick readers, who so often are more picture—mined than print—mined, the subhead serves an important function. It tells the reader quickly what is coming in the copy and enables him to judge whether he wants to continue. In most advertisements, nothing is lost if the subhead causes the reader to skip the following copy. Usually, the headline and illustration, plus the signature of the advertiser, have already enabled the reader to judge whether it's to his self-interest to read the body copy.

A subhead, on the other hand, will most

normally lure the reader into the following copy. In the case of very long copy, it will break up type masses and make the advertisement look easier to read. This is especially true of advertisements that do not sell products but, instead, talk about the company or its point of view. These institutional advertisements, or "corporate" advertisements, usually obtain low readership. Well-written subheads can help make the advertisements look more interesting.

In some places, particularly in department store and other retail advertising operations, subheads are also known as "captions." This is not usually the case, however. "Caption" normally has a meaning all its own, as will be discussed shortly.

The body copy

As its name implies, the body text, or body copy as it is more often known, is that part of your advertisement which tells the entire story. It is the block of words in which you get down to brass tacks with your reader—where you either clinch your sale or lose it. It is the part of copy that puts the "write" in copywriting.

You have probably heard salesmen talk about "getting a foot in the door." Well, your headline is *your* foot. The body copy is the follow-through on that foot. Some advertisements actually have no body copy, from a technical standpoint. That is, they contain no major unit of type. Advertisements built around a comic-strip style, picture-and-caption advertisements, and others, fall into this category. Since the entire story is told in these advertisements by other than the usual means, they will be discussed later as a highly specialized form of body copy.

Captions

Captions are the small units of type used with illustrations, coupons, and special offers. They are generally less important to the main selling points of the advertisement than body copy and are usually set in type sizes smaller than the body text. Now and then you will want to plan an entire advertisement in picture-and-caption style, presenting your sales points by illustrating them and explaining them at the same time, much the way a magazine handles news stories. Here, of course, the caption assumes far greater importance and must be considered as body text.

The blurb

A "blurb," or "balloon," is the advertising profession's term for copy set up so that it seems to be coming from the mouth of one of the characters illustrated in the advertisement. It is most often used, as is the caption, to punch across some secondary feature in the story you are telling, but sometimes it, too, can constitute the complete body text, as in the comic-strip style. Blurbs are often used as headlines. When so employed, they are not changed in any way except to be displayed in larger-sized type and placed at the head of the advertisement. They are still known as blurbs or balloons.

Boxes and panels

You'll hear copywriters and artists referring regularly to "boxes" or "panels." These, as their names imply, are simply captions which obtain greater attention value by being placed in special display positions. A "box" is a caption around which a rule has been lined, singling it out from other copy. A "panel" is a solid rectangle of black or color, in the center of which is the caption, either in white or "reverse" type, or centered in white space.

Boxes and panels are usually used in advertisements using such features as coupons, special offers, and contest rules. These will often be set apart from the rest of the advertisement by means of such devices. Boxes should be used sparingly.

Slogans, logotypes, and signatures

Many times you will meet a client whose company uses a slogan of years' standing and which he insists must appear in every advertisement. Too, almost all advertisers logically demand that their company name be displayed in its familiar form. This display of the company name, seal, or trademark is called a logotype, and is a common part of most advertisements. The term is often abbreviated in advertising jargon to "logo," "sig," or "sig cut." Copyright notices, too, are often required, for legal reasons, and must be included in all copy prepared for such advertisers.

An important point to remember is that everything that appears in print in an advertisement must appear on the copy sheets that he prepares. These sheets serve as a guide to the artists and typographers and other production men who will be working on the advertisement after the copywriter has finished. If the copywriter leaves some element out of his copy, the whole advertisement may be held up later and a publication date missed because the advertisement may need to be reset.

One way to make sure of including the various elements is to set up the copy neatly and logically on the copy sheet by labeling the different elements on the side. Many copywriters are sloppy in their execution. An example of an ideal copy sheet follows. If all copy sheets were handled in this manner, there would be fewer mistakes in production.

Example of properly—executed copy sheet

(illustration occupying approximately top 2/3 of advertisement consists of long, open box of pastels and, propped against the box, a picture presumably executed with the pastels)

Overline: A special introductory offer for only $2.98

Headline: 60 PROFESSIONAL OIL PASTELS

Subhead: New *professional* dustless type

Copy A: A huge assortment of pastels with no two colors the same. These professional dustless pastels can be mixed and blended but never make a mess. They are as convenient as pastels yet have the brilliance and color depth of oil paints. Sticks will not crumble or break easily and can be used on paper, board, cloth, stone or plaster. They are excellent for quick sketches as well as finished drawings and paintings. You may also use turpentine to blend colors and heighten the oil effect. Completed oil pastel paintings do not require fixing and can be framed like a water color painting. Non-toxic composition makes them perfect for adults or young "Picassos"! Great for portraits, landscapes, anything at all. A great gift and a great buy for only $2.98.

Subhead: Offer will not be repeated this season

Copy B: Supplies are limited and orders will be filled first come, first served so we urge you to order right now to avoid disappointment. The price is right and offer will not be repeated this season.

Coupon copy: Mail 10 day no—risk coupon today

Greenland Studios
5165 Greenland Bldg.,
Miami, Fla. 33054

Please send me #9760 Oil Pastel sets checked below. I understand if not delighted, I may return for a prompt and complete refund. Enclosed is check or m.o. for $__________

________#9760 Oil Pastel sets @$2.98 (Add 50¢ postage each)

Name________________

Address________________

City________ State____ Zip______

____Save $1. Enclose only $5.96 for 2 Oil Pastel sets and we will pay the postage. Extra set will make a wonderful gift

Now you have been given all the elements of "copy." They are *all* the responsibility of the copywriter. It is your job, not only to create copy, but to see that it is properly prepared, typed, set, and printed according to the wishes of your clients, your company, store, or newspaper, depending upon what kind of copywriter you are.

It should be pointed out that some agencies and many retail establishments and mail-order houses consider the neophyte copywriter little more than a space-filler. In other words, you may start to work for a company whose policy will not permit you to do much creative thinking on your own for some time. During the preliminary phases of your training you may be asked simply to write the body text, captions, or other parts of advertisements for which the major planning has already been done by others. No attempt is made here to determine whether or not this system is better or worse than that which calls for the beginner to jump into the business of thinking out entire advertisements right from the start. Both have produced, and are still producing, sucessful copywriters. It is somewhat a question of temperament. Some copywriters like to have their assignments blueprinted for them—others find their satisfaction in being their own copy architects.

Broadcast copy must be included, too

All the attention in this chapter has been concentrated on print copy for newspaper and magazines. Most of what has been said will apply to other forms of print such as leaflets, folders, catalogs. For these forms of print, however, more elements may be included. These will be discussed in later chapters.

Also, to be discussed later will be the requirements for broadcast copy in radio and television. The same attention to form must be observed in writing radio commercials and in preparing material for television. In the latter, the writer must think in two dimensions, sight and sound. He encounters an entirely different vocabulary from that used for print. Since, in many advertising agencies, the copywriter creates broadcast commercials as well as print advertisements, he must be equally familiar with the terminology and form required in this kind of advertising.

Is the Copywriter *Really* a "Writer"?

During your copywriting career you will be told many times, particularly by others who earn a living by writing, that your profession is not "writing" at all—that it is wrong to classify yourself as a writer. Newspaper reporters, magazine writers, authors, and poets often comment bitingly that those who write to sell goods aren't "really writing." You will often hear the phrase "prostituting the art."

Don't take these people seriously. Your job of writing not only is *"really writing,"* it is probably one of *the* most exacting forms of writing. You must possess not only the same command of the English language that other writers demonstrate, but you must also, as you have read before in this book, train yourself to be a student of human psychology, salesmanship, merchandising, marketing, and purchasing habits. You must learn to coordinate your writing ability with photography, painting, printing, and engraving. And you must hoard your words—write with a precision and a clarity almost unknown to many other writers.

You are most certainly a writer. As any good writer does, you should strive for perfectionism. But that perfectionism does not always, or even often, translate itself into terms of picturesque prose. From the standpoint of fundamental *selling,* the copy you write must be keyed to the product, the market, the media it is to appear in, and other factors. You will find occasions when the most beautiful piece of writing would be completely at odds with the goal you are striving for.

Notice the difference between these two paragraphs, selected from advertisements appearing in the same publication.

Float on a cloud of loveliness . . . in a luxurious mist of a famous D'Orsay fragance . . . wherever you are. This crystal and gold beauty travels as gracefully as it adorns your dressing table.

HOW SHOULD YOU PICK A BROKER?

In a word—carefully.
Not because there aren't any number of fine firms to choose from—there are.
But even among the finest you still find differences.
Differences in customer service . . .
Differences in physical facilities . . .
Differences in research aid . . .
Differences in personal training and, *most important of all,*
Differences in fundamental policy.

To help you decide about us, we've just prepared a 32-page booklet that explains in detail just who we are, just what we stand for, just what you can expect when you do business with Merrill Lynch.

The first is rhapsodic and dreamy. It is directed toward the innermost emotions of the people it is trying to impress. The other is crisp, matter-of-fact, and informative. Now each of these bits of advertising copy was carefully written and edited to say exactly what the copywriter wished to tell his readers, in exactly the way he wished them to receive it.

Would you say that the first advertisement was any better written than the second? Possibly, by the layman, or by the writing artist, whose main concern would be the well-turned phrase, the picturesque wording, the emotional backdrop, the first advertisement would be adjudged to contain the best writing. Those tricks of a writer's trade are not only unnecessary to the second advertisement, but might even be detrimental to its sales power. It is entirely possible that the copywriter who wrote the second advertisement devoted more time and thought to his copy than did the copywriter who turned out the first. The writing you do must be tailored with precise craftsmanship to fit the job in hand.

Judgment and versatility are other attributes that stand high in the requirements of good copywriting. As an agency copywriter especially, you will be expected not only to pace your copy correctly, but to write copy which differs in approach and feeling as radically as do the above two examples.

COPY OFFERS CREATIVE THRILLS

You may be thrilled when you see your first advertisement in print or hear your first radio broadcast over the air. Don't ever let your job become so routine that you lose that thrill. But try to think of your work as something above and beyond the simple thrill of pride in creative enterprise. If you look at what you are doing in terms of the effect it is going to have on thousands and thousands of people, upon the economy of your clients' operations, upon the selling records of your clients' sales forces and retail outlets, you will discover a creative thrill that few other writers can understand.

One evidence of the right of advertising copywriting to be considered a legitimate example of writing art is in the number of writers of contemporary literature who began as advertising copywriters—especially as advertising agency copywriters. The exactness, the economy of phrasing, the requirement for subtle shadings in word meanings have given many copywriters the precise training they needed for their subsequent literary efforts.

It is not surprising then to discover how many well-known writers spent their early years behind a copywriter's desk. A few of these are such writers as Richard Powell, Cameron Hawley, Sinclair Lewis, and Sherwood Anderson. Many successful writers have, like Richard Powell and Cameron Hawley, produced best-selling novels or plays while they were still employed in advertising. This accomplishment is beyond most copywriters who find all the creative challenge they need in turning out good copy day after day. It is not recommended that persons enter the copy copywriting field as a preparation for producing literary works. It is true, nonetheless, that numerous literary men have found such preparation valuable.

Most advertising men would agree, however, with a highly-creative advertising executive who said: "Advertising copywriting is not a bridge to becoming a great novelist or great dramatist. If you take the work seriously the potential for personal satisfaction can be almost as great in advertising as it is in literature."

Products, Prospects, Purchases.

You've undoubtedly heard stories of the copywriter who wrote the million-dollar campaign as a result of a burst of creative ingenuity that occurred when he woke during the night,or while he was shaving, or while he was scribbling on the back of a napkin in a night club.

Well, it's possible. Such advertising revelations rarely visit the neophyte, however.

If you discover some day the answer to one of your copy problems in this revelatory manner, it will be because you have cudgeled your brain for days working up to it. You have thought so hard that your subconscious mind continued to wrestle with the problem quite apart from more mundane concerns such as bridge, baseball or bills.

A half century ago, when advertising was in its swaddling clothes, it was expected to do little more than keep a product's name before the public. In those days, the answer to the question, "Where does copy start?" would have been "Copy starts with a headline."

Now it's a different story. Advertising has long since proved itself of far more than mere reminder value. Intelligently and capably executed, modern advertising is the most successful method for mass-marketing merchandise and services.

Today's copy "starts" long before you give even the slightest thought to the actual words you will eventually use in writing an advertisement, sales letter, radio commercial, or any other type of selling message. Copy begins with the *basic sales strategy* of the company for which you are preparing advertising. Your copy policy is established when your company or client determines what he has to sell and how *much* of it he must sell to make a profit.

Although this book deals almost entirely with copywriting and the copywriter's duties, you should understand some of the marketing questions that must be investigated and answered before your advertising copy can be fully effective. You must know the basic sales strategy, since it establishes a definite set of boundaries into which you fit your writing and the planning of your writing.

You may never have much to do with the establishment of the basic sales strategy unless you happen to work on a new product promotion; or possibly the product is one that needs a complete promotional overhauling. In either case, you might sit in on meetings during which the sales set-up of the company is established or reorganized. Usually, however, you will do most of your creative work for organizations which have been operating profitably and whose sales strategy is well established.

Part of your job will consist of studying this policy. You will need to understand why it was established. This will be accomplished through a thorough examination of what might be termed "The Three P's": the *product,* the *prospects,* and the *purchases.* To write effective copy, you must know your three P's well. Whatever product you're writing about, consider it in the light of the following analysis:

P IS FOR PRODUCT

1. *Does the product fill a definite need or desire?* An automatic washing machine, for example, fills a definite need. Several, in fact. It enables a woman to wash her family's clothes (1) cleaner, (2) with less effort, (3) in less time, and (4) with less wear and tear on the clothes. If she had been sending her laundry out prior to her purchase of her automatic washing machine, such a machine

will also save her money. Thus, an automatic home laundry can fill five basic needs!

Perfume, on the other hand, does not fill a specific need. It *does* fill a very strong natural desire felt by almost every women—to be more attractive to men. A desire to be a siren (although few women will openly admit it) is so much a part of a woman's nature that it would be hard to find one who doesn't use some kind of perfume. It's as much a part of their "beauty kit" as powder and lipstick. Also, many women use perfume for the same reason men use shaving lotion—to feel better groomed.

Almost all successful products fill either a need or a desire. Unfortunately, however, there always seems to be a continuous flow of products coming on the market which fill neither need nor desire. These are usually spawned by "mad" inventors or by others whose imagination is spent on fashioning the inventions—not in figuring out a real use for their creations. Without seeking competent advice from persons experienced in marketing, they blindly rush into production "before someone steals the idea." Their reasoning, if it may be called that, seems to run something like this: "There's no product on the market like it! Therefore, it's *bound* to be a hot seller!" They fail to see the *reason* there is no similar product—*because there's no real need or desire for one.* Typical of this type of "pre-doomed" product would be a gimcrack like a left-handed shoehorn. Such a gadget might amuse you but you wouldn't buy it. The marketer of such a product would soon run out of prospects because it fills neither need nor desire.

Just the same, there is—and undoubtedly will continue to be—a constant flow of novelty products which manufacturers introduce with the full knowledge that—because they *do not* fill any lasting need or desire—the products can only hope to enjoy flash sales over a short period and then almost die out.

The objective is to whip up a "desire" for their product through its novelty. If it catches on, sales sky-rocket; but they usually plummet a short time later as illustrated by "soapless" soap bubbles and hula hoops which piled up sales for a brief time and then were seen no more. Such products come and go. They're "freaks" and not to be likened to the normal, stable products which are your primary concern as an advertising man.

Once it has been established that your product fills a valid need or desire, the next thing you should want to know is:

2. *Are most users satisfied with the product?* It is a fundamental of marketing that a product must live up to the buyers' expectations if it is to be a successful repeat-sale item. Living up to expectations is probably even more important in the case of low-cost, non-durable products—bread, hair oil, soft drinks—can't attain sustained success—no matter how sound your advertising may, be—unless a good percentage of buyers constantly and quickly repeat their purchases when the initial purchase needs replacement. In the case of the printing press it is important to the continued success of the manufacturer that his product live up to its claims. Repeat orders for $100,000.00 printing presses, however, would come at very long intervals. Few printers would make such a huge investment without first finding out from companies already owning similar presses whether they were satisfactory—thus the buyer of such an item would be satisfied in *advance* of purchase that the product was all right. Regardless of the nature of a product, then, it must represent honest value if it is to obtain lasting

success. Next, you will want to know:

3. *Does the product possess any exclusive features of benefit to the user?* The answer to this question is important. When your product *does* possess exclusive advantage over competition, it often will give you an advantage over the copywriters working on the competitive accounts—a knock-out punch they don't have.

Take for example, the remote control device called "Space Command," introduced by Zenith television. Here was a product development created by the Zenith research engineers which no other television set had, at the time of its introduction through advertising. The copywriter who wrote the copy for Zenith could be sure that the new product offered a benefit that would be of interest to readers, and what's more, one that he could dramatize in terms of the set owner's most basic wants.

Other "firsts" or product exclusives, you'll recall, were the Ford convertible hardtop, Sanka Coffee (caffeine removed), the original Spud cigarettes (mentholated), and many, many others. Speaking of Spuds, although many of you probably don't recall the first time you heard of them, or mentholated smoking, you certainly can see the results of imitation! After a period of time, while tobacco men studied the results, Spuds were followed by a parade of new cigarettes featuring everything from dry ice to creme de menthe.

Many products have exclusive features. Unless, however, their advantages are rather obvious to prospective buyers, these "exclusives" may be difficult to write about and thus less effective as selling tools. That a product differs from competitive ones does not mean, of course, that the difference necessarily will sell more merchandise—the difference must be a definite *plus* value of *demonstrable* importance to the buyer.

Be careful that you are not lulled into a pleasant dream by the glowing description you may get of a product from its maker. Human nature being what it is, almost any advertiser may be overly enthusiastic about what he has to offer. He may endow his product with advantages that actually don't exist outside his own imagination. Only your own close study of the product, independent laboratory tests, or large-scale sampling studies can give an unbiased comparison between two or more similar products-at least insofar as possible consumer reaction and your copy approach are concerned.

Such laboratory tests or samplings, though they may be fairly expensive, often prove to be excellent investments. If, as a result, the product lives up to expectations, buyers will respond more readily to copy backed by impartial comparisons than to copy filled with unproved claims. An example was the well-known "22% Cooler" claim made for Palm Beach suits. Men believed this claim because it was based on actual scientific tests of all leading summer suitings conducted by a completely impartial laboratory. Make this coolness claim without proof and you lose believability.

P IS FOR PROSPECTS

When you have examined the foregoing product considerations you will have explored only one area of the pre-copy approach. Now that you have though about the product, what about the people you hope will buy your goods instead of your competitor's? You must know these people equally well.

In many instances, you will know clearly

who your best prospects are. In many others, what you may consider "obvious" may be wrong. You might think that men would be your best prospects for men's shirts. You may find that they are not. To your surprise you may find that so many wives shop for their husbands that women buy more men's shirts than men do!

Never ride a wild conclusion when determining who are your best prospects. Get the facts—from actual sales studies. Find out:

1. *Are your best prospects men or women?* For maximum effectiveness, your copy must be "aimed" at your best prospects—not at just anyone. Certain copy approaches appeal especially to men, others to women. When you write to women, for example, your copy should be consistently directed to women *only* if it is going to be fully effective. If, as with cigarettes, both sexes are large buyers, your copy will be written to appeal to both. To sum up: Decide whether your product will appeal to men, women, or to both men and women. Having determined this, key your writing to fit the group.

2. *Are they young, middle-aged, or old?* And why is this knowledge of value? Because, as people grow older, as they proceed from grade school, to college, to business, to marriage, to a family, to middle age, and on to grandparenthood, both their needs and desires for products change. Children, certainly, are your *best* potential customers for bubble gum. Children are your *worst* prospects for automobiles—the law and the family budget see to that. Young married couples buy the largest percentage of baby necessities, but they put up strong resistance to the cemetery-lot salesman. Older people (the target is specifically "people over 35") are fine prospects for home improvement products, but would laugh if you tried to sell them boxing gloves or popsicles. So birthdays are important—not only to the people themselves but also to the copywriters who can make money out of birthdays if they key their copy to the age.

3. *Are your best prospects rich, poor, or average?* Who, would you say, would be your best prospects if you were writing an advertisement for fur coats—women of wealth, women of average menas, or working girls? The answer to that question would depend on what *kind* of fur coats you were writing about! You'd know that Park Avenue or Gold Coast women would be your best bets for ermine evening wraps. You would know, too, that the Park Avenue prospect would shudder at the low-priced, dyed-rabbit coat that a low-paid shop girl would go without lunches to buy. Sex, age, and income thus, are important factors in the movement of many types of merchandise. The problem of income and buying habits is a very complex but interesting one and should be studied thoroughly.

4. *Where do most of your prospects live?* If your product is burglary insurance, your best prospects would be among city dwellers, because statistics show that a huge percentage of burglaries occur in cities. Small-town people, on the other hand, would probably be more interested in your copy story on home canning equipment than would urbanites. Farm families, logically, are your audience if you're writing about agricultural equipment. Again you may say, "But all those things are obvious." You're right. Throughout this entire chapter you have been given examples that would be obvious to any thinking person. Why? Because when you, and the next

person, and the next person write copy you tend to forget what was once so obvious to you. You forget the simple truths—the "obvious" thinkings that make your copy sell. You get so wrapped up in technique and the ultra-refinements of the copywriter's art that you forget these obvious truths and facts that sell merchandise. This section, accordingly, has not endeavored to be subtle. You have been told—"when writing to women then write exclusively to women"—"when writing about a home canning product then write primarily to small-town or country dwellers." If you learn these obvious stratagems early in your copy career—and *remember* them—you'll be a better copywriter.

To show you how the obvious can be overlooked, wouldn't you think that it would be a waste of money for an advertiser to take large space in California newspapers to warn motorists to *"Get Set Now for Winter's Sub-zero Blasts!"*? But—one major advertiser did just that! The illustration showed Old Man Winter blowing an icy breath. It failed, however, to chill the sun-tanned spines of Californians, who hooted over this advertisement. The copy pushed antifreeze, tire chains, high-powered heaters, and other arctic equipment—all of which the average Californian has as much use for as he has Florida oranges—— unless he plans to spend the entire winter skiing in the Sierras.

Remember, *where* your prospect lives—his location—has a direct bearing on *how* he lives, and often affects his wants or needs.

5. *What are your prospects' tastes in reading, in TV, in radio?* If you have been able to determine the sex, age, income and habitat of your prospects, you have covered some of the important points of their private lives. You will still want to know something about their *preferences* in reading and in TV and radio. What kinds of newspapers and magazines do they usually read? Do they read the *New York Times, Harper's, Fortune,* and the *Wall Street Journal,* or perhaps a tabloid newspaper, *True Story, Playboy* and *Variety?*

When they watch television do they lean toward high drama or low comedy, sports and news, or westerns? In radio listening are they likely to be hearing your commercials in the car, driving home from work, or at home doing the ironing?

In cross section studies of potential consumers, the equal appeal of a product to different groups often necessitiates diversified radio or television advertising. This wide appeal is particularly true of products such as cereals, which are equally enjoyed by children and adults. You'll agree that a cereal television commercial written for use on a show produced for young children is not likely to have much selling appeal for the TV viewers of one of the cereal maker's adult shows.

6. *How much do your prospects already know about the product?* Are most of your best prospects already familiar with the product, as are most people now familiar with home permanents, for instance? Or is it a new product, whose utility or other benefits must be clearly explained as Toni Home Permanent originally had to be explained? How *much* potential buyers know about the product, and how *well* they know it, will definitely affect your copy "pitch."

Starting your copy in either case will give you certain difficulties. If your product is well-known, you either (1) say the same thing over and over again hoping to sell through repetition, or (2) work for new ways to start your copy. If you use this latter technique, copy will "start" out of your inventiveness and your application of the P's. You'll strain to give an old story a new fascination in each advertisement.

On the other hand, your problem with a new product is that you can assume so little. You're not entirely sure of your prospects, since you cannot tell by any previous sales record, as in the case of an already marketed product, how the consumers react to your product and copy message. The reader will not know your product name, how it works, what it's made of, who makes it, and just what it will do for the buyer. You must explain and sell and you must do your best to gauge your reader's interest in and knowledge of the type of product you are advertising. If he is already acquainted with the type of product, for instance, it will make your copy job easier even if *your* product, is being put on the market for the first time. It may mean that you will need to do less selling of the need for the product. Advertising of similar products may have given your type of product an acceptability to the general public. Thus, you may start off your copy confident that you don't need to stress the need for the product so much as the qualities of *your* product that make it superior to other similar ones on the market.

P IS FOR PURCHASES

You now have arrived at the point where you may think you have done enough analyzing to enable you to create sizzling campaigns that will start a panic at the cash register of every store in the country selling your product. Perhaps you hanker to get your ideas down on paper while you're "inspired"—but wait just a minute! You may know a good deal about your product. You may know fairly well the people who should be your best prospects. There are still, however, some important points you haven't touched—points that affect the actual *buying* of the product.

1. *Where do customers buy the product?* Early in his career every copywriter must reconcile himself to the fact that most people are *not* particularly anxious to buy the products for which he's writing copy. During World War II, when shortages existed, a single whisper from a sales girl to a friend could have sold a carload of nylon stockings. That's because there weren't enough nylons to go around. Normally, in peacetime there's *more* than enough of all commodities. There's plenty of your product and plenty of your competitors'. The public, under normal conditions, won't react to your selling message with a fraction of the mad greed they displayed for nylon stockings a few years back.

Today it is now enough to sell people merely on the *desirability* of your product. You must be a sort of remote-control Pied Piper, and lure them from their easy chairs right down to the store. You must make it as *easy as possible* for them to buy. Unless the product is one that is so well established that everyone knows where he can buy it, you'll want to *tell* him where it is sold—whether at drug stores, hardware stores, grocery stores, or all three! Never leave any question in his mind, since, unless you're selling diamond rings for a dollar, few people will be so anxious to purchase your product that they will be willing to go out and *search* for a place that handles it! *Tell* your readers or listeners where they can buy it! And be as specific as possible. Don't rely on such empty phrases as "sold by leading stores everywhere" or "get it at your nearest dealer's."

The first of those statements possibly has some vague value as advertising. It may enhance the prestige of the product in the minds of a small percentage of prospects. Some people may reason, if they take the trouble, that if leading stores carry it, it must be good. But this type of statement is sometimes no more than an expression of wishful thinking on the part of the advertiser, and it often backfires to his disadvantage. To illustrate, picture a man reading a shoe advertisement in a national magazine. The shoes look good to him, and he wants to buy a pair. The advertisement explains that he can get them "at better stores coast to coast." He concludes from that phrase that Macy's carries this particular brand. Certainly, Macy's is a "better store," so he goes down to Macy's. He finds that Macy's doesn't carry the brand in which he's interested, and what happens? While in Macy's he eyes a pair of shoes by a different maker and decides to buy them instead. The copywriter who wrote the shoe advertisement that appealed to this man actually ended up by making a sale for a competitive brand! Wouldn't it have been much wiser if this manufacturer (as so many do) had clearly listed his dealers in the classified section of the phone book and advised readers to "see the classified section of your phone book for name of your nearest dealer"? Or the maker could run in the advertisement a list of stores in the country that sell the shoes.

Similarly, the phrase "Get it at your nearest dealer's" is meaningless if a prospect doesn't have any idea where his nearest dealer is. He might be 75 miles away for all the reader may know! You have to *tell* him where he can buy all but the most commonplace products. If he can get your brand *only* at Safeway stores, *tell* so. If *all* good stores carry it, *tell* him so. If he can get the name and address of his nearest dealer by calling a telephone number, *tell* him so. If he can order by mail, *tell* him so. Do everything within your power to make it *easy* for prospects to *buy!*

2. *Are purchases primarily seasonal or for special occasions?* Most products sell well all year round. Many are sold as seasonal items. You'd know that snow shovels, Christmas-tree lights, and ice skates aren't bought in June; and you wouldn't be surprised that lawn mowers, flower seeds, and sun shades would sell poorly in winter. But what about electric light bulbs? Do they sell equally well throughout the year? Offhand, if you didn't stop to analyze it, you might well answer "yes" to that question. But, because it is dark earlier to winter—which means more use of electricity and more burned-out bulbs—sales are naturally greater during the winter months.

Similarly, you might reason that because people must know the time every day, watches wouldn't be subject to any sharp rises and falls in sales. But you'd be wrong, because watches—and perfume, jewelry, and candy, to name but a few—are largely bought as gifts for Christmas, graduations, birthdays, and wedding anniversaries. Thus, they are referred to as "special occasion" items.

Why is it important that you know whether the products for which you are writing copy sell more readily in one period than another? Or are bought primarily as gifts? The answer is—to help you avoid misdirecting your copy. For instance, suppose you are an agency copywriter and you are assigned to write copy on watches. The contact man, or account executive in charge of the account, is so familiar himself with the peculiarities of the market that he may take it for granted that you know the slant your copy should take. Without knowing that most people receive their watches as gifts, you might naturally assume that your primary object would be to persuade the reader to buy a watch for his own use. In actual practice, you'd probably have much better results if you told him the watch would make a wonderful gift for his son's coming graduation.

If there's the slightest question in your mind as to whether or not a product falls into one of these specialized categories, ask, don't guess, in order that you can be sure you're aiming at the right market! Be humble and remember that although *you* might think candy bars sell in about the same volume every month of the year, actually they don't.

3. *Is purchase premeditated or impulsive?* Any major purchase, such as a car, fur coat, refrigerator or stereo component system, is usually made only after lengthy consideration. Before buying, people usually debate their actual *need* for a new stove. They ask themselves if, instead of buying a new sofa, they might not have their old sofa repaired. In the purchase of an automobile there is usually a long deliberation as to the family's ability to pay for a car. Even after a decision has been made to buy the super-deluxe, they still take their time before actually making the purchase. Almost any major purchase is made slowly. The buyers "shop around," comparing one radio-phonograph against several others, one pressure cooker against its competitors.

Even some relatively low-priced items are bought this way. Phonograph records, for example. People listen—often to half a dozen or more recordings of the same popular tune—before they buy.

Such sales are made only after the buyer has "weighed the facts." Thus they are termed "premeditated purchases," to differentiate them from what are known as "impulse purchases." In this latter classification falls such merchandise as chewing gum, soft drinks, cigarettes—and any and all other goods people normally buy without going through the long, involved process of reasoning that precedes a "premeditated purchase." A typical impulse buyer is the man who inserts a coin in the Coke dispenser in a service station. He drives in for the sole purpose of getting gas, but, when he sees the Coca-Cola cooler, he decides to have a cool drink. His purchase is completely impulsive.

To show the extent of impulse buying various researchers interested in grocery buying habits, have pointed out that more than 50% of women shoppers buy one-third of their groceries on impulse. Does your product come within this one-third group?

You should learn into which category a product falls if you hope to attain maximum effectiveness in your copy. You can be gay and capricious—and deal in generalities—in an advertisement for a bubble bath. The technique changes when you're persuading a man to part with several thousand dollars for a Cadillac. He wants fact, not foolishness—sincerity, not simpering.

If you want to "win friends and influence people," be sure your copy is always tuned in the right key.

4. *How does the price of your product compare with prices charged by competitors?* If a buyer has a choice between two products he considers to be of equal merit, and equal renown, and finds that one is priced appreciably lower than the other, he is almost certain to take the one that costs less.

Price, especially in times of economic

distress, is an important factor in the selling of merchandise. You are handicapped if you don't know how the price of your products compares with the prices of competitive goods. If your price is appreciably higher, then you will want to explain, as convincingly as you can, *why* it's higher. If it's lower, you'll want to tell your readers or listeners that they not only can get good service from your product, but also that they save money by buying it rather than some other make!

If a copywriter collected personally all the data needed for an analysis similar to the one presented, he would be taking too much time from his writing job. No copywriter would be *expected* to gather it all. Much of it may have been already well-established by previous experience with the given product. Most of the rest will come from research studies. You *can* take an active part by doing what has for many years been popularized as "The Hat Trick." That is, you should put on your hat and go out and do some *first-hand* research on your own hook. Make a representative number of the interviews yourself. Ask questions—not among your own friends, but of the ordinary people on the street. Talk to dealers and wholesalers. Talk to people who use your product and like it. Find out *why* they like it! Talk to people who have tried your product but now use something else. Find out *why* they didn't like your product! Do "The Hat Trick"—often and thoroughly.

Your study of the basic strategy is now completed. And you, personally, have gone out and done enough personal research to give you a good "feel" of the problem.

You now have what seem to be *all* the pertinent facts.

You have determined what seem to be your best selling points. You've identified what seem to be your best prospects. And you've come to a decision on how best to reach these prospects.

You are ready now to start "building" a good, sound advertising program that will sell more of your goods to more and more people.

THE CAMPAIGN THEME

Once the basic sales strategy for any product or service is established, the next step is to develop a campaign theme. This is the "vehicle" in which you "deliver" your selling points to the public. It's the central idea—the imaginative "spark plug"—that will give your advertisements continuity, recall value, and thus, extra selling power.

Your theme is the life line of your campaign, and its development will largely be your responsibility, as the copywriter. So take your time: make sure you develop a *good* theme. The success of the entire campaign may well hinge on the effectiveness of your theme.

Copywriters working on the national level almost always are looking for big ideas, or themes, that can be repeated in many advertisements as part of a long—run campaign. Even on the local level, the copywriters for such organizations as banks and dairies will work mightily to come up with a strong campaign theme that will be used many times with effectiveness. The writer who consistently presents "campaign" themes or ideas is the one who shoots ahead in advertising, not the one who thinks only in terms of "one—shotters." In the following material you will be given some suggestions for utilizing certain basics from which powerful advertising themes spring.

You have already determined from your basic strategy planning *why* people might buy yours and similar products, what they *want* and *expect* for their money. Your first interest is to develop a theme that will, over a long period, influence a large number of people to want and buy *your* product instead of that of a competitor. To accomplish this you want to appeal to *their own selfish interests.*

Just what are the human "selfish" appeals at your disposal? Authorities disagree. Some copy experts cite as many as 24, while psychologists say there are really only three—fear, love, and hunger. Other authorities give varying numbers. Actually, the psychologists are probably correct in stating that all human appeals stem from fear, love, or hunger of one kind or another. In practical use, this fundamental concept is quite limiting. For a workable breakdown, consider the following list, which is comprehensive, yet brief enough for convenience.

As you go over these appeals, evaluate each one as it applies to yourself. Not until you do that can you fully appreciate the wide extent of their power in influencing people to buy the goods you have to sell. You will discover something more in going over these appeals—that they often overlap. Thus, an advertisement will contain several basic appeals. Possibly all of them are equally strong, or it may be that one appeal clearly dominates.

BASIC HUMAN APPEALS

Acquisitiveness — desire for money, power prestige, efficiency, material possessions.

Comfort — desire for physical comfort, rest, leisure, peace of mind.

Convenience — desire to eliminate work, to do tasks more easily.

Curiosity — desire for any kind of new experience.

Egotism — desire to be attractive, popular, praised.

Family affection, togetherness and happy home life — desire to do things as a family unit, to please members of the family, to help children in their growing years.

Fear — of pain, death, poverty, criticism; loss of possessions, beauty, popularity, and loved ones.

Health — desire for good health, longevity, youthful vigor.

Hero worship — desire to be like people we admire.

Kindness, generosity, and unselfishness — desire to help others, one's country, one's church.

Love and sex — desire for romantic love, normal sex life.

Mental stimulation — desire to improve mind, to broaden mental horizons.

Pleasure — desires fulfilled through fun, travel, entertainment, enjoyment in general.

Sensory appeals — desire for any stimulus received through any of the five senses.

As illustrations of how the foregoing may be used in developing advertising campaign themes, following are a number of familiar products whose advertising consistently reflects one or more of these basic appeals. You will recognize immediately the association between the appeal and the product sales story, even though through the years, different words and different slogans and copy approaches have been used to express the idea.

In studying these products and relating their sales stories to the basic appeals you will again be aware that almost all of them employ *multiple* appeals. In many cases one appeal can be made unmistakably dominant. Many advertisements, however, seem to put equal stress on two or more appeals. A Goodyear tire advertisement might, through illustration

Appeal	Headline of advertisement	Product	Advertiser
Acquisitiveness	Any 14 records — $2.98	Phonograph records	Columbia House
	Win Planters Peanuts Discovery Sweepstakes	Peanuts	Planters Peanuts
	Just think, for the price of a Rolls Royce you can own a good watch	Watch	Audemars Piquet
	For those who want the best	Camera	Petri International Corp.
Comfort	Beautyrest. The overnight vacation	Mattress	Simmons
	Bauer Goose Down Guarantees you warm hands and feet	Mitts	Eddie Bauer
	"Fuller cut" comfortable classic corduroy slacks $15	Slacks	Cable Car Clothiers
	Evans makes your feet feel at home	Slippers	L. B. Evans Son Co.
Convenience	The sunny floor that shines without waxing	Floor Covering	Armstrong
	Now the great stores come to you	Shopping by mail	The Kenton Collection
	Introducing Betty Crocker Snackin' Cake (You mix, bake and serve it right in the same pan.)	Cake	General Mills
	Effortless way to go up and down stairs	Stairway elevator	The Cheney Co.
Curiosity	This is our coffee shop. Just imagine what the rest of the place is like	Hotel	Boca Raton Hotel & Club
	Come to Abaco. Away from everything but you. And people like you	Travel	Bahama Islands Tourist Office
	Ontario: Discover us	Travel	Ontario Adventures
	Cormorant fishing, crocodile farms, mouth-watering Babi Goling, and 999 other experiences you could miss in the orient (without this free book)	Travel brochure	Cathay Pacific Airways
Egotism	That great "Touch & Glow" face	Moisturizer	Revlon
	To know you're the best you can be	Hair color	Miss Clairol

	This look was invented for men. But meant for you	Trousers for women	J. C. Penney
	Sarah knows how lovely you can be	Jewelry	Sarah Coventry
Family affection, togetherness and happy home life	The more they eat, the better you feel	Oatmeal	Quaker Oats
	Take your wife and kids to a faraway tropical island. About 8 minutes from Miami	Hotel	Royal Biscayne
	Kids build Lego. Lego builds kids.	Building toys	Samsonite
	Jell-O just introduced Soft Swirl. (So you can treat your family like company.)	Dessert	General Foods
Fear	Two weeks in the hospital can cost you two months in wages	Health care	Aetna Life & Casualty
	If you have a bad break do you have to go broke?	Accident insurance	Commericial Travelers Insurance Company
	Sore eyes may mean styes	Eye medication	
	Maybe you've been brushing your teeth wrong all these years	Toothbrush	Pycopay
Health	Only a dentist can give him a better fluoride treatment	Toothpaste	Colgate
	Kills germs on contact	Lensine	Lensine
	When were you last really fit?	Muscle developer	Bullworker Service
	Sani-Flush wipes out common household germs in 15 seconds	Cleaner	Boyce Midway
Hero worship –	Come to Marlboro country	Cigarettes	
	"My Sears Kenmore sewing machine has 9 different stretch stitches – imagine!" say famous designer Bonnie Cashin.	Sewing machine	Sears Roebuck
	Big Wilt watch	Wrist watch	The Dudley Do-Right Emporium
	Buy Chiquita bananas and get Bubba Smith free	Bananas	United Brands

Kindness, generosity and unselfishness	"Please take care of my sister. . ."	Charity	Christian Children's Fund, Inc.
	You can help save Aurora Cortez for $15 a month. Or you can turn the page	Charity	Save the Children Federation
	Raul lives on 14¢ a day	Charity	Foster Parents Plan, Inc.
	Give them this day their daily bread	Charity	NAACP Emergency Relief Fund
Love and Sex	"At the rate he's moving into the fashion scene, contemporary man is fast becoming an object of sexual delight"	Shirts	Gino Paoli
	Lead him on like a lady. Lead him with Bellodgia.	Perfume	Caron
	All my men wear English leather. Every one of them.	Cologne	Mem Company
	Of all the ways to say I love you, mink is the warmest	Fur coat	Saga Mink
Mental stimulation	The new book of knowledge brings it all home	Book	Grolier, Inc.
	Easy talk tells *your* little learner his favorite story	Cassette records	Sears Roebuck
	This Christmas give their minds pictures and words to play with	Set of books	Field Enterprises
Pleasure	If you want to remember us, just look at some thing beautiful	Hotel	Guam Hotal Okura
	A summer adventure in Chamonix, France	Summer in France	Summer Adventures, Inc.
	Have a more carefree vacation. . .get an AC tune-up now	Spark plugs	General Motors
	I want to go on your Ladies' Home Journal Sunjet holiday	Vacation trip	Ladies' Home Journal
Sensory appeals	The Clairol herbal essence shampoo experience	Shampoo	Clairol
	Lady, be cool	Menthol cigarettes	Brown & Williamson
	Our marriage will cause quite a stir	Whisky and club soda	Early Times Distillers and Canada Dry
	Turkey or Grand Turkey The difference is a spoonful of Grand Marnier	Liqueur	Carillon Importers

and headline treatment, put over a smashing stress on fear. The copy will carry out this theme but will do so through a strong appeal to family love. The father will be urged to protect his wife and children against the hazards of a blowout. A copy section at the bottom of the advertisement emphasizes a strong third point—economy.

In many products you will find it possible to develop a theme that will intermingle appeals so that it is difficult to say just which is dominant. The famous and long-used theme for Pond's Cold Cream, "She's engaged! She's lovely! She uses Pond's!" *primarily* exemplified the hero-worship appeal. With equal justice it could be said to have used an appeal to sex or romantic love. A good case could be made for egotism in this theme also.

Although it is difficult and sometimes impossible to develop a theme which falls unmistakably into one appeal classification, it is best to try to come as close to this goal as possible. A "shotgun" theme which embraces several appeals may often fail to carry out your basic sales strategy by weakening the punch of your copy message.

All advertising, of course, is not built on such attention-catching themes as those given as examples. All advertising, however—even one-time insertions—should be built on a central theme that appeals to the prospect through one or more basic human interests. *The important thing to remember is to choose the appeal or appeals that will have the greatest interest for the greatest number of your prospects.*

U.S.P, suffering points and point of difference

Some years ago Rosser Reeves, a prominent advertising agency executive, stirred the advertising world with his book *Reality In Advertising.* In this short book he made a number of powerful points that caused endless discussion in advertising circles. One of the most important phrases to come from that book was "Unique Selling Proposition," or U.S.P. To paraphrase from the definition in the book, the U.S.P. is a proposition each advertisement makes that is powerful, unique and not offered by the competition. Sometimes the uniqueness lies in the product or in a claim that is made for the product. An example of the latter was Colgate's "Cleans your breath while it cleans your teeth."

What you must do in those minutes or hours before writing your copy is to look for the U.S.P. Sometimes it jumps right out at you. Consider the attributes of the four following products:

Product No. 1:	A power lawn mower that cuts tall grass evenly even when the grass is soaking wet.
Product No. 2:	Canned cream that tastes exactly like real cream.
Product No. 3:	An alarm clock that plays Brahms Lullaby.
Product No. 4:	A magnesium tray that polishes silver without rubbing.

Can you always find a distinct U.S.P. in a product or service? No. If you're ingenious enough, however, you may be able to devise a unique claim such as that mentioned for Colgate. But suppose you can't seem to dig out any usable U.S.P.? Here is where you might rely on the *suffering points* approach.

A suffering point is the need of the consumer that possession of the product will satisfy. Remember that people do not buy products; they buy *uses* of the product that will take care of some problem they have. A product may take care of a consumer's suffering points without having U.S.P.

For example, after Teflon-coated frying pans became common, these products still answered a suffering point — the tendency of food to stick to frying pans. To take another product, a suffering point voiced by millions of non-professional painters was the dripping of the paint and its regrettable habit of running down the paintbrush when the brush was held above shoulder level. DuPont's *Lucite* answered this problem.

Look for your suffering points in every product you advertise and bring them up humanly and believably. Suffer with the reader. Sympathize. Let him or her know that you appreciate the problem and then tell how your product solves that problem.

And then we come to the *"point–of–difference."* While this would seem to be another way of saying U.S.P., it isn't necessarily. It may not be a U.S.P. that makes you different from your competition but merely a quality or product feature that makes it sharper, longer-lasting, cheaper to run. It could be a brighter picture tube in the television set, or a more sensitive tuning device.

Since advertising is so intensely competitive, every copywriter before he begins to write will ask the account executive, the advertising manager, or someone else who should know: "What do we have that's different? *Is* there a point of difference?"

He has a sinking feeling if the answer is "No." If he is given such a difference he immediately, if it's important enough, considers it for use in the headline, the opening copy, and the illustration.

If the difference is not very important, it simply becomes one of the selling points of the advertisement. If it's important enough to be considered a U.S.P. of the product, he will usually build the whole advertisement around it because, of course the best point of difference is a U.S.P.

The most powerful type of advertisement is one that has a strong U.S.P. that is slammed home to the reader by having it stressed in headline, illustration and opening copy. Yet, too often, we see advertisements that stress the most powerful point in headline and illustration but neglect it in the opening copy, or push it in headline and opening copy but let the illustration go off in another direction. All advertisements should have 3-way power..

↓
push headline
open copy
illustration reinforcement

Art and Copy: The Inseparables.

5

Very often you hear it said of an advertising campaign that it's a "copy" campaign, or an "art" campaign. In the former, the copy is so unusual and forceful that the art seems subordinate. Just the opposite is true in the "art" campaign.

The very use of these terms implies a sort of competition between copywriters and artists to see who can play the dominant role in the creating of advertisements. Such a competition exists to some extent but most copywriters are grateful to the artists for providing a showcase for their words, and most artists are content in the knowledge that they have, through their layouts and illustrations, made the copy more effective.

Actually, one of the most important phases of your daily routine is your relationship with your art colleagues. The work of an art director can make or break a copywriter.

You can work up the most effective advertising campaign ever conceived, copywise, and see it fail as a selling tool simply because of inferior layout and art handling. On the other hand, many advertising campaigns presenting no new or fresh copy treatment prove outstanding in selling power because of brilliant art work.

There is no sure way to determine whether the effectiveness of any particular piece of advertising is based on copy or art. One can very rarely stand by itself. Advertising agency graveyards are full of the gravestones of copywriters and artists who never learned the fundamental fact of teamwork.

It *is* teamwork—between you and your art associates—that will result in sound, selling advertisements, properly executed for maximum impact upon readers. Regardless of what some self-styled artist-copywriters may tell you, there is no room for the "I-can-do-it-alone" technique. If you learn quickly how to get along with your art people, you will have taken a major step toward your creative goal.

ARE ARTISTS ADVERTISING MEN?

Among top advertising men throughout the nation, there are some excellent artists who have strayed from their creative field and have assumed positions of importance in executive capacities other than art direction. A few have become heads of advertising agencies, large and small. Others are in charge of the advertising activities of department stores, and other retail operations. Art people will usually deny special interest in any part of the advertising business but their own. The varied and complex business matters which you, as a copywriter, must know to do your part of the creative job properly, have no direct bearing upon the work of your art director *from his standpoint,* though many of them have definite bearing upon the general layout and character of the advertisement itself. Proper emphasis, for example, of certain sales points, or policy matters, are not and should not be part of the art director's responsibility, but yours. If the art director *does* interest himself in these matters—fine, but they are "musts" for you.

WHO'S BOSS?

Probably the most common error that copywriters make in attempting to cooperate with artists, is to assume too much responsibility in "art direction." The average copywriter, in an agency or elsewhere, would bristle if one of his art colleagues tried to tell him how to write his copy, or criticized the manner in which he had already written it. Yet that same writer who has written his headline, has suggested an illustrative device, and has made a very amateurish sketch of what he thinks the layout should look like, will often sit right at his art director's elbow and will try to tell him exactly how to proceed. He will offer advice on styles of artwork, typography, lettering, and decoration. He will insist on photography when the artist believes drawings or paintings to be more satisfactory. He will bullishly reject layouts over which the artist has spent hours because he personally prefers something "just a little different." The result of all this is that he will wind up with an association between himself and his key co-worker that is little less than a contest to see who has the last say.

Remember that you are not an art director. There is no doubt that you can and should offer valuable suggestions about your layouts. From you, the art director must obtain all the essential information about what elements are most important to the ultimate selling job. From you, he can gain the background of the problem—background which he must understand to get the proper "feeling" into his work. Not only can he use this sort of assistance from you, but he can't do justice to his own job without it. If he is capable, and he usually will be, he will almost always turn out a better layout and supervise a better job if he is permitted to use his own imagination without heckling from you.

The goal is to produce advertising of which you both can be proud—you of the thinking behind the advertisement, the power and clarity of the selling ideas, and he of the physical execution of these ideas. This goal can be reached only by mutual recognition of each other's talents and the blending of them in smooth-running cooperation.

Any art director will welcome suggestions from you upon which he may improvise. Artists see, in you, art of another sort. They don't think of you as a dull and uninspired drudge whose ideas are worthless. Most of them will admit that they're glad *they* aren't faced with the responsibility of conceiving the original ideas. Artists are, after all, specialists in translating ideas to layouts and illustrations and they are much better at it than any copywriter or group of copywriters.

Regardless of the type of copy work you do, if your art associates realize that you consider the creation of advertising a job of close and friendly teamwork—if you can establish a method of joint operation with them—you will discover a richness and a satisfaction in the routine of your daily work that many copywriters never find. Such richness will help produce good advertisements. The success of your career as a copywriter depends in a large measure upon your knowledge of human psychology. Don't let that knowledge apply only to the people who read your advertisements. Put it to work in your own personal relations every day. Nowhere will it pay off any more fully than in your dealings with your art directors.

HOW MUCH TO KNOW OF ART

Beginners in copywriting generally feel that a thorough working knowledge of art and layout is a good thing for them to have. Some young men and women, aspiring to be advertising writers, even study art in art schools to better grasp the problems they think will be confronting them. It may be better for a copywriter to know nothing at all of art than to know just enough to make him *think* he knows a lot. Alexander Pope's "A little learning is a dangerous thing" applies very well here.

This is certainly true from the standpoint of economy of effort. Wherever you work, agency, department store, retail shop, direct mail, or mail-order house, you will have available the services of men and women trained thoroughly in the job of making layouts and supervising artwork. It is their responsibility to take your ideas and make attractive and compelling layouts from them. If you, the copywriter, have a wide knowledge of art and layout, you will tend to spend

HAWAII
ALASKA
JAMAICA
SKIING
CAMPING
YELLOWSTONE
SURFING
SWIMMING
Europe
CANADA
SOUND GOOD?
Then join the Big E's all new Bonus Vacation Club.
Have cash for your next vacation. Make 50 weekly payments (you decide the amount) into your Vacation Club and the Big E'll give a bonus of an extra week free for completing your club.
Start your Vacation Club any time of the year and a year later you'll be ready to start out for the time of your life, and cash to pay for it.
GRAND CANYON
lake louise
MIAMI
If you would like to open your Bonus Vacation Club by mail, fill out coupon and mail it to us. We'll send you your Vacation Book by return mail.
the BIG E
the ELMIRA SAVINGS BANK
EAST WATER AT BALDWIN ELMIRA, NEW YORK
1102 GRAND CENTRAL AVE. HORSEHEADS, NEW YORK
MEMBER FEDERAL DEPOSIT INSURANCE CORPORATION
THE ELMIRA SAVINGS BANK
East Water at Baldwin Streets, Elmira, New York
Open a Bonus Vacation Club in my name. Enclosed is my check/money order in the amount of $ ______ for payment Number 1 through payment Number ____. (Please indicate number of payment if more than one payment is made.) Start my club on ______.
NAME
ADDRESS
CITY
STATE
Please Check Club Class Below:
$1.00 $3.00 $5.00 $10.00 $20.00

Fig. 3-1

Effect created by typography.

A careful selection of type faces has helped enhance the vacation feeling desired for this newspaper bank advertisement.

time which should be spent in copywriting, making rough layouts. In all probability these will neither be used nor appreciated by your artists. After all, no two artists will ever see a layout job exactly the same way.

Far better to set your ideas down on paper, *write* your suggestions for illustrations, supply the other necessary elements, such as headlines and subheads, and then forget them until you have something to look at *done by a specialist.* Then, if you have suggestions to make—if you would prefer to see some slightly different style of handling—*and you really feel that your criticisms are justified* for the good of the advertisement—then is the time to take them up. You'll get along better that way with the person it's most important to get along with. You'll have more time for your own job, copywriting. Also, copywriters' roughs often make lazy artists. They are tempted merely to "dress up" copywriters' ideas instead of applying their specialized knowledge of layout to designing the advertisement as it should be designed.

Assuming that you have reasonably sensible taste, that you aren't addicted to wearing chartreuse shirts with lavender ties, all you need to know about art is what you will normally learn working with and around artists.

Fig. 3-2

Thumbnail.

This is a very rough, small sketch that gave the artist a starting point for what you will see in Fig. 3-3 and Fig. 3-4.

Give him something he'll treasure for weeks.

Creative advertising people are notoriously willing talkers, and a question here and there, when you don't understand a term or a problem, will produce the artist's "short course" in that particular subject. If you have the time and inclination, the reading of a book or two on art and layout won't hurt.

Most of your important relationships with the art department, wherever you work, will be concerned with *print* advertising.

Many advertising agencies, however, maintain specially trained and talented art directors whose duties are entirely confined to *television visualization.* In no phase of creative advertising is an individual expected to be so versatile and flexible as in the creating of television "storyboards." Although concentration in this chapter is on the need for copywriter-artist cooperation in turning out good print advertising, the ever-increasing importance of TV creation must be mentioned here lest it be overlooked.

Certain important fundamentals of art which can influence the success of your advertising will be covered very briefly here. At the close of this chapter you will find a short glossary of everyday terms used jointly by copy and art people. Other than learning these few basic facts and terms, you'd better be a copywriter first and an artist last.

LAYOUT

A layout, as its name implies, is the physical grouping of all the elements in an advertisement, as originally conceived by the artist. When you have decided upon a headline, subheads, captions, and illustrative suggestion for any given advertisement, you will present an artist with this material, pointing out which selling points are to get the main emphasis, and in what sequence the other elements of the advertisement should logically follow. From this information, the artist will then arrange the advertisement in an orderly, balanced manner, roughing in your headline and making a very rough sketch of your illustrative suggestion (or a different one, if he thinks it would work better). This is called a *rough layout* (or *visual*), and from it you can determine whether or not the final job will maintain the place you desire, will focus proper attention on the right parts of your message, and, in general, whether your idea is going to "jell." solidify

During your early years as a copywriter (cub, apprentice, or whatever your organization calls you), you will doubtless be working under a copy chief or supervisor, with whom you will be required to clear your ideas before passing them on to members of the art department. When the artist has made his rough layout, you will then discuss it with your superiors, and the three of you will decide whether it is okay to proceed, or whether more roughs are needed. Possibly, especially if you are working in an advertising agency, the rough layout, or layouts, will also be shown to others who are working on the account—contact men, account executives, and, on some occa-

Give him something he'll treasure for weeks.
To Dad

Fig. 3-3

Comprehensive.

This was one of the later steps stemming from the thumbnail in Fig. 3-2.

Courtesy Doyle Dane Bernbach, Inc.

sions, even representatives of the client's advertising department.

Finished and comprehensive layouts

Once the rough layout is approved by all those who are concerned with its formative stages, the artist is ready to do *a finished layout* or *comprehensive layout.* (See Figures 3-3 and 3-6.) Finished layouts are more complete than "roughs." Lettering is done rather carefully and pictures may be sketched. The client can obtain an accurate idea from the finished layout just what the printed advertisement will look like.

The comprehensive is a layout which carries the elements of the advertisement into a more refined stage. It serves two purposes. One is to present the elements to the people who have the final say in okaying them for publication. Two is to solicit new business or to present an entirely new departure for an old campaign.

When advertisements are presented formally, you must be sure that all major elements in the advertisement appear as nearly as possible the way they will actually look in the printed advertisement. Since most of your clients will not possess the trained imagination of you

Give him something he'll treasure for weeks.
CHIVAS REGAL
1801
BLENDED SCOTCH WHISKY
To Dad

Fig. 3-4

Magazine advertisement that came from Fig. 3-2 and Fig. 3-3.

and your art director, they will be unable to visualize the finished advertisement from a rough layout. In finished and comprehensive layouts, therefore, the standard procedure is to letter in carefully the headlines, subheads, and caption headings, and to include a fairly accurate sketch of the illustration. The comprehensive must be accurate enough to be followed easily by two more persons who "get in on the act" of turning out finished advertisements: the commercial artist who creates the "finished" artwork, or photograph; those who handle the printing and engraving and who must know exactly how to position the elements mechanically. (See Figures 3-4 and 3-7.)

Comprehensive layouts are done with extreme care and precision because of their use in presenting a new campaign idea or soliciting new business. Finished layouts, in contrast, are usually just "slick" enough to accomplish the purpose of giving a graphic idea of how the final job should look. When you ask an artist to make a comprehensive layout, he will very often ask *you, "How* comprehensive?" Then, according to the nature of the job, the production time element, and other considerations, you will describe to him just how far he is expected to go. A five- or six-word headline for a comprehensive layout can be lettered in by a good lettering man in a few minutes, but where you wish to show an exact type style or other precision lettering, the job may require several hours.

The thumbnail sketch

A third type of layout often used in advertising operations is called the "thumbnail sketch." (See Figure 3-2.) This is a very rough layout, done in one-half or one-fourth size, by the artist, and is normally used when you are considering several different ideas for a new campaign. From thumbnail sketches, it is possible for you and your art director to determine quickly whether an idea has possibilities. You may find, however, that the various units won't fit and that it would be a waste of time to go into further layout attempts.

In some places, the rule is that you should spend your time writing body copy and captions while the layout is being made, so that your entire advertisement will be ready for study at the same time. You can then take up any final copy-polishing while the finished or comprehensive layout is with the art department.

This "rule" depends, however, on the situation. As mentioned in a preceding chapter you may, when presenting campaign ideas, merely write headlines and suggest ideas for the main illustrations. The body copy can be done later.

If, however, you know what you want to write and you have done the needed background thinking and investigation, you may prefer to write all the copy in the advertisement before you give it to the artist, along with your illustration ideas. By so doing, you will help him since he will know how much space is to be occupied by the copy and can do his layout accordingly.

Sometimes, when the layout technique for a campaign has already been decided upon, you will write the same amount of copy for every advertisement since the illustration size will be the same in every instance and the space for the copy will not vary from advertisement to advertisement. Thus, you might set your typewriter to write 15 lines of 65 characters. While writing copy to such exact specifications can be irksome to some copywriters the practice results in copy that will fit precisely into space allotted.

ARTWORK, PRINTING, AND ENGRAVING

After the layout and copy for your advertisement have been okayed by all those whose approval is necessary, it is ready for *production.*

Production of any advertisement requires the following procedure:

(1) The art director calls in whatever type of commercial "freelance" artist is needed to make the *final art.* Usually this requires a specialist in some particular phase of art, depending upon whether the illustration is to be a careful line drawing in ink, a painting, a cartoon, a photograph, or a wash drawing. (See glossary at end of chapter.) Your art director could *possibly* do this artwork himself, but it is normally the job of a specialist, and in any event the art director probably wouldn't have the time to do this in addition to his other duties. In many agency operations it is the custom for the art directors to "farm out" the actual artwork in this manner. Although some retail advertising departments use the "farming out" method also, some have staff artists who do the final artwork. Except in rare cases, it is the function of the art director to supervise the creation of the final art. He may ask your opinion on certain points, and

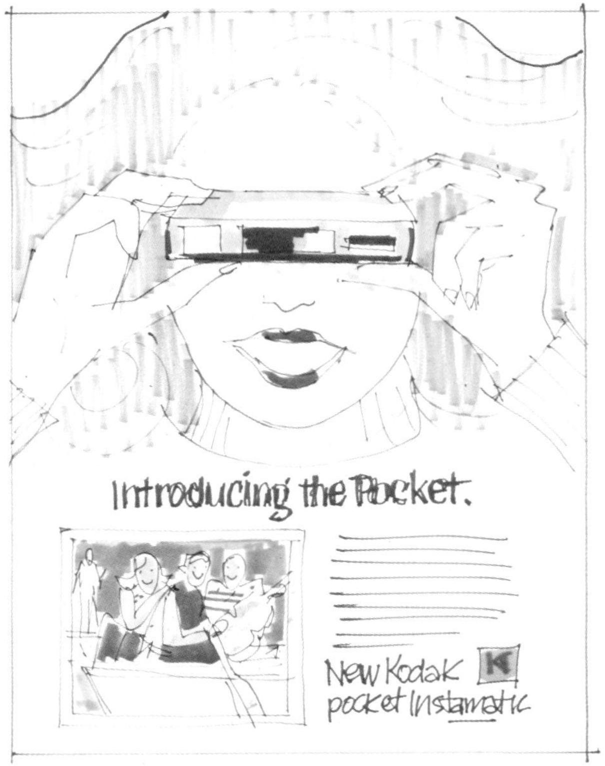
Introducing the Pocket.
New Kodak
pocket Instamatic

Fig. 3-5

Rough layout.

Kodak
Kodak introduces the Pocket.
Little camera. Big pictures.
Now you can take big, sharp pictures with a camera that fits in your pocket.
You get good, clear 3½ x 4½ inch color snapshots with the new Kodak pocket Instamatic camera.
It has a multi-element lens and uses a remarkable new Kodak film.
New Kodak
pocket Instamatic camera

Fig. 3-6

Comprehensive layout.

Courtesy Eastman Kodak Company and J. Walter Thompson Company

Kodak
Kodak introduces the Pocket.
Little camera. Big pictures.
Now you can take big, sharp pictures with a camera that fits in your pocket.
You get good, clear 3½ x 4½ inch color snapshots with the new Kodak pocket Instamatic camera.
It has a multi-element lens and uses a remarkable new Kodak film.
Just drop in the new little film cartridge and shoot. For flash, use a self-powered magicube. Five models, all but one with automatic exposure control.
Pocket a Pocket. At your photo dealer's, from less than $28.
Price subject to change without notice
New Kodak pocket Instamatic® camera

Fig. 3-7

Advertisement as published.

you certainly are privileged to offer any suggestions you may have, but the responsibility for the job rests with the art department.

(2) The art director, in most cases, is also responsible for the direction of type-setting. He will make, or have made, what is called a "type mechanical"—a tissue-paper tracing of the area into which type is to be set. This is attached to the piece of copy to be sent to the printers, and shows the printer exactly how wide and how deep to set the type, specifies the type face and size to be used, and gives the printer all other specific instructions on the job.

(3) Once the artwork is completed and okayed, and copy is set and okayed, the job passes on to the engraver, who makes the plates from which the advertisement is printed. This, again, in most operations, is watched carefully by the art director. In many large advertising agencies and retail operations there are sub-departments which specialize in mechanical production, and which are responsible for all printing and engraving. Even where there are such experts on hand, however, the supervision of the production of the advertisement remains in the hands of the art director.

WHAT ABOUT MECHANICAL PRODUCTION?

As in the case of art, you, as a copywriter, do not need to be an authority on production. It would take years of working closely with printers and engravers to give yourself even the most modest background in the lore of that field. You can and should, however, have a "working knowledge" of the operations of these trades. You should learn exactly what happens to your advertisements after they gain the okay of your superiors and/or clients.

You should know the fundamentals of printing and engraving, the use and production of electrotypes, zincs, mats, and the mechanics of typesetting. You should be familiar with various *styles* of type faces. It will help you to find out the many things that can be done to obtain special effects in the printing of your advertisements. You won't be called upon often to use this information, but it will help you to know just what you can expect in the way of reproduction of your ideas, and to know what is and is not possible from a production standpoint. Also, some copy jobs call for more production knowledge than others.

Don't use too many type faces

If you take a job as a beginning copywriter in a retail store you can save yourself embarrassment if you move slowly in the matter of using a variety of type faces. If your advertisements are set by the newspaper, you will do well to find out how many type faces and families are available to you through the newspaper. Most newspapers don't offer much variety, so if you ask for faces such as Bernhard Cursive, Weiss Roman, or Trafton Script you may be told to limit your type recommendations to faces handled by the newspaper. Actually, a good many retail department stores buy fonts of special faces and keep them at the newspapers ready for use.

A beginning retail copywriter is often inclined to think that his advertisements will gain interest if he employs many type faces and families. If you fall into this trap, climb out fast. You will do much better to avoid showing how many type faces and families you have learned. Many retail people feel that it's undesirable to have more than two type faces in one advertisement and they recommend that the variations occur within one type family. This is the sort of advance information you should get about production in order to do a more intelligent job.

Know typography

In a good many places, of course, your copywriting duties won't require you to specify type. If so, consider yourself lucky, especially as you read the following laments voiced by two young copywriters who found out sorrowfully that they *did* have to know something about type when they started their copywriting careers. After working a couple of months in their new positions, they had some interesting observations to make on the need for knowledge of type. The first excerpt is from a young woman copywriter in the advertising department of a very large department store. She wrote back to her school:

> Because the copywriter here does have a "finger in the pie" as far as layout and type faces are concerned, a sound knowledge of typography is invaluable. I recall that in school I talked my way out of the typography requirement. . . . I rue the day now. To show how type knowledge is always with us, we use a different advertising approach for our basement departments than for the upstairs sections. Type faces are different along with artwork.

The second excerpt is from a letter written by a young man doing copy work for a publisher of two well-known magazines:

One course I could not get into and which I'm sure every advertising student could use, is typography. It would certainly be a big help to me if I knew more about the subject.

An aspect of typography which some copywriters learn automatically and which troubles others is copyfitting. As printers are fond of saying, "Space isn't elastic." If you write 350 words for a copy block big enough for 50 words, you are going to look just a little foolish. As a beginning copywriter you are likely to run into copyfitting trouble much more than the experienced person who has developed a "feel" for how much type will go into a given space.

The rules of copyfitting are simple. Sit down sometime and you can learn in a few minutes the character-count method of copyfitting. It will "pay off" when you stare at your layout and wonder whether the space allotted for copy will take 50, 100, or 150 words. There are methods other than the character-count system for use in copyfitting. Learn *some* method so that you'll be able to save yourself the painful job of rewriting copy just because you had no idea of how much copy you *could* write for the space allowed.

20 BASIC GUIDELINES FOR TYPOGRAPHY

(Condensed from approximately 1,100 words)
Staff Memo at Benton & Bowles

There are exceptions to every one of the following guidelines, but, on the other hand, there is a good solid reason behind each.

In general, the rules of typography follow custom. We find that what we are most accustomed to read is what we read most comfortably and easily.

1. A line should be 1½ to 2 alphabets long. The longer the line, the harder it is for the eye to follow.
2. Body text should not be set in smaller than 10-point. Some folks wear glasses.
3. Use one type fact throughout, for display lines and text. This is an esthetic consideration. An ad looks more homogeneous, less busy, less distracting, when so set.
4. A long copy block must be broken up! This is one rule you will hardly ever want to break
5. Avoid setting the body copy in reverse whenever possible. Reverse type will cut down readership.
6. If the paragraph leads are not indented, more leading is required between paragraphs.
7. Don't print text over tint blocks. It's harder to read that way.
8. Don't print the text over illustration or design element. It is a signal to the reader that the copy really isn't very important.
9. Use lower case instead of caps in display lines. Lower case is more legible.
10. Body copy should always have an even left-hand margin for easier reading.
11. When there are several copy elements, align them wherever possible. This is to avoid a cluttered, busy, look to an ad.
12. Use numerals instead of bullets where possible.
    a. All bullets do is to signal that you have a list.
    b. Numbers do the same job better, add interest, make your list seem more important.
13. Never run a picture without a caption. (Well, hardly ever.)
14. Try to run a cutline under every main illustration.
15. Don't be afraid of "widows"!
16. Use normal punctuation. Commas, semi-colons, periods and dashes serve a useful purpose in guiding the reader through your copy. Leaders (those nasty little dots . . .) usually are merely a crutch for proper punctuation. In addition, they make copy look messy and uninviting.
17. Don't overdo the bangs. Exclamation points are often the refuge of the writer who can't think up exciting thoughts.
18. Keep your sentences short. They make copy look less formidable. They lend a feeling of urgency and conviction.
19. Use italics sparingly. Italics are good for occasional emphasis. A lot of italics in a piece of copy make it paler, look weaker, instead of adding impact.
20. Sans-serif type is better in display than in text. That's because this cleaner, more modern-looking face is easy to read in big size, not so easy in running text.

COLOR OR BLACK AND WHITE?

Unquestionably, advertisements printed in full color normally get better attention than those which appear in black and white. If a rule *must* be given, that conclusion is inescapable. There are, however, certain basic principles which can help you decide whether to plan any advertisement or series of advertisements in full color, one or more colors, or black and white.

Your common sense may tell you that while the generality is often true that "the more color the better," it is *more* true with some types of products than others. The addition of one or more colors to insurance advertising, for example, will probably gain a few more readers, but can scarcely enhance the sales power of the advertisements enough to warrant the extra expense involved. Food products and automobiles, on the other hand, customarily direct their advertising punches directly toward the sensory nerves and are not only more likely to be *noted* if color is used, but are much more *salable.* They're selling "beauty," and there's beauty in color.

Generally speaking, you can let your product dictate whether or not color is to be considered in planning its advertising. That is, you can do so if your advertising budget permits a choice. To use color for attention-value and impact only is mighty expensive. On the other hand, it would be foolish economy *not* to use color if the sales of your product depend upon it. The Armstrong floor covering campaign, to illustrate, has been expensive with its lavish use of color. Yet the use of color is absolutely necessary with this product, which would look dull and lifeless in black and white. Color adds real sales power here.

SOME COMMON ART AND PRODUCTION TERMS

Following is a brief list of terms used almost daily in connection with the art and mechanical phases of advertising production. It is by no means complete, and the definitions offered are far from comprehensive, since this is not a book on art and production. If, however, you become familiar with these few terms and their meanings you will be equipped with a reasonably good vocabulary with which to start your career as a copywriter, whether it be on a newspaper, in a retail store, advertising department, agency, or elsewhere.

Agate—Once merely the name of a size of type, it is now the unit for measuring the depth of advertising space. There are 14 agate lines to the inch.

Air brushing—Blowing a liquid pigment onto photographs or wash drawings. Results in smooth, tinted surfaces.

Ben Day Process—A medium for use in photo-mechanical engraving for adding tints, shading, or stippling to line engravings. The important result is that it gives line plates a halftone tonal appearance. Its use eliminates hand shading of a drawing, thus avoiding irregularities. The ordinary method of indicating on the drawing the portions to be shaded is to attach a transparent flap upon it and mark the areas of each Ben Day with appropriate colors.

Bleed—Printed matter runs right to edge of page. This creates an illusion of size and gives a natural appearance. It also adds considerably to cost—about 10 to 15 per cent in most magazines. It is usually not available in regular press runs of newspapers.

Body type—Refers to type sizes generally used for the composition of body matter. The sizes are 6 to 14 point.

Broadside—This is a large printed sheet used as a circular and folded into a size that can be used for mailing. It differs from a folder in that its printed matter runs across the sheet, regardless of the fold.

Carbro—A carbro is a photographic print in full color, as distinguished from a black-and-white print that has been retouched in color. Carbros are ideal for use as artwork on subjects that are likely to require retouching or idealization. They are not as satisfactory for "snapshot" or "candid" color illustrations because of the length of exposure time needed.

Cold type composition—Copy composed for photo-mechanical reproduction by means other than the use of metal type; usually by the typewriter.

Combination plate—The combining of a halftone and line plate in one engraving.

Contrast—A difference in tonal values in an illustration which gives strong highlights and shadows.

Crop—To cut off or trim an illustration to make it fit into a space.

Cut—Any plate used for printing.

Electrotype—A duplicate of an original engraving or type form. These are used when the same advertisement is to appear in various publications and save the expense of making separate engravings for each. "Electros," as they are called, are useful for long runs, for color work, and for fine engravings. They are electrolytically reproduced from the original type and/or engraving. Since they are expensive to make and costly to ship because of their weight, they are not used as often as mats and plastic plates.

Engraving—A metal plate of copper or zinc upon which is etched the lines from which an advertisement is reproduced.

Face—The printing surface of a piece of type is called its face. The same word is used to describe a style of type.

Font—A complete assortment or font of any one size and style of type. It contains all the characters—capitals, small capitals, lower-case letters, numerals, punctuation marks, etc.

Highlight—Light areas in an illustration. Term is used very frequently in photographic work and is understood to be the opposite of shadow.

Insert—A page, either type matter or illustration, printed separately from the regular sections and tipped in later between the pages. In newspapers these are often called color preprints and are associated with Hi-Fi and Spectacolor process.

Line drawing—Drawings made with pen and black ink are commonly called line drawings. In this class are included drawings made in line, stipple, or brush strong enough in color to be reproduced in the line etching process. In line drawing there is no continuous blending of color from light to dark as in photographs or wash drawings. It consists of solid blacks and pure whites.

Lower-case—The small letters in a font of type as distinguished from the capital letters.

Masking—The use of material to protect or block out certain areas on a proof or plate.

Mat—Abbreviation for matrix. A duplicate of an original engraving, made on heavy paper matting. Used principally in newspaper work. The mat is really a mold. Hot lead is poured over it, thus forming a stereotype. Keep in mind that the printing is done from the stereotype, *not* from the mat. The stereotype can be used only for a limited number of impressions because of lack of durability. A *mat service* provides retail stores with copy and illustrations for ads, or parts of ads, which the store may run in local newspapers over its own name.

Mechanical—When a client approves copy, a "mechanical" is made which explains to the typographers the type faces required and the position of copy in the advertisement. The mechanical is really a tracing of the layout in outline form. The art director dictates the style of type which in his judgment will be consistent with the design of the page. The copy is measured by actual count of characters that can fit into the space allotted on the mechanical. The typographer follows this mechanical exactly.

Mortise—A mortise is a place in an engraving where part of the plate has been cut out to insert type or other illustrative material. Mortising is the cutting away of the part of the block, usually in a space that has been left for the insertion of type matter.

Mounted plate—An engraving plate which is mounted "type high" (0.9186 of an inch). The mount may be metal or wood.

Opaque—A water-soluable paint applied to negatives to block out areas by making them non-transparent.

Overlay—In producing layouts, sometimes alternate suggestions and ideas for arrangements of headlines, copy, or illustration may be desired. A transparent overlay is made and attached to the original, showing these alternates. Very often overlays are made on drawings or paintings to show the engraves the position of lettering, type, or supplementary art to be superimposed when engravings are being made.

Paste-up—When various pieces of art, lettering, design, and typography are ready for final assembly, a paste-up of these units is necessary for positioning. This paste-up is necessary for two reasons: (1) to give the art director a chance to make any necessary adjustments because of changes, corrections, or additions to art or copy after original layout was made; (2) to get the client's approval. If artwork is made up of a number of separate pieces, it shows the advertisement as a unit before plate-making begins.

Photostat—A photostat is a photograph-like copy of any two-dimensional object or print by a special photographic machine. (Very bad distortion will result when three-dimensional objects are used.) Where permanency is not essential, this method of reproduction saves expense and time. The first step is a paper negative which is really a positive, but with values reversed (white on black). The second step is a paper print which has the appearance of a normal photographic print.

Pica—In printing, a pica equals 12 typographical points or 1/6 inch. On a typewriter the key size is either pica, or the small elite size.

Progressive proofs—Made from separate plates used in color-process work to show the printing sequence and the result after each additional color has been applied. They are furnished to the printer by the engraver.

Reproduction proofs—Often called "repro proofs" these are proofs of great sharpness. They can be used for reproduction.

Reverse plate—A line plate in which the whites come out black and vice versa. Thus the letters will normally be white against a black background. Such technique is especially useful in small advertisements that must flag attention. Don't use this for long copy since it is hard to read.

Run-in—To set type without paragraph breaks, or to insert new copy without making a new paragraph.

Script—Script lettering will sometimes bring distinctiveness to headlines or other text as well as provide a style of lettering to harmonize with a special design or special space. It is a continuous form of letters into words. Typographers are able to set type designed especially to imitate a hand-lettered script character.

Set solid—Type composed with no leads between the lines.

Strip-in—Patch placed in an engraving containing correction for original plates. The metal is cut away and new metal, engraved with the correction, is inserted and locked in.

Tooling—Hand-cutting of white areas in engraving for retouching purposes.

Wash drawing—A drawing in sepia, Indian ink, or transparent colors. The color or shading is "washed" on as with a brush. Suitable for halftone. Most wash drawings are made in "black and white"—that is, they are made on white drawing board usually in tones of color running from black to very light grays or pure white in the highlights. In making an opaque wash drawing an opaque pigment is used. The composition is first worked up in masses or all over and then the artist adds lights and shade as may be necessary to emphasize the right detail. This ability to place emphasis where needed makes wash drawings better than photographs for many types of products—especially where great detail is needed.

Widow—A very short line carried over to the top of a newspaper column or magazine page. Sometimes a copywriter will be asked to rewrite a piece of copy in order that the widow can be avoided and a full-length line used instead.

The foregoing list gives you only a few of the terms you will encounter when you are discussing advertising that is to be printed. Advertising television production requires a separate and extensive set of production terms that you will have to learn if you are working with that medium. This knowledge will be picked up easily if you are working daily with television.

Headlines Give You A Foot In The Door (Part 1)

In selling a reading, viewing or listening audience, you will use, basically, the same appeals that a salesman uses to close a deal in person. But there is one very important difference.

When a salesman enthusiastically discusses his product, or his company, or his idea, *he already has the ear of his prospect.* It is true that there may be factors which will prevent his making the sale, but for the time being he has attracted the exclusive attention of the prospective buyer.

You have no such advantage. You must devise a means of attracting the attention of a large and variable group of people who are primarily interested at the moment in something else. The news in the newspaper, the story in the magazine, the music on the air, all are more important to them than your message. These features represent the public's reasons for buying the magazine or turning on the radio. Your job is to distract them from these prior interests long enough to get across your selling points.

Furthermore, you must distract them in a way that will precondition your audience to be receptive to your later selling points. It is poor selling strategy to assume that any attention-getting devices are all right, so long as they gain attention. You should be sure that your "stopper" leads logically into what you have to say.

BEST ATTENTION GETTERS—HEADS OR ILLUSTRATIONS?

There have been thousands of good-natured arguments between copywriters and art directors about which does the best job of gaining the reader's attention—the headline of the advertisement, or the illustration. Nobody has ever won one of these battles because there is no precise answer.

Actually, you have only three ways of shouting "Stop & Read" to your prospects:

(1) Headline alone
(2) Illustration alone
(3) A combination of both

You will find that—often enough to be called standard technique—this last method will prove to be most logical. Headlines fall into certain categories or types. You will see how, in each type, the words and illustration are usually so closely allied to one another that neither the copywriter nor the artist could probably tell you which was the original thought.

Your relationship to your art associates is one, as already discussed, that can and will have an important bearing upon the success you attain. Functioning as a *team* you can contribute immeasurably to the quality of the work the other turns out.

HEADS RESULT MORE FROM WORK THAN INSPIRATION

Contrary to general belief, the best headlines are seldom products of bursts of imagination. Most of the headlines—at least most of the *good* ones—that you read in the nation's magazines and newspapers today are the result of some good honest brain-beating. Headlines, by and large, aren't dreamed—*they're "sweated out."*

For much of your creative time you will be writing headlines that must *start to sell at once,* at the same time that they are attracting attention. You will often use, as attention-getting means, the *sales appeals* of your product. You must stop your audience by offering something they want, thus inviting their interest in further exposition of those appeals.

For example:

YOUR WHOLE WEEK'S WASH DONE IN
30 MINUTES . . . WHILE YOU SHOP!

There is little chance that such a headline resulted from a spasm of creative genius! It tells the entire story—yet is pretty sure to flag the eye of any housewife as it does so.

On the other hand, consider this second one:

WHAT IT'S LIKE TO BE IN LOVE

Also a good stopper for women (and most men!), it could be equally effective as a headline for almost any number of products—perfume, candy, clothes, deodorants, or a travel agency, to name a few. Actually, it is an imaginative and fanciful headline, designed to lure the reader to the copy, where it is discovered that falling in love is highly akin to owning a certain brand of silver.

Most copywriters prefer writing unusual headlines; then they can let their imaginations go really free. They seldom get this chance. Day in and day out, your job will be much more prosaic than that. It will be a matter of stating the facts. stating the facts, stating the facts.

Headline writing varies a great deal with types of markets and types of media. The same techniques that are successful in one may not work well in others. Certain specialized principles apply to each of these fields—fashion, direct mail, catalog, trade and industrial, and retail newspaper advertising. For the moment, consider only the agency copywriter who has a client with a product of national distribution, normal appeal, and reasonable price, and whose problem is to write headlines that will sell the product to the general public through magazine or national newspaper advertising.

CLASSIFYING HEADLINES

Almost every author who has ever written a book on copywriting has devoted much time and effort to the compiling of a list of the various *types* of headlines. As in the listing of the basic human appeals, some name four or five types, while others discover as many as fifteen or twenty. The matter is extremely controversial. Although it is tempting to omit headline classification, it is of some value for the copy beginner to organize his thinking about headlines in some sort of orderly manner. Thus, in this book, too, you are offered a list of headline types.

This list is presented as a means of helping you to understand headlines, their creation and function. It will sometimes serve as a source from which you may pull the right approach to a given advertising problem.

DIRECT OR INDIRECT

In reviewing each of these various basic types of headlines as they are presented in the succeeding pages, try to keep in mind the differences between *direct* and *indirect selling*. *All advertising headlines* definitely fall into one of those two selling categories, regardless of which type of approach or appeal is used.

A direct-selling headline uses one or more of the primary sales features of your product as both attention-getters and sales-influencers. An indirect-selling headline makes no attempt to to do anything but stop the reader and get him to read past the heading.

The two examples given previously illustrate the point perfectly:

YOUR WHOLE WEEK'S WASH DONE IN
30 MINUTES . . . WHILE YOU SHOP!

is direct selling, pure and simple. There, the main attraction or sales potential of automatic washing machines is used to gain the reader's interest. While

WHAT IT'S LIKE TO BE IN LOVE

doesn't sell anything except an intriguing thought.

The question you will immediately ask is "When do you use a direct-selling approach, and when an indirect one?" That depends almost entirely upon what you have to sell. If you can discover features in your product which, in themselves, are strong enough to arouse interest and stimulate sales response, then, by all means, headline them. If you *can* attract your reader by telling him of specific advantages your product has over others, you have a very good chance to make an actual sale. He is enough interested *in what you have to offer* to read further. If, however, he must be caught by a non-selling device, you still aren't sure you won't lose him when you present your sales story.

As you review the types of headlines, note how many of them may be used directly or indirectly. Only in the "news" and in the "slogan, label, logotype" headlines will you find that either one or the other is a *must* . Those two, by their very nature, call for direct selling.

Advertising headlines may be conveniently classified into the following categories (Although many headlines can be in two or three categories at the same time)

(1) News
(2) Direct benefit
(3) Emotional
(4) Gimmick
(5) Curiosity
(6) Directive
(7) Hornblowing
(8) Slogan, label and logotype

Most of these titles are self-explanatory. "News" headlines, for example, are headlines in which the featured offer is handled in the same manner as though it were a newspaper item of timely interest to the reader. "Curiosity" obviously refers to headlines which pique the reader's interest without telling him all.

Generally speaking, it is difficult to boil down a headline appeal into one specific type. Often a given headline will embody two or more of these so-called types. For instance, it is perfectly possible to write a headline that combines both "emotional" and "curiosity" characteristics. It is extremely unwise to depend too much upon *any* breakdown of headlines into types. If you learn to improvise upon a basic approach, rather than try to remember a long list of *possible* types, you will create your own types. You will not be depending upon a list that exists only in some other copywriter's mind.

You will observe two more points as you look over this classification of headlines.
(1) That there are some headlines that do not classify under any heading presented here.
(2) That many headlines have no real meaning, and hence no classification, without being considered with the illustration. Each is wholly dependent on the other for meaning, or classification.

TYPES OF HEADLINES

News

Probably the most common method of direct selling in headline treatment is the *news approach.* As its name implies, this tech-

news headline - outstanding features
- a news story

NDGEL
DHS

nique calls for the same devices used by the man in the "slot" or on the copy desk of a newspaper in preparing headlines for the stories his reporters turn in. That is, to select the outstanding features you have to present them quickly, clearly, and attractively. In writing news headlines, more than any others, a high value is placed on *sentence structure.* This is because you usually have more than one thing to say, and must say it in a minimum of words. Brevity is a powerful virtue in *all* advertising headlines, but you can't afford to be so brief that you omit important sales features or fail to state your case with clarity.

Consider the following headline:

DUST AND SOOT ROLL OFF NEW
SNOW-WHITE CURTAINS AND CHAIRS

This headline immediately followed an illustration showing a salesman demonstrating a chair covered with an easy-to-clean material. It is certainly a headline calculated to attract and hold the attention of every housewife and most men. Although the headline is clear and simple, the writer has not sacrificed the copywriter's prerogative of being imaginative. How much more vivid to say "dust and soot *roll off*" than to use any of the more ordinary phrases that would first pop into his head, such as "easier to clean," "saves time, work," and so forth.

Note one further point about this headline. There is no exclamation point at the end, even though a rather astonishing statement has been made. Probably no other character on a copywriter's typewriter is more overworked than the "screamer." When you are writing a somewhat sensational headline, don't assume automatically that it needs the added emphasis of the exclamation point. In many cases, the character of the headline itself, as in this example, is such that the exclamation point is out of place. If your headline is strong to begin with, there is little need of the additional emphasis of an exclamation.

When you plan on using a news approach, determine quickly *whether or not you really have a news story.* Headlines which announce new features, sensational developments, unheard-of low prices, or any of the other selling points which are called news, *must be backed up.* You cannot afford to write a headline that will attract the attention of your readers because of its news value and then fail to gain conviction as you develop your later copy. If you announce "a new amazingly low price," be sure that your price *is* amazingly low—not just lower than the highest-priced product in the same field, but *low* clear across the board.

Here, for example, are two headlines; each tells a news story, each offers a statistic or two, yet each presents a different degree of that all-important "believability."

DOCTORS PROVE 2 OUT OF 3 WOMEN
CAN HAVE LOVELIER SKIN IN JUST
14 DAYS

Without question, a headline designed to attract the attention of a majority of women, young and old. It tells them something they wish to know, something that they'd *like* to believe, and that doesn't appear to be too impossible. Furthermore, it is a headline which can be backed up by factual evidence, presented in a straightforward manner.

Now consider this statement:

50% FASTER! 100% SAFER!
200% SMOOTHER!

That's a headline about a razor—a product with which most men feel pretty familiar.

Now it is within reason to suppose that male readers of that headline will believe the extra *speed* promise. The nature of the razor seems to make that possible, even though the average man would have trouble believing he could actually cut his shaving time *in half.* But what man, long experienced in using safety razors without decapitating himself, would believe the statement *100%* safer? Very few, probably. It's doubtful, too, if the third part of that headline ever attracted anything more than a hearty laugh. *200%* smoother! In the first place, it's a quality that can hardly be measured. Secondly, the average man is a cynic when the percentage figures climb *too* high. "Shaves smoother" is a statement to be accepted. "Shaves 200% smoother" *asks* for disbelief.

This book does not attempt to debunk other copywriters' efforts. No doubt the man who wrote that headline had reasons for making it bombastic. Just the same, you, as a student of copywriting, must be careful in your presentation of *news* . *It must be believed if it's going to sell.*

In writing news headlines it is well to devote time to the careful consideration of key words such as "amazing," "new," "sensational," "at last," "what you've been waiting for," and others.

There is nothing actually wrong with using these words and phrases *if they are true*. Many copywriters, however, shy away from them as often as possible because they feel such expressions have been overused—clichés that have lost their selling value in modern advertising. Although there may be much truth in the indictment, perhaps the way to correct the situation is to educate copy people to use their heads. If these words are judiciously headlined, in cases where the products they sell actually do bear out their claims, they can and will regain stature as respected elements of good headlines. Certainly in cases where a product (or its characteristics) is in reality "amazing" or "sensational" news to the reader, it is reasonable selling technique to say so.

Here is clearly a product of possible volume sales among the hundreds of thousands of men who use electric razors. It appears to be a product of real news value, unusual, and possessive of characteristics that are both believable and very much desired. The copywriter announces this with the word "amazing" in a key position in his headline. Then he proceeds to back up his contention that it is amazing not only by stating all the facts which make it so, but by presenting the testimony of several men who agree. The whole feeling of the headline is one of important news, but the news is backed up with dignity and credibility.

On the other hand, here is another news headline:

NEW . . . A HISTORY-MAKING ADVANCE IN THE ANNALS OF ELECTRIC CLOCKMAKING!

Sounds as if the least you could expect would be a clock that ran by radar or played Brahms. But, on reading further, the "history-making" advance turned out to be a simple improvement in design, and one which will not be likely to rate with sputniks and moon rockets in posterity's history books.

As you read through magazines and newspapers, give a rating to the news headlines you see. Judge them from the standpoint of how quickly, clearly, and forcefully they slam home selling facts. Grade them on how well you think they perform their primary function—*attract attention while starting*

NDEGC
DHS

direct benefits - product benefit
direct description of benefits - direct sales

to sell. And, finally, notice whether they are *believable.*

EXAMPLES OF NEWS HEADLINES

INTRODUCING BLUSH & SHINE

ANNOUNCING THE WESSON
2-MINUTE DRESSING! MAKE IT YOURSELF—FRESH, PURE, FAST, ECONOMICAL

CAMPBELL'S INTRODUCES NEW
CREAM OF SHRIMP SOUP

WE'VE RE-MADE THE SPREADABLES
FROM THE DRESSING UP

NOW THERE'S A KIT FOR
THE GAL ON THE GO

Direct Benefit

Such a headline, of course, can be combined with straight news headlines, with directive headlines, or the hornblowing type. It is a simple statement of the most important benefit offered by the product to the reader.

One example:
Proof! Albolene Cream cleans
makeup better than cold cream!

When you have a strong benefit such as this, why be cute? Why try to arouse curiosity? A straightforward statement of fact is your most powerful selling weapon.

In today's ingredient-conscious world the following direct benefit head carries a strong message for the reader. Set in big type it commands heavy readership.

Wesson Oil is 100% Pure Vegetable Oil.
No chemicals.
No preservatives.
No coloring agents.

Two more observations can be made about this headline. One is the use of the product name. There are some advertising authorities who declare that *every* headline should carry the name of the product or advertiser. While this statement is extreme it is true that flagging readers with product or company name in headlines will result in higher identification for either, and better "Advertiser-Associated" figures in Starch readership figures described in the chapter on advertising research.

Observation No. 2 is that the use of the subheads strengthened an already powerful and seemingly complete headline.

Beginning copywriters, imbued with the idea that they must *always* be clever shun direct benefit headlines as unimaginative and dull. They forget that a strong benefit is never uninteresting to the reader who reads advertisements for benefits, not for cleverness and entertainment which are strictly by-products.

A man in the car-buying mood will find it fascinating if you tell him directly in your headline that the car you're selling has front-wheel drive that will provide him with better winter driving handling. Nothing dull about this to anyone who drives in the snow-belt areas.

Suppose you have no special advantage over a competing product. Should you, as so many copywriters do, avoid the direct benefit headline in favor of pure cleverness? Not so. You can still use the direct benefit headline but you will combine it with a twist, an interesting phrase, or a different way of expressing the benefit. In that way you can satisfy your urge to be clever while simultaneously giving the reader a strong reason to buy. An advertisement for heat-and-serve salisbury steak demonstrates this two-way type of headline:

"Heat and serve" isn't the best part
(eating is).

Another example of a copywriter's finding an interesting way to headline a direct benefit is offered by an advertisement for a rich looking but relatively inexpensive carpeting. The writer might have written a headline that said:

Here's carpeting that looks
expensive but costs little

Although this headline would attract readers and sales the copywriter preferred a headline that would express the benefit with more flair and imagination. The headline actually used was:

Bigelow's sculptured elegance for the woman
who likes to feel extravagant—but isn't.

Notice once again the use of the company (and product) name in the headline.

A third example of a direct benefit headline that uses the name of the product and incorporates an interesting—and in this case, humorous—twist is the following:

TASTER'S CHOICE®
MAKES FRESH COFFEE
IN SECONDS.

OUR COMPETI–
TION IS STILL
BOILING.

HOW TO GET A LOAF OF GARLIC
BREAD, A COFFEE CAKE OR
A PIZZA PIE OUT OF A BOX OF
PILLSBURY HOT ROLL MIX.

Examples of direct benefit headlines

THE 5-MINUTE
PANCAKE
FOR PEOPLE WHO OVERSLEEP.

HOW TO BROIL A STEAK AS CRISP AND
JUICY INDOORS AS YOU DID OUTDOORS

AMERICOLOR.
IT GIVES OLD WOOD A FUTURE.
AND NEW WOOD A PAST.

SIGHT
SAVERS®
MAKE
YOUR
GLASSES
SILICONE
CLEAN

Emotion

Probably the next most common approach to headline writing is that of capitalizing *directly* upon the emotions of the reader. It could probably be argued that *all* selling, in headlines, personally, in copy and artwork, does this in varying degrees. That is a logical thought. But, for purposes of the grouping here, the subject is discussed only from the standpoint of the headline that goes straight to the heart of the prospect, with one emotional appeal or another.

Unlike the news headline, which usually is used only in making a direct sales presentation, the emotional headline can be either direct or indirect. These two headlines illustrate this point.

HE'LL BE HELPLESS
IN YOUR HANDS
WITH THIS NEW MIRACLE LOTION

ONE LITTLE WHISPER
SHATTERED MY PRIDE!

In one, though it makes capital of strong emotional appeal, both visually and in the headline, a claim is advanced. In the other, the headline has absolutely no direct-selling virtues whatsoever. It does have sales value, believability - human - down to earth.

in that it sets up a situation which, in itself, is representative of the campaign strategy. But, as a headline, it sells only curiosity and attention value. Both headlines capitalize on the reader's interest in anything that can be linked to his or her own personal problems. Certainly love and pride are two strong emotions with which to lure the reader into further examination of the advertisements.

It will be obvious to you that certain products, or types of products, lend themselves particularly well to emotional approaches and you will find that in a great majority of cases the emotional approach is used in their advertising. Your job is one of interpretation. Almost all products used in the initimate daily lives of both men and women are well adapted to this type of approach. In the basic campaigns behind tooth paste, soap, perfume, tobacco, hair tonic, shaving cream, deodorants, and similar items you will find emotional appeals predominant and, of course, headlined.

If you are selling an automobile, a cigarette, a flashlight battery, or a typewriter, a straight emotional headline will be used less frequently. The difference in selling appeal should be clear:

NO GOOD NIGHT KISS FOR CHARLEY!

might present a very good reason why Charley should buy himself a mouth wash—but it would be pretty hard to use it as a sound sales argument for smoking a brand of cigarettes.

In a great many cases, the headlines featuring emotional appeals represent statements from either real or imaginary people. It is easier for the reader to identify himself with a person of some resemblance to himself, who is saying something familiar, than with the impersonal words of an advertiser. Furthermore, your reader is much more ready to apply the sales psychology to himself if someone else is "guilty," than if you come right out and tell him *he* has terrible teeth, or bad breath.

One of the most important points to remember in writing headlines with an emotional slant is that they *must* be realistic. Don't put words in the mouths of characters in your headline that your reader would not say himself. The more human and down-to-earth you can make your headlines, the more attention you will get, and the more believability. If *you* were the reader what would *you* think of the following headlines?

" 'Excello' is the best car I ever owned, regardless of price."

"And for you, pup, good old-time 'Barkies.' "

"It's this Double-Action tonic for my active family."

It should not be assumed that all good headlines of an emotional approach must be testimonial types, or purport to be the words of actual people. There are many, many different ways to reach the reader's emotions—and most of them are good, provided they are based on sound psychology.

You have much more latitude in writing emotional headlines than is possible with the news approach. For example, no woman in the world would actually believe that any lotion on her hands would render her sweetheart "helpless." Still this headline attracts attention. It is not intended by the copywriter to be taken literally by his readers, and they realize that. But they associate the exaggeration with the fact that hand lotion makes hands soft, and soft hands, combined with other things, help to soften hearts.

Certain types of emotional headline writing, on the other hand, must be extra carefully done. Insurance, at least life insurance, represents one of the most common fields of advertising in which the emotional approach is used. Yet, because the subject is anything but frivolous, and because the investment involved is more than the price of a bar of soap, great care must be taken to stick to the facts.

Examples of emotional headlines

OUR ANNIVERSARY
WAS MONTHS AGO.
YOUR BIRTHDAY'S
NOT FOR AGES.
THERE'S NOTHING
SPECIAL TO CELEBRATE .
WHO CARES?

DIAMONDS MAKE A GIFT OF LOVE.

UNTIL NOW, NONE OF US
REALLY KNEW WHAT THE
PIETA MEANT TO US.

YOU CAN HELP SAVE BO SUK
FOR $15 A MONTH.
OR YOU CAN TURN THE PAGE.

EVENINGS THAT MEMORIES ARE MADE OF—
SO OFTEN INCLUDE
DRAMBUIE

(The following head was written in a childish scrawl on a piece of note paper with a child's drawing at the bottom)

DEAR MOMMY,
I HOPE YOU
FEEL BETTER AND
I PROMISE NEVER
TO LEAVE MY
SKATES ON THE
STAIRS AGAIN.

XXXXXXX

AMY

Headlines Give You A Foot In The Door (Part 2)

for products that have few important competitive advantages

Gimmick

During the previous discussions of headlines you have gathered the importance of taking a sane, sound, common-sense attitude toward your creative work. Such advice makes sense particularly when you are writing news and emotional headlines.

But there *are* times when you will be able to pull out all the stops on your imagination and be the kind of copywriter the movies depict. Now and then you will reach that rare state of delight when you can use a "gimmick." What's that?

Well, it's hard to say. A gimmick is a common word in an adman's daily life. It's used to describe practically everything that defies easy definition. Perhaps it's a trick radio idea. Perhaps it's a type style. Possibly it's an art device or a gadget or a spoken phrase. And, it may be a headline. You may not like the word "gimmick," but it *does* describe a headline which is 100% an attention-attracter, and uses for its appeal something that has no apparent relationship to the product involved, even though you eventually discover that there *is* a connection.

You will usually use the gimmick-type headline when you find yourself with a product that has few important competitive advantages to shout as news, and that lacks sales appeal of the emotional type. You can expect to interest many readers who, intrigued by your headline and illustration, expose themselves to your copy story while they linger over your gimmick.

The most important thing to remember in studying the gimmick type is that it is successful only in certain circumstances. Gimmicks should not be used if you can be sure of getting attention through a straightforward approach.

Examples of gimmick headlines:

"Madge said
my hands
should be
in the movies"

(above illustration
of a woman manicure
customer)

"Sure. The
Beast With
Five Fingers."

(above illustration
of Madge the
manicurist)

"Then she
turned in a great
performance
by softening
my hands in
Palmolive®
Dishwashing
Liquid."

(above illustration of
woman customer shown
in the first illustration.
She is now smiling with
satisfaction)

IDEA FACTORY
Johnny drew a
Bird for grandma
to put up in
her kitchen

(headline appears above child's drawing of
bird in bright watercolor, the product
being advertised)

Curiosity

The curiosity headline is closely akin to the

gimmick, but it must be considered in a class by itself.

Every gimmick, whether it be a headline or an illustration, is designed to excite the curiosity of the reader but gimmick headlines arouse curiosity about nothing in particular. Curiosity headlines, on the other hand, definitely arouse curiosity about the product or service they are advertising. For example:

HE WHIRLS A WHITE HOT
"ROPE" OF STAINLESS STEEL

is a headline (and imagine the dramatic illustration with it!) that was written to make the reader curious enough about "a 'rope' of stainless steel" that he would go on and read the rest of the advertisement. Another good curiosity arouser:

C'MON NOW! WHAT OTHER COFFEE
EVER GAVE YOU ALL THIS?

Nothing particularly tricky about that headline, yet it is a curiosity headline. People are not inclined to think of coffee as embodying many varied appeals or advantages. Normally, readers could be expected to read further because they were curious about what was meant.

WHAT . . . NO CORD?

9 reasons not to go to Miami this winter.
There's nothing wrong with Miami. It's a nice place. But every winter?
After all, there are lots of other nice, warm, sunny places in this world. Places you've never been before. Places like the ones listed below. And once you see the prices you'll realize how much you're getting for your money.
Of course, we don't have space to tell you everything about every one of them. Check with your local Travel Agent. He's the first step to the good life. He'll make all the arrangements.
This winter, come with American to the good life.
1. LOS ANGELES Accommodations for 6 days, 5 nights. Visit Disneyland, Knotts Berry Farm and your choice of other famous places you've been hearing about. Includes transfers. (Departures Tuesday through Saturday.) DS-24 $319
2. PALM SPRINGS 7 days and 6 nights at any one of 10 great hotels. A golden opportunity to bask in that fabulous Golden State sun! Price includes aerial tramway ride, city tour, transfers and taxes. IT-PST-4A/4B $330
3. SAN DIEGO 8 days and 7 nights in sunny San Diego. Sightseeing at Sea World, the San Diego Zoo, Skyfari aerial tram, and a Harbor excursion. You need a whole week to see it all! IT-SAN-CV-2 $330
4. SAN FRANCISCO 7 days and 6 nights at the Sheraton Palace in the beautiful city by the Bay. Includes a Hertz car with unlimited mileage to help you see it all. You may never want to go home! IT-WCWS-6 $347
5. CALIFORNIA 7 days and 6 nights at any of 14 Holiday Inns throughout California. See the wonders of the Golden State in an Avis car with unlimited mileage. IT-AHA-C6 $347
6. PHOENIX 8 days of fabulous golfing in sunny Arizona, at any or all of seven great golf courses. Greens fees are all paid. Breakfast and dinners. IT-PG-6 $535
7. TUCSON 8 days and 7 nights of real ranch living—including all those fabulous Western meals! Plus plenty of riding, swimming, tennis, and sauna to help you work up a healthy appetite! Transfers included. IT-TRR-7 $471
8. ACAPULCO 6 days and 5 nights at your choice of 3 great hotels. Cruise around Acapulco Bay in a yacht. Watch the famous cliff divers. Spend the rest of your time soaking up that Mexican sun! IT3-BNIC-TC6 $567
9. HAWAII 15 days starting with a traditional lei greeting at the airport, and continuing with sightseeing tours of the islands. See the best of Hawaii, Kauai and Maui, as well as fabulous Honolulu. IT2-AAI-GOHJ $604
NOTE: All prices are per person, double occupancy, including air fare and tax.
American Airlines
To The Good Life.©

Fig. 5-1

Curiosity headline.

By reversing the usual approach, the advertiser makes it almost impossible for the reader to resist reading the body text.

is a good curiosity headline for an electric iron, yet it sticks with the selling points of the product. So is this one, which offers a selling point for a canned meat:

8 YEARS WITHOUT A MOMENT'S PRIVACY

Both curiosity and gimmick headlines are methods of indirect selling, one a little less indirect than the other. Both should be used when the same general conditions prevail as far as the product's characteristics and appeals are concerned. If you have any means of direct selling at your command—any logical, believable approach to the reader's interest through a straightforward presentation—*use it.* If you have not, if you are selling an idea, an institution, or a product which fails to offer any attention-getting appeals, then it is good copywriting to examine the other means of approach.

Examples of curiosity headlines

THE NAKED LEG

ROSIE'S
GOT A
FRESH
IDEA

PANASONIC'S CRAZIEST COLOR RADIO
AND WHAT TO DO WITH IT.

GUESS
WHAT
WINDEX®
SHINES
BESIDES
WINDOWS
?

NYTOL'S
21 SECOND
STORY.
IT CAN HELP PUT
YOU FAST ASLEEP.

Directive

Now and then you will have occasion to use the command, or directive, approach in writing headlines. This type of headline is more often found in retail advertising, where you wish to get immediate action from your readers. Normally, when you are preparing advertising for national magazines, you will not expect to have your readers leap from their chairs and dash to the nearest drug store or grocery store to act on your sales message. You will not, therefore, have much reason usually for addressing them in such terms as

GO NOW!
DON'T WAIT!
CALL IN YOUR ORDER!
ACT WHILE THEY LAST!

and all the hundreds of other command phrases that are the stock in trade of retail copywriters.

Occasionally directive headlines are effective for magazine advertising campaigns. Directive headlines formed the basis of a long and successful series of advertisements and radio commercials for a soft drink company:

KEEP UP TO DATE! LOOK SMART! BE SOCIABLE!

This is not a command to immediate action, it is true, but it is a definite directive, and one that has a particularly effective tie-in with its product.

Another directive headline, again part of a series designed to increase unit sales, was this one, for a headache relief:

BUY 2 INSTEAD OF 1, AND SAVE

Directive headlines are effective if you can give reasonable support to your command. There certainly is no faster way to tell people to do something than simply to *tell them.*

Directive headlines don't necessarily require prompt buying action

PLAN YOUR HOME FOR FAMILY COMFORT

is a command that cannot immediately be complied with by most of us. Neither can

BANISH "DRAGGLE-TOP"

which was supposedly accomplished by the application of a certain hair tonic.

Here again, there is no formula by which you can determine when and where to use directive headlines. Because they are strong and direct, because they require a minimum of words, and because they often make up in forcefulness what may be lacking in an illustration, such headlines are common in advertising. The directive headline is a general type of headline, and is presented as such. When *you* will use the type, just as with all the others, is something that you cannot be taught. But to give you an idea of just how far the public will go in responding to a directive headline, consider the results they say one California copywriter obtained. He is said to have run an advertisement in a Los Angeles newspaper containing simply his name and address, plus this headline:

SEND IN YOUR DOLLAR TODAY!
LAST CHANCE

So many people are *supposed* to have mailed him dollar bills that he was able to retire with a life income from the annuities he purchased!

Examples of directive headlines

MAKE SOMEONE HAPPY.
MAKE SOMEONE JELL-O.®

FIRST USE VISINE.
IT GETS THE RED OUT.

SUMMERIZE!
. . . THE LIPTON WAY!

THIS FATHER'S DAY,
PUT YOUR BRAND ON HIS B.V.D.'s.

CORNS?
JUST RUB ON
MOSCO

Hornblowing

In this study of headlines, one point has been especially emphasized. When you can be specific *be specific.* If your product has really outstanding selling points, take advantage of them in your headlines. Use them as attention-attracters. If you can find no such headline appeals in the product itself, you may find it advisable to lure the reader with other devices—the gimmick or the curiosity headline.

Sometimes, however, you must decide what to do if neither of these approaches seems to be right. This situation can arise from a number of reasons. The product may compare favorably with all competitive products, in every respect, and still lack any unique qualities. It may actually have some advantages, which, for one reason or another, are not important enough to warrant building an entire advertisement around. It may be that a gimmick or a curiosity-arouser, *per se*, would seem to detract from the dignity of the product or its manufacturer.

In modern advertising, therefore, you will note a great many headlines which simply speak in general terms about the merits of the products they are advertising. These are called "hornblowing" headlines. The term is not used in a derogatory sense. It is true that many such headlines lack power and sales appeal and might be better handled some other way But many, also, are examples of strong selling.

THE WORLD'S MOST WANTED PEN

is definitely a hornblowing statement. It tells you nothing at all about the Parker "51" except that more people want it than any other kind. And, by doing so, instills the feeling that it must be pretty good. So does

MORE PEOPLE ASK FOR MAXWELL HOUSE COFFEE THAN ANY OTHER BRAND

The headline

AMERICA'S LUXURY BACON

doesn't offer you any specific reasons why you should buy that particular brand of bacon, but, combined with a tempting illustration, it helps to implant the feeling of quality that the great name Armour is supposed to stand for.

Automobile advertising and cigarette advertising are two fields in which the hornblowing headline is almost standard procedure. Thumb through a magazine and note the similarity between advertisements for these two products.

MORE POWER	ECONOMICAL
EASIER RIDING	BETTER LOOKING
MORE ROOM	DESIGNED FOR COMFORT

These are expressions that can be found in almost all automobile advertising.

And cigarette ads play follow-the-leader constantly.

HONEST TASTE	GET THE GENUINE ARTICLE
A REAL CIGARETTE	TOPS IN FRIENDLY SATISFACTION

A famous soup manufacturer pictures his product with this headline:

GLOWING WITH HEALTH
BRIMMING WITH FLAVOR

No news there. No curiosity. No command. Yet, because of the power of the name of Campbell prominently displayed, and the appetizing appeal of the illustration, the headline will probably produce the sales response required.

When a beer is advertised as being

PREFERRED FOR MELLOW MOMENTS

or a candy bar because it is

THE CENTER OF ATTRACTION

or a razor because it is

AMERICA'S NO. 1 SHAVER

it is fairly safe to assume that the "idea" department is slowing down. While many hornblowing headlines are part of a carefully worked-out plan, and represent sound thinking and sales strategy, others are only too obviously the result of a failure to discover a better way to do the job.

Remember the function of the horn on your automobile. There are plenty of times when it it the most important part of the car. Used properly and at the correct time, it serves you well. But blowing the horn just for the purpose of making noise can accomplish only one thing —it will wear down your battery.

Examples of hornblowing headlines:

We make our personal products more personal by giving you more choice.

Hormel Ham
an
American
Tradition

the puppy food
with
"total everything"

Fig. 5-2

Lead-in headline.

This headline could also be called a "teaser" headline since one of its chief purposes is to cause the reader to look for the advertiser's bigger advertisement in the same newspaper. The message, however, carries the campaign theme so that nothing is lost if the reader fails to read the other advertisement. This is a cooperative advertisement the cost of which is shared by the advertiser and the local dealer. The bigger advertisement in the same issue is a national advertisement.

ZENITH®
BIG-SCREEN
SUPER CHROMACOLOR®
voted
color tv's
best picture!
FOR DETAILS SEE PAGE 00
Come in
and see the difference
for yourself!
DEALER NAME

Introducing the
the first
really elegant
towel decoration

Introducing: Cup-a-Soup.™
The first real soup you cook up
in a cup instantly.

Slogan label and Logotype

Very often a campaign for the promotion and advertising of a product will have as a basic purpose the getting of as much recognition as possible for either a slogan or the product or the company name. Of course, little will be said here about the various methods of display used, because they vary with every advertisement.

Normally, you might consider that advertisements that feature signatures and slogans as the major display units *still* carry headlines of one of the various approaches already discussed, since subheadings usually carry on and get into the selling story. Such advertisements are frequently found. But if you remember the primary function of the headline—to attract the reader's attention—you will see that these subheads, given less display space, could not be termed headlines in the true sense of the word.

When copywriters use the slogan-label-logotype approach, they do so with one of two ideas in mind. First, they feel that the name of the product or company is, in itself, their most important attention-attracter, or they are willing to sacrifice a potentially more intensive reading to pound home a name or an idea.

A great many highly successful advertising campaigns have been planned and executed upon the principle of name emphasis. An outstanding example of how consistent *name* advertising can pay off as well, if not better, than a succession of clever selling ideas is typified by the Florsheim Shoe Company. For many years, Florsheim has advertised in the nation's magazines, with one main objective, one basic selling idea—an illustration of a good-looking pair of shoes and the name Florsheim. That their theory has been successful is evident from a look at the Florsheim sales record and growth.

Slogan headlines are good devices for both selling and attention provided the slogan is a *selling slogan.* "The pause that refreshes," "Ask the man who owns one," "Time to retire," and scores of other well-known slogans became so synonymous with the products they represented that they gained prompt attention and identification. The Seven-Up Company featured the slogan " 'Fresh Up' with Seven-Up" in every advertising campaign it ran. By constant impact, both the name and the idea were impressed upon the public, with quick sales response.

The slogan-logotype headline is probably best adapted to products whose advertisements depend more upon constant reminder than upon the weight of competitive advantages. That's why you'll find them featured often in advertising for beverages, candy bars, cigarettes, and other items which sell in volume across the counter and for low cost and rarely have any demonstrable superiority over their competitors.

Obviously, you needn't worry about the actual technique of *writing* this type of headline, since it is already written for you. But it does represent a percentage of the headlines that appear regularly, and should be recognized as one of the important approaches.

Examples of slogan, label, logotype headlines:

When you care enough to send the very best

Promise her anything
but give her Arpege

Ontario: Discover Us

Parker
World's most wanted pens

When you're out of Schlitz
You're out of beer

HEADLINE WRITING IS JUST PART OF THE JOB

Your career as a copywriter will give you ample opportunity to prove your ability to create strong selling headlines in each of the categories named. You may discover that your particular temperament and style of writing lend themselves well to one approach and that you don't do so well in others. Many highly paid and competent copywriters have never dreamed up an outstanding "gimmick." Others, whose abilities produce unique and sometimes sensational advertising tricks, may find it difficult to sit down and put together a sound, strong news presentation of their products. The chances are you will often be called upon to do both, and that you will find fun and success in working the problems out. If you do discover that you are better at one type than at the other, ride with the tide, don't buck it. Your copy chief will learn the same thing and will see to it that your assignments correspond with your best capabilities.

You can hardly overestimate the importance of regarding headline writing as a vital part, but not the entire requirement, of good copywriting. Never let yourself get into the habit of thinking of creative work only in terms of headlines.

And always remember that while occasionally you will encounter a problem that may be answered with a burst of imaginative creation, your most-used tools of headline writing will be straight thinking, a recognition of your market and its psychology, and your own ability to write the English language in an orderly way.

Beginning copywriters in school and in business consistently run into the same snags in writing headlines. They invariably ask the same questions. With almost depressing regularity they make the same mistakes. The following section is a discussion of some of these questions and mistakes. This discussion, added to the foregoing material on different types of headlines, should help you in the difficult and important art of headline writing.

Get any group of young copywriters, or potential copywriters, together. Without fail they'll get around to questions on the headline, because headlines are more spectacular than most body copy. Furthermore, every advertising writer has been fed a steady diet of figures relating to the astounding percentage of readers who read nothing but headlines. Here are some of the questions that beginners so often ask about headlines, and the answers to them. Remember as you read the answers that at no time are rules given as inflexible—it is a matter of fitting the answer to the situation, and in the "gimmick" headline, anything goes. You may consider the answers as observations rather than rules.

OFTEN-HEARD QUESTIONS ABOUT HEADLINES

Is the question headline wrong?

No. The "question headline" is very useful. It can get directly to the point that is in the reader's mind. In such cases it serves as a lively opening into the discussion that answers the question. For instance, an Arrow Shirt advertisement that attracted much attention was headed by the question "Which one wears it?" A woman was pictured looking unhappily at three different men in three separate panels who were wearing sloppy collars obviously not Arrows. Each caption explained how an Arrow collar could have improved the man's appearance. Finally, in panel four, a man is pictured wearing the trim Arrow collar. The caption for this panel triumphantly breathes, "A-h-h-h! This one wears it—the Arrow white shirt that has everything! Etc., etc."

The question headline was admirably adapted to this advertisement. It is doubtful whether any other type of headline could have been as suitable for the light touch handled so well in Arrow advertisements. Yet, many capable copywriters tell other copywriters never to use questions for headlines. These writers distrust the question headline because so many copywriters misuse it.

Too often the question is phrased so that the reader can answer it with an impertinent "No!" and, thus losing interest, he goes on to the next advertisement. A question of this type might ask directly, "Would you like soft, lustrous hair?" Many readers, being human, would give the negative answer flippantly and that would end the advertiser's chance to entice them into reading further. On the other hand, the question "Which one has the Toni?" was a strong, interest-compelling headline.

A Camel advertisement asked a direction question:

ARE YOU SMOKING MORE NOW AND ENJOYING IT LESS?

Before you have a chance to say, "you're darned right," the next three words anticipated your answer by telling you to CHANGE TO CAMELS.

The alarmist note is struck in a Wagner Lockheed Brake Fluid advertisement:

ARE YOUR BRAKES *SAFE* FOR SUMMER DRIVING?

Gives you pause, doesn't it! And undoubtedly sold a lot of brake fluid. Another way to handle the direct question is demonstrated by the Dial Soap people:

AREN'T YOU GLAD YOU USE DIAL?
DON'T YOU WISH EVERYBODY DID?

Perhaps the suitability of the question headline hinges upon the ability of the question to draw the reader into the body copy for the answer. If the reader can answer the question without further reference to the advertisement, you'd better look your question over. Be especially careful with direct questions. This warning is doubly emphasized in radio commercials.

All of us have, at one time or another, "sassed" the announcer when he asked directly, "Wouldn't you like to double your income?" Despite the fact that all of us *do* want to double our income, it is hard to resist saying "No" when the question is asked. Keep that in mind when you write your question headline. Also, the question headline is often overused by beginning copywriters. Make sure that the question headline is the best device for putting over your copy message, and be sure to shape your question to get the answer you want.

Should headlines be short?

There is absolutely no firm answer that can be given to this question but it occurs frequently because it has been an axiom of advertising that headlines should be short and that they should not tell too much of the story. There are still many who believe that the headline should say just enough to entice the reader into the following copy, and no more.

If you feel comfortable with the short-headline philosophy, what about the following headlines? Are they wrong?

There are many reasons why
sports car drivers, airplane pilots
and long-haul truck drivers use
shearling seat covers, but year'round
comfort is one of the best. . .

The 1973 Oldsmobile Ninety-Eight Regency.
Walter Hoving, Chairman of Tiffany's, says it's
a car for people with good design judgment.
Maybe you'll agree. Maybe you won't.
But if you're going to invest $5,000 or more in
a luxury car, shouldn't you at least come in and
see?

9 OUT
OF EVERY
10,000
AMERICANS
PREFER
CAMPARI
& SODA.

If some cost-cutting whiz kid
tries to fiddle with our Macaroni and Cheese,
he'll have to tangle with Miss Sampson.

Quick, easy desert for dinner tonight.
Pepperidge Farm's moist Chocolate Fudge
Layer Cake with a big scoop of ice cream on
the side.

You will have to be the judge. A two-word headline might be all you need or you might decide upon a headline and subhead combination such as the following:

Introducing Roast'n Boast.™
It's a whole new way
to cook oven dinners!

Now make deliciously seasoned dishes like pot roast, beef stew—even chicken tomato supreme —with no messy pans to wash and no spattered oven to clean. Read how:

Just remember this, if you begin to worry about the rule "Headlines must be brief". In these days your prospects are assaulted by so much advertising that only those headlines with big, informative, catchy headlines and illustrations may have enough attention-getting quality to make readers pause and partly sell them. Today's headlines do more preselling of the reader than was true in past days when headlines had completed their mission if they had attracted the reader's attention.

Despite all the defense in this section of the long headline, it is desirable normally to write short, interesting headlines that say much in a few words. Certainly if you wish to use large type in the headline you are forced to keep it brief unless you have a big-space advertisement.

There is a certain drama in the punchy one or two-word headline—a memorable quality that is lacking in the very long headline. Volkswagen advertisements over the years have specialized in such headlines achieving an impact that has caused them to be discussed, admired and imitated.

Do headlines always have to use verbs?

Hardly anything must *always* be done in copywriting. That is true of the use of verbs in headlines. Almost every authority in copywriting will tell you that it is usually *better* to use a verb in a headline. Some writers will tell you that every headline should have a verb, or an implied one. Although this book agrees that in the main it is better to use a verb in a headline than not to use one, there *have* been many fine heads that are verbless. The famous war-time headline, "The Kid in Upper Four," which came out in World War II, had no verb but it is one of the best-remembered heads of all time.

Although the following head may not go ringing down through the years, Breck shampoo has used it effectively. Note that it is verbless:

Now . . . both dandruff control
and beautiful hair

Such headlines admittedly lack the vigor of headlines using verbs. There is less life and direct action. There is less chance that the headline will make you move. Just the same, depending upon the campaign, the illustration and the body text, there *are* advertisements for which the verbless headline seems suited.

Even though a defense has been made for the verbless headline—*use a verb as often as you can.* The headline "News about lucite" is pretty drab, for instance, compared to "Lucite makes news" or ' 'Here's news about lucite" or "Lucite *is* news." A headline with a verb seems to go somewhere; a headline without a verb often sits passively in the advertisement. Occasionally, because of its appropriateness with the illustration a headline such as "The Kid in Upper Four" does its job satisfactorily. Usually, however, a headline that is all right without a verb would be better *with* one.

Do directive headlines sometimes cause resentment?

Yes. Americans dislike orders or commands. Printed advertisements and radio commercials are constantly telling us: "Don't scrub your hands with harsh soaps." "Take liver pills for upset stomach." "Don't take chances with your tires."

Orders get under anyone's skin after a while. On the other hand, the average reader is inclined to move only after prodding. What does the copywriter do when he considers that the reader may resent an order but won't make a buying move unless he is given some sort of push? The answer is that the copywriter must pitch his headline in the right "tone."

All through life you have probably found that one person asks you to do something and you do it willingly, whereas another person may ask you to do exactly the same thing and you resent his doing so. Perhaps it was the latter's tone of voice—his *way* of asking—that caused your resentment. It is your *way* of phrasing that causes success or failure in your directive headlines.

Usually you'll do better to suggest than to command. The words "Stop" or "Don't" often sound unpleasant to the reader. From childhood to the grave someone is using those words. If you start your headline with them the reader may react instinctively against your product.

Also, be careful not to offend him by assuming in your directive headline that he is doing something foolish. Headlines of this type would be "Don't waste your money," or "Don't be careless with your child's health."

What about using quotation headlines?

The quotation headline is often a pleasant variant of the straight headline. When you remember that dialogue enlivens almost any book, you can see how quotation headlines can be useful in advertisements.

A headline using a quotation has human interest. It often enables the advertiser to make his product claim more believably; a quotation headline has an element of storytelling about it. Most of us like a story, so when we read the headline—

"It's fun to be a Model Mother!" says Dawn Blake

—we are often hooked into finding out the rest of the story. Who is Dawn Blake? Why does she make the statement?

Testimonial copy is, of course, the most logical vehicle for the quotation headline. Too many of the persons pictured in advertisements seem unreal. The quotation headline can humanize them.

In view of the foregoing, what possible objection can be made to a quotation headline? When it is used by the experienced copywriter, there will usually be no objections, since he will probably use it with discretion. The beginning copywriter, on the contrary, will be inclined to overuse such headlines. Not being able to write effective straight headlines easily, he constantly makes the people in his advertisements do his talking. Since the quotation headline is especially desirable as a change from the conventional headline, the copywriter robs it of its freshness by using it too often. It has been observed in college classes in copywriting that, left to their own devices, the young copywriters would rarely write anything but question or quotation headlines. Such headlines are easy to write and that's that.

Examples of quotation headlines

(Note: All of the first three quotation headlines were used on three successive pages in a women's magazine)

"If you'd rather collect wild flowers than wild outfits, this room is for you"

The totally natural room as interpreted by Armstrong Designer Louisa Cowan

"If you're more at home popping corn than champagne corks, this room is for you"

The traditional room as interpreted by Armstrong Designer Cathy Erb.

"If you want your very first room to be the very last word, this room is for you."

The futuristic room as interpreted by Armstrong Designer Suzy Taylor.

"I can tell you how to place your Long Distance calls so you'll save money.

But I can't help you make them."

avoid "Hanging" headlines

"We do so much for what's inside our packages, why don't we do something for what's outside, too?"

—Our President

"Hanging' ' headlines—should they be used?

First, to make clear what is meant by a hanging headline. It is the type of headline that is not complete unless the reader reads the first words in the body text. An example would be:

Headline: What is . . .

Body Text: . . . the most sensational advance in television today? Why it's the new automatic tuner, of course, etc., etc.

When you examine the foregoing example you see that the headline doesn't make sense unless the reader immediately reads the first words in the body copy. Neither does the body text beginning mean too much if the reader hasn't read the headline.

Now the inconvenient part of all this is that readers fail to follow neat paths in their reading. Some will start with the headline and skip to the logotype. Others will start with the first line of body text, look at the illustration and then glance at the bottom of the advertisement. It is difficult to predict just *how* the reader will read your advertisement.

If you have used a hanging headline, therefore, you may lose much force in your advertisement. The headline reader may look at the meaningless fragment you have written and not bother to find the first line of body text to complete the headline's meaning. He may be irritated if he starts the body text and finds that he must backtrack to the headline to find out what you're talking about.

Even if you lay out your advertisement scientifically, using every possible device to lure the reader from the headline to the first line of body text, you will often fail to do so. This situation is made even worse in lay-outs that separate the head and body text widely by illustrations and other elements.

Generally, therefore, it is sounder practice to avoid hanging headlines. Unless your headline and body copy are completely independent of each other for meaning, and unless each of them will make sense by itself, you will be treating the reader more kindly if you avoid hanging headlines.

6.

Body Copy:
The Selling Part
Of Your Advertistment
(Part 1)

While, as you have seen, much of the selling power of printed advertising stems from its more dramatic components—the headline, the art treatment, blurbs, pictures captions it is the body copy of printed advertisements that puts the "write" in copywriting. This is where you really come to grips with your prospect. Only in the body copy can you *sell* the benefits your product has to offer, can you persuade the reader to buy, can you argue competitive points. Of course you can telegraph these things, and *should*, in your headlines and subheads, but it's only after you have intrigued the prospect into reading the rest of your message that you truly represent copywriting as "salesmanship in print."

SETTING THE PACE

Unlike headlines, which can be broken down into an almost neverending list of types, body text falls into a few well-defined categories. Each category will be used in accordance with the general format and theme of your advertisement. The pace of your copy will be set by the pace of the headline and illustration. You'll find that once you have decided upon a good headline and illustrative device, the selection of style for the body copy will not require much planning. If you use a direct selling, factual headline, your body text will usually be most effective if it, too, is factual—if it starts backing up your headline claims immediately.

Likewise, if you employ a gimmick in your headline and/or illustration, your body copy necessarily should explain the connection before you can get into your selling arguments.

This matter of setting the pace of your body copy is an important one, but simply and logically reached. Common sense, for one thing, will dictate its acceptance, but trial and error, too, will prove the point. It would be next to impossible to write body copy that did *not* fairly well follow the headline and illustration pattern.

BODY COPY TYPES

1. *Straight-line copy,* in which the body text begins immediately to develop the headline and/or illustration idea in direct selling of the product, using its sales points in the order of their importance.
2. *Narrative copy:* (a) The establishment of a story or specific situation which, by its nature, will logically lead into a discussion of a product's selling points.
3. *"Institutional" advertising,* in which the copy sells an idea, organization, service, or product, instead of presenting the selling features.
4. *Dialogue and monologue copy,* in which the characters illustrated in your advertisement do the selling in their own words (testimonials, quasi-testimonials, comic strip and continuity panel).
5. *Picture and caption copy,* in which your story is told by a series of illustrations and captions rather than by use of a copy block alone.
6. *Gimmick copy,* unclassified effects in which the selling power depends upon humor, poetry, foreign words, great exaggeration, gags, and other devices.

Perhaps it would be well here to repeat that this chapter talks about the *primary copy* of advertisements rather than about their general format. For example, the format of an advertisement on Vitalis might call for an illustration of an unhappy young man bemoaning, via a blurb, his romantic failures. If the *entire* advertisement were to be classified in one of the preceding five cateogires, this would come under Number 3 (dialogue and monologue), since the character in the advertisement is doing some of the selling in his own words. The *body* copy, however, in which the young man's plight is amplified and then solved by the use of the product, would probably be Number 2 (narrative).

In many advertisements you will be able to discover more than one type of copy. Pictures and caption, for instance, very often are used as an amplification of the selling ideas, although the main block of copy is straight-line and factual. The same is true of all other classifications.

Copy in any given advertisement can generally be classified under one of the preceding five listings. A recent copy of a national magazine was carefully checked and every advertisement was classified according to this breakdown on copy types. The results are interesting.

The issue contained 140 separate advertisements. Of these, eight contained no body copy at all, being entirely made up of illustration, headline, subhead, and logotype. The remaining 132 were catalogued as follows:

Straight-line	71
Narrative	14
Dialogue and monologue	14
Picture and caption	19
Gimmick	6
Combination	8
	132

Five advertisements of the total featured almost equal emphasis of two or more styles of copy and were classified separately.

BETTER NOT SPECIALIZE

You are going to discover—if you are like most copywriters—that you write one or more types of copy better than you do others. The question then arises: Should you attempt to make yourself a specialist? Should you try to limit your writing to those types of copy you do best? The answer is emphatically no!

In the first place, no matter what kind of copywriting you get into—agency, retail, mail-order, direct-mail—you will find that your daily routine may call for all types of copy. The products you will be asked to sell will not lend themselves to one specific style of copy, or headline-illustration-copy treatment. If you try to specialize, you may have more fun writing what you do write, but you'll soon be writing strictly for fun, and no longer for cash. There are few places for a "one-shot" copywriter in the nation's big advertising operations today. To be more sure of your future, you should be versatile. Naturally the advertisements which you consider your masterpieces—the ones decorating your sample book—will demonstrate the type of copy you write best. Your seniors in the business will certainly recognize your skill in handling certain types of work and will make that recognition evident in the assignments they give you. Just the same, become proficient in writing keyed to all the various categories.

COPY AND RHETORIC

Many beginners ask how much background of English grammar is needed by a copywriter. The answer is—a lot or a little.

No one will deny that a thorough knowledge of the fundamentals of grammar and sentence structure is helpful to a copywriter. This does not mean that the copywriter must be an *expert* in grammar. Usually a *working familiarity* with the principles of rhetoric is sufficient.

You will find that many times a piece of copy will sound better and more sincere if it does *not* quite meet the standards of perfect prose. Remember that most of the people reading your advertisements, who will eventually buy the products you are selling, do not sport Phi Beta Kappa keys. Give them simple talk, not fancy language. But one caution is needed here—usually you will not violate good grammatical usage. Your readers will soon see through your attempt to write "on their level."

The word "usually" was employed in the preceding sentence because some successful advertising has resulted from the copywriter deliberately violating grammatical rules. A celebrated instance of this is the much-deplored but hugely successful "Winston tastes good like a cigarette should" that made the bells ring at the cash register while simultaneously infuriating the grammarians.

Another example is the advertisement that told the readers in the headline that "It ain't hard to speak good English."

Despite these successful violations, most copywriters observe the rules of writing and grammar without being pedantic. Most good copywriting has a conversational tone. While such easy, informal writing might offend the purists and the authors of social science textbooks, it is admirably suited to advertising that communicates with a mass audience composed of people who vary greatly in educational background.

Your writing style in advertising should be interesting, yet simple. It is straightforward, yet subtle. You should abhor dull writing above all else.

One writer had these words about achieving interest through observance of a number of writing niceties.* His hard-boiled, common-sense suggestions should be read very carefully.

"What do I mean by writing style?

Just this. The simple sentence starts with a subject. Then the simple sentence has a verb. Then the simple sentence has an object. The simple sentence ends with a period. The simple sentence gets boring as hell after you've read three or four of them. And you just did!

Let's try again. By hanging a phrase out in front of the subject, you can add an extra thought, and more interest to a sentence. And by starting sentences with a "non-th" word, ("th" words are the, then, there, etc.) you make your copy flow more smoothly . . . read more easily. Of course, ending a sentence with a question mark helps, too, doesn't it? Exclamation points are even better!

If you're the copy-writer, become the copy-reader. Read what you write with a red pencil in your hand. Be brutal. Cut out meaningless words and useless phrases. Combine some sentences and eliminate others. Give the reader a long flowing sentence that combines several thoughts and presents facts which are of average importance. Then use a shorter sentence to quicken the pace for the reader.

And then . . . hit him in the eye! Shock him. It's amazing how short sentences can catch people. They stir the imagination. They create desire. And produce positive action.

Of course, there's more to good writing than varying the length of your sentence. Vary the length of your paragraphs, too.

Like this.

Simple, isn't it?"

*Copy Service Newsletter, International Newspaper Promotion Association, February, 1973, p. 7.

Free-flowing, easy-to-read copy will be more effective than will writing that is self-consciously stiff and precise—whether you're selling cologne or corn plasters—or even a book on English grammar.

Recently a brilliant young Frenchman completing his education in the United States enrolled in a copywriting course at one of our major universities. His scholastic record was high, his personality and imagination exceptional, and his use of the English language impeccable. Yet the university professor whose copywriting course he took was baffled by his work. Every copy assignment the student turned in was a precise and correct piece of prose. He made no grammatical errors and his choice of words was irreproachable. The ideas behind his copy were good. Yet the copy itself simply lacked the vigor, the enthusiasm, the "aliveness" that is evident in the top-notch advertising messages found in our magazines and newspapers today.

"It stopped me," the young man's professor commented. "It was my first experience in criticizing something for being *too* perfectly written!"

Obviously, what was lacking was a familiarity with American *talk*, American *thinking*,

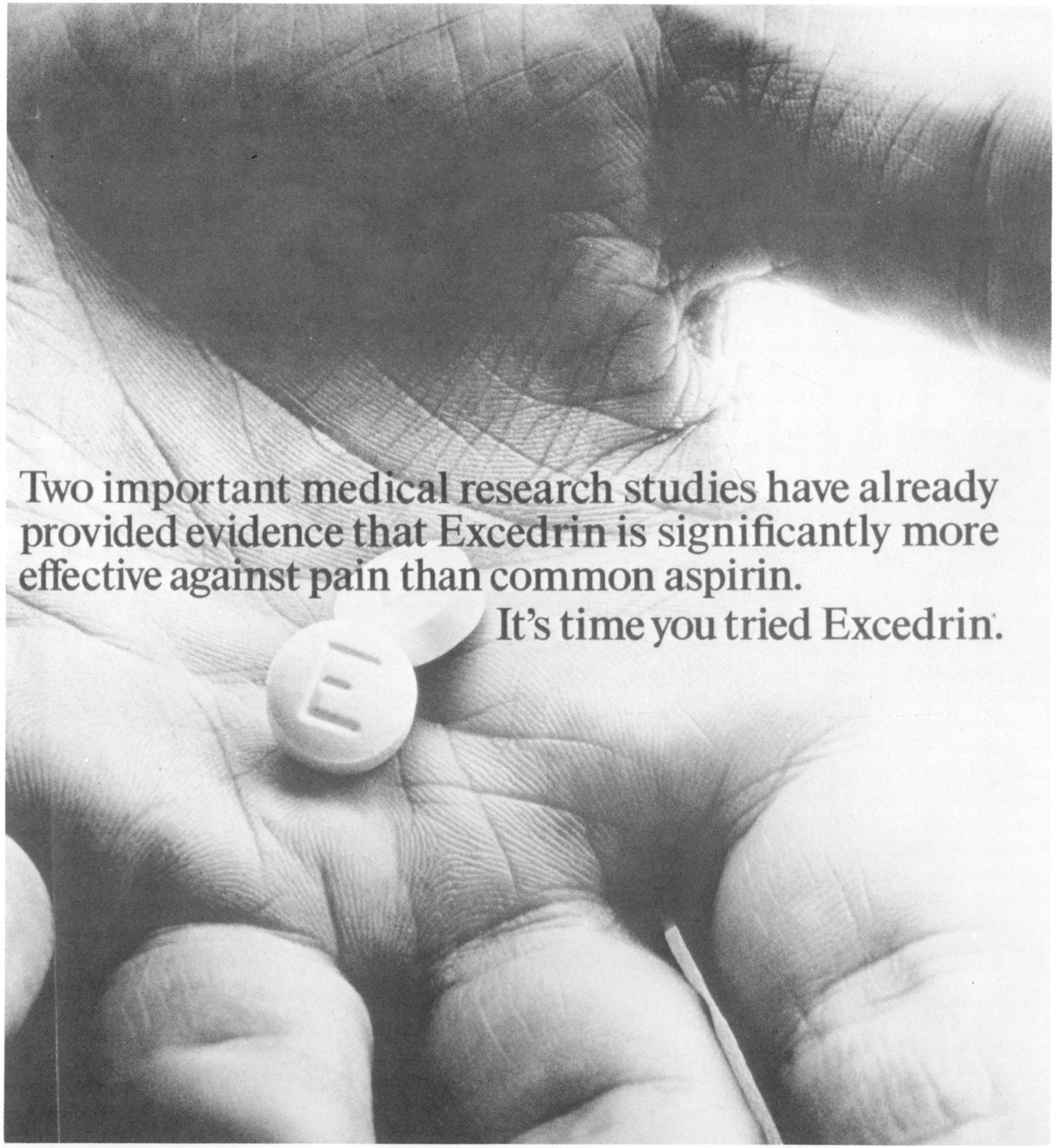
Two important medical research studies have already provided evidence that Excedrin is significantly more effective against pain than common aspirin.
It's time you tried Excedrin.

Fig. 6-1

Straight-line copy.

For a product of this type, a clearly-stated, straightforward product claim is the copywriter's most powerful approach.

speak in "their" language

American *psychology.* The copy was excellent from a grammatical standpoint, but it lacked the humanness, the ease, and the familiar, informal, and idiomatic language written and spoken by the average American.

STRAIGHT-LINE COPY

Straight-line, or factual copy is naturally the most-used type, because, in a majority of cases, magazine or newspaper space is bought for just one purpose—*to tell people about something for sale.* That space costs money—a lot of money! From the standpoint of getting satisfaction for your advertising dollar, straight-line copy is like a white shirt—correct for any affair—whereas testimonial copy, picture-and-caption copy, gimmicks, and the other forms of copy are not always suitable for every purpose. This does not mean that straight-line copy is ideal for all advertisements—simply that it can be used for any approach, whereas the other types have more specialized functions.

Glancing back at the results of the check on a single issue of a magazine, you will note that better than 50% of all the advertisements in this issue fell into the straight-line classification.

Straight-line, or *factual* copy is copy that proceeds in a straight and orderly manner from beginning to end. It does not waste words, but starts immediately to sell the product, on its own merits, and directly following the headline.

When to use straight-line copy

The style or type of copy you write for advertisements must follow the pattern and pace established by your headline and illustration, which are, in turn, paced by the theme idea of your campaign. If you are selling a product that has certain competitive advantages over other similar products, or lends itself to interesting uses, or does something unusual (glows in the dark, for instance!), the chances are that your theme idea will capitalize upon those facts in its plan. Your headline will flag the reader's attention with the most appealing and interesting facts.

The body copy of your advertisement *must maintain the momentum already established.*

All copy—all body copy—regardless of product, medium, or market, must be written to keep alive the interest that the headline and illustration have created. Nowhere is this of more immediate importance than in the straight-line type of copy. Straight-line copy will almost always follow a headline and possibly a subhead *which has used a product feature to gain the reader's attention.* It must not fail to maintain that interest, and yet it cannot logically confine itself to one feature, if the product has *more* than one. This type of copy must be a rapid-fire *form of selling*—starting with *one* idea, or *one* sales point, and quickly putting others across. The most important fact to remember in writing straight-line copy is the "Sunday Punch." Most often, if you have something to say to your readers that you have reason to believe will interest them, it pays to say it at once.

Straight-line copy should normally lead with the "Sunday Punch." Occasionally, however, it is not necessary to do this. The following copy from a magazine advertisement must be considered straight-line, since its primary function is the sale of a product and its overall job is one of telling what the product will do.

> It's Johnson & Johnson quality that has earned for BAND-AID Adhesive Bandages the confidence of millions.
>
> More families use BAND-AID Adhesive Bandages—more doctors recommend them than any other brand.
>
> Every bandage comes to you sterile, sealed in an individual envelope. Keeps out dirt; helps prevent infection, avoid irritation.
>
> Keep one box at home—one at work.

You will notice that the lead paragraph is *not* a powerful direct-selling statement, but a general claim of quality and brand distinction. Actually, from the standpoint of salesworthiness, the second paragraph of this advertisement is far stronger than the first. This product happens to be a recognized leader. Its brand name is almost a generic term. By generic in this case is meant a brand or trade name which, through constant advertising and usage, becomes identified by the public as being the name of a *type* of product, rather than one specific product. Thus people think of "Band-Aid" as *any* small adhesive bandage, rather than the particular one made by Johnson and Johnson. Undoubtedly, the thinking behind this advertisement dictated a policy of protecting that name against the advances of competitors. The selling of the product for its many uses was probably a secondary consideration.

This piece of copy is not discussed for its merits as outstanding copywriting, but simply to illustrate a point about straight-line copy. It is the exception you will always find in any sort of generalization about creative advertising.

Ordinarily, straight-line copy is, as its name

SNIMPG

implies, a series of statements of fact, which will impel the public to desire and buy a particular product for the selling reasons given.

Your thinking must be organized

Straight-line copy, like all other types, demands good, sound preliminary organization before an advertisement is written. By organization is meant a careful review of all the selling points you may wish to get across to the reader, and a close study of the importance of each.

You have probably already gone through much of this operation in the original planning of your advertisement. You have selected the most oustanding feature your product has to offer and have worked out a clear, forceful headline built around that feature. Your opening copy salvo should now be aimed at the feature also. *Immediate follow-through on the headline* is nearly always vital to top-notch straight-line copy. Whether your copy actually fulfills its function and maintains interest and selling power, largely depends upon how you carry on from there.

Practicing copy men and women have various methods of organizing their thinking before writing, depending upon their temperament and manner of working. Some simply close the office door and think. They keep the different angles of their sales story in mind until they develop a clear picture of how it should unfold. Others write a preliminary piece of copy with little attention to sequence, point of order, or emphasis, and then, when they decide what they want, they re-write in order to obtain sufficient continuity and strength in the sections lacking those qualities.

Neither of these methods is ideal for producing the best in copy. One places too much burden on the copywriter's memory, the other often causes a stilted style of writing. Nothing seems to work so well as a *simple check list of selling points.* To see how you may compile such a list, look at an actual advertisement and see what steps the copywriter might have taken in writing it.

Notice that the advertisement will usually follow a list of the points of importance. As a result, it has a continuity and a simplicity that makes it easy to read and understand. It gives primary emphasis to the sales ideas the copywriter wished to feature, yet one point leads to another in logical progression.

Making a list of what you want to tell the reader before you write a word of copy seems like a great deal of extra work, but it will result in clarity and continuity. After you have worked out your campaign and written a number of advertisements within its pattern, the list-making will, of course, be less important, since experience with a given product and a given sales approach will so familiarize you with what you have to say that reminders won't always be needed. In most cases, once you have established your list you need never change it, unless:

(1) Product is improved.

(2) Audience aim is changed. You might have started out with a homeowner campaign and then decided to advertise to carpenters through business papers.

(3) You decide upon an entirely different approach.

For your first attempts at straight-line copy close reference to your check list is an excellent means of keeping your copy *on a straight line.* It is a system used successfully and continuously by some of the nation's most experienced men and women copywriters.

BE BELIEVABLE

One of the most common errors made by

Fig. 6-2

Straight-line advertisement.

This is clear, expository writing that sells the product without any tricks or attempts to be clever. There is much useful information to aid the reader—a characteristic of the advertising of this firm.

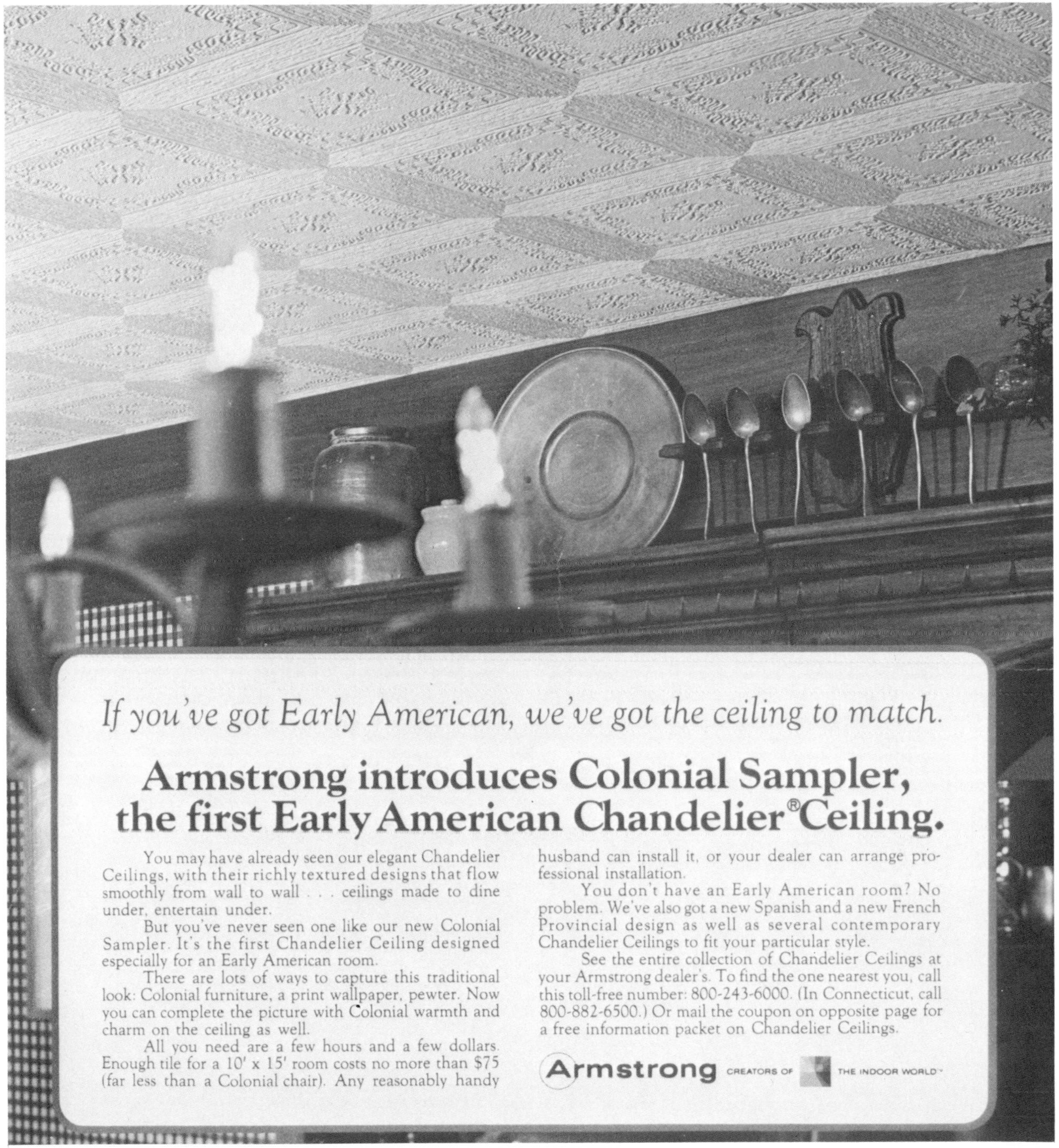

If you've got Early American, we've got the ceiling to match.
Armstrong introduces Colonial Sampler, the first Early American Chandelier® Ceiling.
You may have already seen our elegant Chandelier Ceilings, with their richly textured designs that flow smoothly from wall to wall . . . ceilings made to dine under, entertain under.
But you've never seen one like our new Colonial Sampler. It's the first Chandelier Ceiling designed especially for an Early American room.
There are lots of ways to capture this traditional look: Colonial furniture, a print wallpaper, pewter. Now you can complete the picture with Colonial warmth and charm on the ceiling as well.
All you need are a few hours and a few dollars. Enough tile for a 10' x 15' room costs no more than $75 (far less than a Colonial chair). Any reasonably handy husband can install it, or your dealer can arrange professional installation.
You don't have an Early American room? No problem. We've also got a new Spanish and a new French Provincial design as well as several contemporary Chandelier Ceilings to fit your particular style.
See the entire collection of Chandelier Ceilings at your Armstrong dealer's. To find the one nearest you, call this toll-free number: 800-243-6000. (In Connecticut, call 800-882-6500.) Or mail the coupon on opposite page for a free information packet on Chandelier Ceilings.
Armstrong CREATORS OF THE INDOOR WORLD™

copy people is that of overselling. When you create an advertisement, you have two objectives. One, to wrest the attention of your readers from whatever else they may be thinking about, and two, to persuade them into some sort of action or belief. You job is highly competitive, since you are not only bidding for a sale of your product against the editorial material of the magazine or newspaper, but also against the ingenuity and skill of other trained and imaginative copywriters.

Excited by this competitive situation, it is easy for a copywriter to be foolishly enthusiastic in making claims which simply cannot stand up. He is often encouraged in such extravagances by his clients, who are not unlikely, as mentioned in an earlier chapter, to take a somewhat inflated view of their own product's attributes.

Overselling is certainly not confined to straight-line copy. In almost every one of the major copy categories you can find examples of flagrant violations of good taste and sound selling principles. Copy that is intended to represent the endorsement of someone, real or imaginary, is a particular offender. Since, however, claims for a product seem somewhat less bombastic if they appear to be made by a *user* of the product rather than by its manufacturer, the testimonial is less likely to be weak in the matter of sincerity and believability than the straight-line copy story. Overselling, however, is something to be avoided in every piece of copy you write, regardless of its style.

If you are writing advertisements for a soft drink, for example, be certain that the things you say about that soft drink are things *which people will recognize when they try it.* Straight-line copy simply cannot promise more than the product offers. It must do more than produce a consumer. It must produce a *satisfied* consumer, or it fails to accomplish the job for which it was intended. If you say of your soft drink—

> Once you taste the completely new and different flavor of Gulpo, all other drinks will seem flat and insipid.

—you are guilty of the worst kind of overselling. Your own experience, common sense, and practical analysis of what's in that beverage will tell you that the public will *not* get that kind of reaction from a bottle of Gulpo, or any other drink. If they have been led to suppose that Gulpo has some magical qualities of life and sparkle that other beverages don't have, the disappointment will be sharp when they find that Gulpo is just another soft drink. You will make your first sale, but you will have left the people with a feeling of having been deceived—thus your repeat sales will suffer. You have sacrificed the *good things* your product has to offer for an extravagant claim that can't be backed up. A more modest claim might have led the way to repeat business.

To illustrate the kind of unbelievable, exaggerated statements that cause the general public to say too often "That's just *advertising* talk," here are a few lines culled from national and local advertising. This list could have been expanded by hundreds of examples but the point is made clearly after you read but a few examples:

> "The only way to get anywhere is with a new Comet."
> "Victory employees are the most courteous anywhere."
> "The purchase of a mobile home at Oakridge is the smartest investment a couple can make."
> "Imperial makes any trip more fun."
> "Every meal's a feast when you serve 7-Up."
> "Biggest little treat in all the land."
> "This beer is the most enjoyable companion for any time and any occasion."
> "Chewing Doublement Gum doubles the pleasure of everything you do."
> "Nothing tastes as good as a cold Ballantine Beer."
> "Quality takes a back seat these days unless you shop at Acme."

Not one of the foregoing statements stands close inspection. Not one is illegal but not one is credible to any thinking person. When advertisement after advertisement uses such flagrantly unbelievable, unprovable assertions, it is no wonder that so many of the public look upon advertising practitioners as a bunch of glib "con" men. Occasionally, you would do well to look over this list of statements to remind yourself to keep your copy believable.

Many copywriters suffer from what is called the "Alka-Seltzer complex." That is, they are sometimes inclined to project *immediacy* into their copy that the product cannot substantiate. Alka-Seltzer, or Bromo-Seltzer, or any effervescent salts, can be sold on the basis of the immediacy with which they act to help relieve unpleasant ailments such as headaches of certain types, gas on the stomach, indigestion, and others. To use the same sort of appeal for bacon, cigarettes, beer, or ball point pens would seem to make little sense, yet a glance through any magazine will bring to light plenty of examples in which copywriters have tried to do so.

> *At the first captivating taste* you'll recognize this beer as tops in master brewing.
>
> *Even the aroma* of this marvelous bacon convinces you instantly of its quality.

Just a few words written with this *precision instrument* will prove to you that it's the *peak of pen craftsmanship.*

Are any of those statements true, do you think? You may fancy yourself as an expert on beer, but could you recognize any beer as "tops in master brewing" with one taste? Of course not, so why lead your consumer to think he's going to get a beer so outstandingly different that he'll be able to do so?

Anyone who happened to be in the market for a new pen might be impressed with "precision instrument" and "peak of pen craftsmanship," but do you believe that these abstract boasts could be proved by a few scrawled words on a piece of paper? Hasn't the pen's leakproof quality, or its shape, or its appearance, or its capacity anything to do with such claims?

Don't be a "baloney artist," as copywriters many times are called. Far too many copywriters have already sacrificed believability and sincerity for the *one unit sale* that exaggerated selling can and will bring—men and women who have turned their typewriters into tripewriters! When you write straight-line copy, make sure that it is straight in *honesty,* and in *presentation of product points.* Your job is to build a sales curve of *steady customers* and the only way to do that is to advertise your product for its merits alone.

Straight-line copy is not hard copy to write if you keep straight-line *selling* in mind. Sell, with the words you choose, in exactly the same, direct, uncomplicated, and sincere manner you would use if you were selling in person. Naturally, you should use care and consideration in the selection of the right phraseology—observe the rules you learned long ago that make writing smooth-flowing and smooth-sounding—but remember, in all good straight-line copy the over-all aim is simplicity.

Included in this chapter are examples of straight-line copy. As you study then, remember that copywriters normally do not have a recognizable *style* of writing as do many novelists, columnists, and playwrights. You need not waste your time, therefore, trying to analyze the *style* of any advertisement or advertisements. You will, however, benefit by analyzing carefully how these writers *write*—how they emphasize their selling points, how they maintain clarity and order, and how they stay within the bounds of good judgment in making their claims.

PICTURE-AND-CAPTION COPY

Another common form of body text is that used in picture-and-caption-type advertisements. In an earlier chapter "caption" was defined as being a small unit of type employed descriptively in connection with illustrations and other parts of an advertisement. When such captions are the *principal* means of telling a copy story, the advertisement is said to be a picture-and-caption advertisement. In this discussion, reference is made only to advertisements in which the captions are the sole selling copy.

No rule will tell you precisely when to plan advertisements of a picture-and-caption style. That can depend on the type of product you are advertising, the type of sales features the product has to offer, and the physical space for your story, as well as other factors.

One point to remember is that picture-and-caption advertisements lend themselves much better to sizable space than to small space. Magazine quarter-pages usually don't allow enough room to produce top-quality illustrations in series, together with headline, subhead, caption, and logotype. Even in half-pages, the problem may be difficult unless your captions are so brief as to be almost

Thick and tired of it.
Make peace with snarls and tangles. Hair So New leaves hair easy to comb when it's wet, silky-smooth when it's dry.
One fine mess.
With fine hair, every strand counts. Hair So New sprays away tangles. Helps keep your hair on your head. And out of your comb.
A yard of snarls.
If it takes almost as long to comb as it did to grow, try Hair So New. The spray-on creme rinse that puts your comb on roller skates!
Knotty Marietta.
For a faster fluff that's easier to pick out, spray in Hair So New. (So sheer you can use it between shampoos, too.)
Don't tangle with hair so new®
spray-on creme rinse from Clairol
©Clairol Inc. 1971
CLAIROL
hair so new

Fig. 6-3

Picture-and-caption advertisement.

This advertisement achieves distinctiveness through the use of artwork since most picture-and-caption advertisements use photographs.

classified as subheads. You will find that if you try to put more than one or two illustrations in the space of one-half page or less (still speaking of magazines), you will tend to be cramped for room to give adequate display to your copy, or to say all the things you wish to say. In addition, unless you plan to illustrate something very simple, the illustrations will suffer by being reduced too much.

As a generalization, caption copy goes best in advertisements where you have a page or more to tell your story. Like all generalizations, this statement can be challenged by advertisers who go ahead and defy the principle by using less than page units for picture-and-caption advertisements. Despite this, you would probably do better to plan most of your picture-and-caption advertisements in page sizes—it will be less strain on the ingenuity of your layout people.

The type of product you are advertising may influence your use of caption copy. If you are working out a campaign for an automobile, for example, you'll agree that the reader is likely to be more interested in the looks of the car and more attracted to your advertisement if the predominant portion of it is given over to a large illustration showing

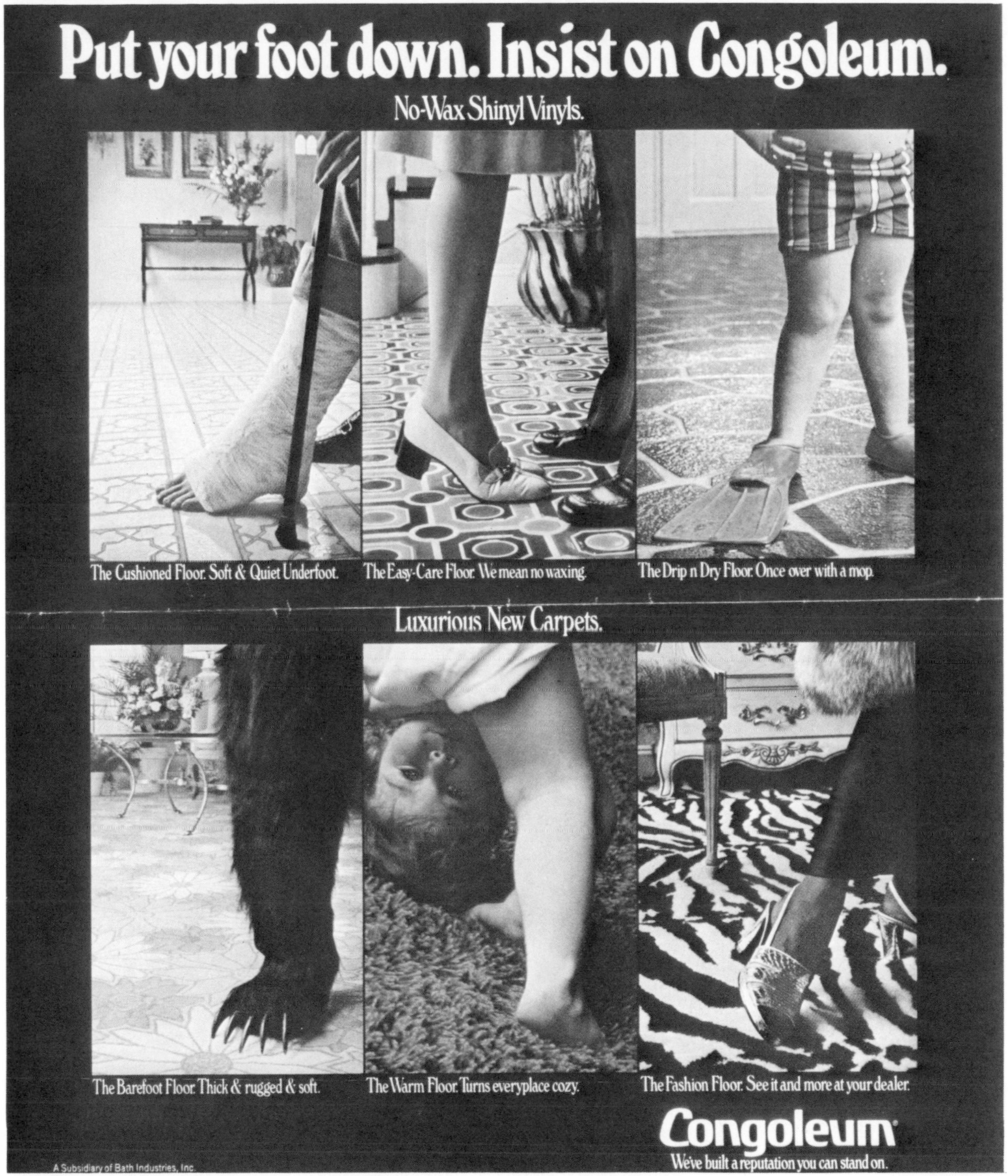
Put your foot down. Insist on Congoleum.
No-Wax Shinyl Vinyls.
The Cushioned Floor. Soft & Quiet Underfoot.
The Easy-Care Floor. We mean no waxing.
The Drip n Dry Floor. Once over with a mop.
Luxurious New Carpets.
The Barefoot Floor. Thick & rugged & soft.
The Warm Floor. Turns everyplace cozy.
The Fashion Floor. See it and more at your dealer.
Congoleum
We've built a reputation you can stand on.
A Subsidiary of Bath Industries, Inc.

Fig. 6-4

Picture-caption advertisement.

This type of advertisement demonstrates a number of advantages quickly and clearly.

the beauty of the car, than if you show a series of illustrations and captions concerning its brakes, mileage, upholstery, and drive-shaft. Shoes provide another good example of products that do not lend themselves particularly well to picture-and-caption advertising. The points of interest to the reader in shoe advertising are primarily style, price, and name. Since illustrations of these features would be dull, the use of picture-and-caption copy is eliminated.

Before you plan to break down the selling points of your product into pictures and captions, be very sure that those selling points will (1) be of personal interest, pictorially, to most of your readers, and (2) that the captions you write for the illustrations back up the promise of the illustrations.

Some time ago the manufacturers of a new-type automotive lubricant inaugurated a series of picture-and-caption advertisements in which the features of this lubricant were highlighted. Illustrations, dramatic and interesting, pictured what happened inside your car when the product went to work. Captions backed up the illustrations with hard-selling copy.

The public response to this campaign was sluggish and disappointing. Finally aid was asked from one of the nation's top advertising men. He had no quarrel with the pictures, and thought the copy was well written and strong. "But," he said, "people just aren't *interested* in the mechanics of what goes on inside their cars."

The reason for this, of course, is that the average person doesn't know enough about motors to understand anything even vaguely technical. He wrote a headline which stated "Cuts Your Repair Costs in Half!" used a big block of straight-line copy telling *how,* and the lubricant immediately became a sensational seller. If you are going to use pictures and captions, be positive that the pictures reflect the self-interest of the readers or your finest copy in the captions will not sell.

Research people will tell you that, generally speaking, advertisements of a picture-and-caption style will get more thorough reading of the copy than will advertisements that contain a big block of body text. This may be true, because people are interested in pictures and will read short captions. It is only true, nevertheless, if the advertisements you are comparing are *both* good advertisements. A good headline and all-type advertisement, for instance, will usually get better reading than a picture and caption advertisement with a poor headline and dull, unimaginative pictures.

Caption writing is easier

You will find it easier, usually, to write captions for picture-and-caption advertisements than to write straight-line copy. The reason is clear. In straight-line copy, you must develop your story in a strong, orderly progression of ideas, one leading smoothly to the other, but you have no such problem with caption copy. Here, once you have selected the specific sales points to be illustrated, your job is to sell each point by itself. You do not have the "transitional" type of writing which carries you easily from one point to another as a straight-line copy.

One of the great weaknesses of beginning writers is that their copy lacks flow and transition. They fail to make their ideas and sentences connect.

If the pictures in picture-and-caption copy have been arranged in a logical sequence the transition is assured. The writer merely writes his captions independently as dictated by the pictures.

An example would be a versatile garden and lawn tool that performs many tasks. Supposing in analyzing its functions you discover that it does the following:

Trims hedges	Shapes bushes
Edges walks	Mulches leaves
Prunes trees	Destroys crab grass
Cuts grass	Cuts branches
Mows weeds	

Now, you devise a headline that stresses the versatility of the unit and points out that it can do nine lawn and garden tasks. You then call for illustrations that will demonstrate each of these nine functions. You arrange the illustrations in a sensible order and write each caption without any reference to the preceding and following caption.

Your advertisement is tied together by the headline that tells of the overall function of the unit—to perform many lawn and garden tasks. From then on, if you have arranged the pictures logically, your advertisement will be a smooth, flowing production.

Major and minor captions

A fairly good rule to observe in planning picture-and-caption advertisements is to evaluate first the nature of the claims you want to make in selling your product. If you discover a single particularly outstanding feature that distinguishes your product from the competition and you are sure that this feature will be

A little philosophizing from Big John about his brand-spankin'new Stew 'n Beef Dinner.
"Beef ought to taste like beef. Vegetables ought to taste like vegetables."
That's not about to happen when everything's been soaking together in one can. But when you keep the beef separate from the vegetables, in 2 cans everything keeps its own distinctive taste and texture.
If you'd like to get Big John to have a tree planted in cooperation with the U.S. Forest Service, pick up his Beans 'n Fixin's. The details are on the outside. Rib-stickin' eatin' on the inside.
BEEF CHUNKS 'N GRAVY
NEW
BIG JOHN'S STEW 'N BEEF DINNER
"True home-made taste doesn't come in a can. It comes in two."
The top can has big, hefty chunks of beef in a rich, dark gravy. The bottom one's got good-sized hunks of potatoes and carrots in a gravy flavored with onions and spices. You just mix, heat, and serve for a rib-stickin' stew you can be proud of.
BIG JOHN'S CHILI 'N BEEF DINNER WITH BEANS
BIG JOHN'S BEANS 'N FIXIN'S
"You don't get to be something over six and a half feet tall without learning a thing or two about eating."
Big John has some other rib-stickin' eatin', too Beans 'N Fixin's and Chili 'N Beef.

Fig. 6-5

Picture-caption advertisement.

This demonstrates the type in which one picture is dominant. It is somewhat more common to make all pictures the same size but either technique is satisfactory.

important to prospects, discard the picture-and-caption idea in favor of a smashing presentation of that certain feature. You can always illustrate other features in minor roles, with captions, but a good strong block of straight-line body copy can do the best job of selling *one* specific.

Picture-and-caption technique is best adapted to products with multiple sales features, no one of which is outstandingly potent.

It is possible, of course, to use picture-and-caption copy and still gain major emphasis on one point in a series of product advantages. The emphasis is gained by displaying the major illustration in larger size than the other illustrations and by running the lead caption in larger-size type. Such treatment may be considered as almost a combination of straight-line copy if it does not confine itself to selling the one feature involved in the picture, and if it presents a complete story. It must be considered a caption, regardless of the length of copy and what size type it appears in, if it does not stand by itself as a complete and all-inclusive sales story.

Avoid covering too many ideas in captions. If you are using a picture-and-caption technique, be sure that your caption completely

Fig. 6-6

Picture-caption advertisement.

Notice how an overall headline has been worked into this technique. Frequently, a picture-caption advertisement lacks a headline. This lack can be a weakness.

Two weeks in the hospital can cost you two months in wages.
America needs action on Healthcare.
If we have our say, you won't have to be rich to be sick. Because the country will have a Healthcare plan that gives all Americans equal access to medical care and the insurance to pay for it.
Actually, Ætna, America's largest private health insuror, has been urging Healthcare for over four years. We've worked with Washington and the insurance industry to develop a total plan that puts our industry in partnership with government. So care will be available to all Americans at a cost that isn't a plague on the taxpayers.
To start with, the whole system of delivering health care has to be significantly improved. (Even if every last cost were covered, there aren't enough facilities or professional people now to take care of everyone.) We need more doctors and nurses. We need trained medical assistants.
We need incentives for medical people to work in places where they don't work now. We need walk-in neighborhood health centers to take a needless burden off the hospitals. And that's just the start.
Ætna
LIFE & CASUALTY
Ætna has a lot to say about Healthcare because we've thought a lot about the way this country should be. And we're doing what we can to move it in the right direction. It's hard work and it puts us right in the middle of public debates. But we think it's right. And in Healthcare, a good many people are coming to agree with us.
You get action with Ætna.

covers the illustrations to which it is keyed and does not wander off into selling other features that have no bearing upon what is illustrated.

Every extra idea that you insert in your individual captions should have a direct relationship to the main point you're trying to get across in that specific caption. Also, each idea maintains the connection with the main selling ideas written in the headline. Use this technique to prevent your advertisements from being disconnected and incoherent. If you have hooked the prospect into reading each caption solely on the basis of what he sees in the picture, don't lose him by failing to give him a direct and powerful sell on *what he is interested in* in the first place (through the over-all theme set by the headline).

Lead-in lines and headings

If you had enough space to work with, every caption would have a headline that highlighted what it was going to say. Rarely can you afford, however, to give that much space to minor headlines. Copywriters, therefore, use three means of gaining immediate attention to key words and phrases. One of these techniques should be used in the writing of every caption.

(1) You may display a word or two as lead-in, running it in heavier, slightly larger type.

(2) You may simply have the first few words of your caption set in bold-face type, or color, if color is used.

(3) Numbering captions helps greatly in increasing readership.

All these devices help the advertisement from two standpoints. They serve to gain just that much more sell, in case the reader looks at the illustration but fails to go on to the copy; and they help dress up the page, mechanically speaking.

When you write your captions, keep this lead-in idea in mind. Put down your most interesting words first, thus giving them the added strength of the extra weight or color.

Body Copy: The Selling Part Of Your Advertisement (Part 2)

DIALOGUE AND MONOLOGUE COPY

In the chapter on headline writing you learned that one of the most commonly used devices in copywriting is to let the people in illustrations do the selling in their own words. Testimonials, when judiciously handled, have proved their ability to produce outstanding results. The trick is to write testimonial headlines so that the message retains its selling power and at the same time is natural-sounding when placed in the mouths of human beings. The same problem is of constant concern to copywriters when they carry the testimonial type of advertising into the body copy.

If you use personalized selling in your headline, whether the statement of a real individual or that of an unidentified person, it does *not* mean that your copy must also continue with personalized selling. Very often you will want to use a testimonial headline from some well-known person as a means of attracting attention, and then develop your own sales message in straight-line copy, captions, or other copy approaches. One of the most famous of all success stories in testimonial advertising, often featured headlined praise from popular movie stars, but confined its selling messages to straight-line copy. When this method is followed, your body copy should be handled no differently than if your headline were a straight selling message.

Often, however, you will wish to use more dialogue or monologue copy than is possible to put into a headline. You may do this by letting your featured character do the complete selling job, clear through the advertisement, or by including additional endorsing remarks in captions.

You will be called upon to write three different types of copy for personalized advertisements: (1) true testimonials, in which you prepare statements for real people to "say," (2) quasi-testimonials, in which you illustrate, by photography or artwork, supposedly real persons, but do not identify them by name, and (3) copy for the blurbs or balloons in comic-strip and continuity-panel advertisements, where obviously fictitious people are speaking. In all three of these types of dialogue and monologue copy, the problems will vary somewhat and must be studied individually if you are going to attain power and believability.

The true testimonial

The longer the statement, the more danger of incredulity—this assertion is almost axiomatic in testimonial writing. You start off fast in testimonials because in the first exposure to the advertisement your audience is influenced by the name and picture of the celebrity. In fact, the "stopping value" of a celebrity testimonial is in the individual's name, not necessarily what he or she says.

After the first statement is cleared, however, and the reader settles down into what purports to be some good plain talk about the product by the testimonial-giver, *good plain talk is absolutely necessary.* Movie stars, lion tamers, baseball heroes, or ballerinas shouldn't be presented as experts on nutrition, engineering, or economics. At least you cannot expect the public to believe they are, or to care very much.

It is entirely possible that thousands of American women will buy a certain brand of soap because a famous movie star says she uses the soap and likes it. In the copy that goes with such a statement the prospect can be reminded that movie stars, to help preserve their beauty, require fine soap, and the fact that movie stars *use* a certain brand of soap is good evidence that it is of fine quality. The readers can be also urged—in straight-line

Fig. 7-1

True testimonial.

A real-life celebrity delivers the testimonial here in a customarily humorous fashion.

copy—to use that soap on the reasonable assumption that it will help them, also, to be more beautiful. Ingredients of the soap and other factors that make it a quality product may be discussed also.

The moment, however, that you attempt to put such selling into the mouth of an alluring Hollywood actress you are injecting a phony note into something that otherwise might be easily believable and salable. There is a huge difference between the following two statements, when you are asked to believe that a screen personality said them spontaneously:

> I think Blank soap is just *wonderful.* It seems to leave my skin extra soft and smooth. I never use any other brand but Blank soap.

That is believable, but who could seriously believe that a person would normally speak in the words of this testimonial:

> Blank soap is the perfect soap. The cottonseed oil in it keeps my skin soft and smooth. None of us in Hollywood would think of using any other soap.

Now notice the difference in those testimonials. In one, the person speaking does not make any claims other than a very strong liking for a brand of soap and her own personal reactions to using it. That is enough to gain

Whenever I think of Scotch, I recall the immortal words of my brother Harpo.

BY GROUCHO MARX

HARPO WAS a man of very few words, except when it came to scotch, horses and ladies.

Actually, scotch ran a poor third. Which wasn't easy considering the way his horses ran.

And the way his horses ran could be summed up in a word.

Last.

He once had a horse who finished ahead of the winner of the 1942 Kentucky Derby.

Unfortunately, the horse started running in the 1941 Derby.

And as far as the ladies go, Harpo's ladies always went.

As a matter of fact, they went a lot faster than his horses. Although his horses were a lot prettier.

But that's a horse of a different color.

Anyway, back to the subject at hand. What was it again? Oh, yeah, scotch.

When it came to scotch, Harpo's words were memorable.

Unfortunately, I forget them.

I remember the thought behind them, however.

The thought was that Harpo appreciated good scotch. Especially one kind of scotch. I know this because one morning I found my liquor cabinet broken into. All the scotch was opened and apparently samples were taken of each bottle. Except in the case of Teacher's Scotch where the case was taken.

I immediately put on my Sherlock Holmes hat, replaced my cigar with a pipe and looked for my thinking cap, but I couldn't find it.

"The Case of the Missing Case," I called it.

Harpo was my number one suspect. He was also my number two and my number three suspect.

The night before I had heard a honking sound in my living room. At first I thought it was a car looking for a parking space in my apartment. (That used to happen a lot until I had parking meters installed.) Little did I know, however, that it was my brother committing one of the most unbrotherly acts since the Andrews Sisters.

So I threw a mackinaw over my Dr. Denton's and dashed off to Harpo's. I must have cut quite a dashing figure.

When I arrived at Harpo's house, there, big as life, were my bottles of Teacher's.

"Why, Harpo?" I asked, lighting my cigar and putting it out on the rug, the one on the floor.

Harpo answered with a honk that was worth a thousand words.

I understood them immediately.

What it boiled down to was that Teacher's tasted better to him than any of the other scotches I had.

TEACHER'S
HIGHLAND CREAM
BOTTLED IN SCOTLAND
SCOTCH WHISKY

I agreed with that. It also tasted better to me. That's probably why we're brothers. After all, scotch is thicker than water.

And, on the subject of brothers, Harpo said he knew enough about scotch to know that Teacher's wasn't one of those scotches everybody and his brother drinks.

I told him he was doing his best to change that.

Then I asked him how he knew that anyway.

Well, to make a long story longer, it seems that he had gone through Gummo's liquor cabinet, too. As well as Zeppo's and Chico's. Before he went through mine. And he said that I had the best taste.

I said, "That's all very interesting, Harpo, but now it's time to play 'You Bet Your Life.' And give me a finger of my own scotch while you're at it."

To show me how generous he was he poured some scotch into a glass and put his whole hand into it. I'd had scotch and water, scotch and soda, but never scotch and hand. But then, Harpo's an old hand at serving scotch. At the risk of beating a hand to death, let me continue. Where was I . . .

At this point I told Harpo I didn't want to hear any more horns.

He honked.

I said, "Say it with strings."

So he grabbed his harp and proceeded to play me to sleep. I snored in accompaniment.

It was while I was sleeping that he uttered those now immortal words. You know the words I mean. At least I hope you do. Cause you couldn't expect me to remember the words somebody said to me while I was sleeping.

But, after all, why harp on that.

86 Proof Scotch Whisky Blended and Bottled in Scotland by Wm. Teacher & Sons, Ltd. © Schieffelin & Co., N.Y., Importers

power from the name of the celebrity as far as influencing the public is concerned. In the second statement, however, the testimonial attempts to take in a lot more territory.

The endorser is claiming more than she could possibly be expected to know. She says "It's the perfect soap." She asserts that the "cottonseed oil in it" is what keeps her skin smooth and soft, yet so far as the public is concerned, she would have no understanding of the action or effect of any of the ingredients, even assuming she knew what they were. After all she's a name star, not a dermatologist. Furthermore, she makes a completely unbelievable claim concerning the soap-using habits of her Hollywood colleagues. There is a big difference between saying that *you* prefer a certain product, and crediting everyone else with the same sentiments.

If you are writing a testimonial for use in cereal advertising, it is perfectly logical to have your endorser say that the product has "finer flavor" or is "crisper" or "stays fresh longer," or even for him to make a general claim about its being "good for you."

It is *not* logical to have the endorser refer to the actual nutritive qualities of the cereal, such as claiming that its wholesomeness comes from "niacin and Vitamin B_1" or that children will thrive on it because it has a high protein content.

Testimonials for candy can certainly indicate a natural perference for its "delicious goodness," its "nutty, crispy, crunchy, chocolaty, chewy, delicate, or otherwise luscious flavor," but they are on thin ice if they present normal citizens talking about "dextrose" or "rich in food energy."

It is very easy to let yourself drift into such errors in writing testinomial copy, because you naturally know more about the products you are advertising than does the general public. If you are responsible for writing advertisements for men's clothing, for example, you undoubtedly know exactly how those clothes are made, what percentage of wool they contain, how they are styled and tailored, and a host of other features that only someone close to the operation could know.

If one of your friends asked you, "What's so good about these clothes?" you would undoubtedly answer with a run-down of the features that most impress you. If the same question were asked of a man who had been wearing one of the suits, he would probably reply in the simply but enthusiastic way in which American men talk—"It fits well," "I get lots of compliments," "I like the style and the price." You can usually avoid this problem of causing your endorsers to talk too expansively and/or technically in testimonial copy by doing two things:

(1) Associate the copy you are writing with *some real person* whom you know well and ask yourself what he or she would say about the product if giving an endorsement. Remember that the individual with whom you identify the product does not know much about it beyond having a high regard for its qualities in general. If you can easily imagine your friend saying what you'd like to have the advertisement say, then the chances are you have created a good, believable testimonial statement.

If you can have this friend actually *make* a statement to you—or read aloud what you have written, you'll be aided even more.

(2) Test your copy on somebody who is not in the advertising business, preferably a person who you know already uses the product you are advertising. Let this person read the statement and tell you whether or not he or she would make such a remark. Only in one or both of these two tests can you be sure

'Why I smoke Vantage.'
I like smoking.
Always have liked smoking.
But I do have eyes and ears.
So I'd be less than honest if I said the critics of smoking didn't have a lot to do with my switching to Vantage.
Every time I'd light one of my old cigarettes they'd make me feel guilty.
Even tried one of those low 'tar' and nicotine cigarettes for awhile, but that was a lost cause.
I couldn't draw any more flavor out of them than I could from a bobby pin.
Vantage?
I took them up about a year ago and I love them.
They taste every bit as good as my old brand. And Vantage has a lot less 'tar' and nicotine.
Well, yes, I could have stopped smoking altogether, only I wouldn't stop smoking even for one day.
Cigarettes simply give me too much pleasure for me to want to quit.
That's something those people who are always knocking cigarettes should keep in mind.
Instead of always telling us not to smoke, you'd think they'd just tell us to smoke Vantage, so we can still get enjoyment out of something we like to do.
Pat Schanning
New York, New York
VANTAGE
MENTHOL
MENTHOL 11 mg. 'tar' 0.8 mg. nicotine
VANTAGE
FILTER 12 mg. 'tar' 0.9 mg. nicotine
Warning: The Surgeon General Has Determined That Cigarette Smoking Is Dangerous to Your Health.
Filter: 12 mg."tar", 0.9 mg. nicotine, Menthol: 11 mg."tar", 0.8 mg. nicotine—av. per cigarette, FTC Report Apr. 72.

Fig. 7-2

True testimonial.

you are not, because of your own vast knowledge of your product, putting words into the mouths of real people—words that sound strained, insincere, or too expert.

Testimonials must be honest

A later chapter gives you background and information on legal questions that have a daily influence on the work of copywriters. It should be pointed out right here, however, that testimonials should never be used simply to gain the name of some prominent person *if that person does not actually use the product regularly and unless he or she subscribes wholeheartedly to the feeling about it you wish to get across.*

The Federal Trade Commission, the various advertising organizations, and other groups interested in better advertising frown upon the practice of writing testimonial statements without regard for the identity of the endorser, and then paying someone a large sum of money for the use of the name and for signing the statement. You may look foolish and dishonest if one of these operations backfires, as they often have, and it is learned that your prize endorser actually uses some rival-brand product. *Know your endorser.* Talk to him, if

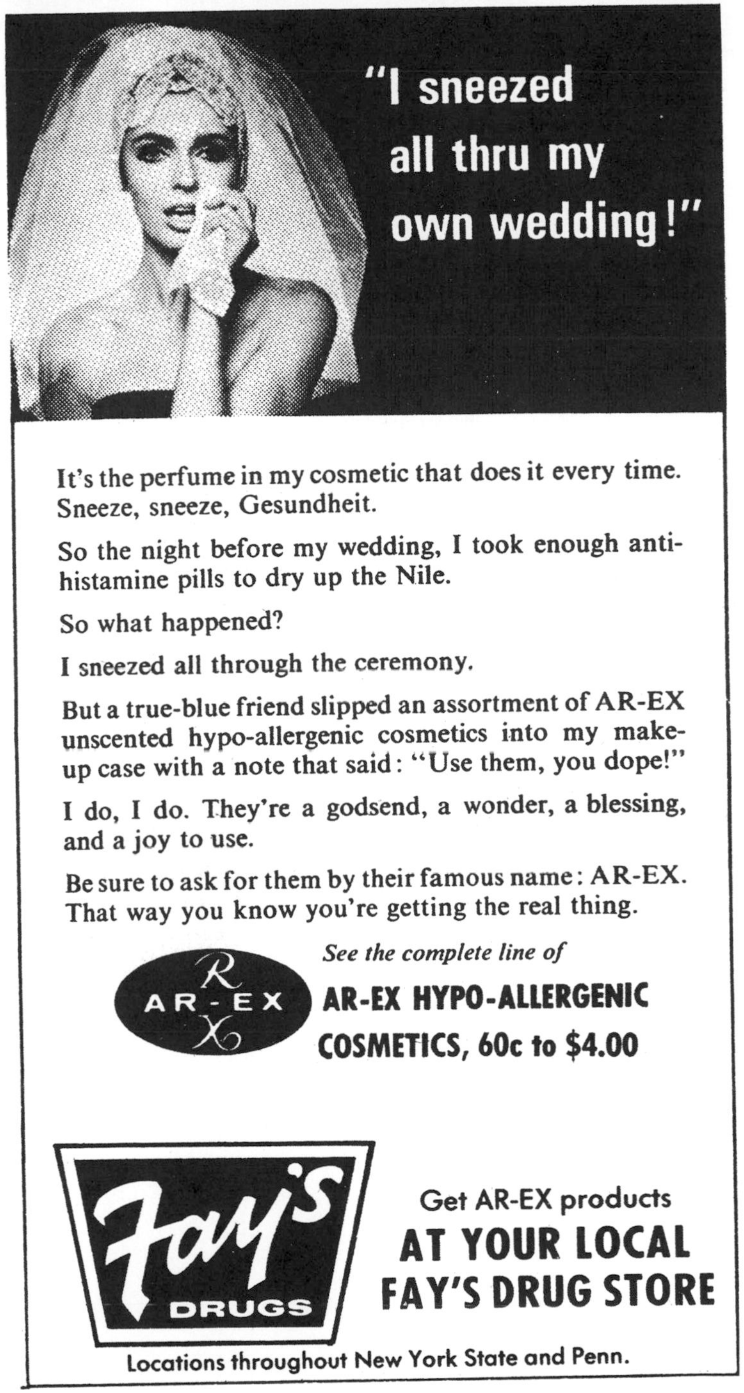
"I sneezed all thru my own wedding!"
It's the perfume in my cosmetic that does it every time. Sneeze, sneeze, Gesundheit.
So the night before my wedding, I took enough anti-histamine pills to dry up the Nile.
So what happened?
I sneezed all through the ceremony.
But a true-blue friend slipped an assortment of AR-EX unscented hypo-allergenic cosmetics into my make-up case with a note that said: "Use them, you dope!"
I do, I do. They're a godsend, a wonder, a blessing, and a joy to use.
Be sure to ask for them by their famous name: AR-EX. That way you know you're getting the real thing.
AR-EX
See the complete line of
AR-EX HYPO-ALLERGENIC COSMETICS, 60c to $4.00
Fay's DRUGS
Get AR-EX products
AT YOUR LOCAL FAY'S DRUG STORE
Locations throughout New York State and Penn.

Fig. 7-3

Quasi-testimonial.

In this case, a testimonial feeling is created by making up a situation and having it described in a testimonial form. This is often done when it would be extremely difficult to find someone in real life to build the advertisement around.

possible—get his own honest appraisal of your product before you write anything. You'll come up with better selling copy and you'll save yourself embarrassment.

You will be responsible, usually, for the writing of the testimonial statements your endorsers sign. On very rare occasions, endorsers have been known to insist upon making their own claims, and refusing to sign anything else. Usually they won't care much, and you will be expected to do the writing for them. Just remember, make all testimonial statements *sound like normal people talking.*

The quasi-testimonial

In planning an advertising campaign for any given product, it may be decided by you and your associates that the story may most effectively be told in the first person—testimonial style. Yet for one of many reasons you may not wish to use the statements of actual personalities. The increased costs of paying for testimonials may be one reason. Availability of well-known people who might be interested in endorsing the particular product may be another. The most common reason for discarding the true-testimonial approach is simply that the product does not lend itself particularly well to the endorsement of a celebrity. In this case, you may desire to use the "quasi-testimonial." In the quasi-testimonial you have a type of copy approach, and also the sort of product (or service) which might be sold by an *unidentified* individual as well as an identified person.

You might have what appears to be an endorsement of a certain type of insurance and an insurance company, by an average-appearing man of late middle age. The headline and practically all the body copy are of testimonial character, with the selling story handled in the first person singular. Yet nowhere is this man identified. He is used solely as a *type,* with whom every man of 55 can conceivably associate himself. It would be worthless to use the endorsement of a well-known individual here, since most readers would not believe that any celebrity could or would "retire" on $300 a month, even though such a person might actually be found in the policy archives of the insurance company.

Secondly, most men who have done so would be reluctant to publish the facts concerning their income, from an annuity or elsewhere. To gain, therefore, the added human interest of the personalized copy, those responsible for this advertisement decided to go ahead and write it just as if this were to be a signed testimonial but to use a photograph of a professional model rather than that of a real endorser.

An interesting slant to this particular advertisement is the fact that the headline is written to capture the personal interest of every reader, while the body text is entirely within the testimonial pattern. If the copywriter had used a headline that stated "How I retired at 55—" he would have sacrificed readership from those men who might automatically say to themselves, "Well, maybe *he* could do it, but *I'll* never be able to retire." The *you* flags interest; the testimonial technique provides believability.

This type of copy is one of the most frequently used and most successful tools of copywriters. Just remember, though, that you must keep such copy material *simple, believable!*

You will have more latitude in writing statements for imaginary people to "say" than for real ones. In the first place, you eliminate all worry lest the endorser not really believe what he says, and actually is not a booster of your product. Secondly, and this is especially true when the illustration of the "endorser" is a painting or a drawing rather than a photograph, the public has become familiar enough with the pseudo-testimonial treatment to understand its motives.

People will not be so critical of the statements of imaginary characters in advertising as they are of those that are supposed to be said by real ones. However, don't let this comment lead you astray. The difference is very, very slight, and you will probably be wise to treat the copy in pseudo-testimonial advertisements exactly as you would if you were writing for a quotation by a real individual. Keep it natural! Keep it simple! Don't try to *sell!*

Personalized copy can sometimes get pretty far afield, far enough so that the foregoing rules don't apply. If you are preparing advertisements for a dog food, you may want to show a talking dog, and let him do your selling for you. You may use an illustration of a baby for a soap or talcum advertisement, putting grown-ups' words in baby's mouth. If you look through magazines and newspapers long enough you can find examples of almost every conceivable kind of object brought to life for advertising purposes—railroad trains, clocks, fish and fowl, vacuum cleaners, and hundreds of others.

Fig. 7-4.

Quasi-testimonial.

Having an animal or object deliver a testimonial obtains high readership, especially if done with humor as in this instance.

I had dingy teeth. And doggy breath.
Nobody kissed me twice.
Even my best friend wouldn't tell me why.
Then I discovered MILK-BONE Dog Biscuits.
Hard crunchy nourishing biscuits that scraped away unsightly stains and tartar (from my otherwise sound and healthy teeth). Removed particles of soft food. Actually helped strengthen my gums. And made my breath almost human again.
And best of all, with Milk-Bone® Dog Biscuits, I got cleaner, whiter teeth in just three weeks!
CLEANER, WHITER TEETH IN 3 WEEKS!
MILK-BONE
BRAND
Dog Biscuits
"How I got cleaner whiter teeth in just three weeks."
© 1972 NABISCO, INC.

These advertisements represent a rather bodacious use of personalized copy, in which the copywriter is working almost strictly for the attention-getting value of the unusual. Naturally, it makes little difference whether you write a statement that sounds believable or not if it is emanating from the mouth of a horse! Among the best examples of this type of copy, judiciously employed as a vehicle for sound selling ideas was Elsie, the famous Borden cow. As in most of the copy in this series of advertisements, the entire piece was a dialogue among the members of the Borden family of bovine salesmen. Nobody would think it particularly unrealistic to have a cow stating "as grand a fit, for instance, as the name None Such is for Borden's None Such Mince Meat. It makes the eatingest, spiciest Thanksgiving pie of 'em all."

At least nobody would think it any more unrealistic than to have a cow stating anything at all! But imagine that quotation placed in the mouth of a typical American housewife!

It all boils down to one thing. If you are writing for human beings, make your copy *human*. If you are writing for cows or codfish, your conscience can be your guide.

COMIC-STRIP AND CONTINUITY COPY

The third type of dialogue and monologue copy falls into the pattern known as comic-strip style or continuity-panel style. The practice of making advertisements resemble comic strips or editorial cartoons is widespread and successful. Researchers have provided considerable evidence that such formats for advertisements often gain greater attention from readers, especially in newspapers, than those designed in a more conventional format.

The success of one format or another in getting closer reading depends upon what is being advertised, where, how, and how often. The number of times you write comic and continuity copy will undoubtedly be few, but there may be occasions when you will have to know the technique. You should be familiar with the ways in which this sort of copy differs from other advertising writing.

There is not much variation between the comic-strip and the continuity-panel advertisement. Both are normally planned to tell a story that stresses the selling features of a product. Both usually involve a character or group of characters whose actions present a problem to be solved. The problem is then solved through purchase of the product being advertised. Both types feature copy displayed in blurbs or balloons, and in many cases this copy accomplishes the entire job of telling the story, reaching the happy ending, and selling the product. Often, however, either a straight-line copy block or selling caption under each panel is used in addition to the balloons.

Newspaper comic-strip advertisements should be designed to resemble as closely as conditions permit an editorial comic strip. They should be of the same size and horizontal shape, if possible, and carry a heading and title just as regular comic strips do.

Continuity-panel advertisements may use a horizontal or vertical arrangement of panels, which tell a type of story similar to that of the comic strips, but which often carry a headline, a large illustration, and a logotype. In many advertisements you will see a series of comic-strip and continuity-panel advertisements of various kinds. Note that there is no set pattern for their construction. Sometimes each type uses the last panel for a display of the product and a straight-line copy story, while others depend on the pay-off of the blurb continuity to carry all the sell.

All these points about this style of advertising are mentioned because in both comic-strip and continuity advertisements your job requires a greater amount of creative ingenuity than is needed in many other forms of advertisement writing. Since success of panel advertisements depends upon a logical, believable story, you must plan the illustrations and the action before you write your copy. In creating most other advertisements you can often count on plenty of help from your art associates to get a good illustrative device, and your main task will be the writing of headlines, subheads, and body copy. In the strip or continuity-panel advertisement, you'll have to go way beyond that. Your job here can almost be likened to that of a movie scenario writer rather than a copywriter, although it is actually a twofold proposition, since in addition to artistic creation you are, of course, trying *to sell something.*

The Bureau of Advertising of the American Newspaper Publishers Association has compiled some very helpful advice to copywriters who are interested in improving their copy for comic-strip advertisements. Following is a discussion and enlargement of some of their suggestions:

1. *Follow editorial style.* If you are writing a comic-strip advertisement, make it look as

I JUST BROWN A POUND OF FRESH GROUND BEEF...
STIR IN MANWICH — IT GIVES THE FLAVOR* AND SAVES THE TIME!
*MANWICH HAS 14 TASTY INGREDIENTS
SIMMER THE DELICIOUS MIXTURE, AND IN 10 MINUTES...
FEED 6 HEARTY APPETITES AT BUDGET HAMBURGER PRICES.
"MANWICH-the secret ingredient in my best homemade Sloppy Joe."
Hunt's. MANWICH SANDWICH SAUCE
Manwich-
Homemade taste without
homemade time.

Fig. 7-5

Continuity strip advertisement.

much as possible like a real comic strip. Do not include panels that look like little advertisements. Do not vary the size of the panels. Remember that you are trying to hook readership on the basis of public familiarity with and liking for comic strips. You will not obtain this bonus readership if your advertisement doesn't *look* like a comic strip.

2. *Keep your first panel interesting*—humorous or action-packed. By doing so you gain impetus in leading your reader along into the next panel and through to the conclusion. Sometimes you will see examples of comic-strip advertisements that beg for further reading, and that do not offer enough excitement about what is coming to lure maximum readership.

3. *Change focus.* Comic-strip artists and writers have discovered that it attracts attention to mix up long and short shots of characters in the strip. The same technique is true of comic-strip advertisements.

4. *Keep blurb copy short.* If you can't set up your situation, develop it, and sell the product in short, natural-sounding blurbs, *don't try to use the comic-strip style.* You will repel the reader if you jam your blurbs with long, involved copy in order to establish

your story. Keep in mind the points already mentioned concerning all types of dialogue and monologue copy. Your characters are actually supposed to be speaking, and the things they say must be things anyone would say in similar circumstances. If they aren't, you will lose selling power even though all the other directions have been carefully followed.

Most of the foregoing comments on comic-strip copy is also applicable to continuity-panel copy, except, of course, for the requirements of staying within the physical confines of the actual comic-strip format. Continuity panels are used when it is felt that the comic-strip technique is desirable, but for one reason or another—usually space limitations—the true size and shape of the comic strip cannot be followed. Continuity panels, for instance, will be used in magazines, rather than the familiar comic strip, since readers of magazines are not accustomed to seeing comics in them and, too, magazines do not sell space the size and shape required for comic strips. The continuity panel is also often used in newspapers when larger space than the standard comic strip is considered necessary.

Both these types of advertising depend, for their maximum effectiveness, upon their ability to *lure* readership rather than to compel it. The closer they can be designed and written to resemble the editorial features after which they are patterned, the better chance they have of succeeding. Much of the foregoing, as previously mentioned, is derived from a study made by the Bureau of Advertising, ANPA.

NARRATIVE COPY

"Narrative" copy, in one respect, is closely allied to most dialogue and monologue copy—in its requirement for setting up a situation or story prior to getting into the selling copy. As you have discovered, most of the personalized copy approaches conform to this pattern. The story, and often the selling as well, are handled in dialogue between the characters in the advertisement, or in a monologue by one character.

When it is necessary to establish a situation or tell a story, you often will *not* wish to personalize the copy. You will then be writing narrative copy.

The most common type of narrative copy establishes a background for the presentation of specific sales appeals for a product.

Your job becomes much broader when you are following a format that requires narrative copy. Your writing problem is no longer one that can be solved with a clear, straightforward, well-organized summary of your product's sales features. You must also create a *preface, a prologue* to your selling story, and one which is not only calculated to select the proper reading audience, but which fits into the over-all sales plans of the product you're selling.

Take, for example, an advertisement for a $200 wrist-watch. The copywriter may reason that $200 watches are not very often sold by simply pointing out how pretty they are or how well they run. He also knows that few men who would be reading his advertisement, in a popular weekly magazine, would actually be live prospects for such an expensive watch, regardless of *what* superlatives he could think of. Neither does he consider as prospects the women who want to give a watch to their husbands or sweethearts. Straight-line copy, accordingly, is out. So is testimonial copy, because while Mr. America possibly will wear a bow tie because a theatrical figure does, he will *not* be likely to spend $200 for a watch because *anybody* does.

No, the problem here is to write an adver-

"John and I found skiing the Alpine rapids sort of like walking on water during a hurricane."
BY APPOINTMENT
TO HER MAJESTY QUEEN ELIZABETH II
SUPPLIERS OF CANADIAN CLUB WHISKY
HIRAM WALKER & SONS LIMITED
WALKERVILLE CANADA
"No matter which way you look at it, walking on water is a miracle. Especially when you tread the raging Salza River in the Austrian Alps. As we slipped on our pontoons, John and I felt we'd really put our foot into it this time.
"Pontoon skiing is a sport that constantly keeps you on your toes. One false step and submerged rocks could have dashed our pontoons to pieces. And you can't make a life raft out of splinters. I kept calm and remembered John's advice: 'Walk softly and carry a big paddle.'
"That evening at the Reinprecht Inn in Grinzing, we celebrated our adventure with Canadian Club." It seems wherever you go, C.C. welcomes you. More people appreciate its gentle manners and the pleasing way it behaves in mixed company. Canadian Club—"The Best In The House"® in 87 lands.
Canadian Club
Imported in bottle from Canada

Fig. 7-6

Narrative advertisement.

This campaign invariably tells interesting stories in its picture-captions.

tisement which will hand-pick those men and women from the millions who read it who could afford a $200 watch. and to offer them a subtle enough sales message to make them wish to do so. The entire selling power of this copy lies in its ability to produce action in a small group of people. By adroit writing alone, this copywriter appeals to the good taste of the successful executive, the ego of the semi-successful executive, the wishful thinking of the newly rich, and the desire of practically every woman to make an impression upon her man.

Narrative copy, in product selling, does not, however, require such unusual products as $200 watches. You will find that narrative structure, while it may be used effectively for almost any kind of product is *best* adapted to products that can be sold on a highly emotional basis. Insurance, deodorants, toothpaste, jewelry, cosmetics, clothing, antiseptics, and similar articles or services may be described in their most appealing light when you can dramatize the results they produce.

HOW DO I WRITE NARRATIVE COPY—LONG OR SHORT?

Copy chiefs in every advertising organization the country over are asked that question almost daily by young writers and other interested people. There is no sensible answer except that copy should be just long enough to do the best selling job. If you are writing an advertisement in straight-line style, be as brief as possible while still giving adequate emphasis to all the sales points you wish to make. If you have only one thing to say and you can say it in three words, then three words is all the copy you should write. If you are preparing a piece of narrative copy, on the contrary, you can't very well confine it to a few words or sentences, although your copy may be every bit as powerful, from a sales angle, or more so, than a terse, telegraphed message.

Don't waste time worrying about whether copy should be long or short. When you have convinced yourself and your associates that the approach is right, tailor the copy to do the job, regardless of the number of words you use.

NARRATIVE COPY IS FUN TO WRITE

Product selling, narrative style, is usually more fun for copywriters than any other type of copywriting because it allows a freedom from rules and regulations that sometimes will heckle you in doing straight selling copy. Few people will argue, for instance, that insurance cannot best be sold to a man who is "in the mood" to buy insurance. You can scarcely get a man in the mood to take on another policy by reciting a cold, hard series of facts and figures to him, unless they are sensationally interesting. You may, however, start him thinking about his insurance needs by painting a word-picture of some of the unplesant events that could happen if he did not have enough insurance. By using (1) an illustration of sufficient strength and human interest that he can easily associate it with himself or his own family, and (2) a poignant story that also could well be his own, you can pre-condition that man to listen to your offer much more receptively than you could if you started in by saying, "Look, brother—I have an insurance policy here that etc., etc."

It's *fun* to let your imagination wander into such writing, away from the fetters of product features, laboratory reports, scientific tests, advertisers' "do's and don'ts," and other qualifying factors which regulate much of a copywriter's daily work. Narrative copy gives you a chance to write a "story."

Emotion isn't always used

Don't get the idea that all product-selling, narrative copy is, or should be, filled with pathos or fear or one of the other great emotional appeals. The only factor that makes narrative copy *narrative* is its requirement for telling a story before selling the product. It doesn't need to establish fear or uncertainty in the minds of its readers. Yet it does maintain a very definite value of self-association for most men. It sets up a situation of normal, everyday nature—notably, self-criticism.

Product selling, in narrative copy, is best adapted to products of a certain type. This, you will probably agree, makes sense, because most such narrative copy is based upon emotionalism. Even the narrative copy for the $200 watch was emotional. Narrative copy can be and is used for every conceivable sort of product in all types of media.

Have fun, but don't forget to sell

Narrative copy, then, for product selling, is fun for copywriters to write. It is a challenge to your creative imagination. It is a fine way to establish a good selling situation—*sometimes.*

Watch out for this—be very sure that the story you tell in your narrative has a quick and easy transition to your selling message, and be sure your selling message *sells hard.*

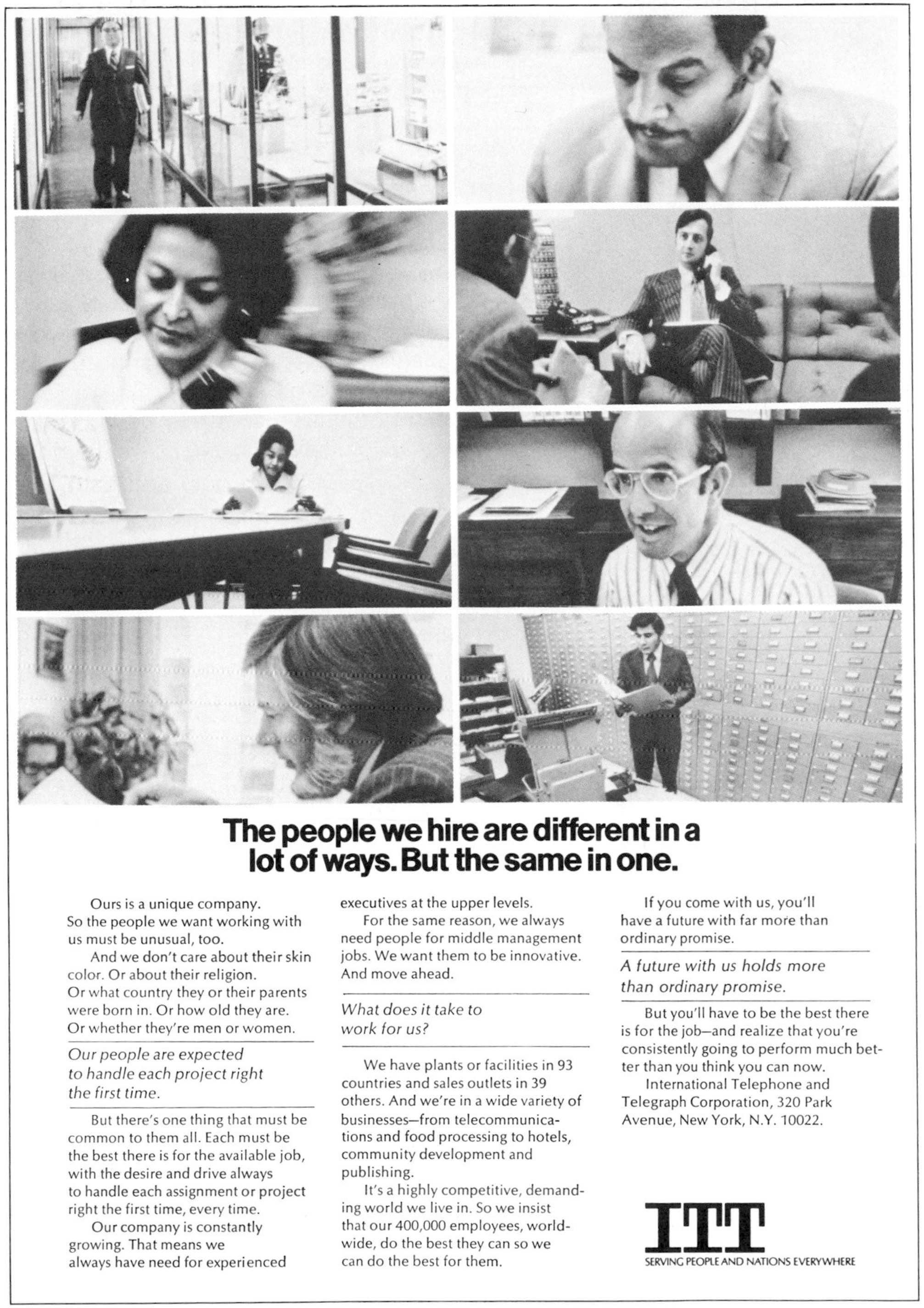
The people we hire are different in a lot of ways. But the same in one.
Ours is a unique company. So the people we want working with us must be unusual, too.
And we don't care about their skin color. Or about their religion. Or what country they or their parents were born in. Or how old they are. Or whether they're men or women.
Our people are expected to handle each project right the first time.
But there's one thing that must be common to them all. Each must be the best there is for the available job, with the desire and drive always to handle each assignment or project right the first time, every time.
Our company is constantly growing. That means we always have need for experienced executives at the upper levels.
For the same reason, we always need people for middle management jobs. We want them to be innovative. And move ahead.
What does it take to work for us?
We have plants or facilities in 93 countries and sales outlets in 39 others. And we're in a wide variety of businesses—from telecommunications and food processing to hotels, community development and publishing.
It's a highly competitive, demanding world we live in. So we insist that our 400,000 employees, worldwide, do the best they can so we can do the best for them.
If you come with us, you'll have a future with far more than ordinary promise.
A future with us holds more than ordinary promise.
But you'll have to be the best there is for the job—and realize that you're consistently going to perform much better than you think you can now.
International Telephone and Telegraph Corporation, 320 Park Avenue, New York, N.Y. 10022.
ITT
SERVING PEOPLE AND NATIONS EVERYWHERE

Fig. 7-7

Institutional advertisement with emphasis on people.

This copy avoids the impersonal approach of many institutional or corporate advertisements by describing the company and its goals in terms of the people who work for it.

Don't waste space to tell a story that does not give you an immediate and powerful springboard into the sales arguments that you wish your reader to hear. Once you make that transition, leave the characters of your playlet to themselves. Do as the veteran copywriter does. Turn your guns on the reader. Get back on the straight-line to show how your product is "absolutely indispensable" to the successful overcoming of the problems you have presented.

INSTITUTIONAL COPY

Even more common than narrative copy is the type of copy you have probably heard called "institutional." In many cases, institutional copy is narrative in style, because under normal conditions you are not trying to sell a *specific* product or service.

At one time this definition of institutional advertising, as referring to all advertisements that attempted to sell the company instead of its product or service, seemed to satisfy advertising people. In recent years, however, the definition has seemed too narrow. Thus, we now have "idea" advertising, "corporate" advertising, "public relations" advertising and "management" advertising. While each of these designations has some merit the term

The phone company wants more operators like Rick Wehmhoefer.
Rick Wehmhoefer of Denver, Colorado, is one of several hundred male telephone operators in the Bell System.
Currently, Rick is a directory assistance operator. "So far, my job has been pleasant and worthwhile," he says. "I enjoy assisting people."
We have men like Rick in a lot of different telephone jobs. Both men and women work as Bell System mechanics, truck drivers, installers and engineers.
We want the men and women of the telephone company to do what they want to do, and do best.
Today, when openings exist, local Bell Companies are offering applicants and present employees some jobs they may never have thought about before. We want to help all advance to the best of their abilities.
AT&T and your local Bell Company are equal opportunity employers.

Fig. 7-8

Institutional advertising with emphasis on an individual.

AT&T has always stressed people in its advertisements thus bringing the corporation down to a level the public can understand.

institutional advertising is still the most-commonly used term by those describing advertising that does not sell goods or services of a corporation.

One criticism of the term, of course, is that a considerable amount of advertising—called institutional advertising—is conducted in behalf of hotels, hospitals, and other organizations that fall under the heading of institutions. In this chapter we are *not* referring to this type of advertising.

Why Institutional Copy is Used

Before a copywriter begins to write an institutional advertisement he must have a clear idea of what it is trying to accomplish. In the usual product advertisement his objective is relatively clear and simple; he is trying to sell the product. Objectives in institutional advertising are not so clear-cut and often are quite subtle. Ordinarily, however, those objectives will fall into one of the three following:

1. To create confidence in the company that will help sell its products. This confidence may be required because:
   a. The company makes so many products that the institutional campaign serves as a sort of umbrella. Thus, if confidence is engendered, it is not so vital that the

Creative Glass.
First you buy it. Then you decide what to do with it.
When Corning set out to make Creative Glass, we had only one thing in mind. To make it beautiful.
The rest, we decided, would be up to your imagination.
So we designed 15 pieces of the most artful, intelligent glassware you've ever seen. Then we made them heat-resistant and cold-resistant. And we priced them as beautifully as we designed them. From $5.00 for a mysterious set of salt and pepper shakers you don't have to turn upside down to shake; to $10 for the Super-Server you see above filled with shrimp and ice.
Creative Glass. We were creative when we designed it. So you could be creative when you use it.
Corning Glass Works • Corning, N.Y. 14830
Creative Glass by Corning. A product of imagination... yours and ours.

Fig. 6-9

Corporate advertising with a stress on products.

The company's creativity is well-expressed in the interesting variety of products it exhibits.

public remember individual selling points for each of the products. Instead, if the institutional campaign has done its job, public reaction will be: "I don't know much about this product but if it's made by the ABC Company it must be good." Such thinking is especially valuable when quick buying decisions must be made by supermarket or drug store shoppers.

b. The company makes the kind of product that will never be bought if the consumer doesn't have strong faith in the reliability, integrity and skill of the maker. Pharmaceuticals, such as remedies and medicines, require such faith. Squibbs, Lederle, and Eli Lilly are advertisers whose great growth has largely developed because of the public trust they have enjoyed through the years.

2. To explain the company management's stand about such pressing matters as a labor dispute, a bad product, or a drastic price rise. Such advertisements have a public relations flavor and very often are tied in with news releases that are published at the same time. Sometimes they are signed by top officials of the company although

Can you find the electric wires in this picture?
That isn't really a fair question.
You'd need X-ray vision to see the electric wires in Columbia, Maryland.
Columbia is a new city, planned in detail before a shovelful of earth was moved. One of the first things planners settled on was underground electricity. General Electric helped the Baltimore Gas & Electric Company do it.
Until recently, underground electricity was economical only for the downtown commercial areas of larger cities.
But that's changed. Greatly. It's estimated that by 1975, 70% of all distribution wires to new construction will be underground.
GE helped bring on the change by designing new kinds of underground equipment. Transformers and cables, for instance, that can withstand harsh underground conditions for years on end.
General Electric is also working on ways to spruce up the looks of overhead power distribution systems. And on nuclear plants to help cut down on air pollution.
Men helping Man

Fig. 7-10

Corporate advertisement.

The company explains in this advertisement how it is improving the environment, a powerful issue in recent years.

written by the copywriter. Exceeding care must be exercised in the writing of such "policy" advertisements which are scrutinized closely not only by the company's advertising department but also by top management, by the company's public relations agency, and by the corporation lawyers.

3. To express the company's philosophy about government, politics, or other aspects of society. Since enlightened management men in a corporation feel keenly the need to speak out on the pressing issues of the day from ecology to the drug problem, or education to slaughter on the highways, advertisements are often used to give voice to these feelings. Once again, a battery of critics will be looking over your work to be certain that it expresses accurately what management intends to convey.

What has probably driven more companies to institutional advertising has been the increasing difficulty of impressing advertising messages for individual products on the minds of prospective buyers. The profusion of brands, coupled with the similar profusion of advertising messages, has made it increasingly

Fig. 7-11

Editorial-type advertisement.

This type of advertisement that looks like an editorial feature can obtain very high readership if the subject matter is interesting. Even the requirement that the word "Advertisement" be placed at the bottom does not hurt the readership.

Share the Secret of Younger-Looking Skin

Women are usually considered unable to keep a secret for more than twenty-four hours. But there's a curious phenomenon. When a woman discovers a beauty secret that makes her look younger and prettier, she is tempted to keep the special knowledge for herself alone. She may be reluctant to pass the beautifying secret along, except perhaps to her very special friends.

But now there's a beauty blend that does such marvelous things to make a woman's complexion look radiant, vital and younger-looking that almost no one could possibly bear keeping the secret to herself. It's a lovely secret, made for sharing. And women in all parts of the world who have enjoyed the blend's beautifying benefits have been passing the wonderful word along.

This precious formulation is known in the United States as Oil of Olay moisturizing lotion. Once you have discovered Oil of Olay with its blend of tropical moist oils at your druggist, and have used it for just a short while, you won't be able to resist telling your friends about it. They will probably be asking what you've done to make your complexion so much smoother, softer and moister.

The natural ingredients in Oil of Olay are compatible with the skin's own fluids and so blend with them easily to help maintain the balance of oil and moisture necessary for a fresh-looking complexion. The beautifying lotion penetrates the surface layer of the skin, helping to ease away dryness that emphasizes wrinkles. So you can't help looking younger. Oil of Olay also helps the skin retain its own moisture, certainly an added beauty advantage.

You'll find Oil of Olay remarkably easy to use. And it never leaves an oily after-feel. Simply soothe on morning and night. Besides moisturizing your skin, the beauty blend is a superb make-up base. It spreads so evenly and penetrates so quickly that your cosmetics stay fresh hour after hour, without ever streaking or discoloring.

Really, now that you think about it, isn't Oil of Olay the kind of secret you want to share? At least with your closest friends?

Beauty Hints

When your complexion has been exposed to excessively drying conditions, treat it to a little extra loving care. Lavish Oil of Olay on the face and neck, and then apply a steamy, moist towel to help the beauty fluid work even more effectively. You will feel extraordinarily refreshed and renewed.

* * *

Your neck needs special pampering if the skin is to look as resilient and youthful as can be. Stroke on Oil of Olay® lavishly, moving upward from the base of the neck to the chinline, with firm but gentle motions of the fingertips. Besides helping to ease away dryness, this nightly ritual will leave you feeling relaxed and refreshed.

(Advertisement)

more difficult for any advertiser to register his selling points. Research of print and broadcast advertising has revealed a dismaying lack of product-point registration and, equally as alarming, poor identification of the advertisers paying for the advertising.

Interesting institutional advertising, not designed to sell but to do one thing only—to create a favorable feeling for the advertiser and hence any product he promotes—has been viewed as a possible way out of the too-many-products, too-many-advertising-messages impasse. Copywriters writing institutional advertising, accordingly, face a stern challenge in their writing task.

Your study must be studied

There is not a great deal to tell you about *writing* institutional copy except that it pays to give extra long and careful study to the subject about which you are to write. If you are going to sell your firm to the public on the basis of its ability to help develop a jet engine, be very sure that what you write about that jet engine makes sense, not only to people you think don't know, but to jet experts. If you are going to go after readership with the story of penicillin, get your information from unimpeachable sources. There is no room whatsoever for extravagant claims in institutional advertising. If you lose believability, you lose everything. Be sure of what you're writing before you start to write, and check it *after you've finished* with the same unimpeachable sources.

In this type of copy, again, the nature of the firm or product you are advertising has a lot to do with the selection of the style of the *format,* and, therefore, your body copy style. Institutional copy is used mainly by three kinds of advertisers:

(1) By organizations such as drug firms that serve the public's vital needs. It lends itself very well to building good will and prestige.

(2) By companies whose products require precise engineering or research, like the oil companies or the automotive industry. Thus, an advertisement based on "creative imagination" sells Chrysler Corporation's ability and ingenuity rather than the separate merits of the individual Chrysler-built cars. These, of course, are advertised in other campaigns built individually for each car.

(3) By advertisers (discussed earlier) who either because they make a great many products themselves, or because they are discour-

Advertisement

How to Speak and Write Like a College Graduate

"Now, like thousands of intelligent men and women who have not had college training in English, you can gain the ability to speak and write like a college graduate without going back to school, says Don Bolander of Career Institute.

"The new C. I. Method makes it easy. In only 15 minutes a day at home, you can bring up your vocabulary, stop making embarrassing mistakes, improve your writing, discover the 'secrets' of interesting conversation."

According to Bolander, "Once you gain a mastery of English, you'll find yourself able to get ahead faster in your job and social life. You'll gain new poise and confidence plus the respect of those around you."

For readers of this newspaper, Bolander has made available a free 32-page booklet that tells how you can gain the ability to speak and write like a college graduate, in your own home. Just send your name, address and zip code on a postcard or letter to Don Bolander, Career Institute, Dept. 576-32, Mundelein, Illinois 60060. (A home Study School).

Fig. 7-12

Editorial-type advertisement.

The copywriter who produces advertisements that read like surrounding news material often finds many readers who shun the more conventional advertisements. These examples are from a daily newspaper but such advertisements are equally effective in magazines.

I Love To Read Fast!

A noted publisher in Chicago reports there is a simple technique of rapid reading which should enable you to increase your reading speed and yet retain much more. Most people do not realize how much they could increase their pleasure, success and income by reading faster and more accurately.

According to this publisher, many people, regardless of their present reading skill, can use this simple technique to improve their reading ability to a remarkable degree. Whether reading stories, books, technical matter, it becomes possible to read sentences at a glance and entire pages in seconds with this method.

To acquaint the readers of this newspaper with the easy-to-follow rules for developing rapid reading skill, the company has printed full details of its interesting self-training method in a new booklet, "How to Read Faster and Retain More," mailed free to anyone who requests it. No obligation. Send your name, address, and zip code to: Reading, 555 E. Lange St., Dept. 576-31, Mundelein, Ill. 60060. A postcard will do.

aged by the difficulty of fighting for recognition against the myriad of advertising products, decide to strive for company-name registration as a form of advertising umbrella.

(4) By "association" advertising, or advertising paid for by a *group* of independent operators in the same industry. Thus the fruit growers of California advertise "Sunkist" rather than their own names. The Washington State Apple Association advertises the merits of the big red beauties grown in Washington. And the National Association of Life Insurance Underwriters uses copy which sells *life insurance,* not that of any particular insurance company. This third category of institutional copy many times promotes sales of a certain type of *product.* A beer advertisement run by the U.S. Brewer's Foundation, even though it cannot describe the good features of any brand of beer, in competitive beer selling, can sell beer, in straight-line copy, and sell it competitively against other beverages.

This is a good example of how impossible it is to lay down a set of rules for you to follow in writing creative advertising. In almost no phase of copywriting is there any rule which dictates either that a certain type of copy *must* be used, or that *any* type of copy *cannot* be used. You are given in this book the most logical and most commonly used devices, and are offered an *idea* of when to use them. You will doubtless be able to find hundreds of examples, similar to this one, which seem to contradict the general principles advanced in these chapters.

Write to reader

Beginning copywriters, and experienced copywriters as well, should beware of the outstanding peril of institutional copy. That peril is the tendency to write in terms of products and sales, and not in terms of prospects and purchases. The writer, especially the beginner, gets so wrapped up in the traditions of the company, in its astounding (to him) manufacturing processes, in the details of its operations, that he completely forgets the reader. The copy becomes chest-pounding in its boasting, and the "you" approach is entirely replaced by the "we."

Such copy often results from the urging of a self-satisfied executive of the advertiser's company who finds it difficult to believe that the success story can fail to be as fascinating to the readers of the advertisements as it is to him. Remember than—keep in mind your

RAISINS
SPRING
A
TASTE
SURPRISE
THEY'LL
REALLY
OPEN UP
YOUR
EYES!
P.S. Raisins—sweet energy-packed fruit—are right to tide a tot over till mealtime. And the little handy packs hold just enough. California Raisin Advisory Board, Fresno.

Fig. 7-13.

Art gimmick—with "poetic license."

reader's interest and never let your reader become subordinated by the urge to let off steam about "us" and "our" and "we."

A poem, deriding institutional advertising, appeared in the magazine *Advertising & Selling* some years ago. This irreverent verse, after pointing out that the advertiser may be interested in his factory and his company history but that no one else is, ended with the following almost bitter admonition:

> So tell me quick and tell me true
> (Or else, my love, to hell with you!)
> Less—How this product came to be!
> More—What the damn thing does for me!

Memorize these words and they may keep you from going the way of a good many copywriters when they tap out institutional copy on their typewriters.

Be interesting

Picture the typical reader of an institutional advertisement. He turns the page, and there is your creation. It has no product that will make his life easier or more pleasant or more profitable. There are no prices to arouse his interest or product selling features to compare with other products.

In short, your advertisement is likely to be viewed as a big fat nothing that offers not one reason for his taking the time to read it. If it follows the lead of too many institutional advertisements it is likely to be dull, self-centered, stuffy, overly-long, and full of "we" and "our" and the board-of-directors language.

You have a vital obligation to be interesting because you won't be read if you're not. Institutional advertising characteristically is at the bottom in readership figures.

To get readership pull out all the stops. Entertain, shock, amuse, fascinate, be unusual and even bizarre. Grab attention with your headline and reinforce it with a different, exciting illustration.

Except for unusual situations, forget dignified prose. Be human. Write relaxed, conversational copy. Concentrate on the people approach. Reduce the awesome corporation to a person—possibly a person who works for it, or a person it serves. The telephone company has done this for years. A.T.&T. is a monstrous corporation in size but the advertising for this company has consistently over the years focussed on people and usually each advertisement spotlights *one* person. The corporation is thus reduced to dimensions to which the reader or viewer can relate, and which he can understand.

From the writing standpoint, to repeat because it's so important, your most vital single job is to be interesting. Then, and only then, will you force readership of your institutional advertisement—an advertisement most readers would rather not read than read.

GIMMICK COPY

If the discussion on "gimmick" headlines is not fresh in your mind, it might be well to review it briefly, since the term "gimmick" is used also for body copy for which it is difficult to find a better term. Any copy not falling into one or another of the foregoing categories may be termed gimmick copy. You are familiar with advertisements written as limericks or jingles or formal poems. Those are gimmicks. So are advertisements in which the copy is set to music or written in pig-Latin or set upside down and sideways.

They are extremely rare because, despite the type of headline treatment you use or the unusual or bizarre illustration you and your art associates may plan, the body copy is usually a place for sober selling. And you can't get much selling out of an advertisement written backwards.

Gimmick copy is seldom used except in cases where you have no need for telling a straight, hard-selling story and you wish to gain added attention and continued interest in an already interesting situation. You aren't shown any fundamentals of writing gimmick copy because there aren't any. It's a case of the fellow with the first idea having the best one—or the worst. At any rate, you won't have many occasions to worry about it.

TO REMEMBER

This section on body copy would be incomplete without a re-emphasis on the importance of simplicity, sincerity, and honesty in *all* the copy you write. If you have the natural ability to write clearly and well, if you have the desire to write, and the needed information concerning your product, you need not spend much time on categories of copy or copy types. As pointed out previously, the style of your body copy will almost always be determined by the style of your advertisement. How you write it depends upon you—*and plenty of practice.*

Important "Extras" of Copywriting.

While most of your creative time will be spent on fashioning headlines, body copy, and illustration ideas, there *are* some other creative tasks that will require your attention. Some of these will take little of your time, others may swallow many of your working hours. Most copywriters learn very quickly that these "odd jobs" of copywriting can sometimes be the most important in a day's work. A copywriter turning out a client publicity story, for example, may discover that sometimes a client may be more impressed by a five-inch publicity story in the newspaper than by his full-page advertisement running in the same issue. He may learn to his chagrin that the same client will overlook the truly excellent creative work in an advertisement if something about the company's signature displeases him. Thus, these "little jobs" that a copywriter does are very frequently "big" when viewed through the eyes of a critical client. Let's look over some of these miscellaneous activities that you, as a copywriter, will be expected to do.

SAY IT WITH SLOGANS?

Americans throughout their political history have been sloganeers. They have made up slogans and have been motivated by them—examples: "Give me liberty or give me death." "Tippecanoe and Tyler too." "Don't change horses in mid-stream."

Slogans have their part in advertising history, too. Any student of advertising soon discovers, for instance, that at the turn of the century slogan-creation was considered the advertising man's most important function. Many stories can be told about the "minstrels" of that era, some of whom became rich by simply conjuring clever, money-making phrases which fascinated advertisers and consumers alike throughout the United States. A lengthy exposition could also be written in explanation of why slogans have since waned in popularity. All this discussion, interesting as it could be, will not be written, since it is a fact that slogans and "sloganeering" are not important in a copywriter's daily life and do not justify more than a superficial study in a discussion of what a copywriter needs to know.

As mentioned previously, many laymen think that the average copywriter spends much of his time thinking up clever slogans and jingles. But this is another advertising canard for which Hollywood must accept most of the blame. Slogans are still used in advertising, certainly. But today the slogan is a "wall flower," not the "belle of the ball" it was in the earlier days of the business.

Today's advertising copywriter spends little time creating slogans. Rarely does he sit down deliberately to write a slogan and, if he did, his chances would be slight for evolving a truly good slogan.

Some of the advertising's most famous slogans have been the result of spur-of-the-moment inspiration, but they are exceptions. Packard automobile's "Ask the man who owns one" was one of the exceptions. Mr. Packard, himself, was credited with the slogan so long identified with the automobile that for many years was a famous name among American automobiles. Back in the early days of the automobile, so the story goes, Mr. Packard was seated at his desk working. His secretary came in to report that a prospective customer had inquired about the merits of the Packard car. When she asked Mr. Packard how she should answer the man, he replied, "Tell him to ask the man who owns one!" Thus was born one of the best-known, most-enduring of all advertising slogans. It was a clever slogan, but could not have endured on that basis alone. Packard's slogan also had "sales power." Sales punch is a "must" for slogans today. Mere cleverness is no longer enough.

Today most of the new slogans coming into advertising are the product of evolution rather than inspiration. Some started out as full-blown campaign themes. After filling the requirements of the time (and losing some of their bright new luster in the process), a new theme was headlined, the former one being retained as a slogan. Among these was "There's a Ford in Your Future" and "You'll Be Ahead with Nash."

Other slogans have first appeared deep in the middle of a paragraph of copy. This is true of Morton Salt's "When it Rains, it Pours." Its copywriter said: "If you want to find a good slogan, write some good copy, and the slogan will pop out at you." Recognized as an especially deft turn of words, a phrase may be picked up and repeated in subsequent advertisements. If it still seems to wear well, it may be used again and again. Finally, it may be displayed apart from the copy block. Eventually it may evolve as a campaign theme that will become a household term. But regardless of how slogans come into being, you should look at slogan writing as just another part of your job.

Certainly, you can probably rattle off ten famous slogans that have stood up under the wear and tear of time. Consider, however, how many would-be slogans have been tried and have fallen by the wayside during the years it took to entrench firmly such standbys as "Good to the last drop," "The pause that refreshes," and "Eventually—Why not now?"

In pre-judging a phrase you think might be an effective slogan, ask yourself these questions:

1. *Does it make a specific claim, or promise a believable benefit?* For example, Hoover's "It beats—as it sweeps—as it cleans" immediately put over a claim you've never heard made for any other vacuum cleaner—a claim that lends a certain "magic" to a Hoover. Colgate's "It cleans your breath while it cleans your teeth" promised you an *extra* benefit, over and above what you normally expect of a toothpaste. Morton's salt's "When it rains, it pours," promises you a remedy for an annoyance you, personally, have experienced.

2. *Does it contain a command to action, a direct appeal to buy?* "Be wiser—buy Kayser," "Say it with flowers," and "Drink Coca-Cola" are good because they make you an active part of the slogan by urging you to take some definite action.

3. *Does it create a favorable identification or image for your product, service, or company?* Newspapers have provided some outstanding slogans that answer this third question. Some of these: *New York Times*—"All the News That's Fit to Print." *Philadelphia Bulletin*—"In Philadelphia . . . Nearly Everybody Reads the Bulletin." *Atlanta Journal*—"Covers Dixie Like the Dew."

Certain writing attributes of slogans appear in the examples that have been offered here. For instance, most of them have a strong sense of the vernacular, of a conversational style that is breezy, informal, and off-hand. A slogan talks "people" language. It is rarely literary in tone and it almost never uses a word that will make anyone reach for a dictionary.

It is rare, too, to find a long slogan. To be memorable a slogan must almost always be brief. A world of copy strength can be packed into a few words as "It's toasted," and "It floats" will testify.

A further aid to memorability is the use of rhyme and alliteration. "Be sure with Pure" is much certain to be remembered than if you wrote "Be certain with Pure" although the meaning is the same for both. If you used alliteration by writing "Pick Planters Peanuts" you'd achieve more memorability than if you wrote "Choose Planters Peanuts."

If your proposed slogan doesn't meet these requirements, see if you can't come up with a phrase that does—if a slogan seems definitely indicated by the particular set of circumstances.

In any event, don't confuse cleverness with selling power; it's a most unreliable guide. Bear in mind, too, that many of advertising's most noteworthy successes have been achieved *without* the continuous employment of slogans! Slogans are by no means a prerequisite for sales. Remember, also, that a good slogan is not always successful nor is a slogan always good. The great usage of a slogan, or the way it is presented, can sometimes establish it in the public consciousness. A successful slogan, accordingly, is not necessarily a good slogan when measured by stern creative standards.

COPY FOR PACKAGES

Another development of modern advertising is the inclusion of selling copy on the packages in which products are sold. Because copy on product packages is infrequently changed, this, again, is an assignment you will be given only on rare occasions. Since package copy, however, is retained for such long periods without revision, it is doubly important that occasional jobs of this type represent your best efforts.

Following is a check list of some of the more important elements of package copy. Some are "musts" for all packages, while others are included only under certain conditions.

1. *Brand name*—This, obviously, is a "must." It's the "headline" of your copy.

2. *Nature of product*—Let buyer know what the product is—whether coffee, cheese, or a mattress.

3. *Specific nature of product*—If product is tea, give exact type—whether green tea, black tea, Ceylon tea, or India tea. If coffee, tell what kind of *grind*—drip or regular. If aspirin, indicate how many *grains* are contained in each tablet.

4. *Uses of product*—If use of the product isn't obvious, give its use clearly. For example, although you might presume that everyone would know that Betty Crocker is used for cake mix the manufacturer doesn't take this for granted. In letters almost as big and bold as the product name itself you'll find the words "cake mix."

If the product has multiple uses, give these other uses. The Cascade package, as an example, points out that Cascade can be used for washing dishes, aluminum, and silver. A package containing a food product ordinarily consumed as a result of further preparation will often carry recipes. Your purpose in listing multiple uses or recipes is, of course, to induce the consumer to "run through" a package of the product quickly, thus hastening the repeat purchase.

5. *Sales claims*—If the product has some definite sales point, highlight it. To illustrate, Comet "bleaches out stains." It's Crest toothpaste "with Fluoristan." Beautiflor wax "cleans as it waxes."

6. *Directions*—If special directions must be given for use of product, state them clearly and simply, avoiding all scientific or technical terms, or any words that might not be immediately understood by a person of limited education.

7. *"Family" products*—If the manufacturer makes other allied products, call buyer's attention to them. You will note that every can of Campbell's soup, for example, lists the

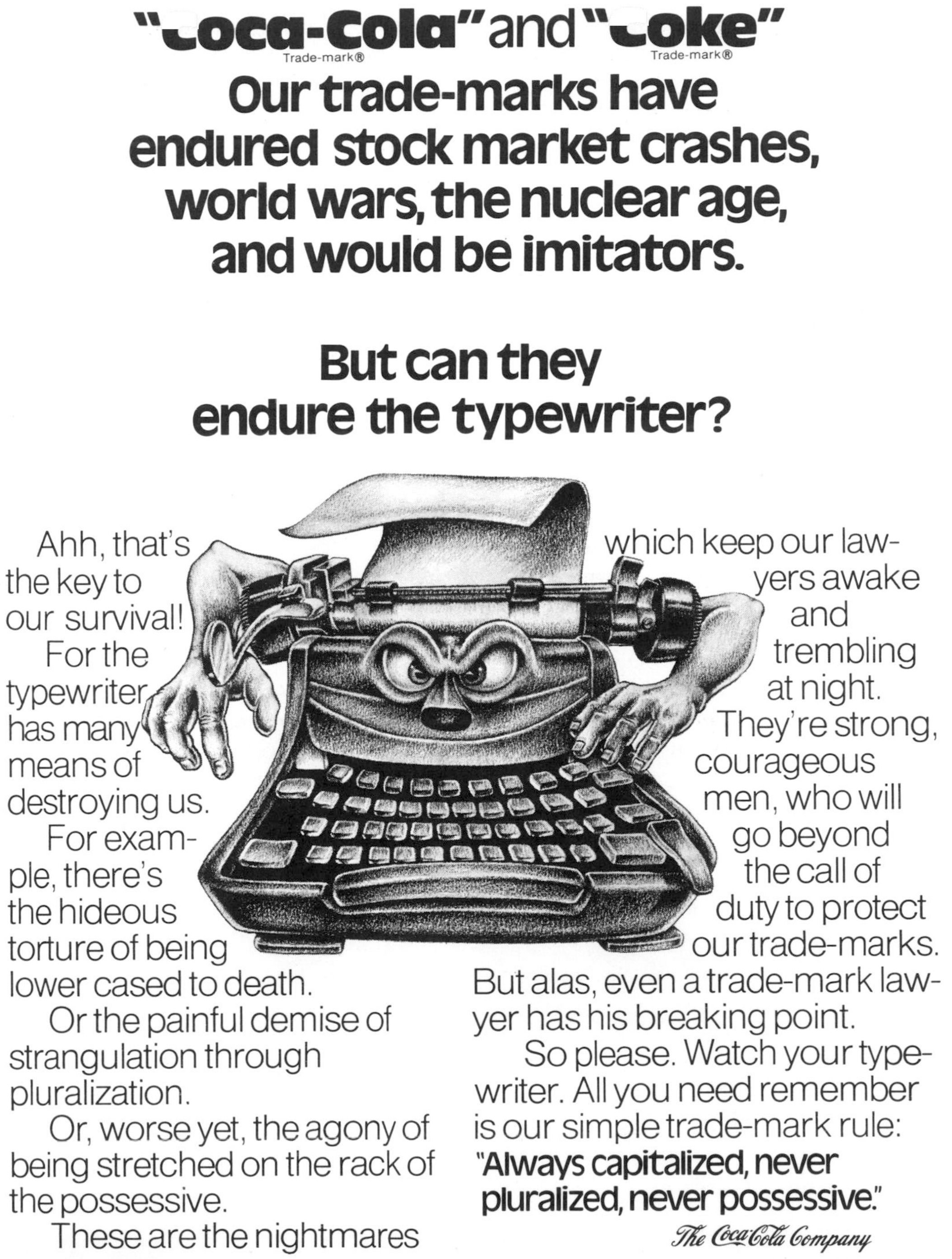
"Coca-Cola" and "Coke"
Trade-mark®
Trade-mark®
Our trade-marks have endured stock market crashes, world wars, the nuclear age, and would be imitators.
But can they endure the typewriter?
Ahh, that's the key to our survival!
For the typewriter has many means of destroying us.
For example, there's the hideous torture of being lower cased to death.
Or the painful demise of strangulation through pluralization.
Or, worse yet, the agony of being stretched on the rack of the possessive.
These are the nightmares which keep our lawyers awake and trembling at night.
They're strong, courageous men, who will go beyond the call of duty to protect our trade-marks.
But alas, even a trade-mark lawyer has his breaking point.
So please. Watch your typewriter. All you need remember is our simple trade-mark rule:
"Always capitalized, never pluralized, never possessive."
The Coca-Cola Company

Fig. 8-1

Trade-mark protection advertisement.

This humorous advertisement makes several serious points. It appeared in publications read by the publishers, editors, and reporters.

other varieties Campbell's sells. Every box of Kellogg's corn flakes mentions that Kellogg also makes other cereals.

8. *Premium offers*—If premiums or contests are being offered by the manufacturer of the product—and he is planning to continue this policy long enough to justify its mention on the package—it's sound strategy to do so, provided the package offers you enough space.

9. *Ingredients*—Food and drug products are required by law to state their composition on the package. Copy of this nature, however, is usually prepared by a lawyer, so is of but passing interest to you.

Probably the best advice anyone can give you regarding package copy is to "make your package a good advertisement." That's what it is, or should be. Don't clutter it with words at the sacrifice of good design, but don't keep your product's good points a secret either. When a woman picks up a can of peas to inspect it, *sell* her with the copy you've written.

TRADE-MARKS AND BRAND NAMES

In addition to writing the types of copy already described, you may even, in isolated instances, be asked to think of a name for a new product for which you will later write the copy. In such cases you are definitely "in on the ground floor," and have the rare opportunity of going through the entire procedure of launching a product, and then seeing it steadily climb in sales—sales your own copy has materially aided in creating.

These product names are commonly known in business as *brand names,* or *trade-marks.* The terms can be synonymous.

Brand names, as we shall refer to them, are not necessarily registered as trade-marks. They may become so, however, once they have been used on goods shipped in interstate or foreign commerce, and provided they violate no governmental restrictions applying to trade-marks. (Pictorial representations may also be registered as trade-marks. These will be discussed later in this chapter.)

Because a new product obviously must be highly developed prior to its introduction into retail channels, its naming is an assignment met more often by those copywriters who work in agencies or for a manufacturer than by writers in the retail field. It is only an occasional assignment at most, but one whose importance cannot be overemphasized. On the brand name rests much responsibility for distinguishing one product or family of products from any and all others; of making a given product (or "line") stand out above the mass of competitive goods or services—in the soap field, for instance, any new name competes with "Ivory," "Dial," "Lux," and the numerous other soaps now being manufactured.

Usually, you will not be charged with the full responsibility of creating a new brand name. You will be asked to get up a list of as many suitable names as you can think of. Other people in your organization will be asked to do the same thing. The advertiser's employees as well as those of his agency—from "top brass" to office boys—may contribute ideas. Sometimes, as an incentive, a bonus rewards the person who offers the name finally selected. The selection of a brand name is so important that getting a good one is worth almost any effort.

Brand names are picked carefully

Selection of a brand name is a serious matter on which a final decision should be reached only after long consideration. Names that come as brilliant "flashes" should be used only after analytical comparison with many suggested alternatives. Experience has shown that even products and services of exceptional merit have little chance of survival, much less marked success, if they are burdened with unappealing, inappropriate, or hard-to-pronounce brand names! Remember that changing a brand name once a product has been put on the market and advertised is a costly and involved procedure. It necessitates writing off as a loss the advertising expenditures made prior to such a change. Satisfied users, accustomed to calling for the product under the abandoned name, must be made aware of the change. Thus if you start with a name you must usually continue with it. You have everything to lose and nothing to gain by choosing a brand name, as old-time aviators used to say, "by the seat of your pants!"

The firm establishment of a distinctive brand name is "insurance" that acts to protect both the consumer and producer alike. In the "cracker barrel" days of not too long ago, great-grandmother had to ask for products in terms applicable to all merchandise of similar nature—the good as well as the bad. (Many types of meats, fruits, cheeses, and vegetables must still be called for by their generic names.

Rapid advancements in the branding and, in many instances, the packaging, of numerous varieties of such "bulk" merchandise are being made, however. Noteworthy among those producers who are making great strides in building brand recognition for this type of goods are Swift, Sunkist, Birds-Eye, and Kraft, to name but a few.)

When great-grandmother needed oatmeal, she could ask for ' 'oat-meal" only by that name and *hope* that it would be satisfactory, not full of chaff, vermin, or other foreign matter. Today grandmother can ask for Quaker Oats and *know* that the quality is high—that every subsequent purchase will meet the same high standard.

Brand names simplify the making of repeat purchases of satisfactory brands and help us to avoid the repurchase of those brands we have found to be unsatisfactory. They insure against the unscrupulous substitution of merchandise of questionable quality on which the retailer's profit margin might be higher. They insure the advertiser from loss of sales that would result from any such widespread substitution for his product. A distinctive brand name further aids the manufacturer by helping to "clinch" for him the sales created by his own advertising. Many of these sales might be lost to a competitor if the manufacturer's product did not possess an easily recalled name the public remembers without effort. Establishment of a brand name, you see, is designed to take the confusion out of buying and selling, and to build a mutually beneficial relationship between the public and reliable manufacturers or service organizations.

HINTS FOR BRAND NAME SELECTING

There are many guide-posts to follow in the selection of a good brand name. There are, nevertheless, numerous brand names now known in every corner of the world that violate many of the suggestions you will be given here. As these come to your mind, remember that they have, for the large part, been constantly advertised over a long period of years. It has taken millions of repetitions and millions of dollars to win for them the eminence they enjoy today. Consider, too, that many of these products might have achieved leadership in their fields more rapidly and at far less advertising cost if those who gave them their names had the knowledge about product-naming that is available now.

Make it distinctive

Since a brand name's first function is to *identify* one product from others, it should be, above all things, distinctive. It should be different, preferably different from *all* other products, but certainly entirely different from the brand name of any product which might be considered even remotely competitive. To be distinctive does not necessarily mean that a brand name must be "clever' ' or "tricky." The name Goodyear is simple and ungarnished. Yet, because it is an uncommon surname, it is distinctive. Many other family names, on the other hand, lack such distinction.

Be careful, when submitting suggestions for brand names, to avoid names similar to those of established products. In the early days of brand names some brand names almost identical to established ones were intentionally chosen. The purpose, of course, was to attempt to capitalize on the established product's reputation; to try to "capture" a portion of a competitor's sales by confusing the public. Actually, such sharp practice has almost invariably harmed rather than helped the imitator. He usually found himself unable to "palm off" any considerable amount of his merchandise

And now a word about Green Giant Cream Style corn
Smoooth!
How does the Green Giant do it? By being pretty smooth himself. First of all, the Giant uses only tall, golden kernels of his very special sweet corn. Secondly, the giant creams it with a process that's so special it's patented. That's why people describe Green Giant Brand Cream Style Corn in a word—smooth. Of course, they often add words like sweet, creamy, delicious.
U.S. PAT. 000
GREEN GIANT
Golden Corn
CREAM STYLE
Save 7¢
on one can of Green Giant Cream Style Corn
Dealer: As our agent, redeem this coupon for 7¢ on the purchase of one can of Green Giant Cream Style Corn. Mail this coupon to Green Giant Company, Box 90, Le Sueur, Minnesota 56058. We will then pay you 7¢ plus 3¢ handling. This offer void in any state or locality where taxed, prohibited, or restricted by law. Fraud Clause: Any other application of this coupon constitutes fraud. Invoices proving purchases within 90 days of sufficient stock to cover coupons presented for redemption must be made available upon request. Offer expires March 31, 1973.
GREEN GIANT and the Giant Figure are trademarks of Green Giant Company. © GGCo.

Fig. 8-2

Trademark identification through use of a cartoon character.

This has become one of the best known symbols in American advertising. Associating a character with a trademark, or making the character itself the trademark, assures memorability.

as being that of his competitor. The similarity in names, in fact, usually confused the public so much that upon reading the newcomer's advertising, people assumed his advertisements were boosting the established product rather than the new one! Purchases were thus made automatically for the well-known brand, defeating the imitator's purpose and causing his advertising to lose a large degree of its effectiveness.

Not only is it dishonest and poor business to trade on an established leader's name, but also costly lawsuits for infringement are almost certain to be instituted. Every possible precaution should be taken to learn whether a proposed brand name has been previously registered by someone else as a trade-mark. Such preliminary checks may be made by contacting any one of the various trade-mark services found in most large cities.

Another possibility is the Trade-mark Bureau of the U.S. Printing and Lithograph Company, Cincinnati, Ohio. This company, for a slight fee, will check its files to see if your proposed trade-mark has been used before. The file is the largest independently owned collection in the country. It must be noted that, while such organizations make fairly comprehensive searches, their findings are not an absolute guarantee that the name is not already in use. This can be officially determined only after the United States Patent Office has passed on the application for trade-mark. The Cincinnati files, however, include U.S. Patent Office trade-marks almost as soon as they are recorded by that agency.

Make it easy to remember

First, as we have pointed out, a brand name should be distinctive.

Additionally, it should be *easy to remember.* If it is not, it will take longer and be more expensive to win widespread public recognition for it. Models of brand names extremely easy to remember are Duz, Seven-Up, and Spry, among many others.

The ease with which a person can remember a brand name is of great importance. To illustrate, let us say that a person goes into a drug store for a hair tonic. The night before, he had read about a certain brand and was impressed by the benefits it promised him, but now that he is in the store, he can't quite recall the product's name. "It's right on the tip of his tongue," but he can't remember it. As a result, Vitalis or Wildroot, gets the sale, a sale a competitor's advertising actually created!

It's unfortunate, but true, that if people have to *think* to recall the name of your product, they will buy a competitive brand bearing a name that comes to mind automatically, *without* requiring any thought!

Make it pronounceable

Still another very important consideration regarding brand names is that they should be *easy to pronounce* by consumers and by announcers in the broadcast media. As the makers of Baume Bengué Analgesique (now simply Ben-Gay) learned, the general public is reluctant, to say the least, to ask for a product whose name it finds difficult to pronounce. There is a very sound psychological reason for this. All of us, without exception, fear ridicule. Consequently, we resist putting ourselves in a position where we might appear ridiculous in another's eyes, even though he may be a completely impersonal drug-store clerk whom we may never again see.

A customer might well hesitate to ask a druggist for Hexylresorcinol. Its name only a scientist might be expected to pronounce with any facility. Recognizing this, the makers of this product wisely gave it an additional name—S. T. 37—which a child could easily remember.

If you had never heard the name Sal Hepatica pronounced, there's a possibility that you might have trouble pronouncing it. Constant advertising, however, has familiarized a huge section of the population with its correct pronunciation. Still, Sal Hepatica may well be losing sales it could make if its name were easier for all people to pronounce.

Even the name Hormel has been subject to widespread mispronunciation. The Hormel family accents the first syllable, but such a large number of people chose to pronounce the name "Hor-*mell*," accenting the second syllable, that the announcers on radio programs the company has sponsored have had to take cognizance of both pronunciations in order to make sure that everyone listening was aware that Hormell was the sponsor.

The peculiar exception to this rule regarding ease of pronunciation seems to be among names of perfumes, cosmetics, and a few other luxury items. Many manufacturers of such products seem to feel that the use of foreign, scientific, or other difficult words—words not ordinarily in the average person's vocabulary—does not handicap sales. They feel, rather, that such names are assets. It would be interesting to check sales figures to see whether the successes of Evening in Paris, Lady Esther, My Sin, Blue Grass, and other luxury items with simple names disprove this theory or not.

Directions are often given for the pronunciation of a product's name. If you feel the need for such directions in connection with any brand name you are planning, you can be reasonably certain that you can find a name that is better if you will dig a little deeper.

Keep brand names simple. Selling, at best, is difficult—don't add further to your problems by shackling the sales power of your advertising with names the public will forget, or shun as too difficult to pronounce!

See that it has pleasant associations

The fourth "must" in the selection of a good brand name is *associations.* Unpleasant associations should be avoided. The initials "D T" might, to illustrate, seem an acceptable name for a coffee made by a man named Daniel Thompson. Here is something short, distinctive, easy to remember, and easy to pronounce. In seeing the name of the product in print, or in hearing it mentioned on the air, however, many would instantly think of drunkenness, not coffee. Others might possibly think of DDT, the insecticide. In either instance, unappetizing mental pictures would be created, instead of the pleasant thoughts which should be associated with the product.

"Balloon" would be a very poor name for a girdle (even though it might be made of balloon silk) because it calls up thoughts of large, ballooning hips rather than the more alluring picture of svelte, slim hips that the woman is thinking of when she buys a new girdle.

Avoid "dating" your brand name

Unless you are trying purposely to establish a product as of old-fashioned vintage—obviously the case in the selection of "Old Spice" as a name for a line of toiletries—brand names that too closely ally a product with a certain era are best avoided. For instance, although "23 Skiddoo" might have been a "stopper" as a name for a mosquito repellent in grandmother's day, the term is now almost meaningless because it is out of vogue. A generation ago a perfume called "It" might well have sold like the proverbial hotcakes. Today, since "it" is no longer used as a synonym for sex appeal, the name has lost its significance. If a cat food named "Hepcat" had been introduced in the 1940's it might have enjoyed success for some time, but as jitterbugging went the way of the bunny-hug and the Charleston, the term would have lost its meaning. The danger of becoming passé is always present in any name adopted to take advantage of a current craze. When the craze is over your name then becomes unintelligible, or "old-hat."

Brand names—new and old

One of the most frequent objectives in the creation of brand names today is to make the name *suggestive of some property or benefit* of the product—an example is "Flit." You can surmise, also, from the name "Filter Queen" that this vacuum cleaner filters the air. It is a benefit in which you can easily see merit, and your name blares forth the virtue. "Mum" or "Ban" are two other examples of desirable names. Such names are of special advantage during that period when a new product is fighting to win wide recognition. This is particularly true if the product is one that is entirely new, or one that has definite properties or benefits exclusively its own.

Once the product has become firmly established, however, the full significance of its name is often lost. Illustrative of this is the fact that when you refer to the brand name "Frigidaire," you aren't actively conscious of the fact that you are, in essence, saying "air that is frigid." At least you aren't if you are like most people. The same principle is true with other such well-known brand names as "Beautyrest," "Kissproof," "Eveready," and "Kolor-Bak."

Some names such as Cellophane, Linoleum, Aspirin, Kerosene, and Shredded Wheat have become so firmly associated with a product that they have become generic—that is, part of the language. When this happens the user often loses the exclusive right to the name. Call it the penalty for having a really excellent name. The only protection is constant watchfulness by the advertiser.

One of the most determined corporations in the protecting of its trade-mark is the Coca-Cola Company. This organization reminds others constantly that when they refer to Coca-Cola in its abbreviated form that they will keep the meaning "clear" if the word *Coke* is spelled with a capital "C." This, the company explains in its advertising, will help protect a "valuable trade-mark." It is obvious that the Coca-Cola Company recognizes the peril confronting its trade-marked abbreviation if editors and others are not reminded that the word *Coke* is the trade-marked prop-

The Bank of New York Company, Inc.

The Bank of New York
The Bank of New York, Albany
The County Trust Company
Endicott Bank of New York
The Exchange Bank of Olean
Metropolitan Bank of Syracuse
Niagara Frontier Bank of New York
Valley Bank of New York

The new corporate symbol of The Bank of New York Company, Inc. symbolizes the unity of purpose of our member banks. We are eight individual banks with eight different names affiliated with the objective of providing all of our customers with the best banking services available in New York State.

Fig. 8-3.

Importance of the trade-mark symbol (or "corporate symbol") is demonstrated by this advertisement that devotes the major emphasis to calling attention to the new symbol.

This symbol could save your life and your property
Look for our Symbol
Your safety, and that of your home, is important to you. It should be. Your concern involves us, too. Has for a long time.
Underwriters' Laboratories is the nation's oldest and largest private testing organization. We started testing for public safety in 1894. We're an independent not-for-profit organization. We have no connection with any manufacturer, nor are we a department of the government. Last year, we evaluated over 37,000 different assignments.
We work in many product safety areas.
You are probably familiar with our work in the field of electrical safety. We also test fire protection equipment and systems, building materials, burglary protection systems, marine products, heating, air conditioning and refrigeration equipment. Even more important, most municipal, county and state authorities recognize our testing and findings.
We test in the laboratory, first.
We have one goal—to see that the product designs we test meet recognized levels of safe performance. Our engineers devise ingenious, and often torturous tests to learn if the product design meets adequate safety standards.
We check factory production.
When we authorize the use of our symbol, it means the product has first passed a series of difficult, demanding tests, then we follow up with periodic, unannounced in-plant inspections to see that the manufacturer is living up to our standards when he produces the product.
You have a responsibility, too.
The UL symbol doesn't mean you can use the product recklessly. Read and follow the instructions, and observe warning markings. Safety is a team effort. Get on the team.
UNDERWRITERS' LABORATORIES, INC.®
TESTING FOR PUBLIC SAFETY
Chicago, Illinois.
Northbrook, Illinois.
Melville, New York.
Santa Clara, California.
Tampa, Florida.

Fig. 8-4

Advertisement emphasizing trademark symbol.

This important symbol is used in connection with hundreds of products. It appears in literally thousands of advertisements and in physical relationship to products entitled to carry the symbol. This advertisement, aimed at consumers, will make the symbol more meaningful when it is seen in product advertising.

erty of the Coca-Cola Company and not merely a convenient, and generic term for a general class of soft drink. (See figure 8-1.)

Even though the true meaning of suggestive names may, after a time, no longer consciously register in the minds of customers, their value in the initial stages of a product's development can be considerable. So long as the benefit or promise contained in the brand name is both important and believable, it is difficult to see how it can be other than an asset in promoting sales.

Following is a cataloguing of a number of famous brand names by classification. With each classification is incorporated a brief analysis of the type of brand name represented. This analysis will indicate why some types of names are usually considered more desirable than others.

Classes of brand names

1. *General designation of quality.* Excel, Royal, Ideal, Perfection, Acme, Hi-Grade, Apex, Superior, A-1, and so forth, are included among those brand names which may be said to give a *general designation* of the quality of the product. These are not the best of names. They are not distinctive. Actually, among the many brands emblazoned with the name "Acme," to name but a few, we find

Acme pencils, Acme paint, Acme oil burners, carbon paper, card cases, fire extinguishers, snap fasteners, shower curtains, scissors, wire, stepladders, thermostats, tables, chair seats, and gasoline. And that list could be enlarged with ease! Another point against such general descriptions is that constant usage has caused the average person to become oblivious to their literal definitions. Thirdly, the claims to superiority implied by such names are so lofty as to lack credibility. In addition, being common words of the public domain, it is almost impossible to protect such names adequately.

2. *Family names.* More numerous, perhaps than those in any other one classification are products named after the founder or owner of the company marketing them. Among those most advertised currently are Parker, Heinz, Borden, Westinghouse, Bendix, Pabst, and Remington.

There are three reasons why it is often well to avoid family names. (1) Often they lack distinctiveness. (2) They may be difficult to spell or pronounce, such as is Ghirardelli, the name of a large West Coast Chocolate producer. (3) They are hard to protect. Any man of the same name can enter business in direct competition with you and use the name you both possess. Sometimes if his so doing will obviously cause damage to your business, the courts will rule against this practice. In the past, however, a number of unscrupulous firms have deliberately hired men having the same names as leading competitors. Giving these men the title (in name only) of head of the firm, they were thus able to use their competitor's name as their own brand name and still argue that they were technically within the law.

3. *Fictional, historical, or heroic names.* Robert Burns, Chesterfield, Victor, Admiral, King, De Soto, Pontiac, Maxwell House, Aunt Jemima, and Bo Peep all fall into this category. There is nothing wrong with such names so long as they fulfill the requirements of distinctiveness (which Admiral and King certainly lack), ease of recall, ease of pronunciation, and pleasant associations. They are, however, difficult to protect. Care must be taken when you choose such a name to make your selection from those characters, events, or places whose durability has been firmly established. If you select the name of some person, place, or event of recent prominence you may find that his fame will have passed in the years to come.

4. *Animals, minerals, vegetables.* Among the first examples of brand names in this classification that come to mind are Camel, Caterpillar, Blue Boar, Walnut, White Owl, and Swansdown. Again, some such names lack distinction and in some cases are difficult to spell, pronounce, or protect. One virtue, however, is that they usually are of more pictorial interest—much more so, for instance, than are brand names based on the name of the company founder.

5. *Familiar objects.* Names based on common objects generally are not so distinctive as some others. In that respect they are like brand names in group number one—Hi-Grade, Acme, Ideal. For example, in addition to Arrow shirts, we have Arrow mucilage, Arrow shovels, Arrow desks, Arrow golf balls, and Arrow needles, to mention but a handful. Such names as Diamond, Anchor, Star, and so forth are similarly duplicated on products of almost every conceivable variety. These names usually do, however, have the advantage, like the animal-mineral-vegetable group, of being translated easily into a pictorial form that increases the recognition value of the name. Nevertheless, they are best avoided.

6. *Numbers and initials.* Many famous

brand names are built on numbers or initials, or both. For example, 3-in-1, S.T. 37, PM, ABC, and ZBT. These are easy to remember, easy to pronounce, and, because of their brevity, allow for a proportionately larger logotype, both in advertisements and on the package itself, than do brand names that are longer. But they, again, are often difficult to obtain as one's own exclusive property.

7. *Geographical or patriotic names.* Columbia, Liberty, American, Hartford, Waltham, and Palm Beach are foremost examples of brand names in this group. Such names have been popular in the past, but, because they lack true distinctiveness in most instances, and are not subject to exclusive proprietorship, they are not considered among the best type for new products.

8. *Coined names.* Another rich source of brand names is tapped through "coining" words. "Coined" brand names may be divided into three types: (1) Those devised by uniting various components of the company name to form a single word. Exemplifying this are Nabisco (*Na*tional *Bis*cuit *Co.*), Alcoa (*Al*uminum *Co*rporation of *A*merica), Duco (*Du* Pont *Co.*) Such contractions or abbreviations, if easy to spell, pronounce, and remember, often make excellent brand names that have the added advantage of calling to mind the full name of the producer. Armco (*A*merican *R*olling *M*ill *Co.*) and Texaco (The *Texa*s *Co.*) are contractions that proved so successful the companies eventually changed their corporate titles and now are known legally by what once were just their brand names. (2) Those such as Tenderleaf, Treet, Perma-Lift, Holeproof, Palmolive, and Rem. These are created in several ways:

a. They may be shortened versions of common words, as is Rem (for "remedy").

b. They may be phonetic spellings, such as Kool and Duz.

c. They may be created by combining two or more words, or parts thereof, employing either orthodox spelling or simplified variations. For example, Spam (from "spiced ham"), Pepsodent, Car-Nu, and Noxema. Among these are many of those brand names which spotlight some benefit or property of the product. Nofade and Pye-Quick promise definite benefits, while Bromo-Seltzer and Pepto-Bismol are semi-scientific descriptions of properties of the products.

(3) Those brand names that are out-and-out inventions, such as Keds, Kodak, Dic-a-Doo, and Drax.

Coined names are today among the most popular brand names. Good ones have numerous advantages. They are distinctive. They have high recognition value, are easy to pronounce, easy to remember, and timeless in their durability. Full legal protection may usually be obtained for them, making them the exclusive property of a single company or individual.

You must beware of certain easily committed faults when coining such brand names. You must, for instance, avoid cleverness for the sake of cleverness alone. Never become so enthusiastic over an ingenious turn of a word that you lose sight of your goal: a name that will help your advertising influence the greatest number of sales to the greatest number of people, a name the public will understand, remember, and respond to.

If you use simplified spelling, make sure that your "simplification" doesn't confuse. Remember that people are used to seeing the word "Quick" spelled in the standard manner. "Kwik" is unfamiliar, and may not be "kwikly" understood. Keep brand names always simple, pleasant, easy to remember, and timeless in their appropriateness.

Worcestershire a winner tonight.
Then enter your recipe in Lea & Perrins contest.
10 First Prizes– one for each of these categories.
1. SEAFOOD
2. MEATS
LAMB, VEAL, BEEF, PORK
3. EGGS
4. CHEESE
5. POULTRY
6. SOUPS
7. SALADS
8. VEGETABLES
9. APPETIZERS
10. "YOU NAME IT"
Let yourself go in the kitchen with Lea & Perrins Worcestershire Sauce. It can make almost any recipe into a winner. Have fun experimenting with your own favorite recipes and you'll see. You can bring out the flavor of all kinds of foods, from chicken to carrots, from salmon to squash. And add a subtle difference to every dish.
Try it. Then send us your own original ways to use the original Worcestershire Sauce. There are 10 First Prizes—one for each of the ten categories. And you can enter any or all, with as many recipes as you like.
There are 50 runner-up prizes, too. And everybody who enters wins a free copy of the Lea & Perrins "Exciting Ideas" Cookbook: 77 things to worcestershire—and every one a winner.
PRIZES
First Prize in each category:
A Minutemaster Microwave oven by Litton Industries. Cuts cooking time by 75%. Lightweight, portable, cooks clean and cool.
Five Runner-Up Prizes in each category:
Ronson's Superflexible "Quintisserie"—a five-in-one unit. Broils, grills, fries, griddles and roasts. Holds roasts or turkeys up to 25 pounds.
LEA & PERRINS
SAUCE
THE ORIGINAL
WORCESTERSHIRE
NET CONTENTS, 5 FLUID OUNCES
200 Honorable Mentions:
A Certificate of Merit from Lea & Perrins acknowledging you as a member of the "Be Original" Culinary Club.
Everybody Wins: The Lea & Perrins "Exciting Ideas" Cookbook.
CONTEST RULES:
1. Entries must be original recipes using Lea & Perrins Worcestershire Sauce, and will be judged on the basis of originality, appeal, consumer usefulness and accuracy.
2. Each recipe must be written legibly in ink, or typed, on one piece of paper.
3. Each recipe must (a) bear name and address of contestant, (b) indicate category title and number in which it is competing, (c) list ingredients and exact measurements in order of use, and (d) give complete directions for combining and completing, including pan size, time and temperature for cooking.
4. Multiple entries are encouraged in any or all categories. Entries must be postmarked by July 31, 1972.
5. Employees of Lea & Perrins, Inc., Creative Marketing Management, Creative Food Service, Inc., their respective advertising agencies and their families may not participate. All entries will become the property of Lea & Perrins and may be altered or advertised without further permission; none will be returned.
6. Judging will be conducted by Creative Food Service, Inc., an independent judging firm. Decision of the judges is final. In case of duplicate winners, duplicate prizes will be awarded.
7. Liability for Federal, state and other taxes is the sole responsibility of winners. This contest is subject to all Federal, state and local regulations.
8. Winners will be announced and notified by mail on or about December 1, 1972, and agree to participate in publicity, advertising and other materials related to the contest, at the sole discretion of Lea & Perrins, Inc.
MAIL ENTRIES TO:
LEA & PERRINS
"ORIGINAL RECIPE" CONTEST
P.O. BOX 560
MONTCLAIR, N.J. 07042

Fig. 8-5

Contest advertisement.

This contest was so successful that the advertiser offered it again less than a year later. See second version in Fig. 8-6 in this chapter.

TRADE CHARACTERS AND PICTORIAL TRADE-MARKS

"One picture," you have read or heard a thousand monotonous times, "is worth 10,000 words." Whether this ratio is entirely fair to the expressiveness of the English language is open to debate. Pictorial trade characteristics or symbols *do,* however, have an extremely high degree of recognition value in advertising. (See figure 8-2.)

Such trade "personalities" or symbols as Aunt Jemima, the Pontiac Indian head, and the Fisher Body coach are often employed to give extra and continuous recognition value to a company's advertising. When such characters or symbols are also affixed to the product or package (as are all four of those mentioned above), they build a close-knit bond between the advertising and the product itself. Application to the product or package, where practicable, helps to create instantaneous recognition in the minds of consumers the moment their eyes alight on the product on the shelf of a store, on the hood of an automobile, or on a gasoline pump in a service station. Many products are actually called for by description of the pictorial trade-mark on the package rather than by name. That is, a customer might ask for "the cocoa with the lady on it" instead of saying "Baker's Cocoa."

The actual designing of suitable trade characters or symbols is plainly a job that requires the talents of an artist. But more often than not, these illustrative devices are based on ideas "sparked" by copywriters. Here are a few "do's" and "don'ts" for you to remember should you ever be confronted with an assignment of this nature. First, review those requisites of grand names which are also applicable to things pictorial. That is, an illustrated trade-mark should be (1) simple, yet distinctive; (2) easy to remember; (3) subject to legal protection. (See figure 8-3.)

You should *avoid* (1) unpleasant associations and (2) current fashions (which might appear ludicrous 10 years hence).

If such a trade-mark can depict a property or benefit of the product without detracting from the mark itself, such inclusion might be advisable. Prominent among pictorial trademarks that do this is the familiar "Iron Fireman"—a robot shoveling coal. If the subject is something the passage of time might make obsolete, it should be avoided. An example is the use of the radiator design of an automobile. Because these designs are changed periodically,

Congratulations to the top prize winners of Lea & Perrins "Original Recipe" Contest.
Seafood Recipe Winner "Washington-State Pickled Shrimp" Mrs. L. Forsgren Seattle, Wash.
Meat Recipe Winner "Sumpshire Spareribs" Mrs. J. Stefanski Ferndale, Mich.
Eggs Recipe Winner "Worcestershire Eggs Fu Yung" Mrs. J. Twomey Phoenix, Ariz.
Cheese Recipe Winner "Cheesey Corncoction" Mrs. G. C. Crispo Quincy, Mass.
Poultry Recipe Winner "Chicken Cherryaki" Mrs. J. Hrvatin Spokane, Wash.
Soup Recipe Winner "Mom's Hearty Cabbage Soup" Mrs. C. Sandblom Naugatuck, Conn.
Salad Recipe Winner "Popeye Spinach 'N Sprout Salad" Miss B. J. Wood Columbus, Ohio
Vegetable Recipe Winner "Onions A La Madrid" Mrs. R. H. Borth Drummond Island, Mich.
Appetizer Recipe Winner "Franks With Beer-B-Que Sauce" Mrs. M. R. Koladije Morristown, N.J.
"You Name it" Recipe Winner "Grand Finale Cake" Mrs. J. R. Hickman St. Petersburg, Fla.
Some Winning Recipes
These three were selected from the wonderful top ten only because our space is limited. If you would like to receive the top ten 1972 winning recipes, please write to: Lea & Perrins, Dept. RC 2, Fair Lawn, N.J. 07410.
Winning Soup Recipe
Mrs. Carl Sandblom, Naugatuck, Conn.
Mom's Hearty Cabbage Soup
½ medium head cabbage, chopped
6 cups water • 1 large onion, chopped
3 Tbsps. sugar • 1 Tbsp. salt
3 peppercorns • 1 bay leaf
4 whole allspice berries
2 Tbsps. Lea & Perrins Original Worcestershire Sauce
1 lb. chopped lean beef
2 cans (6 oz. ea.) tomato paste
Combine all ingredients except tomato paste in large saucepan. Bring to boil; simmer 1 hour. Add tomato paste; cook 15 minutes longer. 5-6 servings.
Winning Salad Recipe
Miss Barbara J. Wood, Columbus, Ohio
Popeye Spinach 'n' Sprout Salad
1 lb. spinach, washed and chopped
1 can (5 oz.) water chestnuts, drained and sliced
1 can (1 lb.) bean sprouts, drained
½ lb. fresh mushrooms, sliced
4 hard-cooked eggs, chopped
8 slices bacon, fried and crumbled
½ cup salad oil • ¼ cup bacon drippings
⅓ cup catsup • ¼ cup vinegar
¼ cup sugar • ½ medium onion, grated
1 Tbsp. Lea & Perrins Original Worcestershire Sauce
Toss vegetables, eggs, bacon in salad bowl. Combine remaining ingredients; heat to simmer. Pour over salad mix. Serve at once. 8 servings.
Winning "You Name It" Recipe
Mrs. J. R. Hickman, St. Petersburg, Fla.
Grand Finale Cake
4 cups unpeeled, diced apples
2 cups sugar • 3 cups flour
2 tsps. baking soda • 1 tsp. salt
2 tsps. cinnamon • 1 tsp. allspice
½ tsp. nutmeg • ½ tsp. cloves
1 cup salad oil • 2 eggs, beaten
1 Tbsp. Lea & Perrins Original Worcestershire Sauce
1 cup chopped walnuts • 1 cup raisins
Combine apples and sugar; set aside 15 minutes. Sift flour, soda, salt, spices together. Stir in oil, eggs, Worcestershire Sauce. Add to apple mixture all at once. Mix well; fold in nuts and raisins. Pour into greased and floured 10″ tube pan. Bake in preheated 325°F. oven 1-1/4 hours. 10 servings.
LEA & PERRINS SAUCE THE ORIGINAL WORCESTERSHIRE
Join the winners! Enter the 1973 "Original Recipe" Contest now.
Worcestershire your own favorite recipe with Lea & Perrins. Then send it to us. Enter any or all categories with as many recipes as you wish. Let yourself go!
10 First Prizes
To each of the first 10 prize winners goes an Amana Radarange Microwave Oven. Cuts cooking time by 75%. Lightweight, portable, cooks clean and cool.
1. APPETIZERS AND/OR DRINKS
2. SOUPS
3. SEAFOOD
4. EGGS AND/OR CHEESE
5. MEATS | LAMB, VEAL, BEEF, PORK |
6. POULTRY
7. SALADS
8. VEGETABLES
9. "YOU NAME IT"
10. SPECIAL PRIZE for young contestants (12 to 18) entering any of the above categories.
100 Runner-Up Prizes
(10 in each category)
An electric Char-B-Que that makes barbecuing easier and better. Portable—use it indoors or outdoors.
200 Honorable Mentions
A Certificate of Merit from Lea & Perrins acknowledging you as a member of the "Be Original" Culinary Club.
Everybody Wins
Just by entering you get The Lea & Perrins "Exciting Ideas" cookbook.
Contest Rules
1. Entries must be original recipes using Lea & Perrins Worcestershire Sauce, and will be judged on the basis of originality, appeal, consumer usefulness and accuracy.
2. Each recipe must be written legibly in ink, or typed, on one side of one sheet of paper.
3. Each recipe must (a) bear name and address of contestant, (b) indicate category title and number in which it is competing, (c) list ingredients and exact measurements in order of use, and (d) give complete directions for combining and completing, including pan size, time and temperature for cooking.
4. Multiple entries are encouraged in any or all categories, but each entry must be mailed in a separate envelope. Entries must be postmarked by April 30, 1973.
5. Employees of Lea & Perrins, Inc., Creative Marketing Management, Creative Food Service, Inc., their respective advertising agencies and their families may not participate. All entries will become the property of Lea & Perrins and may be altered or advertised without further permission; none will be returned.
6. Judging will be conducted by Creative Food Service, Inc., an independent judging firm. Decision of the judges is final. In case of duplicate winners, duplicate prizes will be awarded.
7. Liability for Federal, state and other taxes is the sole responsibility of winners. This contest is subject to all Federal, state and local regulations.
8. Winners will be announced and notified by mail on or about November 1, 1973, and agree to participate in publicity, advertising and other materials related to the contest, at the sole discretion of Lea & Perrins, Inc.
Mail Entries to: Lea & Perrins "Original Recipe" Contest Dept. 20, P.O. Box 560, Montclair, N.J. 07042

Fig. 8-6

Repeat of contest advertisement referred to in caption for Fig. 8-5.

Note the good public relations feature of giving names of winners in the first contest, plus the prize-winning entries.

any trademark showing one would necessarily also have to be changed from time to time, appreciably reducing its recognition value. (See figure 8-4.)

Whether for newspapers, magazines, or a 24-sheet poster, the placing of an illustrated trade-mark is a point to be decided by you and your art associates, usually on a basis to be determined by individual circumstances. It is almost impossible to establish fixed rules for such procedures. Basically, you must remember, it is to be *seen*. Don't put a trademark on a counter display in such as position that it might be blocked by other merchandise.

WRITING ADVERTISEMENTS FOR SWEEPSTAKES (AND CONTESTS)*

Sweepstakes in which sometimes almost fabulous prizes are awarded in exchange for a box top can be tremendously effective sales stimulators. Many advertisers run such sweepstakes year after year after year.

If you should ever be assigned to write a sweepstakes advertisement, there are several points you will want to know. For instance, there are two schools of thought on the subject of such advertising. One believes that a

*Although the more commonly-used sweepstakes are stressed here, the points given apply equally to contests.

fair part of the advertisement should be devoted to the regular copy story on the product itself. The second is convinced the entire advertisement should be used to sell the sweepstakes—the sweepstakes being the "product," in such an instance. (See figures 8-4 & 8-5.)

The first school reasons thus: (1) Every reader isn't going to enter the sweepstakes. You should make an effort to sell such readers the product on its own merits. (2) Straight product copy is necessary to sell that "undecided" segment of the audience. These people who question their chances of winning must be persuaded that they have nothing to lose by entering—that they will get their full money 's worth for what they spend in buying the product even though they don't happen to win a prize.

The second school reasons that more entries (and thus more purchases) are obtained when the entire space is given over to selling the sweepstakes. The inclusion of straight product copy, they feel, *divides* the reader's interest because it presents two separate thoughts for him to consider—equivalent to advertising two different products in the same advertisement! (See figure 8-6.)

Regardless of which of the two foregoing patterns your sweepstakes advertisements take, here are a few copy points worth remembering:

1. Most readers think in terms of winning the first prize—so play up your major prize—*stress* it. Use a big headline to do so.

2. Generally speaking, a long list of secondary prizes has been found more effective than a small group, even though the total cash value in each case is the same. If you have an impressive list of such prizes, don't merely say "50 prizes." Instead, give that fact extra appeal by saying "50 chances to win!"

3. Spot-light total retail cash value of all prizes, if this is an impressive sum.

4. "Win" is a magic word, so headline it.

5. In a subhead, drive home how easy it is to win.

6. In your copy, get over in a hurry how easy it is to enter the sweepstakes.

7. Give examples of jingles, sentences, and puzzle solutions that might be typical of prizewinning entires if you are writing contest copy.

8. List rules simply and clearly, leaving unanswered no question that might come to a reader's mind. Always include the specific date on which the sweepstakes entries close.

9. Be sure to tell the reader he may enter as often as he wishes, if this is the case.

10. Urge readers to enter "NOW."

11. Warn that offers are void where prohibited by law.

12. Make clear that all prizes will be awarded.

PROMOTING WITH PREMIUMS

In considering premium offers, remember that such things as free booklets on the product or samples of the product do not constitute premiums. A premium is normally some item more or less unrelated to your product. It is offered to the buyers of your product either in exchange for evidence of a purchase of the product, or such evidence plus a nominal sum of money.

As with sweepstakes, sometimes an entire advertisement is devoted to the "selling" of the premium. More often, however, such advertisements also include strong product copy. (See figure 8-7.)

Tips for copy on premium offers:

1. Highlight the cash retail value of the premium (if this is sufficiently high).

2. If premium is offered as part of a "combination offer"—as a $2.00 floor mop might be sold in combination with a 59¢ can of

THE NATIONAL PINEAPPLE COOKING CLASSIC!
GRAND PRIZE $25,000
THREE SECOND PRIZES $10,000 EACH
FOUR RUNNERS UP $1,000 EACH
40 Free trips to Hawaii for two! Via the friendly skies of United Air Lines
Use Pineapple! They'll Smile a Lot!
RULES:
YOU'LL STAY AT SHERATON'S FABULOUS ROYAL HAWAIIAN HOTEL.
Your favorite canned pineapple recipe, using chunks, crushed, sliced or tidbits, can win you a trip to Hawaii for two via a giant 747 United Air Lines Friendship in the National Pineapple Cooking Classic. Finalists will enjoy a full, fabulous week in Hawaii and a chance to come home with the cash as one of the big winners. "Male chauvinist cooks" can enter too, so tell the man in your life! Send in your best pineapple recipe now. Easy does it! Be sure to read the rules carefully. See you in Hawaii at the National Pineapple Cooking Classic.
ENTER HERE:
BEFORE APRIL 15, 1973
OFFICIAL ENTRY FORM
The Pineapple Growers Association of Hawaii
NAME OF YOUR CATEGORY
P.O. Box 811
Fullerton, Calif. 92638
Please enter my recipe for ________ in the
NAME OF YOUR DISH
(Category: i.e., Main dishes, Breads, Desserts, Salads)
of the National Pineapple Cooking Classic. I hope I win!
NAME
ADDRESS
CITY STATE ZIP CODE
NOTE: Please write your entry Category (Main dishes, etc.) on outside of envelope.
SPONSORED BY THE PINEAPPLE GROWERS ASSOCIATION OF HAWAII

Fig. 8-7

Contest advertisement.

An interesting aspect of this contest is that the advertiser's product is used in the recipe entries submitted by contestants.

floor wax for a total, say, of $1.59—pop the fact that it is a "regular $2.59 value for only $1.59.

3. Sell the premium—dramatize it, make it appealing.

4. If no money is required, subhead the fact—"Send no money!"

5. Always include statement of time limit for which offer is good.

6. Urge readers to take advantage of offer without delay.

In designing the premium advertisement avoid the trap so many copywriters fall into. Somehow, in order to achieve excitement for the offer, the writer of the premium advertisement often devises a cluttered, frantic sort of advertisement. The layout is messy and the headlines are black, screaming horrors. Keep the layout clean and make the illustration of the offer stand out. Use of color is often useful in getting attention for the advertisement and for making the premium itself more alluring. (See figure 8-8.)

If you are looking for a heavy return of boxtops, about two-thirds of the advertisement should concentrate on the selling of the premium. For fullest effectiveness this copy should be situated at the top of the advertisement.

In the competitive years ahead, premium advertising, already responsible for stimulating billions in premium business, will maintain its present importance. If you are concerned with the movement of low-cost goods to the national market, you will amost inevitably be drawn into premium-promotion activity.

WRITING PUBLICITY STORIES

Publicity is of increasing importance as an adjunct of advertising. You may well, from time to time, be called upon to write publicity stories to be released to newspapers, magazines, and trade papers. Because publicity releases will not be published unless they meet accepted editorial standards, you must write them as straight news stories, avoiding the jargon of the advertising business and any attempt at high-pressure selling. Publicity stories are run free by publications, but only if they are newsworthy *and* if the editor happens to have some space to spare at the time. Don't, above all, attempt to make publicity stories thinly-disguised advertisements.

What kind of situations produce publicity stories of real news value? Here are some: (1) An executive of a company makes a speech of some importance. (2) A company builds a new plant or wins a safety award. (3) An executive is promoted. (4) An old-time employee of many years' standing retires. (5) An employee wins a big national contest. (6) A company makes an important change in a product that is well-known nationally, regionally, or locally. (7) A company announces the introduction of a product totally different from anything on the market. (8) An employee wins a big suggestion-box award.

All these are legitimate news stories. Don't lose sight of that word "legitimate" because any publicity story without real news value is doomed to end in the editorial waste basket. Do you really know what "news" is? An editor may disagree with you in defining the word. He may, in the way of editors, refuse to run an item you think is the story of the century.

What is important to you, or to your client, may be wholly unimportant to an editor because he feels your "news" will not interest enough of his readers. A newspaper editor will refuse a story that a trade magazine editor will accept, and vice versa. Each story, then, must contain news of consequence to the readers of the publication in which we'd like our story to run.

Knowing just what constitutes news is the whole crux of successful placement of publicity material. One test, of course, is to ask yourself this question: "Would I (or anyone) have any interest in this story if I didn't already have a personal stake in it?"

The writing of publicity copy, sometimes disparagingly called "puff" copy, requires a sound knowledge of news procedure. After you have determined that your story has real news value you must prepare it in accepted news style. It should be ready to insert in the news columns as you have written it. If it is a general release going to a great many newspapers, you may send out one version of the story, since in most cases there will be no duplicate readership. The papers may or may not rewrite your copy; it makes little difference here. Say, however, that you are sending a story of interest to the grocery trade and that you send the same version of the story of interest to the grocery trade and that you send the same version of the story to three magazines. All these magazines may have high duplication of readership. If the readers read the same story in the same words in all the magazines they will be bored and disgusted. Furthermore, the editors will be resentful when they discover that you were too lazy to write the story differently for each of the publications.

To be able to write the same story in three different versions and make each version interesting will test your ability in news writing. If you have done some reporting you won't have much trouble. If you haven't, a publicity release may cause you some anxious moments. Principal things to keep in mind:

1. Follow the usual news style, in all but out-and-out feature stories, of putting essential facts high in the story. One way to accomplish this is to use the well-known 5-W's approach; that is, tell who—what—when—where—why early in your story.

2. Remember that because of make-up requirements a story may be cut to fit a space—the space won't be stretched to fit the story. Write your copy so that it can be cut at the end of any paragraph and still make sense—all the more reason for getting important material high in the story.

3. Make paragraphs, sentences, and words short, and write so that it will be easy for the copy desk to dig out a headline for the story—in other words, say something significant and say it quick.

4. Don't worry too much about style rules,

Clam Fondue
No one can resist the taste of sizzling hot, succulent fried clams, all golden brown, plump and crisp. That's why no one can resist the taste of Howard Johnson's Tendersweet® Fried Clams. For the newest way to serve them, try a fondue. For party hors d'oeuvres or snacks nothing's simpler, tastier, or more fun than a clam fondue. Especially when it's made with Howard Johnson's Tendersweet Fried Clams and Planters Oil®
Swiss chefs have always used peanut oil for all their fondue recipes. Fondue without it just isn't authentic. And the oil that will make your fried clam fondue taste the way it was meant to is Planters 100% pure peanut oil. The oil that brings out the delicious flavor of foods, because Planters oil makes cooking . . . cuisine.
Just pour 3 c. Planters Peanut Oil into your fondue pot. Adjust the temperature control setting to medium-high (375°F.). Spear defrosted Howard Johnson's Tendersweet Fried Clams on fondue forks, immerse in hot oil. Fry about 10 seconds, or until golden and crisp. And dip them in your favorite sauce. You'll find several tempting sauce recipes inside of specially marked boxes of Howard Johnson's Tendersweet Fried Clams.
To make your clam fondue even easier, just send $13.95 and the coupon below for a $24.95 value—an electric fondue pot by West Bend® with four color-keyed forks. This dishwasher-safe, 2 quart aluminum fondue pot, colorfully clad in genuine porcelain, has West Bend's Fire-On No-Stick Interior® for easy cleaning. And it's fully automatic with temperature control settings for meats, cheeses and desserts.
Get a $24.95 Fondue pot for only $13.95.
Please send me______ West Bend electric Fondue pots. I enclose $13.95 (check or money order) payable to Clam Fondue Offer plus the cap liner from one bottle of Planters Oil and the ingredient panel from one package of Howard Johnson's Tendersweet Fried Clams for each pot. Allow 4 to 6 weeks for delivery. Offer good only in U.S.A. Offer expires June 30, 1973. Void where prohibited or restricted.
Name
Address
City State Zip
Pimento red
Cheddar yellow
Send to Clam Fondue Offer, Box 218, Rockfield, Wisconsin, 53077.
Orders without zip code cannot be accepted.
© 1972, Howard Johnson Co.
PLANTERS OIL
Tendersweet Fried Clams

Fig. 8-8

Premium advertisement.

In keeping with good premium practice, this offer presents a fine bargain in an enthusiastic way.

but, if in doubt, use a "down" style for newspaper stories since most newspapers are inclining toward that style. (A "down" style uses a minimum of capitals—an "up" style newspaper capitalizes heavily.)

5. If possible, get a picture to send along with the story and write a snappy caption for the picture (8 x 10 glossy prints are best).

6. Avoid too many references to your company or client. If you can put over your idea without any direct mention of your product name or company, all the better. If not, tread very easily. Many editors will throw a story out as soon as a company or product is mentioned.

7. If your story has an interest for a special section of the newspaper, send it to the editor of that section, such as financial editor, or automotive editor.

8. Be accurate—if your facts aren't correct your first story will be your last. Don't kill your chance for future publicity.

Here's an extra note about the 5-W's approach previously mentioned. If you're wondering what elements might properly go under each of the "W's" for a publicity release, here are a few ideas for you. These are, of course, but a few of the many points you might consider.

Sunshine
Let your family enjoy the sparkling taste, the health protection of Florigold Grapefruit, the juiciest package nature ever filled with sunshine! Delicious nutrition for reducing diets—no substitute can ever supply the natural vitamins and minerals of Florida's finest grapefruit, tree-ripened in the sun-drenched Indian River groves.
FLORIGOLD GRAPEFRUIT
FLORIDA'S FINEST FROM THE FAMOUS INDIAN RIVER
Distributed by Seald-Sweet Sales, Inc.
FLORIGOLD INDIAN RIVER
FLORIGOLD INDIAN RIVER
SPECIAL OFFER
Beautiful stainless steel of ultra modern design, the Florigold Grapefruit spoon is the finest ever produced. Its tiny cutting teeth make the difference!
TO: FLORIGOLD SPOONS
P. O. Box 3328, Tampa, Florida 33601
Enclosed is $____ for ____ set(s) of grapefruit spoons @ $1.00 for each set of 4. Allow 6 weeks for delivery. Offer expires June 30, 1974.
NAME ____ (PLEASE PRINT)
ADDRESS ____
CITY ____ STATE ____ ZIP ____

Fig. 8-9

Premium advertisement.

Notice that not only does the offer of the spoons represent a good value but also the premium, in this instance, will be used in connection with the product being advertised. This makes the premium doubly appealing.

WHO—are the people involved in the story?
- (1) Names
- (2) Titles
- (3) Departments
- (4) Interesting history or accomplishments
- (5) Newcomers or old-timers
- (6) Quotes from important people involved

WHAT—has happened?
- (1) Is this the first time?
- (2) Is it a major event in the field?
- (3) Is there anything different about it?
- (4) Does what happened fill a long-felt need?

WHEN—did it happen?
- (1) Has it already happened?
- (2) Is it taking place over a period of time? (How long a period?)
- (3) Is it going to happen?
- (4) Exact date (and time, if necessary).

WHERE—did it happen?
- (1) At the plant?
- (2) Is it local, or did it happen at a number of places simultaneously?

WHY—is it happening?
- (1) What is the story behind the event?

SIGNATURES AND LOGOTYPES

When you are writing copy you will ever be conscious of the signatures and logotypes used in your advertisements, yet you'll have little creative work to do in connection with them. Both are involved with company policy, both are closely connected with layout design, and both remain with little change once established. Yet, each is so important that this chapter would not be complete if a signature-logotype discussion were not included.

The signature

A signature is just what the word implies. It tells you who makes the product that is advertised. Often the maker's address is also included.

The signature, including the address, may be set off by itself to give it prominence, or it may be inserted at the close of a block of copy. There are no inflexible rules on how it is included or where it is placed. The treatment of the signature may be dictated by managerial policy, layout design, space limitations, or any of a number of other factors.

Signatures are used for one or more of three primary reasons: (1) To build greater acceptance for a product or service, which is not already universally established, by acquainting the public with the fact that it is offered by a company of known reputation for quality and fair dealing. (2) To provide the address that must always be included when a sample, descriptive booklet, or any other offer is made. (3) To enable people to write for any further information they may desire concerning the product or service. Such communications are naturally more to be expected in regard to major purchases such as lawn mowers and washing machines than when the product is an inexpensive, day-to-day purchase like canned peas, chewing gum, or adhesive tape. The latter represent such minor investments that few people would trouble to write about them. If additional retail outlets are desired, *both* signature and address should be included to make it easier for interested dealers to write for complete information about product, profit opportunities, and so forth.

The signature is purposely left out in many instances. It may be assumed in such cases: (1) That the product and where it may be purchased are so generally known that there is little likelihood of any reader needing to write to the maker for further information regarding it; (2) That dealers will know where to inquire if they wish to add the product to their stock.

To illustrate: If an advertisement for Absorbine Jr. carried the signature "W. F. Young, Inc., Springfield, Mass.," the inclusion or omission of the company name and address would probably have absolutely no effect on the selling power of the advertisement. Almost everyone knows what Absorbine Jr. is, knows that it is widely popular (so must be satisfactory), and knows where to buy it. The name Absorbine Jr. itself is so well-established that the mentioning of its manufacturer's name could not enhance its reputation to any marked degree.

Every dealer, similarly, knows the facts about Absorbine Jr. and the wholesale trade channels through which he may obtain it.

On the other hand, inclusion of such a line as "Another Fine Lever Brothers Product" on a new item in a well-known company's line would immediately endow it with a certain prestige it might otherwise take years for the new product to win on its own.

The logotype

When an advertisement does *not* carry the company's name, its "signature" is usually the product's name. (With such family names as Campbell and Heinz, the product name is actually part of the company name. That is, the brand name, "Heinz," is derived from the full firm name, "H. J. Heinz Co.")

The style of type or lettering in which the name of a given company's product is displayed sometimes varies from one advertisement to another. Most often, though, it is given a distinctive design and, almost without exception, it is used in this particular style in every advertisement and in all other promotional material, including the actual product label.

When the product's name is thus treated, it is referred to formally as a *logotype* and informally as a "logo." Excellent specimens of such logotypes are those for Sunkist, Palmolive, Larvex, Coca-Cola, Van Heusen, and Valvoline, to cite but a few.

Under most circumstances, it is preferable to use one consistent design in the logotypes. This makes for far greater recall value than when the style of type or lettering is frequently changed. Readers accustomed to seeing the product name in one distinctive "dress" will recognize it more readily when they see it in similar form in subsequent advertisements or on the packages containing the product.

Creation of a logotype, being primarily a matter of design, is not the direct responsibility of the copywriter. As creative "general," nevertheless, you will often make suggestions and offer criticism of logotypes. A little knowledge of logotypes will enable you to tell whether the finished logotype is sufficiently simple, easy to read, and distinctive.

As with company signatures in which the name and address of the manufacturer are given, there are no specific rules that must be strictly adhered to in the placement of the logotype. You will recall, for instance, that in the chapter on headlines, it was pointed out that the "logo" is often used in the headline itself. Customarily, however, it is placed toward the bottom of the advertisement. This is usually for reasons of balance and design, not because it is necessarily more effective saleswise.

Since the logotype is of a distinctive style, and ordinarily unlike the type in which the body text is set, it is rarely included within the actual copy block.

Although you will not design the logotype or the signature, as the copywriter you may want to insist that they be displayed in type that is big enough to be seen easily by readers.

Readership studies consistently show that many readers or print advertisements are unable to recall the name of the advertiser or the product. Quite often this is due to a silly delicacy on the part of the advertiser about displaying his name in a type size that he thinks is vulgar. Possibly the delicacy traces back to the art department that is more concerned with artistic integrity than such mundane considerations as registering company or product names.

Naturally, judgment must be used. An advertisement for Tiffany's, for example, will use restraint in the kind and size of type used for the logotype. For most advertisers and products, however, it is better to be conspicuous than to be delicate and unseen.

In the chapter on research you will find much attention paid to Starch readership studies. One of the measurements used in these studies is the Advertiser-Associated figure, referring to the percentage of readers recalling the name of the advertiser or the product in the advertisements they read. Low Advertiser-Associated figures can frequently be traced back to logotypes or signatures that were set in type too small to be noticeable.

As the copywriter you have a stake in this matter. You have the right to question the inconspicuous logotype or signature. Make your voice heard or that low readership figure will be blamed on your copy and not on that diminutive logotype or signature.

Local Advertising: The Daily Challenge.

Many a retail advertising copywriter has sneered at the copy for national advertisements. Such a copy writer might say: "It'd be a lot easier to write copy if all I had to do is *present* goods. In retail copy I have to *sell* goods and right now—not weeks or months from now."

There's much truth in this hypothetical copywriter's observation. Retail advertising is a dynamic form of selling promotion more concerned with immediate than long-range effects.

If you're the man or woman who wants to see words and thoughts and ideas *work* for you and your organization, you can't ask for a better opportunity than retail copywriting. Retail copy, whether for grocery stores, filling stations, drugstores, or restaurants, is exciting —exciting because it moves goods *fast*. No other phase of advertising permits the writer to deal so directly with his merchandise, and his customers, and to learn first-hand how effective his approach and methods have been. In this chapter on retail copywriting the emphasis is on department-store advertising because it provides the most diversified picture of such copywriting. Most of the principles can be applied to other forms of retail selling, too.

Direct contact with goods and prospective customers of those goods make retail copywriting difficult, demanding, and exhausting. Once you've started to sell Mrs. Jones a house coat at $10.95, or Mr. Smith a new set of seat covers for his car at $29.85, you've tackled a rough job—and your work carries you far from the mere physical procedure of pounding typewriter keys.

You have three bosses in retail advertising—your advertising boss, the buyer who buys the merchandise, and the salesman who stands behind the counter selling the goods you're writing about. If the salesman works on a bonus or percentage basis, his very living may depend upon the skill with which you do your job—that makes you mighty important, too.

In some forms of national copy the copywriter doesn't need to acquire a personal working relationship with all members of his organization. Retail copy can't be written *without* close relationship of the copywriter and the store personnel inside and outside the advertising department. Since no retail department store writer *can* do his job well unless he understands his relationship to the departments and people with whom he must work, you will find in the following material a description of some of the activity going on about you in a typical department store. You will find more details of the work of those people who are so important to you—such as the advertising manager, the buyer, and the comparison shopper.

Examine the organization of a large department store to get an idea of the *extent* of your copywriting duties. Keep in mind, too, that despite differences stemming from the type and size of the store, the advertising budget, and the size of the advertising department, the situation is basically the same in all retail establishments.

Much of the following description of the duties of department store personnel is derived from big stores, but the positions listed carry similar duties in all stores. Other department stores might not use exactly the same organizational set-up but will, in a great many cases, have the same basic pattern.

The Advertising manager: His job is to oversee the entire advertising operation and to plan future campaigns on a top-management level. He is in direct contact with the store manager, in most cases, and translates

Fig. 9-1

Sale advertisement with an institutional approach.

The body copy of this prestige advertisement sells the store as a whole. Only the headlines emphasize the sale, and do so tastefully. For this type of establishment, the absence of prices adds, rather than detracts.

The Annual Miracle on Canal Street...
• Open All Day Washington's Birthday • Final Days • Sale Ends March 3rd. •
The Winter Furniture Sale at
Robert W. Caldwell
HONEST SAVINGS 10% to 50%
All the famous brand names are included: Drexel, Heritage, Henredon, Baker, Kindel, White, Flair, Woodmark, Founders, Century, Milling Road, Barcalounger. Anything and everything for your home. Complete living, dining, and bedroom suites, custom-covered upholstered chairs, sofas, loveseats, sectionals, and occasional furniture. An enormous collection of Debut '73 furniture to choose from.
Caldwell's professional decorators are always on hand to help you design an outstanding room with a practical eye to your budget. You can call on them for help in choosing entire room groups, individual pieces and accessories such as carpets and lamps, or simply to discuss your decorating problem. It's all part of Caldwell's personalized services to their customers.
You are welcome to browse through our six-block long floors. This is Caldwell's 60th year of furniture miracles.
Our Winter Sale also includes Recliners, Rockers, End Tables, Bookcases, and Cocktail Tables.
Visit CANAL STREET—for the largest Collection and Selection. BMT/IRT Subway at corner.
Robert W. Caldwell
MANHATTAN ONLY • 273 Canal Street (just off Broadway) • (212) CA 6-2413.
Store Hours: Manhattan—9:45 am to 5:45 pm, Thursday to 8:30 pm, Saturday to 5:00 pm.
Park your car in nearby City Canal Garage, 349 Canal Street at Wooster.

management's wishes into actual printed or spoken advertising. Many times he is a "yes-man" to management. Other times he may come up with fine ideas which he "sells" to the management.

The advertising manager usually makes up the entire month's advertising schedule in advance—or he might even plan two or three months ahead. All advertising goes through his hands for final approval, whether it's a newspaper advertisement, a television or radio commercial, or a mailing insert. He controls all personnel in the advertising department, including you.

Section chiefs: Large department stores often employ section chiefs or divisional advertising managers to head the various copy sections such as homewares, men's furnishings, downstairs store, fashions, and others. These people are responsible for actual planning within their divisions. They work with buyers and their merchandise managers, check advertisements as they are written by copywriters, consult with the art department on layout suggestions and art treatment. In effect, they are the advertising managers for a group of "clients" within a division of the store.

Merchandise managers: Each major division within the store has a merchandise manager who may control as many as thirty buyers. He is responsible for their buying plans and their spending and sales figures. In an advertising sense, his job is to allocate money from his monthly budget to the various selling departments in his division. He also turns in a tentative monthly schedule to the advertising manager—which is used to make up the entire store's schedule for the coming period.

A merchandise manager passes on individual advertisements for his department, sees that buyers provide full information to the copywriters preparing the advertising.

Buyers: These men and women go into the market to buy the goods you write about. Some of them gladly cooperate with the writers who must turn out selling copy about their goods. They provide "buyer's copy" to tell the writer about merchandise. They give the copywriter every chance to see, feel, try, and test the goods. The buyer is, in a sense, the copywriter's client. You will respect his wishes as long as they result in good advertising.

Regrettably, a good many buyers give copywriters the poorest kind of cooperation. They must be begged for information. Not seeming to care about the copywriter's side, they give information only about the obvious things such as colors, sizes, and prices. Your job will require you to dig for more than these bare facts. Desperately you'll hound the buyer for more help than the scanty facts he gives you in his buyer's copy. Though some buyers will be a real help to you, rely on your own effort and ingenuity to get facts for writing your copy. The buyer has his own problems to worry about and copywriting is not among them. If he gives you complete information—fine. If he doesn't, get it yourself.

Comparison shoppers: Almost all large stores maintain a comparison shopping department to check the truthfulness of statements made in the store's advertisements, to determine whether quantities of merchandise on hand warrant advertising, to act as liaison between the buyer and the advertising department, and to shop in other stores in the community for comparable values and comparative store activity. "Comparison" usually has the final word on all advertising, especially on descriptions that may go counter to policies of the store and trade principles as laid down by the Better Business Bureau.

In addition to being in contact with the buyers, section managers, and the others mentioned, during the advertising day, you will also work closely with the *art director,* who is responsible for layouts, finished art, and photographs; the *production manager,* who marks the type, handles the proofs, enters corrections, and sends all material to the newspapers; the *clerk,* who controls the flow of merchandise that is sent up for sketching or photography.

As you can see, a great many people contribute to the preparation of every advertisement, from the warehouseman who hauled furniture for a camera shot to the clerk who checked copy for accuracy. The combined activity is slanted toward one end—to create advertisements that produce—advertisements that sell!

WRITING COPY FOR THE SMALLER STORE

Of course, the foregoing operation differs in some respects from that of other big stores. The general procedure, however, is similar enough to that of a great many of them that the description will give you a fairly good picture of your duties in the typical big store.

The procedure in thousands of small and medium-sized stores, however, is much different. In a small store you may be a copywriter, advertising manager, production chief, and display manager rolled up into one very busy person. Often, in such a job, you will not write much original copy. A good portion of your writing will consist of revising, shortening, or lengthening the "canned" copy that accompanies your mat material from the mat services or from the manufacturer of the goods you are advertising.

Many small stores depend upon mat services to provide them with layout and copy ideas. Very often, also, small stores let their newspapers do copy-layout work for them. If you land in a store like that you won't find much challenge to your copywriting ability. In other stores, however, you may write much copy, since you will wish to key your advertisements to the local situation. You may use mat material, but just as an occasional help.

One thing you can almost be certain of—in a small store you will usually find that there is not enough copywriting to fill all your working hours. This means you will fill out the rest of the time doing practically anything that comes along.

Take the case of an advertising-school grad-

THE SHOWCASE OF GOOD DESIGN
Our 38th Annual Winter
SALE!
final 4 days
the SALE nobody can afford to miss
Only once-a-year! Storewide reductions on practically every piece in our entire magnificent collection. Teak, Rosewood, Walnut, Mozambique and Pecky Pecan, by the most outstanding American and Scandinavian designers. Including all custom made sofas and chairs . . . in an unlimited choice of designer fabrics! Come now and bring your floor plans. The selection is large, brilliant & exciting. Savings will be more than substantial!
Maurice Villency®
Now on Madison Avenue in N.Y.C.
FURNITURE·DRAPERY·CARPETING·DECORATING
• NEW YORK 200 Madison Avenue at Corner of 35th. Street 725-4840
• ROSLYN HEIGHTS L.I. Exp'way Exit 36 300 So. Service Rd. 621-7537
• PARAMUS New Jersey 685 Route 17 opp. Fashion Center 447-4410
INTERIOR DESIGN SERVICES ARE FREE! • CONVENIENT PAYMENT PLANS
• Daily to 6 · Thursday to 9 · Mon. & Thurs. to 9 in Roslyn Hts. & Paramus
MAURICE VILLENCY INTERIORS

Fig. 9-2

Sale advertisement.

This unusual sale advertisement mentions no prices but creates an air of merchandising excitement along with an aura of prestige.

uate, for instance, who was hired as a "copywriter" in a small retail store. True enough, she *did* write copy. She also did all the layouts, planned the monthly advertising schedules, gave the space orders to the newspapers, and worked with the store manager in determining the advertising budget.

In addition, the "copywriter" helped out on the floor occasionally, filling in as a sales clerk. Regularly, too, she helped put up window displays. She even made talks on fashion trends to local women's groups.

Although all small or medium-sized stores might not expect so much from their young copywriters, you will probably find, if you enter such work, that writing copy will be just *one* of your duties.

STEPS IN EXECUTING A RETAIL ASSIGNMENT

Now to get down to the actual procedure of writing an advertisement. Suppose the buyer of men's shoes has an advertisement on his schedule and that he's supposed to have his "buyer's copy" up to you by a certain date (you usually will work anywhere from 6 to 14 days ahead of publication date). Ultimately, after the buyer has sent his material through his own merchandise manager and then through the advertising manager, you and the other staff members will discuss this advertisement along with others when you confer about advertisements about to be put into work.

Some stores may have such discussion for each advertisement. Others may simply determine general treatment for a group or series of advertisements and leave it up to the copywriter to develop copy for individual advertisements according to this over-all plan. General copy meetings in such stores may be called only for special promotions.

During your meeting, suggestions for treatment may come from any of the copywriters, from the advertising manager, from the art director, from the production manager—from any advertising person at the copy meeting. Perhaps it may be decided that the advertisement is to be hard-selling; that it will emphasize the variety of styles. You and the art director will discuss the tie-in of illustration and copy. You'll agree that the illustration should feature many shoe styles. You are to write captions for the numerous shoes pictured. After much discussion you leave the meeting with a rough idea of the copy and

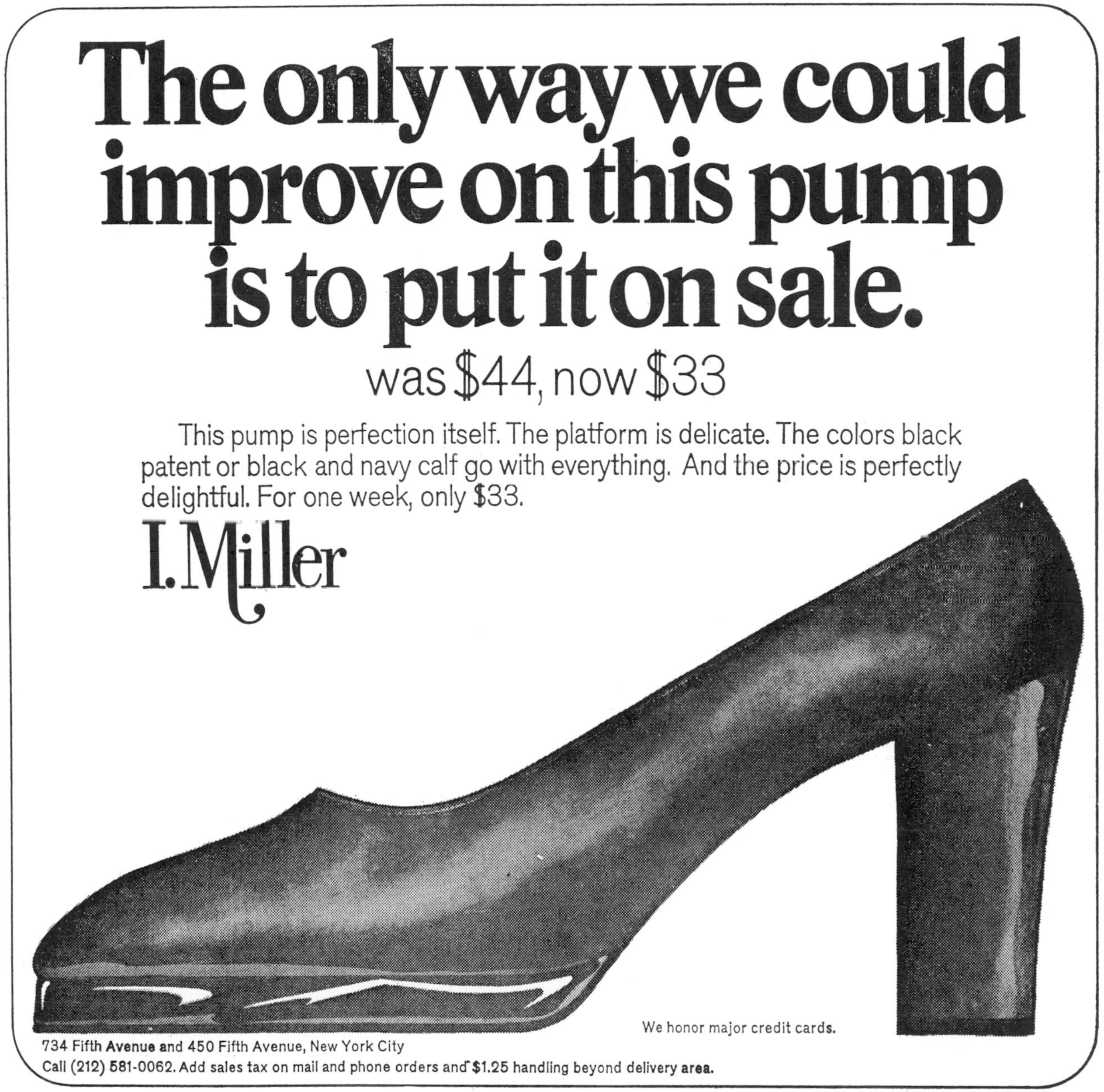
The only way we could improve on this pump is to put it on sale.
was $44, now $33
This pump is perfection itself. The platform is delicate. The colors black patent or black and navy calf go with everything. And the price is perfectly delightful. For one week, only $33.
I. Miller
We honor major credit cards.
734 Fifth Avenue and 450 Fifth Avenue, New York City
Call (212) 581-0062. Add sales tax on mail and phone orders and $1.25 handling beyond delivery area.

Fig. 9-3

Sale advertisement.

This is a good example of how to handle a sale advertisement tastefully. The copy and layout combine in saying "bargain" but in a way that is compatible with the fine reputation of the store.

art approach. You're ready to go to work.

You talk to the art department

One of your most important jobs at this point is telling the art department what sort of layout treatment the advertisement requires. You discuss the merchandise being advertised, suggest type and number of sketches, tell what your headlines and subheads will be—even prepare a rough layout or thumbnail sketch of the advertisement. This last item will be even more vital in a smaller store where the copywriter may be called on to turn in a complete "visual" of the advertisement.

The instructions to the art department are not the final word, of course, since the layout must be approved by the advertising manager before any finished art can be started. Probably the best way to tell the art department exactly what you have in mind is to write the entire advertisement—write every word that you want to have in the advertisement so that the layout person knows how much of a copy block you need, how many and how long the display lines must be, how many items you will have in a listing of merchandise, how many figures must be illustrated, and so on.

Your providing the actual copy assures you that the layout you get from the art department will be much closer to your wishes than if you had merely turned in some vague directions about "large copy block required," or "big display head," or "generous copy space." If *you* were the artist, what would "generous" mean to *you*? Just as you need complete information from your buyer in order to describe the merchandise, the layout people need complete information in order to turn out the right layout for that merchandise.

Remember, however, that many stores do their artwork *first* and *then* the copywriter goes to work. In such stores you would write copy that would fit the character of the artwork, and that would fit into the space that wasn't taken up by illustration. As a copywriter, it is much more satisfactory to work in the situation where you, rather than the illustrator, will be controlling the make-up of the advertisement. Unfortunately, there are probably more stores in which the art treatment comes first. You might as well realize this right now and be prepared to adjust yourself to playing second-fiddle to the art department if you happen to land in a store that gives the art people principal authority in the construction of advertisements.

All right—the layout's made and approved, and the art is to be prepared. This time the shoes were photographed in the photographer's studio after the buyer had delivered them to the studio. In the case of big items, such as furniture, the photograph will usually be taken after hours in the department involved. If you can, it's desirable for you to be around when your merchandise is being photographed or sketched. You might be able to make useful suggestions.

You start writing

While all this art activity is going on, you're supposed to be writing the copy. In large departments you'll be given a copy of the layout as it was actually approved, and the headlines will be represented properly along with copy space and listings. Perhaps you may have some simple adjustments to make. You may need to cut your copy slightly, or change your headline somewhat. The important thing is that this layout is no stranger to you. Most of your planned thinking has been done.

Sometimes, of course, your original ideas may be thrown out completely and you will have to start from scratch when you receive the final layout. Now assume that this is the case with the advertisement in question. You had what you thought was a fine idea but someone along the line—the advertising manager, or sectional manager, or perhaps both—caused your "fine idea" to be dropped into the wastebasket. Now you see the fresh layout in front of you. You're really starting all over again because a new slant has been thrown at you.

You re-check facts

Pick up the buyer's copy—the sheets containing all the information that the shoe buyer had to offer. First ask yourself: What am I selling? No, the answer isn't shoes alone, because everybody sells shoes. What's the *idea* behind this advertisement? What's the story behind all the illegible writing on the buyer's sheet. Dig down into the buyer's copy. Digest what he has given you. Call him up or go see him. Ask to see the shoes. Ask to see any manufacturer's data on the product, or any promotional material. Why does he want to advertise *these* shoes; how does he happen to have this merchandise; is it a new brand, a special price, a new idea? *Get all the facts before you sit down to write!*

You get back to writing

When you're popping with information,

READY FOR YOU THIS WEDNESDAY!

A whole new world of men's clothing! The male equivalent to everything we stand for in women's fashion—the classic and the contemporary—completely consistent with what you've come to expect from us. It's been in the works for over a year. We've transformed the 57th Street length of our Second Floor into a spacious, gracious, intimate atmosphere unheard of outside the Bergdorf tradition. So that this, with our exciting Men's Furnishings on the First Floor and our famous Barber Shop on the Mezzanine, allows us to answer a man's every need. Our emphasis is on total attire, geared to the individual, with total commitment to quality and fit. We run the gamut from the exactingly-finished Oxxford Clothes—the best in the world—to our own private collections of suits, sportswear, outerwear and accessories. We've a team of buyers whose standards of excellence have permitted only the ultimate in craftsmanship, the kind of elegance and taste that used to take all day and many city blocks to get together. Come in, savour the surroundings, sample our service . . . see the superb selections for yourself. Welcome to One West 57th Street, Second Floor. Individualism at last. Bergdorf GoodMAN awaits you.

Fig. 9-4

Men's fashion advertisement.

This advertisement, written in the institutional manner, creates prestige for its offerings without selling any specific items. Only the copy section of the advertisement is reproduced here.

you go back to your typewriter and start to write. First, write the story out for yourself from start to finish. Put it all down on paper so you can go back and refer to it for the facts you'll need. It might be a good idea to make up a check list to use in preparing any advertisement, whether it's newspaper, radio, or direct mail.

Understand that the following procedure represents the ideal. Sometimes you may be so harried with little tasks that you can't find time to go through this suggested process. If you *can*, you'll write better copy. When you first write retail copy you should try especially hard to follow this check list. Later, when you've become adept, you'll do the right thing automatically—it won't make any difference then if you get so busy that you don't *consciously* think in terms of the following check-list points. You'll do the right things by habit. If you're a beginner in retail copy (or any other type), however, you can't help profiting if you check yourself carefully before you start to write.

SOME PRE-WRITING QUESTIONS TO ASK YOURSELF

1. *Who is my customer for this merchandise?* Obviously, if it's a very high-priced pair of shoes, you appeal first to the man who can afford to pay that price. That consideration is going to govern your entire approach to him. Your advertisement is dignified. Your appeal must be to his pride and his desire to wear the best of everything.

If the shoe is a moderately priced item, you know it will have general appeal to all men. If it's a sale item you know again that it will have general appeal, but now you concentrate on the price feature. You will be determining meanwhile whether it's the type of shoe worn by young college men or dignified bankers. Perhaps your market is the rugged outdoor type, or possibly the shoe is the sort of slick stuff the "fancy-dan" likes to wear. These and other factors will be learned from sifting through the material gathered from your buyer and through your own observation.

2. *What benefits does this merchandise offer?* This is part of, yet different from, the actual description of the merchandise qualities. The shoe is described as soft and pliable—these are qualities—but you must translate these words into copy that is meaningful to the man who will wear the shoes. Saying "soft and pliable" doesn't mean so much to Mr.

Smith as saying that the shoes will allow his feet to bend properly, thus easing foot fatigue. Saying that the leather is durable is not the same as reminding the prospective customer that the shoes will take all sorts of rough treatment and bad weather, and that they will last a long time. Saying that the shoes are handsome is not so strong as saying that they're the latest thing out of *Esquire,* or that they'll really make his a stylishly complete wardrobe.

The idea of benefits is tied up with the idea of knowing who your customer is and what he expects to get out of the merchandise you want him to buy. Translate the buyer's cold facts into personal benefits that your reader wants—foot comfort, value for his money, prestige, and admiration.

3. *How shall I attract the reader's attention?* This is most vital, particularly in a newspaper where your advertisement—regardless of whether it's eight-columns full or two-columns by fifty agate lines—is competing vigorously for the attention of the man or woman who paid five cents to read the news stories in the paper. Remember, a good many of your readers did not pay their money to read advertisements, although a considerable number did. Since many people are interested in news, not advertisements, your advertisement itself must be news if you want to interest such readers.

You must get those factual benefits up where they can be seen. You stop a reader with benefits and you can stop him with advertising headlines—just as news headlines catch the reader's eye and cause him to pause for a news story. Your advertising headline is the copywriter's method for stopping the reader and getting him to read your advertisement. Layout and illustration will stop him, too—but merely stopping the reader is not enough. Well-chosen words in the body copy, captions, or subheads must instantly tell him the story of your merchandise and get him to recognize that this merchandise is what he's been looking for; that this merchandise fills a need he has; that this merchandise is what he's going to buy.

Your headline, in this instance, has stopped the reader and has caused him to read in the body text why he should buy these particular shoes—but that's not enough. Your shoes are for sale at one place and one place alone as far as you're concerned. You must convince the customer not only that he should buy *these*

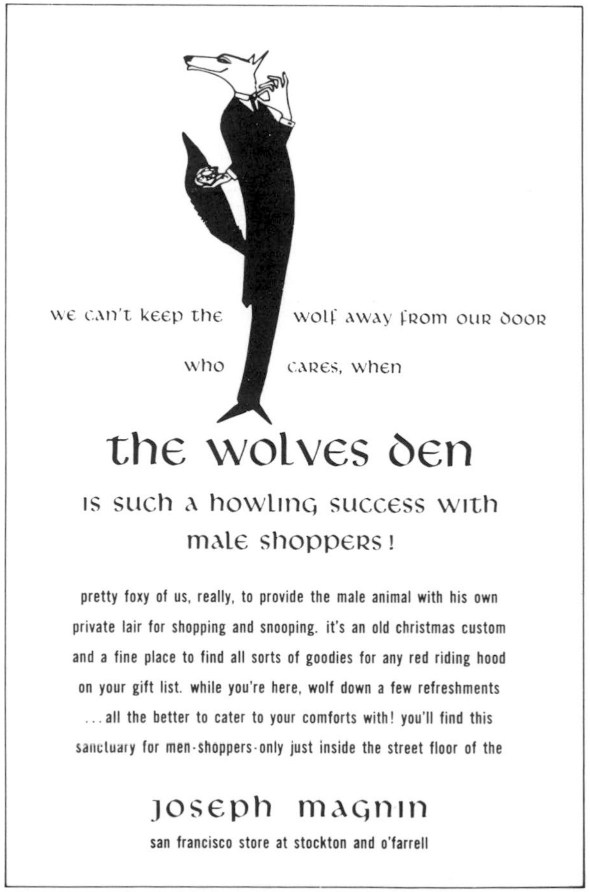
we can't keep the wolf away from our door
who cares, when
the wolves den
is such a howling success with
male shoppers!
pretty foxy of us, really, to provide the male animal with his own private lair for shopping and snooping. it's an old christmas custom and a fine place to find all sorts of goodies for any red riding hood on your gift list. while you're here, wolf down a few refreshments ... all the better to cater to your comforts with! you'll find this sanctuary for men-shoppers-only just inside the street floor of the
joseph magnin
san francisco store at stockton and o'farrell

Fig. 9-5

Fashion-store copy aimed at men.

The copywriter's job is to make the man feel easy about entering a woman's world.

Fig. 9-6

Prestige advertisement.

An offer such as this builds character and personality for a store even if the item may not sell in volume. The copy flatters those who have the sensitivity to appreciate the unusual offering.

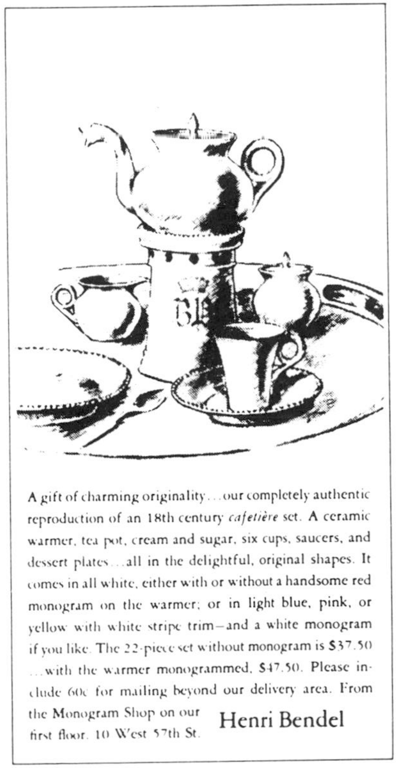
A gift of charming originality... our completely authentic reproduction of an 18th century *cafetière* set. A ceramic warmer, tea pot, cream and sugar, six cups, saucers, and dessert plates... all in the delightful, original shapes. It comes in all white, either with or without a handsome red monogram on the warmer; or in light blue, pink, or yellow with white stripe trim—and a white monogram if you like. The 22-piece set without monogram is $37.50 ...with the warmer monogrammed, $47.50. Please include 60¢ for mailing beyond our delivery area. From the Monogram Shop on our first floor, 10 West 57th St.
Henri Bendel

shoes but also that he should buy them at *your* store.

4. *How shall I identify the store?* Some stores merely put the "sig" or store name logotype at the top of the advertisement and let it go at that. You will usually make your advertisement more effective if you mention the store also in a subhead or lead-in line, and then refer to the store as often as you can in your body copy. In all retail advertising, this matter of identification is vital, because in this day of "famous brands" competitors on every street in town may be carrying the same brands. Without proper identification of your store as the place to buy, you're often merely running an advertisement to help your competitor sell his merchandise.

Your main points then are (1) Determining who your prospective customer is. (2) Presenting the appeals of your merchandise in the form of direct benefits. (3) Presenting those appeals to attract and hold the reader's attention. (4) Identifying the store so that it will be linked immediately with the benefits to be obtained.

Headlines must attract and identify, must feature main appeals, present facts vividly to stop the reader and get him to understand why this advertisement is of personal interest to him. *Body copy* must repeat the main appeals, once again identifying the store as much as possible. Facts should be presented to support claims made earlier, to make your story truthful and believable. The urge to buy the product advertised must be the ultimate end of your copy—to stimulate the reader into coming to your store to buy your goods.

HOW RETAIL COPY DIFFERS FROM NATIONAL COPY

Writing techniques and formulas of the type just given you are only two of the things for you to think about if you do retail copy. Although no one will deny that *all* copy —national, retail, radio, direct mail, newspaper, and magazine—has certain basic similarities, it is also true that retail copy has some characteristics that set it apart. A retail copywriter, especially one who has been familiar with the national field, should be aware of these characteristics along with the beginner who has had no experience. You will find the characteristics in varying degrees in copy for small, medium, or large stores.

Imagine that you have had some experience with other types of copywriting but that you have decided to try retail copywriting. At the moment you are seated across the desk from the advertising manager of the department store for which you are going to work. Knowing your background in other types of copy, he is discussing retail advertising. You realize that he is very diplomatically indicating to you that although you were competent in other forms of copywriting it doesn't follow that you can automatically write retail copy. He is giving you the same briefing he would give *anyone* entering retail copywriting.

It isn't your writing the advertising manager is concerned about; he's aware that you're a good technician. Rather, he's anxious for you to understand the basic concepts of the retail approach—some of the important differences between the writing you have been doing and the kind you'll do in the retail business.

A methodical man, the advertising manager ticks off his points for you. He says, "We're glad to have you with us. Also, *I'm* glad that we have a few minutes now to talk about this retail business. I'm well aware of your background. I know you can write so we'll forget that. What I *do* want to make sure of is that you get something of the retail picture before you type a word of copy. Some of the things I'm going to tell you may be obvious, but they bear repeating because their very obviousness often causes them to be overlooked, even by us who have grown up in retail.

"First of all, and I'm not sure that I wouldn't list this as the one and only point I'll make—*a retail store is part of the community* —a big part. You fellows and gals who write the copy share the community with your readers. You swelter in the same heat and get nipped by the same frost. You enjoy the same football team, and the current crime wave is a mutual worry. The financial ups and downs of your city and county are of acute concern to all of you. The retail business is, except in the case of some very large stores, a 100% local affair. This fact you will feel in all the copy you write. Let's see how this affects your thinking." The advertising manager then makes the following points. He tells you that in retail advertising three facts must be recognized:

1. *Urge to "buy now" is stronger.* There is immediacy in most retail copy. Stores depend upon turnover of stock. The best kind of stock is the kind that is "here today and gone tomorrow." Retail copy, for the most part, should be slightly breathless and urgent. You

Fig. 9-7

Prestige advertisements.

Despite — or perhaps because of — the simplicity of the copy and art in these advertisements, no one would fail to recognize these as advertisements for a first-class establishment.

TIFFANY JEWELRY
The lacey winged bumblebee pin of
eighteen karat gold, richly set with a choice of rubies,
turquoise or sapphires, all with a ruby eye.
Three hundred seventy five dollars,
including federal tax.
TIFFANY & CO.
NEW YORK
EASTER PRESENT
Tiffany's beguiling rabbit clip-pin,
of fur-textured eighteen karat gold
with a heart-shaped cabochon ruby
and cottontail of diamonds pavé.
Three hundred seventy five dollars,
including federal tax.
TIFFANY & CO.
NEW YORK

Fig. 9-8

Baby-clothes copy.

Skillfully the copy and illustration inject the "cuteness" that might be expected, but there is a hard core of factual material to help the buyer.

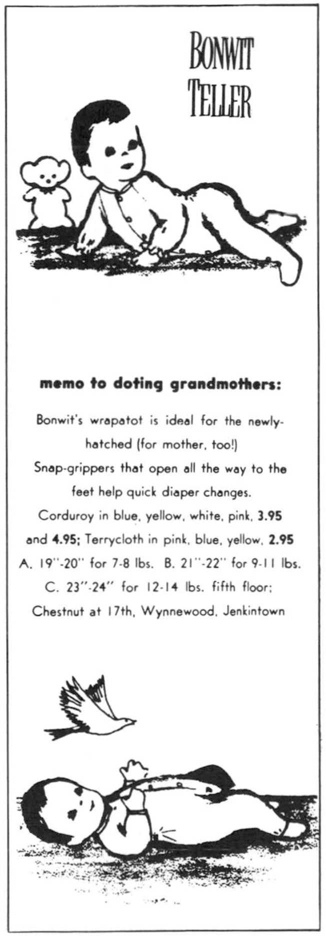
BONWIT
TELLER
memo to doting grandmothers:
Bonwit's wrapatot is ideal for the newly-hatched (for mother, too!)
Snap-grippers that open all the way to the feet help quick diaper changes.
Corduroy in blue, yellow, white, pink, 3.95 and 4.95; Terrycloth in pink, blue, yellow, 2.95
A. 19"-20" for 7-8 lbs. B. 21"-22" for 9-11 lbs.
C. 23"-24" for 12-14 lbs. fifth floor;
Chestnut at 17th, Wynnewood, Jenkintown

should push generally for the quick sale. In retail advertising you expect a quick response to your copy and you *must* get it. Thus, your copy should ever be prodding the customer, sometimes subtly, and sometimes with all the subtlety of a meat-ax. Get the reader to come to the store; get her to telephone; get her to bring her money down for a quick purchase. Phrases like "Come in today," "Buy while they last," "See them today," or "Get yours now while quantities last" are important in retail advertising. Sometimes you push people more delicately, but almost always there is some sort of urge to action—*immediate action.* This urge is much more pointed than in national advertising, which usually doesn't expect or need such immediacy of purchase on the part of the reader.

2. *Readers are more price-conscious.* People who read retail advertising want to know the price of merchandise. They have become accustomed in national advertising to priceless copy, but in much of retail copy, price is all important. Consciousness of cost creeps into all your copy. It weaves a web around the customer until he asks himself, "Can I afford *not* to spend my money?" When you think of price in retail copy you don't just think of price figures. Instead, you look upon your entire advertisement as building justification for the moment when the customer digs into her purse and says, "I'll take that."

There are very few stores that aren't price-conscious down to the last word in the last line of copy. Big stores, little stores, high-price stores, and bargain stores—all of them use price as the wedge for sales. You should get in the habit when you finish a piece of retail copy of looking it over and asking yourself whether your words would make *you* buy if you were the ordinary reader to whom dollars are mighty important. You have few chances in retail copy to forget that all the words you write simply act as background music for that all-important tag line which reads, "Only $00.00 while they last."

3. *Developing of store personality is a must.* Taken as a whole, you probably don't look much different from the people around you. You have the usual number of limbs, eyes, and ears. Compare yourself with the next-door neighbor. Based upon appearance, there isn't much to choose between you, yet you may have many more friends than he has. *Credit your personality.*

Likewise, you can credit successful retail stores with personality. Development of the personality of your store is a never-ceasing copywriting job. Ability to write "personality" copy is something you acquire on the job. You don't learn it the first day. It comes after you have studied your store's advertising; after you have got the "feel" of the place; after you have talked to other store employees; after you have been around a while.

Those saucy Gimbel's advertisements, those dignified productions of Lord & Taylor's, those slam-bang sales-producers of Goldblatt's—they reflect personality. *Personality in your advertising is what makes people come in to see your merchandise instead of going to your competitor's store to see the same merchandise.* Remember that most stores can match goods with their competitors these days. If all you have to offer is merchandise, you may fall back of your competitor who has found a personality and lets it shine through his advertisements. The basis of store personality is found in many things—friendliness, bargain prices, service, dependability, long establishment in the community, size of operation, or perhaps a combination of some, or all, of these.

Personality marks you as different from your competitor. New York City streets are lined with famous stores, each striving to be different from its neighbor. Saks is different from Bonwit Teller. Bergdoff Goodman differs from De Pinna, and Stern's is different from Bloomingdale's, and no one would mistake a Lord & Taylor advertisement with one from Ohrbach's. Each store works hard to be different, especially from its closest rival. A celebrated rivalry exists between Macy's and Gimbel's in New York. Although both stores use effective selling copy, many little differences exist which enable the reader to recognize a Gimbel's advertisement from one out of the Macy copy department.

Personality comes also from the creative technique—from the borders you use, the twist on words, the art treatment, the typography, the repetition of certain copy points or phrases such as the celebrated "Nobody, but nobody but Gimbel's" and the well-known "It's Smart To Be Thrifty" of Macy's.

Companies engaged in national advertising develop personality in their campaign themes but they are not usually *forced* into doing so, as are retail stores. The normal retail store has certain natural rivals who sell the same kind of goods at the same prices to the same type of customers. Rivalry between these stores is very personal. It is a matter of frantic interest to the stores that the stores themselves and their advertising reflect an individual personality which will make the customer differentiate one store from the other.

When you work in a retail store you may find that your toughest assignment is to capture your store's special personality in your copy. It's tough, because the personality is made up of so many little things. Be sensitive to those little things and be observant and one day you'll find that you have pinned down the elusive spirit that spells *your* store to the customers. If you *don't* capture this spirit, you'd better move on.

THE LANGUAGE OF RETAIL ADVERTISING

Your language in a retail advertisement walks a tightrope. Normally, retail copy goes out after the sale. Yet this hard-smacking sales copy must be clothed in friendly, good-neighbor talk because of the personal relationship of the store to its customers.

Note: What is said here does not apply directly to an important segment of retail

Dove of Peace
The most precious gift "Grant us peace," runs a famous prayer. The Dove of Peace, formalized for contemporary tastes in sterling silver. Pendant with chain $10.00
"Also available in 14k yellow gold but allow three weeks for delivery, $110.00."
Do Something Beautiful.SM
LAMBERT BROTHERS
Fine Jewelers Since 1877
545 Madison Avenue at 55th Street
New York
Also Smith Haven Mall • Smithtown
Please send me_____sterling silver dove @ $10.00
send me_____14k yellow dove pendants @ $110.00
plus 75c handling and tax where applicable.
Name_____
Address_____
City_____
State_____ Zip Code_____
Major credit cards are accepted.

Fig. 9-9

Retail mail order advertisement.

This clearly-written advertisement is especially noteworthy for the very usable coupon that makes ordering easy.

advertising—high-fashion promotion. Such copy operates in a rarefied atmosphere that removes it from many of the rules affecting the ordinary retail copy. Certainly it's true that a hat for $2.98 won't get the same copy treatment as will a mink coat. It is also true that many high-fashion writers could often profit from getting back to the less ethereal writing which moves mass merchandise out of retail stores. Regardless of the merits or failings of high-fashion copy, it *is* a part of its little, tightly circumscribed, glittering world. This discussion of retail language does not, in the main, refer to such copy. It *does* refer to the copy for less prosaic merchandise such as hardware, men's shoes, home furnishings, and haberdashery.

The specific words are the ones that sell. If you're selling moderately priced items like hats, "Prices cut in ½" punches harder than "Huge savings." Perhaps the line "Save $5 to $10" may sell the best of the three because it gets even more specific.

A salesperson is specific in talking to a customer—you can be, too. Naturally there is some difference between printed sales messages and those spoken by the person behind the counter. The clerk can be more specific, more pointed, and more down-to-earth because she's not held down by space limitations of a newspaper page. Just the same, a better sale will usually be made if you talk in your copy in the specific language of the salesperson, and not in the words of a copywriter reaching for the "well-turned" phrase and the "empty adjective."

JUDGING HOW MUCH TO WRITE

You'll be faced in retail copy, as in other types of copy, with the problem of how much copy to write. As in other copy, your solution is obvious—write enough copy to do the sales job. For instance, suppose you are writing an advertisement that is describing several items. You have decided to use a main copy block and several subsidiary copy blocks which will serve as captions for the multiple items being advertised. You'll defeat your advertisement if you try to jam too much copy into the main copy block, trying to describe in detail all the sales points for all the items in the advertisement.

In short, here is a case where you would be writing too much copy. You would do a better sales job if you made one over-all sales point covering all the items in an interesting way, thus luring the reader into the specific selling copy in the captions. In such a case, the main copy block might be more effective if it had six lines of copy than if it had twenty.

Judging the right amount of copy is the mark of the skilled, experienced copywriter. As the young copywriter soon finds out, it is often easier to write a page advertisement than a one-column, three-inch advertisement. Most people have more trouble "compressing" than "expressing." You may find it mighty hard at times to keep from writing too much copy. Suppose, for example, you have a really sensational promotion—really "hot" merchandise. The natural tendency is to write your head off. You and your buyers get excited. You load yourself with so many interesting facts that you could write a campaign for the product. Sadly, however, you realize that all these facts, and all this enthusiasm are going to be earthbound by the fact that you have just one advertisement in which to do your sales job.

In such a case, don't lose your momentum. Go ahead—*write* your head off—*then* start the sifting process. Get rid of the fluff. Get rid of the long-winded explanations that attempt to make clear this remarkable value. Tell the story straight, like a newspaper reporter. Remember your customer and his lack of interest in your writing ability. Remember your customer and his desires and wants and needs, all of which you're attempting to stimulate.

Knowing when to stop in the writing of copy is especially difficult in the writing of institutional copy. Such copy, in which you explain store policy, pricing, service, and other facets of store operation, can easily become too long. You can get so wrapped up in the store that you forget the customer. Institutional copy can be fascinating copy, but if you write too much it can easily be the dullest copy for the reader, because you may take many words to talk about something in which he is not basically interested.

SPACE-FILLER OR COPYWRITER?

Copywriters are little gods in some retail organizations. They fill in the spaces on layouts and go home at five o'clock. The next day they fill in more spaces. They have no more contact with the selling process than the man who sweeps the rest rooms. Such copywriters are what advertising men call "hacks."

A *good* copywriter rarely can sit in an office and write about merchandise two floors below—without personal contact with the merchandise. That's why you should school yourself to follow the entire process from start to finish—from the buying of the merchandise, if possible, to the investigation of the effectiveness of the advertisement you wrote. If you can possibly find the time, you should get to the selling department after your advertisement has run. Find out the reaction. If a crowd of shoppers flocks in at the opening bell and rushes to the department using your advertisement, you have a good idea that your copy was effective.

Later, again granting that you have time, check with the buyer and the salesmen to find out what they've sold. At the end of the day, ask again and keep a record of the dollar volume, and the advertised items sold off your advertisement. Some stores will actually require that you attach a form listing these results to a tear sheet of the advertisement. You then turn this in to the advertising manager.

Whether your boss requires it or not, make it your business to keep in touch with your advertisements all the way through. If an advertisement doesn't click, find out why. If you ask the buyers, they'll more than likely say it was a poor advertisement. A buyer might tell you, for instance, that the item is one that is usually bought by the husband and wife together. He might show you rather pointedly that your advertisement is slanted too much on one side—that you failed to recognize that both parties share in buying responsibility.

Perhaps you'll say the merchandise wasn't salable. Puzzle out the trouble. You might even rewrite the copy. Some copywriters have actually rewritten advertisements, asked that they be run again with the new slant, and hit the jackpot on the second running.

HELP FROM THE OUTSIDE

The copywriter in a retail organization does not have to depend on his brain alone for ideas. In small stores, especially, where the copywriter may be a person with a thousand jobs, outside material may be a lifesaver. In big stores or small stores, however, be careful that you don't use so much material from your merchandise sources—often called "resources"—that you forget how to turn out advertising on your own.

Agencies, manufacturers' advertising departments, newspapers, magazines—everybody wants your store to work cooperatively in promoting their products. Magazines will give you tie-in promotional material complete with copy and illustrations for use in your newspaper advertisement. Agencies and company advertising departments will send you brochures full of information, mats, glossy prints, radio spots, copy ideas—and they're all yours to use or discard.

How much you will use and how much you will discard depend upon several factors. The most important factor is the soundness of the ideas offered to you. Sometimes these outside sources forget that you are operating in retail advertising. They seemingly forget that on the retail level, when you talk with your chin right up against your customer's, you must be direct and careful in your use of ideas—often even more careful than in national advertising. For instance, a national campaign on girdles and furs may be built around the distinctiveness of a certain brand—the exclusiveness of its makers. Played up in color, in fine art treatment, such a story may be interesting and effective, and may do much to keep the firm's name connected with prestige and dignity.

On the *retail* level, your customer is primarily interested in how that fur will go with her fall outfit and what that girdle will do for a bulging figure. Out go the fancy words and tricky, cute expressions and vague references. Your language is direct. Chances are that in all the material provided you'll find something to hang your "direct" advertisement on—something about the variety of sizes, shapes, and so on and that will be your springboard.

DIRECT MAIL—A RETAIL SALES-BUILDER

You'll find that most retail organizations think almost exclusively in terms of newspaper advertising. Buyers will talk about a "spread" in their favorite evening paper. Most of the store's budget will be spent in newspapers, because the store can see what it's doing and can depend on reaching a healthy circulation guaranteed by the newspaper. Because it's a proved medium, you'll find that most of your time will be spent writing newspaper advertisements. Such copy will use much of the technique employed in copy for magazines and direct mail. Some differences do exist, however, in the tendency toward greater simplicity, shorter sentences, and use of news style in copy and headlines.

In larger stores you'll find much direct-mail advertising, too. The writing of such copy is discussed in the direct-mail chapter. Some stores have had great success with direct mail. Many have built big orders with simple post cards or bill inserts sent out to inform charge customers that a certain item will be offered. With no other advertising of certain items, some stores have found selling departments jammed with customers who responded to mailing pieces. Stores have also enjoyed great success in response to mailers which invited the customers to phone or mail in coupon orders.

You should understand the basic differences between direct-mail copy and newspaper copy. Though the selling purpose may be the same, your direct-mail piece may necessarily lack the forcefulness of illustration that your newspaper advertisement could command. Size, alone, can make a big difference. A full newspaper page, for instance, has the wallop of a pile-driver—a wallop that direct mail can hardly match. Since newspapers have this "impact" advantage, your words in direct mail, whether in letters, post cards, or insert,

THE J. L. HUDSON COMPANY DETROIT, MICHIGAN • 48226 • PHONE 223-5100

Dear Sir:

Hudson's Men's Store thinks a lot about its year-round customers and because of this, offers you the opportunity to shop for exceptional sale values ahead of the general public. This year the Men's Store Spring Sale starts Sunday, March 12 and runs through Sunday, March 19. But your special advance Courtesy Days are March 9, 10 and 11.

This important division-wide men's wear event occurs only twice a year at Hudson's, and the values are truly superb. This spring the emphasis is on double knits. Suits, sport coats, jackets--even raincoats. Imagine a double-knit sport coat for just 44.99. And there's lots more:

- Big name brands like Kuppenheimer, Weldon, Freeman, Rossi Romano and Gold Toe. For instance, Weldon pajamas, only 4.99.

- Hudson's own brand names including Darwood (double knit suits at just 59.99), Kenmoor, Rockham, Aldrich and Cadre.

The above are only examples of the vast selection in this outstanding sale. You can find everything from fashion suits by Kuppenheimer at 144.99 and designer ties at 4.99 to everyday furnishings like underwear, pajamas and hosiery.

We've listed as many as we could of the sale items on the reverse side of this letter--so you don't have to guess what's included. But the only way to get the entire picture is to visit us at Hudson's Downtown Detroit, 1st and 2nd Floors; Northland, Eastland, Westland, Pontiac, Oakland, Southland, Genesee Valley or Franklin Park. Remember--Courtesy Days are March 9, 10 and 11--and the Sale will be announced to the public March 12.

These sale values are sure to attract many wise shoppers. So I hope you're among the first. If you can't come in, we'll be happy to help you by phone.

Cordially,

J. W. Smith
Divisional Merchandise Manager

Fig. 9-10

Direct mail letters.

The three department store letters shown here demonstrate the importance of the medium where local stores are concerned. Retailers know that their best customers are people who are already customers. Direct mail letters enable retailers to let such customers know about important events and, more important, to let customers know that their patronage is appreciated.

THE J. L. HUDSON COMPANY

Hudson's wishes you much happiness in your new life together. We hope our Brides' Registry helped to make your wedding memorable.

Most new homemakers spend a great deal of time at first getting their "house" in order. If you are one of these, I think you'll enjoy the convenience of a Hudson's Charge Account. With this simple treasure - you can just say "charge it" when purchasing items for your new home, yourself and for each other.

When you shop, of course, you'll receive records of your individual purchases and a complete statement each month. Prompt payment means no finance charge - and more money in your pocket.

I hope you'll fill out the enclosed request form today and return it in the envelope provided for your convenience. You'll enjoy carefree shopping in no time at all.

Cordially,

C. A. Schneider
Credit Manager

Enc.

THE J. L. HUDSON COMPANY DETROIT, MICHIGAN · 48226 · PHONE 223-5100

Dear Customer:

Last spring we staged a Sale of Original 18th and 19th Century Oil Paintings at Hudson's Northland. The interest was so great we began making plans immediately for this year's event. The Sale will be held for just 4 days - Sunday, June 4 through Wednesday, June 7, in the 1st Level Furniture Department at Hudson's Northland.

This year's Sale includes a vast selection of more than 300 original antique oil paintings - some priced as low as $75 and ranging up to $2,500. All by 18th and 19th century artists - the subjects include portraits, landscapes, seascapes, still lifes, sporting subjects and animals.

As in our previous sales - prices are exceptionally modest - considerably below the normal cost for such quality. As you know, originals are excellent investments, increasing in value through the years. Paintings of the 19th Century Romantic School, for example, have quadrupled in value over the past decade, due to increased interest and demand.

We're telling you about this Sale in advance so that you may plan an early visit and take advantage of the selection. Remember the dates - Sunday through Wednesday, June 4, 5, 6 and 7 at Hudson's Northland. An antique oil painting expert from New York will be on hand Sunday and Monday to assist you.

Cordially,

Robert R. Jenkins
Divisional Merchandise Manager
Home Accessory Division

must be even more carefully chosen. Remember, although the newspaper itself had some attraction for the customer (in its news value), your insert comes entirely uninvited into the home—the letterhead or store name itself may be enough to cause it to be thrown away without being read.

Be just as specific as you can. Avoid being cute. Make your letter friendly, newsy, interesting. Get out what you have to say as quickly as you can, catching the reader's eye and imagination with a fact that is of personal interest to him. Avoid printing letters upside down, or employing other such tricks. Devices of that sort only irritate and confuse.

Much direct-mail material can be secured from the manufacturer of the goods you advertise—a fact of great value to the small store, especially. Almost all companies produce mailing inserts for the use of their retail outlets. Some are given to the store free—others can be bought on a cooperative basis. Be sure the store name is imprinted on any mailing piece you buy from a national source, and avoid mailing pieces that lack a local, personal flavor. After all, your purpose is not so much to sell the national brand, but to sell the national brand in your store.

GREY ADVERTISING INC. RADIO

1001 WOODWARD AVENUE, DETROIT, MICHIGAN 48226

CHICAGO - LOS ANGELES - MONTREAL - NEW YORK - SAN FRANCISCO - TORONTO

CLIENT:	Hudson's "Eureka Vacuum Cleaner Offer"	COMML. NO.:	/ (SECS)	F/C/A	☐
PRODUCT:	:10 live Grey Original	TITLE:		FOR PROD.	☐
JOB NO.:	Rev. #1 - Approved (16)	PROGRAM:	/ (NET)	AS REC.	☐
DATE:	March 5, 1973	AIR DATE	3/6-11	WORD COUNT	___

ANNCR: This week only at Hudson's. Buy any Eureka Upright Vacuum and get a regular $12.95 set of attachments at no extra charge. But hurry. Offer ends March 11 (today).

ANNCR NOTE: "Offer ends March 11" airs 3/6-10.
"Offer ends today." airs 3/11 only.

Fig. 9-11

Ten-second live radio commercial selling specific item.

Since this commercial is low cost it can be aired frequently to generate good sales results.

Fig. 9-12

Radio commercial for clearance sale.

Radio is especially useful for sale promotions to create excitement. Such advertisements do not single out individual items but talk in terms of the entire stock.

Follow the same principle with the mats that companies send you. Read them carefully. Make sure that your specific merchandise is described in such a way that your store will be identified as the seller. In fact, it's usually a good idea to use the artwork on a mat—if you like it, or if it's more expedient and economical—and have the newspaper reset the copy matter to conform with the type style and approach of your store. This helps continue the "family" relationship among all your advertisements. It should be followed similarly through direct-mail advertising as much as possible.

Direct-mail copywriting for retail stores may require you to write many things in addition to letters. You may do copy for post cards, illustrated invitations to fashion shows, announcements, and college booklets. You'll find an interesting variety usually.

RETAIL RADIO WRITING

Writing for retail radio is so similar to writing for national radio that there is no attempt to detail how to write radio copy for a retail store. The suggestions found in the radio chapter will apply to retail radio writing.

One caution might be observed, however. You might remember that, as in the case of

GREY ADVERTISING INC. RADIO

1001 WOODWARD AVENUE, DETROIT, MICHIGAN 48226

CHICAGO - LOS ANGELES - MONTREAL - NEW YORK - SAN FRANCISCO - TORONTO

CLIENT:	Hudson's - Oakland "Winter Coat Clearaway"	COMML. NO.:	/ (SECS)	F/C/A	☐
PRODUCT:	:30 live Grey Original	TITLE:		FOR PROD.	☐
JOB NO.:	Approved - Rev. #1 (16)	PROGRAM:	/ (NET)	AS REC.	☐
DATE:	March 7, 1973	AIR DATE	3/8-9	WORD COUNT	___

ANNCR; Gals, now through Sunday, Hudson's Oakland Store only is having a sale you won't want to miss. Now you can save 30 to 50% on Hudson's entire stock of winter coats. See all the fashion looks of the season...from the junior shops...the misses shops...even the Woodward shops...coats from every fashion coat department of every Hudson's store. All in one great place...Hudson's at the Oakland Mall. But hurry...the great coat clearaway ends Sunday.

GREY ADVERTISING INC. TELEVISION

1001 WOODWARD AVENUE, DETROIT, MICHIGAN 48226

CHICAGO · LOS ANGELES · MONTREAL · NEW YORK · SAN FRANCISCO · TORONTO

CLIENT:	J. L. HUDSON'S	COMM'L. NO.: H-F355	/ (SECS)	LIVE ☐ F/C/A ☐
PRODUCT:	QUALITY NAME BRAND CAMPAIGN	TITLE: "SHOWER"		FILM ☐ FOR PROD. ☐
JOB NO.:	177-00-967	PROGRAM:	/ (NET)	TAPE ☐ AS REC. ☐
DATE:	AS RECORDED	AIR DATE		WORD COUNT ______

VIDEO	AUDIO
WOMEN AT BRIDAL SHOWER	
ANNCR:	Ever wonder why you see so many appliances from Hudson's at a bridal shower?
GIRL:	Oh ... it's an Osterizer. How nice. A blender. It's a Toastmaster. Just what I wanted. Oh ... it's Sunbeam. It's terrific. It's a G.E. Peek-a-Perk ...
ANNCR:	A brand name says it's a gift worth having ... no matter how little you spend. And Hudson's has more of the best brand name appliances ... in more styles, models and prices for you to choose from.
GIRL:	It's a...why it's a...a...
OLD LADY LEANING FORWARD:	It's a clock. I knew you'd like it.
SUPER:	Hudson's knows the value of a good name. Just like you do.

Fig. 9-13

Retail television commercial for famous department store.

This commercial, which stresses brand-name products, was prepared for the store by an advertising agency. Most department stores use advertising agencies for their television advertising.

local newspaper advertising, you will do well to capture the local flavor in your radio commercials. You can be a shade friendlier and more intimate. The very fact that you are mentioning a local store in your copy immediately establishes a rapport difficult for the national advertiser to match.

The following commercial with its mention of the local department store illustrates this built-in advantage of the hometown advertiser. This commercial with its frequent push on price was successful in the small town, in which the store is located, in selling 244 pairs of the corduroy pants that were mentioned in the copy.

Mother, does your son play hard? Then shop BIGELOW'S for tough-as-nails corduroy pants, regularly $4.49, now just $3! Yes, for boys who play hard, there's just no substitute for thick-set, long-wearing durable corduroy pants. What's more, he's sure to get extra wear out of these pants—because they have a double knee for extra wear and tear! Choose from navy blue, brown and green, in sizes 6 to 12. And remember, these are a $4.49 value for just $3.00 at BIGELOW'S. You'll also like the cuffs on these pants, the zipper openings and the elastic top with the belt, all for the amazing price of just $3. So, for value that means money saved, for quality that means hard wear, get your son durable, thick-set corduroy pants, regularly $4.49, now at the value-packed price of just $3, in the Boys' department on the Third Floor of BIGELOW'S.

Here is another example of retail store selling through the radio medium. Notice how the writer localized his approach in the beginning of the commercial and then proceeded with his sales talk. Once again the store name adds a localizing touch.

> Every hour of every day fire destroys a home. The recent Elm Street fire shows that it can happen here. And your home could be next. That's why it's so important to have a Protexall fire extinguisher in your home—ready to stop a little fire before it grows to be a home-destroying big fire. You'll find the Protexall featured today in the 4th floor hardware department of Johnson's Department Store. It's made by American La France, world's largest manufacturer of fire fighting equipment. This handsome extinguisher comes in four decorator colors that will fit beautifully into your home design. And the Protexall is as efficient as it is handsome. In seconds, Protexall will put out any type of fire—grease, electrical, or wood. Fire can strike any time so come *soon* to get your Protexall. It'll give you extra peace of mind to know that Protexall is guarding your home and your family. See it today in the hardware department of Johnson's Department Store.

Sometimes a department store that uses radio vigorously will run many spots, long and short and throughout the day. An example of a short spot is the following:

> Your daughter will appear at her perkiest in the over-blouse and skirt look. . . . One dress your size 7 to 14 girl will like is the red printed dress with the red printed over-blouse. The price: $7.98. . . . Dress your daughter in the style she knows is new. . . . From Woodward & Lothrop, Washington. Open today til 6 . . . and Woodward & Lothrop, Chevy Chase, Seven Corners and Alexandria, open til 9:30.

A typical spot of this store includes a description of the item, its price, the department in which it is sold, and the store hours.

High-pressure radio is used less in retail copy than in national copy. The "irritation-type" commercial—the kind that slams the message home over and over again—is not keyed so well to the homespun friendliness of retail radio. Your national accounts don't have to live with their customers. Let them use the sledge-hammer—*you* use a more relaxed approach generally. You'll wear better that way. The push to buying may be in your message, but clothe it in warmth and good-neighborliness for the most part.

Since many retail stores handle radio programs through agencies or through the stations' commercial departments, you may not have a chance to write commercials for a retail radio show. If you do get into retail radio writing there is a good chance that the only kind of commercials you will write will be spot commercials—anywhere from 30 to 60 seconds. A good set of spots can sell a lot of merchandise. You *can* build an institutional story with spot announcements but you'll probably write them in order to put over the quick sale—the unusual bargain—the get-them-while-they-last approach. In these spots you often won't be "relaxed," as suggested previously. You'll find a real challenge, however, in turning out these dramatic, selling spot announcements.

RETAIL TELEVISION WRITING

Although television is being used by many retail advertisers it still is too expensive and too specialized for many other retailers. The retailer using television tends to employ simpler, less costly techniques than the national advertiser. Not for him the expensive animation and elaborate live action film settings used by the big-budget national advertisers.

The retail advertiser is more likely to use live studio shots, or possibly syndicated open-end commercials. More elaborate productions may be possible to him, however, through co-operative arrangements.

Retail copywriters then are very often required to create television within the framework of a limited production budget. This means the retail writer will most often depend upon local station talent and production facilities. There will be much use of slides, stock shots if film is used, and simply-staged studio shots.

Videotape, however, has opened up many

new opportunities for the retailer using television commercials. If his local station happens to have videotape facilities the retailer may, because of lower costs, make more use of television advertising. The writer will find that although his creative possibilities are expanded, videotape used on the local level is essentially live-action studio production except that rehearsals can eliminate the mistakes that have so harassed studio production before videotape was perfected. Too, the writer now finds that optical effects employed with videotape can make the commercials more interesting.

Because the writing of television commercials has so many ramifications, there will be no attempt in this chapter to tell the retail writer just how such writing should be done. If you are writing on the local level it is suggested that you read the chapter on television writing for suggestions. Although this chapter is largely centered on writing for national television advertising, the principles you will find can be applied to retail television.

Fashion Advertising: Different Rules And A Different Language.

A man looks (infrequently) at a fashion advertisement and realizes uneasily that he doesn't understand the language. He senses that same bumbling uncertainty that overcomes him when he cringes his way into the lingerie department to buy dainty garments for his wife.

Even a great many women do not really understand the language of fashion advertising. Instead, however, of being daunted by their lack of comprehension of oftentimes stilted, haughty phrases, they are intoxicated by them. What they can't understand, they can *feel*—and this is where they are different from the uncomprehending and *un*feeling males.

If you have worked up a comfortable set of rules to guide you in copywriting, you'd better drop them in the bottom drawer of the file before you begin writing fashion copy. Good creative techniques for fashion promotion will very frequently be radically different from acceptable techniques for selling ordinary goods and services. You are entering a new creative world when you begin a fashion-copy career.

FASHION COPY COMBINES MOOD AND FACTS

Anyone who enters fashion advertising thinking, however, that it consists of nothing more than creating mood with a series of airy, somewhat zany phrases will soon be disabused of this notion. True, fashion advertising writing uses a flip, mode (or mod) language but the moment of truth arrives when facts must be given and the fashion writer then employs tough, resultful, reason-why copy. She knows that the reader of her advertisement can't make a buying decision if she is served nothing but fluff.

A good example of a fashion advertisement is the following that utilizes a certain amount of the language expected in fashion advertising but which has a hard core of rational, here-are-some-good-reasons-to-buy

COURTAULDS IS ALL AROUND YOU

Crazy Horse bets on Folker's Cape Cod II. A new breed of fabric.

Cape Cod II is a winner. A never-before fabric that's classic looking but no sissy. It's cool and comfortable to wear.

Especially in a shirt-tail jacket and pleated skirt by Karen Saloomey for Crazy Horse, Inc. You can squeeze it, sit on it, rumple it, crumple it—it just will not wrinkle.

You can toss it into a washing machine and dryer—it'll come out crisp, fresh, lively as new. Courtaulds Fibro® blended with polyester gives Cape Code II its thoroughbred character.

The suit comes with a checked blouse. At Lord & Taylor, New York and all branches.

Another example of this same sort of approach in which the fanciful is mixed with the practical is the following. Note that the beginning captures attention through the dream-date reference to the Rolls Royce but notice, too, how quickly the writer gets down to the practical details needed for a buying decision.

"MY LATEST LESLIE FAY."®

When he told me he'd pick me up in his car, I never dreamed it would be a Rolls.

What do you wear in a Rolls? Leslie Fay knows. This dress and jacket outfit was perfect.

MEET DONALD BROOKS IN PERSON AT BONWIT'S—THE ONLY PLACE YOU CAN SEE HIS ENTIRE SPRING COLLECTION! Come meet him at a formal Fashion Show tomorrow, Monday, the 26th, at 3:00 p.m. and see the collection informally modelled Tuesday and Wednesday from 12:00 to 4:00. Here, in the year of the short cocktail dress, Donald Brooks does his own definitive version: a mere slip of a thing covered with blouson'd and deep-sleeved black French lace. Misses' sizes, 365.00 No mail or phone, please. In our Designer Salon, Sixth Floor, it has the Bonwit Teller Touch! Fifth Avenue at 56th Street, New York and all Bonwit stores

It has a navy and white arnel triacetate and nylon knit tank top with a white arnel triacetate skirt pleated all around.

The red linen-like jacket, of 100% polyester, is softened with a drawstring belt.

Also available with red and white tank top, white shirt and navy jacket. Sizes 8-18. About $54.

It's my latest Leslie Fay.® And I love it.

What is fashion copywriting, and how can you learn to write it successfully? Like all other types of copy, it has its tricks. You must learn those tricks. Also, before you can learn to write fashion copy, you must first learn what fashion is. At the outset, then, you will pursue the illusive fashion.

Perhaps you'd better start by thinking of fashion (1) as exemplified in high-fashion periodicals and in advertisements for exclusive stores, (2) as exemplified in volume selling in department and moderate-price stores. When you have thought about these two divisions of fashion you will be ready to absorb a few "do's and don'ts" of fashion writing.

You probably have surmised already that fashion is a capricious commodity. What is and what is not fashion almost defies analysis. Every few years some scholar comes out of his research activities to write a new and learned treatise proving that fashions stem from wars and the general economy of a country. In the broad, over-all view he's probably right. However, in view of fashion's inherent ephemeral quality and because the motives and causes underlying changes in fashion are as subject to change as the fashions themselves, it is of no great importance to pin it down, dissect it and catalog its component parts.

Consider what happened to fashion after World Wars I and II. When women began bobbing their hair after the first war, it was supposedly to assert equality with men by looking more boyish and by affecting the boyish figure. It was even argued that since women had shared the hardships of war as Red Cross workers, nurses, and so forth, they intended to share the rewards. Ostensibly, the generalization to be drawn from this example is that women express their emancipation after a war through more masculine fashions, but this analysis does not work out. Many thousands of women also served in the World War II. Again, when the war was over, they swarmed to have their hair cut shorter. This time the motive was changed. They clipped it off not to look more boyish but to achieve a fluffy, feminine look. The war had made fashion static, imposed regulations, prescribed tailored suits, demanded practical, mannish clothes. The outburst of the new, the curved, the longer-skirted silhouette, as well as of short coiffures, was an expression not for equality, but against the deadly regimentation of war.

Fashion is a female fetish. The approach is so personal that the feeling is strong that it takes a woman to sell another woman. The rare man can understand how important it is to a woman to wear a skirt three inches longer (or three inches shorter) than last season's, but he's at a distinct disadvantage in having to guess how she *feels* in it. A woman knows. She is capable of doing a complete selling job because she knows what it does to her to feel the intimate swish of silk taffeta. She sells the *feel* of fashion, of low waists or high waists, flared skirts or straight skirts, or whatever, almost before she sells the specific merchandise.

Fashion moves in cycles. If you're an aspirant for a top job in fashion copy you'll need to read as much as possible about the clothes of all periods. While you're at it you'll profit also from exposure to the humanities, history, literature, and the economics of the world.

Fig. 10-1
and
Fig. 10-2

Visiting celebrity advertisement.

Retail stores attract many shoppers by using well-known figures from the worlds of fashion, entertainment, and literature. These copy sections of such advertisements demonstrate why the visiting celebrity promotion instills vitality and interest in fashion advertising.

COME MEET LONDON DESIGNER GORDON LUKE CLARKE AND SEE HIS LUKE COLLECTION, EXCLUSIVE AT BONWIT'S IN ALL AMERICA! See the "Luke Look" that's driving Europe wild at a fashion show Tomorrow, February 27th, at 3:00 p.m. and informally modeled Wednesday from 12:00 to 4:00. Here in this country for the first time, Mr. Clarke will present the clothes that are making the world beat a path to his King's Road boutique in London. Softly tailored, his separates can be matched and mated in endlessly beautiful permutations. For 6 to 14 sizes, these shown from 30.00 to 180.00 In S'fari Now, Fourth Floor, they have The Bonwit Teller Touch! Fifth Avenue at 56th Street, New York. And also available in our Chicago and Beverly Hills stores.

Writing fashion advertising is less inspiration than it is a comprehensive knowledge of what made the world turn in Cleopatra's time, and what keeps it spinning today.

Fashion is emotion. You must live with it. It is your job to begin where the photograph or illustration leaves off. Your work is good when you give the reader the feel of fashion, when you make a coming dinner party inviting by letting a woman know how it will feel to appear in an Original by Givenchy.

So much for fashion in general. Now to point up the distinctions between high-fashion advertising and volume-fashion copy.

HIGH-STYLE FASHION WRITING

High-style fashion writing can be fairly formal, as on the pages of *Vogue* or *Harper's Bazaar.* Formal, as it is in the advertisements of Marshall Field's. Informal, as in *Mademoiselle.* Or formal or informal, as in the top fashion advertisements of Lord and Taylor. Whichever it is, this copy is authoritative; it *sets* the fashion.

From these editorial pages and advertisements spring the words and phrases that articulate the fashion. Through the years, the words associated with fashion have been as essential to the fashions themselves as the very fabrics from which they are cut. For instance —the Gibson Girl shirt, the hobble skirt, the Tam O'Shanter, the swing skirt, the D'Orsay pump.

High-fashion copy is designed primarily *to sell the idea of the coat of the moment, rather than a specific wraparound coat in stock.* The importance of this objective must not be underestimated. Writing for this type of advertisement is an exacting job.

Newspapers and magazines from time to time carry striking examples of superb jobs. Quite a number, by their originality and daring, have started whole new circles of advertising thought. In New York, for example, Lord and Taylor runs newspaper advertisements written by copywriters who have distinguished themselves by being able to put down on paper just a few really thought-through words. These writers are masters of the art of saying a lot by writing hardly anything. It isn't easy. Years of apprenticeship and hard work are necessary before a writer can hope to achieve this skill.

Nothing has been said here about the

fashion artist as an important member of the creative team. In many eyes he is more important than *you* in inducing sales. Fruitless and unending arguments can be held on this point since words and illustration must ultimately work together. Each can enhance the other. Make no mistake, however. Recognize that illustration, as important as it is in other forms of advertising, is still more important in fashion advertising in conveying mood and authenticity. Fashion artists are usually superior artists. Such artists will provide you with a strong creative challenge—to do as well with words as they do with art. The test is whether the art embellishes the copy, or vice versa—or does each match the other perfectly?

A study of high-fashion advertisements will reveal these characteristics:

(1) They are directed toward people who set the pace.

(2) Their appeal is prestige.

(3) They speak with authority (usually written in third person).

(4) They strive toward mood and illusion.

(5) Their concern with details, if any, is secondary.

(6) They contrive to make the reader feel she is influencing fashion, rather than being influenced by it.

(7) The copy is usually brief—and always enhanced by dramatic artwork and distinctive type faces.

(8) The words themselves are fresh as an April leaf, highly dramatic and descriptive.

Notwithstanding the fact that good high-fashion advertising has the characteristics described in the foregoing, there is a regrettable amount of high fashion advertising appearing in magazines and newspapers that does not measure up. One criticism is the sameness in the sleek illustrations and the copy's artificial sheen—the bright, insincere patter that has confused shallowness for sophistication.

There is the tendency, too, for fashion advertisers to fall in love with prettiness. Advertisements are judged as "pretty" or not pretty—whether or not they have ideas or selling arguments. The advertisements—copy and art—show and talk about merchandise but make no real attempt to sell it.

The truly difficult art of fashion copywriting—to blend skillfully atmosphere, facts, and selling persuasion—has been mastered by many but still escapes many in the field of fashion copywriting.

FASHION COPY FOR VOLUME SALES

Whereas high-fashion advertising is designed to set the pace, volume-fashion advertising is directed to *selling* the woman who must keep the pace. The student looking forward to a career in advertising will very likely have her start here. This does not mean that volume-fashion advertising is easy, nor does it imply that the techniques involved are less exacting. It does mean that there are more opportunities in this phase of advertising because this is the category into which most advertising falls. The stores and agencies engaged in promotional work to move stocks of merchandise are in the thousands. In contrast, the smart shops and periodicals whose concern is high fashion are relatively few.

No matter how naturally endowed you may be, you must realize that a flair for writing is not enough for writing fashion advertising that sells. You must understand selling techniques, adaptations of style, human nature, and above all, you must have an intimate knowledge of the woman who buys and wears the clothes you are writing about—the woman who does the volume-buying upon which all stores depend.

Fig. 10-3

Men's fashion advertisement.

As is shown here, there is little difference in the mood of a men's fashion advertisement than that aimed for in a woman's fashion advertisement. There is the same stress on designer skill, too.

VIA EUROPA
He saw "The Last Tango in Paris". . . in the rushes.
He's backing a new gallery. His luncheon engagement tomorrow?
Barcelona. The world is his.
His favourite way of spending rainy Saturdays around the globe . . .
visiting private friends in the country. He wants European
fit translated for American shapes. He understands Meledandri
He wears one from our exclusive collection of plaids,
stripes and solids. Wools and wool blends, $165.00 to $225.00.
Via Europa, Escalator Level, New York.
Also available at Bergen County, Garden City, Short Hills
and Stamford. Bloomingdale's, 1000 Third Avenue,
New York, N.Y. 10022. 752-1212.
Open late Monday and Thursday evenings.
the
men's
store

In one sense, your knowledge of women's buying habits, their whims, and their enthusiasms is more important than your writing skill. If you don't have the former, you're just a hack writer spinning out glib, bright patter that fails to convince and thus fails to sell. Although there are vast differences in the markets and in the writing techniques used, a fashion writer and an industrial writer have a lot in common. Each must have an intense personal interest in his specialized field and must be able to turn out copy precisely geared to that field.

You must, above all, be breathlessly intrigued with fashion change and fashion detail. In the illustrative part of your advertisement it must be important to you how a glove stops at the wrist, and where the fake flower is pinned on the dress. It is easy to be wrong in these details. Likewise, it is exceedingly difficult to recover the confidence of the woman who looks over your advertisement and finds that you, seemingly, have less interest in these details than she does.

The writer engaged in volume-fashion advertising must correlate three factors: (1) selling techniques, (2) human nature, (3) forceful style.

Fig. 10-4

Long-copy fashion advertisement.

Written in a light, amusing style this advertisement nevertheless gives all the needed buying information including prices, fabrics, colors and styles.

A Guide to Palo Alto

Since Palo Alto is an unreal place (you could say it's a state of mind), there are no traffic jams, no pollution, no urban blight. Instead, there's an easy informality. Happy day colors. A feel for natural beauty. And certainly no sign of inflation. Maybe all cities should be imaginary.

A Sometimes the best thing to do in an active sportknit is just sit quietly and meditate. Try it in a $7 hot pink sleeveless turtleneck. If the vibrations aren't exactly right, there's always black, white, navy, red, brown, rose, lemon, lime, powder, mint, orchid, yellow, cloud and vanilla.

B The only militaristic note in all of Palo Alto is our tank top. You can have it in our usual endless parade of colors for $6.

Palo Alto

C Or you can have our tank top bodysuit for $8.

D The city mothers have asked all residents to help keep Palo Alto beautiful. (City fathers haven't been doing such a great job in this country, so we have city mothers.) One way to keep P.A. beautiful is to wear a long-sleeved, ribbed bodysuit of Antron* nylon with turtleneck collar at just $10.

E Another way to keep a city attractive is to show up in your magic outfit. The one top that looks like three. Solid body. Striped short sleeves. And white collar. All for $10 in wonderful Antron* nylon. That's magic, too.

F Here's a new arrival in Palo Alto. The versatile shortsleeved top in a very interesting cable stitch effect. No less than 15 colors. And no more than $11.

Palo Alto is just as easy to shop for as it is to wear. All the styles come in S, M and L. And when you see a tag that looks like a road map, you're in the right place. Or write to Palo Alto, subsidiary of Fairfield Noble Corp. 1411 Broadway, New York.

*REG TM DUPONT

The New York Times Magazine/March 4, 1973 21

Effective volume-selling, like other forms of selling, is based on six rather commonly accepted objectives: (1) to attract attention; (2) to hold interest; (3) to create desire; (4) to overcome obstacles; (5) to stir to action; (6) to give satisfaction and pleasant reaction for money spent.

Although the precepts of effective selling can be learned in Psychology 201 or in basic courses on salesmanship, human nature cannot be so conveniently catalogued. Textbooks can give you general knowledge about your woman consumer. *All* people want recognition, want response, work for security, and yearn for new experience. *But*—the woman you are trying to reach considers herself less a member of a particular group and more an individual who is different and has different problems. You must know and understand *this* woman in *particular.* Recognize her problems. If your copy is to sell, you must show her how to dress attractively, but you must be aware, too, that she is concerned with making her budget stretch, and that she is determined to keep her family healthy. You know also that she wants to keep her home attractive—that she wants the honeymoon to last, and

Fig. 10-5

Humorous copy which does not, however, forget to give selling facts. The store was informed after the appearance of the advertisement that the word "hibernate" should correctly be "estivate." This latter word was used as an attention-getter in a second running of the advertisement.

De Pinna
"I think for myself . . .
I hibernate in the Summer
at De Pinna"
• Finest fur storage facilities
• Cleaning, glazing, alterations by experts
• Remodeling by skilled furriers
Write or telephone PLaza 7-9000
FUR SALON, THIRD FLOOR

that, finally, she wishes to have something extra for herself.

Your job is to sell her fashions. Dozens of considerations and economies are pulling against you. Hundreds of commodities are competing with your dress for her attention, and to make your selling job tougher a dozen stores are competing with you to sell her that same $45.00 dress.

If your advertisement is successful, you will attract her, persuade her, and bring her into your store to buy the dress you describe. You will have found a way to say it better. You will have convinced her. You will have succeeded in making your basic black dress her most compelling consideration.

A successful advertisement, you see, is good writing plus a point of view that enables your copy to begin where the reader is.

ELEMENTS OF VOLUME-FASHION COPY

Significantly, the appeals in volume-fashion advertising are quite different from the specialized appeals in high-fashion advertising. The message is toward the woman who must keep the pace. A volume advertisement:

(1) helps a woman to feel she is buying and wearing the new, the smart, that she is *keeping* pace;

(2) assures her that she is well-dressed (Note: not because she is imitating, but because she has the good judgment to recognize "smart fashion");

(3) does not chide her for waiting to be assured that the fashion she is buying is the established fashion; it helps her feel she showed good sense;

(4) emphasizes what is new about the dress you are advertising, and shows her why it will be becoming to her;

(5) indicates that her standard of dressing is parallel to "best dressed" through the merchandising or designing abilities of your store—her store. (*Note:* it's always a good idea to sell the store or the label in addition to the merchandise. In the long run, if the merchandise is good, it will add to sales by making that manufacturer's line, or that store, a habit with the woman you have sold);

(6) connotes fashion in terms of her activities;

(7) answers her implied questions on wearing qualities, washability, and so forth;

(8) tells more of the details—width of seams, fabric, colors, sizes. A woman may be looking for a dress or coat in pink wool. She reads carefully. Nothing is said about color—

nor about the fabric. Remember, by supplying information about the color and fabric of the merchandise you do not necessarily detract from the atmosphere of "style."

(9) gives more stress to price. While you should certainly be aware that price gains more prominence as it drops lower and lower, watch out for basing fashion copy wholly on an economy appeal. ' 'Now—a woolen suit for $39.98" probably will not appeal. Women prefer not to identify themselves with $39.98 even if that's all they have to spend.

Although interesting style is pretty much a personal matter, there are, nevertheless, some precepts and rules that cannot be ignored. Since copywriting is a craft—a workman's job like building a bench or cobbling a shoe—you should think in very clear terms of problem solution. Every block of copy, whether it pertains to mink or walking shoes, has a message to convey. You decide what is to be said and why—and you must say it *exactly* the way it should be said.

You must do justice to the fashion in terms suitable to your reader audience, its age, its tastes, its way of life. The medium and the audience set the slant for the copy. An advertisement scheduled for *Seventeen's* Young pixies must be written to dovetail with their way of speaking and thinking. This is not the way of speaking or thinking of a woman who reads *Vogue* or *Harper's Bazaar.* The fashion writer knows to whom the eyes peering at the page belong.

You must have a facility with words, a sharp ear, attuned to the turn of a phrase, and the perception to recognize gestures, attitudes, and affectations of women. If you're good, you visualize the reader before you attempt to reach her with your copy.

Call attention to designers

Designers are the glamor types of fashion. Fashion advertising, therefore, profits from capitalizing on designers' names. The following copy section from a fashion advertisement of Cotton, Incorporated, demonstrates the technique of utilizing the power of a designer's name.

At a time like this, you'll thank Larry Levine for making it with Cotton.

Sweet-talk time: Time to keep cool under a barrage of compliments. Larry Levine makes the compliments happen. Then helps you keep your cool. He tailored this safari pantsuit in 100% cotton corduroy by Crompton.

Fig. 10-6

Fun in fashion copy.

Most writing for fashion goods is serious. An outstanding exception is the advertising for Orhbach's, a store famous for having a good time while it is selling goods.

Ohrbach's?
Ohrbach's?
What is
Ohrbach's?
Bless our soul! We thought everyone knew! But for the benefit of the lady, we'll explain. Ohrbach's, Madame, is a famous emporium. It's a store that sells high fashion from all over the world. It's a store that insists on "a business in millions, a profit in pennies"... a provident procedure that lets us charge remarkably low prices. It's a store where everything is fresh and pretty and where assortments are so vast, you'll find anything you choose to wear (except lorgnettes!) In short, Madame, this is a store you'll find so agreeable... you'll be telling others what Ohrbach's is!
34TH ST. OPP. EMPIRE STATE BLDG. · NEWARK MARKET & HALSEY · "A BUSINESS IN MILLIONS, A PROFIT IN PENNIES"

Cotton corduroy breathes. Just as you do. So you stay comfortable. Larry Levine knows that 80% of American consumers (like you) think of comfort first when they buy clothing.* Gather all the compliments you can. Cotton keeps you cool. Larry Levine Safari Pantsuit, approximately $64. Poppy red, navy, or champagne. Sizes 5 to 13. At Marshall Field, Neiman Marcus, I. Magnin, Filene's.

FASHION WRITING'S "YEAS" AND "NAYS"

Here are some "Do's and Don'ts" on interesting writing style. You will do well to remember them.

1. *Do* . . . make your caption sound smooth and unstilted.

2. *Don't* . . . rely on a clutter of lush adjectives. When you do use adjectives, make them as specific and fresh as possible. Embellishments like "pretty, marvelous, charming, wonderful, divine" don't really accomplish anything." "Slouch looks, tunnel waistline, popcorn-cardigan, ruffly necklines"—these all give you a definite picture and a definite association. These adjectives have feeling.

3. *Do* . . . whenever possible, use an active verb for description instead of a descriptive adjective. Verbs make a caption stronger, give it movement. NOT: The black skirt has circular bands around it. BUT: Black ribbon bands encircle the skirt.

4. *Don't* . . . use a tired simile. It's even more soporific than the tired adjective. Don't say "crisp as lettuce, sleek as a seal, striped like Joseph's coat." Say "bright, like a fire-engine; fresh as a four-year-old's cheeks; gala as the evening that starts with an orchid."

5. *Do* . . . keep your sentences simple, whether long or short. Be careful that your modifiers fall as close as possible to what they modify.

6. *Do* . . . avoid the phrase that's crushingly last year's. Catch-phrases of the day can be effective, but bear in mind whether you are writing for a daily newspaper or a periodical. The smart phrase that's on everyone's lips now is likely to become completely passé in the long interim between writing and publication of a periodical.

7. *Do* . . . be light and gay and humorous if you can. Don't try to be if you can't.

8. *Don't* . . . imitate someone else's style. Read other people's advertisements for the ideas they contain—but when you have an advertisement to write on the same dress, write in your own way. Be fresh. Remember that fashion is the "Fresh Roses" end of merchandising—and your copy should match it.

9. *Do* . . . digest thoroughly all information on merchandise (study the photograph or layout intensively if you can't see the merchandise yourself) before you put your pencil on paper. You can't write interestingly if you don't write knowingly.

By this point in the chapter you have come to realize that the fashion copywriter must be as subtle as a glance behind a veil, and as direct as a salesclerk in Macy's basement; as factual as a catalog sheet, and as imaginative as a mystery writer. Our fashion writer must have a strong love for fashion, and for glittering, human, persuasive words—and most of all for ideas around which she wraps the words with precision and that mysterious quality called "flair." Possessed of all these qualities she may survive, and even thrive, in the demanding, volatile field that is fashion copywriting.

11

Ask-For-The-Order Advertising: Mail Order (Part 1)

There is a vitality about mail-order copy—a directness—that makes other forms of copywriting seem weak and roundabout. Very often the mail-order writer is likely to view non-mail-order copy as wasteful because it does not ask for, and get, the order. It is easy to see why this viewpoint is held.

If you can remember but one fact about mail-order selling—if you will keep that one fact always in mind—if you will remind yourself of it before you write every advertisement—you can be a successful mail-order salesman. And what is the fact? That every mail-order message you write must do the entire sales job. The *complete* job—capture interest, activate want or desire, overcome objections, and get a signature on the dotted line! In mail-order selling you have no alternative—nothing else to fall back on. If you don't create sales, your employer's or client's sales campaign—and his cash outlay, perhaps his business—go down the drain. If that happens very often—sometimes only once—you'll follow "down the drain," too, right after the campaign, cash, and business.

YOU FIND OUT SUCCESS OR FAILURE—FAST

This direct responsibility for results is not necessarily the curse it may seem to be, since mail-order selling produces such a prompt reaction—or lack of it—that you have an almost instant measure both of the effectiveness of your idea and of the success of your message. If they've proved "pretty good," you may be able to inject into your next message just the right touch needed to make it produce excellent results. If your first message obviously has proved "not so hot," you know at least that you'd better try another version of your idea or even a new idea. You may then, through analysis of the results of the first message, be able to spot the exact flaw.

Of course, you won't ignore the possibility that a poor reaction to a piece of mail-order selling, and the accuracy of any analysis you may make of that reaction, may depend somewhat on two other factors not basically a part of the advertising idea or copy itself. These factors are the same for mail order as for any other advertising-sales effort—"product" and "prospects." If the product is poor or if the prospects are not reasonably well defined (and therefore not reached), reaction is fairly certain to be discouraging. Should reaction be poor even if product and prospects are right, another factor should be considered—whether or not you have had the advantage of pre-testing your copy-sales message. Such copy research is an important subject in itself, as you will see in the chapter on copy research.

SERVICES ARE SOLD BY MAIL-ORDER, TOO

Because of the nature of the selling method—mail-order—the product offered is usually some item of merchandise. When you order something by mail you usually receive in return a package, crate, or shipment containing a tangible item for the cash you sent. A service may, however, be sold by the mail-order method. Examples: a personal income-tax computing service, a manuscript criticism-correction service for amateur writers, and—yes—a mail-order copywriting service (on a fee basis) for small businesses which have no advertising agency or creative personnel of their own. Normally, such a small percentage of mail-order selling is of services—and so much of tangible goods—that throughout this discussion the terms "product," "item," "merchandise," and the like will be used to designate anything sold by mail order.

YOU WRITE TO SUIT THE MEDIUM

As in all advertising, in addition to knowing everything possible about product and prospects, you need the answer to one other major question before beginning to write your mail-order sales message: "How—through what medium—am I going to tell my prospects about my product?" The medium used affects not only the physical requirements of your message—its length, its layout, its illustration, its space for and location of headline, and so forth—but also the handling of your message. This handling may include the approach your copy takes, the use of attention-getting words and copy devices, the relative emphasis of appeals, and the inclusion (or exclusion) of other copy elements. You can see that you *must* ask, "What medium am I writing for?"

MAIL-ORDER KING—THE CATALOG

The "king" of mail-order media—at least the classic one, the "bible" of mail-order selling—is the mail-order catalog. Catalogs vary greatly, one from the other. Most famous are those merchandising tomes typified by the semi-annual "big book" editions of Montgomery Ward & Company and Sears, Roebuck & Company, their lesser "flyers," and other seasonal or special sales books. There are also the slimmer major volumes of the smaller general merchandise firms that sell by mail, together with *their* supplementary catalogs.

Next come the issues of still lesser houses which may limit themselves primarily to definite but still relatively broad fields. The increasingly famed fall and spring catalogs of L. L. Bean, of Freeport, Maine, exemplify this type. Another is Norm Thompson, Portland, Oregon.

Finally come the specialty catalogs limited to one line or type of merchandise, such as seeds. Burpee's and Vaughan's are examples. Sometimes, too, commercial items seldom bought by the layman are offered for sale by mail in catalogs directed to particular trades or groups of potential customers. Frequently such offerings are supplemented by at least occasional personal contact of the prospect by a representative of the firm.

MAGAZINES AND NEWSPAPERS ARE IMPORTANT, TOO

Another important medium of mail-order selling is that of publications—magazines and newspapers—in which the advertiser buys space just as for any other advertisement. The difference, however, is that the mail-order advertiser hopes to receive *immediate* orders as a *direct* result of each individual advertisement, unlike many publication advertisers who build up desire for products over a period of time.

In the magazine field, typical publications in which appropriate items are successfully offered for sale by mail include many that on first thought might not be considered good mail-order media at all—high- and medium-class consumer specialty magazines in the home furnishings and fashion fields. *House and Garden, Better Homes and Gardens, Vogue,* and *Glamour* customarily devote special "shopping" sections to mail-order advertisements. The advertising columns of general magazines occasionally carry successful mail-order offerings, usually in small-space advertisements because of the high rates of wide-circulation publications.

Somewhat more commonly associated, perhaps, with the mail-order selling of specialty types of merchandise, are those magazines appealing to certain classifiable economic, occupational, avocational, and/or social segments of the population. Typical examples of these might be: (1) the pulp groups of movie, romance, adventure, and detective magazines appealing mostly to people of modest education and income; (2) the farming and livestock publications such as *Farm Journal;* (3) comics, and the children's and youth magazines; (4) sports and body-building publications and out-of-doors periodicals; (5) hobby publications such as home mechanics, amateur photography, arts, and antiques; (6) the lower-income and/or small-town and rural women's magazines like *Grit;* (7) publications appealing to specific racial groups such as *Ebony;* and (8) magazines whose paid advertising columns are composed largely of mail-order offers—and whose readers over the years have come to regard them as "marketing places."

This last example, unlike many of the more specialized media that produce best for specific offers, may be expected to produce well on almost any type of offering.

Newspapers offer many opportunities for successful mail-order advertising, especially in comic sections and Sunday magazine pages. The former have been important in reaching the youth market with box-top premium offers. An example of a strong mail-order Sunday magazine is the one that appears in the *New York Times.* A huge variety of mail-order offers appear in the pages of this publication.

MAIL-ORDER SELLING THROUGH DIRECT MAIL

A third general category in the field of mail-order media is that of mailing pieces usually making from one to several offers (a larger number, of course, would become a small catalog). Here is where the two branches of "remote control" advertising meet—in fact, are synonymous. This is direct-mail mail-order selling. By joining the two "mails" you might merely call it "direct-mail-order." Such pieces may take many forms, some of the more common ones being leaflets, circulars, return post cards (nowadays usually with postage payment guaranteed by the vendor), letters, broadsides, booklets, brochures, envelope "stuffers," and the like, or combinations of any two or more of these forms.

These may be sent in reply to a paid (or unpaid) response to some other advertising. Often they go out as individual mailings. At other times they are grouped with similar pieces making other offers, and are sent out to mailing lists either maintained by the merchandiser himself, or rented or bought from a mailing-list service or another advertiser. Often, too, they are used as enclosures, perhaps with a department store's monthly statements to its charge account customers, or possibly enclosed with other purchases being sent from the store, or from a mail-order house such as Alden's, Sears, Spiegel's, or Ward's.

USING THE AIR WAVES FOR MAIL-ORDER

Many successes have been recorded in radio and television mail-order selling. For example, a small farm magazine through radio built up its paid circulation—in just a few months' time—by *several hundred thousand* subscribers. Each subscription was mailed in with a $1 bill. The subscriber lived in thirteen of the poorest states in the country. Radio coverage was only partial in several of the states and was supplied by a *single radio station!*

Individual stations are the mainstay of radio broadcast mail-order selling. Except for occasional premium or similar offers by national advertisers on network programs, most mail-order selling is done over local stations serving relatively limited areas, or, at the widest, perhaps over small sectional networks.

Television has indicated its status as a major

mail-order medium. The manufacturer of a household cleanser, for instance, offered the New York television audience watching its program a costume pin for 25¢ plus a label from its product. More than four per cent of the known television homes reached by that telecast sent for the pin, and the advertiser reported that this represented a greater percentage of returns than that company (long experienced in premium offers) had ever received from a one-time offer in any other medium.

Certainly, in those areas reached by television, and with an offer or product that appeals to the particular audience of televiewers reached by a telecast, television is a potent mail-order medium. It is the only one through which you can: (1) picture your product to your prospects as well as, or better than, in publication display advertising; (2) give them your effectively spoken selling talk (commercial) just as in radio; (3) gain the advantage of action, which you had previously only in a motion picture or a big-city spectacular; and (4) also demonstrate your product in your prospects' homes—and all four of these *simultaneously.*

AS MEDIA DIFFER— WRITING AND PROSPECTS DIFFER

The foregoing brief and admittedly incomplete résumé of major mail-order media is not included as a means of making you an expert on media selection as well as a copywriter. All you actually have to know as a mail-order copywriter is that a desirable mail-order medium offers these two assurances: low-cost circulation and proved results. The subject of major mail-order sales media has been covered briefly here primarily to emphasize how many different forms there are for which you will have to write copy, and at least to imply that you will have to adapt your thinking, planning, and writing to the particular medium for which you are writing. If a pair of decorative wall plaques were to be advertised in magazines such as *House and Garden* and *Grit,* your copy would differ not only because your prospects were of a different economic and social status, but also because your advertising, to be effective in the medium in which it appears, must conform to the make-up of that type of medium. An advertisement planned, designed and written for *Grit* will frequently look out of place if used in *House and Garden,* and vice versa. With few exceptions, an advertisement that is out of its element will not produce successful results.

Assume, similarly, that the same product was being sold by radio or television mail order to different groups of prospects in the same general area. Not only would your programs differ but possibly your time of broadcast and the stations you use. Your copy, likewise, would probably be geared to each group despite the fact that the basic appeal to each group might be almost the same.

Assume for the moment that you are writing commercials for a large phonograph-record retailer, located in a medium-sized midwestern city. He handles a complete line of the records and volumes of all the major recording companies. He does a large mail-order business, but sells at regular retail prices (including postage, however).

It has been decided to push three major types of records—classical music, dance, and hill-billy barn dance. This means three distinct markets must be reached, perhaps at three different times of the day or week. Depending upon the coverage and listening patterns of your local radio stations, you may use more than one of them to reach your markets.

Yet your programs will be similar in that

Inter-State Nurseries
delivers
Hamburg, Iowa 51640
Seven Giant Ruffled
Glads 25¢
Postpaid & Guaranteed
Double your money back if not completely satisfied
New & superior varieties ...if bought by name, they would cost 75¢. Colors range from pink to purple, orange, lavender, yellow, rose. This year we added Red Beauty— one of the brightest glads known. Big bulbs, 1 to 1¾ inches across. Will bloom this summer.
Free Spring Catalog
INTER-STATE NURSERIES
2733 E Street, Hamburg, Iowa 51640
☐ FREE Spring Catalog ☐ 7 Glads 25¢
NAME
ADDRESS
CITY
STATE
ZIP
Glads will be shipped at proper planting time.

Fig. 11-1

Small-size mail order advertisement.

Here is effective use of small space. Many mail order advertisers have made a good living through the use of small space advertisements in big-circulation magazines. This one appeared in Parade Magazine, the Sunday supplement.

all of them will feature recordings (naturally!). So, too, will your commercials be similar, and yet they will vary widely. Your basic appeal to all three markets is almost certain to hinge on one idea—the convenience of getting any recordings you want without the bother of going to a store. Yet, just as you will vary your programs—although all will be music—to appeal to lovers of symphony, to youthful addicts of popular tunes, and to country-dance devotees, so must you vary the appeal in your commercials to suit the varying situations of your audiences:

(1) *To your rural audience:* "Shop from your fireside—no need for a special trip to town; and avoid disappointment—our stocks are always complete."

(2) *To the teen-agers:* "Just drop us a note (or fill in an order blank—if they've been distributed) between classes or in the evening—don't miss that important class meeting, play rehearsal, or basketball game just to come downtown (or into town) to buy a record."

(3) *To the serious-music appreciator:* "A new concert's just as near as your desk (or your phone—if charge accounts are permitted or C.O.D. deliveries encouraged)—avoid a long street-car or bus ride, traffic jams, and parking worries downtown."

To everyone, of course, goes the general story of "same-day" service, of quality products at standard prices *including* packing and mailing costs, of satisfaction or your money back—and perhaps a long-life needle as a premium with each order of so many records, or so many dollars. Most likely you will write even such "standard" parts of the commercials in a different style and in different words for each audience. If you do, then you've adapted your copy to your media, and, other factors being favorable, you should have a set of successful mail-order commercials.

MAIL-ORDER WRITING

Assume, now, that your product is one that *can* be sold to your prospects, and that the medium selected is an effective one for reaching the prospects, and at low cost. The next question is how to induce those prospects to make purchases. What are you going to do that will make the potential customer order? This is the point at which you, the copywriter, really go to work; from here on, the full responsibility for the success of the mail-order offering is yours. The results depend upon how effectively you present the merchandise.

Like running a store by mail

Since *you* are the *salesman,* compare your job with the selling process of the owner of a small specialty shop—of which your mail-order offering is the counterpart. The shop owner first of all creates an inviting window display to attract the casual shopper or passer-by into the store. Assume that he does go in. The shop owner gives him a close-up view of the merchandise—opens it up or takes it apart, giving his sales talk point by point. He answers his customer's questions and meets his objections. Finally, as his customer is about convinced to buy, he presents his final sales point—the clincher—an irresistible reason for not postponing the purchase. Then, ideally, the customer says, "I'll take it," and lays his cash on the counter.

That's the *ideal* sale. It's exactly what you hope to do with your mail-order offering. Your show window that stops your prospect is your display (in type and illustration), or the opening words of your commercial. Your copy (and detailed views, if any) comprise your close-up of the product, and your sales talk. Next, because you're not face-to-face with the prospect, you have to anticipate what his questions and objections are most likely to be, and work the answers into your sales talk (keeping them in a positive vein, of course) as you write. Then you weave in your clincher—why it's important or necessary to order *now*—frequently a matter of limited supply, a special price for a short time, or perhaps a premium for promptness. So far you've pretty well paralleled the retail sales procedure.

At this point your retail customer would say, "Wrap it up" and dig into his wallet. You'd take his money and hand him the change and his parcel. It's not that simple in mail-order selling, since the customer—the prospect—still has one more step to take on his own. He has to make out his order (perhaps getting out paper, envelope, and a stamp), probably write a check (or quite possibly going to a bank or post office to buy a money order), and then mail the order to your firm. Not only do you have to make these extra steps simple and easy as possible, but you must also make your whole offer seem so very attractive that the customer doesn't mind the extra work.

The extra attraction you must weave into your mail-order copy is difficult to define but might be explained by saying that you write in a somewhat "higher key" so that your copy reads or is heard at a higher pitch. Perhaps some of this is the result of your urge to immediate action. This feeling, nevertheless, is often an integral part of the entire advertisement. Perhaps a careful look at each element of the mail-order sale will show what's required to give the entire advertisement its high pitch. Begin with the headline.

Your display windows—headlines

Although you have already read a discussion of headlines, the mail-order headline presents enough individual problems to make it worth some extra attention. Whatever appears in display-size type in your advertisement can be considered headline material. It's the "show window"—the attention-getter—of your "shop." It may be more than merely the first display line; it may consist of several such lines placed in various parts of the advertisement. Most frequently, it includes a large display price—sometimes the most prominent display element of all. Considered alone, this physical handling (layout) of the headline material imparts a large measure of its high pitch—its aura of urgency. Mail-order headlines are frequently written in a more exciting style than for usual consumer advertising. They may be exhortative, like:

"Don't Give in to Gray Hair"
"Save on Farm Income Taxes Before April 15th"
"Look Taller Instantly"
"Make Beaded SEQUIN Lapel Pins—Easy at Home"
"Now! Be Stunning in a Rainstorm"
"Remove Any Stump"
"Treasure Your Baby's Tooth"

Each one is a command to action as well as an appeal to some need or desire.

Others, by brevity alone—a sort of terse *index* quality—impart a feeling of urgency:

"Nylon Parachutes" (not for aviation use)
"Delphinium"
"New Miracle Wall Cleaner"
"Feet Hurt?"
"Gardenia Plants"
"LAW"
"Orchard Fresh Holly" (for Christmas)
"Wrist Watch—Military Style"

Some of these index headings include a selling word or two; others none, except possibly by inference. Display lines in other advertisements rely for their excitement primarily on exclamatory sentences or phrases:

"At Last You Can Throw Away Your Worn-Out Mop for a New All-Purpose DeFold Cleaner"
"Two Bushels of Ripe Tomatoes from One Vine"
"3 Crochet Beauties Easy To Make"
"Lifetime Knife Cuts Anything"
"The Oriental Symbol of Power"
"At Home, Your Own Manufacturing Business"
"For Lusty He-Men"
"Stops Moth Damage for 5 Years or Pays the Damage"

The attention-getter—price

Price is frequently a compelling element of attention-getting display type. Most of the headlines quoted so far have not relied on price display to compel attention. Most of those cited, however, could have done that, too. Probably more mail-order selling is dependent upon price appeal for compelling interest than on any other one factor. A few examples in each of the headline categories cited above will show you how price is an important if not the dominant display factor in much mail-order selling. Price may be a part of the exhortative display:

"Print Your Own Post Cards—Complete Outfit Only $7.50"
"Embroider Add-a-Squares to Make a Priceless Linen Tablecloth—Inexpensive Starting Kit Only $1.00 Postpaid"
"Dutch Bulbs—Plant this Fall!—Dollar Specials" (followed by nine offerings each with "$1" prominently displayed)
"Men! Appear Slim 'n' Trim in Only 5 Seconds with this Amazing Abdominal Supporter Belt! Only $4.98"

The *index* heading is often combined with, or even dominated by, price:

"12 Hardy Phlox $2 Postpaid"
"Hemsticher—Button Holer—Both for $1.00"
"New 'Shooter's Bible' $2.50 Postpaid"
"65 Gorgeous Tulips Only $2 Postpaid"
"Carpenters and Builders Guides—4 Vols. $6.—($1 per mo.)"
(the "$1" alone appears in type almost as high as the headline)

Price often complements the *exclamatory* display treatment and sometimes provides its climax:

"New Easy Way Makes Button Holes, Hemstitches, with Your Own Sewing Machine—Special Offer, Reg. $2.00 Value, Both for Only $1"
(the two attachments offered are listed in small type under "Special Offer.")

Compare this entire display treatment with the *index*-plus-price display for a similar offer:

"At Last! Shirts that Kiddies Can Truly Call Their Own—Personalized Polos—$2.65 Postpaid"
"A Lot of Greenhouse for $264.00"
"For the first time—the design of fabulous earrings costing up to $3300 copied to look like the expensive originals to cost you $1, $2, & $3 pr. Can you tell the difference? (the prices in huge, black type)
"Irresistible Offer! Flowering-Size Darwin Tulips, 100 Bulbs $3.69"

Yes, price is certainly an important display element in attracting attention to a mail-order offering.

"Implying" price is effective

Attractive values or prices are sometimes merely implied in the wording of the display copy—a more subtle method but effective if adroitly handled. Two or three illustrations can make this technique clear:

"Buy Direct from Factory—Seamless Plastic Garment Bags"
"Now . . . a Home that 'Grows With Your Income'—Total Cost of Materials . . . Less than $8,000!" (selling house plans for $2.00 to $5.00)
"Easy to Make Beautiful Rugs from Old Clothing" (a patented hooking-type needle)
"New Direct Mail Plan Saves You Big Money" (for auto seat covers, with their low prices in relatively small display type)

Note the economy appeal implicit in ". . . for your money," "buy direct from factory," ". . . rugs from old clothing," and others.

Naturally, no law or custom dictates that every piece of mail-order display must fall into the exhortative, index, or exclamatory classifications. Not only may plenty of examples of advertisements that stray from these categories be seen any time, but often, too, any or all of them may be combined effective-

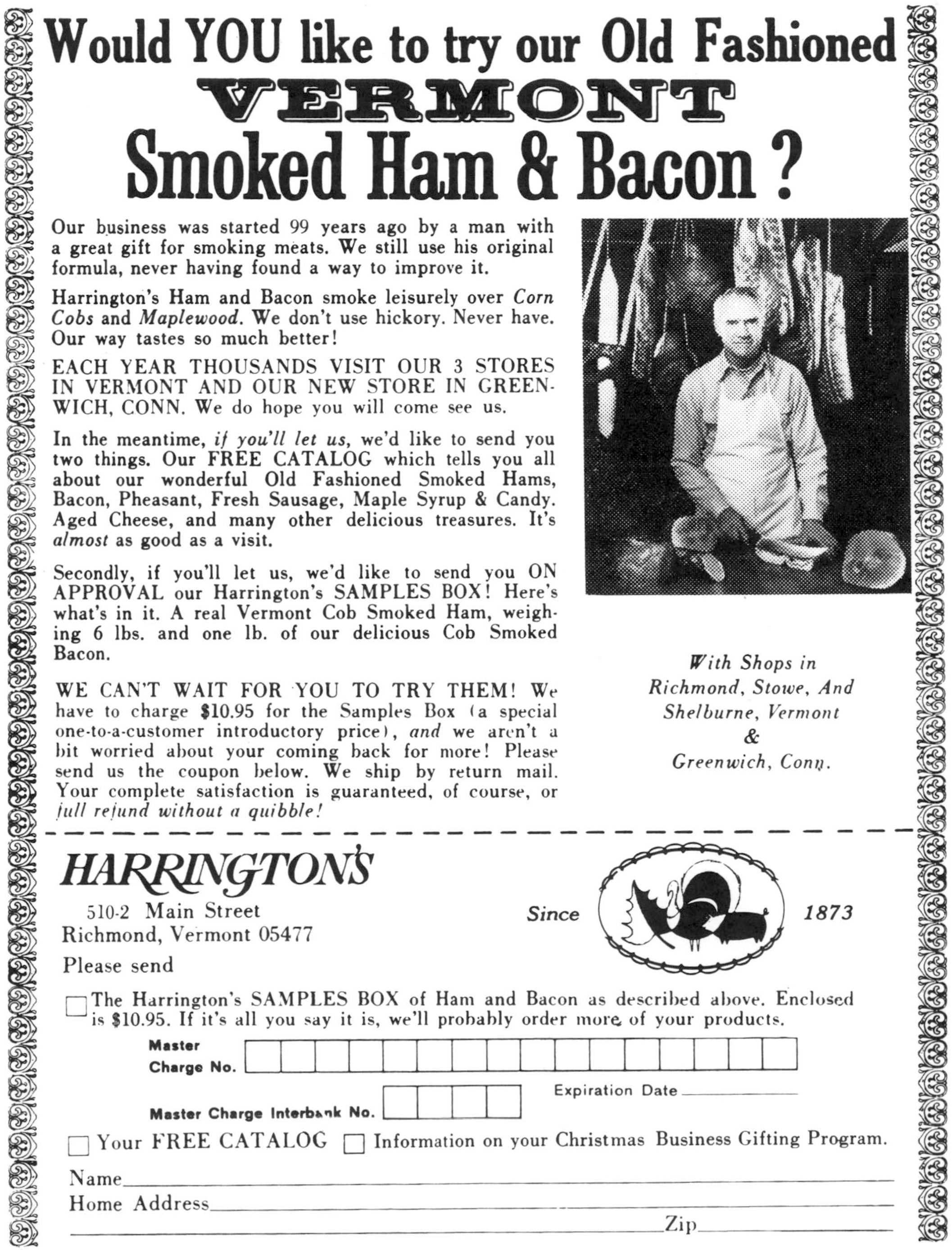
Would YOU like to try our Old Fashioned
VERMONT
Smoked Ham & Bacon ?
Our business was started 99 years ago by a man with a great gift for smoking meats. We still use his original formula, never having found a way to improve it.
Harrington's Ham and Bacon smoke leisurely over Corn Cobs and Maplewood. We don't use hickory. Never have. Our way tastes so much better!
EACH YEAR THOUSANDS VISIT OUR 3 STORES IN VERMONT AND OUR NEW STORE IN GREENWICH, CONN. We do hope you will come see us.
In the meantime, if you'll let us, we'd like to send you two things. Our FREE CATALOG which tells you all about our wonderful Old Fashioned Smoked Hams, Bacon, Pheasant, Fresh Sausage, Maple Syrup & Candy. Aged Cheese, and many other delicious treasures. It's almost as good as a visit.
Secondly, if you'll let us, we'd like to send you ON APPROVAL our Harrington's SAMPLES BOX! Here's what's in it. A real Vermont Cob Smoked Ham, weighing 6 lbs. and one lb. of our delicious Cob Smoked Bacon.
WE CAN'T WAIT FOR YOU TO TRY THEM! We have to charge $10.95 for the Samples Box (a special one-to-a-customer introductory price), and we aren't a bit worried about your coming back for more! Please send us the coupon below. We ship by return mail. Your complete satisfaction is guaranteed, of course, or full refund without a quibble!
With Shops in Richmond, Stowe, And Shelburne, Vermont & Greenwich, Conn.
HARRINGTON'S
510-2 Main Street
Richmond, Vermont 05477
Since 1873
Please send
☐ The Harrington's SAMPLES BOX of Ham and Bacon as described above. Enclosed is $10.95. If it's all you say it is, we'll probably order more of your products.
Master Charge No.
Expiration Date
Master Charge Interbank No.
☐ Your FREE CATALOG ☐ Information on your Christmas Business Gifting Program.
Name
Home Address
Zip

Fig. 11-2

Newspaper mail order advertisement.

This one, appearing in the New York Times, illustrates many principles of good mail order advertising. It offers many good reasons to buy; it has a refreshing enthusiasm; it has a strongly-worded guarantee, and it has a particularly good coupon. Notice, too, the distinctive border that makes this small-space advertisement stand out even on a big newspaper page.

ly. An abdominal belt advertisement display might, for instance, read something like this: "Men! It's Amazing! Send only $4.98 At Once for this Abdominal Belt that Makes You Appear Slim 'n' Trim in Only 5 Seconds! Don't Delay—Act Today!" Corny, sure. Probably effective, too, with certain prospects.

Pulling orders through catalogs and direct mail

Mail-order display lines quoted thus far have been extracted primarily from publication advertisements, but most of them would be "at home" in many direct-mail-order pieces or in mail-order catalogs. In many of these pieces and catalogs, it is assumed that at least a certain portion of the reader's attention already has been obtained. Certainly, in the case of a direct-mail-order piece, hundreds of other items, plus a lot of interesting editorial matter, are not screaming for his attention. As for the catalog, once he's opened the cover, you know the reader has at least some interest in your collection of offerings or he wouldn't have got that far. In such cases, unless price, or perhaps something essentially emotional, is your basic appeal, you will probably use material for your major display that either tells some pertinent fact about your product or else identifies it categorically, and perhaps includes at least a mention of one or two of its features.

A direct-mail-order mailing to a list of businessmen, for example, includes a small six-page folder with the following display (and illustrations) on the first three pages as the piece is unfolded:

(1) "How Will Washington's Next Move Affect *You?*" (Uncle Sam's hand reaches for a knight, presumably on a chess board.)

(2) "It Will Pay You To Know! *Today,* More Than Ever Before, You Need Reliable Facts and Forecasts from the Nation's Capitol." (The Capitol, set on a chess board.)

(3) "Plan *Your* Moves Wisely . . . Safely with the Kiplinger Washington Letters." (Following this is an opening half-page of body copy.)

The salutation on the letter accompanying the folder reads, "This May Be What You Have Been Waiting For . . . ," followed by an "invitation" to accept a special three-month trial subscription offer. Also included in the mailing are a current copy of the forecast, an order card ("We accept your invitation . . . etc."), and a return envelope, postage to be paid by addressee.

A similar mailing—this time a publisher's offering sent out by local bookstores to their own mailing lists—includes a nearly business-letter-size six-page folder (folded once more for mailing)—almost a broadside. Profusely illustrated by extracts from the book being sold, this mailing piece also makes use of dominating type displays which frequently ignore the folds to streak across two or more pages. Heads and subheads comprising the major display elements read like this:

(1) "The Largest, Most Complete Book of Maps Ever Published in America" . . . "Self-Revising Feature" . . . "Actual size 13½" by 20"." (Large illustration of man using the book, its title, *Hammond's New World Atlas,* Prominently displayed.

(2-3-4) "Opens to a Size Much Larger Than Your Daily Newspaper!" . . . "This Atlas Measures Fully 27 Inches Across . . . and 20 Inches Deep! Size Closed, 13½ Inches by 20 Inches." (Most of this three-page spread is devoted to illustration of a typical spread from the atlas.)

In all, this folder-broadside contains only six blocks of body copy and only two of these are large. It relies almost entirely upon display headings, subheads, and illustration to get its message across—swiftly, interestingly, completely. This piece is accompanied only by a return (postage guaranteed) postcard, on its "order" side, in prominent display: "Mail This Card to Secure Your Copy of *Hammond's New World Atlas.*"

If you have seen any mailings of some of the smaller mail-order houses, you will know that the display copy they use can be just as exhortative and exclamatory as the most extreme of mail-order offerings advertised in publications. That this treatment is effective for those prospects to whom such product offerings are most often sent is proved by the fact that the style of presentation has not changed in the years which have seen mail-order catalog advertising, for example, assume a great deal more dignity. The high-key, blatant, attention-demanding type of display, then, seems to have a place, too, in some direct-mail-order selling.

Catalog copy is quieter these days

Mail-order catalog display—especially by the larger houses—is no longer generally typified by the exhortative, exclamatory headlines (except perhaps in special sales editions) so often formerly associated with them. Where catalog display copy now exceeds purely index headings, more often than not it uses the phraseology more typical of many newspaper retail advertisements, or of consumer magazine advertisements by national advertisers. Some examples picked at random from a Sears, Roebuck catalog will illustrate:

"Fit for a little king! Luxury quality Honeysuckle Crib . . . with full, rounded panels, toe-touch drop sides, maple or birch finish"

"*Twice As Warm* . . . double-woven wool fleece overcoats"

"Sears proves that fine bags can be low priced"

"You'll feel lovelier, wearing *Luxurious Lace-Trimmed Slips*"

"Dress Forms . . . Handy Stand-ins to streamline your sewing, make fitting easier"

"Protect your gun from dirt, moisture, scratches"

"Use Sears Laboratory Approved Packaging Materials for freezing foods . . . for freshness, flavor, vitamins"

"It's 'sew' saving to do your upholstering"

"Craftsman Flexible Shafts . . . Many tools in one!"

"Top Carriers save space . . . More comfort inside your car"

"You can now convert 10 back-breaking jobs into fast, easy, profitable farm work" (portable power saw)

"For poultry profits, it's breeding that counts!"

"Blast Horns command attention" "Wash your Windshield while you drive!"

Readers of catalogs have built-in interest

When you write display lines for a mail-order catalog page or item, you still want to attract the interest of your prospects. Yet, they are more truly prospects than are the casual readers of a magazine, because they already are, or want to be, customers of your firm—as is evidenced by their having your catalog. When looking at the catalog, they are usually in a buying mood—at least for a certain type of product. When they turn to that item, then what you've said in your display headings about the product focuses their attention more sharply on it or its features. But if your display fails to interest them, they may turn to your competitor's catalog—or decide to go to a store to shop. *Although lacking competition for attention, you still have competition for the order.* What you say in your headlines (or in major subheads if the main heading is essentially the index type), and in your other display lines, may well affect the prospect's interest and so in turn influence his decision to purchase from you.

Most mail-order copy uses the direct approach

Not only what you say but *how* you say it is important, particularly in reference to the direct vs. the indirect approach. Almost all mail-order display copy is direct and to the point. Whether you say,

"Develop a Torso the Girls Will Admire!"
"Quick-Drying, One-Coat Flat Oil Paint —
One coat looks like two!"

you tell something immediately about the product or the results of its use or application. You do essentially the same thing if you are just a little less direct and write, instead,

"The Girls Never Even Used to Look Twice at Me on the Beach,"
"You Wouldn't Think One Coat of Paint Could Make Such a difference in a Room!"

You'd scarcely, however, write a headline for a mail-order muscle-building course that says, "I'd Rather Stay Home with a Book," or for one-coat wall paint, "I Never Enjoyed Entertaining the Smiths until Tonight." No, you certainly wouldn't use these as major display lines for mail-order selling. They *aren't* mail-order selling. They may represent a technique suitable for a campaign in which you hope to build up an impression over a period of time, but a mail-order sale, nine times out of ten, is an *immediate* sale—often even an impulse sale.

The first caption you write, as you rough out, experimentally, your first draft of copy, may be just as indirect as the last two examples. If so, you'll find yourself hastening almost automatically to add a second display line which tells something much more meaty about your product or the *direct* advantages of its use. Next you discover that you can either eliminate the first line entirely, or at least incorporate its basic idea merely as a minor lead-in element of the second line. It

Norm Thompson reversible float coat ...it could save your life!

You'll be more comfortable and much safer when you're boating, fishing or hunting —enjoying any sports on or around the water —when you wear a Norm Thompson Float Coat. These year-around jackets can be worn anywhere you need a good, windproof, weatherproof, insulated coat. The Norm Thompson Float Coat is really three sport jackets in one:

1. *Well-styled, good looking, reversible jacket.* **2.** *Insulated, completely wind and weatherproof coat that keeps you warm in winter . . . cool in summer.* **3.** *A "Life Jacket" that will keep you afloat if you fall into the water.*

Unique materials make an all-around action jacket

OUTER SHELL: 100% super-strong nylon. **INSULATION:** a remarkable new material called Vinyon®. Vinyon is a vinyl-resin fiber with literally millions of tiny air cells forced into it. These air cells make Vinyon a superlative floatation agent—and also insulate against cold water and wind. (Aside from keeping you afloat in an emergency, this jacket will help maintain body heat.

Hip wader test! This man, fully clothed and wearing hip wading boots, deliberately jumped out of his boat. He swam safely to shore without any assistance, thanks to his Norm Thompson Float Coat!

ALL NYLON ZIPPERS—designed to withstand the corrosion of salt as well as fresh water. **HAND WARMER SLASH POCKETS**—two on inside, two on outside (four in all). **HOODED**—for extra protection. The adjustable hood is tucked away in a zippered pocket under the collar.

Completely reversible in a choice of colors:

1. NAVY BLUE reversing to INTERNATIONAL SAFETY BLAZE ORANGE. This orange is a recognized distress signal everywhere in the world when properly displayed. Any sportsman or boatman should recognize it at once. Knitted nylon collar and cuffs are black. Zipper and draw strings are white.

2. OLIVE GREEN reversing to HUNTER RED—for wear in field and forest. Knitted nylon collar and cuffs, all nylon zipper and draw strings are olive green.

You'll be much safer in a Norm Thompson Float Coat—and you won't have to pay a helluva big price for it. Please specify NAVY/ORANGE or OLIVE/RED colors when you order. Average weight: 36 ounces. Men's even sizes: 36 to 48. Women's even sizes: 6 to 20.

No. 6870 (men) .... **$40.00 ppd.**
No. 6879 (women) .... **$40.00 ppd.**

Carolyn Nelson wears the Norm Thompson Float Coat for winter sports because it's a good looking sport jacket as well as a life-saver around the water any time of year. Safe and sane protection.

The lightweight lifesaver ... the Norm Thompson float vest

This is the life jacket people keep on!

Constructed just like the Norm Thompson Float Coat—except that it's sleeveless to give you even more action freedom. Wear it for protection on your boat. One of the hidden extras about this vest is that your guests won't put up quite as much of a fight when you ask them to wear this vest for safety. If you have a boat, you've already heard all the arguments against wearing life jackets.

A fine vest on the water—the Float Vest also makes excellent insulation when you're out in the open in the winter. Wear it under a heavy wool shirt or sport jacket for windproof, warm protection.

Adjusts for a snug fit

When you wear a life vest it is important that the fit is snug enough so the garment won't slip off in the water. The Norm Thompson Float Vest has a strap at the back to help assure the proper fit.

Colors: navy blue reversing to safety blaze orange with white all-nylon zipper. Olive green reversing to hunter red with olive all-nylon zipper. Average weight: 34 ounces. Men's even sizes: 36 to 48. Women's even sizes: 6 to 20.

No. 6860 (men) .... **$22.50 ppd.**
No. 6869 (women) .... **$22.50 ppd.**

Plenty of freedom for real action afloat in Norm Thompson's neat and trim Float Vest for men and women.

Fig. 11-3

Mail order advertisement from a catalog.

Notice the personal style of the writing that is coupled with all the information needed to make a buying decision. This was a very successful advertisement.

Parma Advertising, for Norm Thompson Outfitters

will then be likely that you've written a display line that's a real stopper—you've set up a "show window" that brings the prospect right into your "store."

Radio mail-order has its show window, too

Radio mail-order selling, too, has its "show window." At first, you may think of the program as the "window," and in many cases that is partially true. But think of the commercials that have no show of their own—the one-minute "spots," the chain-breaks, the trailers—all of them often sandwiched between two other commercials. Think, too, of the listeners who *mentally* "tune out" many commercials that do accompany a program, if indeed these could-be prospects don't literally tune out or turn down the volume on your message. Consider these factors and you'll realize that the opening words, sentence, or thought really comprise the show window—the stopper or attention-getter—of your commercial.

You'll find that many devices are used to attract the listener's attention to the commercial. Sometimes a sound effect, perhaps appropriate in some way to the product being sold, perhaps not. More common is the use of an attention-arresting word or two, "Say, folks . . . ," "Friends . . . ," "Listen, ladies . . . ," and the like. A more original and famous version is the now long-familiar, "Uh, uh, uh, u-uh—don't touch that dial! Listen to . . . ," which of course introduces an entire program. It *might* inspire a commercial copywriter who has a bit of imagination to write a stopper with greater originality than the more trite phrases so often heard. Not only should this satisfy the copywriter's aesthetic ego, but it may also help to overcome the possibly increasing ineffectiveness of phrases which, as they become more familiar to the listener, also may tend to become less attention-compelling.

How to get and hold attention of radio listeners

As in print, you want the show window of your commercial to do more than merely to arouse attention. You want it to inspire interest as well—listener-interest sufficient to *hold* that attention throughout your message. So you write into your next sentence or sentences immediately following your stopper phrase or device some idea or thought that will be of interest to the largest group of prospects among your listeners. This opening thought is the "display" of your commercial. See how these sample opening lines, all of them from successful mail-order commercials, are written to *hold* the attention of the greatest number of potential prospects for the offers which follow:

(1)

"Say, folks . . . you know that beautiful juke box at the corner store? Well, here's the cutest little thing you ever saw . . ." (juke-box bank that lights up when a coin is deposited).

(2)

"Friends, the record you just heard, and *any others* you hear on the ______ [an evening-long program with several co-sponsors], can be bought from ______'s Records-by-Mail. It's the new, easy way for you to buy the records you want . . ."

(3)

"Ladies . . . Here's how you can easily win a complete five-piece bedroom set, a portable electric Singer Sewing Machine, and 101 additional valuable prizes . . ." (quilt-patch bundle offer, a contest entry blank accompanying each bundle ordered).

(4)

"Folks, due to a very special purchase, the makers of the nationally advertised ______ combination cigarette case and lighter . . . for a limited time only . . . will send you a remarkable three-dollar-ninety-five-cent value . . . at the rock bottom bargain price of only *one*-dollar-ninety-eight!"

(5)

"Folks—wouldn't you be thrilled to win a new Ford station wagon or equivalent in cash, just by taking part in a simple, interesting game? . . ." (contest sponsored by rural magazine, each contest entry to be accompanied by $1 for magazine subscription).

(6)

"Say, folks, what musical instrument do you think is the easiest and quickest to learn to play?" (harmonica offer).

An extra "display" line may be inserted occasionally in the middle of your commercial—an additional interest pepper-upper—just in case attention to your message lags a bit after the first excitement has subsided. This is akin to a prominent subhead or second display line like those quoted from the atlas direct-mail-order piece. About a third of the way through the commercial for the cigarette case-lighter combination, for example, we find, "But that's just the *first* half of this sensational offer! Second, you will receive the world's smallest ball-point pen, complete with key chain!" Here the advertiser has reserved part of his offering for use as a midway "headline," perhaps one of the most effective means of renewing interest in any advertisement or commercial.

You'll write headlines and subheads into your mail-order selling for almost identically the same purpose that you'd decorate the show window of your specialty shop—and set up supplementary displays inside—to attract and hold your prospect's attention and interest until he hears your complete message and decides to make the purchase.

Ask-For-The-Order Advertising: Mail Order (Part 2)

DIRECT YOUR COPY TO YOUR PROSPECTS

What is you're a mail-order salesman? You don't have any single customer, nor, strictly speaking, can you assume that there's any one "typical" or "average" prospect, to whom it would be relatively simple to direct your message. Aside from the results of a possible consumer survey all you know about your collective "prospect" is that he or she *is* flesh-and-blood, and probably reacts in a more or less universal way to what generally are considered "normal" flesh-and-blood desires and impulses. Of course, your field or prospects will be limited somewhat by the nature of your product, and perhaps by your medium. A low-priced harmonica, for example, is a child's or youth's product; it probably would not appeal to women (although it might to some men!) except possibly as a purchase to be made for some younger person.

Usually, of course, your common sense and use of general facts can tell you something about the limits of your potential field of prospects—perhaps their sex, age, race, social and economic status, possibly their politics or religion, and so forth. You try to determine into roughly what major field or fields your prospects fall.

Notice the phrase "*field* of prospects." In any category you'll still have a wide divergence from any theoretical norm—as many differences as individuals. So what do you do? You direct your message to as many of your potential customers as you can *without* making your appeal at all to any one—you keep it concrete.

Tell-all copy in catalogs

First, of course, you base your appeal on whichever fundamental desire or desires or your prospects can best be satisfied by your product. Then, imagining the various ways in which the item may answer those wants for different prospects, you try to include as *many* as possible in your message so that you miss as *few* as possible of your potential customers.

Look again, for example, at the Sears catalog headline quoted for a baby crib: "Fit for a little king! Luxury quality Honeysuckle Crib . . . with full, rounded panels, toe-touch drop sides, maple or birch finish." Each of these three features is a selling point that appeals in some degree to almost any mother shopping for a crib.

Why all three in a display headline?—because, even in this limited field of crib-seeking mothers there's no one feature that's going to appeal to each prospect strongly enough to convince her that this is the crib she wants. Three features, in fact, are not enough. At least Sears' experienced mail-order copywriters don't believe they are, for in five lines of telegraphic copy—still semi-display treatment—preceding the main copy block of this offering, not only are these features repeated and expanded, but more are added:

—*So Attractive!* Rounded, full length end panels
—*So Comfortable!* 4-position spring lowers or tilts
—*So Convenient!* Both sides drop with toe-touch
—*So Safe!* Non-poisonous finish in waxed birch or maple
—*So Durable!* Sturdily built of selected hardwoods

Nor are the selling points exhausted in display and semi-display. Those already featured are developed even further in the body copy, and still more are brought in:

Your baby will sleep like cherished royalty in this luxury quality Honeysuckle Crib. Smooth rounded corners on full end panels help keep off drafts, add a smart style note to baby's room. New plastic teething rod firmly attached to top of each side. Four position metal spring raises, lowers or tilts for comfort. Toe-touch release on both sides with automatic safety catch. Casters. Overall size 54 x 30 in.; sides 26 in. high. Shipped freight or express. *Please state finish.*
1 KM 8327—Crib and Spring Shpg. wt. 77 lbs. . . . $37.95
1 KM 8480—Crib, Spring and 1 KM 8210
Innerspring Mattress. Shipping weight
98 lbs. $48.89
Order baby's Crib on Easy Terms . . see inside back cover.

Fig. 12-1

Mail order advertisement from a catalog.

Here is long copy that will be read because it is persuasive copy, because its personal approach is disarming, and because the hard-selling subheads break up the type mass and make the advertising—even though it is long—easy to read. Notice the attention-getting lead-in headline (There just ain't never been no shoe like this shoe before!). This intentional violation of grammar has a stopper effect. Notice, too, that the writer undersells in the copy where he says "Now, we're not going to tell you that Patricks are "perfect" for any one activity or another." Such understatement creates an air of credibility so important in mail order advertising.

Parma Advertising, for Norm Thompson Outfitters

(There just ain't never been no shoe like this shoe before!)

Patricks all-leather boat shoes from France–grip, look, feel and support better

(FOR MEN & WOMEN)

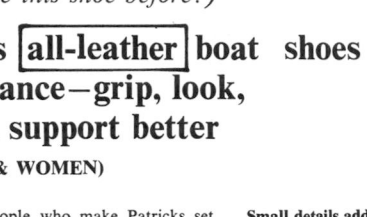

When the people who make Patricks set about designing a new kind of shoe for leisure and sports, *somebody did a lot of thinking.* Better than designed, Patricks were engineered. These questions were asked: What makes feet comfortable in motion? Where does the shoe pinch? How do you make a sole that absorbs shock and is virtually slip-proof? Can strong support be built in without adding weight?

Only after these questions, and many others were answered, could Patricks be made. They're shoes that are *fun to wear* for everyday comfort, for active sports like tennis or boating, and for a *great new look* in casual shoes.

Now, we're not going to tell you that Patricks are "perfect" for any one activity or another. We will say they are comfortable for many of the things you enjoy, such as:

• Tennis • Boating • Walking • Handball
• Shopping • Touring • Beachcombing
• Sight-seeing • Relaxing • Loafing

Foam cushioned at every point of stress!
Around the tops, under the tongue and from heel to toe (including an arch support)—Patricks are *cushioned with foam.* Layers of durable cotton flannel or real glove leather keep foam away from your feet—add their own comforting softness. Uppers are all breathing glove leather so your feet feel cool and stay dry. Toes are squared to give your toes plenty of action room.

Patricks worn with crew length Sportsman's Support Socks, pg. 53.

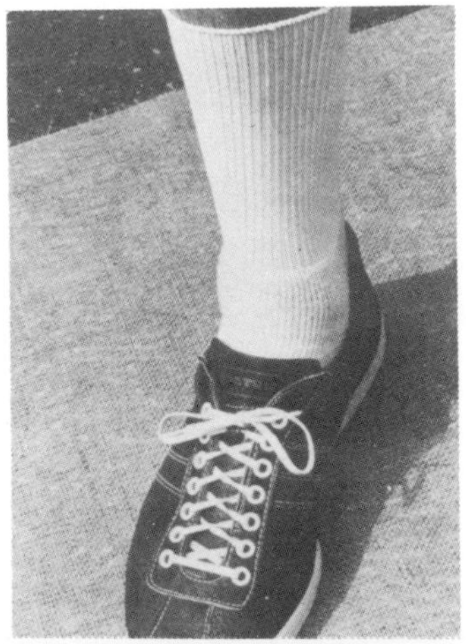

Small details add up to many a mile of comfort!
When you first look at your Patricks, you'll notice that the tops are stitched in a special way. These "decorative" stitches have a purpose: They're put in to *give your feet better support* and keep the leather from stretching out of shape. With modern threads like dacron it is not necessary to add the extra weight of leather stripes to get extra strength and support.

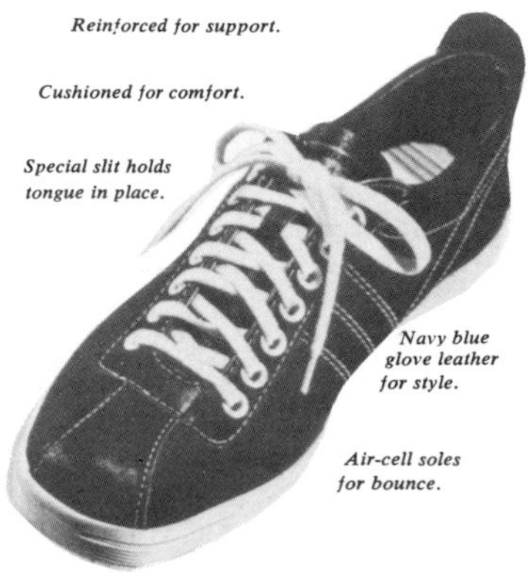
Reinforced for support.
Cushioned for comfort.
Special slit holds tongue in place.
Navy blue glove leather for style.
Air-cell soles for bounce.
Little vacuum cups give you sure grip on smooth surfaces.
Vacuum cup grippers for safety.

Tongue won't slip out of place.
Another example of excellence is the small slit in the tongue. Run laces through it before you tie them—the tongue will stay neatly in place. You'll like this feature if you've ever had the irritation of a side-slipping tongue.

You literally walk on air!
Dozens of specially designed air-cells put new spring and bounce into your step—help absorb those nasty, tiring shocks and jars. These air-cells are separated by thin, strong walls of superior rubber.

Feel like pillows—grip like glue!
Sound contradictory? It's not. Comfortable Patricks are soft and springy—*they're also extra safe!* Patricks cling to a wet deck or fast court with over 100 little suction cups on each sole. These cups create *tiny vacuums* on contact with a smooth surface—*give you extra safety from slips.*

Good looking, practical—easy care!
Fine glove leather used in Patricks is navy blue—a color that looks right with most casual clothes. *Shoes can be wiped clean with a damp cloth.* (Once after some muddy gardening, we just hosed off surface soil). Leather *resists dirt and doesn't need shining.* If you're caught in the rain or have to walk on wet grass, Patricks will also keep your feet dryer than canvas shoes.

Try them at home—at no risk!
Order your Patricks now and *test them at home.* Walk across a freshly washed, wet floor. Take on the family for a fast game of table tennis. If you are not entirely pleased with Patricks, return them to us postage prepaid (in the same good condition you received them) within 2 weeks for a full refund.

Cutaway section shows air cell construction of inner sole and special, springy foam heel cushion.

Materials: Genuine glove leather uppers. 100% cotton flannel interlinings and insoles. 100% polyester foam cushioning. Genuine rubber soles.

Average weight: 29 oz. (men), 24 oz. (women).

Color: Navy blue with white trim.

Sizes: 6-13 (men), 4½-10 (women). Please specify width.

No. 2730 (men) . . . . **$18.00 ppd.**
No. 2739 (women) . . . . **$18.00 ppd.**
Save $2.00 . . . . . 2 for $34.00 ppd.

Note how the sales story is developed, point by point. Repetition is judiciously used for emphasis, until the *complete* selling job has been done—every feature that *many* mothers (collectively, but probably almost never singly) might reasonably ask for in a deluxe crib is pointed out. Every question and every objection they might normally raise are answered—all are included to make shopping by mail as nearly like personal shopping as possible. Even the terse "Casters" is not omitted, although the accompanying illustration shows them plainly. If the copywriter had had more space, he might have added some further copy telling about their construction (perhaps ball-bearing) and how easily they allow the crib to be moved. Not even the reminder that Sears' easy terms are available was forgotten.

Use the language of the prospect

Another type of mail-order catalog offering may be quite different. As was said before, not only must you know what to say to your prospects, but *how* to say it.

Note the illustration and listing from L. L. Bean's catalog. "But," you ask, "where are the major selling points highlighted to attract and interest the reader? There are only small pictures and an index heading!" You must remember that this is a specialty catalog for hunters and out-of-door men and women. Here's one case, admittedly a rather exceptional one, where because of the limited appeal of the class of merchandise, the field of prospects is limited, too. Almost everyone reading this catalog reads nearly every listing on practically every page. Because this catalog enjoys this unique advantage, its manner of obtaining attention and maintaining interest in itself and in its offerings is not as apparent as in other publications.

Another unique advantage which obviates the necessity for any specifically stated claims of quality or value is the reputation of the firm and the integrity behind the name L. L. Bean, which has become synonymous over a period of years with a good buy at a fair price. These are things not easy to acquire, and lucky is the mail-order copywriter in such a situation. Of course, it should also be noted that this firm does not seem to be overly anxious to expand its list of prospects greatly. Therein, perhaps, lies part of the reason for the seeming lack of more aggressive selling usually considered normal for any merchandising house.

Despite its seemingly naive, artless style, the copy sells hard. There is a simple directness that is persuasive and disarming.

Notice, too, the clear-cut, simple explanations that tell all. There is conviction in these words—much more than most "hard-hitting" copy could achieve in pages of superlatives. This is intelligent, mail-order copy. Much of it has been written by men who have tried in the fields and woods most of the products. For these specialized products, offered through this unique medium, to this definite group of prospects this copy is difficult to match.

Advertisements in Publications

Mail-order selling in other media has the same job to do and does it usually through the same copy formula of appealing to as many of the potential prospects as can be reached in any one advertisement without scattering the message so widely that it hits no one. In general publication mail-order selling, for example the copywriter has a considerably more difficult problem than does Bean's in this regard. Unless the publication itself is limited in circulation pretty much to one class of people, or unless some other element in the advertisement (usually the illustration or the name of the product) makes it fairly apparent to what group of readers the advertisement is designed to appeal, your display will have to do the job of attracting the attention and arousing the interest of the particular field of prospects to whom you are writing.

The hemstitcher-button holer index headline cited earlier in this chapter, just by the prominence of these words in display type, almost automatically attracts women who sew, and perhaps some who wish they could, away from what probably are less specifically or more obscurely worded headlines. Then follows immediate this fact-packed selling copy:

HEMSTITCHER—Hemstitch on any sewing machine with this handy attachment. Does two piece, criss-cross, inlaid, circular and hemstitching for pleats; also tucking, smocking and picoting. Makes rugs, comforters, slippers, etc. out of any material. Easy directions included.

BUTTON HOLER—Makes button holes on your sewing machine instead of by hand. Also darns stockings, sews buttons, zippers; and can be used for quilting. Sews in any direction—front, back or sideways.

SEND NO MONEY—Merely send your name, address and pay postman $2.00 plus postage on arrival. Or, send $2.00 with order, and we mail postage paid. You risk nothing. Satisfaction guaranteed or your money back.
[Company name, department, and address.]

Once more—and this time in a 2-inch by 1-column advertisement *including* two illustra-

Fig. 12-2

Order form for catalog.

This is a clear, easy-to-understand, and complete order form. In addition, the advertiser does an extra selling job with the copy on the side.

Parma Advertising, for Norm Thompson Outfitters

ISN'T THERE SOMEONE YOU WANT TO PLEASE AND SURPRISE?

A wonderful, warm way to let someone know you're thinking of them, ***right this minute,*** is a Norm Thompson Gift Certificate. You don't need to wait for a special occasion – though our gift certificates are always welcome on birthdays, anniversaries and special holidays. They make wonderful wedding gifts, too – a boon to those young couples who get "two of everything for the house" – when they really need clothes.

You can make it for any amount from $10.00 right on up. If you want the gift certificate delivered on a special date – let us know, and we'll do our best to insure its timely arrival.

With each gift certificate we send a free Norm Thompson catalog – so you also give the fun of easy-chair shopping and the pleasure of choosing something special.

Now – or any time, let us know what you'd like to send. Please include the name, full address and zip code of the recipient if you want us to mail the certificate and catalog directly to them.

P.S. Handy tip for businessmen: You can order several gift certificates at one time as business gifts. These certificates will be mailed, with catalogs, to your own address.

Norm Thompson ORDER FORM

1805 N.W. Thurman St., Portland, Oregon 97209

Mr.
Mrs.__________
Miss 1st & 2nd initials Last name

Address__________

City__________ State__________ Zip__________

Telephone (Area Code)__________ PLEASE PRINT OR TYPE CLEARLY

Apt., Suite, or Room number if applicable__________

☐ My personal check or money order is enclosed (U.S. Funds only)

☐ Send C.O.D. I agree to pay purchase price plus postage and C.O.D. charges.

Charge total purchase to my. . . ☐ BankAmericard ☐ Master Charge

Card Number __________ *4-digit Interbank number if using MasterCharge*

Your Signature __________ *"Good thru" date*

Qty	Catalog No.	Name of item	SIZE	COLOR	Price

For air delivery . . . add extra charge to your order (see table at right)

Purchase	Add
$ 1 to $25	$1.50
$26 to $50	$2.00
$51 to $75	$2.50
over $75	$3.00

AIR DELIVERY CHARGE

Handling charge of $1.00 for total order *under* $10.00

TOTAL

☐ Send to: (if other than yourself)
Name__________
Address__________
City__________
State__________ Zip__________

☐ I have moved since my last order
My former address was:
Address__________
City__________
State__________ Zip__________

THANK YOU FOR YOUR ORDER

Please use a separate sheet of paper for inquiries not relating to this order.

Tear along perforation, fold and mail in envelope provided.

tions and a display price—is found all the pertinent detail necessary to satisfy any sewer who has $2 to invest in a "satisfaction guaranteed or your money back" purchase. It does, within its physical limits, the complete selling job. No wonder many mail-order advertisements have no white space! In fact, the sales job can be done in even less space, as is proved by this 1-inch by 1-column "Delphinium" advertisement, another of the index headline group (this time without illustration, which is hardly needed to sell non-special variety flowers to experienced gardeners):

DELPHINIUM—Giant flowering magnificent double-type 2-year plants that have bloomed. Gorgeous colorings range from deepest blues, lavenders with pink tints to the wonderful bi-colorings that rival orchids. You will have 3- to 5-foot flowering spikes with flowers 2 to 3 inches across. 6 for $1.50; 12 for $2.50. Cash orders prepaid or sent C.O.D. plus charges. Return at once for refund if not satisfied. GIVEN with $2.50 orders "Million Dollar" Mystery Bloom Peony, $1 value.
[Company name, department, address]. *Clip this.*

A beginning copywriter sometimes feels insulted when he's asked to do a one-inch advertisement. He usually gets over his feeling of injury when he finds out the difficulty of making a *good* small advertisement. It's an art to say a lot in a small space. The best way to get the "wind" out of your copywriting is to do small advertisements.

SPECIAL SERVICES

TO SPEED DELIVERY OF YOUR ORDER

1. ORDER BY PHONE... It's easy, and it may cost less than you think. Dial it yourself, and you can call from anyplace in the United States (except Alaska and Hawaii) from 5 pm to 8 am (your time) for less than $1.00 for the first 3 minutes. (For 1 minute, the charge is only 35¢ from New York to Portland, Oregon.) You can call our ordering number (area code 503) 222-9104, any time day or night, including Sundays and holidays.

2. CHARGE IT... This gives you a number of conveniences. You don't have to fill out a credit application, there are no finance charges, and you deal directly with your bank. We accept both BankAmericard and Master Charge credit cards. This service is available for mail, telephone or telegraph orders.

3. AIR DELIVERY... When you order by phone and use a BankAmericard or Master Charge credit card, you want delivery as fast as possible. We do make a small charge for air delivery (usually much less than the actual amount of air postage). Our rates are on our order form. Norm Thompson air mail service normally takes less than 1 week.

Your Norm Thompson No-Risk, 2-Week Trial Guarantee

When we say pleasing you is important to us, we mean it. Every item in our catalog is guaranteed. If you're not completely satisfied, you have full return privileges. When your package arrives, inspect it carefully. If, by some chance, there is a defect or if you are disappointed in any way, return the item postage prepaid within 2 weeks in the same condition in which it was received.

In addition, we guarantee our advertising claims.

If your purchase doesn't live up to our claims write to us for an adjustment or refund. No ifs or buts. All merchandise must be satisfactory in every respect.

Dear Customer HELP!

We want you to express your individuality but our computer objects! Each time you order, your name is placed in our computer bank so that you'll receive our new catalogs regularly and automatically.

However, if you use initials one time and your first name the next time you order – our idiotic computer thinks you're two different people. Duplicate catalogs jam up your mailbox. So we hope you'll understand these two requests:

1. Please use the order form style of address each time you order. Circle Mr., Mrs., or Miss – add your first initial, second initial, then print out your last name in full.

2. Please check the name and address on the back of the catalog you now have. If it is different in any way from the one you've written on your order form, kindly clip it off and enclose it with your order. We'll give the computer the word.

We don't like conformity a bit more than you do, but we hope you won't mind this time. *Thanks a lot.*

SEND A FREE NORM THOMPSON CATALOG TO A FRIEND OR ASSOCIATE...

You probably know several people who would like to receive it. As a Norm Thompson customer, you know about the ease and convenience of ordering from us by mail – and you're aware of the lower prices we can offer through our direct import program. If we can be of service to your friends, please write their names, address and zip codes on this form, and enclose with your order. We'll do the rest!

(1st & 2nd initials) (last name)
Address
City
State Zip

(1st & 2nd initials) (last name)
Address
City
State Zip

(1st & 2nd initials) (last name)
Address
City
State Zip

(1st & 2nd initials) (last name)
Address
City
State Zip

Fig. 12-3

Back of the order form in Fig. 11-5.

A good mail order advertiser, as this page illustrates, never passes up a chance to sell even when giving ordering, directions, or guarantee information. Observe the maintenance of the friendly, very personal writing style that marks the product-selling copy.

SELLING COPY CONTAINS DETAILS

Department stores, too, know the necessity for giving all the information needed for the prospect to make a satisfactory purchase by mail (or phone). Here are two examples from a group of bill enclosures.

Outstanding Value . . .

Wonderful Wool Fieldbuilt Sweaters for men $12 each

Two-ply French zephyr worsted . . . that's tops in wool! These handsome sweaters are firmly knit, and sized generously. Knit tapes at neck and shoulders reinforce the seams they allow to stretch. Lightweight, warm, in colors for fall: tan, maize, blue, gray or green. Small (38), medium (42) and large (46).

And–

Blue, pink or white wool for your little lamb!
baby blankets
$9.95 each

Keep baby warm in his transfers from bath to bed with this soft blanket. It's made in a lovely weave that is exclusive with our baby-pampering department! It has a deep fringe that actually will not tangle, thanks to an entirely new finish. Big enough for a crib . . . 40 by 48 inches.

Notice how many more factual details are included in these pieces of selling copy than would normally appear in a department store's newspaper advertisement for the same merchandise. Yet the facts are not just listed. Their importance is emphasized and their meaning expanded by an occasional, well-chosen word or phrase that doesn't merely *tell* the reader something—it *sells* him on the merits of the item. The sweater is not "all wool," it's "worsted"—*"Two-ply French zephyr* worsted" at that.

Yet the copy doesn't leave it to your knowledge or imagination to make even this categorical description of the material suffice. It doesn't dare, because the store knows that among its many customers are some who aren't acquainted with this type of wool—or who may not get the full implication of its quality by merely reading even this impressive description. It says in so many words that two-ply French zephyr worsted is "tops in wool!"

What's more, it recognizes that two common faults of sweaters often, paradoxically, are unwanted snugness and a tendency to stretch out of shape, especially around the neck and across the shoulders. Thus, besides the size listings at the end of the copy, it tells you that these sweaters are "sized generously," yet "firmly knit" and "knit tapes at neck and shoulders reinforce the seams they allow to stretch." Now these are some good, positive, product selling points specifically included to answer possible questions and objections by the store's prospects.

So, too, with the baby blanket. The copywriter knows that some of the more experienced shoppers among the prospects may shy away (and justifiably!) from a *fringed* baby blanket—the necessarily frequent launderings may do things to fringe that make it unattractive, but this blanket *has* fringe—deep fringe—as the illustrations show. Does the copy ignore that possible objection? It does not. It turns the objection into an advantage, ". . . deep fringe that actually will not tangle, thanks to an entirely new finish." The fringe becomes another *selling* point.

Tell-all copy works on radio, too

Of course, your radio mail-order commercials, too, must give much important detail about the product, yet probably not one out of ten prospects in a retail shop, where they *can* see the item, would have to have each of the product's features pointed out individually before deciding to make the purchase. Suppose, for example, that you were writing the mail-order commercial to follow the interest-arousing lead-in quoted earlier for the harmonica offer. How best can you (in one minute!) tell your prospects the features most likely to induce them to purchase? What would they want to know about the product? Now, forget you're a copywriter for a minute; instead, you're all the listeners tuned into the station carrying the harmonica offer. You're attracted and interested by the announcer's opening lines:

Say, folks, what musical instrument do you think is the easiest and quickest to learn to play? Well, I guess you'll agree when I tell you that, generally speaking, the harmonica is acknowledged as the easiest musical instrument there is for a beginner to learn to play quickly. In a wonderful offer to [station name] listeners you can get a beautiful harmonica . . .

Ah, there it is! You (the listener) can get a harmonica! "But," you say, "I can't play the harmonica." And that's exactly the point where you (the copywriter) begin to set down the selling points in 1-2-3 order that you're going to use in turning all those prospects into purchasers. Once more you set down the points that you, as a listener want to know about this harmonica:

1. Is it easy to learn to play it?
2. If so, how do I learn? How long will it take?
3. What will I play on it?
4. *How much does it cost?*
5. If it's an inexpensive harmonica, it'll probably fall to pieces in no time, won't it?
6. What is it made of?
7. Aren't harmonicas unsanitary? (Mothers—hundreds of them—will ask this one.)
8. What does it sound like—is it squeaky, tinny, whiney?
9. Can I play high and low notes on it (what's its range)?

10. How much did you say it costs?

11. Suppose I can't learn, or don't like it? How about getting my money back?

12. How long did you say it will take me to learn to play it?

13. How do I get it?

14. How long will I have to wait for it to come?

15. Where do I send for it?

16. How much money, once more, did you say I had to send?

17. Come again—where do I send for it?

Answer all those questions in one minute—if you can. Yes it can be done. And it has been—almost, anyway. Here's the fast-paced commercial as written and used on the air:

> Say, folks, what musical instrument do you think is the easiest and the quickest to learn to play? Well, I guess you'll agree when I tell you that, generally speaking, the harmonica is acknowledged as the easiest musical instrument there is for a beginner to learn to play quickly. In a wonderful offer to [station name] listeners, you can get a beautiful harmonica . . . a book of EASY instructions that guarantees to teach you to play the harmonica . . . 200 songs with the words and music . . . and the entire cost for *everything* is only $2.49! Now let me repeat that slowly. You get a harmonica . . . a book of instructions . . . and the words and music for over 200 songs, all for only $2.49! This mouth organ is unbreakable . . . it's washable . . . it's lightweight, and it has one of the mellowest tones you've ever heard. What's more, it's 100 percent guaranteed. It's also guaranteed that the EASY instructions will have you playing it within five short days . . . or you get your money back. Now here's all you have to do . . . Send no money . . . simply send your name and address to Harmonicas, care of [station and address]. In a few days, you'll receive your harmonica, your simple-as-A-B-C instructions and the 200 songs, and you pay your postman $2.49, plus C.O.D. postage. So act today. Just write to Harmonicas, that's H-A-R-M-O-N-I-C-A-S, Harmonicas, care of [station and address].

The writer of this commercial has answered all but two of those questions, numbers 6 and 9: "What is it made of?" and "What's its range?" Probably those are points the seller didn't care to mention. Yet they might have been made into positive selling points, though, by a resourceful copywriter, had he been given the chance, for, from other parts of the description, it seems likely that the harmonica is made of plastic. He might, therefore, have said, "unbreakable, washable, plastic construction."

If it's a rather small instrument, which it most likely is, he could have said, with some assumption of pride, "A range wide enough for any popular song—two full octaves—twenty-five full and half-notes . . ." (or whatever claim and figures the facts would support). Even with these two omissions, however, we must assume that this was a good selling commercial; at least it is claimed to have been successful.

Perhaps you've noticed one other thing the seller of the harmonica might have done not only to increase attention to, and interest in, his commercial, but to add one more selling appeal as well. This item has the unique (for radio) property of being a natural to demonstrate, if only to have someone (even the announcer) run up and down the scale on it. Here would be audible proof of its mellow tone and its range. For only a little more cash outlay for talent, someone might have been hired to play a bar or two or melody or a few chords to demonstrate the playing ease claimed for the instrument. In fairness to the intelligence and selling ingenuity of the advertiser—or his copywriter—it must be admitted that he may well have considered some such "illustration" of his product in use, but decided against it perhaps because of some inherent limitations in the product itself.

"Show-all"—television's mail-order technique

Television, of course, can go beyond radio in its ability to show merchandise as well as talk about it—and even more important many times—to *demonstrate* it. Your selling principles for copywriting are not changed by television, merely enhanced. Possibilities of television go beyond even illustrations in print, for the product can be shown in actual use, including all views of it and demonstrations of

Fig. 12-4

Catalog copy of a famous mail order company specializing in outdoor equipment.

Notice the complete selling achieved through the offering of full details.

Back Packer Tents

Walls of Urethane coated, 1.1 oz. **per square yard** Ripstop nylon. Floor of 1.7 oz. coated nylon. Construction is weather resistant. An extra top fly **is required** for prolonged rainfall. Four-way ventilation minimizes condensation.

Rear net window with zipper-closed flap inside, net windows on sides with outside awnings, and three-way zipper nylon net door and outside storm door. Lightweight 3-piece aluminum poles and stakes, three guyline pullouts on each side to enlarge interior and one on each end. Packed complete in nylon bag.

Designed for lightness in weight and ample space for two or four men plus duffle. High Visibility Orange color.

Two-Man Back Packer: 5′ x 8′ x 3′6″ center height. Folded 8″ x 18″. Weight complete 4 lbs. 13 oz.
5523 Two-Man Back Packer Tent, $41.00 postpaid.
5524 Top Fly, $15.50 postpaid. (Fly of same material, size 8′2″ x 8′8″. Wt. 18 oz.)
Four-Man Back Packer: 7′ x 8′8″ x 6′ center height. Folded 9″ x 24″. Weight complete 7 lbs. 4 oz.
5525 Four-Man Back Packer Tent, $68.50 postpaid.
5526 Top Fly, $20.25 postpaid. (Fly of same material, size 8′6″ x 14′. Wt. 28 oz.)

Hiker Stove and Cooking Unit

Consists of precision made, self-pressurizing brass stove and combination of aluminum utensils, adequate for a party of 2 to 4 persons. Stove nests in cooking unit, making 8″ diameter x 5″ high package. Weight, Stove and Unit, 2¼ lbs.

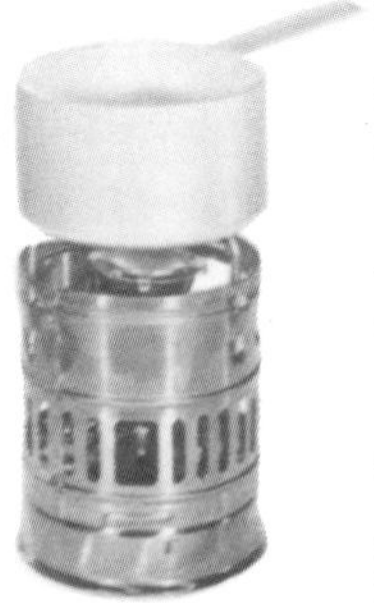

Hiker Camp Stove: Burns ¾ to 1 hour on Coleman fuel or white gasoline. Size 5″ high x 3¾″ diameter. Weight 1 lb. 2 oz.
5325 Hiker Camp Stove, $11.50 postpaid.
Nesting Cooking Unit. Consists of base and windscreen for stove, two cooking pots that can be used as double boiler, deep skillet type lid and pot lifter. Weight 1 lb. 2 oz.
5418 Nesting Cooking Unit, $8.25 postpaid.
Aluminum Fuel Bottle, holds sufficient fuel for 6 refills of the Hiker Stove. Has screw cap with gasket. **Not to be used to hold alcohol.** Size 9½″ x 3¼″. Weight 5 oz.
5326 Aluminum Fuel Bottle, $2.90 postpaid.

Bean's Pack Basket

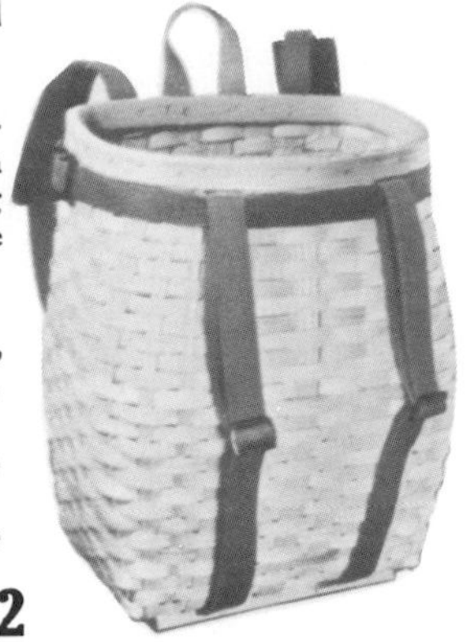

Carefully woven by hand from selected rattan and seasoned white ash. Correctly shaped to fit back. Equipped with heavy adjustable webbing harness with sponge rubber pads. The Pack Basket is the only safe container for carrying breakable goods. Convenient as a storage cupboard for food that should not be kept in warm camp. Leather carrying handle.

Three sizes:
Boys', capacity 2 pecks. Height 15″. **5211 Boys' Pack Basket, with Harness, $9.00 postpaid. 5214 Water repellent duck cover** of our own manufacture, **$3.50 postpaid.**
Men's, capacity 3 pecks. Height 18″. **5212 Men's Pack Basket, with Harness, $13.00 postpaid. 5215 Cover, $4.00 postpaid.**
Extra Large, capacity 4 pecks. Height 21″. **5213 Extra Large Pack Basket, with Harness, $16.50 postpaid. 5216 Extra Large Cover, $5.00 postpaid.**

78 **L. L. Bean, Inc. Freeport, Me. 04032**

its performance. Different models, patterns, or styles available may be shown—and color selections, too, when color telecasting and receiving are commercially in use. In fact, the eventual scope of mail-order selling by air seems unlimited when the possibilities of showing products being modeled or otherwise in use, a full range of styles or patterns—and colors, too—are considered.

Mail-order selling will merely be adapted to suit the medium and the selling advantages it offers, but mail-order selling principles will not—cannot—be eliminated, nor will their fundamental sales psychology be altered. Television's biggest asset as a sales-maker lies in its illustrative advantages, its ability to enhance verbal description—not replace it. Look at a few of the descriptive sales points extracted from the radio mail-order commercial, mentioned earlier, which offers a combination cigarette case and lighter plus the midget ball-point pen premium:

You'll be thrilled with the new _______ cigarette case made of richly finished, lightweight, marble-effect plastic in Hollywood pastel colors. It fits a shirt pocket or purse. IN ADDITION, there is a sure-fire, all-metal cigarette lighter built right into the top of this case. But that's just the *first* half of this sensational offer! Second: you will receive the world's smallest ball-point pen, complete with key chain!

This glittering, all-metal marvel is the mighty midget of the ball-point pens! Small enough to fit a vest pocket or coin purse, it's guaranteed to do a big job of writing. If you order immediately, your cigarette case will be monogrammed with your own initial, in ornamental lettering that glows in the dark. . . .

A pretty fair verbal picture, but translate these sentences into television language—actually not much of a change—and you'll see how some words are replaced or converted to take every advantage of the opportunity of visual illustration provided by the new medium:

Wouldn't you be thrilled to own [announcer produces product in his hand from behind his back] this beautiful new ________ cigarette case? Look at the rich finish [turns case in close-up before camera] or its marble-effect plastic—its Hollywood pastel colors. Notice its light weight [flips case lightly in palm of hand] —how it fits your pocket or purse [slips case in and out of upper vest pocket] . AND LOOK—A sure-fire, all-metal cigarette lighter [flicks flame in close-up, on and off] built right into the top! But that's just the first half of this sensational offer! [Brings other hand, closed, from behind back.] Second, you will receive this [opens fist in close-up] ball-point pen—the *world's smallest*—complete with key chain! [Lets chain dangle and swing momentarily.] This glittering, all-metal marvel is the *mighty midget* [writes large "Mighty Midget" with pen on pad of paper as he says words] of ball-point pens! Small enough to fit your vest pocket [tucks pen into lower vest pocket and removes again] or purse, it's guaranteed to do a *big* job [holds up pad again] of writing. If you order immediately, your cigarette case will be monogrammed with *your own* initial, in ornamental lettering [holds up initialed case as studio lights dim momentarily] that glows in the dark! [Initial glows, then lights come on again.]

Actually, you've changed none of the selling points—and just enough of the words to capitalize on the actual demonstration of your product. In fact, your word count is practically the same. As in your use of any mail-order medium, you've merely used every opportunity at your command to present all your major selling points as graphically and completely as is possible within that medium. You've adapted your copy, too, to suit the medium and to reach as many of the prospects covered by the medium and to reach as many of the prospects covered by the medium as you can. Your word rate is high since the commercial is fast-paced and enthusiastic.

So it is that your body copy, no matter what the medium, is your major factor in convincing the prospect that a purchase of your product is desirable.

Now, to get your prospects to order

Your display has attracted the prospect's attention. He was interested enough to enter your shop, and now you've sold him on making a purchase. Here is where mail-order selling must go an extra step beyond any other kind of selling. Why? Because there's an extra step in the making of a mail-order purchase. As the mail-order salesman you have an extra job to do, too. That job is not merely to ask for the order, but to make the purchase so easy that the prospect is willing to go to the added inconveniences inherent in ordering by mail. He will be glad to write out his order, to remit the purchase price, and to mail the two together.

Ordering directions are important

How do you make ordering simple, easy, or even inviting? There is no single way applicable to all mail-order selling, so first look at the three principal methods of encouraging or inviting the order:

1. An order blank (perhaps with an addressed postage-guaranteed envelope);
2. A return post card (always self-addressed and usually, nowadays, with postage guaranteed) and coupons;
3. Advertisements without coupons; contain mere statements of ordering requirements and mailing address.

Obviously, the first two are definitely *ordering aids.* They remove some of the burden imposed upon the purchaser by the fact that he can't just hand you his money and carry off his purchase. Number 3 relieves the purchaser of none of the effort required to place an order. Which method should you use for any particular mail-order offering? The major consideration is your medium. Mail-order catalogs, for example, usually include an *order blank,* perhaps several, to encourage frequent ordering. Direct-mail-order offerings frequently have a *return post card* enclosed. The *coupon* most often is part of a mail-order advertisement in a publication. *Ordering information* alone is usually used either in mail-order advertisements too small to accommodate coupons or in radio commercials.

1. *Order blanks.* Order blanks usually are the most elaborate of these methods, for several reasons. Because they most commonly accompany catalogs, more than one type of item may be—and usually is—ordered on one blank; this means that often different kinds of information may be required for each item—color, pattern, finish, initials (for monograms), width, length, size, model, price each, per pair, or per set, or what-have-you.

Because general merchandise mail-order houses have so many regular customers ordering several times a season or year, these houses must have a means of keeping up-to-date information on customers' addresses, past and current.

Since they sell on several different sets of terms—cash, time-payment accounts, and open accounts are the three most common—the payment method must be recorded on the order blank. Spaces are provided for such details.

Since weight and bulk of items vary greatly, a choice of shipment methods must be provided on the blank, the customer to indicate his preference. Then such obvious requirements must be provided for as catalog numbers, quantity ordered, name and shipping weight of each item, plus totals on the weights, prices, postage, taxes, and the like.

2. *Return post cards and coupons.* "Miniature order blanks" would be a rather apt description of both return post cards and coupons accompanying other printed mail-order advertising. These are, strictly speaking, too, coupons and post cards are similar to each other, although the customary difference in their sizes may at first mask the resemblance. A study of their mutual requirements will show their similarity:

Very frequently both return post cards and coupons include some inducement for prompt reply—often in addition to any such urge previously incorporated into the accompanying mailing piece of advertisement. One of those you'll find most common is some variation of the magic word "Free":

"Free Examination Postcard"

"Free 10-Day Trial Coupon!"

"Free Sample"

"Free Catalog"

"Don't Wait—Send Coupon Today for Approval Offer"

"Good for *Both Free*"

As a rule these are in some sort of display type—quite often in a "reverse" panel—but sometimes they may be set in relatively small type, especially in small coupons, or where they are subordinated to some other urge to action which receives stronger treatment. Other typical incentives for ordering include such inducements as variations of the common one, "Mail This Coupon Today!" and others a little more original, like:

"Clip This Coupon—Mail Today"

"Order with This Handy Coupon"

"We Accept Your Invitation"

"Mail this Card to Secure Your Copy"

"Complete Crochet Library—Only 10¢ a Book"

"Get the *Facts* by Mail"

"Mail Opportunity Coupon for Quick Action"

"Phone—Wire—Use Coupon"

"This Certificate Saves You $3.00"

All these, of course, besides urging prompt action, serve as well to call attention to the coupon (or card). To accomplish a similar purpose, an arrow or some similar eye-directing device is sometimes incorporated into the advertising layout, although nowadays many layout artists tend to scorn such "corny"

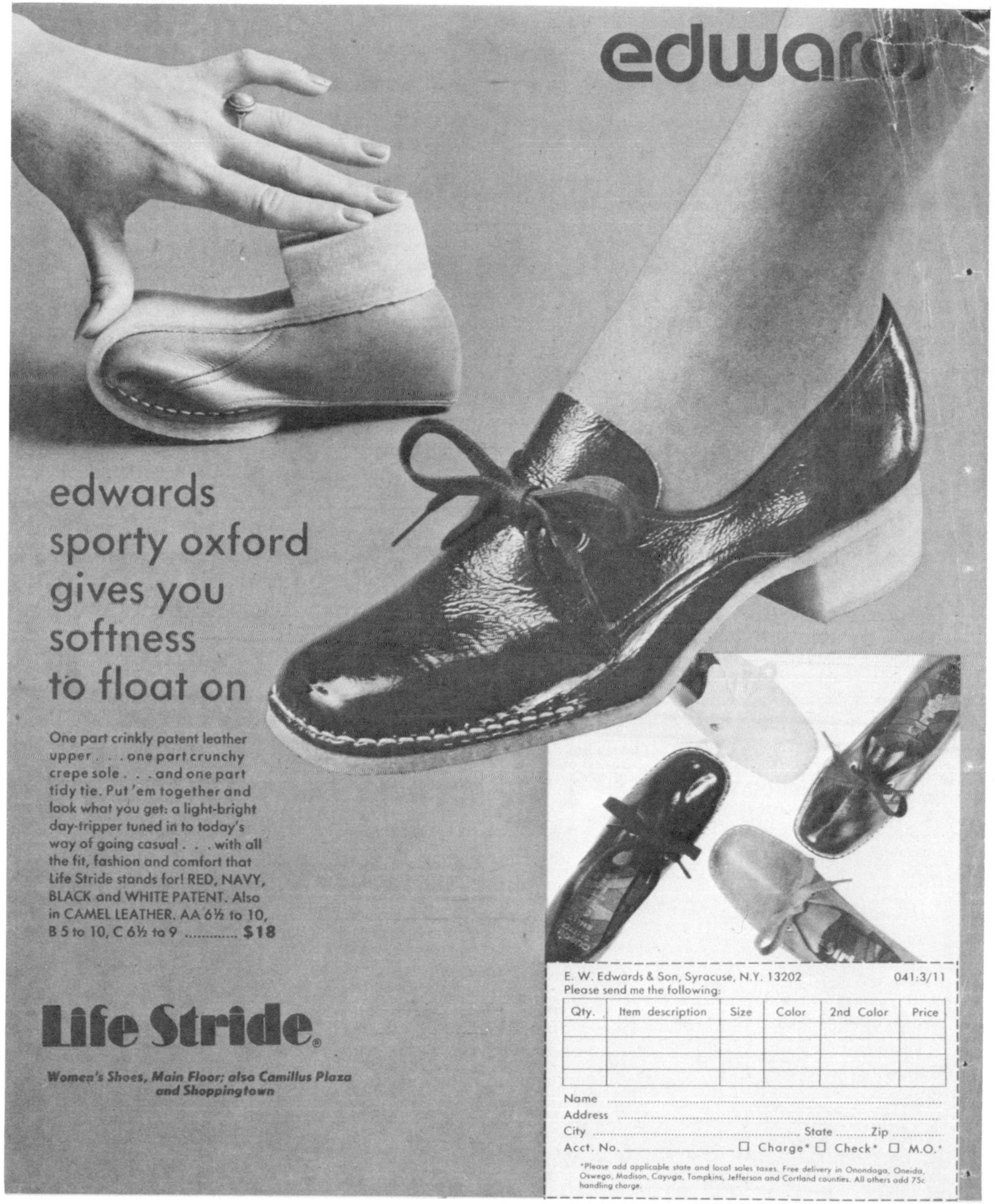
edwards
sporty oxford
gives you
softness
to float on
One part crinkly patent leather upper . . . .one part crunchy crepe sole . . . and one part tidy tie. Put 'em together and look what you get: a light-bright day-tripper tuned in to today's way of going casual . . . with all the fit, fashion and comfort that Life Stride stands for! RED, NAVY, BLACK and WHITE PATENT. Also in CAMEL LEATHER. AA 6½ to 10, B 5 to 10, C 6½ to 9 .... $18
Life Stride®
Women's Shoes, Main Floor; also Camillus Plaza and Shoppingtown
E. W. Edwards & Son, Syracuse, N.Y. 13202
041:3/11
Please send me the following:
Qty.
Item description
Size
Color
2nd Color
Price
Name
Address
City
State
Zip
Acct. No.
☐ Charge* ☐ Check* ☐ M.O.*
*Please add applicable state and local sales taxes. Free delivery in Onondaga, Oneida, Oswego, Madison, Cayuga, Tompkins, Jefferson and Cortland counties. All others add 75c handling charge.

Fig. 12-5

Retail mail order advertisement.

Department stores are among the heaviest local users of mail order advertisements such as this.

treatment, preferring to accomplish the same result more subtly by designing the entire piece to lead the eye "naturally" through the steps of the selling process, ending logically with the final step—the action-inducing coupon.

Another feature that most mail-order return post cards and advertisement coupons share is the inclusion of some sort of statement to make them more personal, as if the purchaser had written them himself. The one you are most familiar with undoubtedly is "Please send me . . . ," or any of its close relatives, followed by a brief restatement of the offer made in the mailing piece or advertisement, again usually phrased in the first person, supposedly the sender's words.

Prospects must know how to pay

Common also to both return post-card and coupon order forms is not merely a restatement of the price but a provision for stating the method of payment chosen. Even where no choice is offered, this is included as a precaution against any misunderstanding by the purchaser. The following illustrations of typical wordings (most of them self-explanatory as to the terms offered) will show you how such statements may be handled:

☐ Charge My Account; ☐ Find Check or M.O. Enclosed;
Please include 3% sales tax on orders in (state)

o o o

☐ C.O.D.; ☐ Money Order or Check; ☐ Charge my account;
(Please do not send currency or stamps)

o o o

☐ Cash ☐ C.O.D. ☐ Charge

o o o

Check for ______ enclosed. No C.O.D.'s.
Check ☐ I am enclosing $______. *Ship Postpaid.*
One ☐ Ship C.O.D. I'll pay postman $______ plus postage.

o o o

Please send me the books checked, at 25¢ each. I enclose ______.

o o o

Mail [*title of book set*] on 7 days' free trial.
If O.K. I will remit $1 in 7 days and $1 monthly until $6 is paid. Otherwise I will return them. No obligation unless I am satisfied.

o o o

Within ten days I will either return the book and owe nothing, or send you $1.50 and the $2.00 a month for three months until the special price of $7.50, plus postage, is paid.
☐ Check here if you send the full price of $7.50 with this card. We will pay the postage. Same return privilege and refund if you're not satisfied.

o o o

☐ Remittance Enclosed; ☐ Please Bill Me;
☐ One Year (26 Issues) $3.50–$3.90 single copy value.
☐ Two Years (52 Issues) $6.00–$7.80 single copy value.

o o o

Enclosed is 25¢ (*in coin*) and the top of a package or sack of your ______. Please send me one of ______.

o o o

Please enroll me as a ______ Book Club subscriber and send me at once "______" as a gift. Also send me as my first selection for $2.00 the book I have checked below:

[four choices listed, each with a check box]

With these books will come my first issue of the brochure "______," telling about the forthcoming ______ selection which will be offered for $2.00 (plus shipping charge) to members only, regardless of the price of publisher's edition. I am to have the privilege of notifying you in advance if I do not wish to purchase any ______ selection. The purchase of ______ selections is entirely voluntary on my part, I do not have to accept a book every month—only four during the year—to fulfill my membership requirement. I am to receive a bonus book for every four ______ selections I purchase . . .
Price in Canada, $2.20.

Many cards and coupons offer return privileges "without obligation," or perhaps a "free trial" offer, restated in the body of the card or coupon, to make sure the purchaser understands that his signature does not obligate him finally and irrevocably to buy.

Addresses must be right

All mail-order return post cards and coupons include the name and address of the seller. The cards, of course, always have them printed on the address side of the card, and sometimes repeated on the order side for the prestige they may lend the offer. The coupons include them primarily to insure that the purchaser has an accurate address for use on the envelope in which he sends the coupon.

One other use is to test the response to the publication in which an advertisement appears, or the returns on each of several mailing lists the seller may be renting. This may be done by "keying" the address. Frequently this key is a fictitious "department" designation. For instance, suppose you are running the same advertisement in *Farm Journal, Successful Farming,* and *Capper's Weekly* magazines, and want to test their relative effectiveness as order-getters. Like the rest of the advertisement, you make the coupon the same in all three publications except for the department in the addresses, which you would most likely designate as, "Dept. FJ," "Dept. SF," and "Dept. CF," respectively.

You do much the same thing in testing rented mailing lists, since you may not be able to secure copies for your own direct check. Most owners of rented direct-mail lists address and send your mailing pieces from their own shops. You can't check returns against the several lists to which your mailings are going out, but you *can* check the effectiveness of each list as a whole merely by keying each group of return cards differently.

One more requirement is common to both return post cards and coupons in any mail-order offering using them. That is the customer's name and address. Illegibility is such a problem that you'll probably use the common request, "Please print." You may also say "Please use pencil" if the paper stock of the card or publication might make ink blot and run. The form and space you provide for the purchaser's address may vary with the classes or groups of people who are expected to respond.

If they are city folks, for example, you'll most likely ask for *street and number* (and perhaps *apartment number*), *city, state,* and *zip.* Perhaps you'll have to designate both, if your offer of your mailing lists or your publications may reach more than one group. In addition, you may want other information about the purchaser:

Is "he" *Mr., Mrs., Miss, Ms.*
(three to be crossed out)?
What is his date of birth?
Does he own a car? What make?
What model? What year?
Is he a home-owner or does he rent?
Does he carry insurance? On himself? On his house? On his car? Other?

Perhaps you need credit references—a bank, names of two business houses where he has established credit, or names of two businessmen who know him. In any case, your card or coupon will have to provide space for any of these additional pieces of information which you require.

One word of caution: *give your purchaser enough space to fill in the information most important to you*—usually his name and address. You'll find it wiser and more profitable, generally speaking, to forego some of the information and might *like* in order to give him room in which to write his name and address. If his name and address is: "Humphrey Stanislavski, Oklahoma City, Okla.," you'll get no reply if you have provided barely enough space for a customer to write: "Ned Hay, Erie, Pa."

Finally, your "miniature order blank" may have to provide spaces for information essential to proper filling of the order, if any choice is involved, or if alternate selections are offered, as in clothing. *Quantity, Size,* and *color* are those you'll probably require specifications for most often. Marshall Field, on some of its coupons or small order blanks, gives even these common requirements the "Field" touch by saying: *"Size?" Color?" "How many?"* and *"Cost."*

3. *Advertisements without Coupons.* What about the mail-order advertisement that doesn't have room enough for a coupon, and what about mail-order commercials? How can you induce everyone who likes your offer to prove it with an order even if a coupon is not provided?

Well, you might just as well make up your mind that you aren't usually going to get so many replies from couponless advertisement as you will receive if you include a coupon. But, you may say, "I *don't* have room for a coupon, and I *don't* have enough money to spend to increase the size of my advertisement sufficiently to include a coupon, but I still have to run an advertisement for my mail-order offering. What do I do *then?"*

One thing you *can* do is to include *adequate ordering information* as a part of your advertisement's copy, exerting every effort to make it sound attractive enough—*to sell it well enough*—so that it brings in a profitable number of orders. A second thing you can do, besides giving *complete ordering information,* is to state the ordering requirements *simply.* And third, you should be certain that the *requirements themselves are reduced to the basic necessities*—that only truly essential elements are included.

Fig. 12-6

Mail order advertisement appearing in a magazine.

Notice the persuasive selling copy, the clear ordering directions and the suggestion that several of the item be ordered. The results of this advertisement were good enough to justify running it several times. The advertiser consistently suggests that readers order more than one item in order to obtain a price saving. The multiple-purchase suggestion is credited with increasing returns 10 percent to 40 percent—this as a result of adding one or two lines of copy.

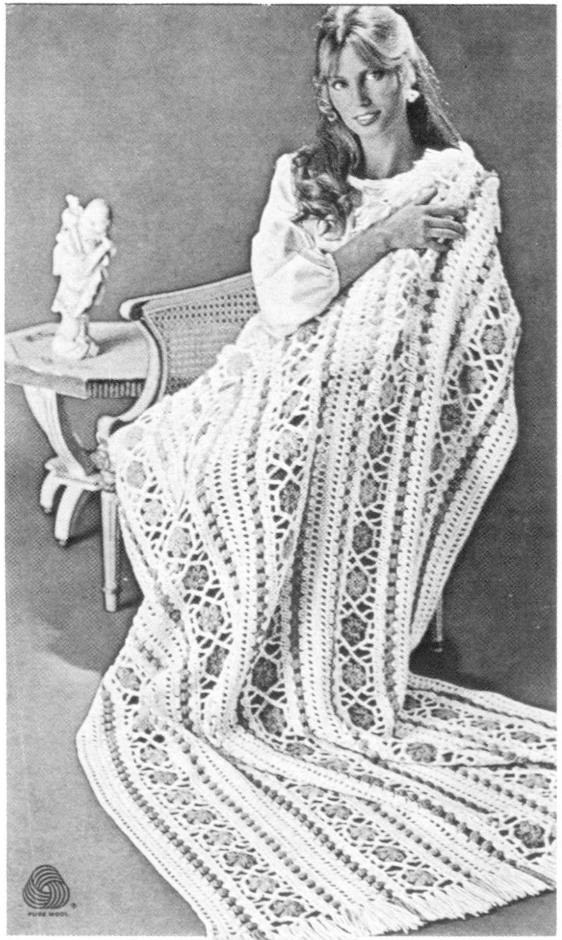

AN AFGHAN TO CROCHET

from Better Homes and Gardens

OUR GUARANTEE

Money back if not completely satisfied.

☐ Please send me ____ blue with white background afghan kit(s), No. 00025. I enclose $____ including postage and handling.

☐ Please send me ____ white and yellow with orange background afghan kit(s) No. 00026. I enclose $____ including postage and handling.

AFGHAN PRICES: $19.95 each plus $1.25 postage and handling. Two afghans for $38.90 plus postage and handling.

ORDER SEVERAL AND SAVE!

Send order and remittance to:
Better Homes and Gardens, Dept. 2M2
Box 374, Des Moines, Iowa 50302

Name____
Address____
City____
State____ Zip____

Complete this kit in a few leisure hours and enjoy it for many years to come. You get more than enough 100% pure Virgin wool to make our big cozy, hand-washable afghan (approximately 45" x 69"). Our really good instructions make it easy to get really good results.

Order several kits. They make ideal long remembered gifts for weddings and other special occasions. The kit is available with flowers in two shades of blue on a white background as pictured above or white and yellow flowers on an orange background (not shown). Please specify your preference.

CREATE A GIFT FROM THE HEART THAT WILL LAST A LIFETIME.

Getting paid—how to go about it

All right, so you're going to cut out all unnecessary ordering requirements from your couponless mail-order advertisements. Logically, you'll start with those elements that most often cause trouble. The biggest trouble-causer is the customer's name and address. Since you certainly can't eliminate those (although it's amazing that customers themselves sometimes forget how important these elements are and omit them completely), you move on to the next most troublesome element—the remittance, or, to speak frankly, money. Cut out the requirement. Heresy! How, you ask, can I stay in business without money?

If you read carefully the quotations from post cards and coupons a few paragraphs back, you'll recall that even *with* these ordering devices some mail-order merchandisers have avoided the need for a remittance with the order. Of course, this is relatively simple for a department store selling either to its charge account customers or making C.O.D. sales locally where its truck drivers can collect for the merchandise at the time of delivery. But the requirement for cash, money order, or check with the order is being omitted by more and more non-local mail-order advertisers who have neither charge customers nor any delivery system of their own. The C.O.D., "pay-postman-on-delivery" type of offer is becoming more and more popular since it eliminates one of the three traditional steps in ordering by mail (writing the order, procuring and enclosing the remittance, and mailing the two together).

C.O.D. orders are not so frequently invited —in fact, are sometimes definitely prohibited —by mail-order advertisers using many of the so-called "class" magazines. Perhaps this is due partially to the fact that readers of such publications are in the middle-to-high income groups. Probably they are primarily urbanites, and therefore more likely to have personal checking accounts. At least they aren't too much inconvenienced by buying a money order. A smaller percentage of the mail-order advertisements appearing in the "class" publications carry coupons than those published in magazines read by supposedly less intelligent or less well-educated folk. Presumably the "class" market advertisers have found that their market shows more comprehension of the need for accuracy in ordering by mail.

Some other ways to get paid

Besides C.O.D. terms, mail-order merchandisers sometimes use other means of making the payment either physically simpler than a full cash enclosure, or at least temporarily easier on the customer's pocketbook or checkbook. One means of doing this is shown in the coupon and post-card examples quoted previously (but sometimes in non-coupon advertisements as well) which offer a "free trial" period, "order on approval," "bill me later," or other similar terms.

Another plan sometimes used—especially with book clubs, sets, or individual books—is a time-payment scheme by which the purchaser remits a payment each time he receives a book-club selection or another book of the set he has ordered. He may also receive the book, or entire set, upon receipt by the seller of a down payment with the order, the balance to be paid in stated installments. In any event, you must state the terms so clearly that any purchaser of normal intelligence cannot misinterpret them.

Be clear and simple

Another consideration in maintaining simplicity in couponless mail-order advertisements is to limit—preferably to eliminate—any alternate items or choices. Usually an advertisement listing more than one offer—or two at the most—will be large enough to include a coupon as well. Some physical means should be given the purchaser to indicate the exact item he wants when a selection is offered. It's the single offering, however, made in a choice of styles or colors or finishes or sizes that cause mail-order grief, effort, and money.

The cure: making clear to the customer the physical means of indicating his choice. Nevertheless, the copywriter—you—will probably encounter some adamant advertiser who won't, or can't, afford the "luxury" of the extra space required for a coupon. In such cases, you must be especially careful to word your ordering requirements copy so that the majority of customers will be fairly certain to include all the information necessary to receive the selection they want. "State choice," "Please indicate model wanted," "Be sure to include all measurements," and similar cautions must be stated—predominantly and preferably in bold face—and stated clearly.

A page margin can be your coupon

One device is sometimes suggested in mail-order advertisements that attempt to make ordering from such advertisements somewhat more convenient. This idea is simply the suggestion that the purchaser clip the advertisement from the publication and write on the adjacent margin his name and address—and any other necessary ordering information. This is an idea you may be able to use advantageously in some cases; but first be sure that your advertisement is of such size of shape that it *will* be next to one of the page margins in the publication(s) in which it will run.

Getting C.O.D. orders by radio and television

As for radio mail-order commercials, relatively little need be added to what has been said couponless advertisements in print. The said about couponless advertisements in print. The same principles apply—only more so. A radio commercial is heard once—it cannot be "reread"—and in that one hearing the offer and all its details, especially the details on ordering, must be grasped completely by the listener. Because comprehension by ear is less thorough than by eye, ordering information in mum." Almost never do you offer a choice of *any sort.* The few exceptions consist almost entirely of colors or sizes where these cannot be avoided. In the matter of payment for the order, more and more radio merchandisers have come to use C.O.D. terms exclusively.

Advertisers-by-air have gone to great lengths to simplify their ordering requirements. They appear sometimes to go to extremes in clarifying other ordering information, too, particularly the address to which the order is to be sent. You'll find the address must usually be given at least twice during even a one-minute commercial, besides the almost inevitable spelling out of the name as well—remember the "Harmonica" commercial earlier in the chapter?

As a further means of simplifying the address, you may imitate many experienced radio advertisers who use the station call letters as an address: "Just write to Harmonicas, that's H-A-R-M-O-N-I-C-A-S, Harmonicas, care of WQXZ, Zenia, 1, Illinois." The station then forwards the mail received (usually unopened) to the advertiser, or he collects it from the station, probably daily.

Here, incidentally, is where television may have another advantage over radio; think how much easier and quicker the television audience may grasp all the required ordering information if much of it is presented visually. Perhaps a sample order, written in the "ideal" form, may be shown—and certainly an envelope correctly addressed should appear on the viewer's screen while the announcer gives the address—perhaps only once!

Mail-order selling in non-consumer fields

So far, almost everything said about mail-order selling has been expressed in the language of merchandising of consumer goods. Remember, however, that commercial, industrial, and technical goods merchandisers, such as many borderline specialty houses (those selling educational goods and materials to teachers or schools exclusively, for example), reach their limited markets by mail-order selling, too. Although the media will differ—and some of the language as well—from consumer mail-order advertising (just as they differ in any regular commercial campaign from regular consumer advertisements), the principles, objectives, and techniques of mail-order salesmanship remain the same no matter who is appealing to what particular group or market. You can carry over everything you know and practice in consumer mail-order selling to commercial mail-order selling. Merely adapt it to suit your product, your medium, and your prospects—exactly as you would to reach any other well-defined consumer group.

You see then that it is unnecessary and repetitive to tell you how to write commercial mail-order advertising. Even the media used fall into similar patterns (catalogs, direct-mail-order pieces, and publications), although patently radio is not used because the coverage wasted on such a nonspecialized audience would prove too costly.

Direct Mail: Copy Aimed At The Individual

In mass-media copy you play a little game with yourself as you write. Although you know very well that you are writing to a mass audience, you try, as you write, to think of one person. This procedure helps you personalize your copy.

In direct mail you do not need to pretend. You *are* writing to one person. Herein lies the great advantage of the medium. A copywriter, in turn, who can capture in direct mail copy the individual approach—call it personal warmth—is almost certain to be a success in the demanding form of writing.

Perhaps the most outstanding feature of direct-mail advertising is its universal use as a means of communication between advertiser and prospect. Of thousands of businesses, only relatively few advertise over the air, in national magazines, or in any but their own local newspapers. Almost every firm, however, uses direct-mail advertising even though it uses other media as well.

One national advertiser, perhaps best known for newspaper campaigns, actually spent twice the amount of his newspaper budget for direct-mail advertising in a recent year. Probably he is doing the same today. You, the advertising writer, may be more likely to exert your creative effort in writing for direct mail than in writing for any other single type of medium.

WHAT IS DIRECT MAIL ADVERTISING?

To define direct-mail advertising: A means of getting your message-in-print personally and individually to a selected group of prospects or customers with whom you want to do business or whose good will you want to establish or maintain. As the words imply, this is a truly "direct" medium, usually conveyed entirely by "mail," as opposed to mail order, which may use radio, television and publication advertising in soliciting mail business.

Some direct-mail pieces are also distributed in other ways. A folder, for example, devised primarily as a mailing piece to accompany a department store's monthly charge account statements, may also be used as a pick-up piece in a suitable spot in the store—probably in the department whose merchandise or service it publicizes. This kind of promotion is sometimes called direct advertising and is considered the same as direct-mail advertising. In this discussion it will be assumed, however, that you are writing to relatively sharply defined groups—in other words, you are creating "direct-mail advertising."

REASONS FOR USING DIRECT MAIL

At one time the Direct Mail Advertising Association issued a list of 49 ways direct-mail advertising could be used as a part of modern merchandising methods. Although many variations in these applications can be—and have been—made, a listing of some of the most common basic uses will give you an idea of the scope of this medium and how greatly you would have to vary your writing to meet the requirements of some of these uses:

1. To sell goods or services by mail. (Although this use does not *necessarily* anticipate return orders *by mail,* its purpose is primarily the same as "direct-mail-order," covered in detail in the last chapter under the general heading "mail-order selling.")
2. To reach all customers regularly with merchandise offers, thereby keeping accounts active.
3. To support salesmen, pave the way for them, thus backing their selling efforts and economizing on their time (and on the prospects' time and patience) when actually making sales calls.

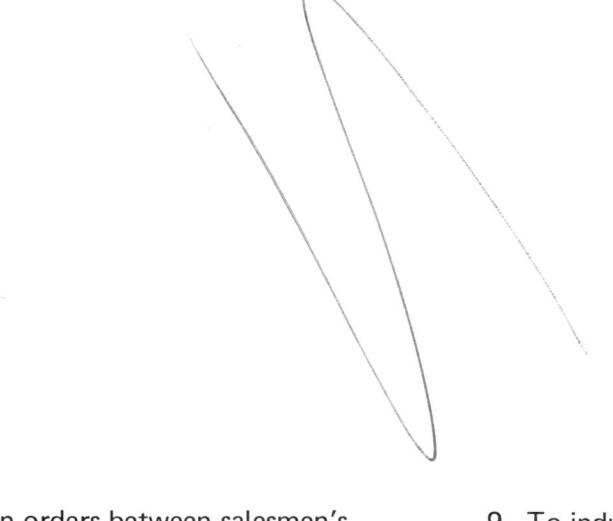

4. To bring in orders between salesmen's calls or from territories not covered by salesmen (or, in consumer selling, areas not serviced through retail outlets), or to open up new territories.

5. To broadcast mailings to and request inquiries from a large group of prospects. Names thus obtained are passed on to dealers, jobbers, or salesmen for solicitation, or are further contacted by additional direct mail. Getting names this way saves the expense of indiscriminate distribution of catalogs, since requests are from definite prospects.

6. To provide news and information about the firm or its products. This might include "education" of stockholders on company products, services, and policies—either from a public relations point of view, or as encouragement of their patronage, or perhaps of their word-of-mouth advertising.

7. To tie up with trade or consumer publication advertising, or to sell dealers on trade paper or consumer advertising programs. Such selling stimulates their cooperative efforts.

8. To stimulate dealer sales by consumer mailings—perhaps by suggesting a visit to the prospect's "nearest dealer." Jobber sales may also be spurred by mailings to dealers.

9. To induce a dealer's own customers or prospects to visit his store—or a manufacturer's customers his showroom—to see some special goods described or illustrated.

10. To overcome competition threatening established customer, or adverse market tendencies. The quick publicizing of a revised price list might fall into this class.

11. To pre-test, on a limited scale, contemplated offers or presentations against each other, using different lists or splitting a single list.

12. To stimulate sales or to increase acceptance of the firm's merchandise or services through enclosures in all outgoing envelopes (with dividend checks or financial statements to stockholders, for example).

13. To request information from prospects to determine their needs. The information will be used as a basis for further mailings or salesman's solicitation. The items will be specifically suited to prospects' requirements.

In this incomplete list, you have a range of jobs to be done that calls for many different types of copy treatment. Yet they offer you one advantage—that of knowing on any individual job the needs and wants of the prospects to whom you are writing. Because of the selective nature of direct mail you write more surely to the prospect's interest than in general media such as newspapers, radio and TV.

HOW PERSONAL INTEREST CAN BE ACHIEVED

One prestige retail clothing chain, for example, mails advance announcements of its seasonal traveling merchandise displays to charge customers and former cash customers. Because this is a very well-defined group of prospects already aware of the company's reputation, styles, and values, the headline of one announcement read merely—

(Company Name) Clothes for Spring and Summer

—almost a pure "index" type headline, with institutional and prestige overtones. Contrast this with another—this one from a non-mail order catalog cover of a chain of retail auto supply stores, based primarily on price appeal (but including some reassurance of quality):

SAVE 25% to 50%
from List Price on
GUARANTEED REPLACEMENT AUTO PARTS

Here is a headline aimed unmistakably at a large—almost universal—but yet quite definite class of prospects, automobile owners, to induce them to visit their local store of the chain where the products listed may be purchased.

Quite another purpose is apparent in a two-fold, envelope-size enclosure on slick, heavy paper, sent to its stockholders with their dividend checks by a large manufacturer of soaps and synthetic detergents. The mailing was sent prior to the break in national media of an introductory advertising campaign for a new shampoo. The company already manufactured a successful liquid shampoo, sold in a bottle, and a transparent "creme" shampoo in a tube had been introduced in a nation-wide campaign within the year just past.

Now that a third shampoo ("beauty cream" shampoo in a jar) was being launched, the manufacturer felt it necessary to explain this seeming duplication of products to its stockholders. The explanation told the readers that research had shown that a definite market for each shampoo existed. The outer fold of this direct-mail enclosure carried the headline (with illustrations of the three products):

Just what customers ordered . . . Three Fine Shampoos

Attention and interest value of the first four words is high because they imply something of vital interest to the particular group addressed—a group whose returns on their stock in this company depend entirely upon how well the company management continues to anticipate the wants of the buying public. To this select group, the entire headline is provocative of further reading to find out *why* and *how* "three fine shampoos" fulfill these wants. And the entire folder attempts to do just the one job—to "sell" the stockholders (owners) of the company on justification of the manufacture and promotion of three apparently competitive products. This single purpose is carried so far that there is not even any encouragement to try any of the products, or to recommend them to friends. The back fold of the enclosure, however, does carry a change-of-address form for the convenience of stockholders who may have moved.

A similar direct-mail piece, mailed separately to stockholders of a large corporation with several diversified manufacturing divisions, tells of the current production and market status of the products produced by three of these divisions for use in the home. Display copy reads:

Outer fold	[Corp. name] PRESENTS PRODUCTS FOR THE HOME
First inner fold	DIVERSIFICATION IN MANUFACTURING [plus explanatory copy]
Inside spread, each subhead followed by explanatory copy	. . . FROM TELEVISION TO HEATING! Radio and Television Receivers Kitchen Ranges Refrigerators Frozen Food Cabinets Kitchen Cabinets and Sinks Residential Heating Units

The final copy paragraph on the first inner fold does invite requests for further information on the products covered. The tone of the entire piece is more product-sales minded than the one on the shampoos. Its purpose is dual—to report company progress, and to sell its line of products to its shareholders by bringing directly to their attention the items it makes. This purpose is rather apparent even in the display copy on the outer fold on the piece.

Making mailings personal

The examples of display copy used in the direct-mail advertising cited thus far have not been personalized beyond the fact that the mailing envelopes were addressed by name. This is generally true of any pieces other than those sent in letter format—and many of *these* do not use prospects' names even in the letters. Others have the name (and sometimes the address) filled in to match (as well as possible) a pseudo-typewritten "circular" letter. Especially in this type of letter, there is usually no display copy—that is, not in display-size type—although sometimes a second color, to stimulate use of a two-tone typewriter ribbon, will be used for important elements of the copy. Yet there are ways of simultaneously personalizing a letter and giving it a tremendous attention- and interest-stimulating impact.

Arousing attention and maintaining interest must be carefully planned to fit the copy treatment. It must avoid attracting so much interest to itself that the major impression remaining with the prospect is that of the physical novelty of the piece. Also, it must avoid any feeling of amateurish handling lest this same impression carry over to the goods or services of the advertiser.

Attention-getters—the gadgets

Another attention-getter and interest-arouser is the "gadget." Chosen and used with imagination it can often help dramatize your message—to get your point across quickly and effectively. Frequently, a gadget is a small copy of a larger, familiar item, but it can be any life-size item—a candy mint wafer, a vitamin pill, a burnt match (never send inflammables through the mails), a golf tee, a pair of dice, a bobby pin, a button, a nail, a bolt-and-nut, or a bottle cork. Samples or pieces of the actual item or product being advertised may also be used as direct-mail gadgets (not, in this case, as samples or swatches to facilitate direct-mail *orders*). Such gadgets may be a piece of wool yarn used in the nap of a rug, perhaps a swatch of the carpeting itself, a sample of printing paper, a page from a new dictionary, or a patented combination washer and lock-nut.

Gadgets generally are attached in some manner to the leaflet, letter, or circular to avoid their dropping out when the envelope is opened. Seldom are they merely loose enclosures. Yet, if the gadget itself contains any part of the message, and if it *does* fall to the floor when the envelope is opened, the recipient's curiosity might be piqued and his interest increased by the part of the message he reads on the gadget as he picks it up. Usually, however, you'll find the gadget fastened on the outside of a folder or near the top of a letter—tied into the copy by a provocative headline or by the lead-off paragraph in a letter.

Sometimes these headline tie-ins are forced to the point of absurdity—pure "corn." This "oldie," actually used—a miniature axe with the headline, "Do you mind if we axe you a few simple questions?"—is not recommended as a shining example of the catchy tie-in, yet some have been written even more insulting to the prospect's intelligence and sense of humor. But, like a famous series of Hart, Schaffner & Marx direct mail-letters—one of which, with two small dice attached, opened, "The luckiest buy I ever made in my life"—most tie-ins attempt to build a natural (no pun intended) bridge from the gadget to the message. Here are a few of the other headlines in the same series which Hart, Schaffner & Marx used so successfully on a cooperative basis with its dealers. The dealer's name was used twice in the letterhead and as the signature:

Gadget	*Lead Copy or Headline*
False mustache	Handle-bar mustaches, like this one, went out of style years ago. And so did the "Zoot Suit"—the peg pants, wide shouldered loose fit clothing for men.
Small spoon	You don't have to be born with a silver [spoon] in your mouth to be able to afford the comfort and luxury of one of our Bench Made Suits.
Full-size pocket comb	We have combed the country for the best coat value we could find.
Blue poker chip	Here's a suit that's a "blue chip" when it comes to luxury and tailoring. Yet you don't have to pay a "blue chip" price for its custom quality!

Sometimes a gadget can be so very clever that it defeats its own purpose—the prospects remember the campaign so well that they forget the advertiser's identity—or confuse it with a competitor's! Sometimes, too, a gadget idea may backfire unexpectedly (or predictably, perhaps, depending upon political views), to wit: An advertiser pasted a new F. D. R. dime (when they first were coined) on a letterhead, suggesting it be used as a partial payment on a return order for the product offered. A number of prospects were indignant at this supposed advocacy of Roosevelt and the New Deal regime.

Here are some cautions in the use of gadgets:

(1) Don't expect a gadget to sell a product that can't be sold on its own merits. A gadget is merely an attention-getter.

(2) Be sure the gadget fits your message and doesn't resort to bad gags or dubious humor.

(3) Avoid the "too clever" gadget that pushes your name and product out of the prospect's mind.

(4) Look for possible ways your gadget may antagonize your prospects, either by its physical connotations or by insulting their intelligence.

(5) Avoid anything dangerous—self-inflammables like matches, sharp objects such as glass, inadequately protected knives, razor blades.

(6) Don't rely entirely on your own personal like or dislike for a particular gadget—or for gadgets in general.

You get results with gadgets

Even though some people may not like them, "good" gadgets do appeal to most people and may well assure high interest in and readership of your message. Gadgets provide showmanship. They personalize your sales message. There are many reasons why any one—or all—of your prospects may have no particular interest in reading your message when it arrives. Possibly his own immediate problems and troubles seem far more important. So, anything you can do—reasonably, that is—to assure his favorable attention and interest, to combat his apathy toward your message, is a boost toward implanting the impression you want him to retain.

Most people, too, have no qualms about tossing a piece of once-read—or unread!—advertising matter into the wastebasket. They aren't so likely to discard an object—a *thing*—nearly so fast. A gadget has physical value, small though it may be. It can be played with, or held, or looked at a little while, especially if it's familiar or useful, or if its size or shape is attractive.

So, go ahead—use gadgets in your direct-mail pieces if you feel a change of pace is needed in a series of mailings, or if you want to assure special attention for an outstanding message. Use a gadget only: (1) *If* you can make it a *logical* and *natural* introduction to your product. (2) *If* you are certain of your prospects. (3) *If* you choose the gadget wisely and use it tactfully and tastefully.

More gadget types—pop-ups and cut-outs

Among other novelty treatments that can be used to gain attention for, and interest in, your direct-mail message are cut-outs and pop-ups. Such devices are not, perhaps, part of the copywriter's province. Yet, the copywriter has a definite interest in them because, like gadgets, they are usually tied in with the copy—either supplementing some part of the message or perhaps providing a springboard for the copy theme.

A cut-out is just what its name implies—some pictorial treatment trimmed to the shape of its outlines rather than having its outlines merely printed on a conventionally shaped background (usually rectangular). It may be used as a loose enclosure with a direct-mail piece, or may be attached to it (perhaps loosely to provide some sort of attention-compelling motion or movability). It may itself comprise the entire mailing, including the message.

Sometimes cut-outs are used to reveal underlying parts or cut-away views of an item, such as a piece of machinery, so that when the cut-out (which may be hinged to the main part of the piece) is lifted, it shows an illustration of the "insides" or working parts of the mechanism. An interest-arousing and action-inviting headline might read: "Under this housing may be the answer to your production problem—lift it and see for yourself."

Another cut-out, somewhat more complicated, and successfully used to dramatize the product and assure reader interest, was a mailing to doctors and hospital buyers which suggested in a letter that they ask the next medical supply house salesman who called to show them the advertiser's new sanitary waste-disposal pails. These pails featured an improved-action foot pedal which effortlessly raised the snugly fitted lid of the pail.

Accompanying the letter was a card that illustrated the pail, and—cleverly cut, inserted, and hinged on a fastening pin—the lid of the pail and the foot pedal were so mounted in the card that the pedal, when grasped by the fingers and moved slightly downward, easily raised the lid. The display copy, laid out to draw attention to the pedal, said: "Step on it lightly—the lid opens wide . . . Release the pressure—the pail's closed tightly." What prospect, receiving a direct-mail piece like this, could fail to play with such a device at least once or twice and, perhaps subconsciously, retain at least some part of the product story?

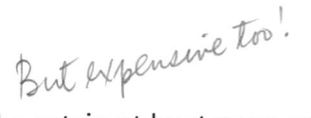

But expensive too!

YOUR BODY COPY MUST GIVE A COMPLETE MESSAGE

As in every other medium of advertising, it's the body copy of a direct-mail advertisement that must tell completely whatever message you want to leave with your prospect.

Unlike mail-order selling, however, direct-mail advertising does not attempt to do the entire selling job, right down to and including asking for the order, except, of course in the case of direct-mail-order selling. Rather, any one piece of direct-mail advertising generally is intended to accomplish only one step in completion of the sale. Referring back to the list of common uses of direct mail, you will find that, while it usually suggests some sort of action—perhaps only passively as in showing willingness to listen to a salesman when he calls—it may actually be used merely to implant a certain idea in the mind of the recipient which calls for no action (for the present, at least) by him. Because direct-mail advertising usually is intended to *further* the sale, and because it is *not* intended to *complete* the sale by itself, the copy you write must be keyed to the purpose for which the mailing is intended—but *must not go beyond it.*

SALESMEN ARE HELPED BY DIRECT MAIL

Suppose that you had the problem once faced by the Simonds Abrasive Company, a Philadelphia abrasives manufacturer. The company's primary market was 33,000 concerns in the metal-working industries—foundries, steel mills, and mass-production metalworking plants such as the Detroit auto industry. Its secondary market covered a wide range of shops, plants, and trades which use grinding wheels for either production or maintenance.

This manufacturer's most economical method of distribution was through 2,000 industrial-supply distributors' salesmen. Distributors' salesmen in the past had turned in a large volume on a few items in the line, sold to a comparatively small number of large consumers. Simonds wanted to get the supply house salesmen to sell more grinding wheels. Only $500 additional sales annually by each of the 2,000 supply house salesmen would mean a million dollars a year additional business for Simonds. How to provide the spark needed to jolt these men into producing even this relatively small increase?

A direct-mail campaign was the solution decided upon. Simonds promotional campaign to industrial consumers was three-fold: business paper and direct-mail advertising and technical publicity in articles written by Simonds engineers for publication in trade papers. What better way to show supply house salesmen the way to increased sales than to merchandise the company's advertising and publicity—to show these men how the company's promotional activities were planned to help them in their jobs, to increase demand for the line, and to provide additional profit possibilities for them?

This was done in a series of five portfolios, sent not only to the supply houses, but personally and individually to each of the 2,000 salesmen (mailed directly to their home addresses) as well. Each mailing was planned to sell the salesmen on only one of the five ways in which the company's promotional efforts helped them sell, but each contained a statement of policy (the same in all five) that repeated the theme of the entire campaign, which might be quoted as "More sales because Simonds helps you sell":

> Simonds Abrasive Co. believes in the Mill Supply Distributor . . . in the service he provides industry . . . in the manner in which he operates.
>
> Our Distributors' salesmen are our salesmen as well. If they are to do a job for us it is our obligation to provide the selling information and sales tools that will make their success possible. That is the reason for sending you the enclosed information.
>
> In Grinding Wheels you have one of the most popular and attractive lines handled by Mill Supply Houses. Widespread use, frequent reordering and good profit margin—these features combine to make Simonds Abrasive a live-wire line for you.
>
> Remember—*Simonds* means top quality! In Grinding Wheels that means we take second place to no one. Our product is right—our service is right and—with your help—we mean to get the business.

Each successive portfolio contained, in a pouch, several examples of the type of promotion that was the subject of that mailing. The titles of the mailings—which were directly to the point in their knowing appeal to salesmen and, therefore, assured the attention and interest of that audience—were, in the order sent:

"Mailing to Your Prospects Helps You Sell"

"Advertising Helps You Sell"

"Trade Press Stories Help You Sell"

"Technical Information Helps You Sell"

"Factory Stock List Helps You Sell" (A stock list, brought up to date monthly, gives salesmen a knowledge of specifications and exact quantities in stock, thus providing accurate ordering and delivery information.)

Use strong copy in each mailing

See how the copy used in the letter (on a special campaign letterhead) accompanying one of these mailings, "Technical Information Helps You Sell," furthers one step in the sale of the company's entire promotional campaign to supply house salesmen:

The test of a good industrial supply salesman is the number of prospects he can develop into good customers—and the number of good customers he can build into regular repeat customers.

A major part of our sales effort is directed toward providing you with grinding wheel prospects in the form of sales leads and inquiries resulting from publication advertising, trade-press articles and direct mail. An even more important result of our advertising effort is the increasing Consumer Acceptance of Simonds Abrasive Co. being built up in the trade—which helps you add to your regular repeat customer list.

Supplementing such a broad program is the need to supply you with actual selling data—to give you the facts about Simonds Abrasive Wheels. The enclosed "Technical Data Sheets" do just that! Note the one on "General Purpose Grinding Wheels"—the most common and widespread type of wheel used—plain straight wheels—coarse, medium and fine—the most simple product we have to sell. Use this bulletin in your daily selling and add grinding wheels to your list of regularly sold items.

Remember sales persistence, combined with product knowledge, is the weapon to break down sales resistance.

Of course, you've noted that this letter reviews briefly the contents of the three previous mailings on direct-mail and publication advertising and trade-press articles. But note, too, how this review leads up to and ties in with the subject of the current mailing, the technical information bulletins, wrapping all these sales helps into one package that carries out the main theme of the entire campaign, "More sales because Simonds helps you sell." Actually then, this mailing has really advanced only one step in the sale of this theme to its audience. It has not diluted its emphasis by incorporating more than *one new idea* in the message.

Avoid giving whole story in all mailings

There is another reason, however, for not "telling all" in many direct-mail pieces, even though they may not be one of a series or campaign, but merely a single mailing. Imagine that you are writing a "one-shot" direct-mail piece for the women's better coat department of a retail store. You are announcing to your store's charge customers, in advance of your general newspaper advertisement, the arrival of a special group of luxuriously fur-trimmed cloth coats, and you are urging the customers' advance inspection of these models for a complete selection.

Your purpose is to get women into the department. Do you tell them, then, all about the coat? Do you list all the colors available? Every kind of fur in the group? Do you illustrate every style? You do not! If you say that dove gray, white wine, forest green, plum nectar, and cinnamon brown, as well as black, are available, some of your prospects won't bother to come in because they may *think* they want a pearl gray, champagne, emerald green, royal purple, or chocolate brown coat. If you say that the fur trims are mink, beaver, and silver fox, some of your potential customers will stay away because they've had in mind squirrel, persian lamb, or blue fox.

If you list draped or boxy styles, some women will avoid your showing because they've been thinking of a swing-back or princess style. Because you *know* that once a woman tries on a beaver-trimmed, dove gray, draped coat she may like it just as well as a persian-trimmed, pearl gray, swing-skirt model, you say, instead, something like "All the season's

BANKERS TRUST
***Photo* BankAmericard®**
P.O. Box 1250, New York, N.Y. 10019

JACK J. BARON
ASSISTANT VICE PRESIDENT

Mr. Robert H. Jurick
1257 Boxwood Drive East
Hewlett Harbor, New York 11557

Dear Mr. Jurick:

It's time to renew yourself.

Your Photo BankAmericard will expire very soon. Of course, we will issue a new card, but we'll need a new picture of you. Times change. Styles change. And so do people. We want your BankAmericard photo to reflect today's you, rather than the you when your present BankAmericard was issued. That way you'll be as current and fraudproof as possible.

Getting your new photo is simple. Just check the enclosed directory and visit any of our conveniently located branches in New York City, Nassau and Westchester counties. (You can even visit selected branches of our affiliate banks in Suffolk and Rockland counties if that would be easier).

No other major credit card in the New York area offers the safety and convenience of a full-color photo. Your Photo BankAmericard is honored in over one million retail, service, and professional establishments throughout the world. In addition, by just showing your card and your face to our tellers, you can cash your personal Bankers Trust checks up to $100 in any of our offices throughout the greater New York area. And remember, with a Photo BankAmericard, you are not liable if the card is lost or stolen.

It's important that you have your picture taken before March 31 so we'll have enough time to process your card and get it to you before the one you now have expires. If it's impossible for you to come in by March 31, we'll issue you a regular BankAmericard that you can use until you are able to get your photo taken.

But we're sure you don't want to be without your photo, so try to come in before March 31. You'll find the most convenient and safest BankAmericard at Bankers Trust.

Sincerely,

Jack Baron

P.S. Imagine someone trying to forge your face!

Bankers Trust
BANKAMERICARD
Mona Lisa

® SERVICE MARKS OWNED AND LICENSED BY BANKAMERICA SERVICE CORP.

Fig. 13-1

Computerized direct mail letter.

Nowadays, with direct mail letters going out to millions the computer has come into its own. The example shown here was very successful.

highest-fashion colors and most-wanted furs, in a range of next year's full or fitted styles flattering to every figure."

You must give certain facts

Of course, there are some things you will *want* to tell your prospects. Sizes, for example. There's no point in making your size-12 or size-44 customer angry at you for wasting her time to come downtown when your size range begins with 14 and ends at 40. In most cases, you'll list the range of prices, too, for much the same reason. If your buyer is a smart merchandiser, he will have attempted to include at least one model in the group that can be priced at a comparatively low figure, perhaps because of a lesser amount of fur used (although probably not a cheaper fur) on a coat which, because of its styling or material, seems otherwise to "belong" with the more expensive models.

Thus, instead of having to admit to a limited price range, say of $175 to 249.50, you may be able to claim that "these exclusive creations begin at the tiny price of $125, while you'll hardly believe we could sell the most luxurious models for their modest price of only $249.50."

Save something for the next step

In all direct-mail advertising that contemplates an eventual sale, remember this strategy —tell enough to interest the prospect—and to keep him interested until you have the opportunity to complete the sale—but don't tell "your all" or you may never have the chance to make that sale. This strategy applies as well to a series of related, progressive-step mailings as it does to a single one—don't weaken your next mailing by telling *its* story before the strategic time. It applies even when your anticipated sale, following a direct-mail campaign, will be requested by mail as well—a direct-mail order.

When you don't follow this strategy—when you rob your following mailings of their impact by anticipating their parts of the sales story early in the campaign—your prospects either become confused by the size and scope of the early bombardment, or become tired and bored with the succession of "old stuff" which comes in subsequent mailings. In either case you have almost certainly lost the sale.

The following letter demonstrates the way to interest without giving away your whole story. Yet the story is complete enough to do its job.

Dear Madam,

Beginning Wednesday, February 18, through February 20, there will be a three day selling of fresh-out-of-the-box CASUAL-TYPE, TAILORED DRESSES in our Sports Room . . . all priced attractively in three groups:

$20.95, $22.95, $25.95

These dresses, by a renowned California maker, are famed for their WONDERFUL FABRICS, FIT AND WORKMANSHIP. Famed, too, for their very fetching, very FLATTERING WAYS. And what better time to start planning your spring wardrobe than now—when you may choose from variety of styles and fabrics.

See these RAYON CREPES in plain weaves, textured weaves, sheer weaves. They're all here—in exciting spring shades, ranging from pastels to brights to basic navy. Do come in at your very first opportunity . . . choose yours from Misses' sizes, 12 to 20 and Women's sizes, 14½ to 22½. And remember—you'll find them in our SPORTS ROOM DRESSES, Sixth Floor, Middle.

Sincerely,

Mailings should be self-sufficient

One caution you should remember, however, in applying this strategy: In any direct-mail campaign—despite the fact that one major impression is all you can expect to get across in any one mailing—each mailing should be complete in itself. It should not be dependent either upon earlier pieces or pieces yet to come. Even though you cannot, of course, tell all of a multi-part story in a single mailing, you must stress adequately the feature chosen for emphasis in that mailing. Know exactly what purpose you want each piece to accomplish, then write your copy to achieve that purpose—and nothing more.

WAYS TO MAKE REMOTE-CONTROL SELLING EFFECTIVE

No book on copywriting—this one included —can hope to anticipate every problem of remote-control sales writing you may be called upon to tackle, in either mail-order selling or direct-mail advertising. A few general pointers, however, not yet emphasized may be valuable to you if followed in planning and writing any remote-control selling job. Only a brief summary of these points will be attempted—you can easily understand them and appreciate their importance without detailed examples being cited. If you like, however, you can readily imagine applications of them as you read.

1. *Keep old customers sold.* One of the most important of these pointers is to remember that the backbone of any permanent success in selling is the retention of the good will and the business of old customers. Much of the responsibility for keeping old customers as satisfied current customers is not the prov-

ince of the advertising copywriter, but rather that of direct salesmen, sales and credit correspondents, and others. At the same time, nevertheless, the firm's advertising also has a share of the job to do in being so planned and written that the needs and wants of the old customers are not sacrificed in the attempt to win new customers as well.

Advertising also frequently plays a big part in the maintenance of friendly relations between seller and customer. During periods of raw material shortages, transportation delays, and other difficulties—even labor troubles—advertising of every sort, including both mail-order and direct-mail, can and does help out in the big job of explaining the situation to customers and retaining their business.

Many firms, both retail and industrial, have adopted the sending of purely good-will direct-mail letters to their entire list of customers periodically. These are sent annually at the New Year or at other appropriate intervals and times—thanking each customer for his business, hoping for uninterrupted "friendship," possibly pledging increased service and improved products, and perhaps requesting ideas for still better fulfillment of the customer's needs. And sometimes just such a simple mailing will make a customer realize that here indeed is a firm interested in *him* and worthy of his continued business.

2. *Use the YOU point of view.* Look at any magazine or newspaper, listen to an evening of radio commercials—with the eye and ear of the *consumer,* the prospect. Which advertisements or commercials have the most appeal? Ten-to-one they're those that say *You!* If this is important, then, in the appeal of general advertising, think how much more vital it is in both branches of remote-control selling.

In mail-order selling it is vital because it is your *only* contact with the prospect, your *only* chance to present your product so that he will want to make a purchase. In direct-mail advertising, it *may* not be your only contact, but at least it is usually your introductory one—the one that must start your prospect thinking favorably about your product.

How best to inspire that favorable thought? By shouting I—me—mine—we—us—our . . . the biggest—the best—the oldest—the newest? Or simply by saying or implying *you* and *your?* You scarcely need bother to answer. Just as *you* as a consumer want to know what the product will do for *you* or how *you* can use it to *your* advantage, so does your prospect want to know what your product will do for him.

It is not important to tell your prospect that your firm is, for example, the oldest or the largest in your field. Your firm's age or size might give your prospect confidence in either the integrity of your house, or the dependability of your other selling claims. But even such a claim can be phrased in *"you"* language, as in: "Your assurance of a quality product is Blank Company's 53 years of building Dinguses for over 81% of the Whatsis Industry." That's written from the reader's—not the seller's—point of view . . . a requisite of good selling copy.

3. *Be truthful and believable.* You may think it superfluous to stress "truth in advertising" any more in the creation of remote-control selling than in that of other types of advertising. You need only to think of the success of the great merchandising houses—mail order in particular, such as Sears and Ward's—as ample proof of the fact that truthfulness pays, and pays well. A close relative of truth is believability. Some mail-order offers seem actually to ignore both these qualities, depending for both their attention value

and selling impact upon startling, even fantastic, claims. These may trap the gullible once, perhaps twice, but no business lasts long when its sales depend upon such a weak foundation.

Not infrequently you may be able to make an advertising claim in all *truth,* but lacking in *believability.* If so, *don't make it,* for your prospects will believe you are not telling the truth anyway. Don't make it, that is, unless, as soon as you do, you back it up with proof, *believable* proof, that can remove any taint of even suspected untruth. This is particularly true of a new product and its advertising, which the buying public always examines with critical suspicion if not outright distrust. Particularly in selling by mail, then, must you create an aura of truthfulness and believability, for oftentimes to your potential customers your product is a new one, because they've never had the chance to see it before.

Some firms even follow the practice—and successfully too—of *underselling* their products on the proved theory that the customer who finds his purchase superior to its claims will be an eager repeat customer, the ideal situation for any merchandiser who plans to *stay* in business. At any rate, avoid exaggeration. "Gushing" over your product only tends to make the reader think you have nothing more concrete than a rush of overworked adjectives to offer him. Statements needn't be weak or unenthusiastic—you can state a simple fact in a way that comes out strong. Stick to the truth, avoid exaggeration, and make your claims believable.

SUGGESTIONS FOR EFFECTIVE COPY

1. Keep your writing style simple and direct. Split up involved sentences. Use words your audience would use if talking about your product, or at least words it will understand. These are usually short words—although where technical language adds to copy effectiveness, don't hesitate to use it.

2. Make your subheads work. Make them attention-getters. Use a lot of them to break up your copy into easily digested ideas. Make them helpful to the reader in grasping quickly the thought you want him to get.

3. Use your two strongest statements at the start and finish of your selling "talk"—the first to arouse attention and interest, the latter to spur whatever action it is that you will ask the prospect to take.

4. Repeat the name of your product frequently—ignoring the niceties of English composition (if that's really how you feel about it) to achieve the repetition which brings with it retention and recognition of that name.

5. Phrase the information in your copy so that it is helpful to the prospect. If it contains more than academic information (which he'll soon forget), but information that is of some real or potential value to him, he'll remember it—and your product—better and longer.

6. Help the feeling infiltrate your copy that your product is the result of exceptionally fine engineering and manufacturing care, from a house of unquestionable integrity. Keep this feeling casual, not heavily stressed, but *don't* be casual about seeing that it's there.

7. Just as with any copy you write, find out from those who know (*before* you start to write) everything you can discover about the product that makes it unique or outstanding in its field. Then, as you plan and write your copy, feature that "different" quality strongly so that your prospects cannot fail to get it.

8. If you have more than one quality or grade of a particular product, you will probably want to "sell up"—to try to interest your prospect in the better item for his own greater

Future Homeowners Club©

a division of t.a. best, inc. □ 42 east genesee street, skaneateles, new york 13152 □ phone (315) 685-5778

Mr. John Doe
7127 Main Street
Anytown, USA 00000

Dear Mr. Doe:

If you've been wanting to buy a home or condominium of your own, but have found it hard to save enough money for a down payment, join the Club!

The Future Homeowners Club is an exclusive service designed to provide a sure, steady way to save for a down payment. It's especially suited for:

. Young married couples planning a family.
. Young singles (men or women) tired of paying rent.
. Married people over 40 who don't own their own homes.

Here's how it works:

You set your down-payment goal, based on income and the kind of home you'd like to build or buy. You can draw on our experience in housing, budgets, and financing to set a realistic goal. We'll prepare a coupon book to help you keep on schedule and to give you a record of your progress. You make regular payment-deposits at whatever interval you choose--monthly, weekly, or every two weeks.

Your Club account will earn a full five percent interest-dividend, compounded daily, from day of deposit until you close your Club.

When you've reached your down-payment goal, we'll make a free appraisal of the property you select, and we can even provide the mortgage under our Assured Mortgage Plan.

Should you move away, or discontinue your Club for any reason, the money you've saved is yours without penalty. In fact, you'll earn interest-dividends until the day of withdrawal. Furthermore, if you move out of our area, we'll be glad to write to a bank in your new area requesting that you be given special consideration for a mortgage.

Owning a home is an exciting idea. Why not start now to make it a reality? Join our Future Homeowners Club and you'll be a present homeowner sooner than you think.

Cordially,

J. J. Smith
President

JJS/mvb

Fig. 13-2

Direct mail letter.

This letter demonstrates all the points recommended to make a letter inviting physically:
a. Short opening paragraph.
b. No paragraph of more than 8 lines.
c. Varied paragraph lengths
d. Type masses broken up.
e. Short closing paragraph.

satisfaction and your greater profit. This situation may occur in any type of remote-control selling, but most likely in mail-order.

The larger mail-order houses have developed a most effective means of trading up their prospects by use of a "good-better-best" technique on all lines where a choice of quality is offered. For some time, they actually tagged many of their illustrations or item headlines with Good, Better, or Best, whichever was appropriate, but when this handling became confusing because of the addition of a fourth, or even a fifth, price line, a refinement of the technique evolved. Now, for the most part, Good, Better, or Best is implied. Illustrations may tell part of the difference between similar items pictorially.

Headlines help too in pointing out differences, and display copy will feature, say, three selling points for a "good" item, five for a "better" one, and perhaps seven for the "best." Body copy (plus price!) completes the comparison. The copy for a "better" product, for example, perhaps even says in so many words that this item includes every feature of item number so-and-so at the left (the "good" item)—*plus* thus-and-so in addition. Selling up to the next bracket, the mail-order houses have found, can be well worth while.

9. Finally, if any other advertising is being used for your product, tie up your efforts to it. Perhaps you are selling a nationally advertised product by mail order in a territory where retail distribution is not feasible or has not been established. Or perhaps your direct-mail campaign is supplementing another campaign in trade journals. In either case, you'll want to take every advantage of the "free ride" this other advertising gives you and your efforts.

Pick up and feature the slogan it uses, its outstanding illustrative treatment, its unique trademark or trade name. If your direct-mail literature is designed to answer requests for "further information" produced by other media, tie your theme and copy in with the advertisement or campaign that inspired the requests. In effect, this again is repetition—so important in establishing your name and position in your chosen market.

THINK OF THE PHYSICAL ASPECTS

Since direct mail takes such a myriad of forms, there is no possibility to discuss the physical aspects of all of them. Instead, we will consider two of the most common types—the letter and the folder.

Physical appearance is of great importance to mailings because the appearance causes the first reaction on the part of the prospect. He may be discouraged in that initial glance to the point where he refuses to go on. Here are some suggestions for attracting him in that first glance.

Letters

There are general rules applying to sales letters. There are many variations possible but what you read here, if applied, can help you avoid some of the great faults of direct mail letters—physically speaking, and quite apart from writing technique. For purpose of this discussion, we will assume that we are talking about one-page letters and that we are using block form in which the type is flush left with no indentations for paragraphs.

- *Short opening paragraph.* Don't smother your reader with the first paragraph. Limit it to a maximum of four lines, and it can be shorter.
- *No paragraph longer than eight lines.* When a paragraph is longer than eight lines, the sales points tend to become buried. Furthermore, the sight of long paragraphs has a depressing effect on the reader—the kind of feeling he had when he was faced with long, laborious paragraphs in his school textbooks. A textbook writer can get away with this because the student *has* to read a textbook; a prospect does *not* have to read a sales letter.
- *Paragraph length varied.* A letter with all paragraphs the same length looks dull and monotonous. This observation applies whether the paragraphs are all long or all short. It is easy to vary paragraph length. Do it. Occasionally, you might want to use a paragraph of a single line, or just several words. This will make your letter more interesting.
- *Type masses broken up.* Why daunt the reader with a whole page of solid, unbroken type? One way to open up the letter invitingly is to use the occasional one-line paragraph already mentioned. Another effective method is to set off important material by indenting it and giving it space above and below. As an example, suppose you want to give a name and address in the letter. The preceding line might read: "When you're in Parkersburg be sure to visit:

  John G. Smelzer
  Smelzer Pottery Company
  18 W. Elizabeth Street

The centering of the name and address creates a pleasing open effect in the letter and focusses the reader's attention on the information.

The same technique can be used when you have several points to make. Supposing you are selling a typewriter. You say: "Consider these useful features:

1. Operates electrically or manually.
2. Has a feather touch.
3. Can be carried easily—very portable.
4. Switching ribbons is simple.
5. Includes all features of standard office typewriter."

Once more, you have opened up your letter and you have centered the reader's attention on important material.

- *Short closing paragraph.* You've said what you had to say, so end quickly. Three or four lines should be sufficient to end any letter.

Folders

One of the most frequently-used mailing pieces is the four-page folder that fits as an insert into a No. 10 envelope. It is used also as a counter piece in establishments from hardware stores, drug stores, and plumbing shops, to banks. Considering the folder page by page, here are some suggestions for physical attractiveness.

Page 1: Use a strong headline physically to catch the reader's attention. An attractive illustration is desirable accompanied by a short copy block. Save the long copy for the inside pages. In many cases, it is desirable to use some technique to create enough curiosity to impel the reader to turn to the inside pages. Your headline might do this as: See the 10 ways this superb tool can save you time and money. Or at the bottom of the page, an arrow can point to the inside pages and an accompanying copy line says: Look inside for profitable details. In short, literally force readers to turn from page 1 to pages 2 and 3.

Page 2 and 3: Treat these pages as one. By so doing, you can use a strong headline that spreads across the two pages and you can use a big, dominant illustration that takes up part of each page. This combination of strong head and illustration will draw the reader's gaze and create a vitality missing if each page is treated separately.

In order to create excitement for these pages, use selling subheads liberally over the copy blocks. If small illustrations are used, along with the dominant illustration, give each a caption. Carry the reader through the pages by directing his reading and by infusing the section with vigor.

Page 4: (back page) Sometimes advertisers leave this space blank. This is a grievous mistake since the back page of folders receives good readership. Treat the back page pretty much as you do the front page with an omission, of course, of any urging to turn the page. Sometimes the back page is a good place to put a guarantee, a special offer, a listing of important points. Make it just as attractive as the front page since often readers look first at the first page, flip the folder over to the back page and then, if sufficiently interested, turn to the inside pages. Make the back page worth looking at.

14

Writing Copy for Business And Agriculture

Discussion to this point has been concerned largely with "consumer" advertising—advertising written for insertion in publications selected to reach persons who will buy and use (consume) the product. You have studied copy written to sell soap and cereal, cars and coats, insurance and cosmetics—to prospects you hope will go to retail stores to buy them for their personal use.

There is another tremendously large and important field of creative advertising which the general public never or rarely sees, and with which many people may be completely unfamiliar. Yet this type of advertising normally takes a great proportion of a copywriter's time and talent, especially copywriters in advertising agencies and in the advertising departments of large manufacturing firms.

Known as "business-paper" advertising, it includes trade, industrial, and professional advertising. It appears not in general magazines, newspapers, on billboards, the radio or TV, but in business papers and business magazines. Almost every field of American enterprise today has one or more of these business-paper publications serving it—a magazine or newspaper that is published periodically and contains news and information of particular interest to those in the industry it represents.

Thus, the *Bakery Production and Marketing* is an expertly managed and edited magazine, circulated to individuals who are vitally concerned with the baking industry. Bakers, large and small, millers, wholesale and retail grocers, and others are familiar with its interesting articles, stories, news items, and advertising, as they are with those of other business-paper publications servicing the bakery industry. *Iron Age* is a famous business paper of the industrial type for the steel industry; *Progressive Grocer* is one of the many business papers of the trade type which serves the grocery field. *Men's Wear* goes to the clothing industry and *American Funeral Director* is read by most of the country's morticians.

HOW IS BUSINESS COPY DIFFERENT?

Now, naturally, all these publications do not stay in business by their subscription income alone, any more than do other magazines and newspapers. They contain a great deal of advertising, often featuring *products* that you see advertised elsewhere in consumer copy. But the copy story behind that advertising may be different—in appeal, in technique, and in intended results.

(1) Advertising in business publications of the *trade* type is designed *to gain the selling and merchandising support of the dealers who offer your product for resale.*

When you write this kind of copy remember to follow the 3-P's formula—product, promotion, profit. Emphasis on one, two, or all three of these elements is characteristic of all trade advertising.

(2) Advertisements appearing in business papers of the *industrial* type enable one industry to advertise to another industry, usually about items that can be used for helping production. Thus the makers of a punch press advertise to the manufacturers of tractor parts and tell the latter how the punch press can help in their production. In contrast to trade-paper advertising, industrial-paper advertising is not concerned with the factor of resale.

(3) The third classification, *professional* advertising, which appears in such publications as *Journal of the American Medical Association, Dental Digest,* and *American Journal of Orthodontics and Oral Surgery,* is aimed at professional people who can do two things for you. They can use your product. They can *recommend* the use of your product.

Fig. 14-1

Trade advertisement with emphasis on display unit.

The importance of good merchandise display is stressed in this advertisement, and many others, in *Hardware Retailing* and other trade magazines.

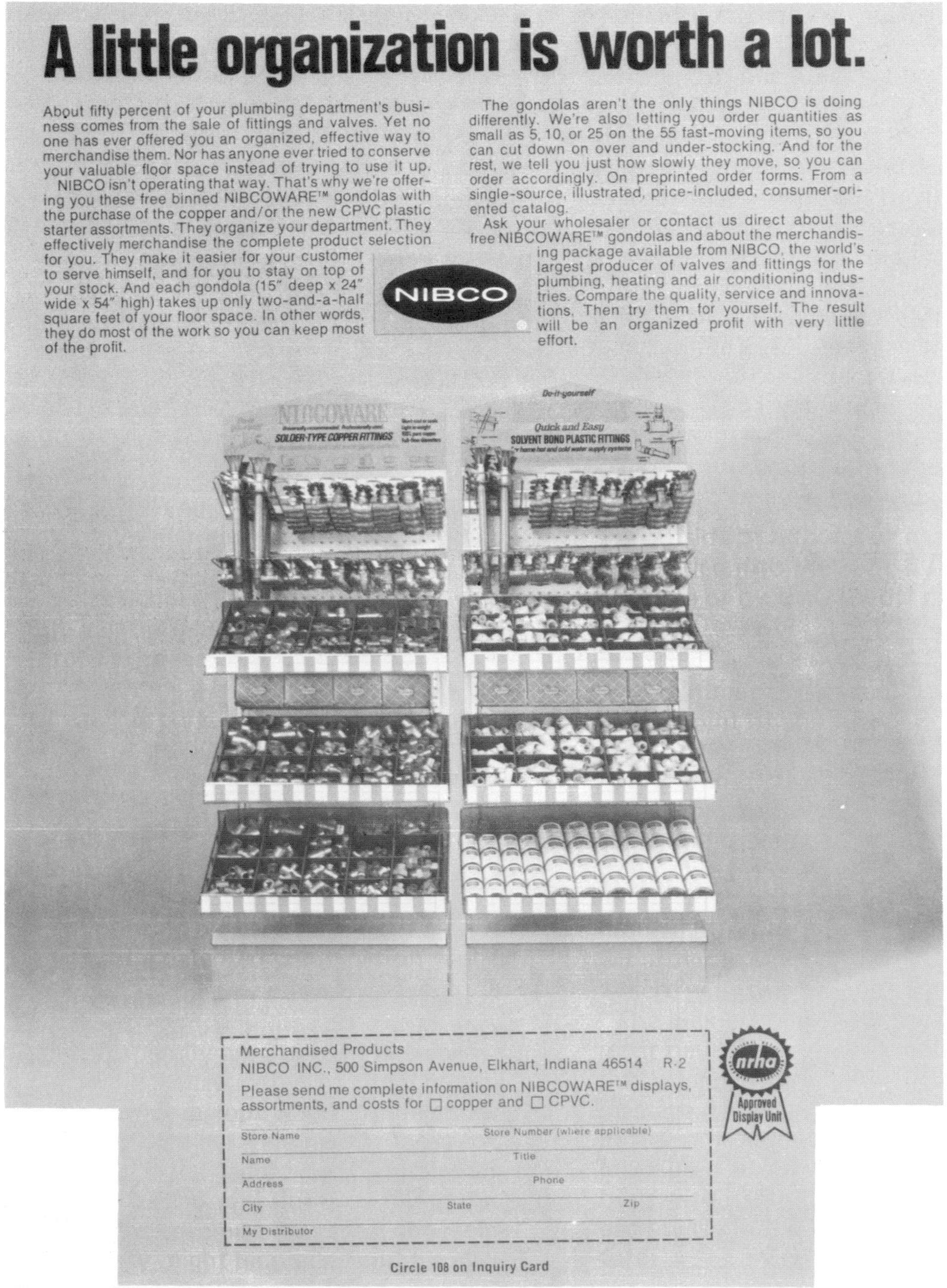
A little organization is worth a lot.
About fifty percent of your plumbing department's business comes from the sale of fittings and valves. Yet no one has ever offered you an organized, effective way to merchandise them. Nor has anyone ever tried to conserve your valuable floor space instead of trying to use it up.
NIBCO isn't operating that way. That's why we're offering you these free binned NIBCOWARE™ gondolas with the purchase of the copper and/or the new CPVC plastic starter assortments. They organize your department. They effectively merchandise the complete product selection for you. They make it easier for your customer to serve himself, and for you to stay on top of your stock. And each gondola (15" deep x 24" wide x 54" high) takes up only two-and-a-half square feet of your floor space. In other words, they do most of the work so you can keep most of the profit.
The gondolas aren't the only things NIBCO is doing differently. We're also letting you order quantities as small as 5, 10, or 25 on the 55 fast-moving items, so you can cut down on over and under-stocking. And for the rest, we tell you just how slowly they move, so you can order accordingly. On preprinted order forms. From a single-source, illustrated, price-included, consumer-oriented catalog.
Ask your wholesaler or contact us direct about the free NIBCOWARE™ gondolas and about the merchandising package available from NIBCO, the world's largest producer of valves and fittings for the plumbing, heating and air conditioning industries. Compare the quality, service and innovations. Then try them for yourself. The result will be an organized profit with very little effort.
NIBCO
Do-it-yourself
Quick and Easy
SOLVENT BOND PLASTIC FITTINGS
SOLDER-TYPE COPPER FITTINGS
Merchandised Products
NIBCO INC., 500 Simpson Avenue, Elkhart, Indiana 46514 R-2
Please send me complete information on NIBCOWARE™ displays, assortments, and costs for ☐ copper and ☐ CPVC.
Store Name
Store Number (where applicable)
Name
Title
Address
Phone
City
State
Zip
My Distributor
nrha
Approved Display Unit
Circle 108 on Inquiry Card

Trade and consumer advertising sometimes alike

Sometimes *trade* advertising and consumer advertising aren't much different. In *Progressive Grocer,* for example, you will find many advertisements offering products used by the dealers themselves, such as paper bags, twine, and business machines. This, of course, is consumer advertising even though it appears in trade publications. Its primary interest to them, however, is a product or service *as a source of profit,* because these people are in business to make money—to earn a livelihood.

Although the beautiful new color of a transparent comb, for example, may be advertised in the *Ladies' Home Journal* in terms of its vividness, glowing good looks, and newness, advertising of the same comb in the trade papers that reach drug and department stores would also tell of the new color idea, but would interpret it in terms of why more people will want and buy the comb; how well it is advertised to create a demand; how store tests showed sales went up quickly when displayed —and increased all other comb sales, as well. And the advertisement might end "If you haven't seen them. . . if our salesman hasn't been around and told you the mighty pretty

Colorite leads in the development of new garden hose.
Because Bob Lustgarten cares.
You can't be on the leading edge of new-product development without knowing what your customers need and want. And that's one area where Bob Lustgarten shines. He's Colorite's Vice President/ Sales. With a vast knowledge of the garden hose industry. He knows precisely what garden-hose buyers want and he's been a guiding force behind the development of exciting new products at Colorite.
We're very proud of Bob. He's one of the many experienced people who work with the most-modern facilities in Colorite's 330,000 sq. ft. plant. His market sensitivity is one very good reason why Colorite has been a consistent leader in bringing out new products. An even better reason is that Bob and his 229 Colorite co-workers care enough to keep searching for better ways to make and deliver garden hose.
Made and shipped by experienced craftsmen who care.
COLORFLEX
COLORITE
PLASTICS COMPANY
101 Railroad Avenue, Ridgefield, New Jersey 07657
© 1972 Dart Industries, Inc. All rights reserved.

Fig. 14-2

Institutional trade advertisement.

Featuring people in institutional advertisements humanizes such advertisements. In this case, the company has carried on the campaign with success by stressing the theme of "experienced craftsmen who care."

profit story we've got to tell, let us know—but quick. Better write or wire right now."

No fancy writing there. Just a straight appeal for action. But don't misunderstand. Trade advertisements can be dramatic, and interesting—and you can employ all the basic essentials of effective copywriting already mentioned in previous chapters. First of all—know what you're writing about, and what you want an advertisement or series of advertisements to accomplish.

Trade advertising, as previously said, is generally confined to products or services handled by wholesalers or retailers for re-sale. Some exceptions might be the advertising of flour and baker's supplies in bakery trade publications—read by wholesale and retail bakers. Another exception is the advertising of certain equipment such as meat cases, frozen food cases, and paper bags, in grocery and meat trade papers. These products while not purchased for re-sale, can very properly be advertised in trade papers as a type of consumer advertising.

Products advertised to the trade are often nationally advertised through magazines, newspapers, radio and TV. When this is true, you may often be called upon to tell the trade

Fig. 14-3

Trade advertisement.

This hard-hitting spread stresses the 3-P's of Product—Promotion—Profit.

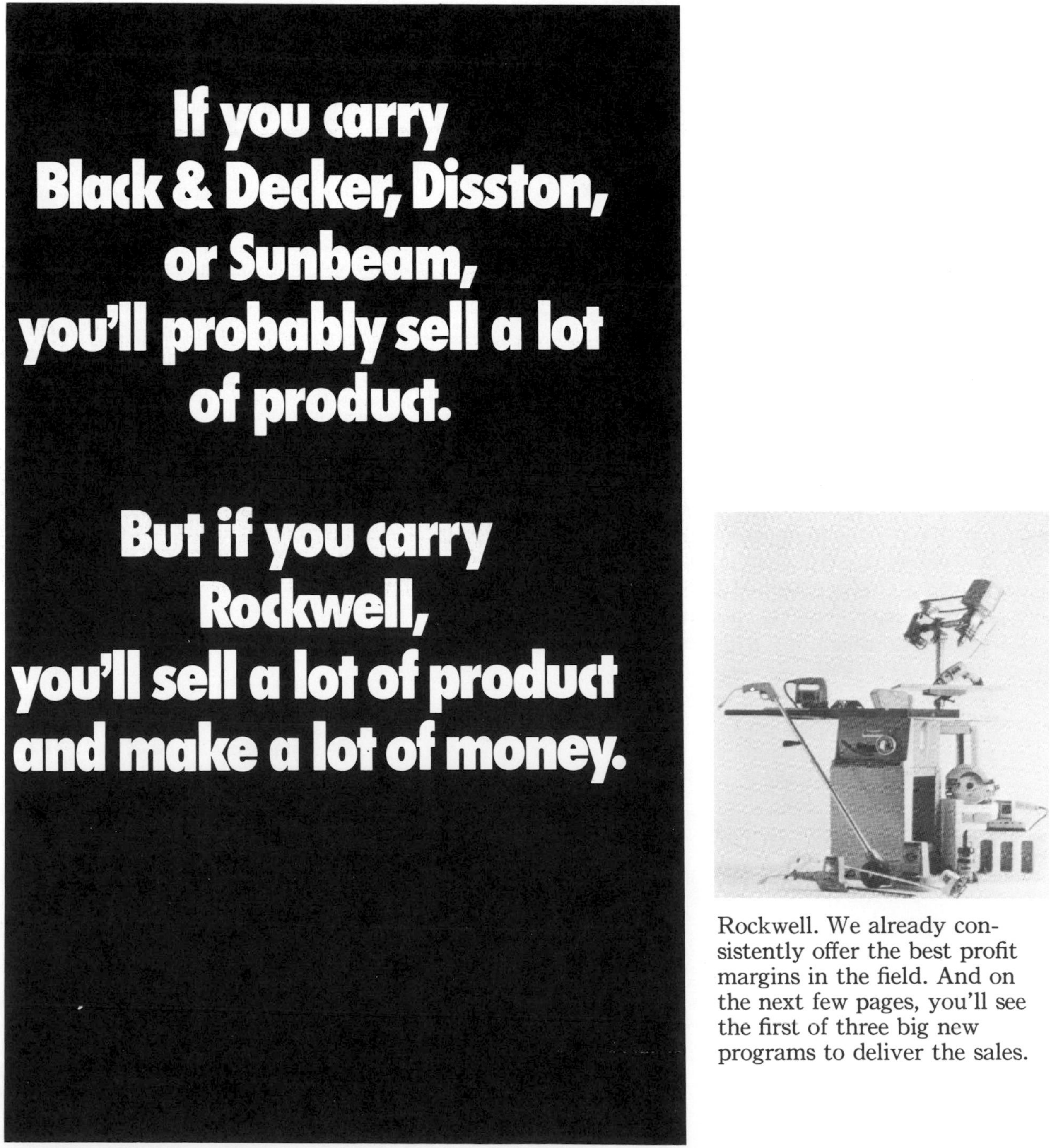
If you carry
Black & Decker, Disston,
or Sunbeam,
you'll probably sell a lot
of product.
But if you carry
Rockwell,
you'll sell a lot of product
and make a lot of money.
Rockwell. We already consistently offer the best profit margins in the field. And on the next few pages, you'll see the first of three big new programs to deliver the sales.

the story of these consumer advertising programs, so dealers will know and appreciate the promotional help the manufacturer is giving through the national consumer campaign.

BUSINESS PUBLICATION ADVERTISING

There's no need for further distinctions between the types of business advertising, since that is not the purpose of this book. To avoid confusion, consider the term business advertising as referring to that kind of advertising that appears in business *publications*—trade, industrial, or professional. Direct-mail, house organs, films, specialized presentations—all aimed at "the trade"—will be eliminated in this discussion. For the time being, so will "collateral"—all the display or point-of-sale materials, training manuals, merchandising presentations, and portfolios—which copywriters are called upon to produce and which usually come under the heading of "trade."

Business advertising is essentially a supplementary selling force that strengthens and meshes with the merchandising and selling program of the advertiser.

Here are *some facts to remember* about business advertising. They lurk behind some of the "do's and don'ts" you'll be asked to observe when you write business copy. Some you'll be told about—frankly. Others will never be seen—but they'll be in the mind of someone who has the authority to set the general pattern of the advertising to be done.

Business publication space rates are low compared with consumer media. Thus, many so-called advertising people—many copywriters—don't consider business advertising "very important." Some agencies don't consider it worth while to hire competent writers skilled in business copy because space commissions aren't high enough. Yet there are notable exceptions to this. One large agency, for example, has a full-fledged vice-president in charge of their business publication operations.

Some advertisers and agencies feel that "consumer advertisements alone can do the job"—that specially designed advertising to trade or industry is not necessary. Such thinking can lead to unsound and wasteful advertising, especially in trade advertising. Any retailer who knows his business can switch customers from one product to another. He can favor one product by displaying it at eye-level on his shelves and putting others down low where women have to stoop to get them. Consumer advertising can and should be supported with a good, heavy program for the trade in most cases.

GETTING RESULTS IN BUSINESS ADVERTISING

"Clever" slogans or gimmicks alone in small space will rarely pay off as business advertising technique. Such thoughts as "Beans by Glick always Click," run time after time in trade advertisements with the assumption that "we're doing a job with the trade," and do not offer a retailer any reason at all for featuring Glick's beans. Tell the trade how it can *make* money with Glick's beans—how *repeat sales* steadily grow—how to display the product more successfully. Tell the retailers what and how store tests show above-normal turnover and shelf-velocity. Isn't that what a good, sharp salesman would ordinarily tell a dealer? He certainly wouldn't come in time after time just chanting "Beans by Glick always Click."

Use as much space as possible. Only then can you give a certain amount of prestige and importance to the product. You *need* that space for fair readership and for a complete sales talk.

Many advertisers and agencies will often turn out poorly produced business advertisements on the grounds that "the budget won't stand better stuff." This is faulty thinking when you have something important enough to say—or when the time is critical (such as during the announcement of a new product, a price slash, and so forth). Get in there and pitch for more color, better art, or more space in your business-paper advertising.

Why does all this concern a writer? Because too often a writer is judged by what *some* advertisements may do. If you don't go on record beforehand with your ideas, you *could* be too handy when the blame for a "flop" is ready for awarding. Look at it this way:

Which is more important—the estimated cost of the advertisements or campaign, or the job to be done? If it's the job, then be sure it can succeed—and that may require much better art and production than were first figured on.

How long should business copy be? Like consumer copy it should be long enough to get over the message—and no longer. That could be 40 words—or 400. Every advertisement must be judged individually. Business advertisements will usually require more copy than consumer advertisements since you will be much more concerned with explanatory

Fig. 14-4

Trade advertisement.

This straightforward advertisement clearly emphasizes two of the 3-P's—product and profit.

AMES: WHO ELSE WOULD MAKE 'EM THIS GOOD.
And sell 'em at these prices.
This year, stretch Hardware Week into more sales and profit with the Ames "GREAT OUTDOORS DAYS" Promotion. Stock these Ames tools during Hardware Week.
SAVE 13%
Ames 19-200 (LR26) Greensweeper Leaf Rake; Dealer Regular $2.67. Special $2.31. Retail Regular $4.00. Special $3.19.
SAVE 12%
Plumb 11-406 (FA16) and 11-419 (FA16R) Hammer; Dealer Regular $4.67. Special $4.12. Retail Regular $7.00. Special $5.49.
PLUMB
SAVE 12%
Ames 23-021 (LS22) Lopper; Dealer Regular $4.00. Special $3.56. Retail Regular $6.00. Special $4.75.
AMES
THE BEST BUY IN LAWN RAKES
GREENSWEEPER
"Better than steel with the bamboo feel"
SAVE 12%
Ames 15-630 (403) Dig-Ezy; Dealer Regular $3.47. Special $3.03. Retail Regular $5.20. Special $3.99.
SAVE 12%
Ames 23-040 (GS40) Grass Shear; Dealer Regular $2.93. Special $2.56. Retail Regular $4.40. Special $3.49.
For more information, write AMES Division McDonough Co., Box 1774, Parkersburg, W. Va. 26101
*DuPont's registered trademark.
® Registered trademark of the McDonough Co.
AMES®
SINCE 1774
FORM NO. 24-844

material. Also, your profit-minded readers are more willing to wade through technical material if they see value in what you say.

WRITING TRADE ADVERTISEMENTS

In the chapter on headline writing you read this:

YOUR WHOLE WEEK'S WASH DONE IN
30 MINUTES . . . WHILE YOU SHOP!

Obviously, that's a headline for an automatic washer. Assume that it is the headline of an advertisement in a campaign ready to break in national consumer publications. Support for this consumer advertising will be provided through a special campaign to reach the trade. Electric appliance stores, department stores, and a few special outlets will be the "trade" in this case.

The people who run these stores handle automatic washers for resale. To them the only value of the claim "Your whole week's wash done in 30 minutes . . . while you shop" lies in the fact that this is a powerful weapon to use in their sales talks. It helps them sell more "X" washers.

Consider the foregoing heading. The thought expressed in it will probably be the basis for other consumer advertisements, and

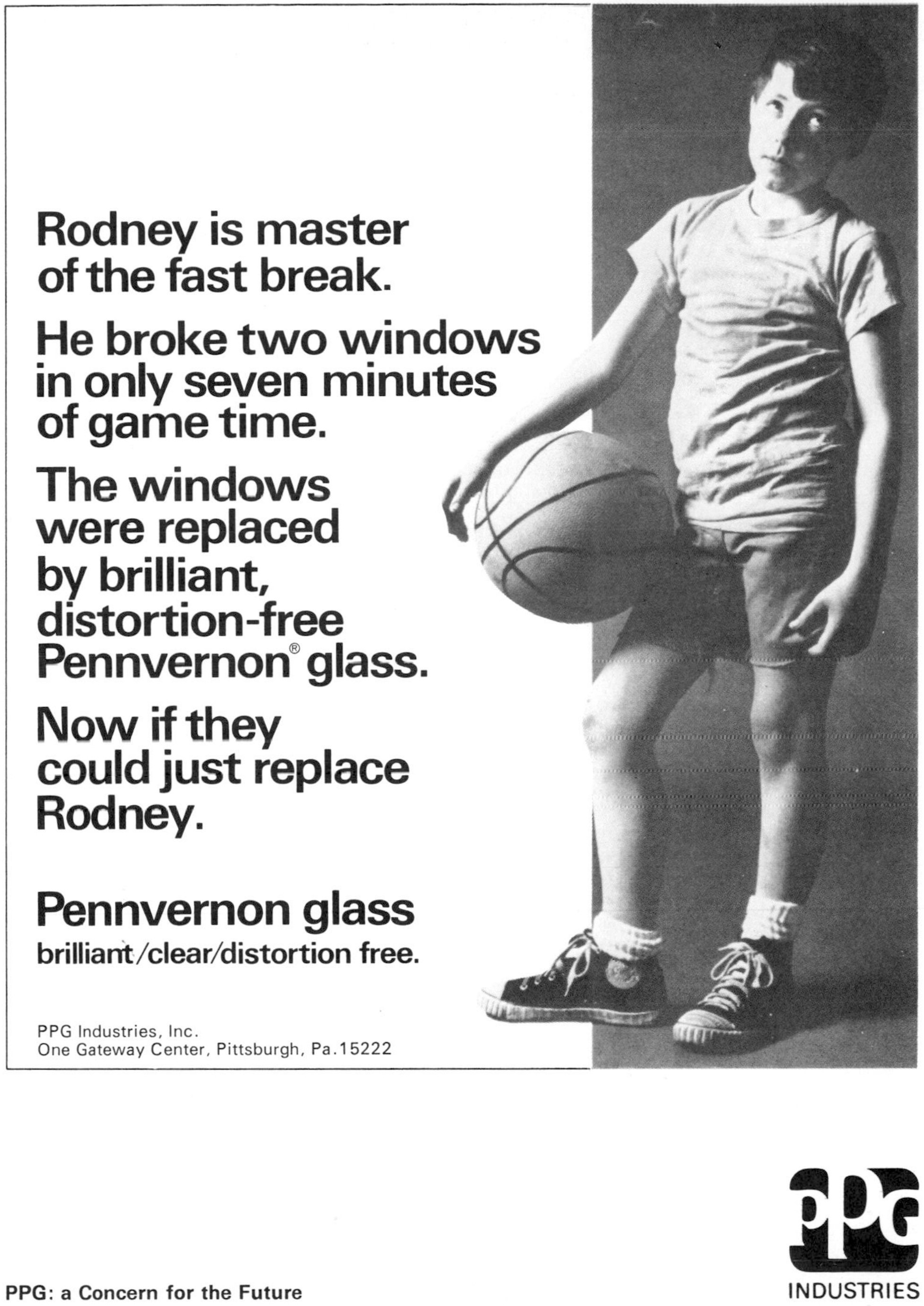
Rodney is master of the fast break.
He broke two windows in only seven minutes of game time.
The windows were replaced by brilliant, distortion-free Pennvernon® glass.
Now if they could just replace Rodney.
Pennvernon glass
brilliant/clear/distortion free.
PPG Industries, Inc.
One Gateway Center, Pittsburgh, Pa. 15222
PPG: a Concern for the Future
INDUSTRIES

Fig. 14-5

Trade advertisement.

Humor is used infrequently in business publication advertisements. If handled well, as in this case, it can be very effective.

will be used to "merchandise" that advertising to the trade. The people who handle the "X" washer—and prospective new dealers—will thus be informed that a comprehensive and effective national advertising campaign is starting; that it will reach people and prospects in every locality; and that, naturally, it will stimulate interest in the washer—and bring people into "your store" for more information or a demonstration.

First of all, a selection of the most effective trade papers would be made. You might or might not have anything to do with the choosing of these, but in any event you would want to be familiar with them in order to adjust your copy style to the magazine and its readers.

The national advertising support

Orthodox treatment might start out this way. First advertisement is a double spread, uses some color, and the type of "news" headline mentioned in the chapter on headlines.

MOST POWERFUL CONSUMER ADVERTISING EVER!
. . . TO HELP YOU RING UP RECORD SALES
ON "X" WASHERS

Subhead: "New, sure-fire, full-page color advertisements run in 5 leading magazines—

aimed to reach more than 65% of prospects in your own neighborhood!''

Second subhead: ''All through the year, these advertisements will appear in *McCall's, Ladies' Home Journal; Better Homes and Gardens.''* Illustrations might show a few typical advertisements, as large as possible, small covers of the magazines mentioned—and possibly a small chart illustrating how 65% (figure used only for example) of prospects are reached by this advertising, for the average dealer.

Copy would explain why the consumer advertisements should be effective, why women are interested in saving time, being able to shop, do housework, etc., while clothes are being washed, etc. All copy would be written from the ''Dealer's side''—how all this advertising is aimed to work for him; how it brings people into the store; how it actually ''pays off at your cash register.'' Such an advertisement might logically ask for action at the end, something like this:

> Continuous advertising support in your own neighborhood is only one reason why the ''X'' franchise is such a money-maker for dealers. A franchise might be available for you. A special ''Profit Table'' that shows sales and profit potentials for your own locality, is yours on request. Get yours —and other facts and figures you should have. Better do it now . . . before your competitor's request arrives first.

Here's some comment on this advertisement. The headlines are quite long. The headlines and the subheads, however, certainly tell the story, and that's always good practice according to highly experienced trade-advertising experts, who say that two kinds of readers see trade advertisements: (1) ''Quick readers'' who seldom read more than the heads and subheads. (2) ''Thorough readers'' (a small group) who will read anything and everything having to do with their business. If, in view of the foregoing, you can get your fairly complete story into your headings, chances are you'll get high readership from both classes of readers. Of course, this reasoning, like so many other facets of advertising, is open to long and thorough discussion. It's the kind of reasoning, just the same, that should be explored by the intelligent copywriter.

The headlines contain some ''you'' element and mention the name of the product. The whole tone of the advertisement is on the ''you''—directed straight to the dealer—and that is an essential in trade advertising, because the writer simply must explain everything the advertiser does, in terms of benefits, profits, help, and so forth, which the dealer-reader can expect from the product or service being advertised.

Stress local effect of advertising

Assuming that the national advertising is the most important message the ''X'' company has for dealers, the next trade advertisement in the series could well treat the ''local'' effect of all the advertising the ''X'' company does—including the new campaign. The heading for such an advertisement might be:

NEW ''X'' WASHER ADVERTISING ''TALKS TO''
NEARLY 7 OF EVERY 10 PEOPLE
RIGHT IN YOUR NEIGHBORHOOD

The whole advertisement might use ''believe it or not'' technique, and with several illustrations and little copy for each, show how the advertising works for every dealer, in his own area. This ''local advertising'' versus ''national advertising'' question is always a moot one. Lately, there has been great recognition of the need to interpret ''national advertising'' in terms of ''local advertising''—since the local readership of national advertising is the only interest any dealer has in it. Boasting that yours is the biggest national advertising campaign ever to hit the magazines just leaves him cold unless you can show him the effect this

Bullard's newest hot wheels
They may just be the fastest movers in town.
Nothing sells like a new idea. Unless it's two new ideas. And we have a two-idea package for your impulse buyers and your toughest value hunters alike.
For all your electric drill-owning customers we have SAND-A-WAY, the newest, hottest selling sanding disc you're likely to see for a long time. It sells because it's different. Unique open mesh design attracts attention and invites trial use. Fits all ¼ inch electric drills. Requires no back-up pad. Won't load up. Gives longer life than sandpaper and provides more sanding uses. Has been known to top its own sales record every month.
For all your portable power saw owners we have JET CUT, the famous metal and masonry cut-off wheels that fit all popular power saws. Your customers cut cement block, brick, marble, flagstone, sheet metal, aluminum, pipe, iron and a hundred other materials with the saws they have at home. And you cut it with your customers for added profits.
These two innovators are hot lines to handle. Attractively packaged to sell themselves with handy display kit as shown. Get onto SAND-A-WAY and JET CUT and watch 'em move. See your nearest Bullard distributor or write us for his name.
GEO.H.BULLARD CO.,INC. Hopkinton Road, Westboro, Mass. 01581, (617) 366-4465

Fig. 14-6

Trade advertisement.

Like many trade advertisements, this one stresses the display units used in selling the product.

campaign will have on his own customers. The eternal question in any alert dealer's mind is, "What does this advertising do for me?"

The next several advertisements in the trade series could well dramatize store tests and store experiences of progressive dealers with the "X" washers. Advertisements would explain how the consumer advertising brought in prospects to find out how a whole week's wash could be done in 30 minutes, and how, with a few little display ideas of the dealer, sales of the "X" washer rose to a new high level. The purpose here, of course, is to persuade the dealer reading about these experiences to think that he can do as well himself.

"TIMING" OF TRADE ADVERTISEMENTS

Time of the year, specific problems that arise at times, and new company policies—all these and more affect trade advertising. What these special conditions are often dictates what the advertisements will say.

A few of them will be shown with special situations—the headlines of advertisements show how the situation might be met.

Suppose, for instance, users had experienced considerable difficulty with the "Swirler"—a patented clothes agitator of the "X" machine. Dealers were getting too many complaints; machines were returned; sales dropped ominously. One effective solution would be elimination of the "Swirler" and introduction of a new-type agitator of proved trouble-free operation. Wouldn't it be big and important news for the trade to know:

REVOLUTIONARY NEW CLOTHES AGITATOR
OF "X" WASHER ELIMINATES SERVICE HEADACHES!

Copy would explain how a "torture treatment," equal to 5 years' normal use, was set up in an independent laboratory, and that 5 machines out of every 100 going through the factory were put through this test. No mention would be focused on the "trouble-free new agitator" that would certainly overcome most of the previous difficulty. The same theme would be used by salesmen making their calls.

Suppose the washing action of the "X" washer is "oscillatory." Other washers use the "reciprocating" action. There is great controversy over the merits of each. If it could be proved in unbiased tests that the "oscilatory" was far superior, tests could be set up in noted laboratories, and results of these tests would make the basis of a series of advertisements. Here's one such headline:

OSCILLATORY ACTION OF "X" WASHER
OUTPERFORMS RECIPROCATING 3 TO 1
IN ACTUAL TESTS

You'd have to be prepared for a big storm of controversy and you'd need to be very sure of your facts, but if the advertiser were strong enough, he could settle the argument positively. He might possibly devise an action that combined the advantages of both—if they were equal in varying respects—and, so to speak, work both ends. Heading:

ADVANTAGES OF BOTH
OSCILLATORY AND RECIPROCATING ACTIONS
COMBINED IN RADICAL NEW
OSCIL-REP ACTION OF "X" WASHER

To the trade that's big news. And as mentioned before—you've got to know the trade, what's going on, what interests dealers—and write "to" them—so *they'll* know *you* know.

CREATING THE PROMOTIONAL PACKAGE

Here is the second way, usually much the preferred, and more effective way, to support the consumer advertising of "X" washers. You will start again with the series that includes the advertisement, headed:

YOUR WHOLE WEEK'S WASH DONE IN
30 MINUTES . . . WHILE YOU SHOP!

Now, you will create "a package" or a "packaged promotion" which will include considerable promotional material, point-of-display pieces, gimmicks, results of store tests, direct-mail and newspaper mats for dealer's use. Also, you'll include a portfolio for the salesmen who call on dealers. The portfolio explains the whole deal. Added to the foregoing, you will also "promote the promotion" to the trade through regular trade publications.

Assume the "Swirler" is an ingenious and exclusive agitator of the "X" machine, and is the main reason why clothes wash so quickly and so clean. Also, the "Swirler" is one important part of the automatic operation which permits women to leave the machine while it merrily goes on with its washing. You'll then dramatize the "Swirler" in every way, bring it into all your promotion and advertising, and introduce a catchy theme that will be the core of your promotion. It is your U.S.P.

You may decide to use the "stop and go" light idea, which is quite suitable for this example. The slogan or keynote will be

Stop Washing . . .
Go Swirling

In the consumer advertising, headlines would

Make it big.
Here's the way we look at money: the more you make, the more we make. And the way for you to make more profit is to make more trouble for competition.
That's where we come in. The IH Troublemakers. We've fielded our most complete line of lawn and garden equipment. From power mowers to riders to tractors. Every one of them with easy features that are hard to beat.
And when you're an IH dealer with the complete line, there isn't a "grass cutter" in town you'll have to turn away.
To make sure you make it big, we've got over a million dollars earmarked for advertising that will tell everyone out there what we make and how easy it is to operate.
Finally, leaving nothing at all to chance, we offer you a co-op advertising program with built-in big results.
In fact, the only thing small about our 1973 program is your chance of not making it big.
Write Don Rigdon, International Harvester Company, Consumer Products, 401 North Michigan Avenue, Chicago, Illinois 60611, for the name of the IH Troublemaker in your area.
International Harvester. Any way you cut it.
Circle 113 on Inquiry Card

Fig. 14-7

Trade advertisement.

This advertisement demonstrates a strong use of the 3-P's approach by talking first of profits, then of product, and finally of promotion.

continue on the time-saving and leisure theme, as exemplified by the headline "Your whole week's wash done in 30 minutes." Copy would explain how this was possible, heavily promoting the "Swirler." Somewhere in the main illustration, or in an illustration of the washer or "Swirler," you might show a gaily waving banner with traffic-signal-light effects and the theme words, *"Stop* Washing . . . *Go* Swirling." Already you can see how this device can be carried through all promotion and advertising —magazines, bill-boards, newspapers, direct mail, display material, trade—even radio, where sound tricks would take the place of the signal lights.

Here's the promotional material you could logically include in your "package"—and which you will promote in your trade advertising (to be explained later on).

1. A series of newspaper mats and radio and TV commercials for the dealer's use, built on the "stop and go" idea.

2. A series of three to six direct-mail pieces for dealers to send to selected prospects, built on same idea.

3. Several large display pieces using the red "Stop" and green "Go" light idea, plus possibly one life-sized cut-out figure of a traffic

Fig. 14-8

Trade advertisement with stress on display units.

Notice the strong emphasis on profit and turnover, too.

policeman with a red and green light above him—(they flash on and off alternately) for use in store window or inside store, next to the "X" washer or washers on display.

4. A series of "how to display the "X" washer" suggestions. This would consist of several illustrations of putting washer on elevated floor platform, placing certain display material around it, casting colored light from a baby spotlight on it in store or window, and other similar ideas.

Then, using the same red and green light technique, all this material or pictures of it will be arranged in logical order in a salesman's portfolio, titled

Stop Wondering . . .
Go Swirling

Next the trade advertising. With all this material ready to help the dealers, and with the attention-getting red and green light treatment, we now have:

1. "A packaged promotion"—complete and available for the dealer, to help him capitalize more effectively on the power of the consumer advertising.

2. A "gimmick"—in the red and green lights and the slogan, which will provide immediately identity in all collateral and trade advertising.

First, the trade advertising could well announce the big consumer campaign already

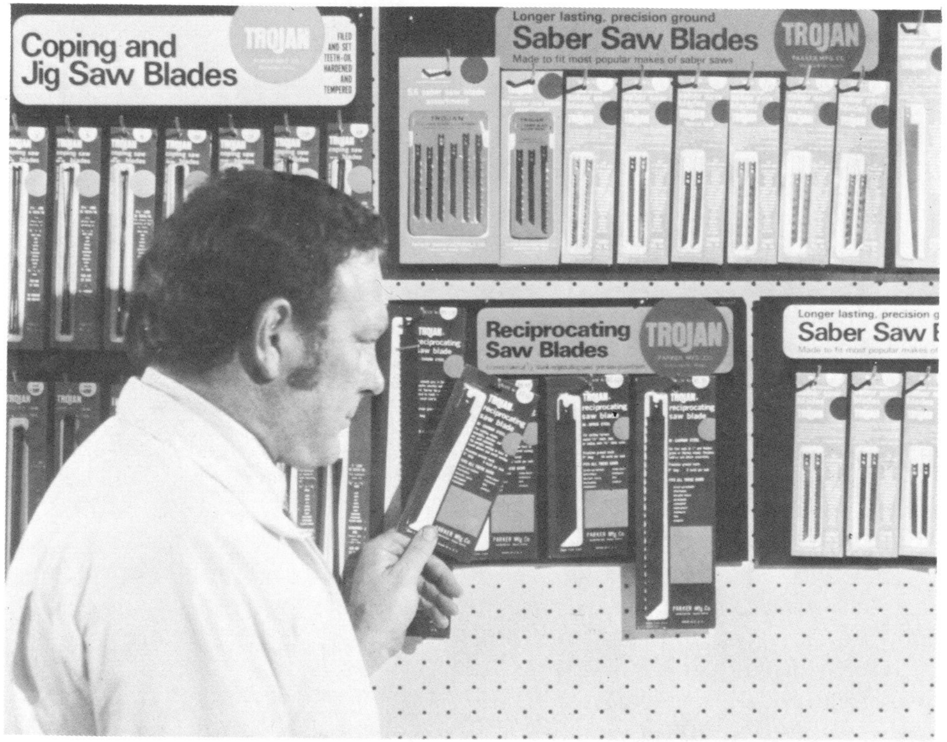

Coping and
Jig Saw Blades
TROJAN
Longer lasting, precision ground
Saber Saw Blades
Made to fit most popular makes of saber saws
Reciprocating
Saw Blades
Saber Saw

Here's why TROJAN displays fill all saber, jig and coping blade needs

Boards are complete blade shopping centers
Profit per display runs up to 49 %
Fast turnover—survey shows most often specified brand
Low dollar investment—quality, yet lower priced
Contain self-selling help, including blade selection guide
Back-up stocks readily available and in small minimums
Catalog sheets and "Helpful Hints" shipped with display
Cards per board are based on actual use ratios

Check below the catalog sheets you need for complete specifications and mail in

Trojan Display	Blade Assortment	Number of Cards	Dealer Cost	Dealer Profit
☐ No. SD-40	7 Saber Saw, 1 Scroll Saw, 2 Kits	64	$36.50	48 %
☐ No. SD-36	7 Saber Saw, 2 Kits	65	36.50	49
☐ No. SD-2	7 Saber Saw	50	23.60	46
☐ No. 1500	14 Coping and Jig Saw	57	19.50	41
☐ No. RSD. 1	4 Reciprocating Saw	30	20.00	35

PARKER MANUFACTURING CO., Worcester, Mass, 01610

Circle 119 on Inquiry Card

mentioned—bringing in the slogan and the red and green light idea in a subordinate way. In every trade advertisement—sometimes large, sometimes small—this plug would always be made: *"Stop* Wondering . . . *Go* Swirling." Use of this phrase would provide a note of recognition when the salesman called with the same device and wording on the front of his portfolio.

Second advertisement in the trade series might be a big play on the central theme of the *"Stop* Washing . . . *Go* Swirling" and explain how, like the proverbial drip of water, this catchy little selling phrase will work and work on the minds of women, wearing down sales-resistance and exciting curiosity. Copy would still devote some words to the big advertising support.

Following advertisements could well run in this order:

1. Big "splash" on all the material available to help dealers sell more "X" machines.
2. Reproductions of telegrams from dealers telling how well the new advertising is working for them.
3. Straight appeal to dealers to "see what's in the big black book the 'X' salesman has ready to show you." This refers to the portfolio, and copy would hint of the "money-magic" that the book brings to readers.
4. Series of advertisements built on store tests, showing how successful dealers used all the material available on "X" machines and how well sales are going. In other words, success stories.

Store tests are important

You've probably noticed that the store tests are mentioned many times. Unbiased store tests are convincing to dealers. First, no dealer can overlook such data when they have to do with his bread and butter. Secondly, not many advertisers are willing to go to the expense and trouble of making the tests (and results may not be suitable for publication). When such test results do appear, they constitute material that is far from common.

All the advertisements mentioned as suitable for this series—whether based on store tests or not—would, of course, always end with a strong urge to the dealer to "wire, write, or telephone us of the 'X' salesman who has been trying to see you—and get the full facts"—or something along that line.

It should be mentioned that when the entire campaign was approved and when the first samples of all the advertisements and material were finally available, everything was timed in order that the whole plan could be presented to the sales organization at convention, so "the boys" could sally forth into their respective territories filled with the fire and fervor of their cause. It's just as important that the *sales force* be sold on your advertising and promotion as the dealers, or "the trade."

WHY DIRECT INSTITUTIONAL ADVERTISEMENTS TO THE TRADE?

Most trade advertising tries to sell a product or service in a very direct way. Some advertisers, however, cannot always do this. Consider Hotpoint. They market many products sold through the appliance trade. If every Hotpoint product division decided to use an aggressive advertising campaign in trade magazines, a competitive free-for-all would ensue. In the case of such multi-product advertisers it is sensible to use an institutional theme. Here, for example, the name "Hotpoint" is promoted and each product is introduced as a member of the Hotpoint family of quality appliances and the selling-theme idea may be expressed as the "quality of Hotpoint."

Merchandising the national advertising, and selling the dealer on promotional assistance and institutional advertising are not, of course, the only means of using trade-paper space. Hundreds of different ideas, plans, deals, promotions, and "packages" are offered to the retailers through trade campaigns. The

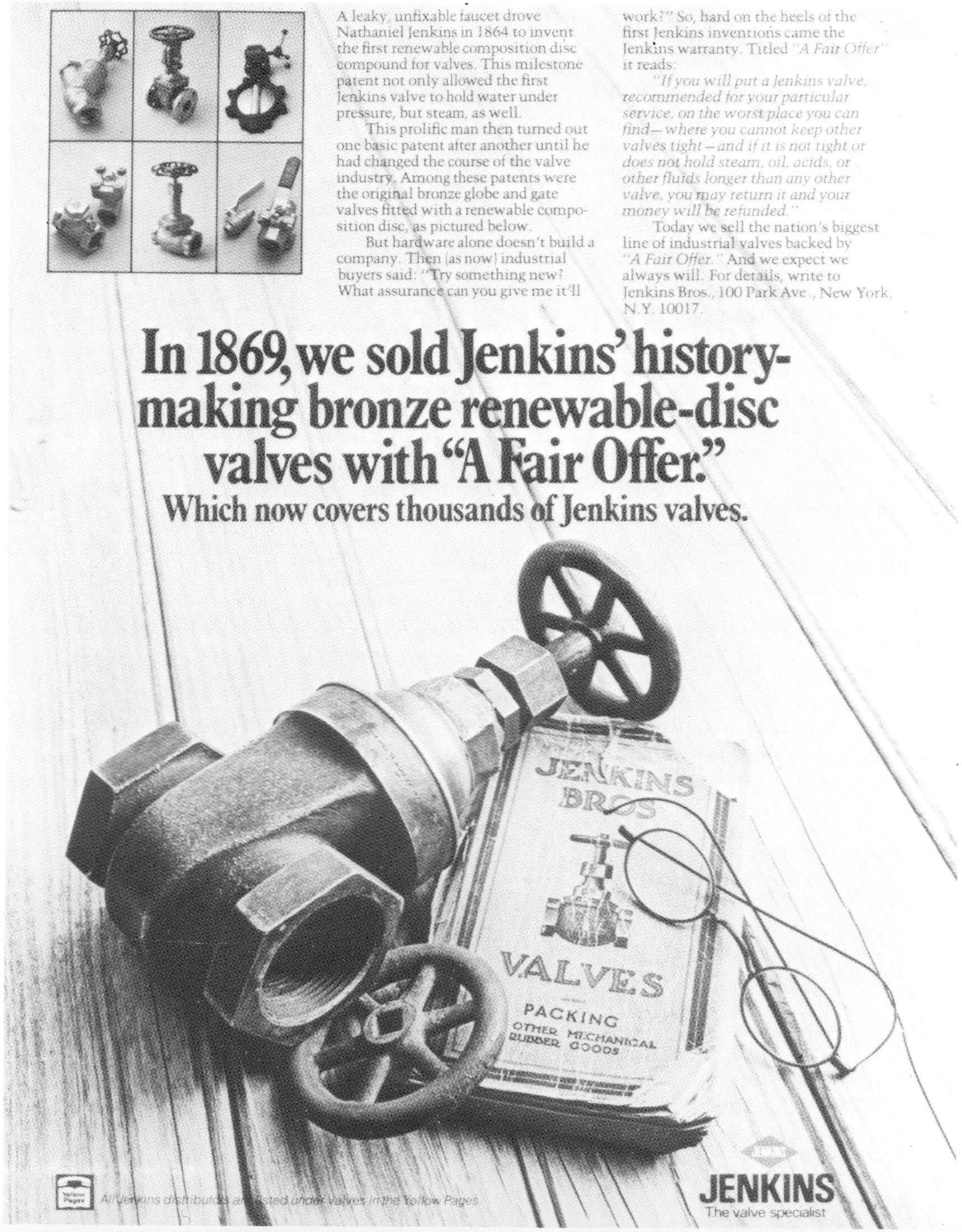
A leaky, unfixable faucet drove Nathaniel Jenkins in 1864 to invent the first renewable composition disc compound for valves. This milestone patent not only allowed the first Jenkins valve to hold water under pressure, but steam, as well.
This prolific man then turned out one basic patent after another until he had changed the course of the valve industry. Among these patents were the original bronze globe and gate valves fitted with a renewable composition disc, as pictured below.
But hardware alone doesn't build a company. Then (as now) industrial buyers said: "Try something new? What assurance can you give me it'll work?" So, hard on the heels of the first Jenkins inventions came the Jenkins warranty. Titled "A Fair Offer" it reads:
"If you will put a Jenkins valve, recommended for your particular service, on the worst place you can find—where you cannot keep other valves tight—and if it is not tight or does not hold steam, oil, acids, or other fluids longer than any other valve, you may return it and your money will be refunded."
Today we sell the nation's biggest line of industrial valves backed by "A Fair Offer." And we expect we always will. For details, write to Jenkins Bros., 100 Park Ave., New York, N.Y. 10017.
In 1869, we sold Jenkins' history-making bronze renewable-disc valves with "A Fair Offer."
Which now covers thousands of Jenkins valves.
JENKINS BROS
VALVES
PACKING
OTHER MECHANICAL RUBBER GOODS
All Jenkins distributors are listed under Valves in the Yellow Pages
JENKINS
The valve specialist

Fig. 14-9

Industrial advertisement of the institutional type.

Such advertisements sell the company's reputation, skill and stature in the industry. This is especially important in products such as valves that come in so many types and specifications that it is difficult in advertising to single out any one valve. When, however, one valve *is* being sold the prospect will have been convinced of its quality through the institutional advertising.
Courtesy Jenkins Bros.

subject matter of your trade advertising will be dependent upon what is the most important message to get across to the trade who will resell your product.

Thus, if you are marketing a brand-new product, through a company with no national prestige or name, perhaps the most important single thing for you to accomplish in trade advertising is to build confidence among the dealers in your company and in its financial background. If you are introducing a new automobile you may wish to inspire such confidence and backing by running trade advertising on your personnel, their experience in manufacturing, designing, and selling cars.

Trade advertising, as you have examined it here, is good for one major result: to gain the selling support of retail merchants. In order to do this, your trade campaigns must offer something to the dealer that will make him want to feature and sell your product. If your advertising fails to do this, you have lost a prime rib in your whole selling skeleton.

TRADE ADVERTISING IS IMPORTANT

There is a widespread tendency among copywriters, artists, account executives, and all other advertising people, to belittle trade

"If you think we're up to something ...you're right."

"We're up to our necks in change . . . more correctly, improvements.

"We've learned that to stay on top you've got to keep up with customers' needs.

"To that end, we merged with W. S. Tyler, Incorporated, a worldwide supplier of screening materials and equipment. Like us, they are an operation of Combustion Engineering, Inc., a widely diversified company supplying equipment, materials, and services to a variety of industries.

"Since both Tyler and C-E Cast Equipment are headquartered in Cleveland, a pooling of resources made considerable sense, further improving our ability to provide a quality line of foundry equipment.

"Now, what do you get out of all this?

"First, SPOmatic machines and allied equipment are being manufactured at Tyler's big plant in Mentor. We believe it's the finest facility in the country for fabricating foundry equipment.

"And our customer service has been streamlined. You can now order exclusive 'maintenance packages.'

"Our engineering capability has been broadened to meet all your needs, including sand and mold handling.

"Our accounting activities have been combined and largely computerized, saving you time and money.

"But we didn't change. You'll find all of the people of C-E Cast Equipment at the same address, same phone number: 7887 Hub Parkway, Cleveland OH 44125, 216-524-9000.

"Yes, now, more than ever, if it's for the foundry business, the only name you have to remember is C-E Cast."

Les Smith

Les Smith
Vice President and General Manager

CAST
COMBUSTION ENGINEERING, INC.

Fig. 14-10

Industrial advertisement.

This corporate advertisement uses the first-person quotation technique to describe the value of a recent merger.

advertising. Copywriters are inclined often to devote much less time to writing and thinking out an advertisement scheduled to appear in a trade journal than they are to one which will run in a national consumer magazine. This is understandable, but bad business. Every trade advertisement you write is just as important a selling link in your chain of promotion as is a consumer advertisement—sometimes even more important. Just because you don't have the same amount of money to spend for art-work and production, just because the space costs much less or the circulation is one-twentieth of a national publication, don't let the value of good trade advertising escape you. When you hear some of your colleagues talking about "Just another darn trade advertisement" to write, remember this: There are many salesmen whose living depends upon their being able to do a selling job on the people who read those publications. The trade advertising you write enable those salesmen to succeed more easily and consistently. The way they succeed can have a material effect upon the total sales of your product, and the way the sales of that product succeed can and will determine how well your advertising is considered to be succeeding.

Fig. 14-11

Industrial advertisement.

Combining a testimonial with a case history approach, this advertisement presents a powerful message for the product. Courtesy of The Minster Machine Company, Minster, Ohio, and ADS Metal Products Co., Long Island City, N.Y.

MINSTER
No. 4

INDUSTRIAL ADVERTISING SUGGESTIONS

Copy to purchasing agents, engineers, and other hard-boiled realists gives the facts, not the frills.

Many of the general principles given for the writing of business-paper copy apply to industrial copy. You will find in the following material some *additional* suggestions for writing industrial-publication copy which might help you approach this market intelligently.

1. *Purchasing agents often aren't so much concerned with immediate cost—but with long-range cost.* Your competitor's metal tubing may cost forty cents a foot but may last only half as long as yours. Your tubing, at sixty cents a foot, would, consequently, be a good buy. Remember that the purchasing agent is buying greater productivity for his firm—that means he is interested in saving manpower and materials. Thus, long-lasting materials and equipment are almost always his first interest.

2. *In your illustration show the product in use.* Much industrial advertising deals with equipment that is dull-looking out of use but interesting when in action. If you can control illustrations for your advertisements, see that

Richard Miller, Treasurer of ADS and President of Marlin Plastics Division, with the firm's newest Minster B1 press. With a new design timing belt driven cam feed and the latest Minster features, this press can run up to 1200 spm.

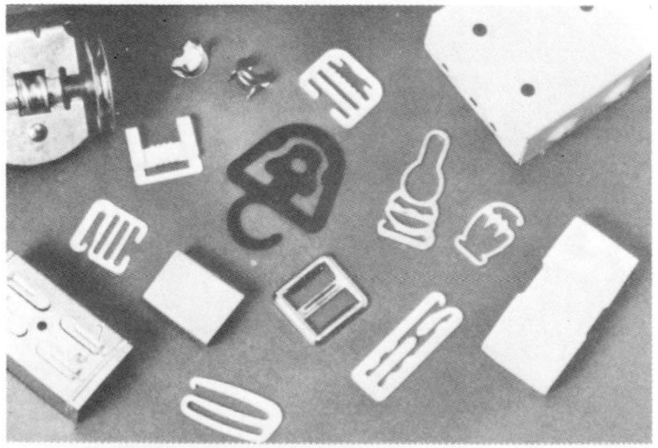

MINSTER

"We replaced all our presses with Minsters"

Kurt Kopf, Plant Mgr., ADS Metal Products, and Vice President of Marlin Plastics division.

Since they bought their first Minster press in 1959 and ran it at 300 spm instead of the 120 spm they had been getting, ADS Metal Products Co. and their Marlin Plastics division, Long Island City, New York, have replaced all of their presses with Minster O.B.I.'s and B1's. Now they get 5 times more production (4,000,000 parts per day) in the same floor space.

The firm designs and makes its own tools and dies and averages press speeds of 600 spm, making over 200 different metal and plastic parts for the garment, venetian blind, electronics and appliance industries all over the world.

Kurt Kopf says, "We get higher speeds, very good accuracy and greater production. Minsters are more durable, easier to service and maintain. They are less complicated in design. We have very little downtime compared to the presses we used to have."

Bulletin 39 contains full specifications and information on B1 presses from 16—60 ton capacities. Look into it soon if you need better press productivity.

your product is not static and make your copy fit the movement of the illustration.

3. *Don't write dull, technical, engineering details that should be in a catalog.* Although industrial copy should be thorough, the readers of such copy are like anyone else in not liking dull, lifeless catalog-type copy. If your material is better suited to a specifications sheet, or parts catalog, save it for those uses.

4. *Write copy with an individual reader in mind.* Have in mind a certain person—engineer, architect, company head. Point your copy message directly at that man's interests. Use his language.

5. *Give complete information.* Talk about your servicing facilities, the construction of the item being sold, the lasting qualities, the type of work for which it is best suited. Tell *why* your product gives better performance. *Why* is the material in your product superior? Remember this also: Your advertisement may be clipped and filed. It may be dragged out later to be placed next to a competitive advertisement. The copy that does the most complete job may get the sale. Industrial advertising, unlike much consumer advertising, is often referred to long after the advertising has run. Make *your* copy worth going back to. The typical industrial-paper reader doesn't shy away from long text—so long as it has something to say.

6. *Use a strong news slant.* Purchasing agents and others who read industrial advertising are constantly asking, "What's new?" The industrial reader is on the prowl for information that will help him or his firm do a better job. Latest developments are his meat—feed him a heavy diet. Your new product, or new use for your product, should be told about in fresh, live news style.

7. *Case histories catch interest.* The usual industrial buyer moves cautiously. Industrial advertising is largely directed to those who buy in big quantities. Successful use by another business of your product makes absorbing reading for the man going over your advertisement. Perhaps, in addition to selling him, you are helping him sell management on buying your product. Your case history of successful use of your product may often be the *only* sales argument that carries weight.

8. *Get into your story quickly.* Although interested readers of industrial advertising are willing to read long copy, they are *not* willing to waste time guessing what the copywriter has in mind. Many of your readers go through mountains of reading matter each day. Although your copy should be complete, it shouldn't be leisurely. Let the reader know immediately through headline, illustration, and first copy block what you're talking about.

9. *Recognize a problem—then show how your product can help solve it.* The reader of industrial advertising is beset with problems. His abrasives don't hold up; his V-belts break; his accident rate is too high—perhaps production is falling. If your advertisement suggests a way out of his troubles, he'll read it like a novel.

TRADE "COLLATERAL"

Closely associated with trade advertising is the writing and production of what is called "collateral." Under this term are included all the special pieces of advertising used in product selling, either by the advertiser's own sales force or by the retail merchant. Such things as special mailing pieces addressed to the trade, portfolios containing promotional aids for the sales force, store display material, and other miscellaneous advertising are called "collateral." Their creation represents an important and volunminous part of almost every copywriter's duties.

Create an intensive or coronary care unit in forty-eight hours.
New construction or general care conversion, Sorgel Modular Medical Walls give you ICU/CCU facilities in a couple of days rather than weeks. Everything is built in and pre-wired in compliance with the latest standards, ready for hook-up. Gas, water, lights, isolated power systems, ground receptacles . . . anything you may require, we can supply.
Every detail reflects Sorgel's concern for high quality. Maintenance is low and front removable panels make future interior modifications easy.
For specific data concerning Sorgel Modular Medical Walls, call your nearby Sorgel or Square D field office. Or write Sorgel Electric Corporation, 838 West National Avenue, Milwaukee, Wisconsin 53204. Phone (414) 384-8100
SORGEL
Subsidiary of Square D Company
SQUARE D COMPANY
Wherever Electricity is Distributed and Controlled

Fig. 14-12

Professional advertisement.

This advertisement is addressed to hospital administrators who read the magazine *Modern Hospital*.

A great amount of material is normally supplied to the product manufacturer's salesmen to aid them in soliciting business from the trade. If you are an agency copywriter, you will be called upon to prepare a considerable amount of this material on behalf of your clients. If you are writing copy for an advertiser, in the advertising department, preparation of such items will occupy an even greater part of your time. It is important for you to consider some of the varied things that salesmen use in their daily calls on the trade. One is the portfolio.

PORTFOLIO—THE SALESMAN'S "BIBLE"

Perhaps the most usable single collateral piece regularly supplied to a sales force is what is sometimes called the "salesman's portfolio," "sales manual," or "sales brochure."

These portfolios are designed to do a threefold job:

1. They are a means of showing the dealers what advertising is being put behind the product, both nationally and locally, what display material is available to dealers for their stores, and how the combination works in pre-selling the product for the dealers.

2. They serve to arouse enthusiasm for the

All of these mammals, except one, can synthesize vitamin C.

Man cannot.

Homo sapiens can neither synthesize vitamin C nor store the water soluble vitamins. They have to be replenished every day.

Normally, man accomplishes this in his daily diet. But under conditions of illness, stress, in convalescence or following surgery, vitamin stores may be depleted or metabolic demands increased.

In such cases, Surbex-T may be indicated. Each tablet provides 500 mg. of vitamin C plus high potency B-complex.

Where nutritional status must be preserved, Surbex-T can help restore what the body can *not* store.

211399

SURBEX-T® **500 mg. of Vitamin C with High Potency B-Complex** ABBOTT

Restores what the body cannot store—the water-soluble vitamins.

Fig. 14-13

Professional advertisement appearing in a medical magazine.

As this advertisement demonstrates, professional advertisements are not doomed to dull creative approaches. The headline-illustration combination here is pertinent, interesting and attention-getting.

product and its potentialities in the dealer's mind, and the same emotions among the salesmen for their own advertising and merchandising promotion.

3. They offer the salesman a complete, graphic, and chronological check list to follow in giving the dealer a "sales talk" over and above the actual merits, price and profit margin of the product, and his company's service features.

There are two very important things to remember in writing a sales portfolio:

One is to *write simply.* A lot of the value that the sales force will derive from your portfolio will not necessarily come while they are actually going over it with a dealer, but in routine conversations with their retailer customers. If you can write interesting, punchy, and informal copy in the portfolios you prepare, the salesmen will often find themselves picking up these expressions and using them in their daily calls. Because salesmen and tradesmen often have a poor view of advertising people and scorn "cleverness" in the material that they themselves are supposed to use, use the kind of talk that the salesman himself would be likely to use. Don't "write down."

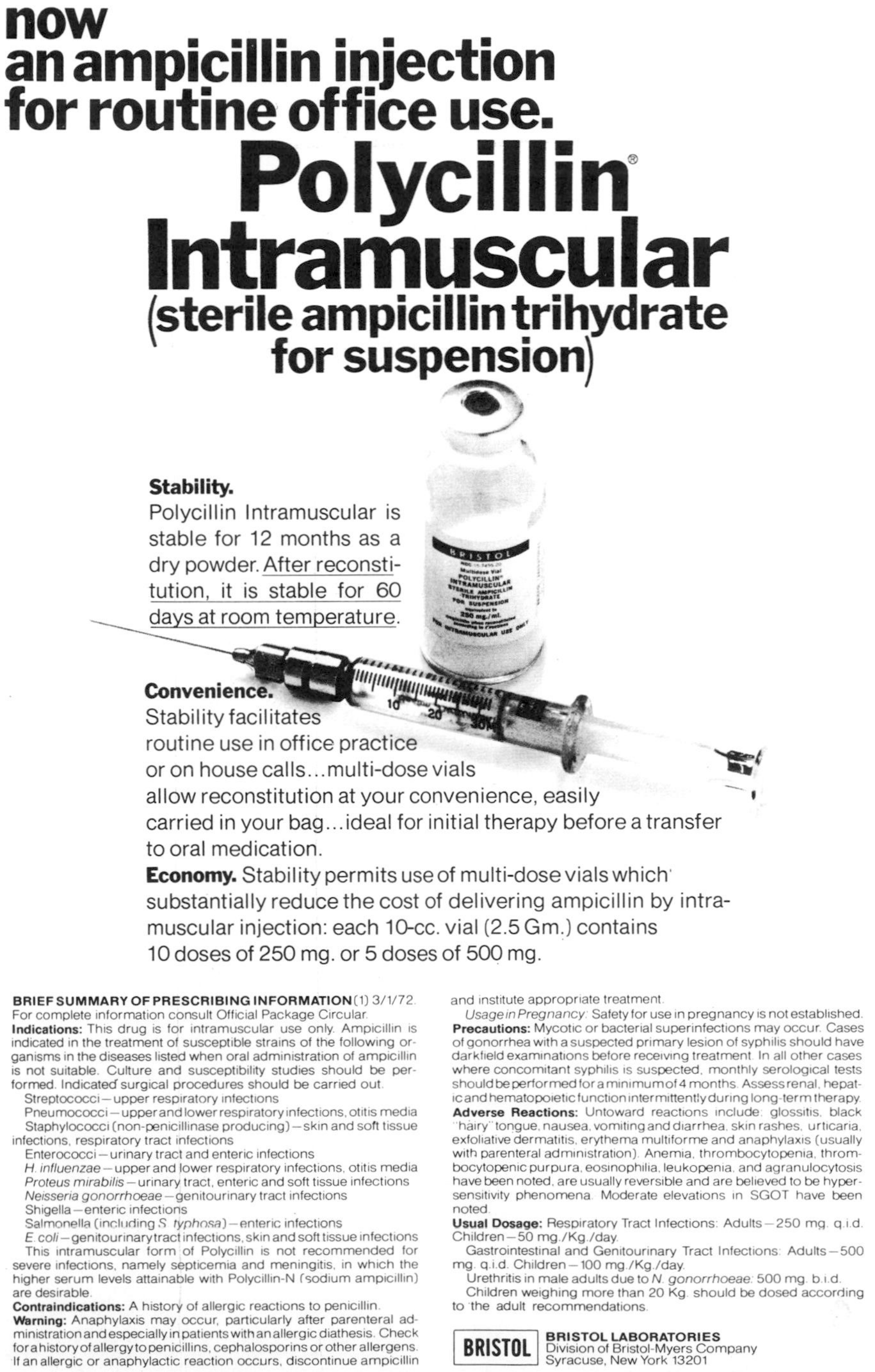
now
an ampicillin injection
for routine office use.
Polycillin®
Intramuscular
(sterile ampicillin trihydrate
for suspension)
Stability.
Polycillin Intramuscular is stable for 12 months as a dry powder. After reconstitution, it is stable for 60 days at room temperature.
Convenience.
Stability facilitates routine use in office practice or on house calls...multi-dose vials allow reconstitution at your convenience, easily carried in your bag...ideal for initial therapy before a transfer to oral medication.
Economy. Stability permits use of multi-dose vials which substantially reduce the cost of delivering ampicillin by intramuscular injection: each 10-cc. vial (2.5 Gm.) contains 10 doses of 250 mg. or 5 doses of 500 mg.
BRIEF SUMMARY OF PRESCRIBING INFORMATION (1) 3/1/72.
For complete information consult Official Package Circular.
Indications: This drug is for intramuscular use only. Ampicillin is indicated in the treatment of susceptible strains of the following organisms in the diseases listed when oral administration of ampicillin is not suitable. Culture and susceptibility studies should be performed. Indicated surgical procedures should be carried out.
Streptococci—upper respiratory infections
Pneumococci—upper and lower respiratory infections, otitis media
Staphylococci (non-penicillinase producing)—skin and soft tissue infections, respiratory tract infections
Enterococci—urinary tract and enteric infections
H. influenzae—upper and lower respiratory infections, otitis media
Proteus mirabilis—urinary tract, enteric and soft tissue infections
Neisseria gonorrhoeae—genitourinary tract infections
Shigella—enteric infections
Salmonella (including S. typhosa)—enteric infections
E. coli—genitourinary tract infections, skin and soft tissue infections
This intramuscular form of Polycillin is not recommended for severe infections, namely septicemia and meningitis, in which the higher serum levels attainable with Polycillin-N (sodium ampicillin) are desirable.
Contraindications: A history of allergic reactions to penicillin.
Warning: Anaphylaxis may occur, particularly after parenteral administration and especially in patients with an allergic diathesis. Check for a history of allergy to penicillins, cephalosporins or other allergens. If an allergic or anaphylactic reaction occurs, discontinue ampicillin and institute appropriate treatment.
Usage in Pregnancy: Safety for use in pregnancy is not established.
Precautions: Mycotic or bacterial superinfections may occur. Cases of gonorrhea with a suspected primary lesion of syphilis should have darkfield examinations before receiving treatment. In all other cases where concomitant syphilis is suspected, monthly serological tests should be performed for a minimum of 4 months. Assess renal, hepatic and hematopoietic function intermittently during long-term therapy.
Adverse Reactions: Untoward reactions include: glossitis, black "hairy" tongue, nausea, vomiting and diarrhea, skin rashes, urticaria, exfoliative dermatitis, erythema multiforme and anaphylaxis (usually with parenteral administration). Anemia, thrombocytopenia, thrombocytopenic purpura, eosinophilia, leukopenia, and agranulocytosis have been noted, are usually reversible and are believed to be hypersensitivity phenomena. Moderate elevations in SGOT have been noted.
Usual Dosage: Respiratory Tract Infections: Adults—250 mg. q.i.d. Children—50 mg./Kg./day.
Gastrointestinal and Genitourinary Tract Infections: Adults—500 mg. q.i.d. Children—100 mg./Kg./day.
Urethritis in male adults due to N. gonorrhoeae: 500 mg. b.i.d.
Children weighing more than 20 Kg. should be dosed according to the adult recommendations.
BRISTOL
BRISTOL LABORATORIES
Division of Bristol-Myers Company
Syracuse, New York 13201

Fig. 14-14

Professional advertisement appearing in a medical magazine.

Full information is given in this long-copy written for the publication's readership.

To give yourself a working background in this trade talk you ought to spend some time on the road with a salesman, going with him on his calls and listening to the type of thing he tells dealers. If you are working in the advertising department of a manufacturing house, you will find that such trips are considered standard procedure. If you are a copywriter with an advertising agency, you may find them a little more difficult to arrange, since the agency will want to keep you busy writing. Few advertising executives, though, will recognize the value of such extracurricular experience for copywriters, so you can get out if you try hard enough.

The second important point to remember in writing sales portfolios is *brevity*. Many copywriters oversell in trade collateral. Keep your ideas simple enough to be covered quickly and easily in a few words. The reason for this is evident when you put yourself in the position of a dealer who is being asked to take time to look over the portfolio, or the salesman whose job is to show it to the dealer. Neither of those men have time to sit down and read a lot of extravagant copy about *anything*. Salesmen will tell you that they can, and do, persuade dealers to "take a

Hospital cuts carpet cleaning costs by 40%.
A Midwestern hospital* had been cleaning their carpet with one of the conventional methods. Cost records showed that it took an average of 12 man hours and two gallons of cleaner to clean a large dining room. In addition, a spotter had to be used prior to cleaning.
Then the hospital switched to Carpetsheen. It took six man hours and one gallon of Carpetsheen to clean the same area. And Carpetsheen did a very thorough job of removing the spots, spills and ground-in dirt. A separate carpet spotter wasn't required.
Consider the savings you could enjoy if you cut your carpet maintenance costs by 40%.
Then, write us and ask us to show you more. We'll send more information on using Carpetsheen, the complete carpet care product, for spotting, traffic-lane cleaning, and renovation. We'll also have a Hillyard Hospital Consultant call to arrange a demonstration at your convenience.
"You know it's right if it comes in the checkerboard drum."
The all-in-one carpet care product.
CARPETSHEEN by hillyard
Professional floor care products worldwide
Corporate offices: St. Joseph, Missouri 64502
*Details on request.
As Hillyard continues to grow, with revolutionary products like Carpetsheen, we find it necessary to seek additional qualified sales personnel. For more information, write Mr. George Roth, Hillyard, St. Joseph, Missouri 64501 and enclose your resume.

Fig. 14-15

Professional advertisement that uses a case history approach effectively.

The combination of persuasive and specific copy, along with a good illustration, should arouse interest among the hospital administrators at whom the advertisement is aimed.

second" to glance at their company's advertising program, or the display material illustrated in a portfolio. But they can rarely pin that dealer down long enough to con a treatise on the subject.

What to put in a portfolio

Any advertiser, agency, or even copywriter will have a personal technique for how best to organize a sales portfolio. There are many different techniques. You can, however, learn a basic pattern that will apply to almost *any* type of product or market. This pattern can be almost standard except for these special points you may be asked to highlight or emphasize:

1. A cover, with an illustration of interest, that tells what the portfolio is all about. If you are giving the salesmen a manual covering their firm's spring and summer advertising, *say so.* Headlines of general interest to dealers and salesmen may be used if desired, but they are not necessary to the effectiveness of good sales portfolios. Usually, however, a breezy headline like *Even MORE Sales Power for YOU This Spring!* is a common device to get interest in the ensuing material.

2. A section devoted to the advertiser's ad-

Dress up your rooms and restaurants in crisp, fresh cottons.
Linen rental service can save you a bundle. Add up the cost of laundry equipment, inventory, space, and labor it takes to run your own laundry and see for yourself. Your linen supplier has the facts and figures to prove it. And he'll also demonstrate how rental service can cut down on customer complaints.
You can't afford a trial-and-error method of maintaining a clean, sparkling appearance. The linens you display for guests in your rooms and restaurants are too critical an area of your business. The answer of course is crisp, sanitary all-cotton items from your linen supplier.
In fact, it's almost like hiring a decorator to have him outfit your establishment with gleaming linens. Tables, beds, bathrooms take on a freshness that says, "Welcome to a place of quality and good taste."
Contact your linen supplier soon and turn your worries over to him.
Reusable cotton rentals reduce litter and pollution build-up.
COMFORTABLE · CAREFREE
COTTON
Cotton Incorporated and Linen Supply Association of America

Fig. 14-16

Advertisement for a magazine serving the institutional trade.

In crisp, direct copy this advertisement in "Hotel & Motel Management" sells a useful service.

vertising-to-come. In this part of your portfolio you will show either reprints of the advertisement, which may be slipped into a "pocket" or flap in the pages, printed right on the pages themselves, or "tipped in"—glued along one edge and inserted in the manual. Normally you will discover that the "pocket" method is best for advertisers who have a heavy and complete schedule of advertisements, since it enables the salesman to carry more advertisements conveniently. It is also much less expensive than printing or "tipping."

In addition to showing the advertisements in your portfolio, you will want to give a complete schedule of where and when those advertisements will appear, and how many readers they will reach. You will also want to point out to the dealers, if the campaign you show is national, that much of the national circulation is right in his town, even in his own neighborhood, so that the advertisements actually function partly as *local* advertising. If the operation is of a type that supplies complementary advertising to dealers for their own local use, in mat form, you will include a page or two of your portfolio to show the dealer reprints of these mats and tell him how to get them. The same is true of all phases of the advertising program—show the whole business, posters, car cards, TV and radio programs, spot announcements, and any other national or local advertising effort that is being put behind the product.

3. A section devoted to *merchandising.* In this part of your manual you will illustrate all the various store and window display material that is made available to the dealer and tell him how to order it. You will point out how this material is designed to "tie in" with the national advertising theme, to provide recognition and recall value, and to give the final impetus to the buyer at the point of purchase.

4. A wind-up page, or pages, where you call for the dealer's support, emphasizing that it means more sales for him to feature your product, and is evidence of his sound business judgment.

Keep this format for sales portfolios in mind. It is not an infallible pattern that can always be used exactly as described, but it is fundamentally the approach that all well-organized sales portfolios should have.

OTHER SALES-FORCE HELPS

In addition to portfolios, you will be called upon to write countless other things de-

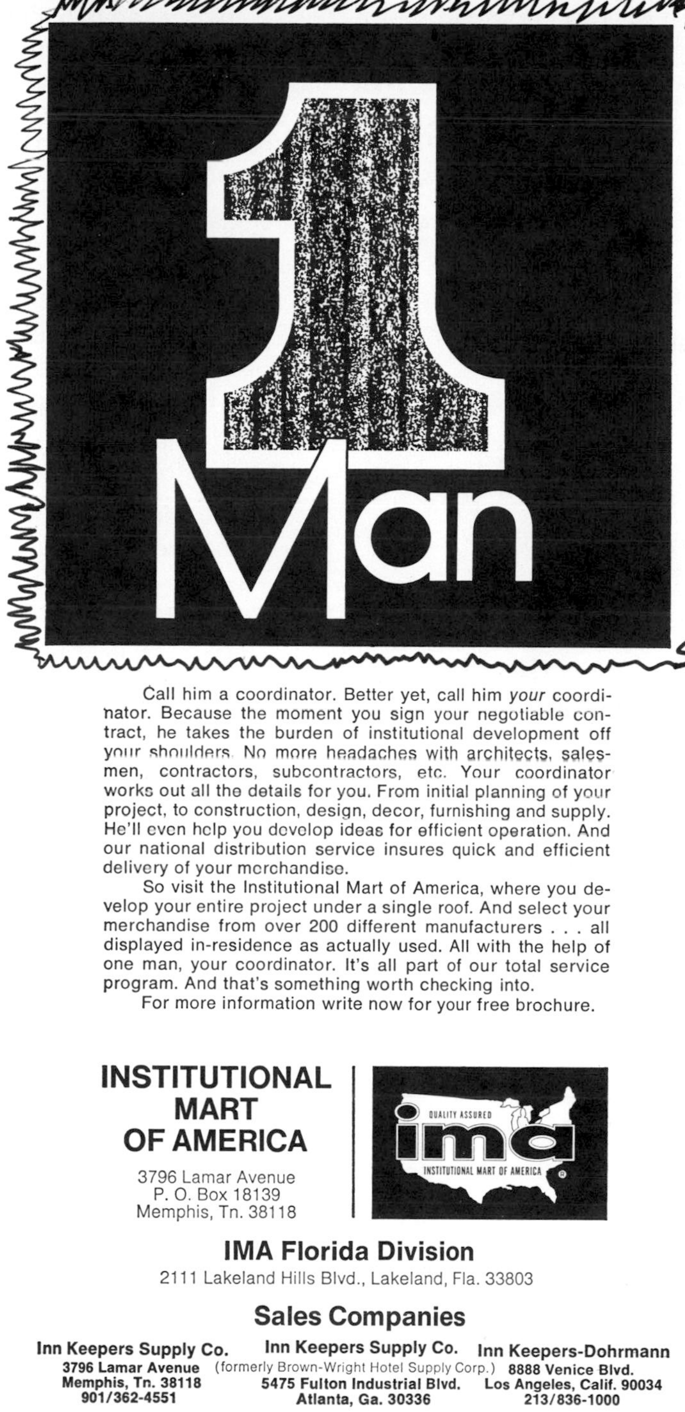

1
Man
Call him a coordinator. Better yet, call him *your* coordinator. Because the moment you sign your negotiable contract, he takes the burden of institutional development off your shoulders. No more headaches with architects, salesmen, contractors, subcontractors, etc. Your coordinator works out all the details for you. From initial planning of your project, to construction, design, decor, furnishing and supply. He'll even help you develop ideas for efficient operation. And our national distribution service insures quick and efficient delivery of your merchandise.
So visit the Institutional Mart of America, where you develop your entire project under a single roof. And select your merchandise from over 200 different manufacturers . . . all displayed in-residence as actually used. All with the help of one man, your coordinator. It's all part of our total service program. And that's something worth checking into.
For more information write now for your free brochure.
INSTITUTIONAL MART OF AMERICA
3796 Lamar Avenue
P. O. Box 18139
Memphis, Tn. 38118
QUALITY ASSURED
ima
INSTITUTIONAL MART OF AMERICA
IMA Florida Division
2111 Lakeland Hills Blvd., Lakeland, Fla. 33803
Sales Companies
Inn Keepers Supply Co.
3796 Lamar Avenue
Memphis, Tn. 38118
901/362-4551
Inn Keepers Supply Co.
(formerly Brown-Wright Hotel Supply Corp.)
5475 Fulton Industrial Blvd.
Atlanta, Ga. 30336
Inn Keepers-Dohrmann
8888 Venice Blvd.
Los Angeles, Calif. 90034
213/836-1000

Fig. 14-17

Executive-management advertisement.

Addressed to the men in the executive suites, this advertisement sells total service. The promise to take care of details is a powerful one in communications addressed to management men who are buried in details.

signed to aid the salesman in making his rounds. Circulars, merchandising folders, sales letters, and post cards are among the type of material referred to. All these items will usually contain highlights of one or more of the basic elements of your sales portfolio—advertising or merchandising. Just remember that their sole function is to arouse interest among the dealers to give display prominence to the product you are advertising, to push it because they are convinced that your advertising is helping them do business.

You will also probably be called upon to write things of direct sales significance to the salesmen themselves, such as sound slide films, skits, and other dramatic presentations to be used in sales meetings and sales rallies, showing these men *how to sell.* Here, of course, you will not be expected to know and plan what goes into the presentations. After all, you are not a sales manager. You will be expected, nevertheless, to understand the information given to you, and to interpret it clearly and forcefully. In a way, you must actually *be* a sales manager. By association with the staff of the sales department, by cultivating their friendship and understanding, you can build a vast backlog of information

Fig. 14-18

Farm advertisement.

Although insurance is bought by farmers and non-farmers, this copy is aimed specifically at farmers. Attention is gained for the advertisement by the unusual art work.

You protect your machinery for a very good reason.

New York Life says your family deserves the same protection.

Like any successful farmer, you spend a lot of time and money on your equipment. You maintain it. You repair it. You insure it. If you didn't, your farm probably wouldn't amount to a hill of beans. Protecting your assets is just good business.

But what about the farm itself? Would your family be able to inherit it intact if you should die? Don't be too sure.

Chances are federal and state taxes, administration fees, outstanding debts and other costs could amount to far more than you imagine. Even force your family to sell off the farm to raise the needed cash.

But there's a good answer. Life insurance. New York Life can guarantee that your family can hang on to the farm intact. It can provide extra money, too, to tide them over. And supplement their income, if necessary.

Your New York Life Agent can show you how you can give your family what it deserves. Financial Security.

We guarantee tomorrow today.

NEW YORK LIFE

New York Life Insurance Company, 51 Madison Avenue, New York, N.Y. 10010. Life, Group and Health Insurance, Annuities, Pension Plans.

on sales problems that will stand you in good stead throughout your career.

Friendship with the sales department is important to copywriters in agencies or advertising departments or even in retail stores. Remember, your lifeline is the sales department. If the sales people don't function correctly, no matter how good your advertising may be, it doesn't *look* good. On the other hand, if *you* don't function correctly, you may make the sales department look bad. The whole business is, or at least should be, a matter of the utmost cooperation.

MATERIAL FOR THE DEALER

Many copywriters make a very serious mistake in giving too little attention to the creation of store display material. Because much of such creation is an art problem—simply adapting advertisements or parts of advertisements, and simplifying them to different proportions—you can easily take the attitude that it does not require much thought on your part. Nothing could be farther from the truth. Many, many sales are lost daily because a copywriter did not understand the nature of the display piece he was building, and made an error that caused his work to be wasted.

For example:

Suppose you are copywriter on a chocolate pudding account. You do a good job of writing and directing an advertising campaign based upon the simply idea of large heads of happy, cute children just about to take a bite of this "Yummy" chocolate pudding. A headline may tell the special good things it has to offer. Following is more short copy and, at the bottom, a picture of the package and a logotype displaying the brand name. The campaign is fine. Everyone likes it. In the magazines or newspapers, it's sure to get lots of attention.

Now the pudding manufacturer wants you to make up a counter display card for grocery stores.

You whip up a counter card, perhaps 12" X 14", which is almost an exact duplicate of your advertisement. That makes good sense, you say to yourself. Cute kid eating the product. That's sure-fire for mothers shopping.

Well, the big hope for counter cards is that they are used together with a counter display of the *product*—card in the middle, packages around it. But big hopes are rarely attained. And all too often, your counter card of soap flakes, candy bars, soft drinks, cereal, or some other product. Where, oh where, is the product identification on *your* counter card when this happens? Yes, that's right—clear down at the *bottom* of the card, completely obscured by other merchandise! It's still a cute picture—still has that important appeal to mothers—but nobody has any idea what you are advertising!

That's the sort of thing that stems from a too hasty examination of what kind of collateral material you are asked to prepare, and an inadequate study of how it is to be used. During your career you may dream up window streamers, counter cards, display easels, wall hangers, over-the-wire banners and pennants, price cards, case display pieces, and other examples of store material. When you are assigned to prepare something of this nature *throw yourself into it.* Don't do it with your left hand while your right hand is writing a color spread for a big circulation consumer magazine.

COPY FOR SPECIALIZED FIELDS—AGRICULTURAL, PROFESSIONAL, EXECUTIVE-MANAGEMENT

Great amounts of copy are written outside of the consumer, industrial, and trade advertising areas thus far discussed in this book. It is impossible to give equal discussion to all the more specialized forms of copy but in the following section you will find a brief discussion of the creative considerations of three of these forms.

Agricultural advertising

To write copy to the man in agriculture you should understand him. He feels isolated, put upon by government, nature, and the inexorable laws of supply and demand that affect the prices he can obtain for what he grows. You must realize that there are wide gulfs between big-business farmers whose acreage is vast and equipment investment enormous, and the small farmer who ekes out a bare living from his few acres. You should know that the problems vary by type of farm, too, since the dairymen have little in common with the cotton grower.

Despite the differences mentioned here, there are some general principles you can observe in writing to the agricultural man.

Watch your language. Today's farmer in a great many instances is no longer the simple son of the soil found in past rural-America. Often he has gone to agricultural school. Even

Fig. 14-19 .

Farm advertising.

Here is a coordinated program utilizing newspapers, radio, and television for the same product. The company also advertises its products in agricultural magazines.

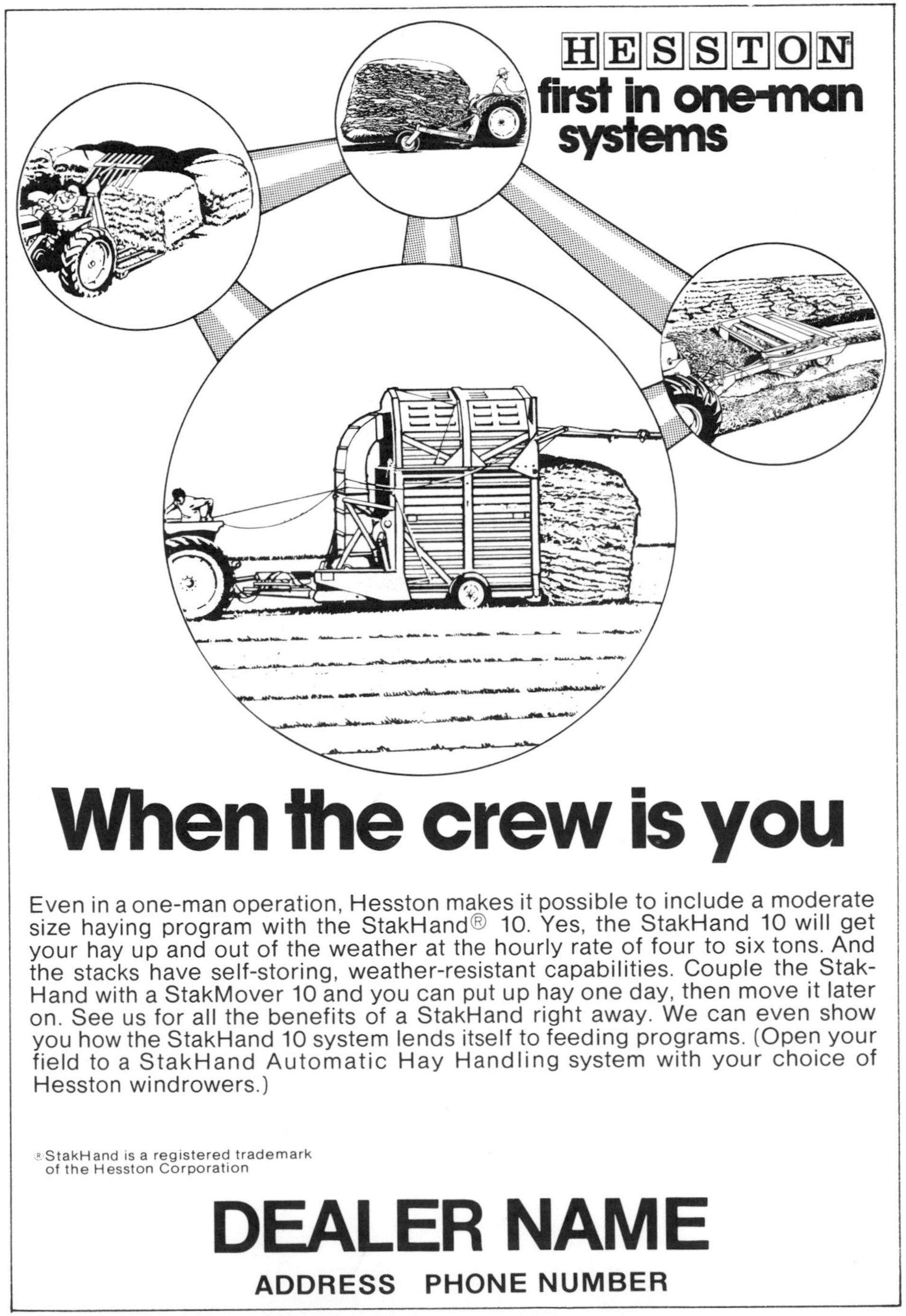
HESSTON
first in one-man systems
When the crew is you
Even in a one-man operation, Hesston makes it possible to include a moderate size haying program with the StakHand® 10. Yes, the StakHand 10 will get your hay up and out of the weather at the hourly rate of four to six tons. And the stacks have self-storing, weather-resistant capabilities. Couple the StakHand with a StakMover 10 and you can put up hay one day, then move it later on. See us for all the benefits of a StakHand right away. We can even show you how the StakHand 10 system lends itself to feeding programs. (Open your field to a StakHand Automatic Hay Handling system with your choice of Hesston windrowers.)
® StakHand is a registered trademark of the Hesston Corporation
DEALER NAME
ADDRESS PHONE NUMBER

if he hasn't, he has learned about antibiotics, animal husbandry, and the fine points of difference in hybrid seed corn. You can use language, therefore, that is any notches above that used some years ago. Be careful, however, that you don't write like a city man trying to talk to a farmer. Use farm language and don't slip. If you do, your copy will be discredited. Remember, too, that although the farmer can be addressed in more sophisticated language than was once true, there are many, many farmers who are not college educated. Avoid a literary flavor and too much urbanity.

Give him proof. Agricultural people have traditionally been skeptical. Alone much of the time and given to introspective thinking, they are cynical about salesmen and their claims. That is true of their attitude about advertising, too.

Testimonials and case histories, accordingly, are useful in agricultural copy is: (a) They relate to the reader's particular interest—hogs, corn, soybeans, dairy herd management, etc. (b) They pertain to the reader's geographic area. The Iowa corngrower, for example, finds little in common with the California corngrower.

Instil a management feel (in some in-

HESSTON RADIO COPY

60-second STAKHAND-10 SYSTEM

(Anncr.) Even when the crew is *you,* there's a *Hesston* StakHand system to fit your haying program. And (Dealer Name in Namc of Town) has it: The StakHand *10* system...ideal for use anywhere you put up just a few tons of hay per season. The StakHand 10 system starts with the Hesston StakHand. And with the StakHand, *one man* can put up one to one-and-a-quarter ton compressed Hesston HayStaks all day long...and never leave his tractor seat. With a StakMover, one man can load the stacks in about one minute, move them where they're wanted, then unload them in less than a minute. And, again, he never leaves his tractor seat. Hesston is first in one-man haying systems, and the StakHand 10 system now makes possible one-man hay handling for the smallest haying program. So see (Dealer Name at Address in Name of Town). Ask him about the StakHand in stover, too.

30-second STAKHAND-10 SYSTEM

(Anncr.) Even when the crew is *you,* there's a *Hesston* StakHand system to fit your haying program. And (Dealer Name in Name of Town) has it: The StakHand *10* system...ideal for use anywhere you put up just a few tons of hay per season. The StakHand 10 system includes a StakHand to put up one to one-and-a-quarter ton compressed Hesston HayStaks and a StakMover to transport the stacks. So see (Dealer Name at Address in Name of Town). Ask him about the StakHand in stover, too.

HESSTON TV COPY

30-second TV Script - STAKHAND SYSTEM

VIDEO:	AUDIO: (Announcer Voice Over)
1. Open on slide of dealer store.	1. If you're looking for the best buy in *one-man* hay handling systems, see (Dealer Name in Name of Town).
2. Cut to slide of dealer beside StakHand.	2. (Dealer Name) is a qualified *Hesston* StakHand dealer...
3. Cut to field action footage of StakHand.	3. ...and Hesston is *first* in one man systems with three StakHands to fit any size haying program. Yes, (Dealer Name) offers one man haying at its most efficient, most economical best.
4. Cut to slide of dealer sign.	4. So, see (Dealer Name) when you're ready for a field demonstration of the Hesston StakHand system.
5. Hold and zoom to extreme close up of dealer name—hold to close.	5. That's (Dealer Name at Address in Name of Town).

stances). This suggestion is made if your product or service is designed for the truly big agricultural establishment where the head man is a businessman as much as an agricultural man. He is buying big-ticket items in combines, tractors, silos and other equipment that runs into heavy expenditures, not to mention fertilizer, seed and less spectacular but still expensive items. Talk to him like a management man.

"Suffer" with him. With some justification the farmer feels that the forces of nature, government, and economics are against him. Let him know that you're on his side and that you know his problems. This can be done subtly, of course.

Professional advertising

Although "professional," might include many activities such as those carried on by lawyers, architects, and teachers, discussion here relates chiefly to medical men. Many of the observations made can be applied to dentists, too. An intelligent copywriter can learn the language and problems of the agricultural man if he is observant and industrious but it is much more difficult to achieve similar success in the medical area. Yet, there are non-medical men and women copywriters who write medical copy, or dental copy. Here are some considerations for such copywriters.

Use the specialized language. Consider this section of copy from an advertisement in a medical magazine: "Verequad provides this help with dual bronchodilating action to relieve smooth muscel spasm of the bronchial tree which usually interferes with the evacuation of bronchi; and expectorant action to thin and loosen tenacious mucus, aiding in its expulsion from the respiratory tract."

If you are writing to doctors, or other professional men, use their language as in the example, not a simplified version of it. Their education has taught them a different vocabulary; it is your obligation to learn it and to employ it.

Avoid overly-personal language. As in industrial advertising, the "you" approach should be avoided. When a doctor reads advertising in his medical journals, he expects to be addressed in a professional manner. Don't write like an advertising copywriter. Medical men, whose writings and talks have been twisted out of shape by promoters of products, are distrustful of advertising men. Thus, they dislike "ad-dy" advertising but will accept advertising written in the style of one

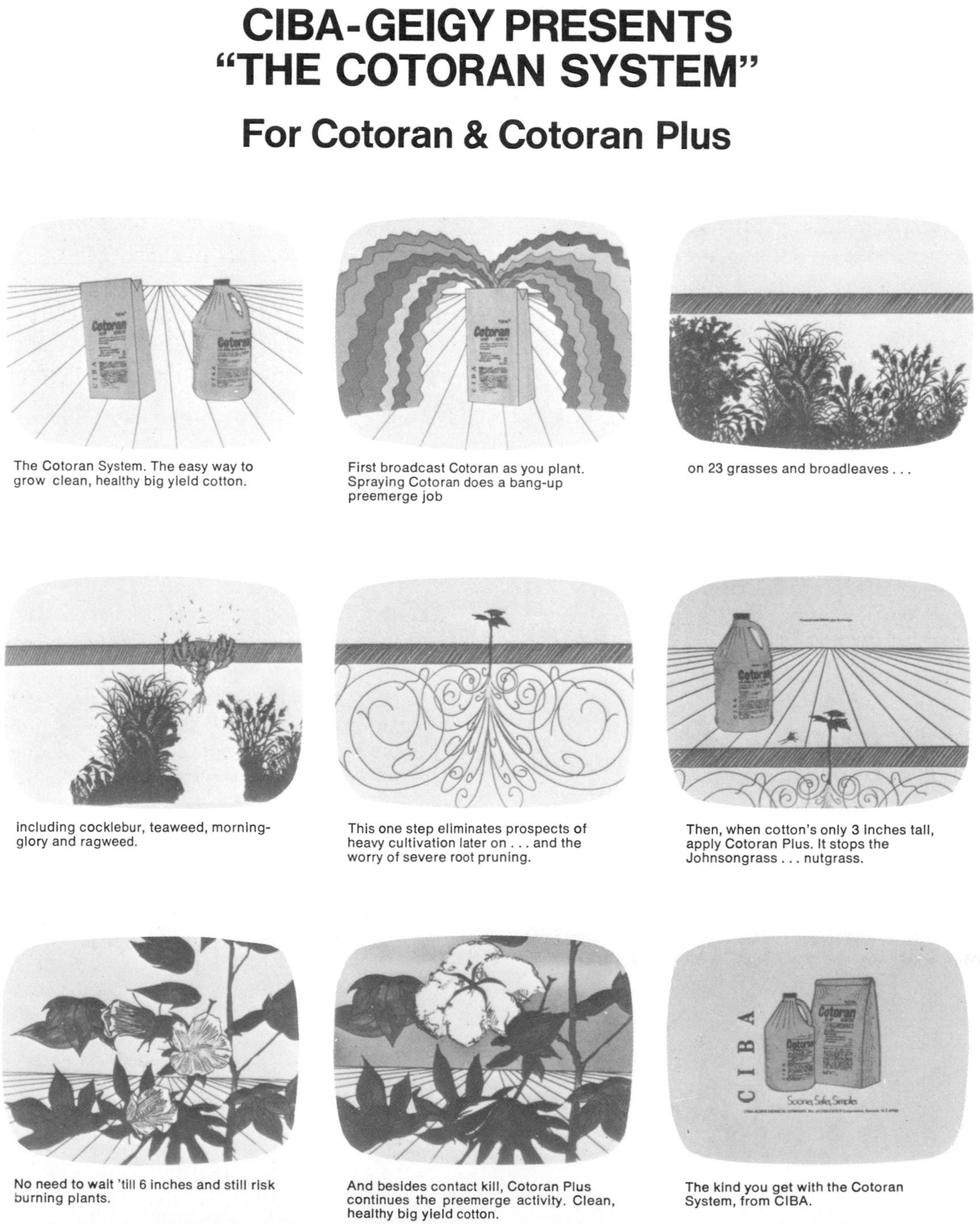
CIBA-GEIGY PRESENTS
"THE COTORAN SYSTEM"
For Cotoran & Cotoran Plus
The Cotoran System. The easy way to grow clean, healthy big yield cotton.
First broadcast Cotoran as you plant. Spraying Cotoran does a bang-up preemerge job
on 23 grasses and broadleaves . . .
Including cocklebur, teaweed, morning-glory and ragweed.
This one step eliminates prospects of heavy cultivation later on . . . and the worry of severe root pruning.
Then, when cotton's only 3 inches tall, apply Cotoran Plus. It stops the Johnsongrass . . . nutgrass.
No need to wait 'till 6 inches and still risk burning plants.
And besides contact kill, Cotoran Plus continues the preemerge activity. Clean, healthy big yield cotton.
The kind you get with the Cotoran System, from CIBA.
CIBA
Cotoran

Fig. 14-20

Animated commercial for an agricultural product.

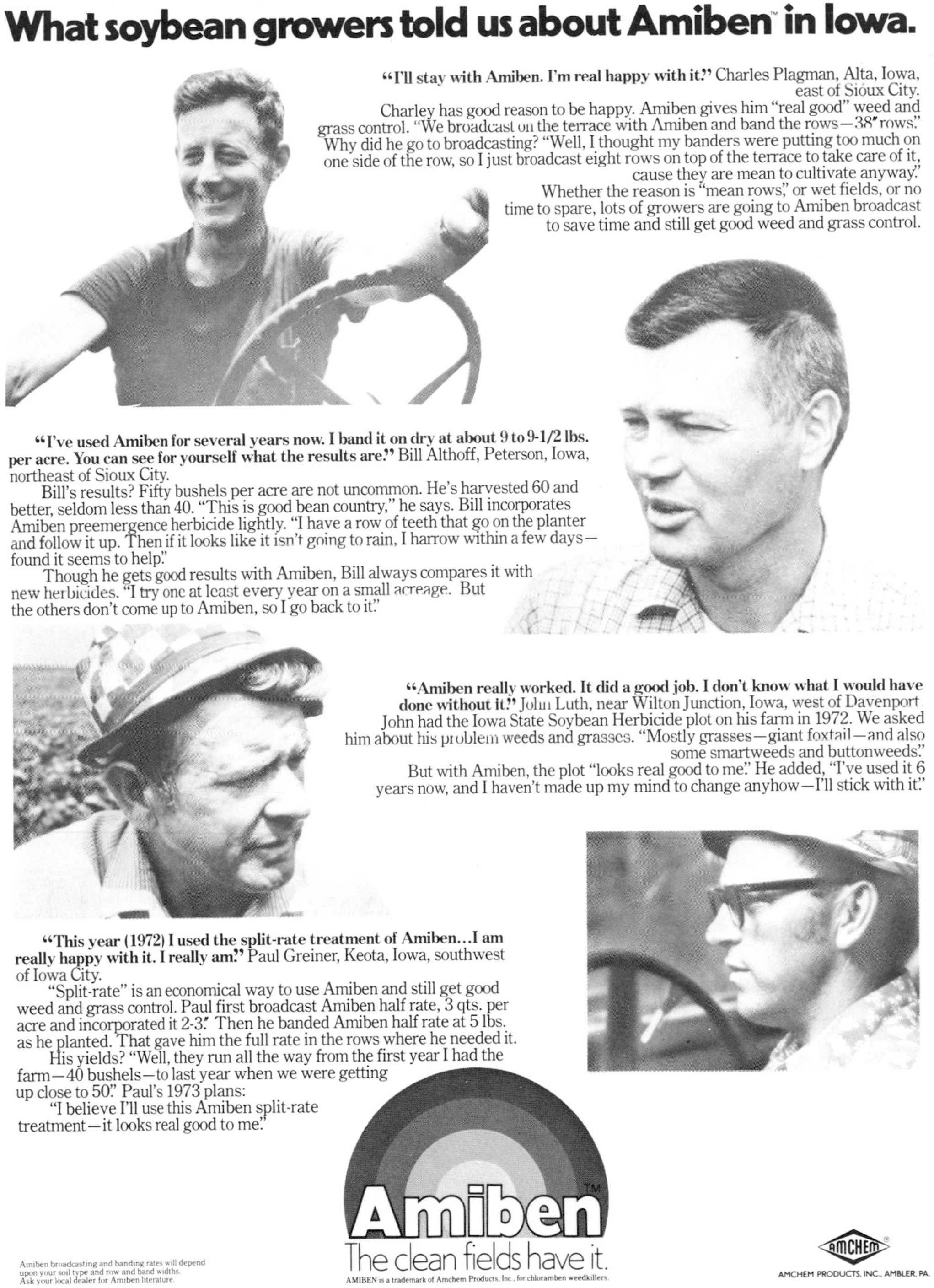
What soybean growers told us about Amiben™ in Iowa.
"I'll stay with Amiben. I'm real happy with it." Charles Plagman, Alta, Iowa, east of Sioux City.
Charley has good reason to be happy. Amiben gives him "real good" weed and grass control. "We broadcast on the terrace with Amiben and band the rows—38" rows." Why did he go to broadcasting? "Well, I thought my banders were putting too much on one side of the row, so I just broadcast eight rows on top of the terrace to take care of it, cause they are mean to cultivate anyway."
Whether the reason is "mean rows," or wet fields, or no time to spare, lots of growers are going to Amiben broadcast to save time and still get good weed and grass control.
"I've used Amiben for several years now. I band it on dry at about 9 to 9-1/2 lbs. per acre. You can see for yourself what the results are." Bill Althoff, Peterson, Iowa, northeast of Sioux City.
Bill's results? Fifty bushels per acre are not uncommon. He's harvested 60 and better, seldom less than 40. "This is good bean country," he says. Bill incorporates Amiben preemergence herbicide lightly. "I have a row of teeth that go on the planter and follow it up. Then if it looks like it isn't going to rain, I harrow within a few days—found it seems to help."
Though he gets good results with Amiben, Bill always compares it with new herbicides. "I try one at least every year on a small acreage. But the others don't come up to Amiben, so I go back to it."
"Amiben really worked. It did a good job. I don't know what I would have done without it." John Luth, near Wilton Junction, Iowa, west of Davenport.
John had the Iowa State Soybean Herbicide plot on his farm in 1972. We asked him about his problem weeds and grasses. "Mostly grasses—giant foxtail—and also some smartweeds and buttonweeds."
But with Amiben, the plot "looks real good to me." He added, "I've used it 6 years now, and I haven't made up my mind to change anyhow—I'll stick with it."
"This year (1972) I used the split-rate treatment of Amiben...I am really happy with it. I really am." Paul Greiner, Keota, Iowa, southwest of Iowa City.
"Split-rate" is an economical way to use Amiben and still get good weed and grass control. Paul first broadcast Amiben half rate, 3 qts. per acre and incorporated it 2-3". Then he banded Amiben half rate at 5 lbs. as he planted. That gave him the full rate in the rows where he needed it.
His yields? "Well, they run all the way from the first year I had the farm—40 bushels—to last year when we were getting up close to 50." Paul's 1973 plans:
"I believe I'll use this Amiben split-rate treatment—it looks real good to me."
Amiben™
The clean fields have it.
AMIBEN is a trademark of Amchem Products, Inc., for chloramben weedkillers.
Amiben broadcasting and banding rates will depend upon your soil type and row and band widths. Ask your local dealer for Amiben literature.
AMCHEM
AMCHEM PRODUCTS, INC., AMBLER, PA.

Fig. 14-21

Farm advertisement using testimonials.

Farmers like to know how others view products, especially if the other farmers are growing similar crops under similar conditions. In this case the subject is weed control and all the farmers are in the same state. This is just one of the pages in a 4-page advertisement appearing in the magazine *Successful Farming.*

doctor addressing another.

Use scientific evidence. Anyone dealing in matters of life and death eschews the casual approach. He wants proof, presented by recognized authorities and backed by careful investigation. Little wonder then that you must draw constantly upon evidence to back any claims you make—and woe to you if the 'evidence' is not supported by proved facts.

Recognize his desire to keep up in his profession. One of the professional man's trials—doctor, dentist, lawyer, architect, teacher—is that new developments occur so rapidly that it is almost impossible to keep up. Thus, the doctor is constantly attending medical meetings, reading scientific journals, exchanging viewpoints with other doctors, and in many ways trying to keep abreast of the latest advances. Your copy should recognize this need to be informed. If you have new features, stress them. If yours is a real breakthrough, make the reader a better professional man, stress it.

Recognize the reader as a user, or recommender. Doctors and dentists, especially, among the professional men, may be viewed in two ways: (a) As persons who will use the advertised product in conducting their profession. A dentist's drill, or a surgical instrument, fall in this category. (b) As persons who will recommend the product's use to patients. A drying lotion for acne, elastic stockings for varicose vein sufferers, or a mild soap for bathing babies fall into this category. Ivory Soap, as an example, has been advertised for many years in medical journals since a doctor's endorsement is so powerful with the new mother anxious to give her baby the best care.

Executive-management advertising

We're concerned here especially with the high-level readers of business magazines such as *Fortune, Wall Street Journal, U.S. News, Business Week* and the business section of the *New York Times.* These men or women feel some sense of kinship with the readers of any magazine addressing itself to management, for example, the readers of institutional magazines in the hotel or hospital fields, or the readers of industrial magazines aimed at management in heavy industry.

Products and services appearing in executive-management publications reflect the broad responsibilities of the readers embracing such widely varying items as computer-calculators, financial services, security-guard protection, high-speed building elevators, business insurance, corporate jets and export banking.

Luxury personal products appear, too, such as high priced automobiles and liquor.

Aim high in the language and subjects you use. High-level, urbane language is much more evident in executive-management magazines than in any other business magazines. A man or woman in the executive suite is likely to be sophisticated, well-educated, and cosmopolitan. Today he is likely to be global in his thinking. He may be in Japan one week and in Yugoslavia for a trade fair the following week.

While he is concerned with ecology and the impact of his industry on the environment he is also concerned with such less broad-gauge management matters as profit-and-loss statements, plant safety, and what the stockholders are thinking. Thus, he is always receptive to advertising that tells him crisply, and sometimes entertainingly about products and services that will result, if used, in a better-run business.

Your language level is not aimed at "the little, old lady in Dubuque" but at a man who appreciates the nuances of good writing. The discussion to this point has centered around the very top management but you might, in the case of many products and services, be aiming at ambitious middle-management men who have heavy responsibilities but not the final word in very top-level decision-making.

If you are consciously aiming at the middle-management executives, your copy may tend to include more facts and figures that the readers may use to arrive at a decision. Advertisements intended for the very top management may, in contrast, be broader and less detailed. The purpose may be to interest the occupant of the executive suite enough to cause him to send a memo down a couple of floors asking a lesser executive "to look into this."

Outdoor And Transit: Copy's Outside Cousins

Men have been advertising with signs for centuries. In the United States, both outdoor and transit advertising have a long history. Of late, each is having its difficulties. The environmentalists have joined other enemies of outdoor advertising to restrict the medium. Transit advertising has suffered a loss of business, especially in the diminished use of inside cards.

Yet each is a lively, vigorous industry for which it is not yet necessary to sing any sad songs. There will always be a place for media that enable advertisers to reach prospects when they are away from home and these two are the *only* media that are wholly devoted to the away-from-home market. They are especially suited for reaching prospects on their way to buying centers.

Despite their many appealing attributes neither medium is very often used as a principal medium. They offer, instead, powerful support as supplementary media. Backing up a campaign in print or television, they can offer effective reinforcement of campaign themes.

Since there are few big budgets devoted largely to outdoor or transit a copywriter usually has relatively few assignments to write copy for these media. When he does, however, he finds it a stimulating challenge since, as is noted later, there are few writing tasks that put such a strain on a writer's creativity. This is especially true if he is not content with mediocre copy and tries for a creative twist that will make his outdoor or transit copy effective, memorable, and different.

OUTDOOR ADVERTISING TYPES

As a copywriter you will probably be concerned with only two major forms of door advertising:

(1) 24-sheet posters

(2) Painted bulletins and painted walls

The 24-sheet poster, the most widely used type of toudoor advertising, is what people are usually referring to when they speak of billboards. Technically, that portion of a 24-sheet poster allotted for the use of the advertiser is 8 ft. 8 in. high by 19 ft. 6 in. wide. Twenty-four-sheets are so called because, when first introduced, they were composed from 24 sheets of paper, each printed separately.

Although painted bulletins are gradually being standardized, painted walls have no standard sizes. Both types are bought and produced as individual units. Like posters they may or may not be illuminated, depending on whether the intensity of the night-time traffic passing them justifies the extra cost of lighting.

Before any further discussion of these major types of outdoor advertising and, more explicitly, the differences between "outdoor" copy and publication and broadcast copy, think of the medium as a whole. What are its advantages? What are its disadvantages?

Outdoor advertising, as the term is ordinarily used in the advertising business, is intended to apply *only*—solely and exclusively—to those companies engaged in *standard* outdoor advertising. That is, the companies represented by the *standard* well-maintained poster boards, the neat, regularly painted bulletins and "well-groomed" units—not the torn and tattered circus, theatrical, and election posters that continue to proclaim their "wares" months after their advertising usefulness has passed—or the rusty metal signs and crude homemade signs still seen "decorating" fences, buildings, and roadside pastures.

Say hello to an
old friend.
GTE
GENERAL
TELEPHONE

Fig. 15-1

Outdoor poster that is part of a corporate image campaign that creates a warm feeling for the company.

It's not
the same old line.
GTE
GENERAL
TELEPHONE

Fig. 15-2

Outdoor poster with clever twist.

ADVANTAGES OF OUTDOOR ADVERTISING

1. People, generally, *like* to read outdoor advertising since it relieves the tedium of the long journey, or the daily commuting trip. This, of course, does not mean that people see and read every sign they pass nor does it mean that the same results would be obtained everywhere. It does, however, indicate that outdoor offers you a huge potential audience for your message—*if you make it appealing enough to arouse the public's interest.*

2. Outdoor advertising offers *continuity.* Your message will remain on the same location for a full 30-day period and may be backing up a copy idea your magazine advertisements have established. Since most people travel and retravel the same route every day on their way to and from their work or shopping, you are able to hammer home your message to the same group of people day after day after day.

An outdoor "showing" of your poster will usually be displayed simultaneously on a number of boards along major traffic arteries. As a person travels down such roads he will often see (and read) the same poster several times before reaching his destination. This constant repetition has a cumulative effect much like that which makes a song a hit. When a tune is introduced, it usually elicits little response, but as you hear it played again and again you find yourself unconsciously humming or whistling it as you go through the day. The repetition, not the song alone, has made a deep impression—so it is with the constant view of the same outdoor posters.

3. Outdoor advertising permits you to use color at relatively low cost. Because newspapers and magazines will not accept color advertisements except in large-size space, many publication advertisers who would like to use color cannot afford to do so. An outdoor advertiser, on the other hand, can easily afford to use color, even though his total advertising may consist of but a single painted wall sign.

4. Outdoor showings of any magnitude greatly impress dealers stocking the advertised product. Day after day they are constantly reminded of the advertising the manufacturer is putting behind his product in order to help him, the dealer, sell more of it.

5. Outdoor advertising is often the *only* medium that can successfully reach an advertiser's best prospects. The hotel posters one sees as he approaches almost every city in an automobile are a good example. They are the only economical means the hotel has at its disposal for reaching the great bulk of the motorists who plan to spend the night in the city.

Because posters are the most widely used form of standard outdoor advertising, and the only type regularly requiring new designs every month, you will deal with them far more than with the others. To win an audience, in competition with all the many other things that may attract a person's attention as he walks down the street or whizzes by in his car, is no easy task. To create a poster that will do this successfully, you have to start with a good *idea!* It doesn't necessarily have to be a *clever* idea; it can be as straightforward as a sermon, but it *shouldn't be dull!* And it must be simplicity itself—usually *so* simple as to be obvious.

KEEP OUTDOOR POSTERS SIMPLE

Simplicity is very evident whenever effective posters are studied to determine *why* they are effective. You will find simplicity mentioned often as an important attribute of effective posters. There *are,* however, some situations in which it is possible to be more subtle in your copy situation—for instance, in a sign on a crowded city street. Such a sign could be read by walkers or slow-moving drivers. Where reading must be done more quickly, however, it is best to use a simple message.

Unfortunately, there is no set formula to follow that will enable you to hit on prize-winning poster ideas regularly. Such ideas are elusive to even the best of creative men.

A pair of quotations might be helpful here as the first guides for your poster-writing efforts. Both are from the pen of the famous nineteenth-century editor and theologian, Tryon Edwards:

> "Have something to say; say it, and stop when you're done."
>
> "Never be so brief as to be obscure."

Having achieved your selling idea, it is extremely important in glance-read poster copy to concentrate attention on your *one* idea. Don't try to make two, three, or four copy points. Be satisfied to slam one point at the readers. If it's tires, it may be safety; gasoline, mileage; bread, taste; soft drinks, refreshment; automobiles, beauty.

Each of the foregoing products has other appeals, but don't use them in combination. *Stick to one idea.*

MOST GOOD POSTERS USE SHORT COPY

Remember, your message must be telegraphic—so concise, yet so clear, that even people with below-average intelligence will "get" it the instant their eyes hit the board. You have *five seconds* to register if the panel is visible at 250 feet and the motorist is going 35 miles an hour.

One study of poster advertising examined 500 posters to see how many words of copy were to be found in each. Here is the way the analysis broke down:

Number of	
posters without words	3.5%
posters with one word	3.1
posters with two words	9.8
posters with three words	16.5
posters with four words	21.2
posters with five words	16.1
posters with six words	11.3

Like everything else in copy, however, the length of poster copy is not to be established through fixed rules. Although it is obvious that keeping your poster copy short is good sense normally, it is possible to find instances of use of longer messages.

Fig. 15-3

Outdoor campaign that uses play on words.

The continuity here is supplied by easily-understood play on words and by the distinctive typography in each poster.

PLUMBERS
ARE ON TAP in the
Yellow Pages
DRY CLEANERS
ARE EASILY SPOTTED in the
Yellow Pages
BICYCLES
HAVE SPOKESMEN in the
Yellow Pages

Fig. 15-4

Outdoor campaign.

Good examples of effective continuity in outdoor advertising. Each poster is different but each has a similarity that provides continuity and quick identification.

Hit us when you're down.
The Arizona Bank Loan Officers
Sock it to us.
The Arizona Bank Savings Tellers
We won't hold you up.
The Arizona Bank Tellers

Readability and comprehension should guide you in determining length of poster copy—not inflexible rules that limit your imagination and originality.

POSTER ELEMENTS

What are the copy and layout elements of a poster? The number varies according to the complexity of the poster, but here is a list that will serve you normally. Posters will generally be made up from some or all of these:

(1) Product name
(2) Principal illustration
(3) Short copy to back up illustration
(4) Package
(5) Selling Phrase

Other elements have been included, but these five are found most often. To keep the list simple, such elements as trademarks, company name, and price were not included.

In many cases the package may well be the principal illustration. A selling phrase may be a slogan or it can constitute the "short copy to back up the illustration." In brief, the elements are juggled around as demanded by the institution, the campaign, or the product itself.

The elements are clear-cut. It is your use of them that results in effective or ineffective posters. Since simplicity is so important to quick reading, attain simplicity by avoiding the mixing of too many elements in one poster. Because there *are* five elements listed in the foregoing does not mean you must use them all. Remember—*strive for simplicity by limiting the number of ideas and elements.*

HOW OUTDOOR ADVERTISING IS BORN

When you receive a request for "one" outdoor poster design, do not be misled by the use of the singular. In order to create a Grade-A poster, you may have to "hatch" a dozen or more ideas—and have several rough, thumbnail layouts of each sketched out on tissue by an art associate.

After these numerous rough tissue layouts are assembled, you and the other persons working on the account will give them a "going over"—discussing and appraising each in detail, and eliminating many. The ideas or designs that survive this first session will be revised and polished, and again be subjected to the close scrutiny of all concerned. You'll repeat the same thing again and again and again, until, finally, you're satisfied you have a poster that will do a job!

Posters are usually (1) direct adaptations of advertisements, using the same headlines and

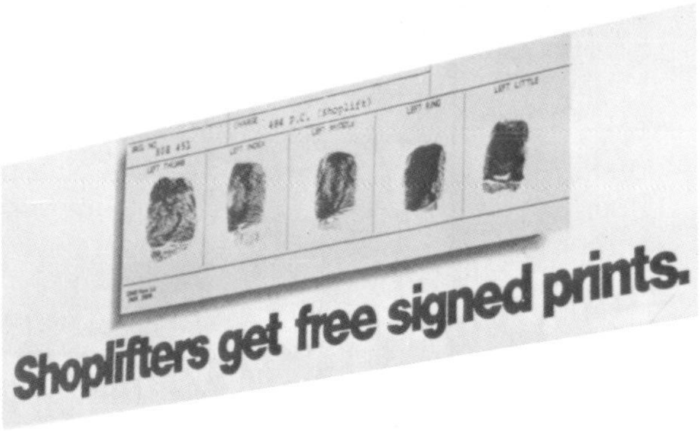
Shoplifters get free signed prints.

Fig. 15-5

Outdoor poster of the public service type.

The humorous twist obtains better readership than if the copywriter had attempted to "lecture."

Fig. 15-6

Public service outdoor sign that carries a dramatic wallop.

The use of the hypodermic needle embellishment gives an extra impact to this outdoor advertising. Notice, too,how the writer has achieved a clever twist in the combination of his words and the use of the hypodermic needle.

POINT OF
NO RETURN
NAEGELE

illustrations used in magazines or newspapers; (2) semi-direct adaptations, in which the theme idea is followed, but which use specially created headlines and/or illustrations; (3) presentations that are completely dissociated from the advertiser's publication or radio copy. In the last type, no attempt is made to tie in with the campaign theme. New ideas are used, but usually a certain family resemblance is maintained.

Outdoor is an ideal medium for publicizing trade-names, trade characters, package identifications, slogans, or any idea that may be quickly stated with perfect clarity. Because it permits the use of color at relatively low cost, it affords an excellent means for putting over appetite appeal. A bowl of corn flakes and strawberries looks like wood shavings and licorice drops when reproduced in black and white. But give it color and it will look so tempting as to be almost irresistible.

PREMIUM ON CREATIVITY

In no other form of written advertising is it more important to be different in imagination and creativity, than in outdoor advertising. That is, of course, because of the nature of posters, the limited amount of space for words and illustration, the need for short,

QUIET AS A FORD

Fig. 15-7

Humorous outdoor poster.

With four words and an amusing illustration, the copywriter and artist have conveyed the advertiser's campaign theme.

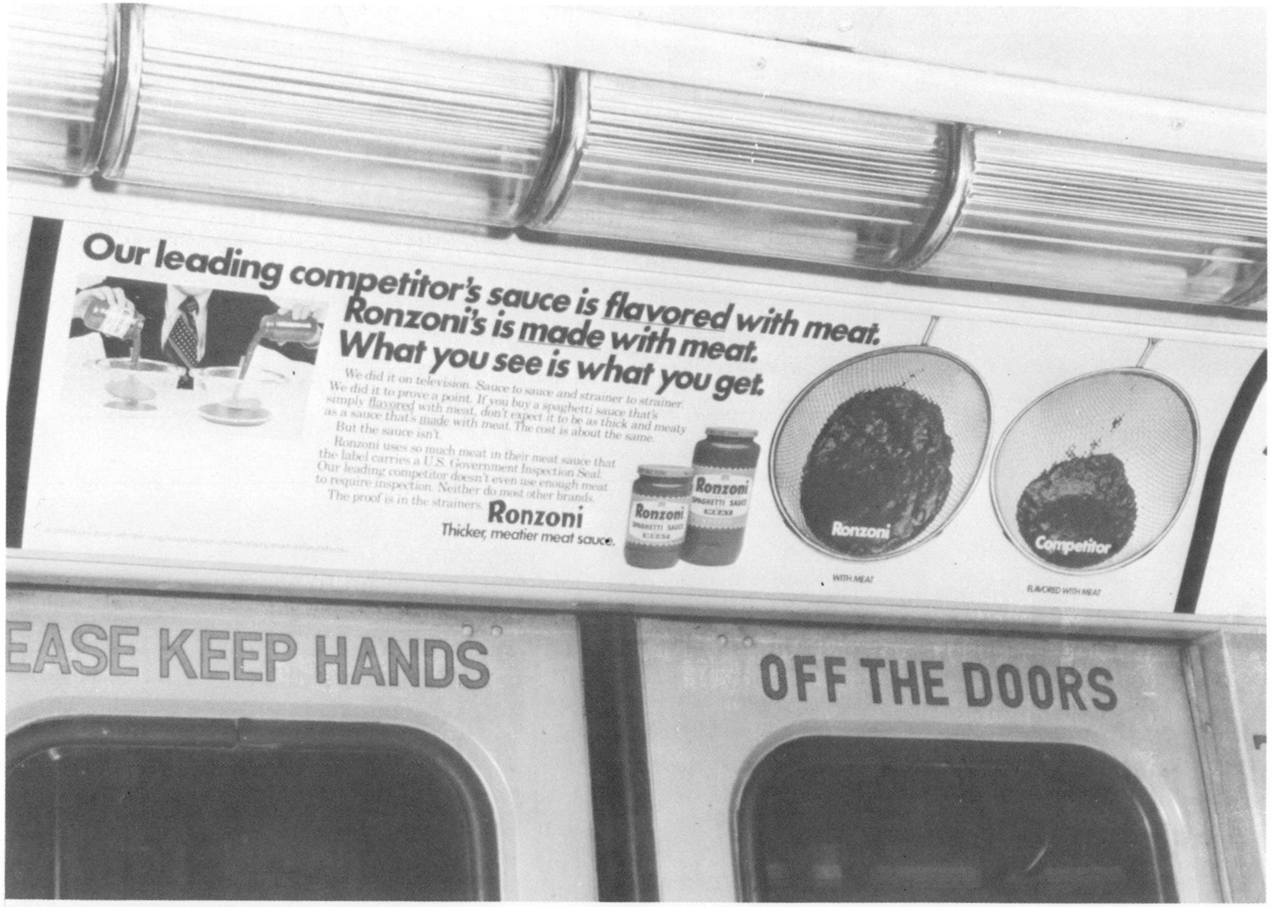
Our leading competitor's sauce is flavored with meat.
Ronzoni's is made with meat.
What you see is what you get.
Ronzoni
Thicker, meatier meat sauce.
Ronzoni
Competitor
EASE KEEP HANDS
OFF THE DOORS

Fig. 15-8

Long copy inside transit card.

This card makes full use of the space and long reading time by: Display of the package. A photo demonstration of the product. Ample copy that gives good reasons for buying the product and that refers to the company's advertising on television.

terse copy, and the requirement of product identification.

The chief function of poster advertising is to serve as a buying reminder to people who are, or will soon be in a position to buy. You are often going after what is called the "impulse sale" when you write poster copy. Since you haven't the time or space to persuade people to buy your product, you have to assume that they have already been sold by some other form of advertising; your job is to remind them of your brand in a bright, memorable and attention-compelling way.

Products such as beer, soft drinks, gasoline, cigarettes and candy are "naturals" for poster advertising. *Your prospect is in an automobile.* He or she is going to stop within minutes. Chances are good that he will purchase one or more of these items, or similar ones, when he does.

It must be equally obvious to you why hotels advertise so extensively on outdoor posters, and restaurants, taverns and other public services. They want to remind the immediate prospect of what they have to offer.

It is often said that the outdoor poster which advertises a grocery store product is a giant point-of-sale display. Food retailers

Fig. 15-9

Long-copy inside transit card.

This card, with its many words and figures, gives the transit riders much to think about. This card demonstrates how much more copy can be written for inside cards than outside cards, or for outdoor posters.

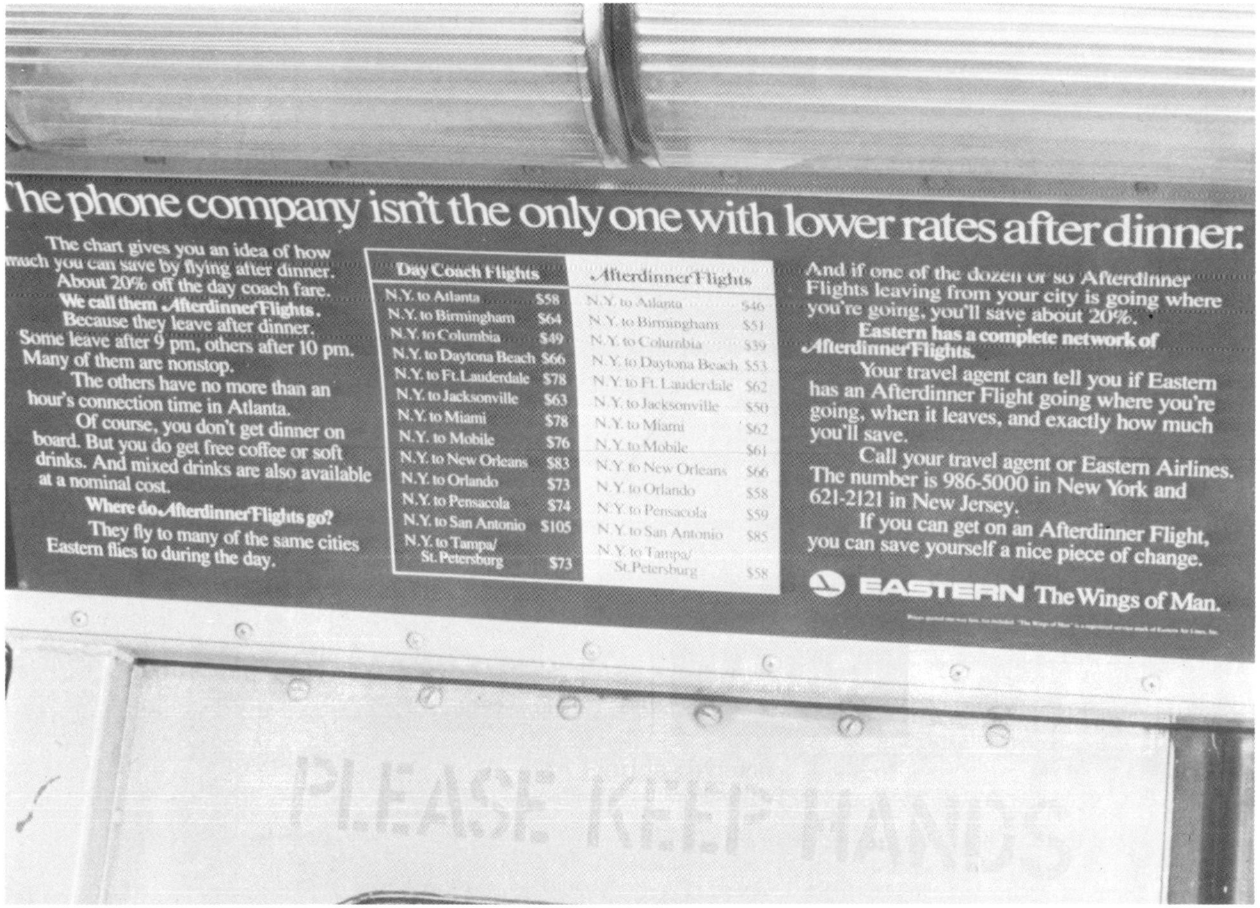
he phone company isn't the only one with lower rates after dinner.
The chart gives you an idea of how
you can save by flying after dinner.
About 20% off the day coach fare.
We call them Afterdinner Flights.
Because they leave after dinner.
Some leave after 9 pm, others after 10 pm.
Many of them are nonstop.
The others have no more than an hour's connection time in Atlanta.
Of course, you don't get dinner on board. But you do get free coffee or soft drinks. And mixed drinks are also available at a nominal cost.
Where do Afterdinner Flights go?
They fly to many of the same cities Eastern flies to during the day.
Day Coach Flights
N.Y. to Atlanta $58
N.Y. to Birmingham $64
N.Y. to Columbia $49
N.Y. to Daytona Beach $66
N.Y. to Ft. Lauderdale $78
N.Y. to Jacksonville $63
N.Y. to Miami $78
N.Y. to Mobile $76
N.Y. to New Orleans $83
N.Y. to Orlando $73
N.Y. to Pensacola $74
N.Y. to San Antonio $105
N.Y. to Tampa/ St. Petersburg $73
Afterdinner Flights
N.Y. to Atlanta $46
N.Y. to Birmingham $51
N.Y. to Columbia $39
N.Y. to Daytona Beach $53
N.Y. to Ft. Lauderdale $62
N.Y. to Jacksonville $50
N.Y. to Miami $62
N.Y. to Mobile $61
N.Y. to New Orleans $66
N.Y. to Orlando $58
N.Y. to Pensacola $59
N.Y. to San Antonio $85
N.Y. to Tampa/ St. Petersburg $58
And if one of the dozen or so Afterdinner Flights leaving from your city is going where you're going, you'll save about 20%.
Eastern has a complete network of Afterdinner Flights.
Your travel agent can tell you if Eastern has an Afterdinner Flight going where you're going, when it leaves, and exactly how much you'll save.
Call your travel agent or Eastern Airlines. The number is 986-5000 in New York and 621-2121 in New Jersey.
If you can get on an Afterdinner Flight, you can save yourself a nice piece of change.
EASTERN The Wings of Man.
PLEASE KEEP HANDS

know that a poster placed on a main traffic location near their store will serve as a quick reminder to shoppers who may very well be on their way to buy from them. These locations, near shopping centers and village business sections, are considered ideal by advertisers whose products sell through food stores.

You'll see much automobile advertising on outdoor boards. While an automobile is not an impulse purchase, nor an immediate-action type of product, remember that a large percentage of the people who see a car displayed on an outdoor poster are driving cars a year or more old. They cannot help being influenced by a sales message showing a beautiful new car. These impressions will multiply to help make the eventual sale.

SELL AND ENTERTAIN

Provided you adhere to the number one rule of *simplicity,* both in illustration and message, you can use cuteness, or cleverness, and the more of either the better! If you're bright enough to make your poster *tell an entertaining story* while it punches home a copy message and product identification you have probably succeeded in creating a good poster. Remember, however, that you have to get the whole thing accomplished in *five seconds.*

Fig. 15-10

Inside transit card that resembles an outdoor poster.

The writer has provided a strong message in few words and made a positive suggestion at the same time.

One of the most famous outdoor posters of all time was the one a number of years ago that read:

THE ONLY CONVERTIBLE
THAT OUTSELLS FORD!

The illustration was a *baby buggy.*

The copywriter who did this poster had a perfect combination of influences. It's simple —just five words besides the name of the product. It gives a selling point of importance —more people buy Ford convertibles than any other, and it says so in a very clever, warmly human, memorable way.

Another great Ford poster violated every rule in the copywriter's book. That was the one which showed the little boy looking longingly into a Ford dealer's window at a new model, and the only brand identification shown was the Ford name on the dealer's window, which was *backward!*

The Morton Salt Company has had many prize winning posters. You may remember their short, simple, but hard-selling line that was used for an extended period:

IF IT'S WORTH ITS SALT,
IT'S WORTH MORTON'S

Get your Campbell's worth!
About 7¢ a 7-oz. serving!
Campbell's
CHICKEN
NOODLE
SOUP
THE DOORS

Fig. 15-11

Inside transit card with humorous twist that catches the attention of riders anxious for diversion.

Fig. 15-12

Inside transit card.

A card written with humor and a directness that will entertain bored riders. Notice, too, that the writer has written a complete message. He has not treated this card as a "baby billboard."

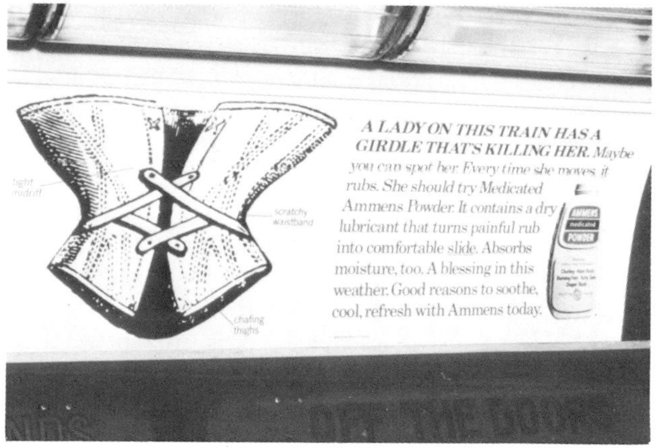
A LADY ON THIS TRAIN HAS A GIRDLE THAT'S KILLING HER. Maybe you can spot her. Every time she moves it rubs. She should try Medicated Ammens Powder. It contains a dry lubricant that turns painful rub into comfortable slide. Absorbs moisture, too. A blessing in this weather. Good reasons to soothe, cool, refresh with Ammens today.

Does the boss ever take a fat girl to lunch?
Yes.
Every Christmas.
D-ZERTA
Better make dessert D-Zerta / the 9 calorie gelatin dessert by Jell-O.

illustrated by luscious vegetables, melons, fruits and other food items commonly improved by the addition of salt.

Standard Oil of Indiana once won a poster competition with a poster which had just one word on it . . . TOPS! It was illustrated only with the cap *worn* by the Standard filling station operator. Ritz Crackers, a national sales leader, used extensive poster advertising that featured puns. One example you may recall—an illustration of a happy man comfortably "settling" back into an easy chair with a package of Ritz and the line

"I'LL SETTLE FOR RITZ!"

You don't *have* to be brilliant, but often it helps a great deal to make your poster sing out from a highway lined with less imaginative efforts.

Whether you elect to be cute or whether your product and problem call for straight selling, above all keep your outdoor advertising *simple, short* and interesting.

You'll see a number of posters in this chapter's illustrations, all of which have won prizes for composition and design, as well as for their copy message. Study them. See how in every case the copywriter and art director

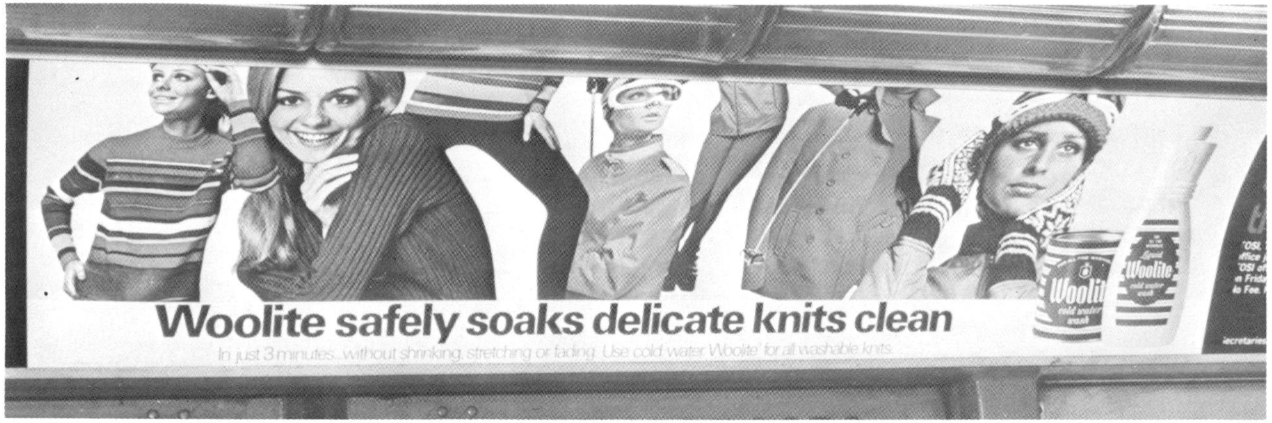
Woolite safely soaks delicate knits clean
Woolite

Fig. 15-13

Inside transit card that puts the headline at the bottom for easier reading.

worked together for a total effect of a fast, memorable impression.

SUMMARY

To sum up, you might keep the following in mind when you write and design posters:

1. Be satisfied generally to put over one idea in a poster.
2. Use as few elements as possible and make those elements count.
3. Be brief, but don't be brief for brevity's sake. If your copy needs to be more than ordinarily long in order to do the job more effectively, then make it longer.
4. Don't be subtle in most posters. Make your poster simple—easy to understand in glance-reading.
5. If you're promoting a packaged product, you can increase package recognition by featuring the package on your posters.
6. Use positive suggestion—although you won't use this technique in all posters, many posters will be stronger if you suggest something the reader can act upon.

TRANSIT CARDS

Although they are not literally located "outdoors," transit cards are often discussed as a branch of outdoor advertising. Most advertising men feel now, however, that transit cards are *not* "miniature posters"!

Some copywriters still look on them as such. If they would but compare transit cards and posters, they would see that except for their shape there is little similarity. Thinking of transit cards as "baby billboards" has caused many copywriters to write poor transit cards. They are not posters, and should not be treated as such.

It is often mistakenly thought that it is necessary for a transit card, like a poster, to get its message over in the flickering of an eyelid. The thought is not sound. Your transit card is traveling right along with your audience, whereas the poster must be read quickly as the automobile whizzes by. The transit card and the reader are relatively stationary. The people you are interested in reaching don't rush by your transit card at a gallop. They sit or stand near it for a long time, 27 minutes per one-way trip on the average, according to studies. The reader can thus linger over your copy, if you have caught his eye and if you have interested him sufficiently to make him want to do so. You don't, accordingly, have to limit your copy to five or six words. Or 50 or 60, for that matter. One important restraining element on the number of words is the requirement that the message be readable three seats ahead or back of the card.

Transit cards can be so designed as to be real traveling salesmen"—selling advertisements that can, by themselves, put over a sale instead of being mere reminders.

As you write a transit card, recall that you are not expecting to reach *everyone* in the car at one time. Passengers aren't going to stretch, and crane, and twist to read your copy. The only people you will usually reach at any single moment are those passengers standing or sitting close to where the card is posted. This is why it is not essential to keep copy brief, nor type king-size. If a person can read your poster from six or eight feet away, readability is all right. A good way to test readability quickly is to place the poster on the ground at your feet. If you can read it easily, the card will probably be readable for riders in vehicles carrying transit cards.

Another thing to remember about transit cards is that they curve. Also that the *bottom* of the card, rather than the top, is closer to the reader's eyes, therefore, is usually easier

Fig. 15-14

Outside transit card with a creative twist.

15 JACKSON HEIGHTS
... A MOUTHFUL IN THE MORNING

to read. More and more this fact is being taken into consideration, which explains why you find many transit card *headlines* at the *bottom*. Because of curvature, the upper inch or so of the card often is practically flat against the roof of the car or bus. If you put *any* of your copy story in these "upper reaches," make it a subordinate line, not your real selling message.

Regarding transit cards, remember—you *may* make them "miniature posters," if you will thus more effectively get over your message, but do not consider such practice as standard. In these days the poster often takes one technique and the transit card another.

OUTSIDE CARDS

In recent years there has been a falling off of the use of inside transit cards and a veritable stampede to the outside cards displayed on the ends and sides of buses. Advertisers using the outside cards obtain readership from pedestrians, motorists, and even from homes as people see the bus going by their windows.

In a sense, the outside cards are a form of traveling outdoor advertising that carries the

Fig. 15-15

Outside transit card on rear of bus.

advertiser's message into all parts of the town. For the copywriter, the outside cards constitute a strong creative challenge since the length of the sales message must be severely limited. Truly, in the case of outside transit cards, the copywriter must consider them closer to outdoor advertising than to the transit advertising represented by inside transit cards.

To write the copy for such cards, the copywriter should, therefore, follow exactly the same suggestions that were made for writing outdoor advertising. Brevity. A single compelling idea. Few elements. Simplicity.

Another form of outside card is the station poster that greets subway and train riders before they step inside the cars. These are treated like outdoor poster except that they are vertical inside of horizontal. Somewhat more copy may be written for these posters than for 24-sheet posters because reading time is longer both by people standing on platforms and by people reading the posters when the transit vehicle is discharging and picking up passengers.

MONEY to the People
OTB

Fig. 15-16

Outside transit card that makes a positive suggestion.

8655
Take us home
The Original
THOMAS'
English
MUFFINS

IDEAS FOR WRITING TRANSIT CARD COPY

Although it has been pointed out that transit cards are not small posters, you should consider that there *are* some techniques that might transfer from one to the other.

1. As in posters, transit cards will usually be more effective if one sales point is made. An attempt to make more than one point will usually dilute your message.

2. Although your reading time is greater for your copy in transit cards, like posters, they should not have too many elements if they are to be efficient and readable.

3. A transit card can use more copy than a poster, but don't go wild. Brevity is still desirable for most cards. The use of a little white space will be helpful sometimes in giving your card a favorable contrast to the crowded cards next to yours.

4. Simplicity is another quality shared by posters and transit cards. Because of your being able to use more copy, you *may* indulge in more subtlety in transit cards, but don't overplay it. The average car rider is usually better sold by a simple message.

Fig. 15-17

Outside transit card with an embellishment.

Esquire Magazine attracted much attention with this Christmas-season idea.

SPECIAL
Esquire
Esquire
Esquire
Esquire
Esquire
Esquire
CHRISTMAS
GIFTMOBILE

5. The featuring of the package is, of course, desirable in transit cards as well as posters—especially so since your card may be the last advertising contact with someone who is about to start her shopping tour.

6. Positive suggestion is a part of transit-card copy, too. As in poster copy, it is not used in every advertisement, but in the right advertisements it becomes a forceful, selling technique.

Thus, in summarizing the essential differences in handling the two—posters and cards—you find that:

a. Unorthodox layout tricks are often used in transit-card designing—the placing of headline at the bottom of the advertisement, for instance, the allowance for the curved surface, and other factors.

b. More latitude is possible in writing transit-card copy since average reading time of transit cards is about 27 minutes, contrasted with the five to ten seconds' reading time of posters. The end result is longer copy and an opportunity for more subtle copy.

16

Radio: Writing For the Ear

In this television era it seems hard to believe that radio was once the "glamor" medium with all the attributes of Hollywood, "big name" stars, and much-heralded shows that kept millions close to their sets each evening. For a number of years radio was everything that television is today. It was the ambition of copywriters to write for radio. To have one's commercials used on the big network shows was to have reached the "big time."

Now, with radio networks reduced to a whisper and the huge-audience shows vanished, the glamor is gone from radio but not the importance. This may be the age of the picture tube but radio is thriving nonetheless. While radio cannot at any one time period command the huge audiences it once did, the medium still reaches a large audience of accumulative listeners—listeners who are gathered during any given week. Although network radio collapsed, local and regional radio has more than made up for the loss.

Radio has become the medium that reaches people while they are doing something (other than purposefully listening to radio). A radio commercial is heard while the "listener" is driving a car, ironing, making beds, milking cows, waiting for service in a restaurant, doing homework, writing letters, eating breakfast. Radio, as the industry reminds advertisers, reaches the audience anywhere and everywhere, no matter what that audience is doing.

Awareness that the radio audience is not immobile and attentive has caused radio writers to change their writing formats. Where once the typical radio listener tuned in to program after program and listened carefully to all of them, he is now a restless, dial-changing listener to whom radio is a background to other activities. His attention must be captured and every device must be used to hold that attention. Some down-to-earth suggestions for keeping attention are given here by a veteran radio writer.

16 WAYS TO CAPTURE AND HOLD ATTENTION FOR RADIO COMMERCIALS

1. PRODUCT-IN-ACTION SOUND EFFECTS: Coffee comes to life in the percolator, as Maxwell House proved in its radio commercials. There are sounds relevant to just about every product, waiting to be employed as creative tools. Beyond the sound itself, how it's used can also make a big difference.

2. MIX 'EM UP: Experiment with various combinations of jingle, dialogue, straight announcement, sound effects, music, etc., all in one commercial. Presented with this kind of variety, the listener is likely to be attentive, wondering what's coming next. The commercial can be a miniature show.

3. SYMBOLIC CHARACTER: Have a distinctive voice represent your product. If it's indigenous to a foreign country, such as spaghetti and macaroni, the voice can hold listener attention by speaking with an accent typical of that country.

4. TIE IN WITH STATIONS' FEATURES: Integrate your commercials with the weather reports, time checks, musical styles, or even the call letters. Any way you can sound less like an interruption to regular programing helps.

5. CALL ON COMEDY STARS: For truly entertaining spots, you can use the guys whose job it is to be funny. But don't let it fall flat; get real comedy material, either from the performer, if he writes, or from his writers.

6. VARIATIONS ON A THEME: Once you hit on the magic jingle, don't be content to present it at one tempo, over and over. See that it gets every treatment from cool jazz to old fashioned waltz.

7. TIE IN WITH CURRENT EVENTS: What's going on in the world that has everyone interested? Is there a world's heavyweight championship fight in the works? Sign one of the fighters for your commercials, if the product lends itself to endorsement by a name from the world of sports.

8. AD LIBS: For the height of realism, why not let your spokesmen call it the way they see it? Foreign actors are most articulate and convincing given the freedom to speak of their country's advantages for radio airing.

9. SPEED UPS—SLOW DOWNS: Often you can capture attention by tampering with the speed of sounds in radio commercials. Caution: take care that important words don't get garbled in the process.

10. REAL LIFE INTERVIEWS: Questioning the man (or woman) in the street about your product can turn up the kind of praise which, captured on tape, can serve to activate the listening audience. Inclusion of actual street noises in the sound tract helps to heighten the realism.

11. ORCHESTRATE SOUND EFFECTS: For greater appeal to the listeners' imagination, let music simulate the

sounds you're after in a commercial. You can establish the real sound, and follow with the musical treatment. The tempo of the product sound can be effectively translated to music.

12. USE REAL KIDS: Where dialogue from youngsters is indicated, you may reach the heights of realism—and charm—by giving the part to actual children rather than character actors. With editing, the little scene stealers have been known to come up with topnotch copy through ad lib.

13. PUBLICITY-HUNGRY STARS: No need to spend a fortune to enlist big names in your radio commercial cause. Check into which show business luminaries are a little short on work, and anxious to get back into the limelight. Chances are you can work out a satisfactory arrangement.

14. AUTHORITATIVE VOICE: Radio listeners are accustomed to accepting the word of the commentators who bring them the news. That same voice—and the authority that goes with it—may be available for delivery of your sales message. Local and regional personalities may be of use.

15. USE A POPULAR OR STANDARD TUNE: If you can get the rights to a familiar tune, you've taken a giant step toward bridging the gap between entertainment and the commercial.

16. CHARACTER SWITCH: Play a trick or two on the listeners now and then to perk up their attention. Try introducing one type of character, say a gentle housewife, and have her enter screaming at her husband; or have a prize fighter talk like Casper Milquetoast.

ENTERTAINING COMMERCIALS SELL

Because of the flighty, inattentive listeners, radio commercials have become increasingly entertaining. Humor, much of the "mad" variety, holds audiences just as well as the surrounding program material. Music is used skilfully to capture attention or to create moods. Yet, despite the increase of various attention-getting and mood-creating techniques, radio commercials have become simpler. The good radio writer knows that in this era of half-listening radio audiences it is vital to give the listener just one principal idea to carry away. He knows, too, that details should be kept to a minimum.

WORDS ARE YOUR ILLUSTRATIONS

Although many commercials do not call for descriptive writing, the ones that do will make you realize that the greatest handicap you face in selling by the spoken word is the inability to *illustrate your product.* This difficulty overshadows the restrictions of writing against time and the dependence upon the imaginations of your listeners. The lack of illustrative possibilities makes commercial writing the most confining form of sales writing. You must be like the storytellers of ancient times who, through ballads and skillfully told tales, made their listeners see the wonders of other lands and other peoples. Many times you'll envy the fashion copywriter who can call for a gorgeous illustration, tag a short line of copy to the art, and be off to the next assignment. If you wrote a radio commercial for the same garment, you would describe the style, the cut, and you'd use all your cunning to make the woman listener imagine how she would look in the dress, or hat, or coat.

The need for visualization in radio influences greatly your commercial writing, since you must choose selling points that can be described readily and convincingly to listeners. No longer can you depend upon artwork or photographs to help you capture and hold the attention and interest of your prospects. If, for instance, you are describing on the air the sales features of a ham, you are missing your most potent sales howitzer—the strongest, most compelling attraction of any ham advertising—a colorful photograph of a big, ready-to-eat, luscious, *ham.* Your job is to make those listening to your commercial *see that ham* through your words alone, smell it, taste it, *want it.*

If you are asked to prepare radio commercials for an automobile, you can't refer gloatingly to the sleek, powerful monster parked alongside your copy in the magazine pages. You don't have that help. You must, solely by the deft use of description, put your audience in the driver's seat of that car—make them feel its surging strength—its ease of handling—make them *see* its handsome lines.

Description is vital in a great many radio commercials. Perhaps you aren't an agency writer concerned with cars and hams and nationally advertised brands. Maybe your job is to turn out radio announcements by the hundreds for use on local stations to bring people into your department store—bring them in to *buy* shoes, and clothes, and radios, and washing machines, and toys. To the housewife listening to the radio as she tidies up the apartment, you aren't going to offer pleasant generalities about the service offered by your store or its courteous sales people and well-lighted aisles. If you want that lady to put on her hat and coat and come downtown to your store to *buy*, you've got to make her *want* the articles you describe. Or at least you have to make the articles so appealing that she *thinks* she wants and needs them. And you have to do it completely with *words.* As you were told previously, you can't draw a picture and then write, "Look, ma'am, isn't this a lovely coat?" You draw your picture with words.

Perhaps no other phase of advertising writing calls for so much unaided writing ability. Sound effects and music are no substitute for

Fig. 16-1

Straight radio commercial.

This retail radio commercial was used as a test. No newspaper support backed the sale. The response was the largest the department had ever enjoyed. The lead-in was given much of the credit for the success of the commercial.

Lando, Inc. ***advertising • marketing • public relations***

☐ 725 LIBERTY AVENUE, PITTSBURGH, PA. 15222 • (area code 412) 281-5887

Radio Continuity

CLIENT:

DATA:

JOB NO: GIMBELS 1-Minute Spot

STATION: GB-8-9252-CA Sealy Promotion

ANNCR: How can you remodel a building with two thousand eighty-three mattresses in the way? Impossible, isn't it? So, when The Sealy Mattress Company started to remodel their warehouse, they offered Gimbels a wonderful buy on all those fine new mattresses. Gimbels snapped it up and the mattresses have arrived, in time for a spectacular one-day sale on the last day of Lilac Time. Savings are phenomenal! A Sealy mattress, twin or full size, will be just thirty-eight eighty-eight tomorrow only at Gimbels. Choose the kind you like -- firm or extra firm, plain or quilted, with felt, hair or foam top. Matching box springs are also just thirty-eight eighty-eight. Larger mattress and box spring sets are a bargain, too. The sixty by eighty queen size is just one hundred nine dollars, and the king size is one hundred forty-nine. Don't miss the Sealy mattress one-day sale -- tomorrow only at Gimbels, last day of Lilac Time. Mellon Square, North Hills, South Hills and Eastland.

even mediocre artwork. In radio the writer is the artist as well as the writer. If you don't think copywriting is really writing, wait until you have written some radio commercials.

Obviously *all* radio commercials don't require great descriptive powers. Neither do all of them demand writing perfection. The appearance of some products does not need description. Why describe an aspirin tablet? Or a cigarette? Or a tube of tooth paste?

Many radio commercials belong to the "see-how-many-times-you-can-get-the-public-to-listen-to-it" school, where the main object is to pound away with your product's name and perhaps one sale idea or buying reminder. Others, such as those for cosmetics, and food products, require explanations and selling on what they can do *for* you, while a third huge category, especially in department store radio advertising and other local operations, feel that they must scream *price.*

TRY THEM OUT LOUD

The one most important rule to learn about writing for radio, whether for commercials or continuity, is that every single word you set down on paper for use over the air *must be*

Fig. 16-2

Straight radio commercial for a children's feature offered by a retail store.

Lando, Inc.* *advertising • marketing • public relations

725 LIBERTY AVENUE, PITTSBURGH, PA. 15222 • (area code 412) 281-5887

Radio Continuity

CLIENT: GIMBELS | DATA: 1-Minute Spot

JOB NO: GB-9-9919-CA | "Children's Book Fair"

STATION: WKJF

TAPE #GBR-5, CUT #3 INSTRUMENTAL MUSIC UNDER THROUGHOUT

ANNCR: Gimbels invites you and your children to meet a dragon. Climb a beanstalk. Sing a song! It's all part of the Children's Book Fair at Gimbels this week. Take your children to Gimbels and introduce them to your old favorites. Like Heidi or The Hardy Boys. And let them introduce you to their favorite characters from The Bumper Book or Richard Scarry's stories. The most exciting part of Gimbels' Children's Book Fair happens this Saturday, December sixth at Gimbels Mellon Square from eleven to three. You can see Marty Wolfson draw cartoons and tell stories at eleven and twelve. Hear Joe Negri play his guitar between one and three. There'll even be a clown with balloons for all the kids. That's this Saturday, eleven to three at Gimbels Mellon Square. But you can choose Christmas books anytime. Use your Holiday Purchase Certificates and you won't be billed till February. Gimbels Mellon Square is open every evening till nine. Branch stores till ten.

ANNCR: It 's Gimbels for Mother's Day. Give her our best! There's something new every day at Gimbels. Like earrings and gloves, and sterling silver thimbles. Charm bracelets, bracelet charms, necklaces and rings. Coffee pots, frying pans, blenders and broilers. Travel irons, place mats, paperweights and pins. Parsley baskets, knitting baskets, garden gloves and swim fins. Golf clubs, tennis balls, cameras, sunglasses, bonbons, tote bags, radios, cologne. Stationery, sugar tongs, cheese boards and goblets. (DEEP BREATH) And a scarf that matches her eyes. It's Gimbels for Mother's Day. Give her our best!

Fig. 16-3

Humorous radio commercial.

Although there is no humor in the words of this 30-second commercial a humorous effect was created by having the announcer deliver the commercial at great speed in one breath.

read aloud by you before you give it your personal approval.

You may not—probably won't—have a private office in which to work. Most beginning copywriters don't. It makes no difference. Even if you have to adjourn to the coatroom for privacy, find yourself an unoccupied corner and play announcer. You see, every writer always relies on *seeing in print* the words that are written. What *looks* very delightful may not *sound* the least bit so.

Embarrassing fluffs by announcers rarely will occur if commercials have been given an advance "out-loud" test. As this book was about to go to press two commercials were heard which illustrated the need for eliminating tongue twisters *before* the announcer is trapped. In both instances, the announcer faltered, started again, faltered and finally gave up, passing over the incident with a quip. The writer had succeeded in making the announcer laugh, but advertisers have a very unsympathetic view of the kind of humor that may cost them product sales.

One of the phrases causing the most trouble was ". . . prepared for *welcoming me in as a.*" Try out this phrase on an unsuspecting friend to see what trouble it can cause when it is rapidly read out loud without rehearsal. The other phrase was "fresh, flavorful, fragrant coffee." Alliteration, as you will read later, is a real trouble-maker. It was, in this instance, and yet a quick reading aloud in advance of broadcast could have resulted in a correction.

To go a step beyond *reading* your own commercials you should *listen* to the announcer as he delivers them. Here's someone reading the commercials who has had nothing to do with producing them. He is not acquainted with the thinking behind them. His reading of your commercials may reveal additional pitfalls not discovered in your own reading. If you can get such a reading in advance—fine. If you can't listen to them until they are on the air, then all you can do is notice the mistakes and remember to avoid those mistakes in your next set of commercials.

Writing errors, found daily in the scripts turned in by advertising copywriters for use on the airways, result from lack of study by copy people of the simplest rules of radio broadcasting and announcing. They are responsible for the lack of sales power in many radio programs and spot-announcement campaigns. By keeping a few rules in mind as you approach writing for radio, you can give yourself a headstart on those who walk gaily into commercial writing with the attitude that it's no different from any other kind of writing.

Regardless of whether or not you observe the various admonitions listed, keep in mind one point. Once more this advice will be emphasized, since it's all-important—*Read 'em aloud!*

LENGTH OF WORDS AND SENTENCES

Short words are usually the best radio words. Regardless of their pronunciation or case of understanding, words that contain more than three or four syllables should be used only when absolutely necessary. Thus "a great car" is better than "an exceptional car"—"lovely" preferable to "beautiful"—"good" to "outstanding," and so forth. Similarly, short *sentences* are usually easier for the announcer than long ones. Sometimes, however, awkward sentence structure can make even short sentences poor radio. Short sentences, therefore, aren't *always* the final answer. A skillfully written sentence that is moderately long but well phrased can often make better listening than a poorly-written short sentence.

Fig. 16-4

Humorous commercial.

Essentially this is a straight commercial but the cave man voice comes in at different points to enliven the delivery.

Rock - 60 seconds.

Mel Brooks voice over -- For thousands of years civilization has searched for a different way to write. First we wrote with rocks. No Good. Just writing "Dear Sir" you could hurt yourself.

Cave Man -- Groan

Mel Brooks -- Then we tried trees. But you couldn't make a lovely W with a tree. You could make a bump, a lump, yes. But not a lovely W. It was a very bad time for man. Now we're modern and lucky. Today we can write with a banana. The Bic Banana. The encompassment of writing progress. It's not a ballpoint. It's a smooth writing, fine line marker beauty. You can write up with it. You can write down with it. You can write colors with it. Get a Bic Banana. Only 29¢. It's a heck of a fruit. A heck of a writing instrument. And this is a heck of a civilization.

Cave Man -- Growl

Cave Man voice over with product

Cave Man -- BANANA

When you make an effort to break up your radio copy into short, easy-to-read-aloud sentences, you will discover another fact about commercial writing—that certain conventional writing practices do not apply. Well-written prose has few sentences starting with the words "And" or "But." Yet these two words are standards openers in radio sentences because they preserve the flowing, conversational quality of the announcer's delivery. Likewise, they stop him enough to keep him from crowding his words and from going too fast or too breathlessly.

The frequent use of contractions is another characteristic of radio writing. In printed prose, contractions may make writing appear overly informal and undignified. In radio copy they often enhance the sincere and conversational qualities of the commercial. If you *read* "Do not miss this chance to . . ." or "You have not tasted candy until . . ." you wouldn't criticize the writer for faulty technique. The writing seems natural.

When these phrases are said aloud, however, they *sound* like prose. They are not phrases that you, or the announcer, or the listener would use. You would *say* 'Don't miss this

Mel Brooks voice over -- Mankind has searched for a different way to write. When the wheel first came out, everybody thought it was a new pen. They all jumped on it and started to write.

Cave Man -- Stop Writing!

Mel Brooks voice over -- They were dumb. Now we are modern and lucky. We can write with a banana. The Bic Banana. A smooth writing, fine line marker beauty. It comes in colors and it's only 29¢. Don't live in the past.

Cave Man voice with product shot -- BANANA

Fig. 16-5

30-second version of the commercial shown in Fig. 16-4.

chance . . ." and "You haven't tasted candy . . ."

Give conscious attention to contractions. They are a definite part of American speaking idiom, and that means that they are particularly good for radio use. As one caution, however, you should remember that occasionally you will want to emphasize a point, and the use of a contraction might weaken your sentence. Suppose, for instance, you are writing copy for a non-skid tire. A claim of "You can't skid" lacks the emphasis of "You can *not* skid." Where a negative element needs emphasis, then you might perfer to avoid the contraction. But in most cases the contraction is desirable.

Likewise, you will find that sentence fragments will sometimes serve better than full sentences in radio. Listen to a conversation some time between two or more persons. Count how many times sentences are not completed. Yet the conversationalists understand each other perfectly. Utilize this conversational tendency in commercials, but use it carefully or you may end up writing gibberish.

Closely associated with sentence length in radio is the use of punctuation. Punctuation, if anything, is more important in radio writing than in writing for print because bad punctuation can mislead the announcer and cause him to make a disastrous mistake over the air. To the radio writer all punctuation marks are important but especially important are the underline, the double dash, and the hyphen.

Underline: The underline should be used sparingly and with purpose. Usually the announcer will know through experience what words to "punch" but here and there you may have a word you wish to stress because of company policy or some other reason. In such cases, underline the word but—and this is important—just the *one* word. Almost never is it advisable to underline two words or a whole phrase: It is almost impossible for the announcer to put true stress on more than one word. Resolutely avoid scattering underlined words throughout a commercial because, by so doing, you overemphasize your message and you make the announcer's job more difficult.

Double-dash: A useful punctuation device is the double-dash which gives a conversational flow to your writing. It gives a dramatic pause that is less abrupt than the full stop created by a period. Used correctly, the double-dash gives a graceful ease to radio writing and aids the announcer in his delivery. An example from a commercial for a savings bank reads: "But a <u>savings</u> balance—that's something else again." Notice not only how the double-dash contributes a natural pause in the delivery but also that the underline gives vigor to the whole sentence. Note, too that all that is needed here is one word underlined. It would have been a mistake to underline "<u>savings balance</u>," since this emphasis would be awkward for the announcer.

Many writers use the three-dot (. . .) punctuation device in radio and print copy. Once a writer has contracted the three-dot habit he finds it difficult to write complete sentences. Avoid this habit. If you wish to make a pause for effect, use the double-dash, but do not overdo that either.

Hyphen: When you wish to join two words in order that they may modify a third word you can use a hyphen. Sometimes your announcer must be guided by the hyphenated words or he will make a mistake in his reading. In the bank commercial previously referred to, the writer used a hyphen in this manner: "Open a dividend-paying savings account . . ." If the hyphen had not been used here the announcer might have read the passage as "Open a dividend." In using hyphens, however, avoid the precious, cute, and artificial combining of words that have given advertising writing a bad name in many writing quarters. Phrases such as "bunny-soft," "cozy-warm," and "baby-cute," illustrate the point.

USE EASY-TO-PRONOUNCE WORDS

Avoid words that are hard to pronounce, even if they are easily understood words. "Indisputable" is a word that everyone would understand, but it could be a stumbling block for a radio announcer. "Applicable," "ingenious," "particularly," ' 'demonstrable," "Naive," and "detectable" would be correctly defined by most high-school students, yet any of them could cause an announcer to hesitate a split second, thus disturbing the natural flow of his words.

Sometimes very innocent-looking words that are simple to pronounce by themselves can become nightmares for the announcer when they are combined with certain other innocent-looking words. A good example is a sentence actually used on the air and which very effectively tied the announcer in knots—"A government order of 22 stainless steel twin-screw cruisers." Too, if you put "in," "an," or "un" next to a word beginning with any of these three sounds you will give almost any announcer a moment of pronunciation juggling—example: "in an unenviable position." Say it fast and notice the mumble that results. It would be pointless for you to attempt to memorize all such sound and word combinations which might cause you trouble. Experience will teach you some of the trouble-makers and reading aloud should take care of the rest.

Beware of adverbs! The adverbial suffix "ly" is a tough one for radio people to pronounce with consistent precision. If you can twist your sentence to gain the same thought without the ' 'ly," you will usually have a better commercial. It is not as good radio to say

> "The shoes that men are increasingly favoring."

as it is to say:

> "The shoes that more men are favoring every day."

And you might wish to say of a cereal product:

> "Nutritionally, too, it's the buy for you."

Much better, radio-wise, to say:

> "For nutrition, too, it's the buy for you."

You don't sacrifice the swing of both, or the rhyme of one—both attributes of good radio commercials—yet you have constructed a sentence that will be easy for the announcers to read without much chance of stumbling.

One fault you must guard against is permitting words to creep into your commercials which are similar, in *sound,* to other words with different meanings. One of these, for instance, is the word "chief." If you are writing a commercial about air travel, you might wish to say "it has many advantages over all other forms of travel, the *chief* one being . . ."

Now *you* know that word is *chief.* You might have used "main," or "outstanding," or some other synonym, but you write "chief." It looks all right to *you*, and it *sounds* fine as *you* read it. Now consider your *listener.* First of all, he's not hanging on your announcer's every phrase. Secondly, he hears the word "chief" only *one time* as it slips past, and he doesn't know, as *you* do, what comes next. It would be very easy for him to think the announcer said "cheap." You'll admit that the difference between the two words is great enough to warrant care in their use whether you're selling air travel or aspirin!

"Breath" and "breadth"; "smell" and

EASTMAN KODAK COMMERCIAL Division: Consumer
Product: Pocket camera Title: Bob's Pocket-60
Length: :60 Campaign: Network & Spot Radio
TV ____ Radio X Air Date: May
Film ____ Tape X Live ____ Orig: X Rev. No. ____
Job No: ____ Code No: EK

Bob Lewis

Kodak introduces "the Pocket":

-- the new Kodak pocket Instamatic camera --

-- the little camera that takes big pictures --

"The Pocket" camera is small enough to fit almost any pocket: jacket pocket, shirt pocket, blue-jean pocket -- ready for the pictures you used to miss.

Now you may think a little camera must take little pictures. But in fact, the pictures you get from Kodak pocket Instamatic cameras are big -- actually three and a half by four and a half inches -- and so sharp and clear you'd think they were taken by a big camera.

The film cartridges are so small you can carry enough for your whole vacation in another pocket. Just drop in a cartridge and shoot!
When you need flash, you just pop on a self-powered magicube.

There are five models of the Kodak pocket Instamatic camera and prices start at less than twenty-eight dollars. See your photo dealer -- for "the Pocket" -- the little camera that takes big pictures -- from Kodak.

Fig. 16-6

Straight commercial.

"swell" and "spell"; "prize" and "price" are other examples of words which might be misinterpreted or given a wrong meaning by the listener. Its just as easy to use a simple synonym and take no chances.

ALLITERATION ALIENATES ANNOUNCERS

The old writer's standby of *alliteration* is the prize example of how radio writing can easily err. Visually the phrase, "Prize-winners in perfectly proportioned peach halves," can't be criticized very harshly. If you saw it in an advertisement, even if you are one of those who reads everything with your lips, you might view it as a nicely turned phrase. Say, however, that you have been assigned to write some radio commercials for "X" peaches and you hit upon that sentence—which looks fine as it leaves the typewriter. Perhaps it looks fine also to those with whom you must clear you copy. It gets an okay and is released to the radio station. Just how do you think it is going to look to the radio announcer who is scanning the copy ten minutes before broadcast time? The way to *find out* how he'll like it is to stand up and *read it* just as you want him to read it. Do that to the peach halves

Fig. 16-7 and Fig. 16-8

Humorous commercials.

Humor is especially well suited to an insect killer. In this case, the radio commercials are adapted from a television campaign of the same type.* Such coordination of the media is highly desirable.

*See example in Writing for Sight, Sound and Movement—Television

atrocity right now. Read it aloud. How does it sound? Doesn't it sound a little bit like a man about to lose his upper plate?

A little bit of alliteration is certainly acceptable in radio writing. In fact, wisely used, it often helps to spark up copy. But alliteration is like dynamite—a little too much is going to blow your commercial apart. Use alliteration if you wish, but be very careful not to overdo it. Your own sense of *hearing* will be your safety valve. If it doesn't sound good to you when you read it aloud, *change it.*

DON'T BARK OR HISS

Another thing you will probably discover, as you stand up and announce your first try-'em-out-loud commercials, is that you have given your copy too many *hissing* sounds. Radio announcers hate the double-ess ending and dislike it even in the middle of words, because it is very hard to say clearly and with force. The word "sensational"—almost a routine part of many copywriters' daily vocabularies—causes announcers to wince. Your commercials would probably sound better if you could manage to write them without ever using the letter "s" or the "z" or the soft "c." Example: while reading the last two sentences,

FOOTE, CONE & BELDING

NUMBER SJ72B5

DATE CLIENT S.C. JOHNSON & SON, INC. TITLE "ESCAPE ARTIST"

AS-PRODUCED PRODUCT RAID-FIK LENGTH 30-Seconds

ANNCR:	And now, Mose Quito, the world's greatest insect escape artist.
MOS:	Tank you. First, I will avoid being hit by one hundred rolled newspapers.
SFX:	THUMP! THUMP! THUMP! THUMP!
SFX:	CHEERS
MOS:	Tank you. And now I will free myself from the throes of sticky fly paper.
ANNCR:	Uh, Mos, there's someone from the audience who would like to challenge you
MOS:	Oh, bring him on.
ANNCR:	It's Raid.
MOS:	Oh, bring him off.
ALL:	RAAAAIIIIDDDD!
SFX:	MAD BUG SCATTER UNDER
ANNCR:	Raid Flying Insect Killer.
SFX:	SLIDE WHISTLE BOMB EFFECT
ANNCR:	With the sweet smelling formula that kills bugs dead.
SFX:	EXPLOSION!
MOS:	There's no escaping Raid!

FOOTE, CONE & BELDING

		NUMBER SJ72B7
DATE	CLIENT S.C. JOHNSON & SON, INC.	TITLE "HALL OF INFAMY"
AS-PRODUCED	PRODUCT RAID-FIK	LENGTH 30-Seconds

SFX: BUG VOICES HAVE SLIGHT ECHO AS IN BIG MUSEUM. HEAVY GANGSTER VOICES - A LEADER AND HIS GANG.

BOSS: Listen, you bugs. 'Dis is da Flyin' Insect Hall of Infamy. The whole history of bad bugs. Heh, heh, heh.

BUG #1: Hey, dere's Mean Gene Mosquito. He was Public Annoyer No. 1!

BOSS: 'Til Raid got him ...

BUG #1: And Fearsome Fly. He flew a suicide mission into a Raid protected kitchen!

BOSS: Tragic story ... tragic.

BUG #1: Who's da big guy, boss?

ALL: It's, RAAAAAIIIIIDDD!

SFX: MAD BUG SCATTER

ANNCR: Raid Flying Insect Killer.

SFX: SLIDE WHISTLE BOMB EFFECT

ANNCR: With the sweet smelling formula that kills bugs dead!

SFX: EXPLOSION

ANNCR: Get Raid Flying Insect Killer.

BOSS: (Weakly) Raid's breaking up that old gang of mine.

C113 SFX: THUD

you are not likely to have experienced a difficulty or unpleasant reaction from the words used. Yet several times in those two sentences, you can find the soft "c" or the "s" sounds. They would not have been pleasant sounding if broadcasted. Were this page to be read over the air, some rewriting would have to be done. Remember, too, that the particularly harsh sounds in the English language do not broadcast well. The sounds "ark" and "ack," "eesh" and "ash," "app" and "amm" should seldom be used. As you enunciate your copy, listen to your voice and try to sift out the sounds that grate on your ear. Assume that the sounds that grate on your ear as you hear them in the solitude of an office or room will sound much worse with even the minimum distortion produced by modern transmission.

SLANG? YES, BUT . . .

When you are urged to "be conversational" in radio commercials, you are being given good counsel, but counsel that might possibly lead you astray, since the conversation of a large percentage of the American people would be unsuitable for radio usage. You will have to use your judgment in deciding what is "conversational" and what slips into the area of poor taste.

The inclusion of a certain amount of slang, informal phraseology, and current jargon will often lend a naturalness and spontaneity that greatly increase the believability and selling power of commercials. Whether to use such devices in your writing and how much to use them, will depend pretty much on what you are trying to sell, and more than that, *to whom* you are selling.

On a sports program, which you could assume would interest a youngish male audience, the most logical types of products to be sold would be such items as men's clothing, beer, shaving soap, or cigarettes. If you were assigned to write commercials for such a show, it would probably be perfectly good technique to use occasional phrases such as "a doggone good buy"—"styles that are really terrific"—"takes off whiskers with the speed of a jet"—and similar masculine-like wordage. Such writing will be helpful in making your audience feel that the commercial is part of the show, written for them alone, and hence will be more likely to take effect—also, they'll feel that the sponsor and announcer are "regular" guys. Needless to say, that kind of talk would not sound very appropriate to a woman listening to a soap opera while she does her housework!

Similarly, a children's program should be liberally sprinked with words currently heard around the schoolyard. If you are asked to write the commercials for such a show, you would be very wise to do some on-the-spot investigating, and pick up phrases and slang which the younger set is using at the moment. Be quite sure, when you do, that you are not writing expressions that mean something only in one locality—one neighborhood —or, if your show is national or your spot announcements are for wide distribution, one section of the country. "Keen," "cool," "swell," "dandy," and ' 'super" are kid-words that are always good anywhere. It may nauseate you to refer to a product as "cool," but it will sound great to the youngsters.

Steer very clear of slang words that might alienate large groups of your audience, even though at first thought they might seem all right. A good example of such a word is "darn." Now you may have used that expression since you were two years old, heard your mother and sister and even clergymen say it often. Yet to many people the word "darn" is simply another way of saying "damn," and even though he may say it himself, you might offend one of your sensitive listeners by putting it in your commercial. There is no need to take chances with words or expressions that have the *slightest* chance of producing a negative effect even on a few people. Those few might otherwise all be easily sold on your product.

"Scram," "blow," "nuts," "oh, yeah," "so what," "screwy," "lousy," "stink," "jerk," "baloney," and other such words should not be included in your radio writing vocabulary. All have either started with, or become associated with, crime and gangster doings, and as such do not represent the clean, healthy slang that makes acceptable, picturesque American talk for radio.

Before using the lighter-type words and phrases in your commercials, try them out on some of your more pedantic friends. If you get a lot of voluntary suggestions to do away with a word or an expression, it's probably wise to do so.

TYPES OF COMMERCIALS

If you are to produce commercials for a radio program—either network or local—there are a number of different techniques upon which you may draw. Some of these are:

1. Straight commercial

This is a straight selling message devoted to the merits of your product, service, or institutional story. It might be compared with a piece of straightline body copy, and is delivered by a commercial announcer, with no outside means of attracting or holding attention.

Many advertisers now look critically at this type of commercial since they feel that inattentive, uninterested listeners will not wait out the announcer for the full period of the commercial. Still, on thousands of radio stations, the selling messages are delivered straight and they are still selling goods and services even though artistically they are not as satisfying to creative people as other commercial types.

2. Dialogue commercial

Here the selling message is put across by means of dialogue between the announcer and others not in the cast of the show. The announcer may converse with users of the product, with experts on one or more phases of the product's manufacture, with dealers, or simply with unidentified parties. Through these conversations the various sales features of whatever is being sold are described. Most commonly used are testimonials.

The principal problem in this type of commercial is to make the dialogue believable and natural. Too often one or the other of the voices becomes a "stooge" for the other.

Suggested ways to make two-voice commercials believable, or at least acceptable:

If a commercial is being delivered by two supposedly real-life people such as two housewives, two husbands, a husband and a wife, or two children, it is almost impossible to deliver a number of product points without making salesmen out of the characters. Generally, such commercials make a stooge out of one of the characters. This one, possibly a housewife will say to the other: "But Kleen-O must cost a lot." The other then replies: "Not at all, Jane. Due to a new manufacturing process, Kleen-O has been able to reduce its price to the low, low price of .78¢. And that's not *all* they've done either. Listen to this . . ."

The easiest way out of the artificiality of the two-voice commercials, as suggested, is to let the characters set the stage by posing a mutual problem. After an exchange of two or three lines, the announcer comes in to do the selling. This is natural because announcers are *supposed* to be salesmen.

But suppose you want to use the real-life characters for the whole commercial? Can you do so successfully? "Successful" here means that you maintain naturalness and believability at the same time that you are putting across enough product selling points to sell the product to the listening audience.

Here are ways to accomplish this:

1. One character reads copy from the package to the other character. By reading the copy, the character avoids being a "salesman."
2. One character reads copy from a product advertisement to the other character.
3. Character talks to a store salesman. The character asks questions and the salesman replies by giving a sales talk for the product.
4. Character talks to a knowledgeable repairman or serviceman—such as a plumber, electrician, etc. The latter points out why the unit works so well, lasts so long, is so easy to repair, or needs to be repaired so infrequently.
5. Character reads directions on the item itself, especially when those directions indicate the ease of operation.
6. Character phones someone qualified to

Fig. 16-9 and Fig. 16-10

Humorous commercials.

As these commercials demonstrate, the two-voice commercials can be effective when it is used with skillful humor. These commercials are entertaining but they also present a good selling message for the advertiser.

talk about the product—a factory man, a dealer, a serviceman. (in television, the split-screen technique can be used for the two characters).

7. Two salesmen are talking about the product, mentioning points that are salesworthy.
8. Sales manager conducts session with novice salesman. He gives a demonstration of the perfect sales talk. This could well be humorously exaggerated.
9. Copywriter gets reactions from his wife about sales points he's putting in his advertisement. She makes pertinent suggestions that give the woman's viewpoint that he has overlooked.
10. Earnest student type telling teacher what he's found out about product assigned as a class study.
11. Same technique as in No. 10 except that professor is telling class and answering questions. Again, there is possibility for exaggerated humor here.
12. Two computers talk to each other. Each discusses product facts in mechanical-sounding voices associated with computers or mechanical men.
13. Man presses button of computer, or of a

SSC and B Inc. *Advertising*

575 LEXINGTON AVENUE, NEW YORK, N.Y. 10022
212·688·1600

BROADCAST

SSC&B JOB NO.
CLIENT S&H
PRODUCT Green Stamps
BROADCAST MEDIUM Radio
LENGTH OF COMM.
DATE TYPED 11/20/

SYLVIA	(WITH HEAVY COLD) Doctor, you came on a house call. You're so dedicated!
DR:	What dedicated. I'm your Uncle and we live in the same building.
SYLVIE:	(COUGHS).
DR:	You're a sick girl. What have you been doing to yourself?
SYLVIA:	Food shopping.
DR:	So?
SYLVIA:	17 stores a day. It's inside, outside, air conditioning, meat freezers, hot chicken rotisseries ... hot, cold, cold, hot ...
DR:	Yes, yes, Sylvia. You're a comparison shopper now?
SYLVIA:	I'm a homemaker. I save a penny here, a penny there.
DR:	Right now, you'll stay in bed and drink lots of hot lemonade ...
SYLVIA:	With lemons six for a dollar?
DR:	I'm coming to that. When you're up again, shop a market that gives S&H Green Stamps. That way you save something every time you buy anything ... specials and everything else! And you don't run yourself into the ground.
SYLVIA:	I feel better already.
DR:	Good. I'll just leave the bill here on the night table.
ANNCR:	Saving money's hard. Saving S&H Green Stamps is easy. It happens automatically ... every time you shop an S&H place. Shop National Tea. It's an S&H place!

SSC and B Inc. *Advertising*

575 LEXINGTON AVENUE, NEW YORK, N.Y. 10022
212·688·1600

BROADCAST

SSC&B JOB NO.
CLIENT S&H
PRODUCT Green Stamps
BROADCAST MEDIUM Radio
LENGTH OF COMM. :60
DATE TYPED 1/23/

SON:	So what do you think of the apartment, folks?
MOM:	So far so good, Sonny. I love your vestibule.
SON:	Mom, this isn't the vestibule. It's the whole apartment.
MOM:	Sonny. Come back home!
DAD:	Now, Mother! He's got everything he needs, right on one wall Stove. Refrigerator. Bathtub.
SON:	Look. This piece of ply wood comes down on top of the tub and presto! It's the dining room.
DAD:	Get a load of the refrigerator, Mother.
MOM:	Hmmm. Canadian bacon. Mushrooms. Sirloin steak!... How can you eat steak on your income?
SON:	Easy. I shop at a place that gives good value and S&H Green Stamps. That way I save something on every thing I buy.
DAD:	Take a leaf out of the kid's book, Mother! He's eating better than we are.
MOM:	That'll be quite enough, Dad. And what are you saving your Green Stamps for, Sonny?
SON:	A charcoal grill. For the patio.
MOM:	The patio?
SON:	Yeah ... Right here on the fire escape.
ANNCR:	Saving money's hard. Saving S&H Green Stamps is easy. It happens automatically, every time you shop an S&H place. Shop National Tea. It's an S&H place.

mechanical man, and gets flood of informantion to each question he asks.

14. If product is intended for a dog, such as a dog food, two dogs talk to each other about it. Or, it could be two cats, two birds, or some other creatures.

The point to remember is that you *can* avoid unbelievable two-voice commercials if you try. Do so because the artificial slice-of-life commercials destroy the credibility of advertising; there is no need for this to happen.

3. Dramatized commercial

This often-used type of commercial may be compared with the narrative-copy approach. A situation is dramatized in a brief playlet, in which the product is introduced as the solution of a problem. Thus, a boy in the first fifteen seconds or so he is horrified to learn that he has bad breath. Thirdly, he hears about a new kind of tooth paste, and in the twinkling of an ear you discover he wins love and romance. Then, in normal routine, the regular announcer closes with a straight product sell, and a plea to buy. Dramatized commercials usually require the hiring of a professional cast, and may range all the way from a few simple, uninvolved lines of script to a full-scale production, with music, sound effects, and lengthy rehearsals.

Like the dialogue commercial the dramatized commercial often becomes artificial and unbelievable. Frequently the action is humorously exaggerated to the point where the advertiser spoofs his product and audience. It can be a very effective technique if enough episodes are presented to avoid boring the radio audience. The same story presented day after day, however, can soon cause great tune-outs.

4. Cast commercial

Many successful programs follow the plan of using only the announcer and the cast to effect selling force. On comedy programs, in particular, one finds the cast often taking part in the commercial, especially when the product is one which can stand a somewhat lighter touch.

If the star is used in a commercial—and that star is popular—much selling power is generated. Usually, however, it is best to add the star for attention value but to let the announcer do most of the selling.

5. Integrated commercial

This is a commercial that has been carefully tailored to a given program. In many cases the commercial is so skillfully woven into the show that the audience is unaware that it is a commercial until the actual selling is being done. Usually, however, the integration is more in the nature of keying the character of the commercial to the character of the program.

Integrated commercials were much more common in the days of the big network shows that used one or more established stars. The technique is comparatively rare in radio these days although it is seen with some frequency in television.

6. Integrated plug

You have often heard radio shows in which a product claim, or "plug," as it is commonly known, has been worked into the regular script of the program. Called an integrated plug, it is one of the most effective of all radio commercial techniques when not overdone. Like the integrated commercial, however, the integrated plug is seldom used in modern radio.

7. Musical commercial

Sometimes this can be a singing commercial in which all or part of the sales message is delivered by some. Whether singing or instrumental music is used in whole, or in part, the musical commercial has become an increasingly common form of radio technique. This growth has occurred despite cries from the public against singing commercials.

"Jingles," as they are so often called, *are* hated when they are bad but among the best-liked commercials are musical commercials that have been done well. Two cautions for creators of musical commercials: (1) Be sure the music is good. Especially try to use music that can be committed to memory—outstanding commercial music, such as the long-lasting Marlboro song. (2) In singing commercials, make certain that the words can be understood. Otherwise, you provide the audience with a pleasant musical experience but no incentive to buy. Make the lyric memorable as well as the music; if you do, you will have a strong selling vehicle for your product or service.

WATCH YOUR TIMING

If you are writing announcements of one-minute length, and you plan them to be straight announcements delivered by an announcer, be sure that each one can be completed within one minute. An average announcer takes about a minute to read, one hundred and fifty to two hundred words. But don't rely on that! Some things are easy to read—some hard. The hard ones take longer to read. Often you will want your message to be given slowly with exaggerated emphasis. Other times it will be desirable to have the announcer read it fast. Do not rely upon a rule of thumb. Read your announcements to yourself —*time yourself* to be sure.

Most straight commercials can be delivered understandably and sincerely at a rate of 160-170 words per minute. Some announcers, however, may be comfortable with a slower or faster rate than this. If you know what announcer will deliver the commercial, pace it to his style. As a rule, commercials to be delivered by women announcers should use a lower word count, preferably around 150.

The character of the offer being made might affect your word count. For instance, an announcement for a sweepstakes is usually charged with excitement. To maintain the excitement the announcer will speed up his delivery and thus you may elect to put considerably more than 170 words in such a commercial. You do so knowing that the listeners' playback of the commercial message will suffer in terms of individual points registered. Still, if you have made the listener aware of the sweepstakes and its glittering prizes, you will have accomplished your objective. You have made him want to enter. He can get full details later from entry blanks in stores or from magazine or newspaper advertisements.

Somewhat the same principle is at work in the frenetic two-voice commercials often heard for local firms such as tire shops. The two-man announcer team announces the message at a tremendous clip without any hope that many points will be recalled but with a very real expectation that listeners will realize that the company is offering something very special in the way of price, a variety of choice, or a dazzling new product.

Two-voice commercials may, on the other hand, be used for supposed real-life conversations between two friends, a man and wife, a sales clerk and a customer, and any number of combinations. In such simulated situations, slow down the word count. Make the conversation natural. Real-life people don't bark out words with machine-gun speed so write fewer than the 160-170 words employed in straight commercials and far fewer than for the two-voice commercials delivered by a team of two station announcers.

If you want to be sure of your timing, count your words *AND* use a stopwatch. Most writers are content merely to use a stopwatch but a person reading his own commercial sometimes tends to speed up his reading pace in order to make the commercial fit the time. The practice of counting the words will help keep him honest. On the other hand, just counting words and not using a stopwatch may cause trouble since a commercial with a fairly low word count may read long because of the use of many multi-syllable words. The stopwatch helps correct for this.

When you become adept in writing for broadcast you may let the number of lines of copy help you determine whether you're writing within your time limitations but this is only a rough guide. You'll always be right if you double-check yourself with the stopwatch and the counting of words. For example, you might be fooled by a commercial that uses several numbers and consequently is short on lines. Each numeral, however, counts as one word. If you give a telephone number and repeat it, you may be devoting as many as

Fig. 16-11

Straight commercial.

There is still a place in radio for the simply-expressed message despite cries from those who sometimes seem to prefer cleverness to sales power.

SSC and B Inc. *Advertising*

575 LEXINGTON AVENUE, NEW YORK, N.Y. 10022
212·688·1600

BROADCAST

SSC&B JOB NO.
CLIENT S&H
PRODUCT Green Stamps
BROADCAST MEDIUM Radio
LENGTH OF COMM. :60
DATE TYPED 11/20/

WOMAN: I try. I may not be very good in math. But I try. Every time I go to the supermarket I try to figure out the best buys -- the best values for the best price. There's just one catch. Did you know there are over 6,000 items in your average supermarket? And maybe half of them cost less than the other half -- but you have to figure out which half? What's <u>really</u> the best value?

You know, you could make a career out of just trying to save money at the supermarket. That's where I was heading, until one day I got smart. Now I shop at a supermarket that gives good value and S&H Green Stamps. That way I know I save something every time I buy <u>anything</u>. Oh, I still try to get the best buys for my money -- but I don't feel so pressured any more. I know even if I goof -- I <u>still</u> get S&H Green Stamps. It's a great feeling.

LOCAL ANNCR: Saving money is hard -- but saving S&H Green Stamps is easy. It happens automatically -- every time you shop at an S&H place. Shop Store Name -- it's an S&H place!

25 words just for this part of the commercial.

In announcements of less than one minute, you may be given a maximum number of *words* to use. These directives are not given to you as a rule of thumb or as a guide or as a suggestion. They are supposed to be followed. Copywriters everywhere are careless about this request from the stations and networks. By ignoring it they cause much worry and trouble for radio production personnel.

From an advertising standpoint, it is far better to limit your message to the words that can be read with sincerity and selling strength than to take liberties with the time and length of your announcement. If you force the announcer to race through your selling message, you lose effectiveness and power.

Timing is especially important when you are taping or transcribing commercials, because once an announcement is recorded it cannot be speeded up or cut. If you send a recording to a radio station that contains a "fifty-word" announcement, but which is actually longer than that, the station producers cannot do as they would in a "live" commercial and speed up the announcer's reading. Their only out is to chop off your story before it is finished, and you can easily see the wisdom of avoiding *that.*

LIVE OR RECORDED?

Announcements are broadcast in two ways. An example will serve to illustrate these methods. Assume you are the manufacturer of a product for general consumption, but being relatively new in the business do not yet enjoy complete national distribution of your product. You must proceed in your marketing strategy by opening up different markets individually until each market has good distribution. You select a new city into which you wish to introduce your product and you allocate money to advertise it there. You decide that newspaper advertisements plus a series of spot announcements make the best combination of local advertising media available for your purposes, and you buy a schedule of spot time on the local radio station. You purchase minute spots, to be extended over a period of six weeks.

(1) You can simply have those commercials typed, along with instructions as to how they should be read, and send them to the radio station, instructing the station representative on which days to read which announcements. Then a local announcer will be assigned to your account and will deliver the spots as you have written them.

(2) You can hire an announcer in your own town (whose voice you like and whose delivery you can control through rehearsals), have a recording made on which you tape or transcribe all the announcements, one after the other, and send that record to the radio station in your new market. They will then play the designated recording at the time you request it, instead of having one of their own announcers read the material.

Both techniques have their advantages. If your messages are simple and straightforward, and do not require a highly dramatic or specialized type of voice, the first way is generally preferred, since it is less expensive.

If you wish to control the *manner* of delivery, in regard to emphasis and pace, the transcription is your answer.

Of course, the first technique, that of sending the station the script for your announcements, is workable only when you have a straight commercial, handled by an announcer only. When you wish your spots to be dramatic, or to contain music or gimmicks, they necessarily must be taped or transcribed. The local radio station could hardly afford to charge you the little they do for a spot announcement of a few seconds, and also stage a musical production for you.

Another situation that will become familiar to you is the writing of a commercial that will be taped or transcribed for a 50-second segment. The last 10-seconds will be delivered live by a station announcer. You will write the 10-second "tag" as well as the 50-second portion.

Sometimes, too, you will have a musical introduction, called "Intro," that runs for a few seconds before the announcer begins talking and you may end with music, too. In other cases, the music will continue under the announcer's voice throughout the commercial and then come up strongly at the end.

NOW–TO SUM IT UP

Although this book does not give you any pat formulas for writing copy in its different forms, it is time in this chapter to put down as guides for radio writing some of the points we have made and to add a couple of additional points. All of these are fundamentals which you should review periodically to be sure you're not straying too far from what we know to be successful elements of radio commercial writing.

1. Keep copy points to a minimum in deference to:
   a. The human mind's incapacity to absorb very much solely through the ear.
   b. The fact that your average radio listener is usually only a half-listener and will have difficulty enough catching one idea, let alone two or three.
2. Make pictures with words. You are not writing for television. If that package you're pushing has blue stripes, suggest to your listener that he look for the blue-striped package. If it's a round container *call* it a "round container."
3. Repeat important words, elements, and names. Remember our inattentive listener. The first time he barely hears you, but the second time he may have that pencil ready to take down what you're saying. Repetition is especially important if you're giving a telephone number. As a general principle, don't bother giving a telephone number unless you plan to repeat it. Ninety-nine out of 100 persons will never catch the number the first time the announcer gives it but there's an outside chance that the number will be remembered, or jotted down, if it is repeated. The same advice applies to the giving of addresses. As for the repetition of product names or the advertiser's name, there is no fixed rule but many writers automatically try to get a name in near the beginning, the middle, and the end.
4. Get attention at the very start. You don't have to scream to get attention at the start but you should come over "big" in some way to distract the listener from what he is doing at the moment, whether washing dishes, polishing the family car, or putting furniture in order. How can you be "big"? Achieve bigness through music, unusual voices, the kind of words you use, the sound effects you achieve.
5. Persuade, don't scream. While a number of success stories—especially in local advertising—have been built by the "screamers," you'll do better in the long run to lead listeners to your way of thinking than to lash them with shrieking messages.
6. Avoid the overworked superlatives and the trite, insincere, glib radio patter. Any comedian working for a laugh can always get it by imitating radio commercials because there are so many that sound ridiculous even without parodying. Does yours?
7. Make dialogue believable and unforced. Again, as in point No. 6, even comedians who are not usually very funny can "slay" audiences with take-offs on radio copy. Finest target is the two voice commercial with two supposed housewives, or with a husband-wife combination. It's almost impossible to deliver a believable, serious commercial with the entire message handled by two actors. Set your stage if you will with the characters from "life" but leave them quickly and let the announcer do the selling. Exceptions to this rule are frankly humorous commercials in which obvious spoofing occurs.
8. Never forget you're writing for the ear. This point, of course, sums up everything previously said about short words, alliteration, unpleasant sounds. Radio writing is not print copy, and it is not television copy. It borrows from both but it has its own unique areas. Above all, radio copy is conversational because the ear is

attuned to the sound, flow, and nuances of conversation.

9. In almost all commercials make your endings strong, positive, and action-suggesting. Naturally, in institutional approaches and certain humorous commercials the big push at the end is inappropriate but in the "let's-move-merchandise-from-the-shelves" type of commercial, *ask for the order.*
10. Watch your word count. Pace your commercial for understandability and sincerity. To be certain that you're not too far above or below your time limitations, count your words and use a stopwatch. You look like an amateur each time your commercial runs over the time. Be *right!*

Writing For Sight, Sound and Movement: Television (Part 1)

A new breed of writers has evolved since television first began commercial operation. The complete television commercial writer not only has the selling instinct needed by any copywriter but also has a whole range of talents not required by other advertising writers.

To practice his craft intelligently he must understand the problems and techniques of the producers and cameramen. This is a whole complicated world in itself. Ideally, he should know staging, acting, and the theater. If he is involved in animated television commercials he should possess knowledge of the complicated art of putting such commercials together but also it is imperative that he have an above-average imagination often tinged with a touch of zaniness because humdrum writers have no part in the humorous and sometimes mad world of animated creation. As the copywriter he may be dealing with producers of animation, an enormously creative group. Without knowing enough about their craft, he cannot command their respect.

One of the problems of television writing is that the writer cannot sit back satisfied when he has turned out his script. On one side he has put down his video ideas and on the other he has written the words to be said by the characters on the video side. Next, a storyboard will be made. The copywriter begins to feel a little more certain of what the completed production might be like but he is still a long way from home. The type of voices, of acting, musical background will determine the final success of the commercial but only when the first prints come back from the producers (called "answer" prints) will writer, client and others have any solid inkling of the finished product. It is apparent that the more the writer knows about all that goes on after he evolves his original commercial script, the less guesswork there will be about the commercial that finally goes on the air.

Contrast all this uncertainty and complication with the delightful simplicity of the average radio commercial, or print advertisement. A print writer does his headline, body copy, gets a rough layout from his artist and the finished advertisement is simply a refinement of what he has already done. At a similar stage in the television commercial script, he has merely begun and by the end of the production process the commercial could be a resounding flop.

Of course, not all television commercials depend upon way-out imagination. Many commercials of the demonstration type are clear-cut from the beginning and may be likened to the straight-line copy described in the listing of body copy types. Probably there are more routine television commercials than highly creative commercials and a writer can make a good living turning out adequate, if undistinguished, television commercials. If he has that creative spark, however, that enables him to come up with the creative point of difference, the rewards for such writing can be enormous. One such idea can make a fantastic difference in the marketplace as shown by the "Don't squeeze the Charmin" campaign of Procter & Gamble.

Make no mistake about it, the world of television commercial writing is a different world. There are new rules, new techniques, and new demands but it's a fascinating world for the truly creative person.

Although it can reach a mass audience of millions at low cost, television's effectiveness is still too often impaired by poor craftsmanship. The medium must become a better salesman, more efficient and responsive, and less prone to the errors once attributable to

SCRIPT FOR ☐ RADIO ☒ TELEVISION FROM DANIEL & CHARLES, INC.

client: CLEP-# commercial title: LINCOLN COL-1-60 date: 12/11/ version no: :60

VIDEO	AUDIO
AGENT SEATED IN OFFICE, ON TELEPHONE. LINCOLN STANDING BEHIND HIM. AGENT SIGNALS FOR HIM TO SIT, FINISHES ON PHONE, HANGS UP, LOOKS AT CARD, LOOKS UP TO LINCOLN.	AGENT: Uh...Lincoln...right?
	LINCOLN: Yessir.
	AGENT: Let's see...you're looking for an executive position. What about college...
	LINCOLN: Well...I've done a lot of reading and studying...sort of on my own.
	AGENT: On your own...(bites sandwich) Look...ah, Lincoln, I know you're a smart guy...but you ain't goin' nowhere without that Sheepskin, Fella. (Agent looks down to card file.)
CU, LINCOLN, LOOKS DOWN; FUMBLES WITH HAT.	
CU, FILE WITH AGENT'S FINGERS RIFLING THROUGH.	

Fig. 17-1

Dramatized humorous commercial.

This commercial makes its point skillfully with the use of ironic humor.

SCRIPT FOR ☐ RADIO ☒ TELEVISION FROM DANIEL & CHARLES, INC.

client: CLEP-3 commercial title: Lincoln COL-1-60 date: 12/11/ version no :60

Page 2

VIDEO	AUDIO
	VO: There you are...an intelligent human being but no college credit to prove it. To help you get it, we're introducing The College Level Examination Program.
AGENT LOOKS UP FROM CARD FILE.	AGENT: Uh...Lincoln, you got a chauffeur's liscence?
LINCOLN SHAKES HIS HEAD, "NO"; AGENT LOOKS BACK DOWN TO CARDS.	
CU, LINCOLN LOOKS TO PHONE BUZZ.	VO: Let us test you. You could be given up to 2 years college credit for what you've already learned without college.
AGENT PICKS UP PHONE, CUPS IT, TURNS TO LINCOLN...	AGENT: Look...you're not really what we call executive material. We'll call if we get sumpin'.
CU, LINCOLN LOOKING DOWN – SUPER FREEZE ADDRESS	VO: Write us. We could help you get college credit for what you've learned in life.

Fig. 17-2

Demonstration commercial.

Notice the effective use of the split-screen technique in the last six frames of this photoboard. Notice, too, the effective build-up to the showing of the full product name in the next to the last frame.

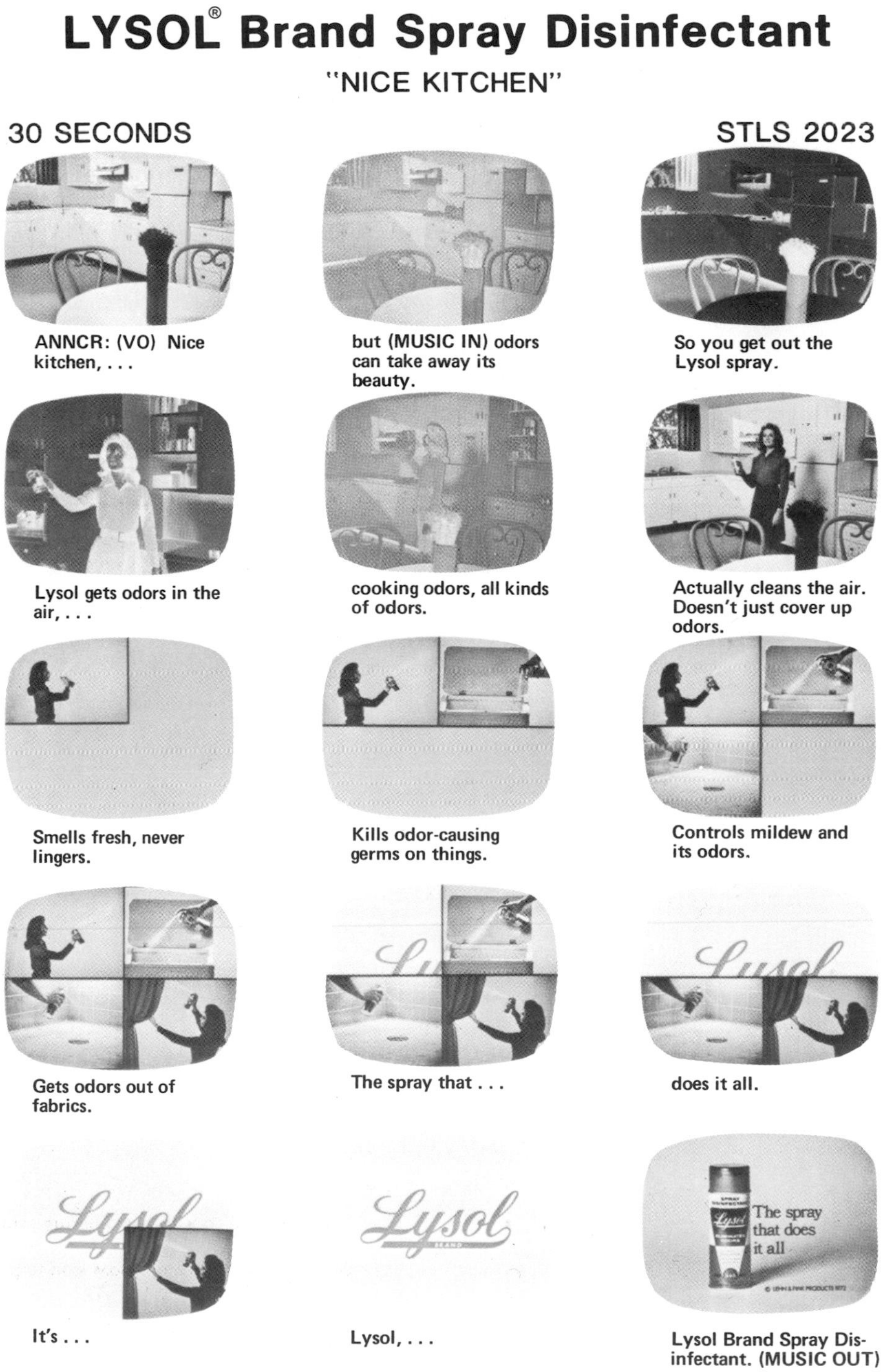

LYSOL® Brand Spray Disinfectant
"NICE KITCHEN"
30 SECONDS
STLS 2023
ANNCR: (VO) Nice kitchen, . . .
but (MUSIC IN) odors can take away its beauty.
So you get out the Lysol spray.
Lysol gets odors in the air, . . .
cooking odors, all kinds of odors.
Actually cleans the air. Doesn't just cover up odors.
Smells fresh, never lingers.
Kills odor-causing germs on things.
Controls mildew and its odors.
Gets odors out of fabrics.
The spray that . . .
Lysol
does it all.
Lysol
It's . . .
Lysol
Lysol, . . .
The spray that does it all
Lysol Brand Spray Disinfectant. (MUSIC OUT)

youthful inexperience. With various creative and technical production factors combining to make the television commercial more complex than any other form of advertising today, there is indeed a critical need for trained, competent television personnel.

NEXT BEST THING TO PERSONAL SELLING

When television first bounced up over the horizon like a giant electronic sun, everyone in advertising, including the clients, wanted to get in the act. Few were ready for it. The possibilities of this new medium for mass communication were irresistible, offering for the first time the opportunity to combine sight and sound, plus sight-in-action. Here was advertising *in action*—the next best thing to personal selling.

Out of the ensuing chaos eventually came a degree of order, with the realization that this form of advertising demanded specialized copy. Not "copy" in the sense of words, for words in themselves are less important in television than in radio or print. All three media do have the same basic aim and strive to make the same basic sense, but there the resemblance ends.

Fig. 17-3

Television commercial that uses words in the video and audio.

The message given in this commercial is part of a campaign.

FOOTE, CONE & BELDING

DATE: June
PRODUCER: MPO Videotronics, Inc.

CLIENT: Zenith Radio Corp.
PRODUCT: Color TV Sets
FILM NO.: ZE72T31R1
FILM TITLE: "Serviceman" (T-2078C R1)
FILM LENGTH: 30

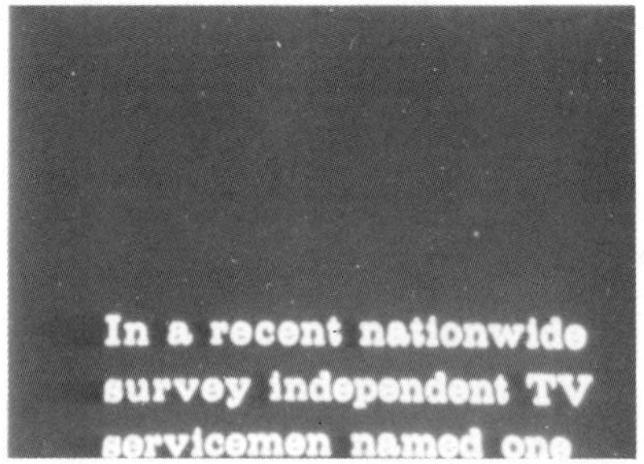
In a recent nationwide
survey independent TV

1. (Anncr VO) In a recent nation-wide survey independent TV servicemen...

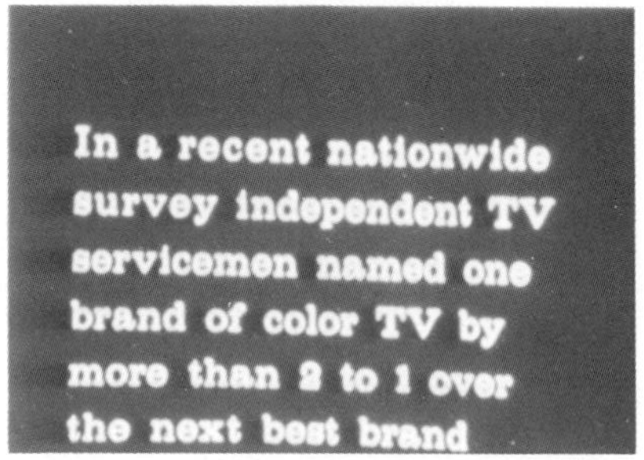
In a recent nationwide
survey independent TV
servicemen named one
brand of color TV by
more than 2 to 1 over
the next best brand

2. ...named one brand of color TV by more than 2 to 1 over the next best brand...

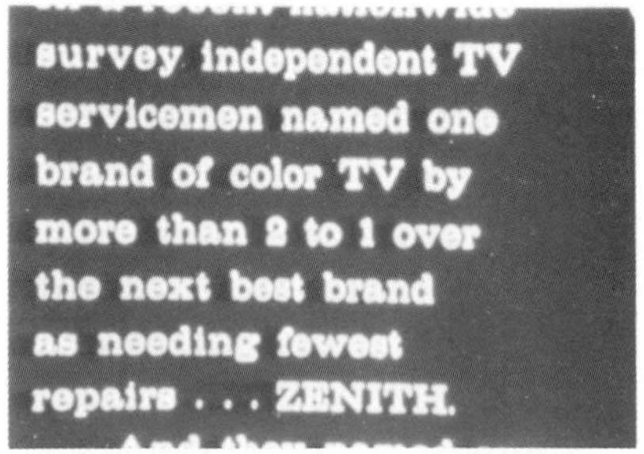
survey independent TV
servicemen named one
brand of color TV by
more than 2 to 1 over
the next best brand
as needing fewest
repairs . . . ZENITH.

3. ...as needing fewest repairs...Zenith.

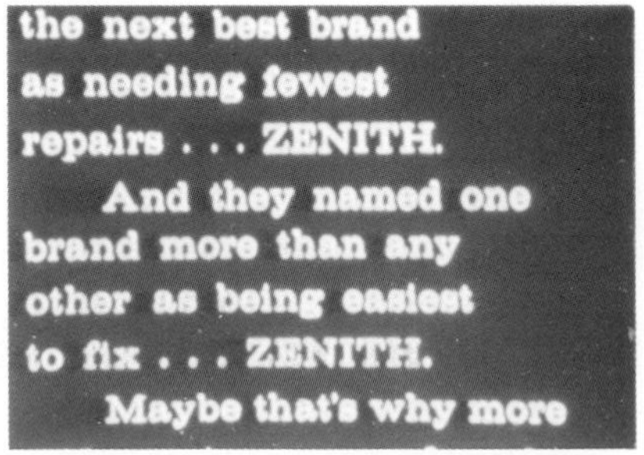
the next best brand
as needing fewest
repairs . . . ZENITH.
And they named one
brand more than any
other as being easiest
to fix . . . ZENITH.
Maybe that's why more

4. And they named one brand more than any other as being easiest to fix...Zenith.

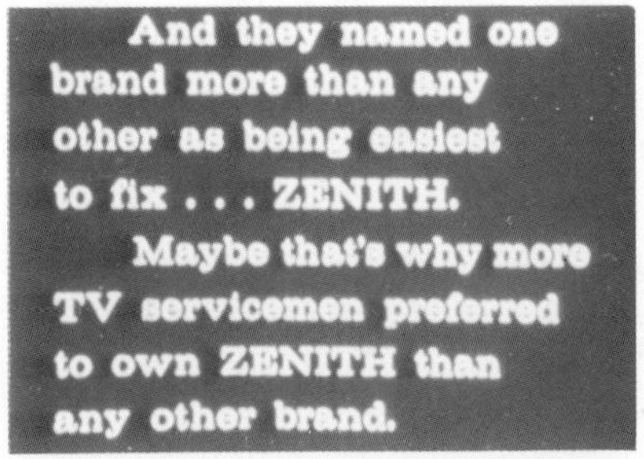
And they named one
brand more than any
other as being easiest
to fix . . . ZENITH.
Maybe that's why more
TV servicemen preferred
to own ZENITH than
any other brand.

5. Maybe that's why more TV servicemen...

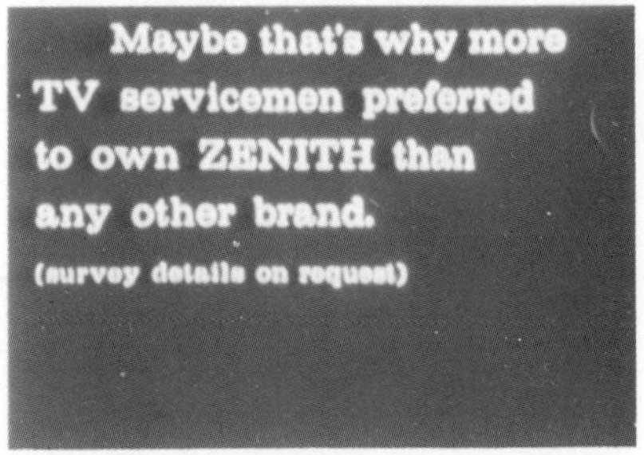
Maybe that's why more
TV servicemen preferred
to own ZENITH than
any other brand.
(survey details on request)

6. ...preferred to own Zenith...

any other brand.
(survey details on request)

7. ...than any other brand.

ZENITH

8. (Music under) At Zenith, the quality goes in before the name goes on.

DANCER-FITZGERALD-SAMPLE, INC.
Client: STATE OF FLORIDA/DEPT. OF CITRUS
Title: "CINDERELLA"
Product: ORANGE JUICE
Commercial No.: FCOJ2610
As Filmed/Recorded: COLOR
Date:
Length: 60 SECONDS
1. (SILENT)
2. BOBBY: It fits! My Princess!
3. GLORIA: My Prince!
4. BILLY: Bring the crown.
5. BOBBY: And they lived happily ever after.
ORANGE JUICE TIME
6. (SFX: APPLAUSE) BILLY: It's Orange Juice Time!
7. ANITA: Perfect timing kids.
8. After that performance, you deserve nutritious orange juice from Florida.
9. BOB: And so does the audience.
10. ANITA: Orange Juice from Florida is more than just delicious.
11. It's rich in natural Vitamin C...which you need to help develop well-formed bones and teeth,
12. and there's nothing artificial or synthetic about pure orange juice.
13. Delicious orange juice from Florida is 100% juice.
14. You can buy it many ways, in many brands.
15. In our house, we enjoy it every day. Because we know, don't we, Princess?
16. That a day without orange juice...
17. GLORIA: ...is like a day without sunshine.
18. JINGLE: Orange juice
NATURAL VITAMIN C
19. with natural Vitamin C
NATURAL VITAMIN C
20. from the Florida Sunshine Tree.

Fig. 17-4

Personality commercial.

This combines live action with a small amount of animation in the tag portion.

FIRST AND LAST, A VISUAL MEDIUM

You, as well as writers experienced in other media, must put your thinking in order when approaching television. This is first, last, and always a *visual* medium. Ideally, your television copy theme should be one that simply puts into words a piece of action seen on the screen. The best television copy is the least obtrusive copy; it does not call attention to itself. In writing it, you are less concerned with copy as such than either the radio or print copywriter. You are after significant action and ways of bringing it about. You are well on your way to achieving these ends if, after writing a final script, you can evaluate it in this manner: block off the audio portion and read through the video to see if it makes an interesting, logical, fluid series of pictures in your mind. If you can grasp a basic, solid message from the video alone, you may indeed make a comfortable living from writing television commercials!

In this medium, however, you will not enjoy the freedom allowed the print writer. For example, his typical advertisement employs a headline, major illustration and subhead to convey the essential sales story. Nor does television afford the set finality of the printed

Fig. 17-5

Production commercial.

Uses music, many scenes and lively action.

M^C^CANN-ERICKSON, INC. | *Television - Radio*

Home Office: 485 LEXINGTON AVE., NEW YORK 17, N.Y.

client Coca-Cola USA
product Coca-Cola
W.O. no. 2-9534 AS PRODUCED
length :60

script title "COUNTRY SUNSHINE"
rev. no.
code no. KOMT2619
date

Long shot of cab on country road	"I was raised on country sunshine
CU of girl in cab	
LS of kids on swing	Green grass beneath my feet
LS of cab	
Kids on horse	Runnin' thru fields of daisies
Kids on tree fishing	Wadin' thru the creek
LS of father on tractor	
Pan of car with girl	You love me and it's invitin'
Shot of hay loft	To go where life is
Mother on porch	More excitin'
Long shot of cab	But I was raised
CU of father reacting to cab	On country sunshine
CU of cab	
CU of girl on swing reacting to cab	I was raised
CU of boy in hay loft	On country
Boy jumps out of hay loft	sunshine. I'm a happy
Mother on porch reacting to girl	With the simple
Long shot of cab arriving at house	Things--a Saturday night dance
Product shot	A bottle of Coke
Girl greets family	The joy that the Bluebird brings I love you please believe me
CU of greeting	And don't you ever leave me
CU of family on porch	Cause I was raised on country sunshine

picture to establish and sustain a mood while your copy carries on at length. It is dangerous in television to rely heavily on a single visual impression. Further, you cannot spread your commercial like a print advertisement, whose full page can accommodate a multitude of sales points, many more than even a two-minute commercial. Too many points are bad enough in print, impossible in television.

Even more difficult are the problems of the radio writer moving into television, for he is accustomed to writing for the ear exclusively, and the ear is much slower than the eye. For radio, each thought transition must be gradual; word pictures must be drawn carefully with clear definition, and verbal over-emphasis is often required to drive home a point.

But television neither needs nor wants these standard radio techniques. In radio then, words have always done the job. To relinquish this to the camera is one of the hardest and most essential things for the radio writer to learn about television. As a television copywriter, you will do well to heed the ancient Chinese admonition: "Don't tell me—show me."

An interesting sidelight on the marked reduction in the need for words to tell what is

McCANN - ERICKSON, INC.
Home Office: 485 LEXINGTON AVE., NEW YORK, N.Y. 10017

Television - Radio

client	Coca-Cola USA		*script title*	"COUNTRY SUNSHINE"
product	Coca-Cola		*rev. no.*	
W.O. no.	2-9534	AS PRODUCED	*film or et code no.*	KOMT2619
length	:60		*air date*	

CU of kids drinking Coke	It's the real thing
Product shot	Like Coke is
Guy getting out of truck	That you're hoping to find
Girl and guy embrace	Like country sunshine, it's the real thing
Couple on swing	Coca-Cola
SUPER: It's the real thing	

Lyrics Copyrighted (C) 1972 by The Coca-Cola Company

"Coca-Cola" and "Coke" are registered trade-marks which distinguish the same product of The Coca-Cola Company.

happening on a screen is provided by the motion picture industry. In the era of silent pictures, from 1914 to 1928, there was a steady decrease in the number of explanatory titles used in movies from three titles per reel in 1914 to three titles per ten reels in 1928. You can profit by the experience of motion picture producers by using sound in its true function: to support, emphasize, drive home and clarify the message.

NEED FOR TRAINED CREATIVE WRITING

Most helpful to you in creating effective television commercials will be a clear, keen, and imaginative visual sense, in order to develop and exploit to its fullest, the great potential of television for imagery and its unique capacity for product demonstration. Your creative writing talents will determine the extent to which you can communicate ideas with imagination, using words and pictures your audience will readily understand. This translation of ideas demands precise knowledge of the audience to be reached, for unless you understand the viewer he will never understand your message. People buy ideas, not things. Behind each product must lie the idea of what it will do for the buyer: an honest promise. Your idea developed with freshness, originality, and imagination will result in a more effective commercial—an idea which will be retained and acted upon by the viewer at the point of sale.

"Originality," however, is a quantity to be reckoned with, according to Rosser Reeves, once board chairman of Ted Bates & Co., a New York agency with a huge percentage of its billings in television. In his book, *Reality in Advertising,** Reeves raised warning signals about the preoccupation with originality that can lead writers to absurd extremes. In searching after the different, the clever and the unusual, or in attempting to imitate some *truly original* approach, writers can forget that an advertising campaign is not designed to express their individual ego or talent for entertaining. Rather, it is a functional tool whose purpose is to fully inform the public via maximum projection of the message. Forget the aesthetics and deal with the realities. Bring the brick and mortar of the basic claim to life with ideas, information, and specific visual interpretations that speak convincingly about why your product is better.

This is *trained* creative writing. The more of it you can develop and use, the better quarterback you will be on the creative team. Also, it is necessary to understand the value of simple, honest, persuasive copy with powerful graphic interpretations. This calls for a knowledge of your product, your product's market, consumer research, company policies, and whatever taboos the client has stipulated. A familiarity with any competing products is helpful. In addition, you may also be required to coordinate television with the client's print campaign.

COPYWRITER AS TEAM QUARTERBACK

If you are a heads-up quarterback for your creative team, you will be able to prevent most of the failures and eliminate much of the waste and extravagance in the production techniques and their application to the television commercial, the greater service you will render—and the larger salary you'll be able to command. In making a one-minute commercial on film, you may well be the hub of a 100-man task force, which means working with account executives, television directors, actors, producers, cameramen, technicians and union personnel. You will be expected to know at least a reasonable amount about many things which today fall outside the scope of most copywriting jobs.

Naturally, you will have plenty of expert assistance from specialists in each of the many fields, but to handle your part of the production—the commercial—you should learn the important features of these other fields. A knowledge of your co-worker's expectations and capabilities is essential.

BUDGET BUGABOOS

In this business, you can not afford to detach "ivory tower" luxury from the realistic factor of cost. While your agency's television director will usually control production and costs, this does not give you license to turn out "brilliant" ideas without regard to limitations already imposed by a given budget. It is not always easy to burden one's thinking machinery with an extra such as an adding machine, but you will learn by experience that it is wiser in building your commercial to avoid costly scenes that will invite price-cutting surgery later and thereby endanger the continuity of the whole script.

Another factor that now complicates cost control is the mechanics of union negotiations on payment of actors, announcers, and

Fig. 17-6

Dramatized commercial that uses a product-comparison approach.

JOHN F. MURRAY ADVERTISING AGENCY
685 THIRD AVENUE, NEW YORK, N. Y. 10017

CLIENT: AMERICAN HOME PRODUCTS
PRODUCT: ANACIN
TITLE: "SUPERMARKET WEDGE"

COMMERCIAL NO. AHAN3150
LENGTH: 30 SECONDS
DATE PRODUCED:

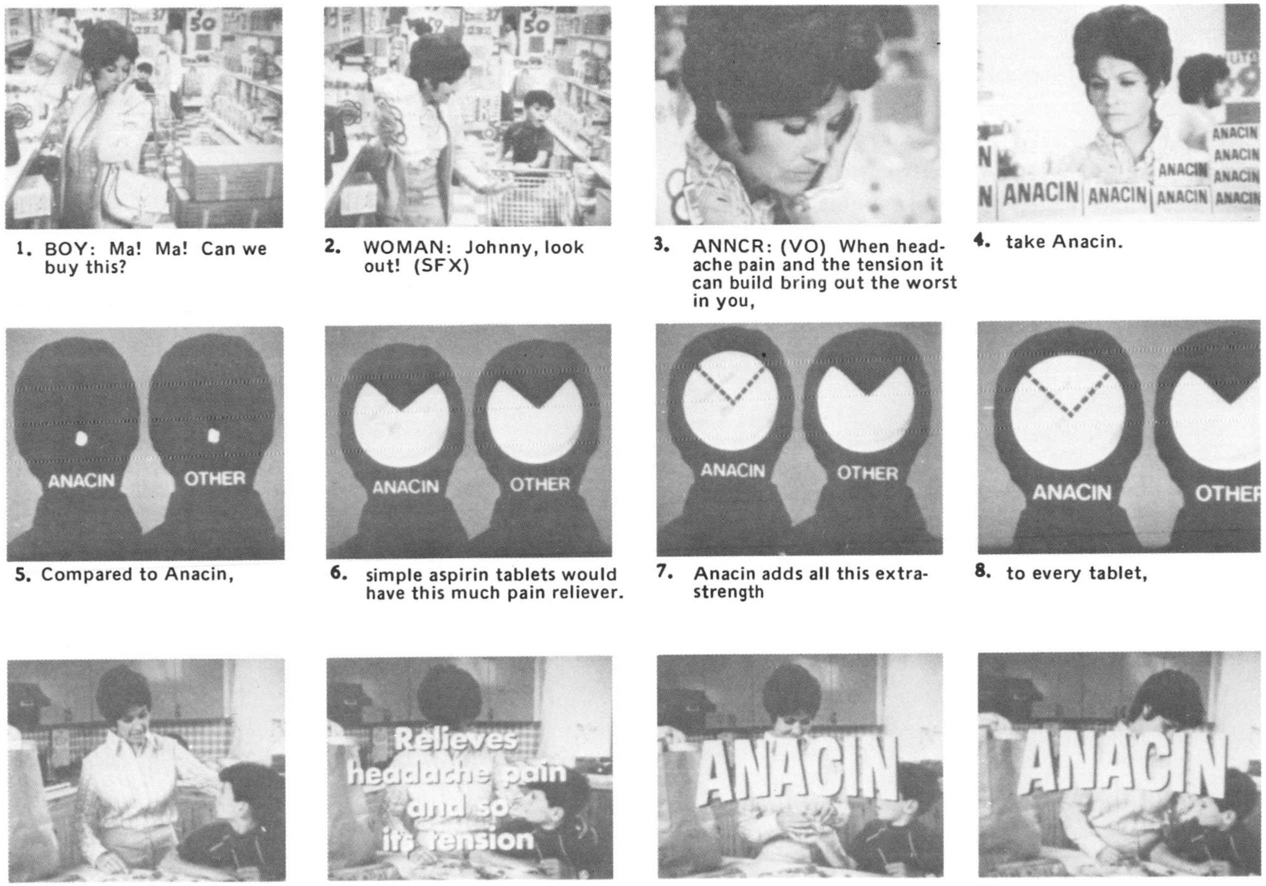
ANACIN
OTHER
Relieves headache pain and so its tension
ANACIN

1. BOY: Ma! Ma! Can we buy this?
2. WOMAN: Johnny, look out! (SFX)
3. ANNCR: (VO) When headache pain and the tension it can build bring out the worst in you,
4. take Anacin.
5. Compared to Anacin,
6. simple aspirin tablets would have this much pain reliever.
7. Anacin adds all this extra-strength
8. to every tablet,
9. rushing relief power to your headache.
10. Anacin relieves headache pain and so its tension fast.
11. Anacin.
12. BOY: Feeling better now Mom? WOMAN: Oh yes, I feel a lot better.

vocalists in television commercials. Codes of the SAG (Screen Actors Guild) and the AFTRA (American Federation of Television and Radio Artists) now call for original "session" fees plus repayments to talent, depending on where and how many times a particular commercial is used. Unless this detail is carefully calculated at the start and budgeted accordingly, it can cost the sponsor many times his actual production investment. All in all, it is said by some authorities, that when you pull the final script out of your typewriter you should know the cost of producing your commercial within ten per cent.

Only with experience, of course, can you learn such rapid calculation, and you may never be required to do any such figuring. But, the fact remains that the accomplished television copywriter is a many-faceted being—salesman, psychologist, dramatist, film craftsman and bookkeeper. And as such, you may take part in planning sessions, production briefings and many of the various stages of actual production. You can make all of these efforts more productive and efficient from the beginning with good writing—the best insurance against faulty interpretation and costly production.

ADVANTAGES OF THE MEDIUM

Among television's advantages, as noted, is the doubly vivid combination of action in sight, plus sound. This can assure greater impact and retention value, two hallmarks of a superior television commercial. With this medium, you also have the advantage of controlling the sales story, step by step, as in personal selling. You can rely on the proved AIDA formula (Attention, Interest, Development of sales points, and Action bid) and lead your audience through your story to a forceful closing. This is a technique which newspapers and magazines cannot confidently apply, because readers may begin a print advertisement at any one place and thus by-pass many salient points.

Another of television's strong points on which you can rely, and which you should strive to exploit, is its dramatic quality—ideally suited to quick, efficient demonstration of products to mass audiences. Combine the powerful elements of sight-and-sound, step-by-step control of the sales story, and television's very "personal" nature, and you have at your command a medium that can project an advertising message with enough impact to assure deep penetration and long memorability.

AND THERE ARE DISADVANTAGES, TOO

With all its attributes, television is still ideally suited for every advertiser. In the eyes of many advertisers, there are several drawbacks which make this medium unattractive or unusable. Unless the advertiser is an adventurous type, television can be expensive in comparison with the results that can be expected from using other media. It can be wasteful, too, if a product does not possess a fair return potential in the medium. Even relatively low-cost items with widespread use-appeal can miss the mark in this field where experience and judgment are priceless assets in the planning and execution of an advertising campaign.

The transitory nature of the television commercial can also discourage many advertisers whose product may require extensive explanation of its function and merits. Time is the culprit here, because television does not provide a second look at your message, as is the case with print. On the other hand, while there may be *immediate* second look, there may well be as many as 50 looks at a particular commercial within all too brief a period from the viewpoint of the audience. If the commercial is anything but first rate, your effort may be resented or may cause boredom.

Television, in spite of its phenomenal growth and almost universal appeal, is subject to much criticism, and perhaps justly so. For years the viewer was taken for granted, because he was easily pleased with what he saw and almost as easily moved to buy what he was shown and told on the magic screen. Soft-soaped, tricked and confused by a mass of contradictory claims, the viewer is finally developing an increasingly mature and critical judgment about commercials.

ELECTRONIC SORE SPOTS

Unfortunately, from the standpoint of viewers, many commercials are addressed to them at the psychologically inopportune moment—when the hero is hanging from the cliff by his fingertips. This intrusion is resented and, when the offense is compounded by a boring, irritating or even insulting commercial, it is little wonder the television commercial has become one of America's favorite whipping boys.

Never approach your audience as though it were obligated to pay attention to your mes-

BIC BANANA INK CRAYON
OPEN ON MAN DRESSED IN MONKEY SUIT. HE HAS THE VOICE OF CHARLES NELSON REILLY. HE IS STANDING IN TYPICAL ARTIST'S LOFT IN FRONT OF AN EASEL.
Monkey: Hi, humans! Today I'm going to instruct you in the art of drawing and coloring with bananas.
CUT TO CLOSE-UP OF PACKAGE OF BIC BANANA INK CRAYONS. HE TAKES ONE AND DRAWS WITH IT.
Monkey: These are the bananas of which I speak. Bic Banana Ink Crayons.
MEDIUM SPOT OF MONKEY HOLDING UP BIC BANANA.
Monkey: You don't peel them. You draw and color with them.
HI MOMMY
THE SOCIAL LIFE OF THE SNAIL
HE HOLDS UP COLORFUL DRAWING.
Monkey: This is just one of the many masterpieces I did with the ten bright colors of my Bic Banana Ink Crayons.
HE HOLDS UP A CARD WITH A DRAWING OF A FEMININE-LOOKING GORILLA WEARING A FLOWERED HAT. THE CARD SAYS: "HI, MOMMY!"
Monkey: This one is a Mother's Day card I designed.
HE HOLDS UP A BOOK REPORT COVER WHICH READS: "THE SOCIAL LIFE OF THE SNAIL."
Monkey: This is a book report I did.
BIC BANANA INK CRAYONS
HE HOLDS UP WHAT APPEARS TO BE A VERY REALISTIC DRAWING OF A BANANA.
Monkey: And this....is my lunch.
HE BEGINS EATING THE BANANA.
CUT TO DOUBLE PRODUCT SHOT.
VO: Bic Banana Ink Crayons. In ten bright colors. The only fruit you can draw with.

Fig. 17-7

Storyboard for animated commercial.

sage. To demand rather than to ask; to abuse rather than to disarm, is violating every precept of salesmanship. You should be aware that television has been charged with blatancy, repetition, poor taste, misrepresentation, coarseness and deception. It is still difficult, at this writing, to watch a full evening of television without being assailed by commercials discussing human plumbing, underarm deodorants, nasal passages, sore feet and other matters of questionable taste. Artificiality of the worst type results when these commercials, offensive enough in subject, are delivered by the obviously fictious "authority" used to create professional status and knowledge.

These offenses constitute a serious indictment against television in the eyes of the American viewing audience. Yet, there is no need for these crimes to be committed. There is nothing startlingly new or magical about the appeals that reach, motivate and win the loyalty of your audience, selective and skeptical as it may have grown. The "you" approach, always effective, can be even more personal with television. Products can be related directly to one's life experience. This, of course, embraces the family and the desire for the better life.

Fig. 17-8

Humorous man-on-the-street dramatized interview commercial.

Fig. 17-9

Humorous animated commercial.

Paint selling is ideally suited to presentation on color television as this commercial demonstrates.

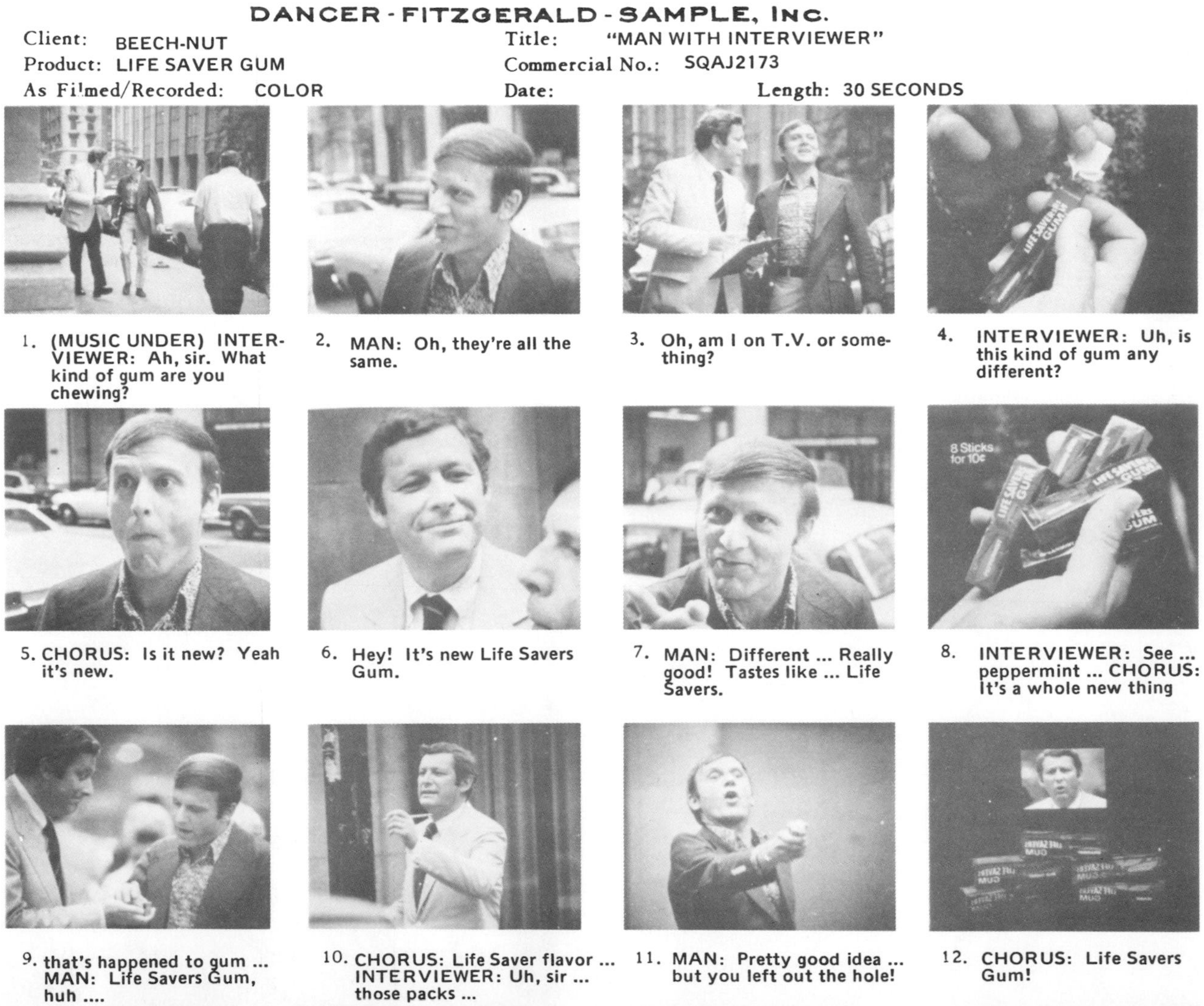
DANCER - FITZGERALD - SAMPLE, INC.
Client: BEECH-NUT
Product: LIFE SAVER GUM
As Filmed/Recorded: COLOR
Title: "MAN WITH INTERVIEWER"
Commercial No.: SQAJ2173
Date:
Length: 30 SECONDS
1. (MUSIC UNDER) INTERVIEWER: Ah, sir. What kind of gum are you chewing?
2. MAN: Oh, they're all the same.
3. Oh, am I on T.V. or something?
4. INTERVIEWER: Uh, is this kind of gum any different?
5. CHORUS: Is it new? Yeah it's new.
6. Hey! It's new Life Savers Gum.
7. MAN: Different ... Really good! Tastes like ... Life Savers.
8. INTERVIEWER: See ... peppermint ... CHORUS: It's a whole new thing
9. that's happened to gum ... MAN: Life Savers Gum, huh ....
10. CHORUS: Life Saver flavor ... INTERVIEWER: Uh, sir ... those packs ...
11. MAN: Pretty good idea ... but you left out the hole!
12. CHORUS: Life Savers Gum!

Your viewer is also looking for the "new" in your product or service in order that he can be up to the minute with progress. He is interested in the good deal, if you can give him convincing justification for purchase. In keeping with his powers of more critical appraisal, your viewer will appreciate a well-presented commercial, devoid of trickery, ambiguous language and "talking-down."

Talking-down is a particular sore spot in television commercials, along with excessive repetition, artificiality and extravagant claims. Remember, television dramatizes and, in so doing, it can exaggerate even the exaggerated. Your sophisticated housewife and career girl seriously doubt that Hollywood's glamour girls use all the products they so glibly endorse. Today's motorist wonders if there is really any appreciable difference among motor oils, and even the young sports fan is on to the fact that his hero gets paid for those breakfast cereal commercials.

Yes, viewers resent poor commercials—long ones, loud ones, the hard sell and the similarity. All these are familiar complaints and, in spite of efforts to overcome such trouble spots, they will probably always be with us. The alternative to them, pay-as-you-go, or

THE PITTSBURGH PEACOCK "COLOR DYNAMICS"

(PEACOCK WALKING PAST REGIMENTED PEOPLE ON A BUSY CITY SIDEWALK).

PEACOCK: Pardon me, I understand there's a Pittsburgh Paint store around here somewhere.
MAN: Yeah, I've seen it but I forget . . . hey, what kind of a bird are you?

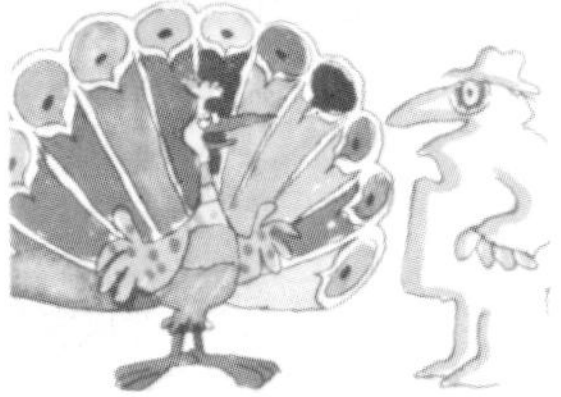

PEACOCK: I'm the Pittsburgh Peacock! I mean what else would I be?

(THE BRILLIANT COLOR OF HIS PLUMAGE IS SO STARTLING. THAT IT BEDAZZLES THE GREY-TONED PASSERSBY.)

MAN: What happened?
WOMAN: Where am I . . . I can't see . . .
TEENAGER: All of a sudden these fanTAStic colors.

(HE WALKS AROUND THE CORNER . . .)

(AND SPOTS A TRAFFIC COP DIRECTING TRAFFIC DURING RUSH HOUR).

(HE DARTS OUT QUICKLY THROUGH TRAFFIC).

EXPRESS

PEACOCK: Pardon me officer, I'm looking for a Pittsburgh Paints dealer.
OFFICER: Right around the . . .

OFFICER: Whattaya think YOU'RE doin out here?
PEACOCK: I'm the Pittsburgh Peacock and . . .

(THE DAZZLING COLORS HOPELESSLY SNARL TRAFFIC . . .)

PITTSBURGH
PAINTS

PEACOCK: You'd think they'd never seen COLOR before.

(HE WHIZZES PAST THE PITTSBURGH PAINT STORE AND SCREECHES TO A HALT).

(HE RUNS BACK INTO THE STORE AND UP TO THE DEALER AND OPENS HIS PLUMAGE).

(THE DEALER DOESN'T BAT AN EYE).
PEACOCK: Here I am!
DEALER: Good

PEACOCK: At a Pittsburgh Paints dealer, they understand dynamic color.

PITTSBURGH

(AS THE PEACOCK MOVES INTO POSITION, A WOMAN RUSHES IN . . .)

WOMAN: That's the shade I want for my living room! And THAT one right there for my den!
PEACOCK: Whatever's right.

PEACOCK: Now, where would you like me to work?
DEALER: A little to one side actually.

PEACOCK: (MOVING ASIDE) Oh, I'm sorry. I did it again.

pay-TV, has thus far been rejected by a majority of viewers.

Before leaving this department of discontent, make a note that one of the quickest ways to bring up your viewer's defense is to attack negatively his way of life or habits. If these are to be changed or improved, shame is not the instrument to accomplish the change. An elderly woman once addressed herself to this matter in a statement noteworthy for its articulate and philosophical quality. She found television lacking by reason of its "contempt for the fragileness of life and disregard for the long time it has taken the race to climb up."

While it has been remiss in discharging its duties and obligations in the past, television is growing more responsible, responsive and self-critical. With changing times come new problems, the challenge of increasing costs and competition, and the demise of the weak commercial.

TRENDS

Paramount among the signs of the changing times is the strong trend to believability, in claims for and demonstrations of products. The honest promise of a believable benefit, the proferring of simple, useful information couched in a message within the viewer's understanding and experience is overtaking the extravagant, unsubstantiated claim and the excess of gimmicks and optical tricks once employed. Unnatural situations and artificial-sounding dialogue, the too-perfect result of product demonstration effected by use of film trickery, are now readily spotted as "phony" by viewers. The average family it is said tunes in to some 350 commercials a week, so don't expect them to be naive babes in the woods when it comes to accepting rash claims. Nor is this a captive audience, although if you can gain their attention, hold their interest and validate solid claims with honest pictorial proof—then you may have a *captivated* audience.

The paid testimonial, as indicated earlier, is a device that sorely tries the viewer's believability quotient. When used, it must strike a happy marriage between the product and the personality to whom its sales message is entrusted. Viewers are legion who think motion picture stars will endorse anything, and this is a definite liability to any product so advertised. Simple fact is that movie stars are skilled in creating *other* characters on stage or screen and, therefore, have difficulty being themselves and lending conviction to their selling job. Somewhat akin to this type of commercial is the aforementioned use of the "medical authority."

The move, then, is always from bombast, brag and boast and the simple, useful and believable. This calls for better understanding of the viewer and better public relations, with the aim of building good will and developing loyalty.

IDEAS, THE START OF THE COMMERCIAL

Where, then, do *you* begin in writing a television commercial? The first step, as noted earlier, is the evolution of the idea—the first, but often overlooked, principle of successful advertising in any medium. Your idea must strike at such basic motivations of the viewer as: love, ambition, self-preservation, economy. It should be developed with imagination and tempered with a knowledge of the medium and the advertiser's needs, as well as the consumer's desires. By applying simple reasoning, you will find that the product to be advertised contains within itself such sources of ideas as: what is new about the product; what benefits it offers to the user; the experience of these consumers with the product; its advantages over competitive products; and its price of value.

These facts now give you the substance of ideas which, through creative thinking, can be used with imagination to penetrate the viewer's mind. In an effective presentation, you must touch upon the right motivational button and stimulate desire for the product and its benefits. In short, you must enunciate a basic formula stated by Horace S. Schwerin of the Schwerin Research Corp:

Sales Idea x Strength of Presentation = Commercial Efficiency. (The motivating force of the sales idea, multiplied by the strength with which it is put over, equals the effectiveness of your commercial effort.)

Throughout this discussion and in your own preparation of television commercials, keep in mind that the greatest opportunity this medium offers is that of *demonstration—demonstration* to sell. Demonstrate the new feature, the benefit, the advantage, and, where applicable, the price. Show the product; how it works; how it saves; how easy it is to use; how it makes one more attractive or more popular. When price is an important factor, superimpose it on the screen to make it seem even more of a bargain and to make it that much more memorable.

Another point to recall at this point is the element of simplicity. While advantages of the product are important to enumerate, don't try to make your television commercial a catalog of all these advantages. If it has a dozen or more advantages, that's great for the advertiser, but not for his commercial. Time is needed to put across a point, which means the selling story must be boiled down to one principal point, or possibly two of three. Just be sure the selling story has enough time to register on the viewer's mind, and that there is time at the conclusion to sum it up with a convincing repetition.

DEFINING THE PROBLEM

Television commercials vary in length, cost and production techniques, depending on the specific jobs they are intended to perform. Such variations call for definition of the problem, a matter that may or may not lie within your province as copywriter. The problem deals with such factors as over-all sales objectives, location and identification of primary customers, and the limitations of budget. Are you going to hit targets singly or in number? Your commercials should be designed with a basic sales objective in mind: winning new customers; holding regular ones; increasing use per capita; forcing distribution; improving dealer relations; building prestige and good will; and even impressing stockholders.

PROGRAM OR SPOT?

Design-wise, your commercials must also take into account whether they are to be used for *program* or *spot* presentation. In order to present his commercial in what he feels is the proper environment, an advertiser will often buy (through his advertising agency) a specific type of entertainment or information *program,* network or local. This program can run from five minutes to more than an hour. Very often, the advertiser and his product become identified, for better or worse, with the program and/or its star. Commercials used within these programs are usually a minute or longer and can be "live" or on film or tape. Some advertisers follow the practice of using live commercials with a live program and film picture quality as seen by the viewer. However, with the advent of television tape and its live quality, this problem is easily overcome.

	VO: Introducing one of the best kept secrets in Detroit.
MAN RUSHES FROM HOTEL INTO A CAB	MAN: (OUT OF BREATH) Follow that car!
	TAXI DRIVER: What car?
	MAN: The Matador!
	TAXI DRIVER: What's a Matador? (CUT)
TWO MEN ON STAGE. ONE IS M.C.WITH MICROPHONE, OTHER IS WINNER OF GRAND PRIZE.	M.C. With me is Mr. Herb Kepke, the winner of the Grand Prize which this year is..... (DRUM ROLL)
CAMERA ZOOMS BACK. CURTAIN SWINGS OPEN. AUDIENCE GOES AHH OHH	1973 Matador.
C.U. ON 2 MEN	M.C. Mr. Kepke do you have anything to say?
	Mr. KEPKE: Yes, what's a Matador.
MAN HANDS A TICKET TO A PARKING LOT ATTENDANT.	MAN: The white Matador please.
	ATTENDANT: Yes sir.
ATTENDANT IS IN THE MIDDLE OF THE LOT	ATTENDANT: (FROM A DISTANCE) Hey mister, what's a Matador?
	ANNCR VO: The Matador is an American Motors car that gives you...
	more rear seat leg room, more hip room, and more trunk room than any other car of its class,
	And only American Motors makes this promise:
	The Buyer Protection Plan backs every '73 car we build.
	And we'll see to it that our dealers back that promise.
ATTENDANT HAS FOUND CAR AND PULLS IT TO GATE	
MAN DRIVES AWAY, SECOND ATTENDANT COMES UP TO FIRST ATTENDANT.	SFX: CAR DRIVES AWAY.
	SECOND ATTENDANT: Hey Pete what kind of a car was that?
	FIRST ATTENDANT: (CONFIDENTLY) A Matador.
	SECOND ATTENDANT: Oh that's a Matador.
	American Motors Corporation. We back them better because we build them better.

AMC Matador
We back them better
because we build them better.

Fig. 17-10

Dramatized commercial.

Following are a script, storyboard, and photoboard for the same product. Name registration is a primary objective of the commercial.

CUNNINGHAM & WALSH INC.

CLIENT: AMERICAN MOTORS CORP. **PRODUCT:** MATADOR **DATE:**

FILM TITLE: "WHAT'S A MATADOR" **FILM NO:** AOOM3046 **FILM LENGTH:** 60 SEC.

1. ANNCR. (VO): Introducing one of the best-kept secrets in Detroit.

2. MAN: (OUT OF BREATH) Follow that car!

3. TAXI DRIVER: Which car? MAN: The Matador!

4. TAXI DRIVER: Right...

5. What's a Matador? (CUT)

6. M.C.: Mr. Herb Kepke, you have just won the Grand Prize (DRUM ROLL)

7. ... a 1973 Matador.

8. M.C.: Mr. Kepke, do you have anything to say? MR. KEPKE: Yes, what's a Matador? (CUT)

9. MAN: The white Matador, please. ATTENDANT: Right.

10. ATTENDANT: (FROM A DISTANCE) Sir, what's a Matador?

11. ANNCR. (VO): The Matador is an American Motors car

2. with more hip room, more rear seat leg room, and a bigger trunk

13. than any other car of its class.

14. And only American Motors makes this promise:

15. The Buyer Protection Plan backs every '73 car we build.

16. And we'll see that our dealers back that promise.

DAY PARKING

17. SECOND ATTENDANT: Hey, Artie, what kind of car was that? FIRST ATTENDANT:

18. (CONFIDENTLY) That's a Matador. SECOND ATTENDANT: Oh, so that's a Matador.

AMC

19. ANNCR. (VO): American Motors Corporation.

AMC Matador
We back them better
because we build them better.

20. We back them better because we build them better.

Fig. 17-11

Personality salesman commercial.

This "extreme example" type of demonstration commercial holds audience attention while providing convincing proof of the product's ruggedness.

arwick, welsh & miller, inc.

TELEVISION
February 28,
:90
UTTT1911
"Espadon (Front)"

TIMEX CORPORATION
ESPADON

VIDEO	AUDIO
1. WIDE SHOT OF ESPADON IN SURF.	1. SWAYZE VO.O.: This is the Espadon 422 - a boat designed for rescue work in rough surf.
2. DISS. TO SWAYZE STANDING NEXT TO THE ESPADON.	2. SWAYZE O.C.: Ladies and gentlemen, John Cameron Swayze for Timex. In a minute, the Espadon is going to take a Timex Marlin watch for a ride in that surf out there.
3. CUT TO ECU OF WATCH.	3. SWAYZE V.O.: We've attached the watch to a ring on the front of the boat.
4. PULL BACK TO BOAT BEING CAST OFF INTO SURF.	4. Our driver's ready...let's see if our Timex can take it!
5. SHOT OF BOAT HITTING WATER HARD.	5. Every time that boat slams down, remember, our watch is right there.
6. DISS. TO SHOT OF BOAT RACING TOWARDS SHORE.	6. Laboratory tests show the Marlin can withstand an impact of 2,000 G's and still run accurately.

Spot television advertising, on the other hand, is that which is placed by advertisers on a market-by-market basis, originating in the individual market where it is telecast. The advertisement may consist of an 8-second to 10-second commercial announcement known as an "ID" (for Station Identification). It may also be a 20-second, 30-second, or even a 40-second commercial between programs; a 60-second announcement between programs; or within a local program or a network participating program in which a number of advertisers have bought spot time. Spot commercials are almost always on film or tape. They come at the viewer from all angles and in all forms and, because many of them are irritating, they are the kind of advertising people usually complain about when they point an accusing finger at television commercials.

Whether they are irritating or amusing or whether they are viewed attentively or only vaguely heard above the sound of running water, the growth of spot television has been a phenomenon in the advertising business.

PROGRAM OR SPOT: ADVANTAGES AND DISADVANTAGES

There are advantages to the advertiser in

7.	ZOOM IN TO WATCH.	7.	O.K., let's see how our Timex did. There, it's still going. See the sweep second hand? You know the Marlin has to be rugged to take punishment like that!
8.	CUT TO PRODUCT SHOT OF THREE MARLIN WATCHES. SUPER: "FROM $10.95."	8.	The famous water-resistant Marlin, ladies and gentlemen. Also available with an automatic calendar. Or, with a day and date indicator.
9.	DISS. TO 3 SHOT OF SPORTSTER WATCHES.	9.	And, for smaller wrists, the Timex Sportster.
10.	CUT TO REPRISE OF ESPADON. SUPER: "TIMEX"	10.	Well, you saw it. No wonder more people buy Timex than any other watch in the world.

both program and spot presentation of commercials. A network program offers an advertiser prestige and a huge framework within which he can sell his individual products. He is also provided with a kind of mirror that reflects the total philosophy and public relations effort of the company itself. Network program commercials assure the advertiser of the same quality of presentation and emphasis in each market. These programs lend themselves readily to "merchandising" to dealers and distributors in order to impress them with the extent of national advertising support behind the products they handle. Network television, well positioned as to time and type of program, is a franchise that can secure large audiences and a loyalty that may carry over into consumer loyalty to the products advertised on the program.

Such advertising calls, however, for a large investment and, moreover, the important elements of time and program may not be readily available. There is also the further disadvantage of a long-term commitment that is required, the minimum being 13 weeks, with some time-and-talent combinations asking for 26- and 39-week commitments.

Spot commercials have the great advantage

of extreme flexibility with regard to market, station and time selection. Once the spot schedule is established, it may be used to rotate various products of the sponsor and thus permit multiple brands to support the over-all budget. Local, regional and seasonal sales drives may be supported as required by the product marketing problems. Spot announcements can be merchandised to a sales organization, as well as by that organization at the local retail level. Spots deliver maximum efficiency per advertising dollar, especially for the advertiser with an established, frequently-purchased, brand name product. His dollar is spent almost entirely for circulation, with no major program expenditure to achieve that circulation. Spot announcements develop a high degree of audiency- and sales-penetration through their greater frequency daily and weekly. They are primarily "reminder" advertising and are also effective selling tools for advertisers who wish to change their campaigns with the season or weather.

Spots are the choice when budget or the availability of broadcast time on networks prevents use of programs. In this respect, the cost factor in SAG talent fees for programs often discourages an advertiser, and turns him to using spot commercials. The advertiser who does this must expect lower recall of both his brand name and sales points.

COMMERCIAL LENGTH VS. EFFECTIVENESS

Sixty in seconds is not a magic number in terms of commercial effectiveness. Optimum effectiveness has been measured at from 71 to 100 seconds, with a sharp falling off beyond that point. Very good performance is attained however, by shorter-length commercials especially the now dominant 30-second commercials. In terms of audience appeal, the pattern has changed, with viewers apparently preferring the shorter commercial.

This raises a point of caution about the construction of 20-second commercials. While these are often built into the longer 60-second commercial in such a way that they can be extracted *in toto,* the job must be done skilfully to avoid the feeling that the 20-second version has been cut off in mid-air without a closing shot of the package or the traditional injunction to buy. Such "cold cuts" not only make the commercial tend to lose effectiveness, but appeal as well. Whenever possible, it is wiser to produce the shorter commercials as units in themselves than to extract them from existing lengthy commercials.

Determination of a commercial's length must take into account the theme, approach, and specific product advantages. Different sales stories vary in their basic natures; the degree of their complexity; and the ease with which they can be absorbed. If you choose a 60-, 30-, 20-, or 10-second spot at random, you may run the risk of putting an elephant in a phone booth or a mouse in a grand ballroom. The most intelligent approach is to realize that any length may be right for your particular product and story. The length that best balances effectiveness and appeal is most likely to be discovered by combining judgment and investigation.

HOW MUCH REPETITION?

Having decided on program as opposed to the spot presentation of your commercial, it is well to keep in mind certain principles about another factor: repetition. Viewer knowledge increases with repetition up to a certain point, when indifference or psychological deafness and blindness set in. It is difficult, if not impossible to measure at what point this mental tuning-out takes place, but there are four factors that seem to relate specifically to any commercial's life expectancy: (1) its frequency of broadcast; (2) its content as it affects the viewer; (3) variety of presentation in a given series; and (4) techniques used in commercial construction.

Since the first authorized spot commercial was televised (by the Bulova Watch Company) in 1941, many advertisers have been successful with a minimum of well-constructed and oft repeated messages. Skilfully built and judiciously scheduled, a spot can be used for many months, even years. Another can run its course in a few weeks in a heavy saturation campaign, yet still have been effective and economical. Kellogg's Rice Krispies ran a $3,700 cartoon jingle 50 times in a row on a children's program and burned it out like a meteor. Yet it served its purpose well, at a cost-per-showing of less than $75.

How acceptable a commercial is refers not to how much a viewer likes it but to its "what's-in-it-for-me" content and how well it entertains, informs and holds forth a promised benefit. A film series should focus on a central theme for greatest impact throughout the series, but *varied* repetition is the key here, particularly in the manner in which the commercial begins. Beer commercials are much the same in any given series, but the variety of ways in which they capture attention at the outset makes for interest. Singing jingles combined with animated cartoons are a combination with long life expectancy, especially if the commercial spot is used intermittently. You cannot, however, expect to repeat too often live action films in which memorable characters or settings are featured, since viewers tend to pick apart your commercial with each repetition.

The various production techniques (cartoons, live action, stop motion, etc.) which affect a commercial's life expectancy will be discussed later in the chapter.

STATION BREAK SPOTS

Let's examine more closely at this point the shorter of the spot commercials, the 10- and 20-second station break television spots, which can best be viewed as the rifle bullets of this medium. Here you encounter the challenge of brevity, plus the need for simple, clear-cut selling ideas expressed with visual impact. It is probably much simpler a task to write a five or ten minute film script than a 10-second television spot. This difficulty was spelled out succinctly by a noted literary figure who, at the conclusion of a lengthy letter, is said to have noted: "Please excuse the great length of this letter. Given more time, I would have made it shorter."

You will be tempted in building spot commercials to crowd too much material into both audio and video presentations, which will only result in a confused and meaningless jumble of words and scenes from which your viewer will derive little. Again, concentrate on the video or visual in your commercial, since this is what must remain with the viewer after your brief message. Remember, however, the sound or audio plays an important role, too, enabling the viewer to hear you even if he has left the room.

Advantages

Both the 20-second commercial and the 10-second Station Identification (called "ID") spot have the advantage over a one-minute commercial in their ability to sustain a much stronger sales pitch and the fact that they can be repeated more often than their longer cousin. They are also easier to schedule for more intensive coverage on a number of stations, and thus are effective in coping with local sales problems.

CLAIROL, Inc.
EARTHLY DELIGHTS
30-Second Commercial

Fig. 17-12

Animated commercial.

In 61 words and full animation this 30-second commercial does a thorough job of product identification and sell.

Clairol invites you into a garden of earthly delights . . .

the most beautyful shampoo experience on earth . . .

with Clairol's Herbal Essence Shampoo with Natural Protein.

Made with the essence of

herbs and flowers

it makes your hair clean, and conditioned,

and smelling like the first day of spring.

clairol herbal essence shampoo
with natural protein

Introduce your hair to Clairol's Herbal Essence Shampoo.

Your hair will get very excited.

The ID spot, chiefly a "reminder" type of advertising, can be built in two ways: the *"shared"* ID which is on the television screen for a full 10 seconds, but shares its picture with the station's call letters in the upper right corner; it gives you 8 seconds of sound. Advertisers generally prefer the *"full screen"* ID, which does not share its video with the station; however, the picture is only 7¼ seconds long, with 6 seconds of sound. (The 20-second station break commercial permits full-time use of video, with 18 seconds of sound.)

Disadvantages

The ID is a commercial form that must fight hard for identity and leaves small margin for error. Its brief moments of sound-and-picture glory are almost always preceded by the closing commercial of the preceding program and a 20-second chain break. It is immediately followed by the first commercial of the next program. In spite of its physical limitations, the ID can do a fine selling job as both a reminder for impulse-type items and as a supporting element for concurrent campaigns for big-ticket advertisers in television and other media.

To detract attention from surrounding commercials, station break commercials often employ cartoons, which are particularly effective because they "read" well. They also simplify the problem imposed by screen layout, since then the commercial message is confined to 75 per cent of the total area. Since this is primarily reminder advertising, the sponsor's name must be indelibly identified, probably along with a slogan or an important selling point. It is better not to resort to camera tricks, such as dissolves or wipes, where action on the screen is involved. Stay with a basic setting and be content to move component parts in and out for the sake of fluidity. Hold to the premise, if possible, that the sponsor's signature or logotype should be on-camera for at least half, if not more, of the allotted 10 seconds.

BUILDING A GOOD STATION BREAK SPOT

While the ID can be a single spot repeated often, or part of a family series, there seems to be a fairly basic structure involved in writing a successful version. This usually calls for a headline or principal "reason why"; and once this is set it is a matter of using it in the audio and dramatizing it in the video. One of the outstanding examples of effective use of the ID spot was made before the abolition of TV cigarette advertising, by Kool cigarettes with audio that stated: "Don't be chained by the hot cigarette habit. Break the habit with Kools." Video presented the Kool cigarette pack breaking through (with a clank) the links of a heavy chain. The basic story of this cigarette continued to be told in a series of ID's that dealt with the cooling effect enjoyed by smoking this brand. Such commercials are in contrast to those contrived and complicated by local advertisers who seek to make major productions out of the precious 7 to 8 seconds allotted by the ID. It is enough to succeed in registering one salient point strongly in even a one-minute or longer commercial, let alone trying to do more in an ID.

In constructing the 20-second commercial, select the dominant sales point from among the several that may be included in a 60-second version and simply polish that point to its finest. This commercial has the ideal length for the cartoon singing jingle, which thus makes it a good opening or closing for a one-minute spot. While the point is often made that the one-minute should be constructed so that 20-second commercials can be edited from it, you will be safer in writing the shorter version first, in its own right. Having done this well, the minute version will readily permit amplification of sales points made in the shorter length commercial, with possible addition of secondary points. The use of the established 20-second jingle, either at the opening or closing of a series of one-minute spots, can serve as an institutional or identification bridge that maintains continuity and recognition for the series.

The success stories of advertisers who have used the station-break spot to understanding advantage are numerous, and many of them have achieved this success with little or no other advertising. One of these, a watch company, revealed this formula:

> Buy 5 or 6 spots a week on a station and hold them for all year use. Try to reach the entire family by buying spots in prime time (8:30 p.m. to 10:00 p.m.) with adjacencies to good shows, if possible.
>
> Buy a volume in spots commensurate with the company's sales in the particular market.

Another advertiser who had done a strong selling job with spots summed up the situation: "Spots give us more coverage with the flexibility to handle sales problems peculiar to different areas. We can adjust our product commercials according to regional preferences in flavor, for instance." While minutes give an advertiser more elbow room and more prestige, selling can be done effectively in many instances with the 30- and 20-second spot and the 10-second ID. Just as many advertisers have succeeded using the full page, so can television advertising succeed using full, traditional one-minute commercial, in spot or program framework.

DEVELOPING THE TELEVISION COMMERCIAL—THE STORYBOARD

Where do you, as the writer, start to develop a television commercial script? There is no better method of script presentation and description than that of a storyboard, the technique used by virtually all advertising agencies and successful film producers. The storyboard is a series of small sketches with accompanying description of action plus audio copy that gives an advertiser an approximate conception of what his commercial will be upon completion. It is a sort of halfway point between the birth of the original idea and the finished film.

Storyboards are preferable to written scripts for a number of reasons. Since the commercial will be presented through a medium in which the visual image is paramount in importance, it facilitates production to think in terms of pictures from the beginning. Furthermore, since a number of people may read and be called upon to approve a script, it is probable that each will have his own personal visualization of how the story will appear on the screen. If a storyboard is prepared, all concerned will think in terms of the pictures shown. Each can check the staging and action as the commercial is actually shot. Also any errors in visualization from the standpoint of company policy or product value will be apparent, and can be corrected before actual production begins.

A properly designed story can also be utilized as a shooting script that suggests camera angles and staging, as a preliminary layout for set designs or backgrounds, and as a guide for the film editor when the film is cut. Close-ups, camera moves and optional effects can all be indicated. The director is also aided by the storyboard as he plans the action and staging of the film to obtain the desired dramatic effect.

Storyboards can be too detailed

A word of caution is needed here to point out that too detailed and rigid a storyboard is not always the best one. Much depends on the type of producer who will take over from your storyboard to put the commercial on film. If he is a truly creative producer, you will be short-cutting your commercial by imposing too exacting directions upon him. He may have ideas about enacting some of your scenes in a manner to make them much more forceful. Or he might have suggestions on how to cut costs by repeating the use of a certain setting or dropping a bit of action that lends only minor support to the story. Such a producer can be a tremendous asset, so it is best to give this talented team member a green light with a storyboard that leaves him room for his own creative contributions.

Only through experience with such a producer or by his long standing reputation can you know when to construct a loose storyboard that takes advantage of this "bonus" talent. Other producers, you will learn from bitter experience, will follow you too unquestioningly, investing no creativity of their own in the commercial. Storyboards for these producers must spell everything out in minute detail. If you know, therefore, with what producer you will be working, build your storyboard to get maximum utilization of his talent. You may even want to consider, if you are working with an unimaginative producer, using a "third column" in your script in which to analyze and explain objectives and to elaborate on the handling desired in the video and audio columns.

BALANCE OF VIDEO AND AUDIO

A basic problem in writing your television commercial, regardless of its length, is the proper balance of video and audio. Do not pace the visual side of the commercial too fast and use too many scene changes. The main trouble, however, lies not with scenes being too long or too short, but with uneven pacing. Long scenes too often are followed by jet-speed, short ones. This uneven pace stems from approaching the commercial's sales points with words rather than pictures. You may find one point easy to express in a few words and then accord this point a correspondingly short visual. The more involved points get prolonged visuals. This is working the wrong way. The brief copy point should either not be visualized at all or its audio should be extended sufficiently to cover a visual of comfortable length.

It must be remembered that it is a mistake to pace your audio for television as fast as you would for the typical hard-sell radio commercial. Your audience in television has to follow video as well as audio, which makes it difficult to grasp a television sound track that is paced too fast. This pacing problem is particularly acute in film commercials where the announcer succeeds in getting in the full message only by racing through the script at breakneck speed.

HOW MANY? THE WORD COUNT

Most radio announcers read comfortably at 160 to 170 words a minute, and others considerably faster. A governor of Nebraska was once clocked at 487 words a minute in an election campaign speech. Obviously, such verbal fluidity is well beyond the speed of the television viewer's understanding. You will find that 135-140 words a minute will fit nicely into many live-action film commercials, although for the most part you will need fewer than that. Recommendations often range from 80 to more than 160 w.p.m., but experience has shown that a rule of thumb of two words per second usually works out consistently well.

Delivery rate is rather hard to define because of pauses and the fact that many commercials use more than one speaker. One study of 350 one-minute commercials by word-count analysis compared this data with effectiveness results for the same commercials. The most effective commercials ranged in word count from 101 to 150, demonstrating that a moderate speaking pace was desired over extremes of too many or too few words a minute.

Having a certain delivery rate, however, is no assurance of successful commercial writing. (The Texaco commercials without words, shown earlier in this chapter, are valid testimony to this fact.) A sensible speaking pace can be a contributing factor, of course, but the important thing is the quality of your words, not their quantity. Quantity, as it applies to the shorter commercials, would be: 20 words for the 10-second spot; 40 words for the 20-second spot. The one-minute commercial will usually take well with 120-135 words; but if the announcer is on camera give him less to say and, if he must demonstrate, still less than that. The ground rules say that a 20-second sound track cannot run over 18 seconds, nor a one-minute track over 58 seconds. You will be safer aiming for a shorter count, such as 16 or 17 seconds on the short spot, and 55 or 56 seconds in the one-minute version. This will permit an easier pace and more flexibility in your commercials. Remember, too, in production it's much simpler to stretch than to tighten.

AND NOT TOO MANY SCENES, EITHER!

What has been said here about pacing the audio holds true for the video portion of your television commercial. Don't confuse your viewers with too many scenes or those that are too busy and distract from your sales story. You can avoid cutting scenes too short by allowing a minimum of 3 seconds for viewers to orient themselves to any new scene. Scenes can also run too long, so keep in mind that after 6 seconds something had better move, or perhaps the viewer will. Either a different camera angle or some action within the scene can provide movement to prevent a scene from becoming static.

A single scene that is properly plotted out for action and camera angles can sustain interest for 20 or 30 seconds in a commercial (even for minutes in a movie). Ordinarily, however, you will want to think in terms of 5 or 6 seconds or more per scene. For more important visuals such as establishing a person, demonstrating, or major copy point, you will want to use 10 to 20 seconds or more.

One television researcher found that the average "poor" commercial had one scene per 7 seconds, while the average "good" commercial (one that increased brand preference) had one scene per 13 seconds. Also, too many voices, as well as too many scenes, cut down remembrance.

There is no firm rule about the number of scenes in a commercial, but here are a few general measures that will serve to guide you: No more than two scenes in a 10-second spot; four in a 20-second spot; and ten in a one minute spot. Keep in mind that to the viewer a closeup from a previous shot is not considered a new scene.

18

Writing For Sight, Sound and Movement: Television (Part 2)

TYPES OF COMMERCIALS

What, then, are the various *types* of commercials you may be required to write? Some are classified today as *soft* or *hard sell*—labels which refer more to the tone of copy rather than to the commercial's effectiveness. One might also set up classifications such as *reason why* and *emotional* commercials. In order to be more to the point in typing commercials, break them down according to their *source of authority:*

1. Straight sales pitch
2. Personality salesman
3. Dramatization
4. Demonstration
5. Testimonial
6. Production (song-and-dance)

The first of these basic, live-action types is the so-called "stand-up" commercial, in which the announcer, seated or standing, delivers a *straight sales pitch,* usually stressing price advantage or reason-why claims. The speaker is unknown to the majority of his audience and he uses no mood or other atmosphere setting to slide into his story. He needs a well-constructed story and probably some props, charts, graphs or other attention-getting visual devices to help put across the story effectively. The straight salesman will deliver the commercial in one of three ways: (1) Punchy, fast-paced and repetitive in the manner of the "pitchman" role. (2) Informally and conversationally, like a friendly sales clerk talking over the counter; (3) Casually, even ad-libbing, like a neighbor discussing the weather over the backyard fence. Which technique will work best? Very often this will be determined at rehearsals where you, the copywriter, must be ready to adapt and revise your script on the spot to whatever changes in copy or delivery seem called for at the time.

The *"personality" salesman* is quite another type, for here is a star with a certain name, fame and following, and it is expected that his audience will lend a very receptive ear to whatever he says or sells. These personalities seldom work directly from the commercial scripts provided by the sponsor's agency. Instead, the agency simply supplies a fact sheet about the product to be advertised, and the personality (or his staff) will expand on this material in his own style.

Arthur Godfrey, during some 35 years that saw him climb from a local radio wake-up man to the biggest billings attraction in the network business, sold practically every product category available to radio and television. He had this to say about commercials: "It takes me a half a minute to say hello, so rehearsed, well-written commercials are not for me. I believe in my product and I give my audience credit for having brains of their own. I imagine how I would feel in the listener's or viewer's place. I established part of my reputation by poking fun at the carefully prepared scripts of ad agencies and at some of the silly ideas used to trick people into trying the product. But I never razzed the product—it was the guy who wrote the commercial that I was after."

Also classified with this personality group are the *"star" salesmen* who, although not performers on the program, have built a name and following of their own, often in other entertainment fields.

It is the naturalness and believability of such sales personalities that make their commercial endorsements effective. They must have established themselves as known and likable characters, with appealing appearance, voice and mannerisms in order to build a loyal audience. In using such personalities in a television commercial, it is important to avoid being so glib, expert and perfect in presentation of the message that the individual sacrifices his qualities of warmth and naturalness.

Dramatizations are akin to "personality" commercials and are most often used on comedy, musical and dramatic programs. These commercials are usually done by lesser-known members of the show's cast and may be done straight or dramatized in the roles these people play on the program.

Demonstrations get to the very root of television's impact, and there are several kinds of demonstration that can be used as part or all of a given commercial:

Product versatility—to acquaint viewers with new and interesting uses

Product in use—to show its works, what it does

Before-and-after—to prove results in use

Extreme example—dramatic proof of margin of quality, as in Timex watch commercials that subjected a watch to rugged treatment to prove it "takes a licking and keeps on ticking." Torture tests on proving grounds likewise aim to prove superiority of one make of automobile over another.

Wells, Rich, Greene, Inc./767 Fifth Avenue/New York, N.Y. 10022/Plaza 8-4300

RADIO • TELEVISION

client Bic	code no. WBBM 2302 rev. no.
product Bic Banana	length :30
title "Blueberry"	job no. 3301-001TV

VIDEO:	AUDIO:
WE OPEN ON CLOSE UP OVER THE SHOULDER OF YOUMAN MAN WRITING WITH A BLUEBERRY.	MEL BROOKS VOICE OVER: Don't write with a blueberry.
CUT TO ZOOM IN ON YOUNG MAN IN DEN WITH A BASKET OF BLUEBERRIES AND PAPER IN FRONT OF HIM ON DESK.	With your blueberry you're gonna get a half a T, a piece of Y.
CUT BACK TO OVER THE SHOULDER.	Besides, it would take you two boxes of blueberries to write one postcard.
CUT TO MEDIUM SHOT OF YOUNG MAN AT DESK. HE PICKS UP BIC BANANA AND STARTS TO WRITE.	That's how small they are. If you must write with a fruit,
CUT TO OVER THE SHOULDER CU OF HIM WRITING WITH BIC BANANA.	write with a BIC BANANA. A smooth-writing, fine line marker beauty. It comes in a lot more colors than a blueberry.
CUT BACK TO MEDIUM SHOT AS HE REACTS.	And it costs a lot less money than a car: 29¢.
CUT TO PRODUCT SHOT WITH HAND WRITING NEXT TO PRODUCT "THE BIC BANANA. A DIFFERENT WAY TO TO WRITE."	The BIC BANANA.

Fig. 18-1

Script for dramatized commercial.

Fig. 18-2

Use of puppet.

Cleverly constructed puppet makes a good presenter of the virtues of the product.

Campbell SOUP Company

"VEGETABLE MAN NO. 1"

(MUSIC UNDER)

VEGETABLE MAN: You know, there are two things I know of with 16 vegetables:

I'm one; Can you guess the other?

Give up?

Vegetable
SOUP
It's Campbell's Vegetable Soup.

CONDENSED
THE ALPHABET SOUP
Vegetable
MADE WITH BEEF STOCK
SOUP
The alphabet soup.

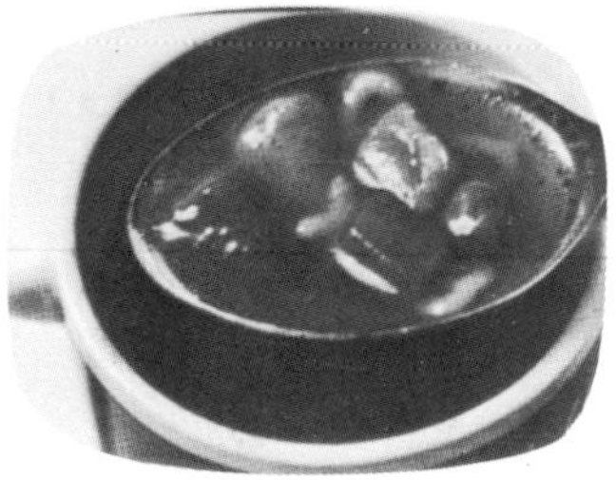
The only thing I know with 16 vegetables, . . .

Campbell's
Vegetable
SOUP
not counting me.

Campbell's
(SINGING) M'm! M'm! Good!

M'm! M'm! Good!

Campbell's
CONDENSED
Vegetable
That's what Campbell's Soups are, . . .

M'm! M'm!
Good!
M'm! M'm! Good!

Competitive tests—to show superiority over competitor, as in various washing or sudsing tests that seek to show that one brand of soap or detergent produces whiter washes

Demonstration commercials rely heavily on film tape production in order to cover periods of time necessary to illustrate points of superiority in use. The full application of a home permanent can be filmed or taped and then simply edited to required length, showing key sales points. Film and tape also permit use of split screens and other optical devices to lend additional impact and drama to before-and-after and competitive-test commercials of the demonstration type.

In recent years, the Federal Trade Commission has insisted that product demonstrations be literally true. In the past, in contrast, glycerine was substituted for ice cream because the latter melted before scenes could be shot.

Under the new rules, if the product being advertised is ice cream, then ice cream must be used in the scene, not a non-melting substitute. This means that the ice cream must be kept cold until the last seconds before shooting, and then rushed on to the set for a quick shot.

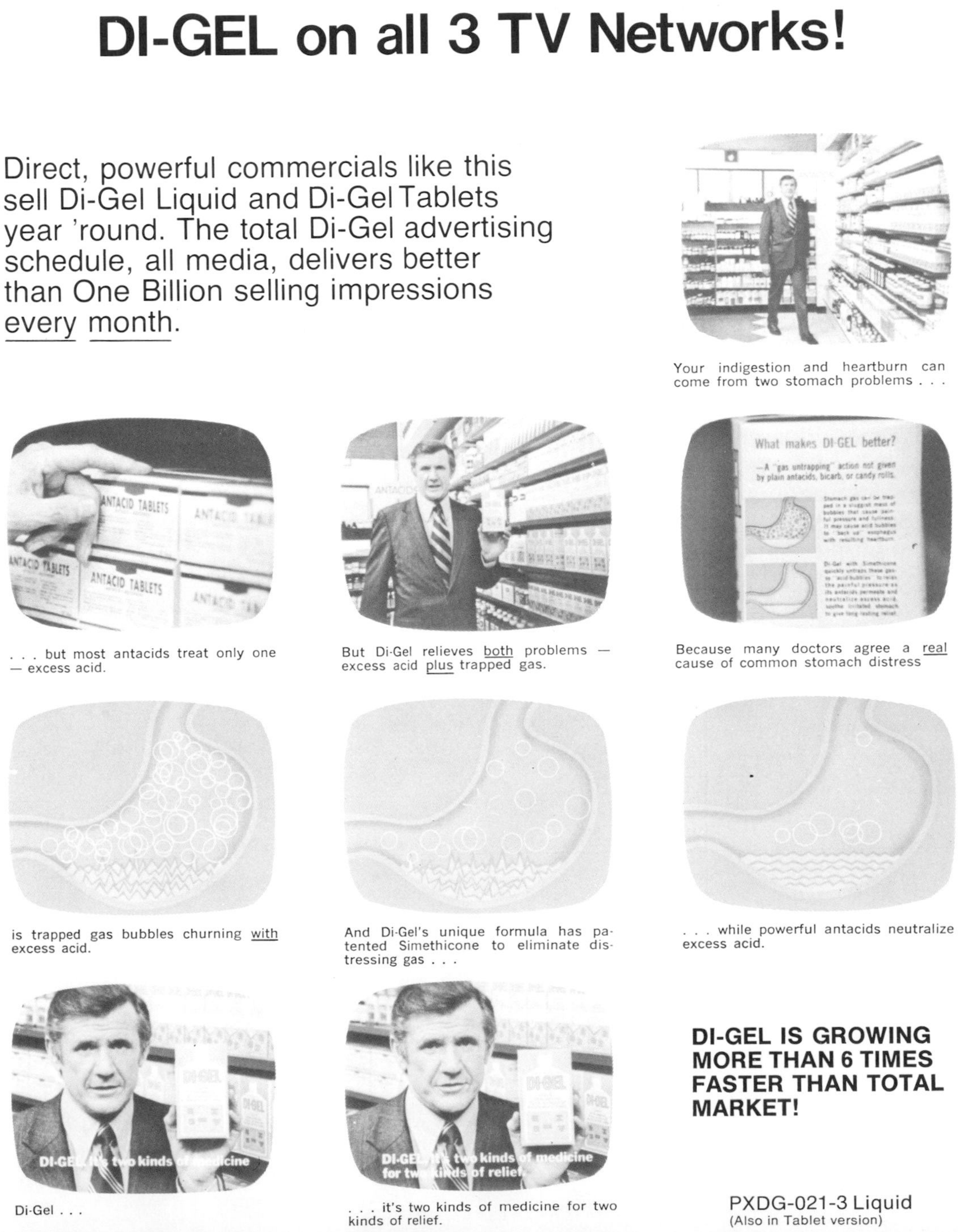
DI-GEL on all 3 TV Networks!
Direct, powerful commercials like this sell Di-Gel Liquid and Di-Gel Tablets year 'round. The total Di-Gel advertising schedule, all media, delivers better than One Billion selling impressions every month.
Your indigestion and heartburn can come from two stomach problems . . .
. . . but most antacids treat only one — excess acid.
But Di-Gel relieves both problems — excess acid plus trapped gas.
Because many doctors agree a real cause of common stomach distress
What makes DI-GEL better?
is trapped gas bubbles churning with excess acid.
And Di-Gel's unique formula has patented Simethicone to eliminate distressing gas . . .
. . . while powerful antacids neutralize excess acid.
Di-Gel . . .
. . . it's two kinds of medicine for two kinds of relief.
DI-GEL IS GROWING MORE THAN 6 TIMES FASTER THAN TOTAL MARKET!
PXDG-021-3 Liquid
(Also in Tablet version)

Fig. 18-3

Straight selling commercial.

This photoboard is used as a promotional piece by the sales department.

Such literalness has greatly increased the cost of shooting many commercials. Every copywriter writing for television must keep in mind this requirement of literal honesty in every product demonstration he calls for. This is in contrast to television's earlier days when a maker of glass for auto windows demonstrated the clarity of the product by removing the windows. This supposedly gave the viewer a true idea of just what it was like to be looking through an auto window using the advertiser's glass. The courts ruled against the advertiser in a court case and said that future commercials must use the window glass.

At one time, because of the difficulty of showing many products on television, production short-cuts were taken and given legal approval. Those days are gone. Write accordingly.

Testimonial commercials are a proved type of television selling in which screen stars, sports heroes and prominent figures from all walks of life are used. The main problem in this type of commercial is to avoid staginess and artificiality. The viewer is all too ready to disbelieve the words of your prominent personality unless you phrase the message in comfortable, conversational language that fits your star salesman. Keep the testimonial brief, natural and believable, for even professional actors are not always capable of adjusting to selling roles. The same precautions must be observed in testimonials featuring satisfied users or so-called passers-by in the interview type of testimonial commercial. Don't ask these obviously ordinary people to speak, complicated and unreal sounding "advertising" phrases in praise of your product. It simply will not be swallowed by your viewers.

Exercise care in the casting of these commercials, too, of you have a voice in the matter. Try to use people who are not too beautiful or handsome, but who have faces with character that can quickly win over viewers. In television, there is not always time for the viewer to take his eyes off the attractive girl and to get in step with your message. Use familiar, comfortable settings well within the experience of the viewer so he does not have to reorient his mind to an unsual setting before grasping your message. If your commercial is filmed or taped, get enough footage of a particular interview to catch facets of personality and unexpected conversational phrases that no prepared script could ever conjure up for the non-professional performer. Subsequent editing can then cull the highlights of the interview for commercial use.

Song-and-dance productions, often with extensive choreography and original music, are a type of commercial that only the large, blue-chip advertisers can afford. Most often they are used by advertisers of soft drinks, beauty preparations and automobiles, and they are definitely an art form that skilfully combines entertainment values with emotional selling. With its sweeping movement, intricate dance routines and the need for synchronization with lip movements, this type of commercial is usually produced on film or tape, preferably the latter, in order to insure a professional job.

LIVE, FILM OR VIDEOTAPE?

Throughout this chapter we have been using the terms "live" and "film" and "tape" as methods of telecasting commercials. Let us look now at the advantages and disadvantages of each as they relate to your job: *creating a commercial.* "Live" deals with action seen on the television screen as it takes place right in the studio before the television camera. "Film" commercials are those shot in a studio, on location outdoors, or wherever there is a suitable site for the desired action. The action is recorded by a sound motion picture film camera; the film, after any necessary editing, is then transmitted over the air via the television camera. Film commercials can be either live-action or animation. "Tape" or videotape is a system that records both sound and pictures simultaneously on magnetic tape. Because it offers such amazing fidelity and can be played back immediately, it has been called "instant film," blending the best of live and film techniques.

"Live" television production offers, first of all, the advantage of generally lower cost for the one-time commercial. It can also be produced in less time than film, from the written script to the actual production on camera. Live commercials can, of course, be changed in wording or action at the very last minute, a not insignificant advantage to many an advertiser, particularly in a keenly competitive situation. It is also said that the talent and production personnel involved in creating the live commercial find the excitement and unpredictability of "doing it live" a stimulant to superior effort. There is also the claim that live commercials are more acceptable or preferred by the viewer than those on film, al-

Fig. 18-4 (A and B)

Dramatized commercial in 30-second and 60-second versions.

The drama is achieved without the use of people. This was an award-winning commercial.

OGILVY & MATHER INC.

2 EAST 48 STREET, NEW YORK 10017

MURRAY HILL 8-8100

Client: MERRILL-LYNCH

Title: "BULLS"
Commercial No.: XMUM1033 (:30C)
Date Approved:

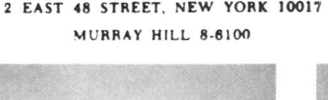

1. (SFX)

2. ANNCR: (VO) America... Merrill-Lynch is bullish on America.

3. In the years ahead, we see America growing in many different ways.

4. That's why we've moved into different kinds of investments.

5. Not just stocks but bonds, mutual funds, real estate,

6. a lot of ways

7. to put your money to work.

8. (SFX)

9. (SFX)

Merrill Lynch
is bullish on America.

10. America...Merrill-Lynch is bullish on America.

though this is subject to serious question in view of the high quality of film commercials presented these days.

Film television production is the logical choice when plans call for repeated telecasting of the commercial. The filmed commercial can also be reviewed before broadcast to eliminate fluffs and to insure a smooth-flowing production. It is easier to arrange shooting dates with film so as to take advantage of the availability of talent and production people. An important consideration here is that talent favors doing commercials on film because of residual payments due them when film are used again on networks or local stations. Film, of course, presents the opportunity to achieve greater realism through "on location" shooting, especially with outdoor scenes. Film also simplifies programming of commercials on stations in different time zones. Wider latitude in production values, with a variety of sets, optical tricks and careful editing, is another considerable advantage of the film commercial.

To the viewer, it probably matters not whether a commercial is live, film or tape. At their best, the various methods of producing commercials are virtually indistinguishable.

1. (SFX)

2. (SFX)

3. ANNCR: (VO) America...

4. Merrill Lynch is bullish on America.

5. In the years ahead,

6. we see America growing in many different ways.

7. And we want you to share

8. in America's growth.

9. That's why we've moved

10. into different kinds of investments.

11. Not just stocks but bonds, real estate, financing and more.

12. Merrill Lynch has a lot of different ways

13. to put your money to work.

14. (SFX)

15. (SFX)

16. (SFX)

17. (SFX)

18. America...

Merrill Lynch
is bullish on America.

19. Merrill Lynch is bullish on America.

Merrill Lynch
is bullish on America.

20. (SFX)

Fig. 18-5

Musical television commercial.

CANOE
SBPN 2133
STANDARD BRANDS
PLANTERS NUTS
AS PRODUCED

VIDEO

1. BOY AND GIRL IN CANOE EATING PEANUTS.

2. SEVERAL QUICK CLOSEUPS OF PEOPLE IN SPOT

3. COP DIRECTING TRAFFIC HOLDS OUT HAND. PASSING GIRL PUTS PEANUTS INTO IT

4. FATHER WATCHING TV WITH KIDS LOOKING OVER SHOULDER. FATHER STRETCHES, KIDS PUT NUTS IN HIS HAND.

5. BOY AND GIRL EATING NUTS AT ZOO. ELEPHANT TRUNK REACHES OVER AND STEAL SOME

6. THE SCENE SHRINKS TO ½ SIDE PRODUCT APPEARS ON BLACK WITH MR. PEANUT

AUDIO

Music and Singers

There's a good feeling in the air.

Touching everyone, everywhere

Today's as happy as a handful of

Planter's Peanuts.

And that's as happy as anyone

could ever be.

Today's as happy as a handful of

Planter's Peanuts.

V.O. Nutritious Planters.

Dry roasted using absolutely no

fats or oils.

The viewer wants simply to see a commercial that holds his interest and will reward him for the time invested in watching it. What is closer to the core of the *live* vs. *film* question is the fact that too many writers of commercials have tended to specialize in either one area or the other, often being departmentalized into rival camps within a given agency. With the advent of videotape and its many production advantages, a new breed of writer must evolve who knows well the potentials of both live and film techniques.

VIDEOTAPE: THE MAGNETIC MARVEL

What are the magical qualities of this continuous, 2-inch wide, plastic ribbon with its coating of magnetic iron particles? Someone once enumerated 84 advantages of tape recording, but, confining them to the field of the television commercial, we find an even dozen creative advantages:

1. *Mistakes eliminated.* The foolproof commercial will, of course, result in more efficiency down the line, but caution must be exercised not to seek perfection too earnestly. "Nit picking" at minor flaws can destroy warmth, personality and spontaneity. Try to make a good commercial within the first three takes.

2. *Immediate playback.* Tape enables you to see it *now,* to adjust lighting and camera angles, and to work on changes in dialogue. Time is money and an aid to creativity, all of which tape affords.

3. *Picture-and-sound quality.* The potential for higher quality in both sound and picture lies with tape. Tape is easier to work with because it is made *for* television and is electronically linked throughout, in frames-per-second speed and in its high-fidelity magnetic recording track. Tape can be duplicated many times over unlike film which loses quality with each optical step.

4. *Production values.* Tape can provide special effects, optical tricks and big production values at low cost, quickly. This includes such tricks as using a simple postcard as a background for an announcer, or combining cartoons and live action, or superimposing titles and other special effects.

5. *Lower costs.* An hour's tape may cost about $250; an hour's film may be about $435, with processing adding another $600. An even bigger saving is in time and in cutting costs in terms of creative man-hours and agency supervisory time. Tape can record and store a month's worth of commercials in one day. Sets can be struck as soon as the playback shows a good take. Talent can be called only for the day needed. Savings in rental items—props, equipment, etc.—are possible as a result of tape's shorter production time.

6. *Rehearsal and correction.* Tape provides a mirror in which talent can check performance for minor faults that might be tolerated in a regular film commercial rather than set up for another shooting session. This advantage of immediate playback check has made it possible to attract many big-name stars to the television commercial who previously were reluctant to expose themselves to this new field without some form of "performance insurance."

7. *Approval by client.* Before a commercial is finally approved by a major advertiser, it usually goes through numerous hands, all of which consumes valuable time. Tape makes it possible for many, if not all, of those concerned with passing upon a commercial to be present and to make necessary revisions immediately, thanks to quick playback.

8. *Alternate versions.* Two or more versions of a given commercial are easily permitted with tape. Changes in settings or new approaches suggested on the spot are less costly.

9. *Testing.* With alternate versions, a commercial can be quickly pretested via research before actual telecast to determine the most effective approach. Some of the larger videotape production houses now employ "closed circuit" testing facilities for just such purposes.

10. *Man-hour savings.* Tape affords efficiency and convenience in achieving maximum utility of personnel. Time schedules in the pre-tape days of live and film television commercial production limited the capacities of both creative and technical people. Now this talent can be utilized more efficiently within the compact time schedules of tape and can then move on to the next assignment without any old problems outstanding.

11. *Last-minute changes.* Modern, fast-paced selling and marketing demand the flexibility which tape gives to an advertiser's commercials. New scenes can be inserted in existing spots in an hour, and sound tracks can be erased and recorded anew in less time than that. Tape thus puts television ahead of newspapers in the all-important factor of advertising flexibility.

12. *"Tranquilizer."* Tape takes the "heat" off production schedules and dispels the gen-

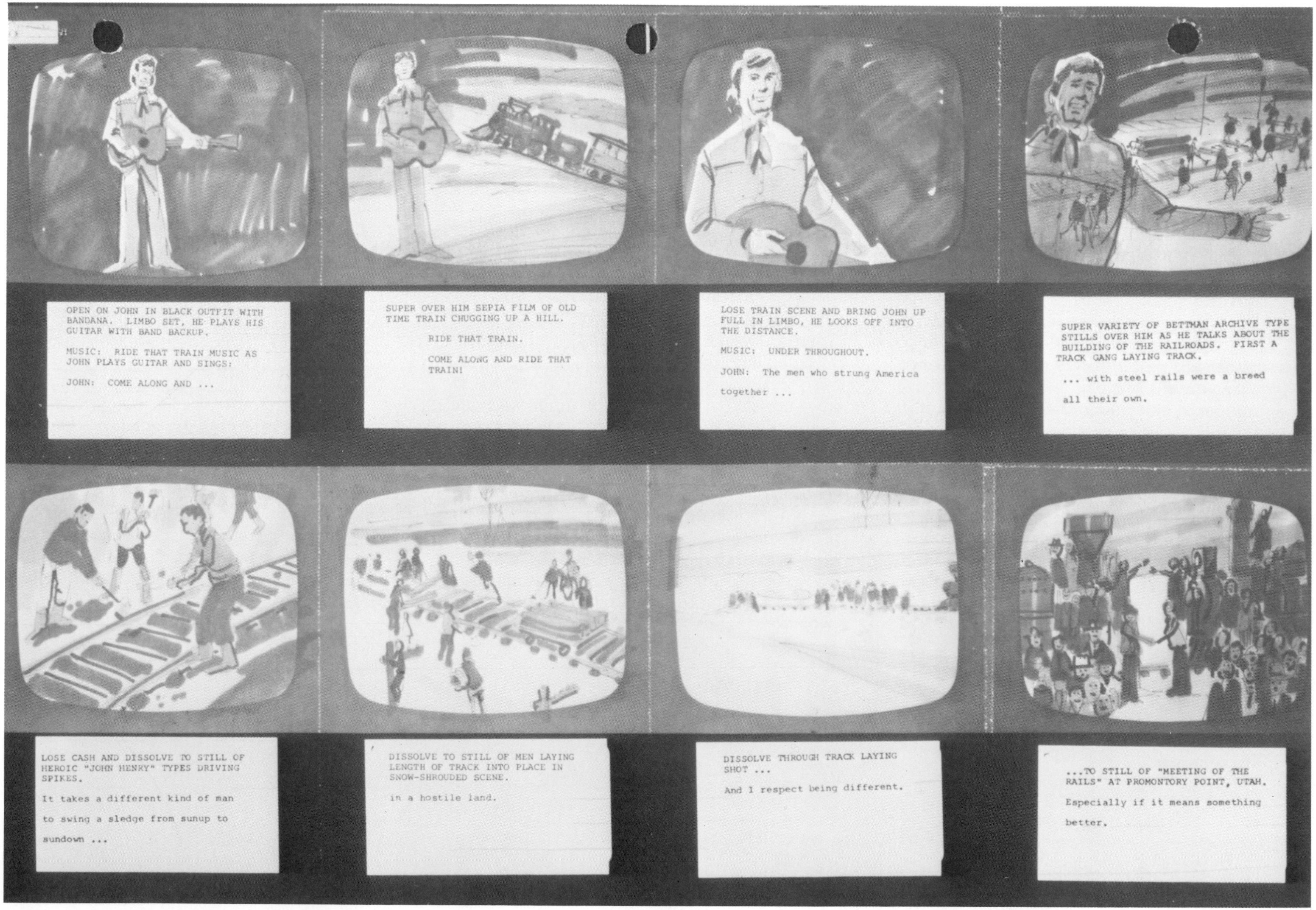
OPEN ON JOHN IN BLACK OUTFIT WITH BANDANA. LIMBO SET, HE PLAYS HIS GUITAR WITH BAND BACKUP.
MUSIC: RIDE THAT TRAIN MUSIC AS JOHN PLAYS GUITAR AND SINGS:
JOHN: COME ALONG AND ...
SUPER OVER HIM SEPIA FILM OF OLD TIME TRAIN CHUGGING UP A HILL.
RIDE THAT TRAIN.
COME ALONG AND RIDE THAT TRAIN!
LOSE TRAIN SCENE AND BRING JOHN UP FULL IN LIMBO, HE LOOKS OFF INTO THE DISTANCE.
MUSIC: UNDER THROUGHOUT.
JOHN: The men who strung America together ...
SUPER VARIETY OF BETTMAN ARCHIVE TYPE STILLS OVER HIM AS HE TALKS ABOUT THE BUILDING OF THE RAILROADS. FIRST A TRACK GANG LAYING TRACK.
... with steel rails were a breed all their own.
LOSE CASH AND DISSOLVE TO STILL OF HEROIC "JOHN HENRY" TYPES DRIVING SPIKES.
It takes a different kind of man to swing a sledge from sunup to sundown ...
DISSOLVE TO STILL OF MEN LAYING LENGTH OF TRACK INTO PLACE IN SNOW-SHROUDED SCENE.
in a hostile land.
DISSOLVE THROUGH TRACK LAYING SHOT ...
And I respect being different.
...TO STILL OF "MEETING OF THE RAILS" AT PROMONTORY POINT, UTAH.
Especially if it means something better.

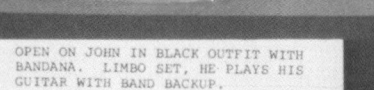

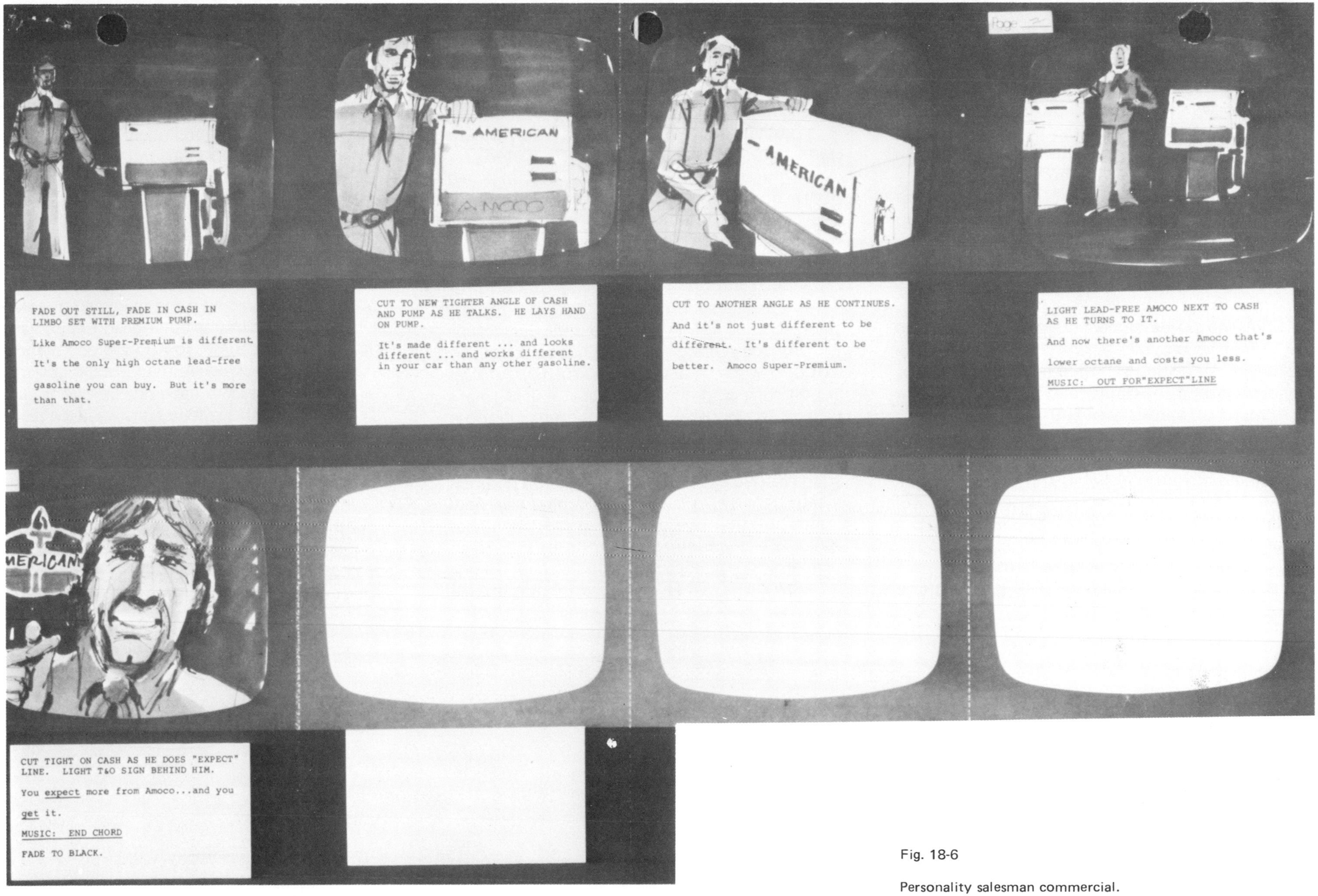
AMERICAN
AMOCO
AMERICAN
FADE OUT STILL, FADE IN CASH IN LIMBO SET WITH PREMIUM PUMP.
Like Amoco Super-Premium is different. It's the only high octane lead-free gasoline you can buy. But it's more than that.
CUT TO NEW TIGHTER ANGLE OF CASH AND PUMP AS HE TALKS. HE LAYS HAND ON PUMP.
It's made different ... and looks different ... and works different in your car than any other gasoline.
CUT TO ANOTHER ANGLE AS HE CONTINUES.
And it's not just different to be different. It's different to be better. Amoco Super-Premium.
LIGHT LEAD-FREE AMOCO NEXT TO CASH AS HE TURNS TO IT.
And now there's another Amoco that's lower octane and costs you less.
MUSIC: OUT FOR"EXPECT"LINE
AMERICAN
CUT TIGHT ON CASH AS HE DOES "EXPECT" LINE. LIGHT T&O SIGN BEHIND HIM.
You expect more from Amoco...and you get it.
MUSIC: END CHORD
FADE TO BLACK.

Fig. 18-6

Personality salesman commercial.

A popular personality can be very effective in putting across a commercial message.

erally frenetic atmosphere and tension that builds up in shooting a film commercial. Tape provides that second chance that relaxes everyone, safe in the knowledge that fluffs can be erased on the magnetic tape.

To make a baker's dozen of this list of advantages, there is also tape's role in making practical the re-entry into television of the local advertiser. In smaller cities and towns, this advertiser has been severely restricted in obtaining good commercials for reasons of budget and scarcity of talent. Now, with tape, his costs of producing commercials are much less and he can apply tape's immediate playback advantage to the task of getting the best possible performance out of local talent employed in making his commercial.

TO ANIMATE OR NOT TO ANIMATE

You, the writer, in originating the story idea for a television commercial, must decide which approach is best suited to the product or service being advertised. Your job, of course, is to choose the approach that will initiate the greatest number of sales and develop good will for the sponsor-client. You must also decide, probably with the help of others, what production technique will show your chosen idea to best advantage. Each assignment calls for individual treatment; a story or technique that proves successful in one case may be a failure in another. It is hoped that you and your producer will have had enough experience in the field to know what can or cannot be animated, and whether the idea or product can be shown to advantage by the use of such a technique. You'd be surprised how many times you'll have to answer *no* to animation as the best possible method for advertising your product. If you're undecided about using animation as opposed to demonstration, use demonstration if your product *has* to be demonstrated for full sales effectiveness. Don't substitute cuteness for sales impact. If you decide that animation is the right method for the job, keep the following creative elements of that technique in mind:

Product character of trademark. Animation should fit the trademark or trade character naturally, without being forced. If your character is a Disney-type cartoon—full-animation drawing with rounded lines, full shading and natural features—it won't fit well with a highly stylized, modern art treatment. Work with your producer to develop animation characters that will save you time, money and are well suited to the story you want to tell.

Setting and staging. Keep it simple and inexpensive, yet effective, for setting and staging for animation are as important as for live-action films. Your message is on the screen only briefly, so give your cartoon characters and product full attention by eliminating distracting backgrounds. Use simple lines, for instance, to denote cabinets for a kitchen scene. Staging is equally as important as background so, if your action can take place in one location, don't have characters chasing through many different scenes. If you want special effects, such as opticals that make products glow, sparkle or change, write them into your original storyboards. Extra production charges are made if you want to work them in later.

Movement of characters. Try to keep the movements of animated characters similar to those of a human being in the same situation. Remember that movement in animation *should* be exaggerated to be appreciated by viewers. Be sure they see that your character's wink is a wink, that his look of surprise is *very* surprised, lest these pieces of action be missed. Allow sufficient time for the move-

1. (Voice effect of words in balloon: gibberish. Speeded-up, high, mechanistic effect. Up, then under)

2. (Anncr VO--hold gibberish under) If you need more than words, (Fade gibberish out, slowly)...you need more than a pen.

FLAIR!

3. You need Flair.

4. (Music punctuates, narrates from here on)

5. Flair writes feelings.

light bulb

6. Flair writes ideas.

7. Flair writes colors.

8. Flair writes music.

9. (Music up)

10. Flair writes...

11. ...emotions.

Pictures

12. Flair even writes pictures!

13. Man does not live by words alone.

14. Man needs Flair...

FLAIR
12 SUPER HUMAN COLORS

15. ...in 12 very human colors.

Fig. 18-7

Imaginative 30-second animated commercial.

ment to be grasped by viewers. Try to plan your animated spots rather loosely so that there is time for little bits of side action that can give your commercial added interest and longer life.

Copy and narration. Consider the soundtrack of your commercial as consisting of two parts: the voice or narrative, and the music and sound effects. The best animated spots are written with a maximum of 85 to 100 words, rather than the 135 to 150 live-action count. This leaves room for the previously-mentioned bits of action that can enhance your effort. Give your character time to speak effectively, and write copy to fit the character's intended voice, rather than try to bend a character to fit copy.

Music and sound effects. These lend mood, action, tone and emphasis that can "make" your animated commercial. If you are using offbeat or stylized art treatment, make the music suitable. Be sure the tempo of the music blends with your type of animation. Sound effects give impact and originality to your spot. If you want them, be sure to leave enough time for them in your script. They seldom fit when you try to squeeze them in later.

Fig. 18-8

Fast-paced, dramatization commercial.

This one gets attention with its lively action and the strong visual attraction of the exaggerated package of gum. This was an award-winning campaign.

1. VOCAL: Wrigley's Spearmint Gum-Gum-Gum.

2. Wrigley's Spearmint Gum-Gum-Gum.

3. Wrigley's Spearmint Gum-Gum-Gum...

4. Carry the big fresh flavor--...

5. ...wherever you go...whatever you do.

6. It's the finest pack of flavor--...

7. ...wherever you go...

8. ...whatever you do.

9. Wrigley's Spearmint Gum-Gum-Gum. Carry it with you.

10. Wrigley's Spearmint Gum-Gum-Gum.

11. The big fresh flavor.

12. Wrigley's Spearmint Gum-Gum-Gum.

13. Carry it with you.

14. Wrigley's Spearmint Gum-Gum-Gum. The big fresh flavor.

WRIGLEY'S
SPEARMINT
CHEWING GUM

15. (Music under, Anncr VO) Flavor this big...

(CONTINUED)

Timing the entire spot. Don't drag or zoom through your commercial. Good timing usually means writing a minute spot for 55 seconds, leaving some precious seconds available for consumption along the way. It is difficult to time an animated commercial because of the need to consider copy, music and action. There's no surefire solution, but one of the safest approaches is to act out the commercial in its entirety.

Product package and logotype. With *simple* handling, animation (and stop-action photography) can do great things for your package or product. If your package has illustrations that are not in character with your style of animation, use artwork representation rather than the real package. You can use a matching dissolve from the artwork to the real package or logotype at the end of the spot. Emphasize important features of your package by bringing the elements off the box to full screen, as with a logotype that bounces off the package and then back on.

RECOMMENDED: ANIMATION PLUS LIVE ACTION

It is the consensus of almost all those who have worked with animation over a long per-

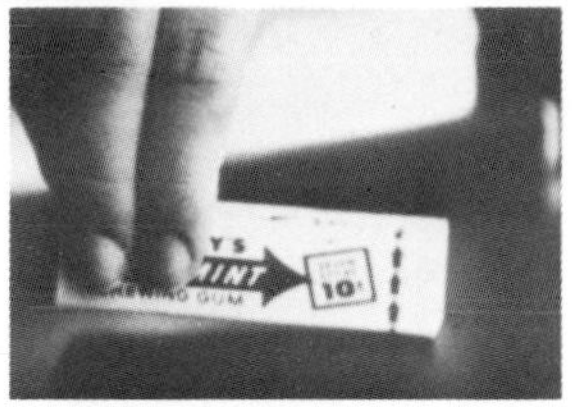

16. ...shouldn't be left behind.

17. So wherever you go...

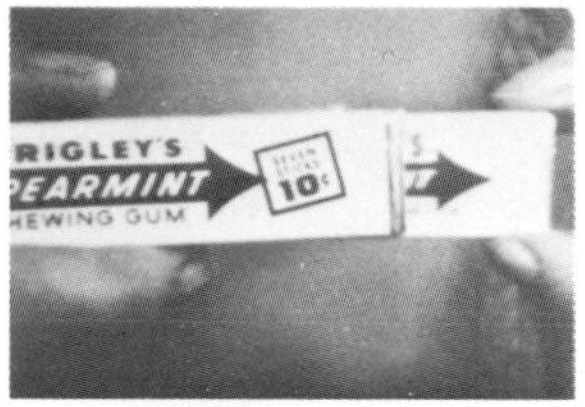

18. ...carry a pack...

19. ...of Wrigley's Spearmint Gum.

20. That way you'll never be without its big,...

21. ...fresh clean flavor.

22. Wrigley's Spearmint Gum.

23. VOCAL: Carry the big fresh flavor--...

24. ...wherever you go... whatever you do.

SEVEN STICKS 10¢

25. It's the finest...

26. ...Spearmint flavor--...

27. ...the great Wrigley taste...

28. ...delicious to chew.

29. Wrigley's Spearmint Gum.

Carry the big fresh flavor

30. Carry it with you. Wrigley's Spearmint Gum. The big fresh flavor. Wrigley's Spearmint Gum... (Fade)

iod that the all cartoon commercial should be approached with caution, for its promise generally outruns its performance. The main danger of pure animation is its over-commitment to entertainment at the cost of sacrificing copy ideas. The viewer is beguiled into enjoyment without being sold. The judicious use, however, of animation *in conjunction with live action* has much to recommend it. There are two basic types of this "hybrid" commercial: (1) an opening animated segment (often comic or clever but containing the germ of the product story) is followed with a live straight sell; and (2) a straightforward sales presentation that moves into animation after a live opening, usually to illustrate a product's "reason-why" story. The first type is best exemplified by commercials that often use an animated character with a catchy jingle, as an opening and then move into live-action scenes of the product in use. The second hybrid type is most often seen in commercials for patent remedies, which often employ diagrammatic views of visceral plumbing to illustrate the nature of their internal action. In either case, the flexibility of the live-plus-animated commercial allows the advertiser to blend exaggerated hyperbole or humor with naturalistic

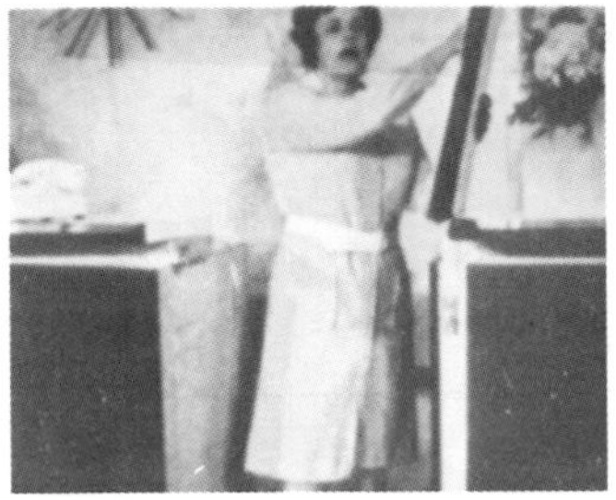

1. HELEN KUTCHER: I'm Helen Kutcher

2. and I have a large family.

Kutsher's Country Club
Monticello, New York

3. I'm owner of Kutcher's Country Club in Monticello, New York.

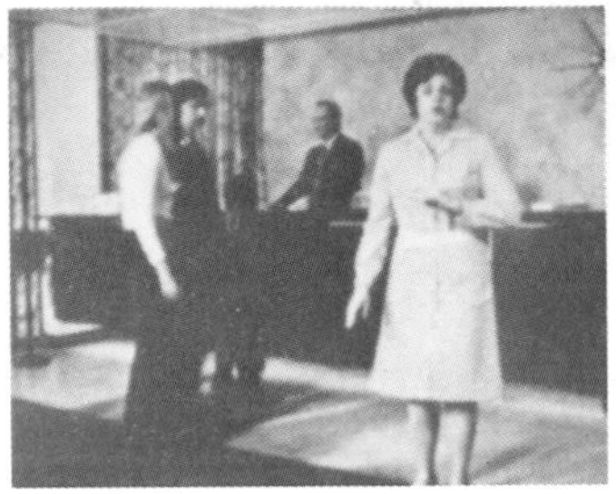

4. And our hotel is a busy place with people coming and going all the time.

5. That's why I'm conscience of keeping everything thoroughly clean

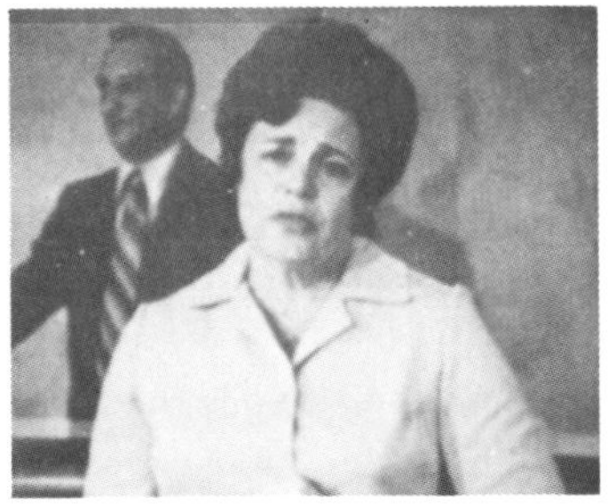

6. and as germ free as possible.

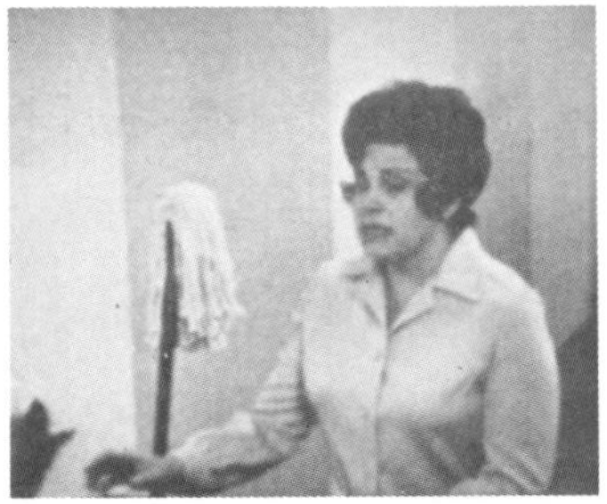

7. And that's why I agreed to try new Listerol's Spray Disinfectant.

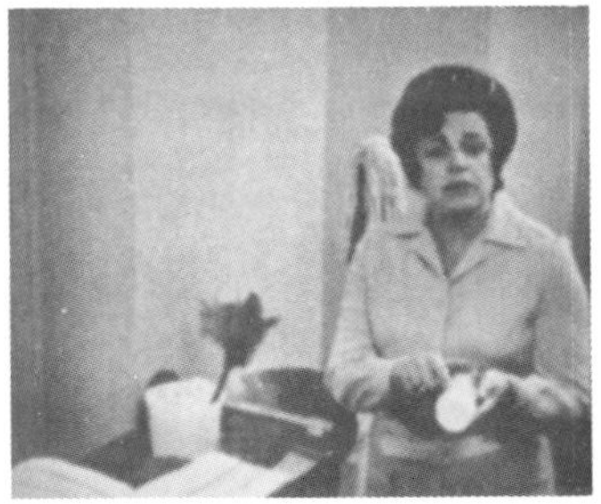

8. It says here, that Listerol kills odor causing germs,

9. so I tried it in all kinds of places.

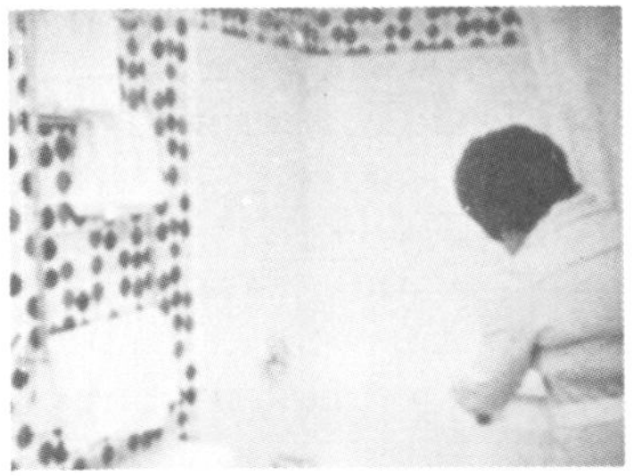

10. I used it in the bathrooms

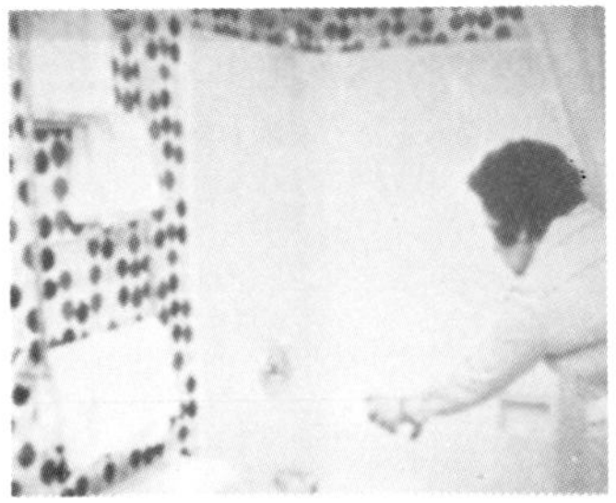

11. to prevent mold and mildew

12. and I sprayed all over to eliminate odors,

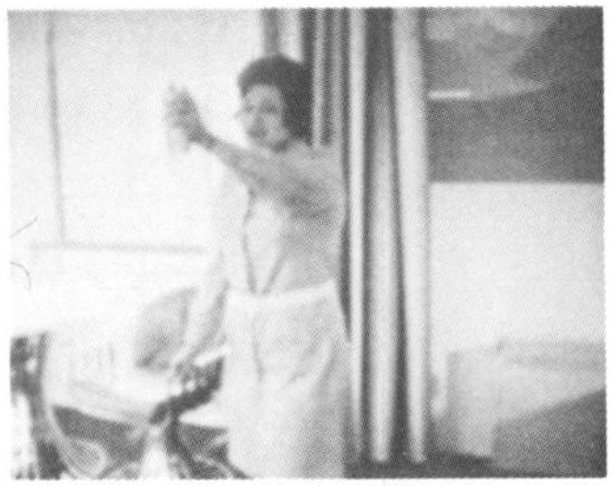

13. to freshen the air.

14. I like Listerol better than the product we've been using.

Listerol
LISTERINE

15. And knowing that it's put out by the makers of Listerine Antiseptic gives me confidence.

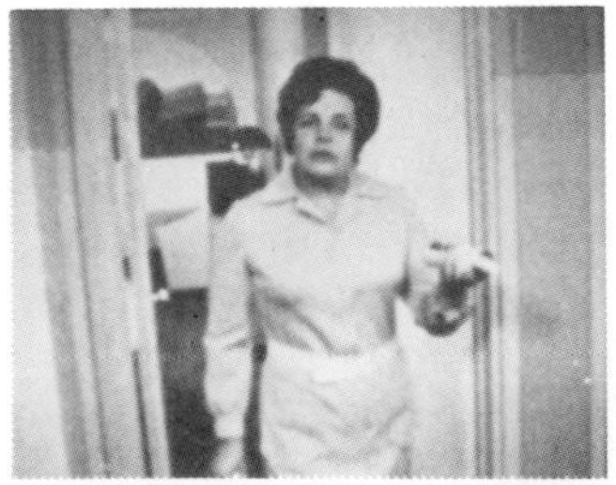

16. I'm making it standard equipment around here.

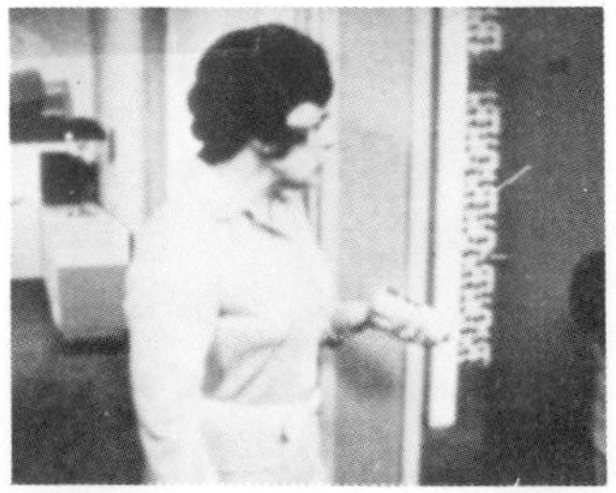

17. After all,

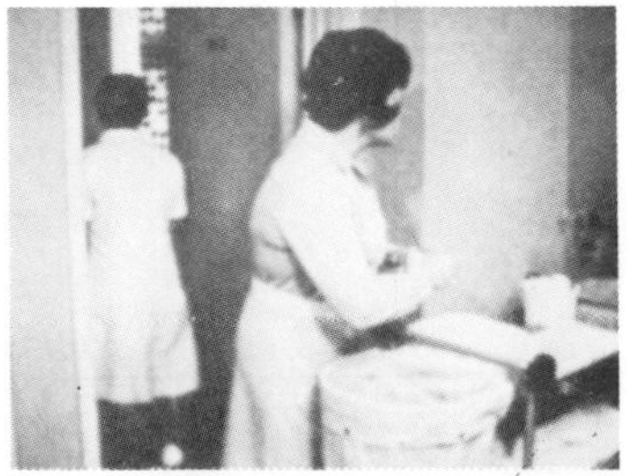

18. I have some pretty important people to take care of.

19. ANNCR: (VO) Listerol Spray Disinfectant.

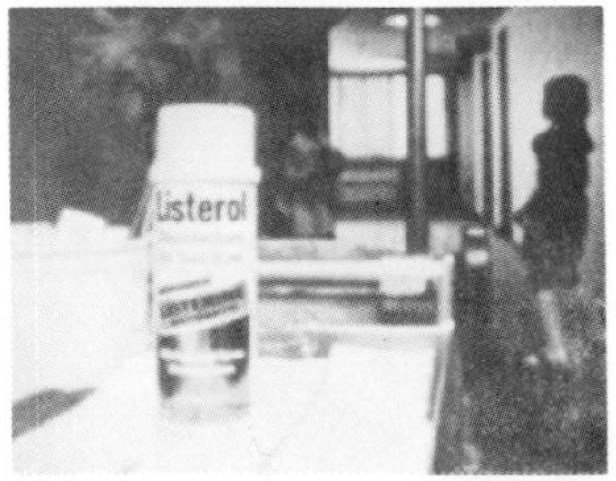
Listerol

20. It took the Listerine people to introduce a spray disinfectant this

Fig. 18-9

Dramatized problem-solving commercial.

This can also be classified as a product-testimonial.

demonstration, to charm the viewer while selling him.

Combining live action and animation is definitely effective, but can be expensive. An economical method is to use animated characters over still-photo shots of your product, giving you the depth of live action with the adaptability of animation. Another way of reducing expense is to use the same segment of animation to open or close an entire series of film spots. This lets you use your budget for animation of better quality or for more spots.

In trying to determine whether to use "live on film" or animated commercials for your particular product, there are some general considerations you'll recognize as helpful. Food products normally lend themselves better to television presentation with live action. The realism which can be gained by showing real people preparing and enjoying meals will almost always sell better than the cartoon characters with whom the housewife cannot identify herself. The sales points of a new car, likewise, can best be demonstrated by actually showing a real person driving it, rather than showing drawings of the car.

Cosmetic selling usually needs the realism of beautiful girls whose hair, lips, complexion and over-all charm cannot possibly be captured in animation. On the other hand, many times you will be selling a service instead of a branded product. Sometimes when doing so you can expect more memorability and attention if you invent an animated character to tell your story. Insurance selling, gasoline advertising, and bank and loan association commercials all lend themselves to the use of animation.

PRODUCTION TECHNIQUES

Assuming you are committed to the use of film (or tape) television commercials, there are five basic production techniques available to you:

1. Live action
2. Cartoon
3. Stop motion
4. Photo animation
5. Puppets

Live action is similar to human, personal experience and is the most believable technique in television commercials. The viewer can identify himself with the action on the screen and relate your commercial message to his own experience. While cartoons and puppets are figments of a fantasy world, and stop motion and photo animation are products of camera trickery, live action has the quality of genuine reality. There are two main types of live-action commercials: (1) narrative style, with the voices off-screen; and (2) dialogue style, with one or more persons speaking on screen, to each other or the audience.

The narrative style is less expensive, yet it has longer life expectancy because the speaker or speakers are not seen repeating the same story over and over, and thereby suffering loss of credulity. Narrative live action lends itself best to: *demonstration*, where the product is shown in use, with a voice presenting the sales story from off-screen; *exposition*, to set a scene quickly; *human interest*, to show family or other emotional settings; and *appetite appeal*, to show tempting dishes, as in the well done Kraft commercials with the announcer's voice off-screen.

Dialogue has particular advantages for: *personality commercials* in which a name star or well-known announcer does the selling, job; *testimonials* by actual users; *key copy lines* spoken by an actor as one part of a longer commercial.

Fig. 18-10

Demonstration commercial.

This dramatic demonstration insures good memorability for the commercial and the point being made.

Video	Audio
Ms of side of fire truck and fireman (wide enough to recognize fire truck)	SFX: on camera EFX (rasping sound of ax being removed from steel clamp)
Ms axes being driven deep into plank	SFX: Anncr. (v.o.): Sharp cutting steel versus the Goodyear Custom Power Cushion
Super: "The Goodyear Custom Power Cushion Polysteel Tire."	Polysteel Tire, the 40,000 mile tire engineered for American Cars.
LS truck beside ramp. Red car, ostensibly Fire Dep't. Auto, starts up on ramp and axes.	
ECU tire rolling over ax blades.	Watch as we demonstrate the penetration resistance of steel cord belts under the tread.
Dissolve to tire in animation as two Polyester cord's weave across tire.	Inside, a polyester cord body to soak up shocks,
Super: "Polyester Cord"	
(Ax) steel belts slide around tire.	and double steel belts for strength.
Tire begins to roll, approaches fire axes.	
Super: Forms "Polysteel" as axes penetrate tire. Dissolve out of animation.	Polysteel
Ms tire rolling over ax blade.	
Ms car receding off ramp.	Cut upon cut. Yet the Goodyear Custom Power Cushion Polysteel Tire keeps going.
Dissolve to stationary tire in animation as polyester cord weaves across tire.	A flexible polyester cord body...
Super: "Polyester Cord"	
Double steel belts slide around tire. Super: "Double Steel Belts." Dissolve out.	And double steel belts. (SFX: Sliding Steel Belts)
Tire rolls up on polysteel letters.	
Super: "Goodyear Logo & Logotype" "Facts about demonstration available on request."	Polysteel. The 40,000 mile tire engineered for American Cars. Only from Goodyear.

The cost of live-action films, narrative or dialogue, varies a great deal because of the many factors involved: cast, settings, props, location trips, etc. Here again the matter of the SAG code and residual fees to talent used in live-action commercials has tended to switch some advertisers to other techniques. The move away from live action is not always wise, for its basic reality and faculty for reaching out to meet the viewer on common ground makes live action the most useful technique in television commercials.

Cartoon as a television technique is fun. It is high in viewer interest and it is probably lowest in cost per showing. While it wins interest quickly, it nonetheless lacks depth of penetration because it sacrifices credibility. Because viewers enjoy cartoons, but don't believe them, most experienced advertisers will follow the cartoon segment of their commercials with real people using the product and repeating its benefits.

Cartoons are most effective for: *gaining interest,* at the opening of a spot by presenting some whimsical or fantasic situation, or an unusual character; *trademark character,* either the actual company or product trademark or one devised for purposes of a given campaign;

personalizing the product, whereby a can of wax takes on life and personality with a cartoon face; *fantasy,* which enables just about any character or thing to do just about any type of action—an exercise in exaggeration to stimulate the imagination; *singing jingles,* because bouncy rhythms and cartoons are "naturals" that comprise one of television's longest lived types of commercials.

There are three grades among cartoons: full animation, limited animation, and "grow" or "scratch-off" cartoon, in order of decreasing cost and effectiveness. Cost depends largely on what "moves" in your cartoon, since as many as seven artists may work on each frame of a full-animation cartoon. At 24 frames per second, this means as many as 1,400 drawings may be needed for a one-minute spot. It thus behooves you to use no more characters than absolutely necessary in your commercial, and to work closely with your animation director to make maximum use of "cycles" of the same sequence of pictures wherever possible, especially for backgrounds. Limited animation, which costs about half as much as full, makes full use of cycles, often shows only extremes of facial expression and relies heavily on camera movement and lens tricks. The "grow" cartoon cuts costs in two again. It works with a single drawing, photographed from the rear as lines are scratched off on successive frames. When projected in the opposite direction, the cartoon seems to "grow" or be drawn on the screen.

Cartoons are honest fun and, as such, can do a selling job for impulse-purchase types of products. Where there is substantial reason-why for the purchaser to buy, cartoons need support from live action, as previously discussed.

Stop motion is the ingenious technique that makes inanimate objects come to life. This type of animation is accomplished by using a camera adjusted to move one or two frames at a time. Between exposures the objects are moved slightly or changed with the thought of continuous action when projected at normal speed. Stop action should be confined to inanimate objects, since actors cannot remain in one position long enough for this type of shooting. This technique provides an impressive way to introduce packaged products. For example, a number of packages shown unevenly spaced on a table suddenly assemble themselves into a neat display. The scene cuts to a close-up, then one package unwraps itself and out hops the product. Automobile doors open and close by themselves, or packages march across the screen.

The advantages offered by stop motion relate to: *personalizing the product,* as in the marching cigarettes or other products that are made to fly, dance, walk, zoom or take themselves apart; *mechanical action,* as in fitting parts of a motor or showing how attachments are used on appliances; and *demonstration,* without human hands, as in a commercial showing a wall oven that opens itself and a roast slides out. In the first of these advantages, stop motion shares with cartoons the ability to personalize a product, while in the last it vies with live action in its faculty for demonstration. It seems advisable here, too, to combine stop motion with a follow-up live action, pairing up the interest-rouser with the realistic demonstration.

Photo animation is the technique that sends bottles spinning and boxes zooming across the televiewer's screen. It is the method that the low-budget advertiser can use to excellent advantage to achieve impressive effects, largely through the camera's movement and optical tricks. It has been called "Fotan" by many producers and the technique lends itself best to: *special announcements,* in which titles and tricks are the main elements, as in coming attractions for movies; *signatures* at the end of most commercials in which the package, logotype or slogan pop on to the screen, often in synchronization with voice copy; *retouching products,* as in appliances of chrome and glass, using still photographs which are then reproduced on motion picture film with dissolves or other optical tricks to achieve a dramatic effect; *catalog of products,* where an inclusive line of related items can be presented quickly, clearly and, again, with startling pop-on effect.

Photo animation is not advisable to use with live action, for it works only with separate still photographs or drawings. To move an inanimate object in a live-action scene involves costly optical treatment. An example of Fotan at work was shown on behalf of a liquidizer that made tomato juice out of tomatoes, cole slaw out of cabbage, and crushed ice out of ice cubes. Still photos of the original items were shown at top left of the screen. They moved in procession to the center and were whirled downward in the appliance and finally emerged at bottom right as completed dishes. Truly graphic!

Puppets have enjoyed only a fair success, as a television production technique, for the creation and manipulation of them, usually as trade-mark characters, have been too limited to achieve best results. There are three types of puppets used for television commercials: string, hand, and stop-motion puppets, the latter made famous by George Pal. The first two types require the continuity of a regular program to establish viewer interest. "Kukla, Fran and Ollie" were one of the few notable successes among hand puppets, principally because of their creator's skill in investing them with all the characteristics of human beings. The frame-by-frame or stop-motion puppets created by George Pal achieved most renown in this area for they showed expression, animation and characterization without the need for manipulation by hand or string and without the limitation of one-expression faces. These puppets operated within miniature scale settings and were photographed one frame at a time, with the doll's body being moved and its head changed to match the next move called for in the commercial.

SUMMARY OF BEST USES OF TECHNIQUES

(1) CARTOON (*Full animation*) is best used for developing trademark characters, personalizing products, exaggeration and fantasy, singing jingles.

(2) LIVE ACTION (*Narrative*) is best used for demonstration, human interest, exposition.

(3) LIVE ACTION (*Dialogue*) is best used for testimonials, personality commercials, dramatic spots, key copy lines.

(4) STOP MOTION is best used for demonstration, mechanical action, personalizing product.

(5) PUPPETS (*Stop motion type*) are best used for trade-mark characters and singing jingles.

(6) PHOTO ANIMATION is best used for titles and signatures, retouching products, and catalog of products.

SOME FINAL POINTS OF EVALUATION

Before concluding this chapter, it may be profitable to imagine that you have a finished television commercial script in front of you. How can you size up its potential? Its creative worth? Its practicability from a production standpoint? Here are a few telegraphic queries on areas of your commercial that have been discussed in this chapter and which you'll do well to keep in mind in reading and evaluating the scripts which you may soon be writing:

Does the video tell the story without audio, and how well?

Is the video fully graphic (specifying technique, describing staging and camera action)?

Does the audio "listen" well (language, pacing)?

Do the audio and video complement each other and are they correctly timed for each other (act it out)?

Are there too many scenes (can some be omitted)?

How well have you identified the product?

Does your script win attention quickly and promise an honest benefit?

How well have you *demonstrated?*

Have you provided a strong visualization of the one major claim that will linger in the viewer's memory?

Could a competitive brand be substituted easily and fit well? (Better not.)

Is it believable? (*Always* ask this.)

Are you proud to say you wrote it?

SUMMARY

Nobody can tell you exactly how to write a television commercial. Nobody can tell you exactly what to say or what to show. These are things that can come to you only with time and experience. In this chapter you have been given an idea of what kind of things you will be expected to know about television commercial writing and, to a lesser extent, production.

Remember, however, that as television matures, both technically and creatively, the scope of your activities in the field will broaden and the challenge to your resources will be greater. Only by increasing its effectiveness can the television commercial pay the ever-increasing bill. This will increase your responsibility considerably.

On the following pages is a glossary of some of the more frequently used terms in preparing and producing a commercial. As you study these, keep in mind that this is a book about copywriting and not television production. For those interested, there are detailed texts on television production.

A Brief Glossary of Frequently Used Television Terms

Across the board—a program scheduled three, five or six days a week at the same time.

Ad lib—impromptu action or speech not written into script or, in music, to play parts not in the music.

Adjacencies—shows (on same station) immediately preceding and following the program referred to.

AFM—American Federation of Musicians.

AFTRA—American Federation of Television and Radio Artists.

Angle shot—camera shot of the subject taken from any position except straight.

Animate—to arrange and film static drawings or objects so that when the photographs are shown cinematographically they produce the illusion of movement.

ASCAP—American Society of Composers, Authors and Publishers, which licenses public performances of music of its members and collects royalties.

Background or rear-view projection—special technique whereby a wanted scene drawn from special photo or stock library is projected on a translucent screen which acts as a background for a studio set.

Back-time—to time a script backwards from end to beginning, with running time indicated every 15 seconds or less in the margin of the script, to keep the show "on the nose."

Balop—short for balopticon, which is a projection mechanism used in television to project objects, photographs and still pictures on to the mosaic element of television tube.

Billboard—announcement at the beginning of show which lists people starred or featured.

Bit—small appearance or few lines in show. One who plays it is called a "bit player."

BMI—Broadcast Music, Inc., competitors of ASCAP.

Boom—crane-like device for suspending microphone or camera in mid-air and moving it from one position to another.

Bridge—slide, picture, sound effects or music used to cover a jump in time or other break in continuity.

Camera or cue light—red light on front of camera which is lit only when camera is on the air.

Camera right-left—indication of direction in a setting as viewed from the point of view of the camera or televiewer.

Camera shots—(Referring to people) Head shot, only the head; Shoulder shot, shoulders and head; Full shot, entire person. (Referring to objects) CU, close-up or narrow angle picture limited to object or part of it; no background; MCU, medium close-up; TCU, tight close-up; LS, long shot in which figures are smaller than frame and sensation of distance is achieved; FoS, follow shot in which camera follows talent; RevS, reverse shot in which same object already on one camera is picked up from an exactly opposite angle by another camera; DI-DU, dolly in and up. DO-DB, dolly out and back.

Clear a number—to get legal permission to use specific musical selection.

Cover shot—wide angle television picture to alternate (for contrast) with close-up.

Cow-catcher—isolated commercial at start of show which advertises a product of the sponsor not mentioned in program itself.

Cut—to switch directly from one camera picture to another and speed up action for dramatic effect.

D.B.—delayed broadcast of a live show by

Dissolve—fading out of one picture as another fades in; to denote passage of time and present smooth sequence of shots.

Dolly—movable fixture or carriage for carrying camera (and cameraman) about during taking of shots.

Double spotting—also triple spotting. Station practice of placing a second or third commercial right after the first.

Down-and-under—direction given to a musician or sound effects man to bring down playing level and sneak under dialogue lines that follow.

Dubbing—mixing several soundtracks and recording them on a single film.

E.T.—electrical transcription, usually 33-1/3 rpm's.

Fanfare—few bars of music (usually trumpets) to herald start of show or commercial.

Film cue—performation in film to indicate time remaining.

Fluff—any mistake, action, word or phrase accidentally included, resulting in an imperfect sound or picture.

Hiatus—summer period, usually 8 weeks, during which sponsor may discontinue his program, but thereafter resume his time period until the next hiatus.

Highlight—emphasizing a subject or scene by special lighting or painting to make it stand out from the rest of the picture.

Hook—program device used to attract tangible response from the audience; e.g., an offer, a contest, etc.

ID—TV station identification or call letters (or 10-second commercial)

Idiot cards—cue sheets attached to the front of camera, or blackboard and printed reminder sheets out of camera range to prompt talent in delivering lines.

Inherited audience—portion of a program's audience which listened to preceding show on same station.

Kill—to strike out or remove part or all of a scene, set, action or show.

Lead-in—words spoken by announcer or narrator at beginning of show or commercial to set a scene or recapitulate some previous action.

Lip sync—direct recording of sound from scene that is being filmed; usually refers to film commercials in which actors can be seen with lips moving.

Live—"on the spot" television of events or people in contrast to transmission of film, videotape or kinescope material.

Local—show or commercial originating in local station as contrasted to network.

Make good—offer to sponsor of comparable facilities as substitute for TV show or announcement cancelled because of emergency; or offer to repeat a commercial, without charge for time, because of some mistake or faulty transmission.

Monitoring—to check show or spot content and transmission with on-the-air picture.

NARTB—National Association of Radio and Television Broadcasters.

Optical—trick effect done mechanically, permitting the combining of two or more pictures in one, creating wipes, montages, dissolves, fades and other effects.

Package—special show or series of shows bought by an advertiser, which includes all components ready to telecast.

Pad—to add action, sound, or any other material to fill the required on-the-air time.

Pan—gradual swinging of camera to left or right across a scene to see segments of it as camera moves.

Participating program—a single TV show sponsored by more than one advertiser.

Play-back—reproduction of a soundtrack in studio during film shooting to enable action or additional sound or both to be synchronized with action; also, playing or recording for audition or reference purposes immediately after spot is made.

Plug—mention of a name, show or advertised product; or, loosely speaking, the commercial announcement.

Process shot—film combining real photography with projected backgrounds or model sets or drawings.

Projectors—used in TV for still material. They include: Balop, which takes cards or opaques (no transparencies); balop card size is usually 3" x 4" or 6" x 8". Also, Projectall, which takes both opaque cards and transparencies or slides; card size is 3" x 4"; slides, 2" x 2".

Punch it—to accent or emphasize an action, sound effect, music or line of dialogue.

Rating—percentage of a statistical sample of TV viewers interviewed personally, checked by telephone or noted in viewing diary, who reported viewing a specific TV show.

Residuals—payments (required by the Screen Actors Guild) to talent for each broadcast of each film commercial on each network program. Per 13 weeks' usage. If same commercial is used in spot markets, payment is additional per quarter.

SAG—Screen Actors Guild.

Segue (Pronounced *seg*-way)—usually the transition from one musical number to another without any break or talk.

Sets-in-use—per cent of all TV homes in a given locality whose sets are tuned in at a specific time, regardless of the station being viewed.

Share-of-audience—per cent of viewers watching a given

show or station based on the total sets-in-use.

Slide—usually refers to still art work, titles, photographs or film which are picked up or projected upon camera tube. Slides are of two types: transparent or opaque, their size varying according to station projection method used.

Sponsor identification—percentage of viewers of a show or personality who can identify the name of the sponsor or are familiar with specific data about the product advertised on TV.

Spot TV—market-by-market buying of TV time (programs, announcements, participations, station breaks). It affords flexibility in adapting a TV ad campaign to time zone, seasonal variations, special merchandising plans, etc.

Station time—portion of a station's schedule not normally available for network programs; totals 3 out of every 6 clock hours.

Stop motion—film taken by exposing one frame instead of a number of frames at a time. Objects are usually moved by hand a fraction of an inch for each exposure according to a set pattern.

Take—single shot picture or scene held by TV camera; also, command to switch directly from one picture or camera to another, as "ready one—take one."

Talent cost—expense or cost (for music, talent, etc.) of a show or commercial aside from the time charge.

Telefex—rear-view projection system for special effects, backgrounds, etc.

Teleprompter—rolling script device for talent who have difficulty in learning lines. Lines are printed large enough to be read at distance on sheet which revolves, keeping pace with show's action.

Transcription—recording of highest quality, usually at 33-1/3 rpm, especially made for telecast or broadcast.

Under—show that does not use all its allotted time; also, to sustain and subordinate one facet of the drama or situation under another.

Videotape—a system that records both sound and pictures simultaneously on magnetic tape; offers great advantage of immediate playback plus exceptionally fine picture fidelity. In one day commercials can be completed on tape that previously took three weeks in running through film processing.

VO or *voice-over*—narration-type recording as opposed to lip sync or live sound; also, voice-over narration where voice talent is not seen.

Wipe—transition from one scene or image to another in which new scene replaces old one in some gradually increasing geometric pattern, i.e., circle (circle in, circle out), square (expanding square), fan, roll, etc.

Word count—number of words that will fit comfortably into a commercial of a specific length. Rule of thumb for television commercials is 2 words per second, although count will vary depending on type of commercial. Word count for radio is higher, approximating 170 words per minute spot.

Zip-pan—effect obtained by swinging camera so quickly around from one point of rest to another that between the two the picture is blurred.

Research: An Aid To The Copywriter's Intuition

There was a comfortable period not too many years ago when advertising copywriters drew upon experience, judgment and intuitive sensitivity to judge whether a piece of copy would be effective. These three qualities are still needed by copywriters but a fourth dimension has been added—knowledge of research findings and methods. Research has become almost a tyrant in the big corporation-big agency level of advertising. Many are the sighs in the business for the simple days of advertising when a copywriter was able to function without consulting psychologists, sociologists, and statisticians to determine if his copy made sense. On the lesser levels of advertising—in the small and medium-size agency, for example—research has not yet become as important as in the upper levels but still there is much talk of adhering to principles worked out by research.

It almost seems as if the copywriters, resentful sometimes, of the shackles imposed by research, are the last ones to pay any attention to what research has to say. Confident of their ability to turn out smooth reading copy, copywriters are often uninterested in methods of pre-checking or post-checking the copy's effectiveness. Copy testing, readership tests, and check lists, they may contend, are something for the "research boys" to worry about. Yet, it is doubtful that you the copywriter can reach full effectiveness unless you have some knowledge of techniques for measuring copy's effects. You don't need to be a scientist. You *should,* however, know enough about copy research to have a reasonable idea of the "why" behind the success or failure of a piece of copy. You should know the best methods for discovering that "why." You should know good from bad research. More and more everyone in advertising is expected to know the "why" as well as the "how." Copy research supplies some of the answers for the copywriter. Perhaps you will set up your own "homemade" research method. Many copy men do. The retail field for instance, has devised so many individual copy-checking systems that this chapter does not attempt to deal with them. Some are very good—some are very bad.

COPY EFFECT HAS ALWAYS BEEN UNCERTAIN

Since the first piece of copy was written, there has never been any real certainty regarding the effect of copy upon the consumer prior to its actual publication. There have been many uncertainties. From the start it was known that consumer reaction to advertisements was variable. An appeal that worked during one year might fail the next year. Even on a day-to-day or week-to-week basis the success of advertisements is uncertain. There have been attempts to take the uncertainty out of advertising. "Foolproof" systems have been devised to eliminate guesswork in copy. The consumer and his reactions to copy appeals, headlines, and illustrations have been studied as scientists study the beetle and his activities. It would be pleasant to relate that the research has been completely successful—but it hasn't. There are still uncertainties. As long as man himself is so uncertain, there will always be a quantity of "by guess and by gosh" in copywriting. The weather, the political picture, the news, epidemics, and a thousand other variables can affect the success of a piece of copy. If any one of the variables is hard at work, the most scientifically conceived job of copywriting can fail.

Most copy-researchers admit the variables. They admit that it is difficult to predict the exact degree of success or failure for any single piece of copy. They can merely predict that the copy *should* be successful or unsuccessful. Meanwhile, a huge field of copy research has developed. Copy research is greatly concerned with development of techniques for measuring copy's effectiveness *before* its appearance in print or in radio commercials—and then with analyzing why it failed or succeeded *after* its appearance. Confusion has sprung up about the measuring techniques. A new terminology has developed. Some smart advertisers are high-readership advocates. They reason: "If they don't read it—they won't buy it because they don't know about it." Opponents say: "If a thousand persons read but only one buys, high readership means nothing. Advertisements pay off on conviction, not mere readership." Many advertising people believe in check lists. Others ridicule their use. Some say that only in returns from mail-order advertising can copy effectiveness be measured. Many will refute the assertion by pointing out the innumerable variables that will affect results even in this situation. There are, therefore, many measuring techniques for copy but certainly no complete agreement on them.

As a copy writer you should know what's going on. You should know the merits and faults of the different testing techniques. The term Communiscope, for instance, should be more than a name; you should know that it is a method for testing advertising readership. You should know what's going on but you must be careful to avoid two dangerous traps:

1. Don't let yourself become so sold on any one method of copy research that you are blinded to the merits of other types of research. Remember—there is no perfect research method.

2. Don't get so bogged down in the mazes of copy research that you forget to write copy that is vigorous, spontaneous, and alive. No check test has ever been invented that can substitute for the warm, human writing that digs down deep into the consumer's desires and makes him want to buy your product—just because you've produced persuasive copy born out of humanness, intuition, and plain, good writing. You can't be *too* scientific in your copy approach and tangle yourself in formula.

It is useful, however, to make *some* pre-publication and post-publication analysis. Such research often: (1) stops the advertiser from plunging into an expensive but foolish campaign; (2) indicates need for a change in a current campaign. You can save much money and effort if you understand proper research techniques.

Think of the copy-research techniques as falling into two general groups: (1) before-publication; (2) after-publication.

Both groups are lashed by loud-voiced critics, but it is your job to learn all sides of the arguments. On the *before-publication* side you can apply such tecniques as: (1) consumer panel, (2) split-run, (3) check list, (4) Flesch formula, (5) eye camera, (6) motivational research.

On the *after-publication* side: (1) readership study (recognition, identification, recall, impact method), (2) Communiscope, (3) sales test.

RESEARCHING COPY BEFORE PUBLICATION

Consumer panel

Sometime, if you haven't already done so, you will probably "try out" some copy on other students, your wife, your secretary, your mother, or strangers. "Just trying to get consumer reaction," you'll explain. The consumer panel is a more elaborate way to do the same thing.

Instead of arbitrarily selecting one person

as your guinea pig, you will select a number of persons. Each will be a typical potential buyer of the product for which you are testing the copy. In addition to being "typical," panel members must also be "interested"—that is, "interested in the product." Copy for "Model" chewing tobacco should not be submitted to panel members who have not, and never will, use this type of product. The panel's rating of your advertising helps you determine possible reader-reaction in advance of publication. If the panel members can never be interested in your product, they are not competent to rate your advertisements, since what would appeal to them would not, in many cases, appeal to the regular or potential user.

A consumer panel "ranks" different advertisements for the same product. Two or more advertisements are presented to the individual members who are asked to indicate, "Which of these advertisements do you like best," or "Which of these advertisements would be most likely to make you want to buy the product." All advertisements are thus rated until they are ranked in order of preference. This is sometimes called *order-of-merit* ranking.

Another method is the *paired-comparison* technique, wherein advertisements are judged in pairs. The respondent picks what he thinks is the better advertisement in each pair. Then, through elimination, the best of all the advertisements is selected. Usually this system is used for choosing an approach, format, or theme rather than individual advertisements in one pattern.

Many times different elements of the advertisements are rated. For instance, your advertisements might be identical except for the headlines, which will be rated in comparison with each other. The next rating will compare illustrations, the next copy appeal, and so on.

Why the consumer panel method is used

Although the consumer panel method has been useful for indicating how an advertisement might fare in the final published form, it has faults mixed with its virtues. On the plus side of the consumer panel method:

1. *Good results.* In many instances there has been a satisfactory correlation between consumer-panel ratings and selling power of the advertisements rated. This correlation has been good enough, despite the formidable list of faults of the method, to justify the continued use of consumer panels in pre-testing copy.

2. *Speed.* Once the panel has been selected, the job of rating the advertisements can ordinarily be done speedily and easily.

3. *Moderate cost.* A few interviewers equipped with photostats of comprehensive layouts can do the whole job. A good many advertisements or separate advertising elements can be rated in one session, thus reducing the cost per unit tested.

4. *Consumer viewpoint.* You tend to overlook the consumer in some forms of copy research. You think of appeals, copy approach, or the "market." The consumer panel makes you think of the "market" in terms of individuals who view advertisements with like, dislike, or indifference. If you follow the ratings of a consumer panel, you are being guided by the preferences of a representative segment of your consumer target rather than by your personal, and possibly isolated, judgment. Too, your respondents are classified as to age, work, income, and other aspects. As in the case of most copy research methods, it is easier to pick flaws in the consumer panel than to find virtues. The following list doesn't condemn the method as useless but provides

you with some reservations. It should also indicate to you some weaknesses to avoid should you attempt to set up a panel.

Consumer panel testing has its difficulties

1. *Respondents.* Finding the right person to serve on a consumer panel is vital to the success of the method. Determining just what is "typical" and then finding persons who fit that description is likely to be a slow, tedious task. The requirements that such persons be "interested" in a particular product provides a double complication.

2. *Difficult to make conclusions.* The questions usually asked of a consumer panel fail to obtain a final answer. Examine the two questions again: "Which of these advertisements do you like better?" "Which of these two advertisements would be more likely to make you want to buy the product?"

The first question has nothing to do with sales potential. The respondent may like the advertisement because the illustration features a beautiful girl. The rest of the layout may please him; he might even read and like the copy. All this, however, might not have the slightest influence in making him buy the spark plugs being advertised. His favorable answer for a particular advertisement was based upon subjective factors having nothing to do with influencing him to buy.

The second question, although it is aimed more at determining buying behavior, asks the respondent to indicate how he *might* act. There is a great difference between a person's intentions and his actions. Some copy evaluators have combined the answers to the two questions. The combining is not practical. One question measures liking for an advertisement on a basis entirely removed from buying behavior. The other attempts to measure buying potential. Combining these two unlikes is tricky and conclusions thus derived would be questionable.

3. *Separating elements is dangerous.* Although there is some value in dissecting advertising elements and letting the panel judge headlines, illustration, and other items individually, the process is somewhat unrealistic. A person thumbing through his magazine is looking at advertisements, not headlines or illustrations. The general rating seems to be more accurate, according to the findings of the Advertising Research Foundation. Probably the best procedure is to use both methods—individual element rating *and* general rating. Both should then be analyzed carefully before the findings are accepted. It seems dubious in any event that final judgment of an advertisement should be based on a rating of the separate parts. Remember, some women taken feature by feature are not attractive. Assemble the features and you may have a charming result. An advertisement taken by sections may not be noteworthy. Combine elements and the result is often a persuasive, compelling advertisement.

4. *Panel members become copy "experts."* Almost everyone feels competent to criticize advertisements. Persons selected for consumer-panel service frequently forget their consumer function and begin to act like copy chiefs. The tendency causes real trouble, since the panel members thus are no longer "typical" consumer prospects. Instead, they have become professional critics. When they no longer view the advertisements with a consumer's eyes, their usefulness as panel members has ended.

5. *Hard to compare more than two advertisements.* Although many consumer panels are asked to compare more than two advertisements at a time, it is often questionable that more than two should be compared—at

the most three. The fewer the elements to be considered, the more reliable the judgment is likely to be. Thus the paired-comparison method may be preferable to that which gives the respondent the task of giving rank order to six different advertisements. If he does his job conscientiously, the respondent will probably be confused as he considers all the elements found in six advertisements. It is difficult enough to obtain reliable opinions from consumer panels without complicating the task further by confusing them. The paired-comparison method at least eliminates some of the confusion.

6. *Size of the sample.* Although the trend has been toward small samples, the sample size may often have to be varied for different types of products, or if the voting is so close on certain advertisements that the advertiser must ask for additional votes. One hundred or less opinions have been considered enough by many advertisers using the consumer-panel method but, again, don't accept this figure as final.

7. *Impractical for certain items.* Some products of infrequent purchase like figure skates or short-wave transmitters are not suitable for consumer-panel testing. Such products call for unusual promotions; ordinary testing procedures are not so suited to them as to ordinary items of everyday purchase like cereals, milk, or coffee.

8. *Prestige factor is operative.* The consumer panel, like any procedure requiring decision on the part of a respondent, is often inaccurate because of the respondent's pride or vanity. The respondent, not wanting to admit that a sexy illustration is appealing to him, will vote against it although under actual reading conditions the same illustration would win his delighted attention. Intellectuals might be unwilling to admit that moving-picture star endorsements attract and convince them. As long as people are subject to vanity, the prestige factor will be at work in situations like that set up by the consumer-panel copy-testing procedure.

9. *Test measures standings—not quality of advertisements.* Respondents are asked to rate advertisements in 1-2-3 order. This system is followed whether advertisements are good or bad. In some tests all the advertisements might be poor. The rating would simply indicate which was the least objectionable. The No. 1 advertisement might be used because the panel voted for it, not because it had merit.

10. *Campaigns are overlooked.* Most national advertising is campaign advertising. One advertisement, by itself, might not have the push and appeal that it has as one of a series of advertisements. Yet the consumer panel may be asked to judge an individual advertisement, ignoring the cumulative effect of the campaign. For instance, a *Ladies' Home Journal* advertisement featuring the campaign idea "Never underestimate the power of a woman" becomes powerful through repetition, as does the *Philadelphia Bulletin* advertisement which tells you that "In Philadelphia nearly everyone reads the Bulletin." Although it is unlikely that such advertisements would ever be used in consumer-panel testing (since they are not for consumer products), they provide a good illustration of the point being made here.

In both campaigns, the usual reader, when he glances over a particular advertisement, is *not* reading one advertisement but is receiving the smashing impact of all the advertisements of a given series. Perhaps he was half-sold before he read this last advertisement, which acted as a sales clincher. He has been sold by

Fig. 19-1

Typical page from Readex Reader Interest report.

Readex measures interest, not observation. Readers report only what they found of interest.

READEX, INC., Reader Interest Research,
140 Quail Street,
St. Paul, Minnesota 55115.

ADVERTISING ACHIEVEMENT AWARDS — Readex calls special attention to and has prepared special award certificates for the following advertisements which have achieved outstanding reader interest in comparison with all other ads in this issue.

INTEREST	SIZE	PAGE	ADVERTISER
53%	2c4	14-5	AMERICAN HOIST & DERRICK COMPANY
39	2c4	12-3	TEREX DIVISION OF GENERAL MOTORS
38	2c4	10-11	CLARK EQUIPMENT COMPANY
38	1c4	5	WARNER & SWASEY

ADVERTISEMENTS BY PRODUCT CLASSIFICATION IN ORDER OF INTEREST.

INTEREST	SIZE	PAGE	ADVERTISEMENT
1. TRACTORS, LOADERS, SCRAPERS, WAGONS & ATTACHMENTS			
39%	2c4	12-3	Terex 82-40T Crawler
35	2c4	36-7	Allis-Chalmers HD-41
33	2c4	66-7	John Deere JD544-A
30	2c4	46-7	MF Equipment
27	2c4	50-1	Trojan Loaders
25	1	125	Ateco Attachments
24	2c4	88-9	Long 5-N-1 Super 16
23	2c4	28-9	Int'l. Harvester 25C Crawler
23	1r	75	New Holland L-35 Loader
18	1c4	2	Caterpillar Wheel Loaders

69% Total Reader Interest in one or more ads.

77% Highest Total Reader Interest Recorded in 12 Reports (October 1970).

49% Most Interesting Single Ad in 12 Reports (July 1972).

INTEREST	SIZE	PAGE	ADVERTISEMENT
2. - SHOVELS, DRAGLINES, BACKHOES, BACKHOE/LOADERS & ATTACHMENTS			
38%	2c4	10-11	Clark Lima 945

(CONTINUED)

INTEREST	SIZE	PAGE	ADVERTISEMENT
2. - CONTINUED			
38%	1c4	5	Warner & Swasey Gradall

47% Total Reader Interest in one or more ads.

69% Highest Total Reader Interest Recorded in 12 Reports (July 1971).

55% Most Interesting Single Ad in 12 Reports (October 1970).

INTEREST	SIZE	PAGE	ADVERTISEMENT
3. - CRANES, HOISTS & ATTACHMENTS			
53%	2c4	14-5	American Hoist Cranes
36	1c4	30	Northwest Truck Crane
31	1c4	2C	Link-Belt Speeder Crane
28	1c4	16	Grove RT Cranes
18	1c4	113	Koehring 1510 Skytrak
5	1/4	139	Equipment Systems Products

63% Total Reader Interest in one or more ads.

84% Highest Total Reader Interest Recorded in 12 Reports (July 1971).

59% Most Interesting Single Ad in 12 Reports (February 1971).

KEY TO SYMBOLS: Under the Heading of "SIZE", Numerals indicate Ad Size. Letters following Numeral show Color. No letter following indicates Black & White.
EXAMPLE: 1b - 1 Page Blue; 1/2 g - 1/2 Page Green; 2c4 - 2 Page 4 Color.

b - Blue	c4 - 4 Color	ϕ - Orange	y - Yellow
br - Brown	g - Green	r - Red	

Under the Heading of "PAGE", the Letters "a, b, etc." indicate an Insert following the Page Mentioned.

the campaign. Any *one* advertisement in the campaign might not have sold him. Yet the consumer panel judges *one* advertisement in an attempt to answer the question "Which advertisement would be most likely to make you buy the product? That one advertisement might fit in very poorly with the campaign, and with most national advertisers the campaign is the important consideration. That is why, in many cases, national advertisers will continue to emphasize a campaign even though it is tempting to put all the emphasis on a current prize contest. Long-run considerations, however, are not necessarily a part of a consumer panel's thinking.

11. *Conditions are not natural.* No matter how skilled the interviewer, or the phrasing of the questions, the conditions under which the consumer panel operates are not normal home-reading conditions. The panel member cannot help being less casual than in his reading in the home. He is on the alert for faults; the very act of comparing is unrealistic. Certainly, the usual reader will not match advertisements against each other. Also his reading under panel conditions allows him to give undivided attention to the individual advertisements. Under more usual conditions, there would be

the competition from surrounding advertisements. There would be unfavorable position. In finished, printed form one advertisement might gain over another through better type, use of color, and other mechanical factors.

Summary of consumer-panel method

To sum up, the consumer-panel method is used so widely that you should know how it works. You should know that it has some virtues and many faults. Let it guide you, but have the proper reservations. Get in the habit of questioning the results of the consumer panel or any other copy-testing method. They are all fallible. All the eleven faults will not be present in each use of the consumer-panel method. Clever researchers can eliminate nearly all the difficulties. The test will never be free from *all* the faults, however—a fact to keep in mind.

Check lists*

Although the consumer panel has its critics, it evokes sniffs rather than snorts from the opposition. Much of the sniffing, actually, is done by the very people who employ the panel method. They see the inadequacies but they use the system anyway because it *does* provide useful information. Like the faults in a friend, the faults in the consumer panel are tolerated because of compensating virtues.

Check lists, however, bring out snorts—if not bellows—from the nonbelievers. The check list has been obnoxious to hundreds of copy people. Other hundreds defend its use. Certain check-list systems, such as that of W. S. Townsend's rating evaluation, have caused excited controversies among advertising men and have actually caused splits between advertisers and agencies that had been operating amicably previously.

Before *you* engage in the check-list squabble, you had better clarify the meaning of the term. Practically everyone who has written copy has used a check list at one time or another. Usually, the list will be a simple little affair—a casual reminder to put in certain important elements like the slogan, price mention, and selling conditions. Other check lists bring in more elements to watch for. They keep the copywriter on the track without attempting to provide any scientific pre-evaluation as to the effectiveness of the advertisements.

The check list, in its ultimate form, goes beyond "reminding." It attempts, as in the case of the elaborate systems worked out a number of years ago by Townsend, or by Dr. Charles M. Edwards, Jr., to serve as a yardstick for pre-evaluating the effectiveness of advertising. So confident were the proponents of check-list evaluations that they made assertions such as Mr. Townsend's that through use of the Townsend system you could tell a good advertisement from a bad advertisement before publication in 9 minutes flat.

Some of the opponents, however, hoot when check lists are mentioned. They assert that: (1) originators of check lists or pre-evaluation techniques are engaged in a meaningless battle of points with each such originator simply trying to outdo the other in dreaming up new point lists; (2) that check lists or pre-evaluation methods hamstring, originality; (3) that copywriters use points by instinct; (4) that personal judgment is overemphasized in the check-list system. Since, sooner or later, you will probably be engaged in a discussion of check lists, these four arguments are examined here.

Check lists—no!

1. *Check lists degenerate into a battle of points.* The Townsend system was originally based upon 27 points of evaluation for national advertising. They were:

*See Appendix for example of checklists.

1. Identification
2. Attention
3. Interest
4. Proof
5. Timing
6. Good quality
7. The proposition
8. Consumer acceptance
9. Personality—you
10. Sincerity
11. Focus
12. Poor quality
13. Loss (if prospect doesn't buy)
14. Who (testimonial of prominent user)
15. The request for action
16. Association
17. The command to act
18. Aim
19. The main appeals
20. The instinct for life
21. The instinct to reproduce life
22. The instinct for bodily comfort
23. The instinct for personal importance
24. The instinct to enjoy the five senses
25. Layout and illustration
26. Sequence
27. Type

The 27 points were subsequently reduced to nine points for retail advertising. Here is the shortened list:

The Townsend Nine Standard Method for Rating Retail Advertising

A. Headlines and subheads
   No. 1 Identification—memory
   No. 2 Main appeals—featured
   No. 3 Reasons why—subheads

B. Copy
   No. 4 Main appeals—copy interest
   No. 5 Quality—proof—belief
   No. 6 The proposition—action

C. Layout and illustration
   No. 7 Sequence
   No. 8 Main appeals—illustrated
   No. 9 Identification—style

The Townsend backers said that the 27 points were not "created," but were simply identified as basic to all copy and each was given an approximate value. Thus, a copywriting novice could tell quickly whether his, or someone else's copy, had the elements to make an effective advertisement.

Dr. Charles M. Edwards, expert in retail advertising research, in turn worked out a complicated formula using 671 points for checking retail advertising. This formula was not for the novice but for the skilled researcher. Yet it is often mentioned among the check-list systems. It was used extensively for evaluating copy of the R. H. Macy department store in New York City, but Dr. Edwards felt that in most stores no more than 14 to 22 points were of vital significance.

Another check-list system that received wide attention was the Thompson-Luce method, which used 35 factors assertedly controlling reader interest.

The factors were assembled on the basis of exhaustive analysis of readership studies. Each one of the 35 was consistently present in high-readership copy, according to the method's originators. For instance, news interest might appear five times as frequently in high-ranking advertisements as in low-ranking advertisements. A picture of a famous man might appear three times as frequently. A forecast of the probability of success was made on the basis of proper incorporation of the points.

Even from this brief discussion of check lists, you may see some aptness in the term "battle of the points." Although there was merit in each of the systems, it was difficult for copy people to know just which system was the best or whether *any* such system was

Fig. 19-2

A magazine page that shows the readership figures obtained by Starch researchers for the different parts of the advertisement.

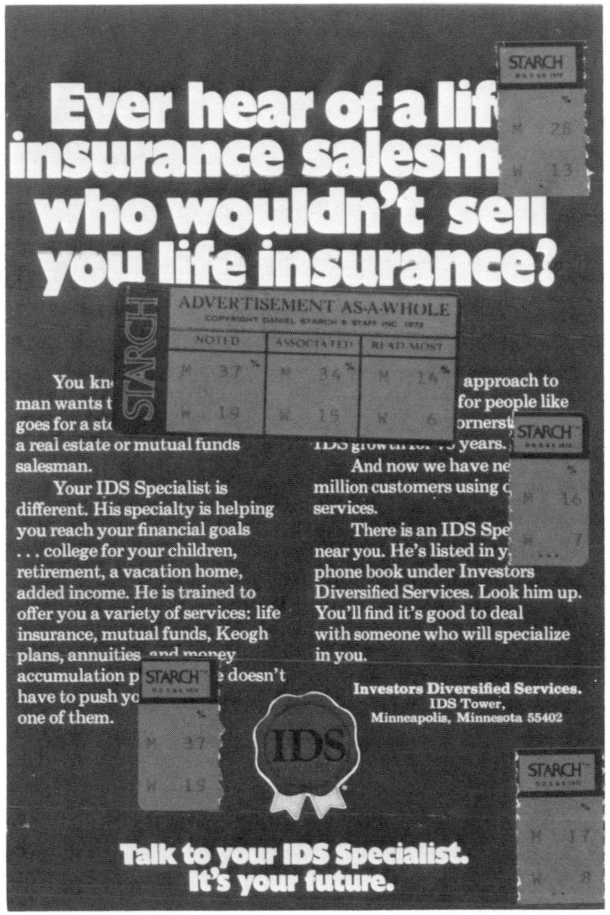

Ever hear of a lif
insurance salesm
who wouldn't sell
you life insurance?
STARCH
ADVERTISEMENT AS-A-WHOLE
NOTED
ASSOCIATED
READ MOST
M 37
M 34
M 14
W 19
W 15
W 6
M 28
W 13
M 16
W 7
M 37
W 19
M 17
W 8
You kn
man wants t
goes for a st
a real estate or mutual funds
salesman.
Your IDS Specialist is
different. His specialty is helping
you reach your financial goals
. . . college for your children,
retirement, a vacation home,
added income. He is trained to
offer you a variety of services: life
insurance, mutual funds, Keogh
plans, annuities
accumulation p
doesn't
have to push yo
one of them.
approach to
for people like
ornerst
years.
And now we have ne
million customers using
services.
There is an IDS Spe
near you. He's listed in y
phone book under Investors
Diversified Services. Look him up.
You'll find it's good to deal
with someone who will specialize
in you.
Investors Diversified Services.
IDS Tower,
Minneapolis, Minnesota 55402
IDS
Talk to your IDS Specialist.
It's your future.

sound. Confused by the point battle and the involved methods of evaluation, a great many copywriters dismissed every system.

2. *Check lists hamstring originality.* "Creative work cannot be written according to a cut-and-dried formula. The check list provides a mechanical crutch for the copywriter which, if followed, generally would tend to make all advertisements look the same." So go the comments of many copywriters. An illustration of how intensely some advertising men feel about this is provided by the example of one very large agency which threw one of its biggest accounts out of the "shop" when the account insisted on adoption of a check-list system by the agency copywriters working on the account's copy.

Check-list originators deny that their systems choke newness and sparkle in copy. Rather, they say, using a good check list as a guide, the original writer can produce freely, confident that his writing is channeled more effectively for sales-getting. The check list merely systematizes a job that often has no system but much originality, according to the check-list backers.

3. *Copywriters use points naturally, so check lists are useless.* Most copywriters argue that they incorporate the necessary points in their writing without using any "system" to stultify their naturalness of expression. They suspect the check list as an attempt by research men to invade the copywriter's field. "Possibly all right for beginners but not for the experienced man" is a frequent comment about check lists. The comment is valid in the case of many copywriters who, through long practice, automatically use attention-getting, selling points in everything they turn out. Other writers—beginners and some old hands—might well adopt some system to keep them on the track in their thinking. The best copywriter in the field might occasionally use a check list to remind himself of the fundamentals that sometimes slip away from him as he becomes more advanced in his job. Since check lists contain nothing new, but simply present ever-constant, faithful sales points, they can be a great comfort to the beginner and an occasional aid to the skilled copywriter. You would do well to find for yourself just how the different systems operate. You may not want to adopt any, but you will learn to analyze your copy's use of basic selling factors. Check lists aren't all bad or all

good. You will profit from discovering that, too.

4. *Personal judgment is overemphasized.* Any check list, say the critics, is basically a personal judgment on what elements are needed to make an advertisement successful. *Any* copywriter can, they continue, evolve his own list. Even in using a check list to evaluate an advertisement, the interpretation is a matter for individual judgment. That this criticism has some truth is borne out by situations wherein persons using the same checklist evaluating system arrive at radically different results in their ratings of the same advertisement. In short, one person many have more skill in applying the check list than another, or both may be equally skilled but differ entirely in their use of the system. The method then becomes no better than the ability of the persons who use it. The defense against the statement is, of course, that although actual application of the check list may be subject to varying interpretations, the check list itself is rooted in solid, tried fundamentals that are commonly accepted as basic to effective copywriting.

About the most conclusive thing to say of the check list is that it's up to you. It's a quick, inexpensive way to evaluate an advertisement—one of the quickest and most inexpensive. If you use a check list be sure that you don't let it make you write like an automaton, and that you retain your good judgment.

Whatever you use—a simple system or the most refined method—don't let it substitute for your own original thinking.

Testing by inquiry results

The idea behind inquiry testing is simple. You run advertisements and you judge their relative effectiveness by the number of inquiries they bring. These inquiries may result from a hidden offer buried in the copy, or from a coupon offer, openly made, inviting purchases or inquiries.

The hidden offer rids the advertiser of professional coupon-clippers and inquiries from the curious. It also indicates extent of reading, but results in less inquiries or sales than does the coupon offer.

In the usual inquiry test different advertisements are run at different times in the same publication, or at the same time in different publications. Results are then compared. Another version of the inquiry test is the split-run test. This test has some of the advantages or disadvantages of the usual inquiry test plus some advantages and disadvantages of its own. Most of the discussion here will consider the split-run technique.

The split-run test

Split-run refers to the practice of testing advertisements by running two or more versions of the same advertisement on the same press run but on different presses of a newspaper or magazine. Thus, Advertisement A may be exactly like Advertisement B except for the headline. Each advertisement in the case of a newspaper will go out on the same day, in the same position in the paper. From the response to the advertisement, the advertiser can tell which of the two headlines was more effective. In the case of a magazine, as many as four versions of the same advertisement will go out and each may be distributed in a different area. Response will be judged by the coupon return, or by the replies to a hidden offer—one or the other is usually employed in such tests. Any element of the advertisement may be checked—copy, illustration, headline. In some instances, the advertiser will test four entirely different advertisements.

You may wonder why this form of testing

is not classified with the after-publication copy-testing techniques instead of the before-publication list. It could be. It is placed in the before-publication group simply because such testing usually precedes general use of the winning advertisement or advertisement elements. Normally, the advertisements would not have been run before the split-run test. In this sense, therefore, the test is a before-publication test. A fact you should realize, too, is that although several hundred newspapers offer split-run service only a few magazines offer split-run, so such testing is quite limited in its scope for magazines.

What split-run offers the researcher

1. *Parallels running conditions.* The trouble with so many copy-testing methods is that they are unrealistic. The researchers set up situations which are artificial despite all efforts to make them otherwise. The consumer-jury method is a good example. The split-run test, on the other hand, gives the advertiser an almost perfect simulation of conditions under which the advertisements will be run. There will be no tampering with actual reading conditions; there will be no dependence upon the skill of interviewers. Instead, the advertisement readers will read as they always do—right in their homes and unaware that they are taking part in a test. Their response to the advertisements will give an excellent, although not completely reliable, comparison of the effectiveness of the test advertisements.

2. *Test itself produces business.* An obvious advantage of split-run testing is that the test pulls in business, unlike other tests which produce nothing but information. A split-run test may promote the product just as well and bring in just as much business as any other advertising used for the product.

3. *Checks geographical differences.* That sections of the country, or even sections of a city, vary in their response to different products, copy appeals, and so forth, is well known. Magazine-reading habits, for example, differ greatly in different cities. One tomato-sauce manufacturer found that his sales were very good in one city while very poor in another. A TV star who gets a good rating on the West Coast may fare poorly in the South and Midwest but will get a good rating on the East Coast. This is the sort of thing that will vex you or any other advertising man. The split-run test can help you out since it provides a means of checking the power of your appeals in four different sections covered by a magazine. The split-run provides you with a method of making such a check. As one magazine man, whose publication offers split-run testing facilities, has explained it, split-runs make possible: "Pre-testing before general release, eliminating ineffective advertisements; comparison of campaign theme and ideas; development of the presentation; evaluation of different headlines; measuring various illustrative treatments; comparing 4-color to black and white or to black and one color; exploring different layout techniques; comparison of the relative values of various hidden offers."

Watch out for these weaknesses in split-run testing

1. *That the coupon or inquiry return from a set of split-run advertisements is not necessarily a true measure of the relative effectiveness of the advertisements.* Here are some considerations:

a. It is difficult to use split-run for measuring effectiveness of general advertisements. The method is suited to mail-order advertisements. To make a mail-order advertisement out of a general advertisement for purposes of the test can distort the true picture of reader reaction to a general advertisement run under normal conditions.

b. Since most of your readers *won't* reply to your test advertisements, respondents may not give a fair indication of your readership. Also, you learn nothing in the split-run about people who *don't* send in the coupon.

c. Mail returns may not give a true evaluation of potential store sales. The kind of people who reply to your coupon or hidden offer often are not typical of the kind of people who come into a store to buy the product. Children, professional "coupon clippers," and many women make a business of replying to advertisements carrying offers despite the fact that they have no real interest in the product. Split-runs using hidden offers can avoid this difficulty somewhat.

2. *Unlike some other copy-testing methods, the split-run reveals nothing about the readers.* You know nothing about the way they read the advertisement, their economic or social status, or whether anything in the advertisement actually appealed to them or whether they were just "curious."

Split-run advantages mentioned in the preceding discussion apply to conventional inquiry tests, too, except for the checking of geographical differences. The split-run, however, wins over the conventional inquiry testing in its control over position and time elements. With all test advertisements running at the same time in the same position, you can get a better idea of the comparative drawing power of the copy and other advertisement elements, since extraneous variables are thus reduced. As for the disadvantages, they are essentially the same for conventional inquiry and split-run testing.

Testing for readability

Some years ago, United Press, worried that they were writing "over" their readers, made a thorough study of their wire stories. They found among other things that out of 100 United Press stories going out in a single day the average sentence length was 29 words—the average length of lead sentences was 33 words. Yet comfortable reading for the mass of the population is a sentence length of around 20 words. The U.P. found that although they were averaging around 30 words for their sentences, current magazines ran about as follows:

MAGAZINES	AVERAGE SENTENCE LENGTH
Time	16 words
Reader's Digest	18 words
Atlantic Monthly	24 words

United Press editors found that in addition to writing long sentences their writers were also using too many long, complex words. Alarmed by the trend, the wire service began a writing reform within the organization. Sentences were shortened, language was simplified, and readability, according to tests, increased noticeably and quickly.

What was true of United Press has been true of almost every organization writing to the public—magazines, newspapers, advertisers. Sentences have been too long, words too long, and the writing impersonal. The three factors make a marvelous recipe for low readership. During labor-management difficulties, publications are usually crowded with good-sized advertisements from both sides explaining their viewpoints. In such issues, involving the general public welfare, it can be assumed that both sides are anxious that the greatest possible number of people read their messages. Controversial advertisements of this type, you would think, would be designed for easy digestion. Not so. Most of them are ponderously written. The language level is beyond the ordinary reader. They are written like treatises on economics. Neither labor nor management seem able to speak the language of the people—nor to write that language so that the majority of people are convinced and will respond.

Thanks to readership studies you know that Advertisement A gets 55% readership and Advertisement B gets 20%. But why? It might have been the headline, illustration, or position in the publication. There are many ways to account for the difference. One of the most important is this matter of readability. Was the copy a chore to read or did it run off smoothly under your glance? What made the difference in readability between A and B? How do you actually measure readability? At least *some* of the answers to these questions have been supplied by a former Vienna lawyer, Dr. Rudolph Flesch, whose readability formula you can learn and apply quickly to your copy or anyone else's copy.

Basis for the formula are four elements as they appear in 100-word samples of writing: (1) Average sentence length. (2) Average number of syllables. (3) Per cent of personal words. (4) Per cent of personal sentences. These are no magic ingredients—Flesch has simply expressed mathematically what writers have always known—that short words and short sentences make for easier reading. In sentences, for example, the Flesch table points out that about 88 per cent of the population can understand without difficulty sentences that fall in the *Fairly Easy* category. Such sentences average 14 words; their syllable count is 139 per 100 words. *Very Difficult* writing, in contrast, is suitable to only about 4.5 per cent of the population. Here the average sentence runs 29 or more words and the syllable count soars to 192.

An interesting facet of the Flesch formula is the stress on the use of personal words and personal sentences in order to achieve what is termed a high "interest" factor. Words such as *people, folks* (plus personal names and personal pronouns) are classified as "personal" words. Personal sentences include spoken sentences set off by quotation marks; questions, commands, and other sentences addressed directly to the reader; exclamations; and incomplete sentences whose meaning must be inferred from the context. A classification of Dull writing has no personal sentences and contains only two per cent or less personal words per 100 words. Typical users of such writing are scientific magazines which, however absorbing to their limited audience, would be found dull by the mass audience. *Highly Interesting,* in contrast, has 10 personal words and 43 per cent of personal sentences.

For years, young writers have been told—"write simply." "Write on the level of your readers." It is not easy to decide what kind of writing is suited to the different levels. Because a "Li'l Abner" advertisement gets a good Flesch rating, and thus can be read by most of the adult readers, does not mean that all advertisements must be written in "Li'l Abner" style. Certainly, if you are selling a mass-appeal item write in the way that will appeal to the biggest possible portion of that market. If you are writing *New Yorker* copy for a very expensive product you will *not* be addressing a mass readership. The readers you want to reach will have a lot of money in their pockets, and appreciation of precision instruments. They will have an educational background which enables them to surmount easily a "Difficult" Flesch rating of the advertisement. By no means should a copywriter write consciously to the Flesch or any other formula. The system is simply a device to tell you whether or not your writing is geared in readability to the various segments of your readership. That the method has some practi-

Fig. 19-3

Another advertising page that has been "Starched."

STARCH
ADVERTISEMENT AS-A-WHOLE
NOTED
ASSOCIATED
READ MOST
M 25%
W 24
M 23%
W 21
M 12%
W 13
STARCH
M 23
W 21
Birthday
STARCH
M 13
W 13

cality is evident in its adoption by a number of advertising agencies, and publications. The formula is applicable to any kind of writing and, as a matter of fact, has been used widely to determine readability of the editorial content of magazines and newspapers.

Some advocates of the Flesch system assert that they have learned quickly to write at a lower index level than previously. A good example was furnished by the magazine *Wallaces Farmer.* The publication asserted flatly that as a result of experiments, during which they adopted the Flesch system, they increased their readership by many thousands over a period of a few months.

A significant point coming out of the Flesch formula is the degree of correlation between Flesch rating results and readership studies such as the magazine reports of Daniel Starch, and the Continuing Study of Newspaper Reading.

The principal danger in the use of the Flesch system is that writers might adopt it too literally. It would be oversimplification to believe that all you must do to write good copy is to write short words, short sentences, and throw in a personal reference now and then. Thought and writing skill must still be used by the copywriter. The Flesch formula does nothing but wave a warning when the copy begins to clank. Because a copywriter can read his copy easily often makes him forget that others won't have a similarly easy time reading it. The Flesch system acts as a siren to scream: "These sentences are too long"—"Only half your readers will understand this."—"Don't forget your readers are human; they like personal references to themselves or other human beings."

Secondly, be cautioned that the Flesch formula cannot be applied literally to radio or television writing since a good radio announcer can make material that looks difficult to the eye seem "hearable" when he reads it out loud. Through skillful phrasing and intonation the announcer breaks long sentences into easily assimilated phrases. Even long, unusual words that would daunt the reader of a printed page will "sound easy" when delivered by a good announcer or actor.

In conclusion, don't use the Flesch system as a mold for your writing. Flesch doesn't measure literary excellence or selling effectiveness, but how well you reach your audience. A formula should not be used constantly if you are to maintain elasticity in your writing. Use it occasionally as a sort of check-up on your writing. Employed in this manner, it can help your writing to be more consistently readable—especially if you are writing to a mass market.

What do the eyes reveal?—Eye camera testing

A film record of the path of the eye over an advertisement is made by the eye-camera. Not only does the eye-camera indicate eye direction but it indicates, also, how long a reader's glance remains on any one section of the advertisement. Although the eye-camera is probably more suited to long-range advertisement research than to copy testing individual advertisements, it can be useful in the latter activity. It can, for example, indicate the relative pulling power of the various advertisement elements. It can answer the question as to whether the subject is merely a headline reader or whether he reads body copy, too. Also, the eye-camera may reveal the extent of reading, although under the test conditions necessary for an eye-camera test the subject is rather far away from home-reading conditions. Undoubtedly the instrument can reveal the mechanics of eye-flow. The greatest use for the eye-camera is in determining the correct mechanical structure of the advertisement. It tells nothing of what the subject thinks about the advertisement, or how he might react to it. It simply indicates how to arrange the advertising elements for the most logical, thorough, and easiest readership. In this sense it may be considered even more useful as a layout-testing device than as a means for testing copy. It *can* be argued, however, that interest in copy can be indicated by the length of time the eye rests upon it. As a counter-argument, it may be that the subject had to spend much time on a particular section because it was so difficult to understand.

Daniel Starch, in his *Factors in Readership Measurements,* has said: "Photographic records of eye movements measure precisely where the eyes look and how long they look while they read. Such records are probably affected to some extent by the artificial conditions that attend laboratory reading. However, it seems reasonable that eye-camera tests broadly measure the relative amounts of text that would be read under normal conditions."

Continuing to talk about eye-cameras, Starch pointed to strong correlation between eye-camera results and magazine readership test results. Thus, if an advertisement checked in a Starch readership study was classified high in "Read-Most" results ("Read-Most" refers to those readers who have read 50% or more of the reading matter of an advertisement), it tended to be scanned a longer time during eye-camera tests. You can see how this works when you examine the following table:

	Read-Most Readership		*Eye-Camera Reading Time*	
	Per cent	*Rank*	*Seconds*	*Rank*
Swans Down Cake Flour	15.2%	1	4.9	1
National Dairy Products	7.0	2	3.2	3
Grape Nuts Flakes	6.3	3	2.7	4
Ivory Soap	4.2	4	2.3	5.5
Palmolive Soap	2.5	5	2.3	5.5
Tavern Home Products	2.4	6	4.0	2
Trushay Lotion	2.0	7	2.2	7
Elizabeth Arden	1.0	8	1.7	8
Jolly Pop Corn	0.8	9	1.0	10
Chevrolet	0.4	10	1.1	9
Everglaze Chintz	0.3	11	0.6	11

Probing the mind—motivational research

Any researcher knows that very often the answer he can obtain from a respondent is not the true answer to the question that was asked. The true answer is hidden in the subconscious. Even the respondent is not aware of it. An advertising researcher, therefore, in probing for reactions about a product or a campaign may, if using ordinary research techniques, obtain a set of answers that will not reveal the real feelings of the respondents. To dig under the surface advertising has, in the last few years, used increasingly motivational research, a form of investigation that draws heavily upon (1) psychology—laws underlying thinking, learning, and actions. (2) sociology—the study of mass behavior. "MR," as it is familiarly called by advertising men, has been used before or after campaigns have been run; thus, it fits into post-publication copy research as well as pre-publication. Also, it must not merely be thought of as a copy research tool since its findings are used to establish a rationale for the whole marketing process.

A motivational research practitioner usually proceeds on the assumption that he does not know what his investigation may uncover since irrational behavior, drives, impulses, fears and desires may cause people to act as they do toward the product or situation being studied. Out of his study may come reasons respondents could tell the ordinary researcher but probably will not.

Most motivational research is concerned

Fig. 19-4

Page from Starch Readership Report that shows male readership of a number of advertisements. Notice the cost figures in the two right-hand columns.

STARCH
READERSHIP REPORT

PAGE 1

44 ADS
READER'S DIGEST JANUARY

MEN READERS

PRODUCT CATEGORIES			COST	RANK IN ISSUE		PERCENTAGES			READERS PER DOLLAR			COST RATIOS		
PAGE	SIZE & COLOR	ADVERTISER	PENNIES PER READER	BY NUMBER OF READERS	BY COST PER READER	NOTED	ASSOCIATED	READ MOST	NOTED	ASSOCIATED	READ MOST	NOTED	ASSOCIATED	READ MOST
		COMMUNICATION/PUBLIC UTILITY												
7	1P	BELL TELEPHONE SYSTEM L D L	1.7	19	19	25	23	12-	64	59	31	98	102	182
		BANKING/FINANCE												
9	1P2B	INVESTORS DIVERSIFIED SERV	1.2	8	9	37	34	14	90	82	34	138	141	200
		FIRE/CASUALTY INSURANCE												
192	1P2	COLONIAL PENN INSURANCE CO	2.3	30	31	20	18	12	48	44	29	74	76	171
210	1P	ALLSTATE AUTO INSURANCE	1.1	8	7	35	34	17	90	87	44	138	150	259
		PASSENGER CARS/VEHICLES												
38	1P4	OLDSMOBILE CUTLASS CARS	.8	3	3	63	58	23	135	124	49	208	214	288
48	1P4B	FORD MAVERICK CARS	.7	1	1	68	66	21	145	141	45	223	243	265
170	1P4B	MERCURY MONTEGO CARS	.7	2	2	65	63	19	139	135	41	214	233	241
		COMMERCIAL TRUCKS/LEASING												
180	1P4B	FORD PICKUP TRUCKS	.9	4	5	53	52	17	113	111	36	174	191	212
		PASSENGER TRAVEL												
14	1S4	BOEING/BRANIFF/PAN AM/UNITED EASTERN/TWA & AMERICAN	2.3	6	31	44	37	14	52	44	17	80	76	100
		COSMETICS/BEAUTY AIDS												
19	1P4B	VASELINE INTENSIVE CARE LOT	2.1	23	29	26	22	5	56	47	11	86	81	65
		PERSONAL HYGIENE PRODUCTS												
37	1P4B	SOFT & DRI ANTI-PERSPIRANT	3.8	41	41	14	12	3	30	26	6	46	45	35
43	1P	COLGATE DENTAL CREAM	2.4	33	35	21	16	4	54	41	10	83	71	59
172	1P4B	DENTU-CREME DENTURE CLEANSER	2.9	33	39	24	16	4	51	34	9	78	59	53
215	H1/2P	ORAFIX DENTURE ADHESIVE	1.5	37	13	21	14	1	98	66	5	151	114	29
		BATH/MISC. TOILETRIES												
22	1P2	WET ONES POP-UP TOWELETTES	2.2	25	30	22	19	6	53	46	15	82	79	88
		HAIR PRODUCTS												
2C	1S4B	MISS CLAIROL NATURAL WEAR	5.3	25	43	37	19	1	37	19	1	57	33	6
13	1P4	TEGRIN MEDICATED SHAMPOO	1.7	14	21	32	27	4	68	58	9	105	100	53
		MEDICINES/PROPRIETARY REMEDY												
3	1P4B	CONTAC COLD CAPSULES	1.2	5	8	43	39	8	92	83	17	142	143	100
4	1P	SOMINEX TABLETS	1.7	19	19	24	23	12	62	59	31	95	102	182
16	1P4B	BUFFERIN TABLETS	1.3	7	10	37	36	8	79	77	17	122	133	100
24	1P4B	ROMILAR III COUGH SYRUP	1.7	13	17	32	28	6	68	60	13	105	103	76
26	1P B	GERITOL	2.0	25	26	27	19	12	69	49	31	106	84	182
28	H1/2P2B	DI-GEL ANTACID LIQUID/TABLET	1.9	41	24	16	12	6	70	53	26	108	91	153
29	H1/2P4	ASPERGUM	1.0	16	6	26	25	6	101	97	23	155	167	135
30	3/4P4B	SINAREST NASAL SPRAY	1.7	24	17	23	21	11	66	60	31	102	103	182
153	H1/2P2B	PREPARATION H SUPP/OINTMENT	2.3	43	31	14	10	4	61	44	18	94	76	106
155	1P2	ANACIN TABLETS	2.3	30	31	23	18	5	56	44	12	86	76	71
158	H1/2P	VIVARIN STIMULANT TABLETS	1.6	38	16	15	13	5	70	61	23	108	105	135
159	H1/2P	SERUTAN LAXATIVE	1.3	33	11	20	16	6	94	75	28	145	129	165
166	H1/2P2	TEGRIN MEDICATED CREAM	1.8	38	23	14	13	6	61	57	26	94	98	153
167	H1/2P	BEN-GAY LOTION	.9	18	4	26	24	9-	122	112	42	188	193	247
174	H1/2P	BLISTEX & BLISTIK LIP BALM	1.4	36	12	15	15	6	70	70	28	108	121	165

- FEWER THAN 50 WORDS IN AD.

with the subconscious level in which there are strong motivating forces that the individual respondent does not recognize. Other thinking levels, of course, are the outer level that those about us can see, and the conscious inner level of personality, a sort of private dream world. This, too, is an area for motivational probing.

Although there are many ways to obtain information, a good portion of motivational research depends upon three techniques: (1) Depth interviewing. (2) Focused group interviewing. (3) Projective approaches. *Depth interviews* are not, of course, the exclusive province of motivational researchers; all types of researchers have conducted depth interviews for years. Such interviews may last one or two hours during which questions are asked that seem, and often are, quite indirect but which, nevertheless, center around the problems investigated. Unsuspected motivations are often unearthed through these interviews. *Focused group interviews* do in the group what depth interviews do on an individual basis. A group leader introduces various stimuli (advertisements, parts of advertisements, products, packages) thus stirring an informal discussion among the six to twelve

Fig. 19-5

The Photo-Graphic Brandt Eye-Camera.

The light on the subject's head hits the area observed by the reader but, since it is infra-red, cannot be seen by the subject. The 16mm spectoscopic film in the camera, however, records both content observed and the infra-red spot. Thus the exact location, duration, and sequence of every fixation are recorded.

Courtesy Dr. Edmund W. J. Faison, President, Visual Research International.

persons in the group. An interesting result of group interviews is the sometimes startling frankness with which group members will discuss subjects that could hardly be approached in the individual depth interview. Likewise, because group members usually try hard to contribute, it will often be found that the group will contribute more points and more talk than will be obtained from the individual interview.

Projective approaches, more strongly identified with motivational research than the other techniques, use (a) Free word association. Typically, respondenst are given lists of words, one at a time, and asked to respond with the first word that comes to mind. Judgment is made on the basis of the frequency with which a word may come up, or how long it takes for the word to appear. (b) Sentence completion. Respondents finish a series of incomplete sentences. A respondent will be guided along a certain direction but, if correctly handled, he will not know what data is to be obtained. (c) Picture responses. An illustration is shown to the respondent who then interprets the illustration or tells its story.

A sort of madness overcame portions of the advertising industry when motivational research first appeared as a tool of advertising researchers. Swiftly people began using motivationai research who had no knowledge of its meaning or techniques. Many times ordinary consumer surveys might have obtained more information for them, and at considerably lower cost. Of late, however, the fever has subsided as advertising men have become aware of the limitations of "MR," as well as its virtues. While much hitherto buried information has been obtained through motivational research, its use brings up questions among the companies, advertising agencies, and the media that employ it. For example, who is going to validate the results among the average businessmen who pay for the research? How can these businessmen judge the validity of the work conducted by psychologists? Too, the businessmen ask how they are to judge the accuracy of the techniques used when arguments persist among the motivational researchers themselves, not only about the techniques for getting the information but about the interpretation of the results obtained.

Regardless of the doubts and queries and the uneasiness of businessmen suddenly wading in the esoteric terminology of the psychologist, motivational research, properly conducted, is here to stay. It will remain in some form or other because it helps reduce guesswork in advertising creation by giving copywriters answers to those eternal questions: "What do they *really* like or dislike?" "What do they *really* want?" "What do they *really* think?"

The absorption of creative advertising men with these questions is illustrated by the use during the past few years of such techniques as psychogalvanometer testing, and hypnosis. The former, utlizing an instrument greatly akin to the "lie detector" police work, has been used to measure involuntary reactions to various advertising stimuli. A number of media and large companies have tried this form of testing. Both galvanometer testing and the use of hypnosis, like the use of motivational research, evidence the advertising man's discontent with the surface answers obtained through conventional survey methods.

RESEARCHING COPY AFTER PUBLICATION

Who reads the copy?—readership studies

The advertisement has been published. No advertiser alive can help wanting to know certain things about that advertisement. How many persons read it? How thoroughly did they read? How much advertiser and product identification was created? How well do the readers remember the advertisement? What features of the advertisement obtained the best readership? All these questions and more are answered to a degree by readership studies undertaken after publication of the advertisement. A great argument has raged about readership techniques from the time they were first used. Advertising men have shouted at or for the various methods. You may be sure of one thing, however. You will always have some form of readership study. Like them or not, you will need to know the various methods, and you should determine which one you believe in most firmly. You should learn readership terminology and the mechanical procedures for detecting misleading readership research.

The readership report, like radio and TV ratings has become an obsession in some circles. The magic percentage figures of readership studies are hypnotic. They lull the advertiser into satisfaction with his advertising or they goad him into anger. With many advertisers a high percentage of readership is the final test of an advertisement's success. "The readership reports say we're on the right track," says the man who produced the advertisement. The advertiser leans back satisfied. Yet, there are so many variables to consider in readership reports that you will be a very wise copywriter never to accept a readership report at face value. Look behind the figures. Don't let the mesmerizing effect of good readership keep you from setting off on new copy trails. An evil of the reports is that they encourage "status quo" advertising. "We're woing along fine," cries a cautious executive. "The readership reports are good. Why endanger our success with that new technique?" The hesitancy is understandable. Yet, new ideas are the life of advertising. New ideas are responsible for increased sales and higher manufacturing output. If you rely too slavishly on readership reports, you will find a good formula, and you will never leave it. Some advertisers have done well under that system. Most advertising, however, has been flexible. Most advertisers have been willing to try for the greater reward—have been willing to experiment.

Many good advertising ideas would have been lost had smug, satisfied executives refused to experiment. Yet such refusals are frequent when readership figures for present campaigns are good. A bit of the gambler is needed to desert the high readership campaign for the bold, new idea.

Assume, as you read now about readership study techniques, that there is misinformation in the best of them—and some good in most of them. What you find—good or bad—will depend upon your capacity for objective analysis.

Testing by recognition

"What do you usually read?" "What advertisements did you see in yesterday's paper?" This type of recall questioning was used for years to determine advertisement reading. Opinions were obtained, but not actual behavior. As mentioned before, you will find a big area between what people *say* they do and what they *actually* do.

Recognition testing (which is based on presenting published material to find out what has actually been read) ignores opinion. Actual reading behavior is measured. A widely known newspaper-readership study using the recognition principle was the Continuing Study of Newspaper Readership.* In magazine readership studies, Daniel Starch and Staff are probably best known among research organizations using recognition testing.

*The Studies ended in 1952 because by then it was felt that further studies would simply duplicate information already obtained but individual newspapers using the same

A quick glance at the technique used in the Continuing Study and the Starch study will show you how newspaper and magazine studies are conducted. Some of the essential differences in analyzing readership of the two media will be uncovered. Other prominent studies that employed the recognition methods were the Continuing Study of Farm Publications, and the Continuing Study of Magazine Audiences conducted by Crossley Incorporated. Both introduced new twists in the procedure, but the recognition principle guided their technique.

Continuing Study of Newspaper Readership—method

An interviewer went over a newspaper with a person who said that he had read the issue of the newspaper being tested. The reader pointed out every news item, picture, and advertisement he had read in the test issue. Reading of local advertisements was recorded in terms of how many men and women read the advertisement. National advertisements were checked also for reading of headlines, illustrations, and copy blocks. Reading totals for the approximately 450 men and women interviewed for each study were totaled and added to the accumulative totals for the more than 100 Continuing Studies that were made for newspapers before the studies were discontinued.

Advertisement Readership Service—by Daniel Starch and staff

Interviewers check respondents on reading of advertisements one-half page or larger in a number of national publications. Respondents are divided equally among men and women. The advertisement as a whole is checked on a three way basis:

1. *Noted*—reader has seen the advertisement.
2. *Advertiser-associated*—reader has seen or read the advertisement enough to know the product or advertiser.
3. *Read-most*—reader has read 50% or more of the advertisement's reading matter.

Parts of the advertisement—headline, subheads, text units, illustrations, and logotypes are also checked for observation and reading.

In addition to determining per cent of reading for advertisements and their component parts, the Starch service also provides cost ratios of the advertisements and ranks them in terms of dollars spent to obtain readers. These figures are refined to the point where the studies tell the advertiser just how much it costs merely to get his advertisement seen, or seen and associated, or read most. Thus you might get a high cost for the "seen" classification but your copy may be read so well that a high percentage of those who read the advertisement read most of the copy. Your cost ratio for "read-most" would then be low.

The real value of recognition studies is in cumulative studies. It would be foolish to let one study entirely influence an important decision. You can compare that one study, however, with other studies. The cumulative figures can show you whether your copy was "on" or "off." The principal strength of readership studies is in the long-trend aspect. As study piles on study, you see certain appeals pulling consistently. Certain ideas pull every time—others fail consistently. The studies attempt to give the "why."

Weak spots in recognition testing

1. *Poor memory, dishonesty, false pride*—either in combination or singly—reduce the believability of readership figures. Sometimes magazine researchers attempt to measure the effect of the three factors by setting up a "confusion control." Thus they ask people to

point out advertisements they have read in a certain magazine. The advertisements have not yet appeared in any publication but have been so cleverly inserted in the test issue that the respondents think they are already-run advertisements. The researcher finds out how much the reading of such advertisements totals and makes a statistical allowance for this confusion factor in his final figures. So many people become honestly confused in readership tests that an allowance *must* be made for this "honest" confusion. Marlboro advertisements, for example, have a strong family resemblance. It is easy to think that you have seen a specific Marlboro advertisement when actually you are remembering not that advertisement but the impression created by the series. Other persons, ashamed to admit they read certain items, skip by them when being interviewed. Thus the accuracy of the readership percentage is reduced.

2. *All reading is not reported.* Often respondents will say firmly, "No, I didn't read that advertisement." Quite often the interviewer will accept the negative answer instead of making certain that the respondent has not actually read the advertisement. Much reading is not declared by the respondent. If respondents fail to tell you what they *have* read, you are helpless. There is no way to correct for this factor, nor to validate your findings. The man conducting the test has nothing to work from. As one researcher has ruefully said, "If certain product advertising get no more readers than the surveys sometimes report, the products would have to be pulled off the market."

3. *The recognition study measures memory or observation—it does not indicate sales or conviction power.* This is probably the strongest objection to readership studies as a whole. Proponents of recognition studies, such as Daniel Starch, have attempted to show that there is a relationship between high readership and high sales. Starch has said, (*Factors in Readership Measurements*) "In general, the more readers an advertisement attracts and the more completely it is read, the more sales are produced by that advertisement —except that some types of copy treatment actually repel buyers. The more reading there is of such advertisements, the less buying there is." Opponents point to many advertisements which obtained low readership but which pulled big coupon returns—and vice versa. "You can't sell 'em if they don't see your advertisement" is the usual report. The answer to that is, of course, that a thousand persons may see your advertisement yet no one will buy the product.

Many times, too, short copy will rate higher in Starch's "read-most" figures than will long copy. Yet the lower-rated long-copy advertisement will often far outsell the other because the readers it sells it "hooks."

In a sense, high readership and sales might be in opposite corners of the ring. You may have devised your advertisement for high readership. Tricky, unusual features may get you your high figures, but you may have worked so hard for attention that you crowded out a powerful selling message. You may be full of pride when you see the Starch reports, but your sales manager may feel a different emotion as he looks over his falling sales.

The *real* readership is the readership of your sales story by people who may subsequently *buy*—not general, casual readership. You should ask, "How many *prospects* read our message?" A diamond advertisement might get high readership among fat matrons sighing for their pre-marriage romance. The diamond salesman will trade a dozen fat matrons, however, for one slim, young bride-to-be—*she* represents prospect readership.

Recognition testing has its good points, too

1. Regardless of the lack of conviction-measuring, *recognition studies do give an adequate (if not entirely reliable) idea of the observation and reading obtained by a particular advertisement.* Even hard-boiled mail-order men—the kind always screaming for "direct results"—use a form of advertising which they didn't try generally until readership studies proved it effective—the editorial technique. Yet mail-order men scoff almost in unison at readership studies. "Sales, not readership" is their motto.

2. As already mentioned, *the recognition study measures actual reading behavior*—a more reliable measurement than that obtained through opinion or what the respondents *say* they have read.

3. *The method is useful for comparing readership of different campaign advertisements, or competitors' advertisements, too.* Unlike mail-order advertising, newspaper or magazine advertising may run a long time before sales results show that advertisements are not being read. A readership survey gives the advertiser a reasonably quick and accurate method of checking advertising effectiveness. Poor format, for example, might discourage readership. One advertiser provides backing for this point. Readership was poor on an advertisement he felt certain contained effective copy. When he examined the advertisement critically he discovered the trouble—the format was dull, conventional, lifeless. Using the same copy but giving it a new dress, he tried again. This time he inserted several lively illustrations instead of one drab one. Copy was broken into small doses. Captions were plentiful. The advertisement was a success!

A warning should be made here. When comparing readership results, say in a Starch report, you should compare products in the same group. You most valid comparison in readership is made with your competitor's advertising. Comparing your readership with that of a non-competitor is a meaningless sort of activity.

Other recognition techniques

1. *Measurement of separate advertisements.* Respondent is shown a number of advertisements cut out from a newspaper or magazine. He selects advertisements he thinks he has seen published. He is then asked detailed questions about each of the advertisements. An advantage of this method is that the interviewer can thus lessen the influence of nearby editorial matter on the reading of advertisements. Often in recognition tests, a respondent will answer that he has seen an advertisement simply because he has read the editorial matter near it. Also, since the advertisement is taken out of the usual reading sequence of the magazine, there is no chance for this factor to inflate the claimed reading. The method, of course, still has the usual disadvantages found in recognition testing.

2. *Controlled recognition testing.* A number of techniques have been worked out to correct the interview error occasioned by respondents' dishonesty or faulty memory. Some of these techniques require control groups. In a typical situation one group has seen the advertisements, the other has not. Reading differences are then balanced.

Another technique—the system of "confusion control" already described—uses the standard procedure of showing advertisements that have been run and others that have not. By using a simple formula the researchers can weed out the unreliable interviews and come out with a close estimate of actual readership. The formula for this type of testing runs like this:

1. 100 persons are interviewed.
2. 3 persons claimed readership of an advertisement not yet published.
3. 33 persons indicate readership of an advertisement that *has* run.
4. Subtract 3 from 100—equals 97.
5. Subtract 3 from 33—equals 30.
6. Readership is 30 persons out of 97—equals 30.9%.

This method, used in magazine and newspaper studies, has also been used by the Traffic Audit Bureau (TAB) in analyzing poster reading.

Recognition testing—good or bad?

Results from recognition studies have pointed the way to many techniques now used by copywriters. Recipes in food copy, for example, were shown from the first readership study to assure almost good attention from readers. Editorial techniques—shown by readership studies to get high readership—have been used more and more. Questions on layout and position have been settled through recognition studies. Such fundamental questions as "Will people read long copy?" "Does small type stop reading?" have been answered by recognition studies.

Not one, but many, studies have provided the answers. Questions are still being settled. A mass of evidence is becoming available as recognition studies pile up. Admitted that the conclusions are averages; they cannot be projected to every individual case. Still they point the way. The long-range value of the studies is obvious. Consider vitamins, for instance. For years advertisement copy that could squeeze vitamins in somewhere had almost automatically good readership. Then it was noticed through recognition studies that vitamins were not catching so many readers—the vitamin honeymoon was over and food advertisers began to think of other appeals.

Recognition studies are usually praised by those advertisers whose advertisements get high readership. They are often called unrealistic and silly by advertisers who happen to produce low readership advertising. Despite the latter group, you will profit from the findings of recognition studies. They have been useful to advertising men for some years now. They can help you.

Identification testing

A typical identification test proceeds like this: You are shown an advertisement in which all identifying features have been inked or pasted out. You are then asked to identify the advertisement by indicating what company, product, or service is being advertised. The rest of the advertisements in the newspaper or magazine have been "masked." Whether the results from identification testing is debatable. Some advertisers feel, however, that high identification of their advertisements gives an important clue to the success of the advertising—especially in campaign advertising, since the advertiser wants assurance that his campaign idea and format are going over.

Recall tests

A recall test tries to determine what you remember about an advertisement. Unlike in the recognition test, usually no advertisement is shown. The recall test aims at determining the positive, lasting impressions made by an advertisement some time after it has run. Brand-consciousness is probably measured better through recall testing than through any other method. Since no advertisement is shown, the respondent must yank up facts about the advertising out of his mind without help from his visual sense. This form of testing is best administered by research experts, since the posing of the questions and interpretation of results are jobs for a specialist. Three forms of recall testing dominate: 1. Unaided recall. 2. Aided recall. 3. Triple associates.

1. *Unaided recall.* This form of recall testing is used very little. It consists of asking questions that provide no starting clue on which the respondent may base his answer. Information obtained from the vague questions that must be asked yield vague results. For instance, you might be asked: "What radio commercials do you remember hearing lately?" The same question might be asked about advertisements you have seen. Without any assistance from the interviewer, you are thus forced to pull out into the light some of the hundreds of advertisement impressions jostling themselves in your mind. Trying to attach some meaning to the answers is a nightmare for the researcher. On an individual basis it is almost impossible to isolate the factors that would cause you, as the respondent, to name some particular advertisement and not some other advertisement. On a mass basis, it would take a terrifying number of interviews to bring out any usable facts. Supposing, for example, you were asked, "What recent advertising copy has impressed you most?" Picture the possible answers to this question. Think of the interviews needed to develop any worth-while facts. Then think of the countless variables that might have brought the answers. For practical copy testing you may forget the unaided recall.

2. *Aided recall.* Advertisers spend millions to create brand-consciousness. This "burning" of the brand on the consumer is one of advertising's most important jobs. "How well is our advertising putting our brand across?" is a question of quivering interest if you want consumers to walk into a store to ask for Wheaties, or Ivory Soap, or of Philco. One of aided recall's particular jobs is to indicate what brand a consumer thinks of when a certain type of product is mentioned, such as: tooth paste—Pepsodent; tires—Goodyear; canned soup—Campbell's. Perhaps you feel that testing brand-consciousness is quite apart from copy testing. In a sense your feeling is justified, since such testing doesn't delve deeply into the copy as to Flesch tests, readership tests, and check lists. Lack of brand-recognition may, however, indicate that little association is being created between a type of product and a certain brand. Poor copy may be one of the reasons for lack of identification. Other reasons might be faults in the position of advertisements, illustrations, media, timing, and campaign continuity.

What is the principal *importance* of the aided recall test? Simply this: It indicates at least the beginning of an association between the brand and a product. Scientific illustrating, expert copy, and page advertisements are useless if such association isn't made. If, when you want a blanket or chewing gum, you don't think of brands to fill your requirements like North Star or Wrigley's Spearmint—then the copywriter, artists, and other advertisement creators have wasted their time. If they have succeeded, the recall test will indicate not only the success of your advertising but also the relative failure of your competitors in obtaining brand-consciousness.

The aided recall using a question such as—"Can you name a brand of shaving cream you have seen or heard advertised recently?"—is virtually useless for single advertisements but can be useful for measuring campaign impact. From the answers, you learn whether the campaign is moving forward or is failing to impress consumers.

One of the more interesting forms of recall testing is provided in *Impact* testing in which respondents "play back" for interviewers what they remember of advertising they have seen in magazines read in a recent period. Gallup & Robinson, a well-known advertising research organization has led the field in impact testing. The company has some of the biggest names in American advertising as clients. These clients, who pay substantial fees for impact testing of each product they advertise, are informed by Gallup & Robinson what has been good and what has been bad about their advertising as revealed in each impact testing procedure that has been carried out. This information is given to clients on a regular basis in "clinics" that are usually conducted by Gallup & Robinson men in the client's offices.

The test itself consists of a long interview that lasts one or two hours. A person is approved as a respondent after he has first proved that he has actually read the magazine being used for test purposes. He is then shown names of all products which have been advertised in full page or double page advertisements. His next job is to tell what he remembers of the advertisements that he thinks he remembers seeing in the magazine issue. When he tells what he remembers he is, in research parlance, "playing back" the advertiser's message. What the advertiser hopes will appear in the playback are:

(a) Sales points or arguments
(b) The advertiser's principal message
(c) Reasons for buying
(d) What ideas were obtained
(e) What went through the respondent's mind as he read

It is obvious from a glance at these points that impact testing goes considerably beyond recognition testing in that its objective is to measure the effect of exposure to advertising rather than to determine mere reading of the copy message. Idea registration and buying urge may often be determined from impact testing. While the aims of impact testing, like those of motivational research, are to dig deeper than the surface to determine what to put into advertising or to determine what makes advertising work, the method has its difficulties. Expense of such research is one factor since costs of the method limit its use rather generally to the larger advertisers with big-budget campaigns. This limitation is unfortunate since many smaller advertisers are thus frozen out and, as is very often the case, they are the ones who could profit most from using impact testing.

Another criticism, often expressed by researchers, is that the method is too difficult—that the procedure is "under-stimulating" which means that the clues given for recall are so weak that an advertising impression has to be massive before it can be recalled. Those who criticise impact testing in this manner, on the other hand, often call the recognition method, as used by Starch, "over-stimulating," meaning that exposure to advertisements during interviews is often more intense and longer than during normal reading of the magazine. Although there is some validity in the charge that the impact method is difficult, the fact remains that a great amount of copy guidance is obtained from impact interviews. Advertisers who employ impact research use it for long periods and seem satisfied.

Speaking of aided recall testing in general, it must be conceded that a single advertisement has so little chance to catch attention and sink the brand harpoon into the reader that you might well think of aided recall as used mostly for campaign testing. Yet the very success of a campaign destroys, to some extent, the chance of using aided recall testing to measure the effect of the campaign copy. Take Lucky Strikes, for instance. If you were asked what brand of cigarettes you had seen advertised recently the answer might pop out, "Lucky Strikes." Actually you may have seen more advertising by Marlboros, Winstons, or Chesterfield. Over the years, however, Lucky Strike had possibly built more impact than any other single brand. Your answer, then, was not impelled by recent observation but from the piled-up impressions of years. To use aided recall testing for current advertising of a leading product such as Luckies you would need to refer to some unusual feature that had not been used in past years—a slogan, illustration, or headline. This kind of testing, although a form of aided recall, has been given a more impressive title—the triple associates test.

3. *Triple associates test.* Suppose someone came up to you and asked, "What automobile advertises 'Big car quality at lowest cost.' " If at the time Chevrolet was so advertising, and you answered, "Chevrolet," you would have made the three-way connection sought in the triple associates test. Here are the three factors:

(a) Product—low-price automobile.
(b) Brand—Chevrolet.
(c) Copy theme—Big car quality at lowest cost.

As you can see, you are given two elements—the type of product and the theme. Then you supply the brand, thus making the third association. You might not be given the theme exactly as it is used. The question might read, "What automobile advertises that it gives the value of a big car at a lower cost?"

Finding the extent of the association of brand with copy theme is the principal goal of the triple associates test. The information is used for determining *campaign* effectiveness only. Although the advertiser wants to develop high identification of his copy theme, he is even more hopeful that the triple associates test will connect *brand* and *theme.*

Consumer recognition of the theme for itself is of little value. In some campaigns, actual harm has been revealed when it was discovered that consumers associated the copy themes with the wrong products. The uncovering of such misinformation is another value of the triple associates test. If the advertiser discovers that a high percentage of the consumers are identifying his copy theme with his competitor's product, then he'd better scan his advertising carefully—especially if the campaign has been running for some time.

Sales increases may be due to many factors other than the effectiveness of current advertising. A rising sales curve may be the final result of good advertising that appeared a number of months ago. It may, also, be due to improved selling methods, a change in the price levels, a more favorable business climate.

Should your triple associates test show bad results, you might, in view of the preceding, do some worrying about your advertising even though sales curves are going up. The upward trend might exist *despite* the advertising.

As in aided-recall testing, you must be careful if you are the dominant advertiser. To illustrate, imagine that you are the first peanut advertiser to promote vacuum-packed peanuts. Imagine further that you are the *only* really big peanut advertiser. Suppose for your triple associates test you ask, "What peanuts are vacuum-packed?" How much reliability could you place in the findings when many persons could *guess* your brand—if they didn't *know.* To get around this difficulty, you can ask the consumers to indicate by brand which of *several* products are vacuum-packed. In this list you might name such products as coffee, soup, pickles, peanuts, and shoe-string potatoes. If the respondent included peanuts among the several products vacuum-packed, you would know that your advertising of the feature was making an impression. Similar testing conducted at regular intervals should tell you whether your campaign theme and brand recognition were becoming stronger or weaker.

To sum up—think of the following in connection with the triple associates test: (1) It is an excellent way to determine brand and theme association in *campaign* advertising. (2) Through this test you can often obtain a more reliable indication of the success of your advertising than you will get from rising sales. Many times, moreover, you will find a strong correlation between sales and high brand- and theme-awareness—and vice versa. (3) On the negative side, don't forget—as in so many tests of copy, the results don't necessarily measure conviction or selling power. You can establish superb recognition of theme and brand but the consumers may buy your competitor's product. Often it's easier to capture attention than conviction—especially if you depend on "irritating" consumers into becoming aware of you. In such cases the triple associates test results may look good despite what consumers may actually think of your product and your advertising.

Communiscope testing

In the section on impact testing it was mentioned that critics have called the Starch technique "over-stimulating" and the impact method "under-stimulating." An answer to these asserted weaknesses was, according to its sponsores, Communiscope testing. This form of testing was begun because its originators believes neither recognition nor impact testing provide measurements sensitive enough to produce statistically significant differences among most printed advertisements.

A long-used testing device—the tachistoscope—provides the principal means for Communiscope research. This device is a slide projector hooked to an electric timer. In the test situation, advertisements on slides are flashed rapidly before respondents who then play back what they have seen. Backers of the Communiscope method assert that a respondent will be stimulated enough to remember whether he has seen the advertisements and what he remembers about them—but he will not be "overstimulated" by having been given so much time to look that he "learned" the advertisement while the test was administered.

Test reports will give three types of information to clients: (1) percentage of adults in the United States who recognize and recall the advertisement checked; (2) what impression and meaning was derived from the advertisement; (3) respondent's emotional reaction to the advertisement.

A criticism of Communiscope testing by those who favor recognition testing is that it is impossible to measure exposure to advertising and the influence of the advertising on those exposed to it at the same time. These critics add that the importance of memorability has been overstressed since it cannot be assumed that the reader who can play back the contents of an advertisement has necessarily been favorably influenced by the advertisement—nor does failure to play the advertisement back prove that the advertisement has had no influence.

From the viewpoint of supporters of the impact method, Communiscope testing fails to supply the interpretive data and analysis supplied by the former.

Copy testing through sales tests

You will find sales tests mentioned in many books as a form of copy testing. It *is* true that the efficiency of different copy approaches is discovered in sales tests. *Also,* it is true that packaging, pricing, choice of media, labor conditions, income trends, salesmen, inventory controls, and other elements affect results of sales tests. The form of advertising—position, advertising size, frequency—are tested as much as the copy itself. Since copy is just *one* of the forces being examined in sales tests, it does not seem necessary for this book to dip very far into the subject. Copy has been the principal object of analysis in other copy-testing procedures—since *you* are close to such tests. The sales tests, on the contrary, are closer to the market-research man, or the sales department. You will probably not have actual contact with such tests except to supply the original copy for the campaign. After that, you lose sight of the test as the sales and marketing men move in. A sales test, briefly explained, goes something like this:

You decide to test the effect of your advertising in two markets. One of the market areas is considered a "control" area. The other is the "test" area. Three or more cities are usually found in each area. The new campaign will be used in the test section. In the control area you will either: (1) run no advertising or (2) continue to run your old campaign. Sales results in the two areas will then be compared by checking store inventories in selected stores before, during, and after the advertising is run.

Possibly you will run a different campaign in each of the test cities. The results will enable you to compare the campaigns against one another as well as against the control cities.

Some advertising men believe only in a sales test, because they look upon the test as operating under "actual" conditions as opposed to "artificial" conditions of other forms of copy research. Yet many factors make the sales tests extremely difficult to control. Results must be examined with great care to avoid erroneous conclusions. Some of the difficulties:

1. Selection of appropriate control and test cities.

2. Sales ability of salesmen in the different areas. Poor salesmen in the test cities and good salesmen in the control cities might throw the whole test off, since the new campaign might thus show poor sales despite effective advertising.

3. Dealer reaction. Unless dealers cooperate equally in all the test areas, sales variations will occur quite apart from the advertising.

4. Competitive advertising and sales efforts may vary from city to city during the test period.

5. Media differences are hard to control. Some newspapers and radio stations are much more aggressive than others in their merchandising promotions. They do a vigorous job of backing up the advertisers. Also, they may vary greatly in the amount of reader or listening interest they command.

6. Unusual weather conditions during the test may affect sales results. A paralyzing snow storm affecting one of the cities might affect its sales record negatively.

Think of the factors named. When you realize that there are many *other* variables and that, in addition, a sales test is expensive and time-consuming, you can see why it is not of great concern to you.

Testing—general conclusions

An effort should be made to keep up with research methods and organizations—some of which have been discussed in this chapter. Any alert copywriter should know about the many studies performed for business publication advertisers, as well as the complicated world of television research.

There are, in addition, others that may or may not be important to you depending on the nature of your work and where you work. Do not let the virtues of any one system blind you to its faults. Be everlastingly critical. Do not let testing replace good sense. Good sense must be used in analyzing and applying copy testing. Consider the Flesch formula, for example. Your copy will, according to the readability formula receive an equally high rating if the copy is printed backwards or if the sentences are jumbled. Since the word count, affixes, and personal references are the same in either case, the readability score will be the same. Good sense is the final determinant of copy effectiveness in this case—as it is in every copy-testing method.

Your judgment of sales points, human nature, and effective writing style are *the* important factors in copywriting. The copy tests are your assistants—they'll never be your boss. The best businessman and the best copywriter get off the track occasionally. Copy research is valuable if it does nothing but reduce the margin of error in the guesses of advertising men. It can unkink the thumb in the famous "rule of thumb" measurement you have heard so much about. When you lose touch with the market and the consumer, copy testing may bring you back. If you were to be asked the principal values of copy testing you might answer:

1. To determine in *advance* of publication what copy style, copy approach, or copy appeals are likely to obtain the greatest readership and/or sales conviction.

2. To determine *after* publication the quantitative and qualitative aspects of readership and thus to indicate what copy techniques should be continued, discontinued, or modified for future use.

3. To obtain through cumulative findings a body of information about copy that advertisers may use to produce advertising of the greatest efficiency—advertising that will cost the advertiser less in time, effort, and money because it avoids the mistakes of the past.

Copywriting And The Law

Any discussion of the legal problems in advertising copywriting is likely to appear discouraging in the first instance because it almost necessarily will read like a list of prohibitions. The resources of the English language, however, are almost infinite. Millions of words of copy are written every year without running afoul of any legal difficulties whatever. It is the purpose of this chapter to point out situations in which legal problems may arise and to show how they can be avoided by proper advance planning. The alternative might be serious and costly court proceedings in which the agency could be held responsible along with the advertiser.

The single most important principle is to get the facts and make certain they are correct. Any attempt to write copy about a product or service without knowing in complete detail exactly what it is and does will invite legal difficulties. It must be emphasized, though, that even telling the absolute truth is not always enough. Each sentence in an advertisement, considered separately, may be literally true and yet the entire advertisement as a whole may be misleading. This can come about because statements that ought to be made are omitted, or because the advertisement is composed or set up in such a way as to create a misleading impression. If the copy can be understood in two different ways, the advertiser is not excused just because one of its meanings can be sustained as accurate.

It is essential to bear in mind also that most consumers are trusting and unsophisticated people. It is not a defense to a charge of false advertising to show that a particularly intelligent and acute reader should have been able to figure out the true meaning of the copy. The standard to be applied is not the level of intelligence of the average purchaser, but of someone even less knowledgeable than that.

Television creates its own special problems for the copywriter. The visual portion of a TV commercial may be misleading even though the off-camera voice is telling the exact truth; or the audio may be the means of misrepresenting the picture that appears on the screen. Product demonstrations, in particular, must be genuine, and the accompanying dialogue must be honest and accurate.

There is no point in trying to be tricky when writing advertising copy. Short term gains in sales possibly might result, but in the long run such a policy can do only harm to the advertiser. This can come about through loss of good will from disillusioned customers even though no government agency ever may get around to commencing a legal proceeding designed to force the discontinuance of the misleading copy.

Thus far in this introductory section, we have been dealing with the category of what generally are called "product claims." To show that the law is not completely arbitrary, there is another recognized category known as "puffery" or "puffing." Under this heading come the harmless exaggerations that are expressions of opinion rather than claims of some objective quality or characteristic for the product. For example, even the most gullible consumer is considered capable of grappling with the fact that such statements as "the best of its kind," "the most beautiful" or "the finest" might not be literally true. This does not mean that a false objective claim can be legalized by disguising it in the form of a statement of opinion. If an automobile will not get 50 miles to a gallon of gas, the advertisement still will be misleading even if the statement is put in the form of the manufacturer's opinion that, "I believe this car will get 50 miles to the gallon."

The difference is between a representation that induces the purchase and one that does not. The consumer who buys "the funniest book you ever read" rightfully can expect to be amused, but he doesn't really expect the advertiser to be able to prove the superlative.

Product claims and statements of opinion, of course, are not the only areas in which legal problems arise in advertising. Permission to use copyrighted material, defamatory statements, the right to use a person's name or picture, proper trade-mark usage and idea piracy are just some of the other areas where an awareness in advance of the possible legal pitfalls may save a great deal of trouble and expense that otherwise might be encountered. An attempt will be made here to discuss those topics that are most likely to affect the work of the copywriter.

FEDERAL TRADE COMMISSION

The one government agency most concerned with problems of advertising is the Federal Trade Commission. This agency, under the Federal Trade Commission Act, has broad authority to proceed against "deceptive acts or practices" in almost all kinds of commercial activity. The theory of the law is that false or misleading advertising, like other deceptive acts and practices, is an unfair method of competition. If a false advertisement succeeds in its purpose, it will give the advertiser an unfair advantage over his truthful competitors. But false advertising is an offense even though no competitors are hurt, because the Federal Trade Commission Act is also designed to protect consumers. The FTC constantly brings numerous cease and desist proceedings under this law.

The FTC also functions in several other and different ways. It issues advertising guides, trade practice rules and standard rules. In addition to the Federal Trade Commission Act itself, which is phrased in broad general terms as indicated above, the FTC administers several special statutes dealing with particular fields of commerce, including margarine, wool, fur and textile products.

FALSE AND MISLEADING ADVERTISING IN GENERAL

The Federal Trade Commission is concerned with so many different varieties of false and misleading advertising that it is almost impossible to categorize all of them. There are, however, certain specific areas of difficulty that constantly recur in advertising cases brought by the FTC. Some of those with particular interest to advertising copywriters are discussed in the succeeding sections.

Guarantees

There seems to be a common temptation to use the word "guaranteed" rather loosely. It is a very rare occurrence when an advertiser actually guarantees his product unconditionally, but that is the way the word "guaranteed" will be construed legally unless any conditions that may be attached to the offer are stated clearly in the advertisement.

If, for example, the advertiser means that he merely will replace a defective article rather than refund the purchase price, then the advertisement must say so. If the guarantee is limited in terms of time, then this must be stated clearly. If the guarantee applies only to defective parts rather than to the entire article, then the advertisement should make this clear. Frequently there are extra charges, such as shipping expenses for the defective merchandise or the return of the repaired article; these conditions must be set forth clearly in the advertisement.

A "money-back" guarantee means that the customer is entitled to a cash refund, not just a credit slip or an exchange of merchandise. The expression "satisfaction or your money back" should not be used unless the advertiser is willing to let the customer himself be the sole judge of whether or not he is satisfied.

Similar words such as "warranty" or "warranted" also require the same treatment as "guarantee." The word "bonded" signifies something more. This should not be used in advertising unless an actual bond has been posted by the advertiser to insure that the customer will get what he is promised under the terms of the guarantee or warranty.

An example of a suitably stated guarantee with certain limitations might be, "Guaranteed against defective materials and workmanship for 90 days." But this guarantee would not be fulfilled merely by shipping a replacement part under circumstances where the customer had to pay an installation charge, shipping expenses, or the like. In all cases the true nature of the guarantee must be disclosed clearly; there should be no doubt about what the advertiser is willing to do and what, if anything, the customer will have to do in order to obtain the benefit of the guarantee.

Premiums

When an article of merchandise is offered as a premium, it is essential for the copywriter to learn as much as possible about the premium, just as he must learn about the product of the advertiser itself. A misdescribed premium is the responsibility of the advertiser, not of the manufacturer of the premium merchandise.

The most common problem arising out of the use of premiums is a misrepresentation of their value. Sometimes advertisers who are extremely careful when making claims about their own products are somewhat less careful in describing the premiums that they offer. If an advertisement states that a premium is worth a certain amount or has a value of a stated sum, that amount should be the price at which the premium merchandise actually is sold customarily when offered for sale on its own.

Premium offers also raise a multitude of problems under separate state laws. In order to make it practical to use premiums in national distribution, it is common to take two precautions. In the first place, premium coupons have a cash value assigned to them. This ordinarily is a nominal sum like one-tenth of a cent, but the manufacturer must be prepared to redeem the coupons in cash at that rate on demand. Secondly, the coupon traditionally carries what is called a "nullification clause" reading somewhat along the following lines: "This offer void in any state where prohibited, taxed or otherwise restricted."

Any premium offer on a large scale also may raise serious questions under federal and local tax laws, but these are not the responsibility of the copywriter and obviously are outside the scope of this discussion.

Contests and lotteries

A true contest is a perfectly lawful advertising method. Legal difficulties arise in two principal ways. The first is when the advertiser fails to give the full details of the contest. In that case it frequently turns out to be some sort of a "come-on" device that will cost the reader much more than he ever anticipated in extra fees for tie-breaking puzzles or some other hidden requirement. The second is when it is not a true contest at all, but a lottery, because the element of chance is present. This not only violates the Federal Trade Commission Act as an unfair method of competition, but also is an offense under numerous other laws, state and federal.

Just as in the case of a guarantee, the key to proper contest advertising is to make certain that all of the details are given clearly and unequivocally in the advertisements. This means more than a complicated list of rules in a small type that a highly intelligent person might be able to figure out with close attention to detail.

One famous contest case went all the way to the United States Supreme Court. The advertisement gave the impression that it was a rebus, or picture puzzle, contest with an entry fee of three dollars. Actually, when you examined the fine print, you could find out with very careful analysis that there was a required nine dollar entrance fee and, in addition, that it might be necessary to pay as much as a total of forty-two dollars in order to continue with the tie-breakers. On the basis of the advertiser's own past experience, it was clear that this really was an essay contest to break the ties that were bound to develop. The statistics showed that 90,000 people had submitted answers to the first eighty puzzles. Of these, 35,000 solved all eighty. The first set of tie-breakers was completed by 27,000 people. Eventually it was necessary, under the osbscure language of one of the rules, to write a competitive letter on the subject. "The Puzzle I Found Most Interesting and Educational in This Contest."

This particular contest was involved in a Post Office Department fraud order case rather than a Federal Trade Commission cease and desist proceeding. The general principles, of course, are the same. The key finding of the Postmaster General which the United States Supreme Court upheld was that the advertisements for this puzzle contest had been "deliberately contrived to divert readers' attention from material but adroitly obscured facts."

A lottery is not a contest at all; it involves a payment (or other legal consideration) in exchange for the chance to win a prize. All three elements of consideration, chance and prize must be present or the promotion is not a lottery.

There ordinarily is no difficulty in determining whether or not a prize is involved. If no prize were offered, there would be no legal problems because there would be no contest.

Chance means that the participant has no way of controlling the result. It may be understood as the opposite of skill. An essay contest in which awards are given for merit by impartial judges is perfectly satisfactory because there is no element of chance present; but a baseball contest that requires listing the standings of the teams in both the American and National leagues at the end of a particular month is something completely outside the possibility of control by the participant. It is guess-work, or chance, and not skill.

Consideration generally is found in the entrance requirements. For example, buying some breakfast cereal in order to get the coupon from the back of the box is enough to constitute consideration. It does not matter that the price of the cereal was not increased when the coupon was added to the back of the box. The consumer bought that particular box of cereal when otherwise he might not have purchased any, or have purchased a different brand, and that is sufficient to satisfy the requirement of consideration. The familiar provision for using a "reasonable facsimile" of the entry blank is included in order to avoid a violation of the lottery laws by eliminating the element of consideration.

If there is absolutely no charge or obligation of any kind, then a prize lawfully may be awarded by chance. So-called "sweepstakes," with coupons distributed free to all comers, fall in this category. Conversely, if a prize is given for true skill as distinguished from chance, then it is not unlawful to charge a consideration for permission to enter the contest.

Good purpose, incidentally, does not excuse a lottery. Although enforcement officials rarely crack down on fund-raising drawings for charities, enterprises of this sort technically are lotteries just as if they were operated for advertising purposes or for private gain.

Testimonials and endorsements

An advertiser cannot escape responsibility for a false or misleading product claim by putting it in the mouth of an endorser. Testimonials and endorsements must be true and free from misleading statements. Merely because someone is willing to write a letter saying that a particular drug cured his disease does not mean that this necessarily is so, even though the author of the letter believes it to be true.

The Federal Trade Commission will take action against advertisements containing testimonials given by people who are not competent to pass judgment upon the accuracy of the statements of opinion that they are making. There is a great deal of difference between a baseball player saying that he eats a particular brand of bread and likes it, and the same baseball player saying that eating a particular brand of bread has a beneficial effect upon his health.

There is nothing wrong about paying for a testimonial. The fact that the endorser receives some compensation for giving the testimonial need not be disclosed in the advertisement.

It is improper to take words or sentences out of context. A testimonial should be given in its entirety; or at least the portion that is used should not create a different impression from what the complete text would have implied if given in full.

When testimonials are used in advertising they must be genuine. The natural tendency of any reader of an advertisement containing a testimonial or endorsement is to believe that a real person gave it. A fictitious endorsement, therefore, is an unfair trade practice.

The use of a testimonial also implies automatically that it is reasonably current. If the endorser no longer uses the product or if the product has been so changed since the date of the testimonial that the endorsement no longer fairly applies to the product which is advertised, then the testimonial should be discontinued.

A public opinion poll or market survey is the equivalent of a testimonial on a mass scale and its results must be used with corresponding care. In addition, reference to a poll or survey in advertising copy will be construed as a representation that proper sampling techniques were used and that the sample was of meaningful size.

ADVERTISING GUIDES

On several occasions, the Federal Trade Commission has issued what it calls "Advertising Guides." These are detailed statements that constitute basic policy developed by the Federal Trade Commission in specific business areas and compiled essentially for the use of its own staff. They are released also to the public, particularly for the guidance of advertisers, in the interest of obtaining voluntary cooperation and avoiding legal proceedings.

Deceptive pricing

Claims of special savings, extra discounts, less than the usual price and reductions from ticketed prices, have been among the most troublesome problems faced by FTC enforcement officials. The Deceptive Pricing Advertising Guides go into these problems in explicit detail. Examples of both approved and disapproved types of statements are given, along with the basic principles that will satisfy Federal Trade Commission requirements. A statement, for instance, that there is a reduction or saving from a specified retail price, or from the advertiser's usual or customary retail price, is improper if an artificial mark-up has been used to provide the basis for the claim of a saving. The claim is equally improper if it is based on infrequent or isolated sales, or on a price that was charged some substantial time in the past, unless, or course, these facts are stated clearly and adequately. The saving or reduction must be from the usual and customary retail price of the article in the particular trading area where the statement is made, and the saving or reduction must be from the advertiser's usual and customary retail price charged for the article in the regular course of business.

Certain words and phrases are recognized as representations when an article is being offered for sale to the consuming public at a saving from the usual or customary retail price. Obviously; these should not be used unless the claim is true. Examples of words or phrases of this type are "special purchase," "clearance," "marked down from stock," "exceptional purchase," "manufacturer's close-out" and "advance sale."

Pre-ticketing with fictitiously high prices comes in for special attention in these advertising guides. No article should be pre-ticketed with any figure that exceeds the price at which it is sold usually and customarily in the trading area where it is offered for sale. In this connection, the FTC points out that those who distribute pre-ticketed price figures are chargeable with knowledge of the ordinary business facts of life concerning what happens to articles for which they furnish the pre-ticketed prices. The same basic principle applies to the use of the pre-ticketed price in advertising copy. The manufacturer may be held responsible for exaggerated prices in national advertising even though it is the retailer who misuses the figures; and the retailer will not be excused merely because it was the manufacturer who first advertised the fictitious price.

"Two for the Price of One" sales are prohibited unless the sales price for the two articles is the advertiser's usual and customary retail price for the single article in the recent regular course of his business. Similarly, half-price sales or one cent sales are improper unless the represented saving in price is true with relation to the advertiser's usual and customary retail price for the article in the recent regular course of his business. If the special offer is conditioned on the purchase of additional merchandise, then all terms or conditions imposed must be disclosed conspicuously in connection with the offer.

The key point to remember is that the word "price" itself constitutes an implication that the figure given is the usual and customary price charged by the advertiser in the recent regular course of his business in the trading area reached by the advertisement. This rule must be the starting point for all price advertising.

Tires and tubes

The Federal Trade Commission advertising guides for tires and tubes grew out of a long series of proceedings involving misleading terminology and various types of exaggerated product claims in this industry. One of the guides, for example, states that manufacturers should not use deceptive designations for the different grades of their products. If the first line tire of a particular manufacturer is designated "standard," then the same manufacturer's tires of a lower quality should not be designated as "super standard." If discontinued models or obsolete designs are offered, those facts must be stated clearly. Used products must be described adequately, so that it is clear they are not new. Terms such as "nu-tread" and "snow tread" do not constitute sufficient disclosure of this fact.

The unqualified use of absolute terms such as "skid proof," "blow-out proof" and "puncture proof" is improper unless the product really affords complete and absolute protection under any and all driving conditions.

The term "ply" is defined in technical detail. Tire advertising should contain an adequate statement of the identity of the fabric or other material used in the construction of the ply. Statements implying that tires possess a specified number of plies are not to be used unless this is the fact. The term "ply rating" is an index of tire strength and does not necessarily represent the number of cord plies in a particular tire. If a term such as "eight ply rating" is used to describe a tire containing fewer than eight plies, then the statement must be accompanied by a conspicuous disclosure of the actual number of plies in the tire.

These technical provisions are included here as an illustration of the degree of detail into which the Federal Trade Commission goes on appropriate occasions. Obviously, it would be foolhardy to write copy for automobile tires without studying the FTC's Tire Advertising Guides carefully.

TRADE PRACTICE RULES

Still another function of the Federal Trade Commission is the promulgation of trade practice rules. Typically, these are quite complex and detailed sets of regulations worked out by members of the Federal Trade Commission staff in conference with representatives of a broad segment of the industry affected. They put the requirements of the Federal Trade Commission Act into concrete form as applied to that particular industry.

Over the years, trade practice rules have been issued by the Federal Trade Commission for dozens of different industries. A few will be referred to here, largely for the purpose of indicating by example the fact that it is highly important for any copywriter to determine whether trade practice rules exist in the industry with which he is concerned and to make certain he is familiar with them in detail if that turns out to be so.

Watches

A watch either is waterproof or it is not. In order to describe it as waterproof, the case must be of such composition and construction as to be impervious to moisture through immersion for the life of the watch. The FTC trade practice rules include details of a specific test that requires complete immersion for at least five minutes in water under atmospheric pressure of 15 lbs. per square inch and for at least an additional five minutes in water under atmospheric pressure of at least 35 lbs. per square inch without admitting any water. If a watch does not pass this test, it may not be described as waterproof, although, possibly, it may be described correctly as "water-resistant" or "water-repellent." Here, too, a specific test has been promulgated by the FTC.

Similarly, the terms "shock-proof," "jar-proof," "magnetic" and "regulated" are defined carefully. Improper use of any of these terms will be considered a violation of the principles of the Federal Trade Commission Act.

Radio and television sets

One of the problems peculiar to this industry is the number of tubes in a radio or television set. Rectifier tubes, so-called ballast tubes, lamps used only for illumination, resistors of the plug-in type and other devices must not be counted in stating the number of tubes.

When describing the size of the picture tube in a television set, the horizontal measurement is required. The trade practice rules permit the use of the diagonal measurement only if it is also stated, in immediate conjunction with that figure, that it is a diagonal measurement and if the horizontal figure is given in addition. Only a tolerance of plus or minus one-eighth of an inch is permitted in quoting the figures for the dimensions of the picture tube.

It is an unfair trade practice to sell any radio or television set as a discontinued model unless the manufacturer has discontinued it entirely and replaced it on the market with a new set or model. This means a new model embodying specific, material changes in appearance, mechanical design or function, with the addition of new features to perform new functions.

The terms "rebuilt" and "factory rebuilt" also are discussed in detail. It is improper to use such words unless the product has been dismantled and reconstructed, with badly worn and defective or missing parts either repaired or replaced with new parts. If the term "factory rebuilt" is used, then the rebuilding must have been done at a factory or under the supervision or control of the factory of the original manufacturer.

Fountain pens and mechanical pencils

The use of the word "gold" creates a number of problems in the industry. The unqualified word "gold," or its abbreviation, cannot be used alone unless the part of the product so described is composed throughout of gold of 24 kt. fineness. The word "gold" cannot be used at all to describe an alloy of less than 10 kt. fineness. When the gold is more than 10 kt. but less than 24 kt., the karat fineness must be shown in immediate conjunction with the word "gold."

Terms such as "duragold" or "goldene" may not be used unless the article is made of pure gold or of an alloy of at least 10 kt. fineness. No phrase or representation indicating the substance, charm, quality or beauty of gold may be used properly unless the article is of at least 10 kt. fineness.

"Gold filled," "rolled gold plate," "gold flashed" and similar terms also are described in terms of their technical definitions. It is an unfair trade practice to use any of these terms under circumstances where they do not meet the requirements laid down in the trade practice rules.

Correspondence schools

A school may not adopt a name which gives a misleading or deceptive impression. Under specific FTC rulings, for example, the word "college" cannot be used by a school unless it is an institution of higher learning empowered to confer degrees and possessing a faculty of instructors in various branches of learning. The faculty and equipment of the school must not be misrepresented by illustration or otherwise. Words such as "federal" and "national" may not be used in such a way as to represent by implication that the school has any connection with the federal government. The word "foundation" is improper as part of the name for a private commercial school.

It is an unfair trade practice to make deceptive statements concerning probable earnings or opportunities in any vocation for which the school offers a course of instruction. It is improper to claim that taking a particular course necessarily will bring about a certain result, such as learning to play a musical instrument, or learning to perform a particular trade skillfully. It is also unfair to indicate in advertising that only qualified applicants are accepted when the fact of the matter is that anyone paying the purchase price will be received as a student.

Luggage

The correct name of the material from which the luggage is manufactured must be stated. Luggage not made of leather, of course, must not be misdescribed. It is also an unfair trade practice to use trade names that are misleading because they suggest the presence of genuine leather in a product made from imitation leather, or the presence of one variety of leather in a product made from a different variety.

Even genuine leather frequently is processed in such a way as to indicate that it is leather of a different type. The words "genuine," "real," "natural," and the like may not be used to describe leather that has been embossed or processed to simulate a different kind, grade, type or quality. The facts must be disclosed in detail when the product is advertised. For example, "top grain cowhide," "imitation pig grain" or "split cowhide, embossed design" are appropriate terms that explain what the leather is and what finish has been applied to it.

Top grain leather is the best grade. The trade practice rules provide specifically that leather from which either a layer of the top surface or grain, or a so-called "buffing," has been removed shall not be considered top grain leather. In addition, terms such as "waterproof," "water repellent," "dust-proof," "warp-proof" or the like should not be used unless they are literally true of the product.

STANDARD RULES

In connection with its trade practice conference work, the Federal Trade Commission has published two standard rules with the announcement that they are prescribed for inclusion in every set of trade practice rules issued thereafter. It is clear that these can be taken as expressions of the Federal Trade Commission's policy and the standard rules therefore are treated as having general application.

One of these rules deals with push money, that is, payments by manufacturers to retail sales clerks. But copywriters have very little concern with it. The other rule deals with the tricky question of the proper use of the word "free," and this is of considerable interest to copywriters.

The Standard "Free" Rule prohibits the use of the word "free" under circumstances where there has been a reduction in the ordinary and usual price of the product, or its quality, or its quantity or size. This applies to the merchandise that is required to be purchased in order to obtain whatever it is that the advertiser is offering "free." In other words, neither the price, the quality nor the quantity of the regular merchandise can be juggled in order to absorb some or all of the cost of the supposedly free merchandise.

In addition, if the free merchandise is not truly an unconditional gift, then all of the conditions or obligations affecting its acquisition must be set forth clearly and conspicuously "so as to leave no reasonable probability that the terms of the offer will be misunderstood." A disclosure in the form of a footnote is not considered sufficient compliance by the Federal Trade Commission. The rule specifically requires that this disclosure must appear in close conjunction with the word "free" wherever that word first appears in each advertisement.

SPECIAL STATUTES

As indicated above, the Federal Trade Commission is charged with the duty of enforcing a group of special statutes dealing with specific products or industries in addition to its general powers under the Federal Trade Commission Act. During the past few years, it has become increasingly common to find specific statutes of this sort introduced into Congress and there may be more of them from time to time. Each of the principal ones now in effect will be discussed briefly.

Oleomargarine

A special law provides that no advertisement for oleomargarine (or margarine) may contain a representation by statement, word, device, symbol or any other method that the oleomargarine offered for sale is a dairy product. This means that dairy terms may not be used in writing copy for margarine. Specific examples of prohibited advertising statements are "churned to delicate sweet creamy goodness," "always country fresh" and "the same day to day freshness which characterizes our other dairy products."

The law specifically permits a truthful, accurate and full statement of all the ingredients contained in the oleomargarine. On this basis, some manufacturers have added actual butter, apparently for the principal purpose of being able to advertise that fact. The Federal Trade Commission prohibits any emphasis in margarine advertising on an unstated percentage of butter content. If butter is added, the percentage must be set forth clearly and conspicuously or the advertisement will be considered misleading in a material respect.

Wool products

The Wool Products Labeling Act defines "wool," "reprocessed wool" and "reused wool." It requires a clear and explicit statement of the true composition of any wool product, and also a statement of other fibers in addition to wool if there are any such contained in the product. Although this law deals specifically with labeling, the same principles are applied as a matter of policy to the advertising of wool products and the rules and regulations under the Wool Products Labeling Act should be consulted in preparing advertising copy for any product containing wool.

"Wool" means the fiber from the fleece of the sheep or lamb, or the hair of the angora or cashmere goat. It also may include the so-called specialty fibers, which derive from the hair of the camel, alpaca, llama or vicuna. Accordingly, it is proper to use just the word "wool" or terms such as "alpaca," "camel hair," "llama," "vicuna," "cashmere" or "mohair" if in fact the fiber is that type of wool. If, however, the fiber is reprocessed or reused, those words also must be included in order to avoid misleading the public.

The key facts that must be shown are the kind of wool involved and its percentage by weight. In addition, if 5% or more of any other fiber is included in the total fabric, the presence of this fiber also must be disclosed. And the weight of any non-fiber that is used as loading or filling must be disclosed with its proper percentage stated prominently.

Fur products

The Wool Products Labeling Act was followed by a Fur Products Labeling Act. Unlike its predecessor, this statute does apply to advertising by its terms.

Since there are so many different types of fur and they come from so many different parts of the world, the principal objective of the Fur Products Labeling Act is to make certain that the true type of fur is named and that the country of origin is given in all instances. A Fur Products Name Guide has been issued by the Federal Trade Commission in which the name of the animal can be looked up and checked according to its scientific designation. The country of origin, of course, must be determined and disclosed.

The Fur Act also contains detailed regulations about disclosures of the method of construction. Terms such as "pointing," "bleaching," "dyeing" and "blending" are defined and the circumstances under which they may be used are set forth.

Trade names or trade-marks may not be used if they might create a misleading impression concerning the character of the product, the name of the animal producing the fur, or its geographical or zoological origin.

Textile fiber products

The most recent special statute in this series assigned to the Federal Trade Commission for administration is the Textile Fiber Products Identification Act. Like the Fur Act, this statute specifically applies to advertising as well as labeling.

If any fibers are mentioned at all, the correct generic name of each fiber present in the amount of more than 5% of the total fiber weight of the product must appear. Detailed regulations have been issued by the Federal Trade Commission including a list of definitions of generic names for manufactured fibers.

In advertising any textile fiber product, all parts of the required information must be stated in immediate conjunction with each other, in legible and conspicuous type or lettering of equal size and prominence. The generic names of the fibers that are present in amounts of more than 5% must be listed in the order of their predominance by weight. If any fiber is present in an amount of 5% or less, then the list of ingredients must be followed by the designation "other fiber" or "other fibers" to make this fact plain.

Specific examples of various types of approved expressions are given in the regulations. The following statements, for instance, would be appropriate for use in advertising: "60% cotton, 40% rayon, exclusive of ornamentation"; "all nylon, exclusive of elastic"; and "all cotton except 1% nylon added to neck band."

An imported textile fiber product must be marked with the name of the country where it was processed or manufactured. This requirement applies where the form of an imported textile fiber product is not basically changed even though it is processed in the United States, such as by finishing and dyeing. However, a textile fiber product manufactured in the United States from imported materials need not disclose the name of the country where the textile originally was made or processed.

"RED FLAG" WORDS

The watchful eyes of the Federal Trade Commission's alert staff are particularly sensitive to certain "red flag" words. The copywriter, too, must learn to recognize the danger signals. This does not mean that these words may never be used, but only that particular care is required because they are so easy to misuse. The presence of a red flag word frequently is an indication that the entire basic thought of an advertisement is wrong from the legal viewpoint. Of course, it is entirely possible to violate the Federal Trade Commission Act without using a single word on this list, but experience has shown that these are the ones most likely to create legal difficulties.

It would be futile to attempt a complete list of red flag words; there is no such thing and, even if there were, the passage of time would eliminate some old ones and add others. A few important examples will be discussed to illustrate the general principles involved in avoiding trouble. The fundamental idea is to make sure that you know just what the words mean and that your product can fulfill the promises contained in them.

Two such words have been discussed already—"free" and "guarantee." They are such trouble-makers that they have been treated separately. The following are some additional sources of difficulty. Notice that a good many of these red flag words apply particularly to drug and cosmetic copy. Advertising for such products is watched with special zeal because these products affect physical and mental welfare. At one time, the Federal Trade Commission analyzed 915 of its cases and found that from all the different classifications of commodities, 65.5% of the questioned advertising copy related to drug products and 14.4% to cosmetics. In other words, almost 80% of all questioned copy fell into these two classes.

1. *Banish, Rid, Stop, Correct, End.* Each of these five words says to the consumer, "This is the last of your trouble—it's all over now—permanently and forever." There *may* be times when you can use these words in their literal meaning. Too often, however, the Federal Trade Commission finds them used inaccurately—if not dishonestly.

Words in this group probably have been more used and abused in drug copy than in any other type of advertising. See if the following examples don't look familiar: "Banish sleepless nights." "Rid yourself of constipation." "Stop psoriasis." "Correct sluggish liver conditions." "End headaches." Each of these statements promises relief to sufferers—*permanent* relief. It is the permanency feature that makes the Federal Trade Commission balk. Permanent relief means cure, and drugs seldom cure.

Cosmetic copy often uses these words carelessly, also. It is too easy to write: "Acne sufferers—rid yourself of unsightly pimples." "Ashamed of your hands? Banish roughness."

To generalize—think before you use these words. Consider whether your claims are truthful. Ask yourself, "Can my product cure, fix or remedy *permanently* the condition under discussion?" If you can't answer that it does, you'd better use a different word, or qualify your statement with "can help rid you of . . ."

2. *Cure, Remedy, Therapeutic, Curative.* Millions of people suffer chronically from myriad ailments—ulcers, varicose veins, eye trouble, headaches, arthritis. Each of these afflicted persons is anxious for relief. Some of them swallow gallons of patent medicines led on by unthinking or untruthful copywriters who promise "cure" or "remedy."

Unfortunately, real cures are rare. The proper procedure for the copywriter is to find out what the product actually has accomplished and claim only that it will relieve specific symptoms—not cure the disease (unless the manufacturer is certain that it really will).

"Remedy" is put in the same class as "cure" by the Federal Trade Commission. "Therapeutic" and "curative" are eyed suspiciously also.

Drug copy isn't the only type using these red flag words. Cosmetics, soaps, tooth pastes and foods are only a few of the other products that slip one of these words into their copy on occasion. All four of them are alarm signals.

3. *Blemish-free, Clear, Smooth.* There are

few forms of mental suffering so acute as that felt by girls or women who have bad complexions. Since they are so extremely susceptible to advertising promising them skin that is blemish-free, clear or smooth, the Federal Trade Commission has been especially critical of such copy. Here are some points to remember in writing copy for a product used for skin care. If the product is applied externally and you promise that it will make the skin blemish-free, you must: (1) establish the fact that the skin is blemished because of external factors and not because of a systemic condition; (2) indicate that the product can be effective only if the cause of the blemishes *is* external; and (3) be sure your statements are based on *proved* facts. If the product is taken internally, then reverse the procedure of (1) and (2).

Clear, as applied to skin, is interpreted as blemish-free. Think of this definition when you use the word. Then set up conditions as you do when you use the expression "blemish-free" itself.

A smooth skin normally is difficult to promise unless you establish the fact that: (1) The skin is already rough because of some specified treatment or condition; and (2) The regular use of your product will bring a change. Be sure that the manufacturer has support for your claim. It is better, incidentally, to stick to the comparative in this case. An outright promise of smooth skin through use of a product is easy to make but very difficult to fulfill. Many complexions will never become smooth through use of *any* product, but they may get smoother than they were. Be satisfied with that.

4. *Safe, Harmless.* When you say unqualifiedly that a product is safe or harmless, you are asking for trouble. Humans have a fiendish capacity for proving you're wrong whether you're writing about drugs, electrical apparatus, machinery, or even baby products. To say that a product is safe or harmless under all conditions is like saying a gun is unloaded. Too often you're mistaken.

Suppose a drug product is advertised as "safe" or "harmless." The Federal Trade Commission immediately wants to know: (1) Isn't it possible that certain persons may be allergic to one or more of its ingredients? (2) Can *all* persons reading the statement rely on the fact that the preparation will not harm them?

Improper use of these red flag words in copy is more than just false advertising. Suppose a person *does* suffer from using the product because it turned out not to be safe or harmless. There is the basis for a possible damage claim.

So far as the law is concerned, when you say your product is safe you don't mean safe to a certain degree. You mean completely safe. The same thing goes for "harmless." If you're not sure, don't use either of the words.

5. *Science, Scientific, Test, Evidence, Proof, Research.* Use these words, singly or in combination, and the credulous public conjures up visions of test tubes, microscopes and long hours spent in the laboratory by white-coated men with Vandyke beards. If what you are writing is a television commercial, the picture may be right there on the tube to reinforce the impression created by the words. Yet this group of red flag words probably has been the most abused of all.

Scientists themselves use these words with great restraint. They imply a careful, systematic investigation conducted under unbiased conditions by experts who are trying to find out the truth, not to prove that their employer's brand has a slight edge over its competitors in some particular respect. Perhaps your company's laboratory discovers something about a product that you can translate into a copy claim. Do the findings of a couple of chemists become "science"? Because an informal poll of ordinary practicing physicians shows a slight favoring of your product, does this constitute "overwhelming scientific proof" that your product is superior? When you stop to think about the fact that even eminent scientists often honestly disagree, you can realize how extremely inaccurate and misleading an impression can be created by the careless use of these red flag words.

Approach "science" with humility and use "proof" and "evidence" sparingly. If you have substantial evidence to back you, and if your use of the terms is literally true, then, of course, you would be foolish *not* to employ this very strong copy approach. Otherwise—be careful.

6. *Doctor, Laboratory.* These red flag words have much the same kind of built-in trouble potential as the group last discussed. A doctor's recommendation is considered a precious asset for any kind of product that can either help you or hurt you, and "laboratory" goes right along with it because that is where the doctor frequently gets his inspiration. But beware of the temptation to be anything but scrupulously accurate in your use of these terms. The Federal Trade Commission, knowing how gullible the public is about doctors' recommendations, is hypersensitive to copy of that type.

If you want to keep your "doctor" copy out of legal turmoil, here are a few points to bear in mind:

(a) Make sure the "doctor" to whom you refer is a genuine physician—licensed to practice medicine by a recognized governmental authority.

(b) If he is not such a doctor, then make it very clear just what kind of "doctor" he *is*—for instance, a doctor of naturopathy or chiropractic.

(c) Avoid the unqualified representation that a preparation is "a doctor's prescription." If true, the statement "formulated in accordance with" a doctor's prescription is acceptable. But be sure of your facts.

(d) Don't make a blanket statement of medical approval for your product based upon an informal survey which asked doctors for their personal preference or for a "less harmful than Product X" type of statement; these and similar limited expressions of opinion actually don't amount to recommendations.

(e) If an analysis by doctors reveals an insignificant advantage for your product over your competitor's product, don't blast forth with a claim of superiority. In the past, cigarette advertising sometimes was characterized by this kind of magnification of infinitesimal differences, without revealing to the public the fact that all brands contain substantial quantities of the substance involved in the analysis. Such things make cynics of the doctors and the public.

Often the word "laboratory" is used simultaneously with "doctor." The principal caution to observe with this word is that you must not refer to "our laboratory" when the client does not operate a control or research laboratory in connection with its organization. At the same time, don't mention laboratory and doctor together unless the doctor actually did his research in the laboratory from which you assert he obtained his facts—otherwise, you may have him approving research which he would not have endorsed according to his own ideas of research methods.

The word "laboratory" is viewed suspiciously whether or not doctors are mentioned in the same advertising copy. The strict attitude of the Federal Trade Commission is shown by a series of cases in which manufacturers were forbidden to use "Laboratories" as part of a trade or corporate name because they did not actually operate any laboratory.

7. *New.* The Federal Trade Commission usually won't believe that, if a product has been used for a time, it can be restored entirely to its original state through the use or application of your product. Whenever your copy asserts that the product stays "just like new" despite age, use and abuse, get ready to defend your statements. "New" to the Federal Trade Commission means fresh—no different from the day you bought it. Remember that picture when you write "looks like new." Also keep in mind that the phrases "works like new" or "lasts like new" are subject to cynical legal scrutiny.

The scrutiny becomes especially watchful when the advertiser says that his process will make something old work like new. A "better performance" claim may very well be accurate and do a good selling job without ever getting attention from the Federal Trade Commission, while the little word "new" in the copy is waving the red flag and asking for trouble, which frequently comes.

Although no more "red flag" words will be discussed, there are, of course, many more than have been presented here. The purpose in providing this partial list is twofold: to make you cautious in the use of these specific words; and to alert you to the necessity for honesty and accuracy that is the basic legal guide to all copywriting.

FOOD AND DRUG ADMINISTRATION

The Food and Drug Administration exercises control over a tremendously wide area of the entire American economy. Food is our country's largest single industry. Drugs are among the most widely advertised of all items. In addition, the Food and Drug Administration has jurisdiction over "devices," which are defined as instruments or apparatus for use in the diagnosis, cure or treatment of disease or to affect the structure of function of the body of humans or animals. This includes everything from a fever thermometer to a message machine. And last but by no means least come cosmetics, which the law defines to include articles intended to be "rubbed, poured, sprinkled or sprayed on, introduced into or otherwise applied to the human body or any part thereof for cleansing, beautifying, promoting attractiveness or altering the appearance"—with the single exception of soap.

The Food and Drug Administration is concerned primarily with the false or misleading labeling of products under its control. From the standpoint of the advertising copywriter, the principal problem, therefore, is package copy. Any literature, however, that accompanies a product has been ruled to be part of its "labeling" and leaflets, brochures or the like also come under the jurisdiction of the Food and Drug Administration when they are designed to accompany the product as the time and place of sale. Other types of advertising for products controlled by the Food and Drug Administration are supervised by the Federal Trade Commission under its general powers over false and misleading advertising, but obviously it would be inviting trouble to make a statement in advertising copy that would go against the prohibitions of the Food and Drug Administration if it happened to appear on a label.

The statute under which the Food and Drug Administration operates deals specifically with the question of labeling that becomes misleading by failure to state what should have been included. The law provides that, in determining whether labeling is misleading, there shall be taken into account not only representations made or suggested, but also the extent to which there is a failure to reveal facts which are material in the light of any representations that are made. There also is a specific provision that any information required to be on a label must be placed prominently, with such conspicuousness and in such terms as to make it likely to be read and understood by the ordinary individual, under customary conditions of purchase and use, for the particular product involved.

Numerous detailed provisions are made for a great variety of specific products, some in the law itself and others in the voluminous regulations that have been issued from time to time by the Food and Drug Administration. Particularly worthy of mention is the fact that the statute provides for the Food and Drug Administration to issue definitions and standards of identity for foods, and many such have been published for a great variety of edible products. These definitions and standards of identity typically prescribe minimum quality standards that a product must meet in order to be entitled to bear that name. If the particular product for which you are writing copy fails to satisfy these standards, then it is not proper to use what you might think is its ordinary name. For example, if cocoa contains less than 10% of cacao fat, it must be sold as "low-fat cocoa"; and only if it contains more than 22% cacao fat can it be called "breakfast cocoa." Obviously, this is the kind of factual detail that must be checked before copy is prepared.

If no standard of identity has been established for any particular food, then it must be labeled to disclose each ingredient by name—except for spices, colorings and flavorings, which may be declared simply as such. There are provisions also for exemptions from these requirements, and the Food and Drug Administration has exempted various foods for various reasons. In a number of instances the indications are that these exemptions are only temporary and definitions and standards of identity may be issued at a later date.

Drugs and devices must be labeled with adequate directions for use. Special mention must be made where a drug is liable to deteriorate. New drugs may not be offered for sale at all unless they have been tested adequately and approved. Drugs listed in standard formularies such as the United States Pharmacopoeia must be labeled with their official names, and any differences of strength, quality or purity from the official standards must be stated conspicuously on the label.

Cosmetics are subject to misbranding and false labeling restrictions similar to those affecting foods, except that there is no provision for definitions and standards of identity with respect to cosmetics. It should be noted that a product may be both a drug and cosmetic. The claim on the label made by the manufacturer concerning its function will determine which set of legal requirements the product must fulfill. It is possible that the identical product can be sold under two different labels for two different purposes, in one case as a drug and in the other as a cosmetic.

POST OFFICE DEPARTMENT

The Post Office Department exercises control over advertising in two main areas. The first of these affects advertising that depends on the use of the mails. This includes both direct mail advertising and mail order advertising. For example, a lottery or any fraudulent scheme, that is, a plan for obtaining money or property through the mails by means of false pretenses, is a violation of the postal laws. The Postmaster General need not even take the offender to court. He can conduct an administrative proceeding and, if he finds a violation has been committed, the Postmaster at the local office is directed to stamp the word "Fraudulent" on all mail addressed to the offending party and return it to the sender. Postmasters also are instructed not to pay any money orders drawn in favor of such a party.

Secondly, in addition to this direct method of control, the Post Office Department exercises indirect control over advertising carried in any publication that goes through the mails. This comes about because of the very valuable second-class mailing privilege which amounts to a government subsidy in favor of periodicals that have what is called a "public character," that is, that contain news, literature, scientific information or the like, and have a legitimate list of subscribers. The Post Office Department has the power to revoke second-class mailing privileges if the periodical fails to maintain its so-called public character. It is theoretically possible that advertising misrepresentations might be sufficient to warrant this type of extreme action, although there seems to be no record of it ever having been done.

The particular concern of the copywriter with the second-class mailing privilege is that, while any periodical which has this privilege may contain advertising, the advertising must be clearly indicated as such. If an advertisement is written and set up so that it gives the appearance of being editorial matter, then the word "advertisement" itself must appear as an identifying symbol in sufficiently conspicuous type and placement so that it will be readily noticeable to the reader. Failure to comply may lead to revocation of the periodical's second-class mailing privilege.

FEDERAL COMMUNICATIONS COMMISSION

The Federal Communications Commission also exercises an indirect type of control over advertising. Radio and television advertising is subject to the general supervision of the Federal Trade Commission just as advertising in print media is. The FCC, however, licenses every radio and television station and it is one of the over-all conditions of such a license that the station must operate in what the law calls the "public interest, convenience and necessity."

If the Federal Communications Commission should find that, because of advertising misrepresentations or any other reason, a station has not been operating within this quoted statutory purpose, then it has the power to revoke or refuse to renew the station's license. This power obviously can be a potent one.

While the Federal Communications Commission has criticized false and misleading advertising, it is the FCC's general policy not to take any specific action with respect to this type of offense, but rather to bring the matter to the attention of the Federal Trade Commission. But the FCC has indicated its disapproval of advertising by physicians, clergymen and persons offering advice on marriage or family matters. It also has disapproved advertising of lotteries, contraceptive devices and hard liquor. All such advertising practices jeopardize the licensee's chances of securing a renewal of his license, which ordinarily runs for a period of only one year at a time.

The Commission has been known to bring to the attention of a station (informally) what it considers objectionable advertising. This method of procedure can be extremely effective since few stations would care to risk the loss of their broadcasting franchises and some would be unwilling even to risk the publicity of a public hearing in connection with a renewal application.

BUREAU OF ALCOHOL, TOBACCO, AND FIREARMS

The Bureau of Alcohol, Tobacco and Firearms is charged with the responsibility, among other things, of administering the Federal Alcohol Administration Act. On this basis, the BATF imposes on the liquor industry what is almost without doubt the most detailed and severe set of controls that any industry in the country must face in its advertising practices.

The BATF exercises supervision over distilled spirits, wine and malt beverages. Its control starts basically with the labels to be used on the products. There are detailed regulations setting forth what must appear on the labels and no label can be used on an alcoholic product unless it has been approved by the BATF in advance.

The next step is direct control over the advertising of the products. The class and type of the beverage must appear in every advertisement. These must be stated conspicuously, and the designation in the advertising copy must be the same as that on the approved label for the product. Detailed information about alcoholic content is required for distilled spirits, but statements of alcoholic content are prohibited in advertisements of malt beverages and wine. The name and address of the company responsible for the advertisement always must be included. It may be the distiller, the distributor or the importer in proper cases. The name and address of the advertiser, the class and type of the product and the alsoholic content (in the case of distilled spirits) are the so-called "mandatories" in liquor advertising.

The BATF regulations also prohibit certain types of advertising statements specifically. These include false or misleading statements; disparagement of competing products; obscene or indecent statements; misleading representations relating to analysis, standards or tests; guarantees which, irrespective of their truth or falsity, are likely to mislead the consumer; statements indicating authorization by any municipal, state or federal government; the use of certain words such as "bonded" (unless the product in fact is bottled in bond), "pure" and "double distilled"; claims of curative or therapeutic value; misleading statements as to place of origin; and many others. In particular, no statement concerning an alcoholic beverage may be used in advertising if it is inconsistent with any statement on the labeling of the product itself.

OTHER FEDERAL LAWS

There are certain specialized industries in which still other Federal agencies exercise specific control over advertising. For example, the Securities and Exchange Commission has the power to stop the sale of a security if its advertising contains an untrue statement of a material fact, or if it fails to state a material fact necessary in order to make the advertising not misleading in the light of all the circumstances. The Federal Aviation Agency has control over advertising by airlines of their passenger and freight services.

There are other federal statutes that apply to particular products and some of them contain labeling and advertising controls. Among these are the Economic Poisons Act, which governs insecticides, fungicides and similar products; and the Federal Seed Act.

Another group of statutes deals specifically

with the use in advertising of particular symbols or representations, including the laws which prohibit the use of the American flag, the Red Cross symbol, the 4-H Club emblem, "Smokey Bear" as originated by the U.S. Forestry Service and a number of others. A leading advertising agency once had to scrap a filmed television commercial because the magic letters "F.B.I." were mentioned in a flippant manner; the Federal Bureau of Investigation called the agency's attention to a law making the use of those initials in advertising a misdemeanor.

These statutes are so specialized in nature that it would be impractical to discuss all of them in detail. They are mentioned primarily to indicate the necessity for checking in each instance to find out before preparing copy whether or not some special law deals with the subject.

OBSCENITY

It is hardly necessary to point out that obscene advertising is improper. However, there are legal as well as moral objections to obscenity. The problem here is one of definition. Standards of taste vary from community to community and even more noticeably from time to time. Nevertheless, a writer should have no great difficulty in drawing the line between obscenity and acceptable copy. Although poor taste is not in itself unlawful, it certainly is disapproved by most advertisers. A copywriter who avoids poor taste almost automatically will avoid any question of violation of the obscenity laws.

COPYRIGHT

We are not concerned here with the technique of protecting an advertisement under copyright laws, but rather with the problem of using somebody else's copyrighted material as part of your advertising copy. There are many misconceptions about the right to use such material, whether in quoted or paraphrased form.

A copyright does not protect the basic idea of the author. An advertising copywriter, therefore, is privileged to use the basic ideas contained in anything that he may read. But copying the exact language, or closely paraphrasing the way in which the original author expressed his idea, is an infringement if the original work is protected by copyright. The same rule applies to art as well as to copy.

It is sometimes thought that copyright infringement occurs only when the fact of copying is concealed; that is, when the copier attempts to pass off the work as his own. This is not so. The mere fact that the source is acknowledged does not prevent the use from being an infringement of copyright. Actual consent of the copyright owner must be secured. A fee frequently is charged for this privilege, but that is something that must be arranged in advance, because the copyright owner may decide to withhold permission altogether.

The one basic exception to this rule is the doctrine of what the law calls "fair use." It is this exception that makes it possible, for example, for a reviewer to quote passages from a book that he is reviewing and for a scientist to copy from the works of others in the same field in order to be able to comment on scientific developments. It is important, however, to bear in mind that the purpose for which the copyrighted material is to be used is a definite limitation of the scope of the doctrine of fair use. Specifically, to take even a small extract from a copyrighted work and use it in a commercial advertisement is not fair use. This point was made unmistakably in a case involving the Liggett & Myers Tobacco Company which copied, although not in exactly the same words, just three sentences from a doctor's book about the human voice which made some favorable comments about the use of tobacco. Specific credit was given for the source of the quotation, but no permission had been obtained to use it.

The case went to court and the decision was in favor of the copyright proprietor. There must be "substantial" copying to constitute infringement, but this does not necessarily mean a large quantity. The court decided in this case that even three sentences amounted to a substantial copying under the circumstances because of the relative importance of the material that was taken. It was decided also that the use was not a "fair use" because it was for a purely commercial purpose.

Another common misconception has to do with music, which is also subject to copyright if the proper formalities are observed. There is a widespread impression that so long as no more than eight bars of a popular song are borrowed, there can be no infringement of copyright. This is clearly wrong. The same basic standards apply to the infringement of a musical copyright as to a literary copyright. In other words, was the part taken from the copyrighted work substantial and was the use a fair one? The distinctive characteristics of the melody or the lyrics of a popular song can be expressed in fewer than eight bars. It is, therefore, not safe to use the words of a song unless permission has been granted or it has been checked and found to be in the public domain.

Copyright does not protect the title of a work. On the other hand, this does not mean that everyone necessarily is free to use a title. The practice of commercial tie-ins of all types is so common today that titles of books, plays, motion pictures, songs and even comic strips have become highly important commercial properties. Although it does not constitute a technical copyright infringement to use someone else's title, this may be prohibited by general principles of unfair competition in order to protect its exploitation values. The legal test is whether the public is likely to infer that there is some connection between the title as used in advertising and the work on which the title originally appeared. If so, the title may not be used without permission.

LIBEL

To libel somebody means to injure his reputation by making a false statement that will subject him to ridicule or contempt in the community, particularly if it would tend to cause damage to the victim in his business or profession. The penalties for libel can be severe. It is a complete defense to a charge of libel if the defamatory statement can be proved true in fact, but the possibility of such a situation developing out of advertising copy is remote. Most of the litigated cases in which individuals have been libeled by means of advertising involved false testimonials.

Libel can be committed by a radio or television broadcast as well as by a printed advertisement. Libel also can be committed by pictures. The use of a professional model is no assurance against a suit for libel. The usual form of model release, which will be discussed in the succeeding section, does not waive any rights under libel laws. One particularly well-known case involved an advertising photograph. The angle at which the picture was taken and the way in which the light fell created an obscene impression that was not noticed by the people who prepared the advertisement. The model sued on the theory that this was damaging to his reputation and the court agreed that the photograph was libelous. Protection against this unfortunate kind of result can be secured by having the model approve the finished layout.

It is possible to libel a business or a product as well as a person. While this is difficult to establish as a legal proposition under the laws pertaining to libel, disparagement of competitors and their products also constitutes an unfair method of competition within the meaning of the Federal Trade Commission Act and, therefore, may bring on an FTC proceeding.

RIGHTS OF PRIVACY AND PUBLICITY

The use in advertising of the name or picture of an individual without his consent constitutes a violation of his right of privacy. In New York State, this right is created by specific legislation which requires that the consent be in writing. In most other states, the same rule of law prevails through decisions of the courts, although oral consent may be enough. Utah and Virginia have specific statutes similar to that of New York. The New York statute, however, is limited to living individuals. Utah and Virginia go further and give the heirs of a deceased individual the right to complain about the unauthorized use of his name or picture. When preparing copy for national advertising, obviously the most restrictive of all these laws must be taken into account.

It is this right of privacy that makes it necessary to obtain a release from every model who poses for artwork or photography. Similarly, an endorsement or testimonial cannot be used without a release from the individual whose name is to appear in connection with it. Anyone less than twenty-one years of age is legally an infant and his or her parent or legal guardian must sign the release in order for it to be valid.

Releases frequently are limited in their scope. A model release, for example, may permit only the use of the picture of the individual and not his or her true name. Furthermore, the right to use a picture does not always carry with it the right to use words in connection with the picture indicating that the model endorses a product or service. Even a release from an individual permitting his name to be used as an endorser does not necessarily include the right to create a statement praising the product and attribute it to the individual as though it were his own words. In addition, as indicated in the preceding section, the possession of a model release in the customary form does not excuse libel, so that a photograph covered by a release might be used in conjunction with libelous words in such a way as to violate the legal rights of the model.

Decisions of the courts have recognized that the right of privacy is somewhat out of step with the facts of modern commercial life. For example, figures in the entertainment and sports world frequently have no desire for privacy in the same way that an ordinary citizen does; they seek publicity actively. As a result of court decisions, therefore, the right of privacy of such individuals has been limited on the theory that the individual has given up his right of privacy by making himself into a public figure. This does not apply, however, to strict commercial uses such as advertising. A magazine or newspaper can use a publicity still of a motion picture star for editorial purposes, but it cannot be used as part of an advertisement without a release.

T
In Teletype®, the "T" is always capped.
Teletype is a registered trademark used to identify the products manufactured by Teletype Corporation.
Therefore, our name should always be used as an adjective as in "Teletype terminal." It should never be used as a noun or as a verb.
Thanks for helping us keep our name straight. By always remembering to cap the "T."
TELETYPE
Teletype is a trademark registered in the United States Patent Office.

Fig. 20-1

Trade-mark advertisement.

Notice the warning not to use the name as a noun or verb — also, the suggestion to use a capital "T."

In recent years, the courts have considered the right of publicity as something distinct from the right of privacy. Only a public figure possesses this right of publicity. It is the law's recognition of the fact that the name and picture of a personality in the entertainment or sports world has a definite commercial value for endorsements, testimonials and the like. Accordingly, the use of the name or picture of such an individual for advertising purposes without written consent may give rise to a claim for substantial damages.

It will be desirable, occasionally, to use a personal name in advertising and the copywriter may devise a fictitious name for that purpose. This always creates the risk that unknowingly the fictitious name will turn out to be borne by some real individual who will make his complaint known. It then becomes a difficult it not impossible task to prove that the name in the advertisement did not refer to the actual living individual. In order to avoid such problems, some agencies maintain files of cleared names, generally individuals on their own staffs or working for their clients who have consented to the use of their names in advertising. Even if a duplicate of such a name should turn up in the form of another living individual, the advertiser or agency always can go to the release file to establish that the cleared name is the one that was used in the copy. This will not, of course, excuse the use of a celebrity's name even if by coincidence the agency has an employee bearing the same name who is willing to sign a release.

PROPER TRADE-MARK USAGE

Basic trade-mark principles have been discussed earlier. The purpose of this section is to describe the proper ways of using trade-marks and brand names in advertising in order to avoid the possible loss of the valuable legal rights that a trade-mark represents. Some trade-marks have become associated so completely with the products to which they are attached that they are treated by the public as merely a name for the product rather than an identification of one particular brand of that product. When a trade-mark literally becomes a household word in this way, it has ceased to be a trade-mark and no single manufacturer any longer has the exclusive right to use it on his product. The tremendous investment that may have gone into establishing the trade-mark and creating a brand image through extensive advertising has been lost to the advertiser. The question is an important one for advertising copywriters because the improper use of a trade-mark in advertising can give the public the impression that it is a generic term instead of a brand name, and that is what it will become very quickly under such circumstances.

Another indication of the seriousness of the problem is to list a few well-known products whose commonly accepted names today once were the valued trade-marks of particular manufacturers. These include aspirin, lanolin, milk of magnesia, celluloid, kerosene, shredded wheat, linoleum, cellophane and escalator. In order to preserve a trade-mark, it must be kept in mind that it indicates only one particular variety of the product and is not the name of the product itself.

Grammatically, a trade-mark is a proper adjective. A trade-mark must be identified as such in all advertising, which means that at a bare minimum it requires an initial capital letter. There are many other typographical methods by which to give distinctive treatment to a trade-mark so that there will be no doubt of what it is. It may be run, for example, in all-caps or placed in quotation marks, it may be set in a distinctive type face, or the manufacturer's logo may be included in the body copy.

A trade-mark should be so designated by actual notice to that effect at least on its first or most conspicuous appearance in any given advertisement. If the trade-mark has been registered in the United States Patent Office (and this requires a legal check) use the official circle-R notice or the abbreviation Reg. U.S. Pat. Off. If it has not been registered, then use the abbreviation TM or the word "trade-mark." The notice may be in the form of a footnote referred to by an asterisk.

Another way to indicate clearly that a trade-mark is not merely the name of the product is to use the word "brand" in connection with it. When the copy talks about the "XYZ brand" of a certain product, there can be no doubt that XYZ is the brand name or trade-mark and not the generic name of the product itself.

Furthermore, if you use the generic name of the product every time you refer to the trade-mark, you will avoid the possibility of creating a situation where the public will start the loose usage of the term that eventually leads to its loss of trade-mark significance. If aspirin had been sold as aspirin pain-relieving tablets instead of just as aspirin, the trade-mark might have been preserved.

A simple way to test your copy for this purpose is to omit the trade-mark from the sentence in which it is used. A complete thought still should be expressed. For example, "See the latest XYZ toaster at your local appliance store"; not "See the latest XYZ at your local appliance store."

A good trade-mark exists only in one form and the copywriter should stick to it. Don't make up fanciful words containing the trade-mark and don't use it in the wrong grammatical form. As stated above, a trade-mark is a proper adjective. It should not be used as a noun, in the plural, as a verb, in the possessive or as an adjective that describes some quality of the goods.

It is not uncommon for trade-marks to be used under license agreements from their owners. Under such circumstances, the licensee's package and advertising copy should contain an appropriate legend stating the facts in order to preserve the legal rights of the trade-mark owner. A typical notice for this purpose would be in the form: "Manufactured by

XYZ Corporation under authority of ABC Company."

Many companies publish manuals giving specific directions on how their trade-marks are to be used. These manuals are prepared very largely for the use of advertising copywriters and it goes without saying that you should follow such a manual if one has been issued by the advertiser on whose product you are working.

COMPARATIVE ADVERTISING

Direct reference to competitive products or services in advertising once was a rarity that people considered in bad taste or even morally reprehensible. In recent years, following a period when veiled references to "Brand X" were in vogue, a substantial amount of advertising has appeared in which competitors are mentioned specifically. No longer is a product or service simply "the best on the market"; instead, many advertisers do not hesitate to identify the competition and make direct comparisons. Philosophical questions of morals or ethics are outside the scope of this chapter, but does comparative advertising raise any legal questions?

In order to identify a competitor in advertising, it almost invariably is necessary to use his trade-mark so that the public will understand the comparison. For that reason, the legality of comparative advertising has been tested most often in the framework of lawsuits claiming trade-mark infringement. In one extreme case, a manufacturer of low-priced domestic perfume advertised that his product duplicated the exact scent of "Chanel No. 5," a famous and expensive brand of French perfume. When this use of the Chanel trade-mark was attacked, the court responded by ruling that there was nothing wrong about referring to a competitive product by its trade-mark, provided that the comparative advertising was strictly accurate.

In accordance with this ruling, the prevailing view is that comparative advertising is legally permissible so long as there is no misrepresentation. But if inaccurate or untrue statements are made, the advertisement can be attacked as false disparagement of the competitive product or service as well as trade-mark infringement and substantial damages might be awarded. It has been pointed out repeatedly that strict accuracy is the basic legal requirement a copywriter must bear in mind; this brief discussion shows why that requirement must be observed with special care when the advertisement makes a direct reference to competitive products or services.

IDEA PIRACY

It was explained above that a copyright does not protect the basic idea of any literary or artistic work. Nevertheless, some ideas are treated as property by the law and, like other forms of property, they can be stolen.

One of the constant problems that plagues advertising agencies and advertisers alike is the unsolicited idea. An astonishing number of people constantly are engaged in attempting to present what they consider novel merchandising ideas, catchy advertising slogans and similar helpful thoughts which they confidently expect will bring them substantial remuneration. The fact of the matter is that professionals are much better at thinking up advertising ideas and slogans than amateurs. Even if the unsolicited idea has merit, it frequently turns out to be simply a duplication of an idea that is already in the company's files as the result of studies by its own staff or the staff of its advertising agency. Yet it is sometimes an impossible task to persuade the member of the public who submitted the unsolicited idea that it was not his particular brainchild that was stolen.

Idea piracy suits are a nuisance and can be extremely expensive. As a result, many large advertisers and advertising agencies have set up standard procedures by which they attempt to protect themselves from receiving unsolicited ideas in the first place; or, if they do, to receive them only when the submitter of the idea has signed a written release in advance that will protect the agency and the advertiser from the risk of any litigation. It is important for the copywriter to learn just what system his own employer follows for dealing with situations of this kind.

The copywriter may very well be exposed to friends or acquaintances from outside the profession who are sure they have a "wonderful idea" to submit. When faced with such a situation, the copywriter would be well advised to refuse to listen to the idea, but explain as politely as possible that his employer has a standard policy either not to consider ideas from the outside at all, or to consider them only when submitted in writing and accompanied by an appropriate standard form of signed release, whatever the case may be. Considerable difficulty, expense, and eventual hard feelings can be avoided through this precautionary technique.

STATE LAWS

The greater part of our discussion thus far has dealt with federal laws. These, of course, apply to all national advertising. They also apply to a great deal of local advertising because either the advertising itself or the product crosses state lines, and thus involves interstate commerce which is under the control of the federal government.

It is necessary to know in addition that practically all of the states have their own individual laws dealing with advertising in one way or another. Writing copy for strictly local advertising, such as that for a retail store to run in a local newspaper, obviously involves the law of the particular state. Unfortunately, the situation is even more complicated than this, for states have the right to pass judgment on advertising that affects their local interests even though the same advertising simultaneously may be subject to federal controls. To take one specific example, a number of states have their own advertising requirements for liquor. Advertising copy to appear in such a state must comply with the regulations of the Federal Bureau of Alcohol, Tobacco and Firearms and also, with the requirements of the local authorities.

Most of the states have enacted laws, based on the model statute recommended by *Printers' Ink,* prohibiting untrue, deceptive or misleading advertising. These are criminal statutes which provide for a fine and imprisonment, as distinguished from laws such as the Federal Trade Commission Act under which the typical penalty is an order to cease and desist. Because of the severe punishment, these state laws are not enforced very frequently. Local authorities seem to be reluctant to proceed criminally in such cases.

Some states are even stricter than the federal government in their legal approach to the lottery problem. There are parts of the country where the offering of a prize by chance is prohibited even if no payment or other consideration is required from the entrant. The theory of these state laws is that awarding prizes by chance is a form of gambling, which they consider both immoral and illegal whether the chance must be paid for or not. As these laws are interpreted, the required legal element of consideration is found in the benefit derived by the sponsor.

The typical state also has a miscellaneous collection of other statutes covering specific areas of commerce, that generally deal with advertising along with other phases of the business involved. Among the industries regulated in this manner in many states are small loan companies, employment agencies, optometrists and opticians, barbers and hairdressers, and real estate brokers. In addition, many states have their own Pure Food and Drug laws and practically all states prohibit obscene or indecent advertising. Intoxicating beverages are a special case, as already indicated, and the specific law of each state must be checked if liquor advertising is involved.

CONSUMERISM AND THE COPYWRITER

Sometimes laments are heard from creative people about the maze of legal regulations that have grown out of the consumerism movement. Fear is expressed that creativity will suffer as copywriters attempt to work within the limitations of the ever-increasing rules, guidelines and prohibitions.

An agency executive, Allen Rosenshine, vice president of Batten, Barton, Durstine & Osborn, had these words of comfort for creative people:*

"Maybe the legal restrictions have become so stringent that we just can't do product demonstrations anymore.

Well, I don't believe that.

What I DO believe is that we are tending to shy away from the legal problems rather than trying to meet them head on. If we look long enough and hard enough we will find something meaningful about the product that is worth saying, and can be said legally.

If we can't, then we have a basis for a client recommendation to the effect that a product improvement is necessary. And even if it isn't the big breakthrough product improvement that will bring competition to its knees, as long as it makes sense conceptually, there is no reason why the creative department can't advertise it dramatically, but within the bounds of legal propriety.

That's exactly the kind of creative imagination that clients have been paying for in the first place.

And even if we can't make open ended comparisons anymore; even if we CAN'T say a product is "better" without saying "better than what," that is not the end of advertising.

Even if we CAN'T say "our product is the best you can buy," that's not the end of advertising either . . .

I suggest we spend our time more productively if we work out our own set of guidelines that would enable us to work within the current—or even projected—legal restrictions."

*Speech delivered to the Eastern Regional Conference of the American Association of Advertising Agencies, June 5, 1972, New York City.

INFLUENCE OF THE CONSUMERISM MOVEMENT

During the past several years, pressures exerted by consumer interest groups and the addition of some activists to the FTC staff have influenced the adoption by the Commission of new techniques for dealing with false and misleading advertising, particularly requirements for corrective advertising and for the substantiation of product claims. As this book goes to press, the developments are so recent that they have not yet been tested in court proceedings; it is probable that the legal basis for the imposition of these requirements will be challenged by some advertisers or agencies.

Orders requiring corrective advertising are based on the theory that false and deceptive claims have a residual effect on the consumer so that conventional orders to discontinue the misrepresentations are insufficient to protect the public. Instead, the FTC now requests in many cases (and some advertisers have agreed to supply as part of the settlement of FTC complaints against them) positive statements that will dissipate the misleading claims. A typical order requires that 25 per cent of advertising expenditures for the product in question for a period of one year must be devoted to advertisements, approved in advance by the FTC, stating that previous claims were subject to misinterpretation and giving the true facts;

for example, that "Profile" bread is not effective for weight reduction.

The Federal Trade Commission's advertising substantiation program was launched by a resolution adopted in 1971 that is based on the FTC's statutory authority to require the filing of special reports to aid its investigations. Orders calling for the submission of documents, including test reports and testimonials, to support advertising claims concerning safety, performance, quality and competitive prices, have gone out to various manufacturers of such products as television sets, air conditioners, pet food, electric razors, toothpaste and detergents. These orders refer to specific product claims for which substantiation must be furnished, for instance: "Sani-Flush kills common household germs in 15 seconds"; "Tabby Canned meets 100 per cent of a cat's daily nutritional needs"; "Ajax Liquid contains more ammonia than any competing product." The FTC reserves the right to make public any of the materials submitted in response to these special orders and also to release reports of its own to inform the public about the response or lack of response to its requests for substantiation.

CONCLUSION

It may very well seem that the task of keeping up with this enormous array of legal requirements is beyond the capacity of any single individual. Fortunately, the basic responsibility ordinarily is not the copywriter's alone. This is true particularly in a large advertising agency, which either will have its own staff of lawyers or use the services of an outside law firm to check copy for compliance with legal requirements.

It is, nevertheless, of great importance for the copywriter to have at least a minimal familiarity with the kinds of legal problems that do exist. A conscientious copywriter not only will acquire as much information as possible about the product or service on which he is working, but also about the kinds of legal restrictions that may apply to the particular industry involved.

The fundamental source of information about the product or service, of course, is the advertiser itself. The details may come directly, or more likely indirectly—through the account executive or supervisor in his place of employment. In the case of an advertising agency, information about legal requirements can come from the agency's own staff or from the client. In addition, many industries have trade associations that provide tremendous quantities of helpful information. Better Business Bureaus also are sources of extremely valuable assistance. The National Better Business Bureau, Inc. publishes *Do's and Don'ts in Advertising Copy,* an excellent loose-leaf volume that is kept up to date with monthly revisions.

A number of industries have their own self-imposed codes of regulations. As a practical matter, although these do not have the force of law, it is essential that they be followed. Some well-known examples are the codes of the National Association of Broadcasters, The Distilled Spirits Institute and the Motion Picture Association of America.

The copywriter should strive to be informed in order that legal difficulties may be avoided. Two basic rules that the Federal Trade Commission likes to emphasize are enough in themselves to constitute a condensed code of principles for advertising copywriting: (1) Laws are made to protect the trusting as well as the suspicious; (2) Advertisements are not intended to be dissected carefully with a dictionary at hand, but rather to produce an impression upon prospective purchasers. Keeping these simple rules in mind will solve many of the legal problems in advertising copywriting.

Reflections On Copywriting: A Summing Up

At times, almost any copywriter would be glad to exchange places with just about any other type of worker—salesman, carpenter, druggist. He will at these times feel rejected, underpaid, overworked. At other times, he would not exchange jobs with anyone. Flushed with creative excitement and gratified by the results obtained from his creativity, he feels that no other work could provide the heady challenge and satisfaction of copywriting. Few other jobs are likely to shoot a person so rapidly from the heights to the depths, and back again. Let's examine why this is so.

COPYWRITERS—ARTISTS OR BUSINESSMEN?

Purple drapes, a cathedral-like hush, and sweet violin music playing softly in the background—these were provided (the story goes) to create the right mood for one temperamental advertising-agency copywriter in the fabulous 1920's.

During this period, when advertising billings were beginning to zoom, the copywriter could do no wrong. If he wanted "mood background," the indulgent advertisers let him have it. The copywriter was a favorite actor in a dizzy drama of lush profits.

Today's copywriter is likely to be less coddled than the copywriter who worked during the period from the end of World War I until the 1929 crash. He was credited then with the sensitivity of any other "artiste." He was a littérateur who condescended to work at the prosaic job of selling soap, automobiles, and washing machines.

When the crash came, advertising emerged from the golden haze. The era of advertising research began. Advertising became a serious, painstaking business instead of a madcap adventure. The copywriter pulled down his purple drapes and looked out soberly upon the smoky city below. He was no longer an artiste with taken-for-granted temperamental rights. He was a businessman.

Not all copywriters, admittedly, have given up the idea that they are apart from the ordinary businessman. Generally, however, most of today's copywriters think of themselves as businessmen—not artists.

MUCH MORE THAN SLOGAN WRITING

Most people in the general public have only the vaguest idea of a copywriter's work and some of these ideas have been colored by exaggerations of motion pictures and trashy novels that "tell the truth" about the advertising business.

Very deep-rooted is the idea that the usual copywriter is a glib "sloganeer." A sizable portion of the public, including many businessmen who should know better, think of copywriting in terms of writing clever slogans. Countless persons, desiring entrance into advertising and the copywriting field, have been armed with nothing more potent than a firm belief that they could "turn out slogans"—"99-44/100% pure," "Say it with flowers"—and others, have become a part of the American vernacular, has helped create the illusion that copywriting is basically slogan writing.

The duties of a copywriter, although practically unknown to most persons, do not discourage advertising aspirants. Individuals who might, for example, question their ability to do satisfactory work in the research department or the media department of a company will apply very confidently for a copywriter's position. Without advertising knowledge or experience, applicants will try unhesitatingly to enter this tough, competitive field. When their applications are received indifferently or without too much serious consideration, the applicants are hurt and amazed.

BEING A GOOD WRITER ISN'T ENOUGH

Just what is there about copywriting which makes it seem easy and desirable? The answer is that there is almost 100% ignorance among nonadvertising folk of just what a copywriter is supposed to do—and what he gets paid for doing it. They have no comprehension of the hard work and supplementary knowledge that must accompany a copywriter's expected ability in writing.

Advertising managers, like newspaper editors, are continually squashing the hopes of applicants who have little else in their personal sales kit than an alleged flair for writing. Because of letter-writing ability, or a succession of "A's" on high-school or college themes, the youthful men and women of self-asserted literary merit feel that writing advertising or newspaper copy is merely an extension of the writing they have already done. Everyone thinks he can write because everyone has to write at one time or another. How many times have you looked at an advertisement and said to yourself, "And they call *that* copywriting! Why didn't they do it *this* way?" The world is filled with people who feel they could do a better job of writing advertisements than the men who make their living as copywriters. Under the delusion that they "could do it better," the uninitiated approach the copywriting field eagerly and confidently.

WHICH IS HARDER—COPYWRITING OR REPORTING?

Reporting and copywriting demand ability, knowledge, and experience far beyond a surface facility in writing. Requirements for the two occupations are similar in some points. In both, for instance, it is vital to understand people and to use that understanding in the fashioning of lucid material.

A copywriter, like a reporter, must be analytical, observant, and thorough. Each has specialized knowledge fitting him for his work. Where, for example, the aspiring reporter might find it advantageous to obtain a background in political science and labor economics, the future copywriter might acquire a knowledge of sociology and mass psychology.

Despite certain points of similarity between the two occupations, it is perhaps more difficult to prepare for a copywriter's job than for that of a reporter. A journalism school, granted normal intelligence and aptitude on the part of the student, can teach the student the celebrated "5 W's" formula. Having mastered the rather stylized forms of newswriting, the intelligent journalism school graduate can do a creditable beginning job for most newspapers.

The fact that copywriting is less precise than newswriting and less amenable to "formula" writing makes the task of teaching copywriting in school somewhat more arduous than the teaching of newswriting. Take the writing of crime stories. Any reporter who has worked a police beat has developed a format for crime stories. Depending on his ability, he can vary the writing within his format, but essentially he follows a rather definite writing pattern. His work is made easier and faster if he follows the pattern. You have no such "formula" to help you in copywriting. You cannot use as a crutch any mechanical style of writing to make your job easier—each advertisement is custom-built to time or space requirements and to the product.

What makes your preparation for copywriting work even more difficult is the fact that the copywriter as a businessman must know business matters. Before you set down at the typewriter you should have a background of business experience that enables you to write copy intelligently and competently. The knowledge of selling, of merchandise, or of general business procedure gained from this experience gives you confidence.

The copywriter adds another element to his writing that is not present in the news story. This is the element of persuasion. Whereas the reporter gives the facts without embellishment, the copywriter while also giving facts must add words and sentences that will cause his readers to take action. His words must create a mood, an excitement, and a desire for the goods or services he is selling. Not for him is mere recital of facts. He must sell, as well as tell. As anyone knows who has done face to face selling, persuading a reluctant prospect to a course of action can be difficult. Yet this is what the copywriter must do in every advertisement he prepares.

To sum up, copywriting like reporting demands much more than facility with words. Whether it is more difficult to become a good copywriter than a good reporter is debatable, but there is no debating the assertion that copywriting calls for hard and extensive preparatory work.

COPYWRITERS—"ANONYMOUS" BUSINESSMEN

Although a copywriter may write top-flight copy, may develop slogans, trade names, and descriptive phrases that become a part of the nation's idiom, he may never be identified with his work. Copywriters are anonymous. They are among the thousands of businessmen who do their jobs day after day—efficiently and unknown. Here again the copywriter is removed from the class of the "artiste."

Not for the copywriter is the acclaim of the "by-line" newspaper reporter or of the motion picture scenario writer. If the only satisfaction you get out of writing is the glow you feel when people talk about your work, then copywriting will give you only limited satisfaction, since the only people who will know what you have written are those who are associated with you in business. As a copywriter you are just another salesman peddling merchandise and ideas.

WHAT YOU CAN EARN

Salaries for copywriters are generally thought to be much higher than they are. Although top agency copywriters draw very high pay, many beginning copywriters start with salaries little better than that of office boys.

Skill in copywriting, however, is rewarded as well as in any other business activity. Some advertising agency copy chiefs, to illustrate, are paid huge salaries, but for every high-salaried man there are hundreds of copywriters who earn modest salaries. The high salaries paid to relatively few copywriters have, unfortunately, been so widely publicized that the beginner is led into thinking that all copywriters are paid bountifully.

If you are able to check the salaries paid to copywriters in the different kinds of advertising activity—retail, agency, newspaper, business concerns, or radio—you will soon discover that such copywriters are paid no better and no worse than are persons of comparable skill in most other fields of business activity. A few make the top-bracket figures—most make average salaries.

HURRY! HURRY! HURRY!

Like the newspaper reporter, the copywriter is hounded by a deadline. If he is a nervous type, he will find the work taxing. Day after day, month after month, he will be hurried, always conscious of publishing or broadcasting dates. What field of advertising is *most* trying on the nerves of the copywriter? It is difficult to say.

The retail field, in which the artists, copywriters, and production men are just a step ahead of the publishing date, is full of worry for individuals who like to do thoughtful, careful work. As one retail copywriter said, "There's an empty feeling in turning out copy this way. I'm always haunted by the consciousness that this hurried, 'rush-rush' work is not my best work. I'd like to work in an agency where the deadlines are farther apart."

The retail copywriter typically sighs for the green fields of agency copywriting. All the way down the line, the agency copywriter is envied. But what is the situation with the agency copywriter? Is his job relatively easy? Actually, he voices almost exactly the same complaint heard from the retail copywriter. True, his deadlines are not usually "daily" deadlines, but he is seemingly always behind the schedule. Then, there is always the unexpected presentation, the new account, or the quick revision. All these call for "hurry-up" writing dashed off to the accompaniment of the impatient jigging of the copy chiefs or clients waiting for the copywriter to get through.

Copywriting provides little quiet, leisurely writing. The copywriter is a businessman who writes under hard-driving business conditions for other businessmen who have no time for creative temperament. The copywriter produces work quickly—and good work, too, or out he goes.

Still, many successful copywriters feel that they do their very best work when under extreme pressure. Like athletes who come through when the "chips are down," you may often find inspiration when circumstances force you to do the "impossible." If you're the type who can rise to the urgency of the moment, you will find the pressure stimulating.

NEEDED—MENTAL AND PHYSICAL STAMINA

The drain on a copywriter's creative talent is considerable. Where a successful magazine writer might make a good living turning out a few articles or stories a year and have a chance to "rest up" between efforts, the copywriter must turn out a quantity of good writing daily. Each day he searches for new ways to write his headlines, slogans, body copy, commercials, and direct-mail pieces.

If you, as a copywriter, are assigned miscellaneous accounts, you must adjust yourself rapidly to each new product that you write about. You are expected to give a fresh twist to your copy in order that you may satisfy the probing and skeptical examination by executives of the client company. Such quantity writing puts a great strain on your "freshness" and originality.

The working hours of copywriters are likely to be irregular. When an emergency arises (and emergencies are always arising), you are expected to stay on the job day and night until your part of the work is done. Overtime is a part of creative work. Then, too, as a conscientious copywriter, you are likely to take your work with your wherever you go. As you walk down the street you may see new uses for the products that you write copy about. You jot down the ideas before they escape you. At night you squirm in your bed, musing over a new approach for a current campaign. Finally, unable to get back to sleep, you snap on the light, sketch the idea, and wait impatiently for morning in order that you may give your "sizzler" the test of daylight examination.

The combination of irregular hours and work which creates nervous tension makes good health an important requisite for copywriters. Obviously, you don't need the muscles of a Samson but if you can bounce out each day fresh and vigorous—all the better. Health and an ability to take each new assignment as it comes are important in the profession.

Unless you reach top levels, you cannot expect pampering in your working conditions. You are more likely, as an average copywriter, to work in a crowded little cubicle piled high with proofs, unfinished work, and samples of products about which you are writing. Some copywriters, in fact, seem to work best in an office that many persons might consider hopelessly littered. If you're the usual copywriter, you cannot expect specialized work to bring specialized working conditions. Although your work may be important, you are just part of the business of creating advertising that will sell, and you carry on your function in a business office.

REWARDS OF COPYWRITING

Up to this point, the "cold water" approach has been employed in discussing the career of a beginning advertising copywriter. Any copywriting book must describe the negative aspects. Such frankness is necessary because of the general misconceptions regarding copywriting. When you start your first copywriting job you should do so eagerly but not with a feeling that you are about to enter a "never-never" land divorced from the usual business world.

Before discouraging you further, however, it is only sensible to point out that there are agreeable sides to the life of a copywriter. To those who can stand the pace, the work is deeply satisfying. A copywriter may grumble, threaten to quit, fight with the boss, but he knows deep down that it would be difficult to find any other work that he would like so well.

The lure of the copywriter's job is compounded of varied factors. Some of these factors mean more to one person than to another. You, for example, might experience a never-ending thrill in the creative side of the work. Seeing "your stuff" in *Life* magazine or *The New Yorker* or hearing "your" commercial over a national network—these moments are your bonus for the hours of word-hammering. Reading your writing in print is a satisfaction whether the words appear in a country weekly, a huge metropolitan daily, or a national magazine. Although much of the copywriter's work is mere common sense put into selling words, some of his efforts fall into the classification of sheer creativeness. Such work is a joy to perform, never routine, always satisfying.

GOOD COPY SERVES A VITAL FUNCTION

Another copywriter might derive his satisfaction from the important part he has in the movement of goods. He realizes that all the manufacturing skill and marketing genius behind a product are wasted unless *his* words convince the customer he should buy the product. To this copywriter comes a sense of usefulness in the business picture—the feeling that he is a "mover of goods."

This feeling of being useful is vital to the copywriter. Your work is better if you can feel that it is of service in the social and economic sense. Admittedly, the utility of many products is so questionable that you feel no glow in having written the copy that makes goods move from the producer to the consumer. On the other hand, if the product is beneficial to the user, you are gratified that you can inform the user about the product and that you can cause him to buy it. One of your real pleasures is to see the sales curve rise as a result of a successful advertisement or series of advertisements. You soon discover that if your copy doesn't sell, it represents so much wasted effort. The successful copywriter and the sales department are never far apart.

If you feel that you are part of business, if you see your work as contributing to the marketing pattern, you are likely to be a better copywriter. You then see the marketing pattern as it is concerned with the product research and sales plans behind the goods advertised. You include in your working knapsack some knowledge of the manufacturing difficulties and even the legal aspects such as the patent rights, trade-mark details, and the Fair Trade regulations affecting the distribution of the products you write about.

YOU'RE PART OF THE TOTAL EFFORT

You are aware, too, of the many things that happen after you have punched out copy on your typewriter. You know that untruths or careless wording may cause trouble with such groups as the Radio and Periodical Division of the Federal Trade Commission, or the Better Business Bureau, or the Federal Security Agency administering the Federal Food and Drug Act. Possibly your words might cause consumer "kickback" which will make the sales department storm and ask angrily, "Who wrote this?" Copy, you realize, is a sharp-edged business tool, part of the marketing process involving you, salesmen, wholesalers, retailers, consumers, manufacturers, researchmen, and all others engaged in business. You have an obligation to all of these and especially to the consumers who, like you, are entitled to honest, competently written copy in order that they may make the best possible use of their money when they purchase goods.

It is very necessary for you to obtain a feeling which has been described aptly as "togetherness." Without the feeling, you write copy in a void. With the consciousness of the whole job, you attain unity in your copy.

In a sense, you must also look upon yourself as a merchant who has goods to sell. Your words either take the place of salesmen or make the salesman's job more productive by acting as the "door opener." They tell the truth about the goods but they tell the truth persuasively—so much so that the reader is given a reason to buy. Again, you must, above all, become a part of the vital business of moving goods.

THE RETAIL COPYWRITER IS A MERCHANT

The feeling of being a "merchant" must be especially strong in the department store copywriter. True, some of these writers merely sit in their tiny offices in the advertising department. By preference, these "sitters" deal with goods—not with people, and not with the big, dynamic selling process of modern retailing. They become wrapped up in their task of writing words—countless words—about merchandise. Such copywriters are not businessmen-writers. They have the writer's viewpoint only. It is not enough.

The retail copywriter—the good one—*must* be a part of the retail business. If you write newspaper advertisements for an aggressive department store, you have the privilege of learning merchandising in its most vigorous form. Some of the best copy in any business activity is turned out daily at such stores as Marshall Field & Company, Macy's, Pogues', and Bullock's. Do the men or women copywriters turning out these words learn to do so by spinning them out in their offices, far removed from the bargain-hunters in the basement? No! These writers become a part of the business scene. They get out of their offices and into the store.

They talk to buyers. From them they can learn merchandising, fashions, trade-talk, prices, and customer likes and dislikes. The topnotch retail copywriters learn the jobs of other people in the store, too. The salespeople, in direct contact with the customers, can provide much grist for copy. A personal service shopper can be "pumped" for comments made by customers who talk to her. In the retail trade, the learning of all the functions and services of a department store is known as acquiring the "whole-store" viewpoint. The acquisition of such a viewpoint by you, the retail copywriter, is a part of your training as a businessman and hence—a better copywriter.

IF YOU'RE GOOD, YOU HAVE PRESTIGE

Lastly, if you have become a good copywriter, you will derive satisfaction from your standing in the business community, and in the firm for which you work. Although it has been pointed out that good copywriters are not coddled as artists, they are definitely treated with respect as an important type of worker.

If you are in an agency, you are one of a relatively small group of specialists. To picture this, assume that XYZ agency has lined up a new account through the work of its new-business man. The account executive who is to service the account has been approved. The agency's financial stability and business integrity have been found satisfactory by the client. Despite the foregoing—the fast-talking and persuasive new-business man, the charming and efficient account executive, the firm's unquestioned integrity—all these will mean nothing if the agency cannot, through you, furnish good *selling* copy. Copy is a last and very important link in the manufacturer-agency-consumer chain. As the welder of the link, you are an important individual. Yours is the final responsibility.

A retail copywriter has the same sort of prestige. The men and women who write the copy for Ohrbach's, Wanamaker's, Hudson's, and Famous-Barr are solidly established in the business community. In addition to having developed the ability to write selling copy, they have stored in their brains an accumulation of valuable knowledge about products, merchandising, and other general business facts. So long as advertising is used in the mass distribution of goods, there will be need for skilled copywriters, especially in retail advertising—the biggest field of all.

Mediocrity in copywriting brings the usual reward of mediocrity. Skill in the profession enables you, the possessor, to "name your ticket" in the advertising world.

ONE LAST WORD

Now that you have been pummeled by rules, warned against this, and told to do that, you might think back over what has been said. If you do, you'll find that the following are some of the principal conclusions:

1. *There is no easy road to copywriting ability.* Throughout the book we have made a sincere effort to deglamorize copywriting. You were told that copywriting is not Hollywoodish; that as a copywriter you will not be a petted, pampered artist. You will be a businessman in a business office. You'll be important—yes. You will not, however, have special prerogatives and working conditions. If you think of yourself always as a businessman, you'll be better off. You're expected to know how to write but you must remember that your writing is a tool of business, not a stepladder to literary prominence. If copywriting ability were easy to acquire, there'd be no need for this book, for advertising copy courses, for the slow apprentice system so often found in agencies and retail stores—nor

would copywriters be paid so well. But copywriting is *not* easy to learn. It's an exacting craft which a very few learn easily and the great majority learn through trial and error, perseverance and instruction. Some never learn it.

2. *Skill in one kind of copywriting does not automatically transfer to other types of copywriting.* Competent copywriters can usually write all kinds of copy. An agency copywriter, for example, because he handles diversified accounts, often attains proficiency in almost every type and style of copy. The fact remains, however, that a person who has done nothing but radio or television copy has learned different techniques than has the copy man who has spent all his time on magazine or newspaper copy. The retail writer who began in department store copywriting and has remained in it is in a little world of her own which has its own problems.

Even within the same field, there are pronounced differences. In Chicago, for example, Carson, Pirie, Scott & Company, the widely known State Street department store, develops the "Carson" copy approach. Copy and art treatment are distinctive enough to identify advertisements as "Carson's" advertisements, establishing the store's character and individuality unmistakably. The store's copy people, ever mindful of their great rival, Marshall Field & Company, strive constantly to be different from Field's. The same thing is true of nearly all big cities—big stores through their copy and art treatment build up individuality. Thus a successful writer for one store may be so thoroughly indoctrinated into certain copy techniques that she must consciously adapt herself to the general approach used by another store if she changes jobs.

Then, look at mail-order and fashion copy. The first is stripped of nonsense. It's direct, detailed, and slugs the message home. The customer gets up from the floor groggy with facts. He knows just how to order. He probably even knows how many seams were put in that pair of overalls he's asked about. Fashion copy, on the other hand, is normally light, fluffy, and inclined to substitute atmosphere for facts . Perhaps each writer could take over the other's job. In a good many cases, however, it is doubtful that such a switch-over could be made without considerable flexibility on the part of the copywriter.

As a last "clincher" on the point that a certain adjustment is needed in order to switch from one kind of copy to another—think about the industrial magazine advertising writer. Consider the technical knowledge needed to write industrial advertisements. Think again, then, of your fashion writer, or your average writer of consumer copy. The airy, nonsensical touch of the fashion copywriter would be out of place in a hard-selling advertisement for steam boilers. Some writers can do both types of copy. Others never can.

To sum up: Each copywriting job makes use of the basic human appeals, but differences in writing style, media, and subject matter make it difficult to say that because you have mastered one copywriting job you can necessarily master tham all—no more than a master steamfitter can become a grade A carpenter even though both of them are in the building trade and are "handy" with tools.

3. *Copy research, like copywriting, has no final answer.* You have probably noticed that this book handled copy testing as if it were capable of blowing up in the authors' faces. Copy testing and other forms of research *are* explosive. Some of the most violent advertising arguments are concerned with research methods. If you picked up the idea that we don't espouse any one kind of copy testing;

that we find some good and bad points in all the methods; that we think copy testing is very important and that you should learn some of the methods—then the research section did its job. Most of all, we hoped that you would decide, after finishing the chapter, that you would always keep an open mind about copy testing, always looking for the good and bad points of each system.

4. *Education, work experience, and personality are important elements in copywriting success.* Although there are and have been successful copywriters with no more education than one might pick up from McGuffey's Fourth Grade Reader, education—especially college education—*is* an advantage to copywriters. You must gather that there are certain courses of study that are more stuied to a copywriting career than others, *but* this doesn't mean a copywriter can't profit from almost any course of study. Although advertising, newswriting, and such courses are directly applicable to a copy career, a course in history, economic geography, or sociology might provide a background that could be very useful some day.

As for work experience, we *depart* from American tradition by suggesting that you try several jobs. Work experience, is ideally composed of writing and selling, with an accent on diversity of experience. A sort of composite reporter-salesman may have floated before your eyes as the ideal pre-copywriter. That's *our* ideal, too.

Quite a stress must be placed on the copywriter's personality. Of course, you can find some good copy men who shy from human contact. They're the exceptions. Unless you like people, and share the usual enthusiasms, annoyances, and disappointments of most people, you are handicapped as a copywriter. And, too, if you are overly sensitive to criticism of your work, you'll suffer as your fellow-workers or bosses roughly and caustically give you "the business" in criticizing what you consider your choicest copy. Also, your personality must be adaptable to the creative demands of copywriting. You work hard, long, and fast in most copy jobs. Unless you are willing, and capable of doing so, we advise you to think carefully before you enter copywriting.

5. *Your conscience and good taste should make you an "honest" copywriter.* There have been so many high-sounding and painfully moral treatises turned out under the title of "Honesty in Advertising" that we've decided to be different. We assume that you have been well indoctrinated into the ethics of truth and honesty in advertising. Our approach is to point out that it's just plain *silly* to write untruthful copy. We believe this firmly. On one side, you have the law ready to pounce if you transgress. We hope very earnestly that the sections involving points about which the Federal Trade Commission is very sensitive will help you avoid trouble with that body. On the other side are the consumers of your products. Their buying power is an effective inducement to honesty. Sooner or later the cheat and fraud is discovered and, when he is, he loses sales.

We have discussed the "practical" inducements to honest advertising. When you are dealing with the public—the very young and the very old—the shrewd and the feeble-minded—the very poor and the very rich—your own conscience, also, should dictate honesty. In your person-to-person contacts you wouldn't cheat a subnormal or a charity case out of one cent, yet, through their copy, a lot of your copywriters can bilk thousands of people. It's a matter of extending your conscience beyond what you're writing and visualizing the undiscerning people who will buy your product because you tell them to. The saying "Let your conscience be your guide" can be most apropos in this instance—only be sure to put your conscience in order before you write copy.

As a closing note, remember that nowhere have we said, "this is the way and the only way to write copy." If you put any of the book's principles to work, remember that each copy job is just a little different from the one before. Learn what we have said and then make allowances and adjustments when you apply our ideas to your individual situation. Among the copywriter's greatest assets are his flexibility and skill in adjusting to the needs of the individual copy assignment.

Appendix

What you find in this section should be useful on many occasions. It is material for the working copywriter, or for the student who is working at *learning* copywriting. Too often material in a book appendix is never looked at. In this case, such neglect would be a pity since every item in *this* appendix should be useful to you at one time or another.

Copyfitting

Even experienced copywriters can write too much copy for the space. Beginning writers consistently do so. Seldom does anyone write too little copy for the space, but this can happen, too.

There are complicated copyfitting systems that require mathematics, or call it arithmetic, that will help you. Then, there are crude word-count systems that are based on an average number of words per line, multiplied by the number of lines to achieve the total.

The first system is too time-taking for the impatient copywriter, and the second too inaccurate. On the latter point, for example, "honorificabilituditadibus" is counted as one word. So is the letter "a". Radio writers can be thrown off by multi-syllable words, too.

Fig. A-1 is a page from a type specimen book. You are given in this page type sizes from tiny 5 pt. type all the way to 36 pt. Body type usually ends at 12 points. For newspaper copy 10 to 11 pt. type is desirable with 11 pt. type being especially good for easy reading.

You must remember if you use this type specimen page as a guide that a 10 or 11 pt. type in one face may take more or less room than 10 or 11 pt. type in another face. Still, if you're careful enough to be guided by the pages reproduced here your chances of being markedly wrong in your copyfitting for the usual advertisement are remote.

For a quick idea of how much copy you should write, find out the length of lines in your body text. Let's say that the line is four inches long. Assume, too, that you've decided upon 11 pt. size. Since you discover that 11 pt. type fits 15 characters to the inch, four inches will take 60 characters. Set your typewriter for 60 characters and then type away.

Naturally, you'll have to determine how many lines deep your copy is to go. Decide that and multiply 60 by the number of lines to get the total number of characters. Usually, however, all you need to know is the character count per line and then you simply type the number of lines needed. You normally don't worry about the total number of characters although sometimes you may be told to write a piece of copy with a limit of 780 characters, or 900, or some other figure.

Remember these type specimen pages if you're in doubt about how much copy to write. They can save you much reworking of copy, not to mention the embarrassment of having your copy returned for pruning.

Proofreading

You'll be asked to "proof" your own work, and sometimes that of others. Likewise, someone may be "proofing" yours. When you use the standard proofreading symbols and methods, you're using a common language of the writer, editor, and printer.

In Fig. A-2 is a simple listing of proofreading marks. For most copywriters this listing is sufficient. If, however, you find that you need a proofreading guide more elaborate than this, write to Mergenthaler Linotype Company, Mergenthaler Drive, P.O. Box 82 Plainfield, New York 11803.

An incidental piece of information that might be useful to you is that there is no proofreading symbol for the underline. When you underline a word, a printer automatically will set it in italics. To make sure that he

Century Schoolbook Bold

Fototronic—Century Schoolbook Bold

5 pt. Printing has performed a role of achievement unparalleled in the revelation of new horizons, and in emphasizing t
he potentials of social and cultural development. The invention of printing stands at the peak of man's broad civiliz
PRINTING HAS PERFORMED A ROLE OF ACHIEVEMENT UNPARALLELED IN THE REVELATION OF NEW
PRINTING HAS PERFORMED A ROLE OF ACHIEVEMENT UNPARALLELED IN THE REVELATION OF NEW HORIZONS 1234567890
Printing has performed a role of achievement unparalleled in the revelation of new horizons, and in emphasizing in th
PRINTING HAS PERFORMED A ROLE OF ACHIEVEMENT UNPARALLELED IN THE REVELATION OF 123

5½ pt. Printing has performed a role of achievement unparalleled in the revelation of new horizons, and in emph
asizing the potentials of social and cultural development. The invention of printing stands at the peak of m
PRINTING HAS PERFORMED A ROLE OF ACHIEVEMENT UNPARALLELED IN THE REVELATION
PRINTING HAS PERFORMED A ROLE OF ACHIEVEMENT UNPARALLELED IN THE REVELATION OF NEW 1234567890
Printing has performed a role of achievement unparalleled in the revelation of new horizons, and in emphas
PRINTING HAS PERFORMED A ROLE OF ACHIEVEMENT UNPARALLELED IN THE REVEL 456

6 pt. Printing has performed a role of achievement unparalleled in the revelation of new horizons, and
in emphasizing the potentials of social and cultural development. The invention of printing stand
PRINTING HAS PERFORMED A ROLE OF ACHIEVEMENT UNPARALLELED IN THE REVEL
PRINTING HAS PERFORMED A ROLE OF ACHIEVEMENT UNPARALLELED IN THE REVELATION O 1234567890
Printing has performed a role of achievement unparalleled in the revelation of new horizons, and
PRINTING HAS PERFORMED A ROLE OF ACHIEVEMENT UNPARALLELED IN THE R 789

6½ pt. Printing has performed a role of achievement unparalleled in the revelation of new horizo
ns, and in emphasizing the potentials of social and cultural development. The invention of
PRINTING HAS PERFORMED A ROLE OF ACHIEVEMENT UNPARALLELED IN THE
PRINTING HAS PERFORMED A ROLE OF ACHIEVEMENT UNPARALLELED IN THE REV 1234567890
Printing has performed a role of achievement unparalleled in the revelation of new horizon
PRINTING HAS PERFORMED A ROLE OF ACHIEVEMENT UNPARALLELED IN 123

7 pt. Printing has performed a role of achievement unparalleled in the revelation of new
horizons, and in emphasizing the potentials of social and cultural development. Th
PRINTING HAS PERFORMED A ROLE OF ACHIEVEMENT UNPARALLELED IN
PRINTING HAS PERFORMED A ROLE OF ACHIEVEMENT UNPARALLELED IN T 1234567890
Printing has performed a role of achievement unparalleled in the revelation of new
PRINTING HAS PERFORMED A ROLE OF ACHIEVEMENT UNPARALLE 456

7½ pt. Printing has performed a role of achievement unparalleled in the revelation o
f new horizons, and in emphasizing the potentials of social and cultural develo
PRINTING HAS PERFORMED A ROLE OF ACHIEVEMENT UNPARALLE
PRINTING HAS PERFORMED A ROLE OF ACHIEVEMENT UNPARALLELED 1234567890
Printing has performed a role of achievement unparalleled in the revelation of
PRINTING HAS PERFORMED A ROLE OF ACHIEVEMENT UNPARA 789

8 pt. Printing has performed a role of achievement unparalleled in the revelat
PRINTING HAS PERFORMED A ROLE OF ACHIEVEMENT UNPARAL
PRINTING HAS PERFORMED A ROLE OF ACHIEVEMENT UNPARALLE 1234567890
Printing has performed a role of achievement unparalleled in the revelatio
PRINTING HAS PERFORMED A ROLE OF ACHIEVEMENT UNP 123

8½ pt. Printing has performed a role of achievement unparalleled in the re
PRINTING HAS PERFORMED A ROLE OF ACHIEVEMENT UNPA
PRINTING HAS PERFORMED A ROLE OF ACHIEVEMENT UNPA 1234567890
Printing has performed a role of achievement unparalleled in the rev
PRINTING HAS PERFORMED A ROLE OF ACHIEVEMENT U 456

9 pt. Printing has performed a role of achievement unparalleled in th
PRINTING HAS PERFORMED A ROLE OF ACHIEVEMENT U
PRINTING HAS PERFORMED A ROLE OF ACHIEVEMENT U 1234567890
Printing has performed a role of achievement unparalleled in the
PRINTING HAS PERFORMED A ROLE OF ACHIEVEME 789

10 pt. Printing has performed a role of achievement unparalleled
PRINTING HAS PERFORMED A ROLE OF ACHIEVEME
PRINTING HAS PERFORMED A ROLE OF ACHIEVEM 1234567890
Printing has performed a role of achievement unparalleled
PRINTING HAS PERFORMED A ROLE OF ACHIE 123

11 pt. Printing has performed a role of achievement unpara
PRINTING HAS PERFORMED A ROLE OF ACHIEV
PRINTING HAS PERFORMED A ROLE OF AC 1234567890
Printing has performed a role of achievement unparal
PRINTING HAS PERFORMED A ROLE OF AC 456

12 pt. Printing has performed a role of achievement un
PRINTING HAS PERFORMED A ROLE OF AC
PRINTING HAS PERFORMED A ROLE OF 1234567890
Printing has performed a role of achievement unp
PRINTING HAS PERFORMED A ROLE OF 789

14 pt. Printing has performed a role of achieve
PRINTING HAS PERFORMED A ROLE
PRINTING HAS PERFORMED A RO 1234567890
Printing has performed a role of achievem
PRINTING HAS PERFORMED A RO 123

Characters per pica: 5 pt-4.5; 5½ pt-4.1; 6 pt-3.8; 6½ pt-3.5; 7 pt-3.2; 7½ pt-3.0; 8 pt-2.8; 8½ pt-2.7; 9 pt-2.5; 10 pt-2.3; 11 pt-2.1; 12 pt-1.9; 14 pt-1.6; 16 pt-1.4

Fig. A-1

Type Specimen sheets.

Courtesy Rochester Monotype Composition Co.

Fig. A-2

Proofreaders' marks.

Courtesy University of Chicago Press, ''A Manual of Style'', 12th Edition

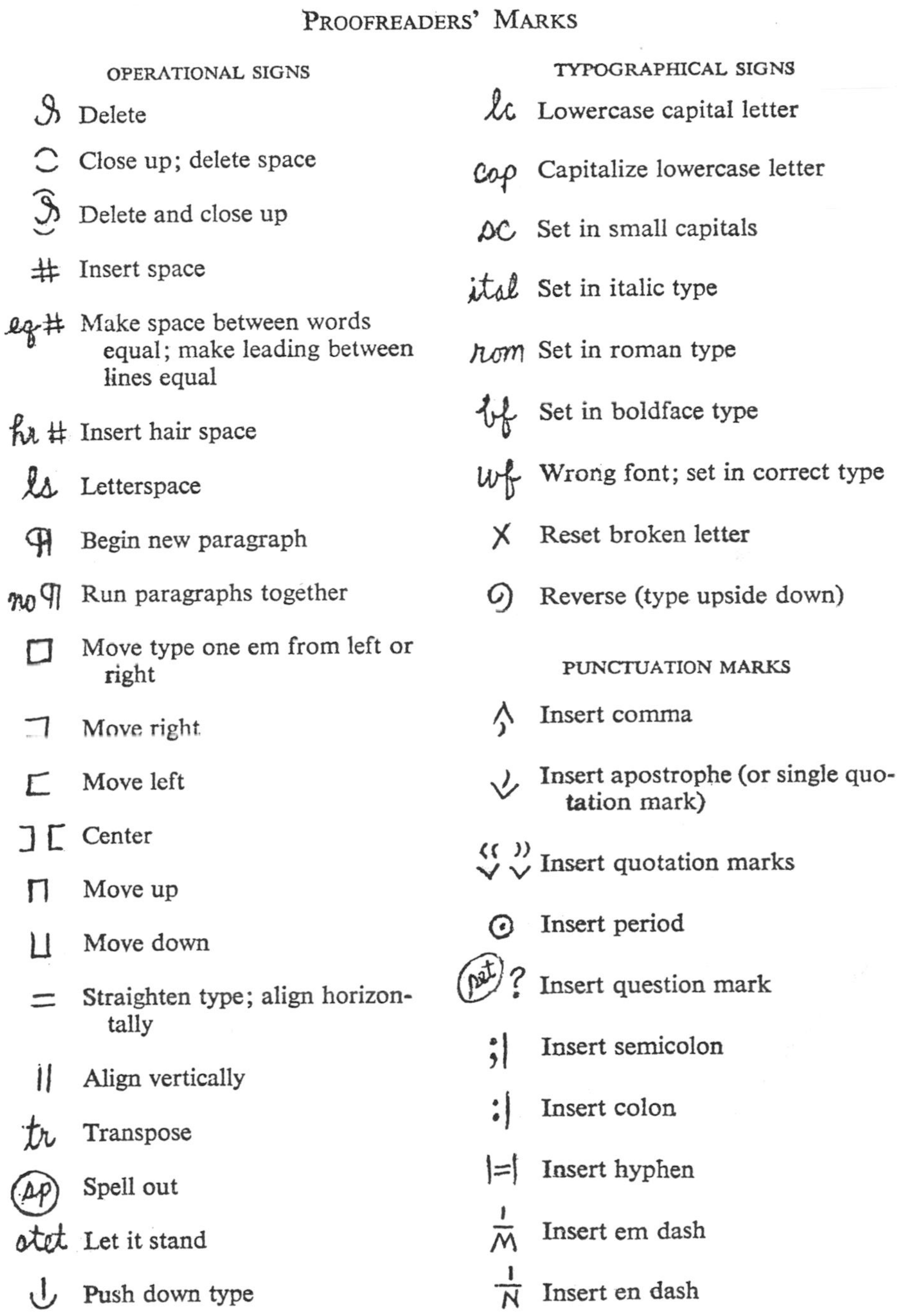

PROOFREADERS' MARKS

OPERATIONAL SIGNS

Delete
Close up; delete space
Delete and close up
Insert space
Make space between words equal; make leading between lines equal
Insert hair space
Letterspace
Begin new paragraph
Run paragraphs together
Move type one em from left or right
Move right
Move left
Center
Move up
Move down
Straighten type; align horizontally
Align vertically
Transpose
Spell out
Let it stand
Push down type

TYPOGRAPHICAL SIGNS

Lowercase capital letter
Capitalize lowercase letter
Set in small capitals
Set in italic type
Set in roman type
Set in boldface type
Wrong font; set in correct type
Reset broken letter
Reverse (type upside down)

PUNCTUATION MARKS

Insert comma
Insert apostrophe (or single quotation mark)
Insert quotation marks
Insert period
Insert question mark
Insert semicolon
Insert colon
Insert hyphen
Insert em dash
Insert en dash

understands that you want an underline, put a line under the word or phrase and then on the side of the sheet use these words: ''Printer. Underscore, *not* italics.''

Check-lists, rating systems and evaluation methods

In the chapter on advertising research you read about check-lists. For the usual copywriter a check-list is merely a simple list of product points. For instance, if he were writing about a flashlight he might list:

- Floats.
- Casts beam half mile.
- Waterproof.
- Shatterproof plastic.
- Three long-life batteries.
- Lightweight.
- Can be focussed.
- One-year guarantee.

For the conscientious copywriter ever anxious to improve performance, there are many systems and methods that have been written by men in agencies and companies. Most copywriters pay little attention to these. This is unfortunate since much is to be gained by using these suggestions either before, or after, writing copy.

Following are a number of systems. Perhaps one or more might be of great help to you.

No. 1

Some years ago, David Ogilvy, noted advertising man and author, offered the following scoring system for rating the mechanical or physical aspects of an advertisement. His suggestions are as valid today.

To use this, assume that the advertisement begins with a score of 100. Then deduct points according to whatever transgression has been committed. It is dubious that any advertisement will obtain 100 points when you rate it in this manner. The scoring system has much merit, however, in making the copywriter and artist painfully aware of some very important principles.

Rating System Based on Layout and Printing Factors

1. If the graphic technique obtrudes itself between the copywriter and the reader, deduct 17 points.
2. If the illustration is lazy — if it does not work hard at selling the product, deduct 11 points.
3. If it requires more than a split second for the reader to identify the kind of product being advertised, deduct 10 points.
4. If the brand name is not visible at a glance, deduct nine points.
5. If the layout looks more like an advertisement than an editorial page, deduct seven points.
6. If the illustration lacks "story appeal" — something interesting happening — deduct six points.
7. If a drawing is used instead of a photograph, deduct six points.
8. If the layout is cluttered or complicated, deduct five points.
9. If there is more than one place to begin reading, deduct four points.
10. If type is used self-consciously for purpose of design, deduct four points.
11. If the body copy is set in reverse, or in a tint, deduct four points.
12. If any illustration appears without a caption, deduct three points.
13. If the illustration is defaced in any way, e.g., by having the headline run into it, deduct two points.
14. If the illustration is any shape other than rectangular, deduct two points.
15. If the headline is set in more than one type face, deduct two points.
16. If the body copy is set in a sans serif face, deduct two points.
17. If the measure is wider than 40 characters, deduct two points.
18. If long copy is not broken with crossheads, deduct two points.
19. If the first paragraph is more than 12 words, deduct one point.
20. If the paragraphs are squared up, deduct one point.

On the content side, Mr. Ogilvy decries (1) any advertisement which is obviously dishonest, (2) an advertisement which would obviously be considered indecent or blasphemous by more than five per cent of the readers of the publication in which it appears, and (3) any advertisement which is an obvious imitation of another advertiser's advertisement.

No. 2-A

You will find the following suggestions in two parts. In 2-A you'll find major considerations to think about in your advertisement. By the way, this material applies to newspaper or magazine advertisements but the section in one question about including telephone numbers and hours would apply specifically to newspaper advertisements.

In 2-B, the scoring sheet enables you to determine how well the six major considerations have been applied.

WARNING. Don't apply this two literally to *all* advertisements. In fact, you can't apply it to all advertisements. For example, there are splendid corporate, or institutional advertisements that would rate poorly if judged by this system. There are image-building advertisements that would fare badly, too. In short, before you use this system, be sure that your subject matter, technique, or objective is suitable. If so, use. If not, don't use.

The six things to look for in an ad:*

1. *A theme*—can the sales message in the ad be stated in a simple declarative sentence?
2. *Headline*—a good headline normally includes the company name and a reader benefit. It should also be selective so the reader knows whether or not the ad is directed at him. And, of course, the headline should be simple enough to be clearly understood.
3. *Illustration*—the illustration should attract readers and help tell the story or reinforce the main sales point of the ad. If possible, it should show the product in use.
4. *Text or body copy*—the text should follow the headline, amplifying user benefits, explaining and offering proof that the product or service being advertised is a good one. And the text should end with an action close. It should tell the reader what to do next and it should make it easy for him to do it.
5. *Signature*—the ad should end with the company name clear and visible. Address (complete with zip code), phone number and hours open for business should be included.
6. *Ad layout*—the ad layout is nothing more than the arrangement of items two, three, four, and five. It should be planned to draw readers into the ad, guide them through it and visually present the image the advertiser wants to present.

*From Sales Management, Sept. 18, 1972. "Best Way To Judge Your Company's Ads: Score Them" (No Author)

Scoring sheet for evaluating an advertisement*

Item	Score
Can the main sales point bc stated in a simple declarative sentence	1 point
Does the headline mention company or brand name	1 point
Does the headline promise a benefit	2 points
Does the headline select the people the ad wants to talk to	1 point
Is the headline simple and easy to understand	1 point
Does the headline promise something new	1 point
Does the illustration show the product in use	1 point
Is the illustration attention-getting	1 point
Does the illustration show user benefits	1 point
Are there supplemental photos, drawings, or charts to add interest and help sell the product	1 point
Does the text repeat the benefit in the headline and amplify on it	1 point
Does the copy back up claims with proof	1 point
Does the copy present the whole story	1 point
Does the ad have an action close that tells the reader what to do next	1 point
Is the company name, address, phone number and hours included in the ad	1 point
Does the ad attract the reader's attention	1 point
Is there a logical visual path through the ad	1 point
Does the ad convey the company's image	1 point

16 or more points	excellent
13 to 15 points	good
10 to 12 points	fair
9 points or less	poor

*From Sales Management, Sept. 18, 1972, "Best Way to Judge Your Company's Ads: Score Them"

No. 3

One major corporation established the following "communications checkpoints" as criteria for its review-rating program. The objective was to determine whether an advertisement was above average, below average, or average in qualitative terms. Many company advertising departments establish such guidelines to judge their own output and that of their advertising agencies.

Checkpoints In The Ad Review

1. Does the advertisement offer a reward for the reader's time and attention? A benefit to the user? News? Service? Does it entertain or amuse?
2. Does the advertisement avoid the necessity for mental work by the reader? Is the headline specific, clear and direct? Does the illustration work hard to support the sales message? Is the layout simple and orderly, avoiding clutter?
3. Does it provide validation and support for the sales claim? By demonstrations? By tests? By case history or testimonial? By guarantee?
4. Does it exploit the principle of repetition? Is the story told in the headline? Again

Fig. A-3

The ten essentials of a good ad.

in the illustration? Again in the copy?

5. Does the treatment avoid the stereotype? Is it arresting? Fresh? Non-everyday?
6. Is the total effect modern and advanced?

No. 4

In Fig. A-3 you will find material aimed especially at the copywriter who is creating newspaper advertising, especially advertising for retail stores. The basic ideas and the copy came from the Bureau of Advertising of the American Newspaper Publishers Association. The material had been published in the Bureau's annual Retail Advertising Plan Book. It was also used as a mailer sent out by one newspaper to help local merchants and others prepare better advertisements. It is reproduced here as it appeared in the February 1973, International Newspaper Promotion Association Copy Service Newsletter, edited by James B. McGrew, of the Lancaster Newspapers, Inc., Lancaster, Pennsylvania.

Dear Advertiser,

The increasing complexity of retailing — such as the rapid growth and diversity of competition, changing customer shopping habits and the continuing squeeze on profits — has made it vitally important that merchants get full value from their advertising dollars.

The newspaper ad is the retailer's best store window and salesman. Nearly everyone reads a daily newspaper, and readers shop the newspaper for good values. Yet, the effectiveness of advertising varies widely. In terms of readership and sales results, some ads are far more successful than others.

The most important single factor determining how many people will read any newspaper ad is the skill and technique used in preparing the ad.

The following suggestions for copy and layout are drawn from several studies. When effectively used, these techniques and rules generally increase readership

LANCASTER NEWSPAPERS, INC.
8 W. King St., Lancaster, Penna. 17604

essentials of a good ad

make your ads easily recognizable 1

Advertisements which are distinctive in their use of art, layout techniques and type faces usually enjoy higher readership than run-of-the-mill advertising. Make your ads distinctively different in appearance from the advertising of your competitors. Then keep your ads' appearance consistent. This way, readers will recognize your ads even before they read them.

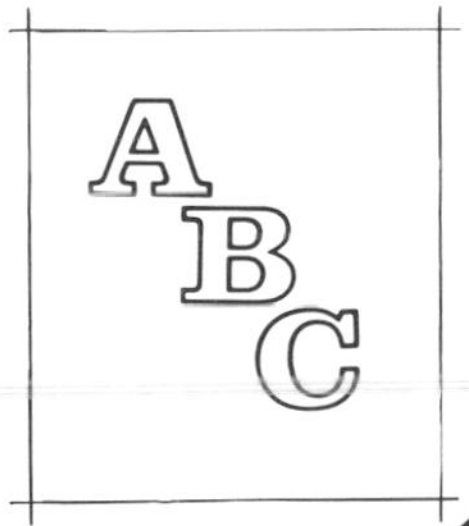
A
B
C

use a simple layout 2

The layout should carry the reader's eye through the message easily and in proper sequence: from headline to illustration to explanatory copy to price to your store's name. Avoid the use of too many different type faces, overly decorative borders and reverses. These devices are distracting and reduce the number of readers who receive your entire message.

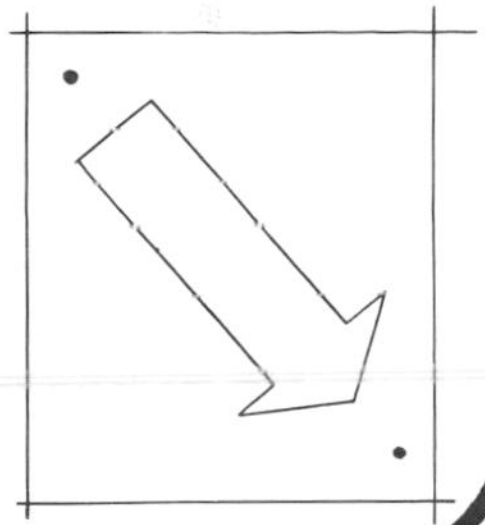

use a dominant element 3

— a large picture or headline — to insure quick visibility. Photographs and realistic drawings have about equal attention-getting value, but photographs of real people win more readership. So do action pictures. Photographs of local people or places also have high attention value. Use good art work. It will pay off in extra readership

use a prominent benefit headline 4

The first question a reader asks of an ad is: "What's in it for me?" Select the main benefit which your merchandise offers and feature it in a compelling headline. "How to" headlines encourage full copy readership, as do headlines which include specific information or helpful suggestions. Your headline will be easier to read if it is black-on-white and not printed over part of an illustration.

SAVE

Intelligencer Journal. LANCASTER NEW ERA SUNDAY NEWS

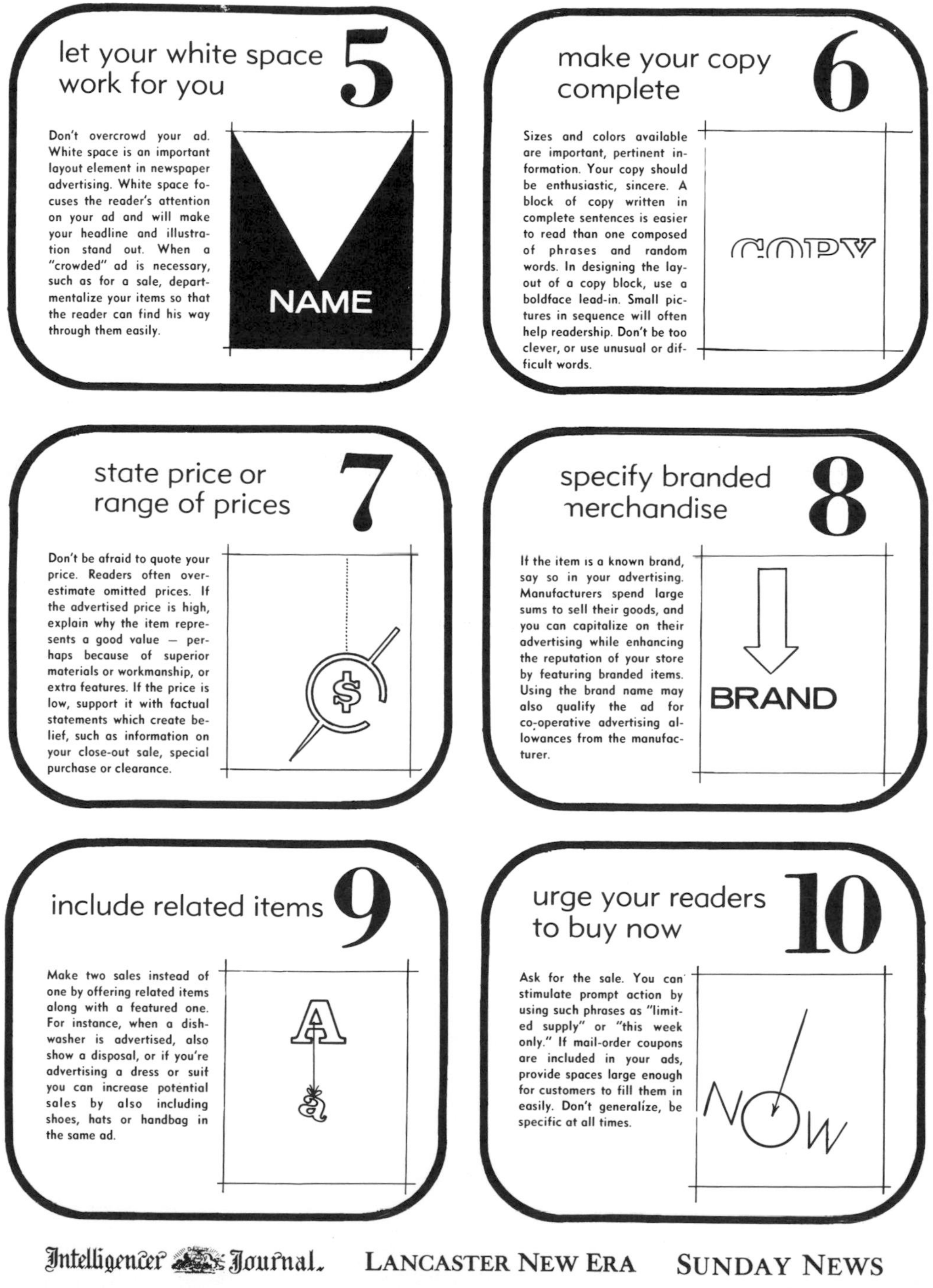
let your white space work for you
5
Don't overcrowd your ad. White space is an important layout element in newspaper advertising. White space focuses the reader's attention on your ad and will make your headline and illustration stand out. When a "crowded" ad is necessary, such as for a sale, departmentalize your items so that the reader can find his way through them easily.
NAME
make your copy complete
6
Sizes and colors available are important, pertinent information. Your copy should be enthusiastic, sincere. A block of copy written in complete sentences is easier to read than one composed of phrases and random words. In designing the layout of a copy block, use a boldface lead-in. Small pictures in sequence will often help readership. Don't be too clever, or use unusual or difficult words.
COPY
state price or range of prices
7
Don't be afraid to quote your price. Readers often overestimate omitted prices. If the advertised price is high, explain why the item represents a good value — perhaps because of superior materials or workmanship, or extra features. If the price is low, support it with factual statements which create belief, such as information on your close-out sale, special purchase or clearance.
$
specify branded merchandise
8
If the item is a known brand, say so in your advertising. Manufacturers spend large sums to sell their goods, and you can capitalize on their advertising while enhancing the reputation of your store by featuring branded items. Using the brand name may also qualify the ad for co-operative advertising allowances from the manufacturer.
BRAND
include related items
9
Make two sales instead of one by offering related items along with a featured one. For instance, when a dishwasher is advertised, also show a disposal, or if you're advertising a dress or suit you can increase potential sales by also including shoes, hats or handbag in the same ad.
A
urge your readers to buy now
10
Ask for the sale. You can stimulate prompt action by using such phrases as "limited supply" or "this week only." If mail-order coupons are included in your ads, provide spaces large enough for customers to fill them in easily. Don't generalize, be specific at all times.
NOW
Intelligencer Journal. LANCASTER NEW ERA SUNDAY NEWS

No. 5

In the following pages you will find a fairly elaborate advertising evaluation check-list that can be used: (a) To check your own work. (b) To check the work of someone else and thus give him a valuable critique. Used in this way, it would eliminate the infuriatingly vague type of comment expressed in the words: "I don't like it but I can't tell you exactly why."

This check-list, thus, can be used by the copywriter or by the copy chief. It is not, as you can see, a casual, once-over-lightly evaluation since it embraces headlines, body copy, layout, illustration, and typography.

The person using this evaluation system on a regular basis might wish to work out a point-scoring system and evolve a total for the "perfect" advertisement. Thus advertisements could be judged in terms of how far or how close they are to a perfect rating.

Advertising Evaluation Check-List

Headline

	10-8	7-5	4-0	POINTS
Over-all, is the headline:	Strong	Average	Weak	
	____	____	____	______
1. Does the headline relate to the product?	Closely	Fairly	Poorly	
	____	____	____	______
2. Does the headline contain a benefit?	Strong	Fair	Weak	
	____	____	____	______
3. Is head lively and full of action?	Lively	Fairly lively	Static	
	____	____	____	______

4. Is headline tied in well with opening copy?	Very	Slightly	Not at all	
	______	______	______	________
5. Is headline tied in well with illustration?	Very	Slightly	Not at all	
	______	______	______	________
6. Is headline aimed directly at prospect-reader of publication?	Very directly	Fairly well	Not at all	
	______	______	______	________

Miscellaneous Comments

Body Copy

	10-8 Strong	7-5 Average	4-0 Weak	
Over-all, is the body copy strong, average, weak?	______	______	______	________

____

____

____

1. Is copy well-organized in progressing logically from beginning to end?	Very well organized	Fairly well organized	Poorly organized	
	______	______	______	________

____

____

____

2. Does copy start out fast and interestingly?	Very well	Fairly well	Starts slow, uninterest-ing	
	______	______	______	________

____

____

____

3. Copy identifies company and/or product?	Strongly	Fairly well	Not at all	
	____	____	____	______
4. Copy stresses main benefit?	Strongly	Moderately	Poorly	
	____	____	____	______
5. Copy stresses subsidiary benefits?	Strongly	Fairly well	Poorly	
	____	____	____	______
6. Copy written in language of prospect-reader?	Very much so	Fairly well	Not at all	
	____	____	____	______

7. Can copy be called helpful?	Very helpful	Fairly helpful	Not helpful	
	______	______	______	________

____

____

____

8. Are copy claims believable?	Quite believable	Fairly believable	Not believable	
	______	______	______	________

____

____

____

9. Copy ending urge to action or some other positive manner?	Strong	Average	Weak	
	______	______	______	________

____

____

____

Miscellaneous Comments

____

____

____

____

Layout, Illustration, Typography

	10-8	7-5	4-0	
Over-all, is the total physical effect of the ad effective in achieving sales objectives, campaign objectives, or other objectives?	Very	Fairly so	Not at all	
	____	____	____	______
1. Is headline strong enough physically to achieve impact?	Strong impact	Fair impact	Little impact	
	____	____	____	______
2. Is main illustration strong enough physically to achieve impact?	Strong impact	Fair impact	Little impact	
	____	____	____	______
3. Is main illustration interesting to prospect-reader?	Very interesting	Fairly interesting	Not interesting	
	____	____	____	______

4. Is copy typographically easy to read? | Very easy ____ | Fairly easy ____ | Hard to read ____ | ____

____

____

____

5. Is size of ad space suitable to accomplish ad objectives? | Very suitable ____ | Fairly suitable ____ | Not suitable ____ | ____

____

____

____

6. Is layout technique (drawing or photo) suitable for purposes of ad? | Very suitable ____ | Fairly suitable ____ | Not suitable ____ | ____

____

____

____

7. Does logo stand out? | Very well ____ | Fairly well ____ | Poorly ____ | ____

____

____

____

	Very well	Fairly well	Poorly
8. Does layout "track" well in leading the reader logically through the ad?	____	____	____

Miscellaneous Comments

No. 6.

The copywriting marking code that follows has been used for some years to grade advertising campaigns turned in as term projects. On the paper of the student will be placed the code letter and number to tell him the nature of his transgression.

It is included here as a guide to warn of the many faults to be found in advertising copy and layouts. The "Analysis" referred to on the bottom is the market and creative analysis each student provides. This analysis is done before the copy is written.

Copywriting Marking Code

Layout and Typography

L-1 sloppy lettering
L-2 poor balance
L-3 coupon badly-designed (crowded, too little room to write, no sell)
L-4 headline and/or logo too small to get attention
L-5 headline is jammed against top
L-6 illustration idea dull, or not appropriate
L-7 too empty looking
L-8 just generally amateurish

L-9 use some small illustrations to liven up your ad, or to better explain the product
L-10 your layout has no focal point
L-11 your illustration is too small
L-12 your layout is sloppy
L-13 copy lines are set in too wide a measure
L-14 copy blocks are too small
L-15 layout (or certain sections of it) looks crowded
L-16 too much solid, unbroken type
L-17 too much material run together. Don't obscure points by running them together. List for easy reading.
L-18 layout cut up into too many elements

Copy

C-1 poor writing
C-2 skimpy copy treatment
C-3 illogical writing; doesn't fit in well, or doesn't make sense
C-4 writing is confusing
C-5 take too long to get started
C-6 writing is awkward
C-7 trite, worn-out, or cliche-ridden language
C-8 too fancy or literary for audience
C-9 needlessly negative
C-10 language is artificial, unnatural, or stilted—or all three
C-11 you don't make clear just what you're selling
C-12 your writing is too impersonal
C-13 you don't get excited enough
C-14 don't jam too many ideas in one sentence or paragraph
C-15 dull, lifeless slogan
C-16 poor product name
C-17 you don't stress the U.S.P. or point of difference
C-18 copy isn't geared well to the medium you're using
C-19 you fail to stress the most important point
C-20 too sweeping a claim
C-21 statement is misleading
C-22 unbelievable
C-23 exaggerated

Technical and Grammatical Faults

C-24 unsupported comparative
C-25 grammar is incorrect
C-26 antecedent is not clear
C-27 bad punctuation
C-28 use paragraphs
C-29 your writing lacks transition
C-30 use active tense
C-31 avoid this backward "newspaperese"
C-32 write complete sentences
C-33 I'd prefer more cohesive writing rather than a mere listing of points a la catalog copy
C-34 wrong spelling

Headlines

C-35 weak headline—doesn't interest or doesn't sell
C-36 head (or copy) lacks benefit or direct personal appeal to reader
C-37 not a good tie-in of headline and opening body copy
C-38 you should use some subheads
C-39 headline isn't specific enough
C-40 headline doesn't involve the reader

General Faults

C-41 you fail to use principles taught you this semester (in writing, merchandising techniques, in physical form, copy style, etc.)

C-42 wrong form
C-43 too much copy for space (or paragraph, or point being made)
C-44 too much "we" or company viewpoint
C-45 company's promotional backing out sold hard enough, or specifically enough.
C-46 you're emphasizing the weaker appeal
C-47 not enough difference between your various ads
C-48 need more product details
C-49 need fewer product details
C-50 should use product name here
C-51 weak ending
C-52 doesn't end with urge to act

Analysis

A-1 superficial ideas or execution
A-2 you've aimed at wrong market(s)
A-3 analysis is badly-written
A-4 you haven't done a thorough job
A-5 no discussion (or not enough) of differences for different media
A-6 you fail to pinpoint your market(s) definitively
A-7 reasoning seems faulty here
A-8 too dogmatic here
A-9 you don't dig deeply enough

INDEX

U

V

W